PEARSON CUSTOM LIBRARY

Strategic Cost Analysis
Horngren, Datar and Rajan 15th edition
B60 ACC 5002/5012
Olin Business School

PEARSON

ISBN 10: 1-269-78557-5
ISBN 13: 978-1-269-78557-0

PEARSON

Table of Contents

Chapter 1

The Manager and Management Accounting

From Chapter 1 of *Cost Accounting: A Managerial Emphasis,* Fifteenth Edition. Charles T. Horngren, Srikant M. Datar, Madhav V. Rajan. Copyright © 2015 by Pearson Education, Inc. All rights reserved.

The Manager and Management Accounting

All businesses are concerned about revenues and costs.

Managers at companies small and large must understand how revenues and costs behave or risk losing control of the performance of their firms. Managers use cost accounting information to make decisions about research and development, budgeting, production planning, pricing, and the products or services to offer customers. Sometimes these decisions involve tradeoffs. The following article shows how companies like Apple make those tradeoffs to increase their profits.

iTunes Variable Pricing: Downloads Are Down, but Profits Are Up[1]

Can selling less of something be more profitable than selling more of it? In 2009, Apple changed the pricing structure for songs sold through iTunes from a flat fee of $0.99 to a three-tier price point system of $0.69, $0.99, and $1.29. The top 200 songs in any given week make up more than one-sixth of digital music sales. Apple began charging the highest price ($1.29) for these songs—songs by artists like Adele and Carly Rae Jepsen.

Six months after Apple implemented the new pricing model, the downloads of the top 200 tracks were down by about 6%. But although the number of downloads dropped, the higher prices generated more revenue than the old pricing structure. Because Apple's iTunes costs—wholesale song costs, network and transaction fees, and other operating costs—do not vary based on the price of each download, the profits from the 30% price increase more than made up for the losses from the 6% decrease in volume.

Apple has also applied this new pricing structure to movies available through iTunes, which range from $14.99 for new releases to $9.99 for most other films.

To increase profits beyond those created by higher prices, Apple also began to manage iTunes' costs. Transaction costs (what Apple pays credit-card processors like Visa and MasterCard) have decreased, and Apple has also reduced the number of people working in the iTunes store.

---

[1] *Sources:* Bruno, Anthony and Glenn Peoples Variable iTunes pricing a moneymaker for artists. Reuters, (June 21, 2009); http://www.reuters.com/article/idUSTRE55K0DJ20090621" The long tale? *Billboard* (November 14, 2009); http://www.billboard.biz/bbbiz/content_display/magazine/features/e3135ed869fbd929ccd cca52ed7fd 9262d3?imw=Y" Savitz, Eric,Apple Turns Out, iTunes Makes Money Pacific Crest Says (2007); Subscription Services Seems Inevitable. Barron's "Tech Trader Daily" blog, April 23. http://blogs.barrons.com/techtrader-daily/2007/04/23/apple-turns-out-itunes-makes-money-pacific-crest-says-subscription-service-seems-inevitable/ Apple, Inc. "Frequently Asked Questions (FAQ) for Purchased Movies. Accessed May 1, 2013; Nekesa Mumbi Moody, "Adele, Carly Rae Jepsen Top iTunes' Year-End Sales," *Billboard* (December 13, 2012).

By studying cost accounting, you will learn how successful managers and accountants run their businesses and prepare yourself for leadership roles in the firms you work for. Many large companies, including Nike and the Pittsburgh Steelers, have senior executives with accounting backgrounds.

Financial Accounting, Management Accounting, and Cost Accounting

Learning Objective 1

Distinguish financial accounting

...reporting on past performance to external users

from management accounting

...helping managers make decisions

As many of you have already learned in your financial accounting class, accounting systems are used to record economic events and transactions, such as sales and materials purchases, and process the data into information helpful to managers, sales representatives, production supervisors, and others. Processing any economic transaction means collecting, categorizing, summarizing, and analyzing. For example, costs are collected by category, such as materials, labor, and shipping. These costs are then summarized to determine a firm's total costs by month, quarter, or year. Accountants analyze the results and together with managers evaluate, say, how costs have changed relative to revenues from one period to the next. Accounting systems also provide the information found in a firm's income statement, balance sheet, statement of cash flow, and performance reports, such as the cost of serving customers or running an advertising campaign. Managers use this information to make decisions about the activities, businesses, or functional areas they oversee. For example, a report that shows an increase in sales of laptops and iPads at an Apple store may prompt Apple to hire more salespeople at that location. Understanding accounting information is essential for managers to do their jobs.

Individual managers often require the information in an accounting system to be presented or reported differently. Consider, for example, sales order information. A sales manager at Porsche may be interested in the total dollar amount of sales to determine the commissions paid to salespeople. A distribution manager at Porsche may be interested in the sales order quantities by geographic region and by customer-requested delivery dates to ensure vehicles get delivered to customers on time. A manufacturing manager at Porsche may be interested in the quantities of various products and their desired delivery dates so that he or she can develop an effective production schedule.

To simultaneously serve the needs of all three managers, Porsche creates a database, sometimes called a data warehouse or infobarn, consisting of small, detailed bits of information that can be used for multiple purposes. For instance, the sales order database will contain detailed information about a product, its selling price, quantity ordered, and delivery details (place and date) for each sales order. The database stores information in a way that allows different managers to access the information they need. Many companies are building their own enterprise resource planning (ERP) systems. An ERP system is a single database that collects data and feeds them into applications that support a company's business activities, such as purchasing, production, distribution, and sales.

Financial accounting and management accounting have different goals. As you know, **financial accounting** focuses on reporting financial information to external parties such as investors, government agencies, banks, and suppliers based on Generally Accepted Accounting Principles (GAAP). The most important way financial accounting information affects managers' decisions and actions is through compensation, which is often, in part, based on numbers in financial statements.

Management accounting is the process of measuring, analyzing, and reporting financial and nonfinancial information that helps managers make decisions to fulfill the goals of an organization. Managers use management accounting information to:

1. Develop, communicate, and implement strategies
2. Coordinate product design, production, and marketing decisions and evaluate a company's performance

Management accounting information and reports do not have to follow set principles or rules. The key questions are always (1) how will this information help managers do their jobs better, and (2) do the benefits of producing this information exceed the costs?

Exhibit 1 summarizes the major differences between management accounting and financial accounting. Note, however, that reports such as balance sheets, income statements, and statements of cash flows are common to both management accounting and financial accounting.

Cost accounting provides information for both management accounting and financial accounting professionals. **Cost accounting** is the process of measuring, analyzing, and reporting financial and nonfinancial information related to the costs of acquiring or using resources in an organization. For example, calculating the cost of a product is a cost accounting function that meets both the financial accountant's inventory-valuation needs and the management accountant's decision-making needs (such as deciding how to price products and choosing which products to promote). However, today most accounting professionals take the perspective that cost information is part of the management accounting information collected to make management decisions. Thus, the distinction between management accounting and cost accounting is not so clear-cut, and we often use these terms interchangeably in the text.

Businesspeople frequently use the term *cost management*. Unfortunately, the term does not have an exact definition. In this text we use **cost management** to describe the activities managers undertake to use resources in a way that increases a product's value

| Exhibit 1 | Major Differences Between Management and Financial Accounting |

	Management Accounting	**Financial Accounting**
Purpose of information	Help managers make decisions to fulfill an organization's goals	Communicate an organization's financial position to investors, banks, regulators, and other outside parties
Primary users	Managers of the organization	External users such as investors, banks, regulators, and suppliers
Focus and emphasis	Future-oriented (budget for 2014 prepared in 2013)	Past-oriented (reports on 2013 performance prepared in 2014)
Rules of measurement and reporting	Internal measures and reports do not have to follow GAAP but are based on cost-benefit analysis	Financial statements must be prepared in accordance with GAAP and be certified by external, independent auditors
Time span and type of reports	Varies from hourly information to 15 to 20 years, with financial and nonfinancial reports on products, departments, territories, and strategies	Annual and quarterly financial reports, primarily on the company as a whole
Behavioral implications	Designed to influence the behavior of managers and other employees	Primarily reports economic events but also influences behavior because manager's compensation is often based on reported financial results

to customers and achieves an organization's goals. In other words, cost management is not only about reducing costs. Cost management also includes making decisions to incur additional costs—for example, to improve customer satisfaction and quality and to develop new products—with the goal of enhancing revenues and profits. Whether or not to enter new markets, implement new organizational processes, and change product designs are also cost management decisions. Information from accounting systems helps managers to manage costs, but the information and the accounting systems themselves are not cost management.

Decision Point

How is financial accounting different from management accounting?

Strategic Decisions and the Management Accountant

A company's **strategy** specifies how the organization matches its own capabilities with the opportunities in the marketplace. In other words, strategy describes how an organization will compete and the opportunities its managers should seek and pursue. Businesses follow one of two broad strategies. Some companies, such as Southwest Airlines and Vanguard (the mutual fund company), follow a cost leadership strategy. They have been profitable and have grown over the years by providing quality products or services at low prices and by judiciously managing their costs. Other companies such as Apple and the pharmaceutical giant Johnson & Johnson follow a product differentiation strategy. They generate their profits and growth because they offer differentiated or unique products or services that appeal to their customers and are often priced higher than the less-popular products or services of their competitors.

Learning Objective 2

Understand how management accountants help firms make strategic decisions

...they provide information about the sources of competitive advantage

Deciding between these strategies is a critical part of what managers do. Management accountants work closely with managers in various departments to formulate strategies by providing information about the sources of competitive advantage, such as (1) the company's cost, productivity, or efficiency advantage relative to competitors or (2) the premium prices a company can charge relative to the costs of adding features that make its products or services distinctive. **Strategic cost management** describes cost management that specifically focuses on strategic issues.

Management accounting information helps managers formulate strategy by answering questions such as the following:

- *Who are our most important customers, and how can we be competitive and deliver value to them?* After Amazon.com's success selling books online, management accountants at Barnes & Noble outlined the costs and benefits of several alternative approaches for enhancing the company's information technology infrastructure and developing the capability to sell books online. A similar cost–benefit analysis led Toyota to build flexible computer-integrated manufacturing plants that enable it to use the same equipment efficiently to produce a variety of cars in response to changing customer tastes.

- *What substitute products exist in the marketplace, and how do they differ from our product in terms of features, price, cost, and quality?* Hewlett-Packard, for example, designs, costs, and prices new printers after comparing the functionality and quality of its printers to other printers available in the marketplace.

- *What is our most critical capability? Is it technology, production, or marketing? How can we leverage it for new strategic initiatives?* Kellogg Company, for example, uses the reputation of its brand to introduce new types of cereals with high profit margins.

- *Will adequate cash be available to fund the strategy, or will additional funds need to be raised?* Procter & Gamble, for example, issued new debt and equity to fund its strategic acquisition of Gillette, a maker of shaving products.

Decision Point

How do management accountants support strategic decisions?

The best-designed strategies and the best-developed capabilities are useless unless they are effectively executed. In the next section, we describe how management accountants help managers take actions that create value for their customers.

Learning Objective 3

Describe the set of business functions in the value chain and identify the dimensions of performance that customers are expecting of companies

…R&D, design, production, marketing, distribution, and customer service supported by administration to achieve cost and efficiency, quality, time, and innovation

Value-Chain and Supply-Chain Analysis and Key Success Factors

Customers demand much more than just a fair price; they expect quality products (goods or services) delivered in a timely way. The entire customer experience determines the value a customer derives from a product. In this section, we explore how a company goes about creating this value.

Value-Chain Analysis

The **value chain** is the sequence of business functions by which a product is made progressively more useful to customers. Exhibit 2 shows six primary business functions: research and development (R&D), design of products and processes, production, marketing, distribution, and customer service. We illustrate these business functions with Sony Corporation's television division.

1. **Research and development (R&D)**—generating and experimenting with ideas related to new products, services, or processes. At Sony, this function includes research on alternative television signal transmission and on the picture quality of different shapes and thicknesses of television screens.

2. **Design of products and processes**—detailed planning, engineering, and testing of products and processes. Design at Sony includes deciding on the number of component parts in a television set and determining the effect alternative product designs will have on the set's quality and manufacturing costs. Some representations of the value chain collectively refer to the first two steps as technology development.[2]

3. **Production**—procuring, transporting, and storing ("inbound logistics") and coordinating and assembling ("operations") resources to produce a product or deliver a service. The production of a Sony television set includes the procurement and assembly of the electronic parts, the cabinet, and the packaging used for shipping.

4. **Marketing (including sales)**—promoting and selling products or services to customers or prospective customers. Sony markets its televisions at tradeshows, via advertisements in newspapers and magazines, on the Internet, and through its sales force.

5. **Distribution**—processing orders and shipping products or services to customers ("outbound logistics"). Distribution for Sony includes shipping to retail outlets, catalog vendors, direct sales via the Internet, and other channels through which customers purchase new televisions.

6. **Customer service**—providing after-sales service to customers. Sony provides customer service on its televisions in the form of customer-help telephone lines, support on the Internet, and warranty repair work.

In addition to the six primary business functions, Exhibit 2 shows an administration function, which includes accounting and finance, human resource management, and information technology and supports the six primary business functions. When discussing the value chain, we include the administration

Exhibit 2   Different Parts of the Value Chain

Administration

Research and Development	Design of Products and Processes	Production	Marketing	Distribution	Customer Service

---

[2] M. Porter, *Competitive Advantage* (New York: Free Press, 1998).

function within the primary functions. For example, included in the marketing function is the function of analyzing, reporting, and accounting for resources spent in different marketing channels, whereas the production function includes the human resource management function of training frontline workers. Each of these business functions is essential to companies satisfying their customers and keeping them satisfied (and loyal) over time.

To implement their corporate strategies, companies such as Sony and Procter & Gamble use **customer relationship management (CRM)**, a strategy that integrates people and technology in all business functions to deepen relationships with customers, partners, and distributors. CRM initiatives use technology to coordinate all customer-facing activities (such as marketing, sales calls, distribution, and after-sales support) and the design and production activities necessary to get products to customers.

Different companies create value in different ways. Lowe's (the home-improvement retailer) does so by focusing on cost and efficiency. Toyota Motor Company does so by focusing on quality. Fast response times at eBay create quality for the online auction giant's customers, whereas innovation is primarily what creates value for the customers of the biotech company Roche-Genentech. The Italian apparel company Gucci creates value for its customers by building a prestigious brand. As a result, at different times and in different industries, one or more of these functions is more critical than others. For example, a company such as Roche-Genentech will emphasize R&D and the design of products and processes. In contrast, a company such as Gucci will focus on marketing, distribution, and customer service to build its brand.

Exhibit 2 depicts the usual order in which different business-function activities physically occur. Do not, however, interpret Exhibit 2 to mean that managers should proceed sequentially through the value chain when planning and managing their activities. Companies gain (in terms of cost, quality, and the speed with which new products are developed) if two or more of the individual business functions of the value chain work concurrently as a team. For example, a company's production, marketing, distribution, and customer service personnel can often reduce a company's total costs by providing input for design decisions.

Managers track the costs incurred in each value-chain category. Their goal is to reduce costs and to improve efficiency. Management accounting information helps managers make cost–benefit tradeoffs. For example, is it cheaper to buy products from a vendor or produce them in-house? How does investing resources in design and manufacturing reduce costs of marketing and customer service?

Supply-Chain Analysis

The parts of the value chain associated with producing and delivering a product or service—production and distribution—are referred to as the *supply chain*. The **supply chain** describes the flow of goods, services, and information from the initial sources of materials and services to the delivery of products to consumers, regardless of whether those activities occur in one organization or in multiple organizations. Consider Coke and Pepsi: Many companies play a role in bringing these products to consumers as the supply chain in Exhibit 3 shows. Part of cost management emphasizes integrating and coordinating activities across all companies in the supply chain to improve their

Exhibit 3   Supply Chain for a Cola Bottling Company

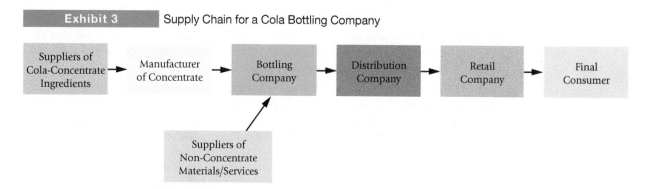

performance and reduce costs. For example, to reduce materials-handling costs, both the Coca-Cola Company and Pepsi Bottling Group require their suppliers (such as plastic and aluminum companies and sugar refiners) to frequently deliver small quantities of materials directly to their production floors. Similarly, to reduce inventory levels in the supply chain, Walmart requires its suppliers, such as Coca-Cola, to directly manage its inventory of products to ensure the right amount of them are in its stores at all times.

Key Success Factors

Customers want companies to use the value chain and supply chain to deliver ever-improving levels of performance when it comes to several (or even all) of the following:

- **Cost and efficiency**—Companies face continuous pressure to reduce the cost of the products they sell. To calculate and manage the cost of products, managers must first understand the activities (such as setting up machines or distributing products) that cause costs to arise as well as monitor the marketplace to determine the prices customers are willing to pay for products or services. Management accounting information helps managers calculate a target cost for a product by subtracting from the "target price" the operating income per unit of product that the company wants to earn. To achieve the target cost, managers eliminate some activities (such as rework) and reduce the costs of performing activities in all value-chain functions—from initial R&D to customer service (see Concepts in Action: Trader Joe's Recipe for Cost Leadership). Many U.S. companies have cut costs by outsourcing some of their business functions. Nike, for example, has moved its manufacturing operations to China and Mexico, and Microsoft and IBM are increasingly doing their software development in Spain, Eastern Europe, and India.

- **Quality**—Customers expect high levels of quality. **Total quality management (TQM)** is an integrative philosophy of management for continuously improving the quality of products and processes. Managers who implement TQM believe that each and every person in the value chain is responsible for delivering products and services that exceed customers' expectations. Using TQM, companies design products or services to meet customer needs and wants, to make these products with zero (or very few) defects and waste, and to minimize inventories. Managers use management accounting information to evaluate the costs and revenue benefits of TQM initiatives.

- **Time**—Time has many dimensions. Two of the most important dimensions are new-product development time and customer-response time. New-product development time is the time it takes for companies to create new products and bring them to market. The increasing pace of technological innovation has led to shorter product life cycles and more rapid introduction of new products. To make new-product development decisions, managers need to understand the costs and benefits of a product over its life cycle.

  Customer-response time describes the speed at which an organization responds to customer requests. To increase the satisfaction of their customers, organizations need to meet their promised delivery dates as well as reduce their delivery times. Bottlenecks are the primary cause of delays. For example, a bottleneck can occur when the work to be performed on a machine exceeds its available capacity. To deliver the product on time, managers need to increase the capacity of the machine to produce more output. Management accounting information can help managers quantify the costs and benefits of doing so.

- **Innovation**—A constant flow of innovative products or services is the basis for the ongoing success of a company. Managers rely on management accounting information to evaluate alternative investment and R&D decisions.

- **Sustainability**—Companies are increasingly applying the key success factors of cost and efficiency, quality, time, and innovation to promote **sustainability**—the development and implementation of strategies to achieve long-term financial, social, and environmental goals. The sustainability efforts of the Japanese copier company Ricoh include energy conservation, resource conservation, product recycling, and pollution prevention. By designing products that can be easily recycled, Ricoh simultaneously improves its efficiency and the cost and quality of its products.

Concepts in Action

Trader Joe's Recipe for Cost Leadership

Trader Joe's has a special recipe for cost leadership: delivering unique products at reasonable prices. The grocery store chain stocks its shelves with low-cost, high-end staples (cage-free eggs and sustainably harvested seafood) and exotic, affordable luxuries (Ethiopian Peaberry coffee and Thai lime-and-chili cashews) that are distinct from what traditional supermarkets offer. Trader Joe's can offer these items at everyday low prices by judiciously managing its costs.

At Trader Joe's, customers swap selection for value. The company has relatively small stores with a carefully selected, constantly changing mix of items. While typical grocery stores carry 50,000 items, Trader Joe's sells only about 4,000 items. Recently, it has been removing non-sustainable products from its shelves, including genetically modified items. About 80% of the stock bears the Trader Joe's brand, and management seeks to minimize costs of these items. The company purchases directly from manufacturers, which ship their items straight to Trader Joe's warehouses to avoid third-party distribution costs. With small stores and limited storage space, Trader Joe's trucks leave the warehouse centers daily. This encourages precise, just-in-time ordering and a relentless focus on frequent merchandise turnover.

This winning combination of quality products and low prices has turned Trader Joe's into one of the hottest retailers in the United States. Its stores sell an estimated $8 billion annually, or $1,750 in merchandise per square foot, which is more than double Whole Foods, its top competitor.

Sources: Based on Beth Kowitt, "Inside the Secret World of Trader Joe's," *Fortune* (August 23, 2010); Christopher Palmeri, "Trader Joe's Recipe for Success," *Businessweek* (February 21, 2008); Mark Mallinger and Gerry Rossy, "The Trader Joe's Experience: The Impact of Corporate Culture on Business Strategy," *Graziadio Business Review* (2007, Volume 10, Issue 2); and Allessandra Ram, "Teach Us, Trader Joe: Demading Socially Responsible Food," *The Atlantic* (August 7, 2012).

The interest in sustainability appears to be intensifying among companies. General Electric, Poland Springs (a bottled-water manufacturer), and Hewlett-Packard are among the many companies incorporating sustainability into their decision making. Sustainability is important to these companies for several reasons:

- More and more investors care about sustainability. These investors make investment decisions based on a company's financial, social, and environmental performance and raise questions about sustainability at shareholder meetings.
- Companies that emphasize sustainability find that sustainability goals attract and inspire employees.
- Customers prefer the products of companies with good sustainability records and boycott companies with poor sustainability records.
- Society and activist nongovernmental organizations, in particular, monitor the sustainability performance of firms and take legal action against those that violate environmental laws. Countries with fast-growing economies, such as China and India, are now either requiring or encouraging companies to develop and report on their sustainability initiatives.

Management accountants help managers track the key success factors of their firms as well as those of their competitors. Competitive information such as this serves as a *benchmark* managers use to continuously improve their operations. Examples of continuous improvement include Southwest Airlines' efforts to increase the number of its flights that arrive on time, eBay's efforts to improve the access its customers have to online auctions, and Lowe's efforts to continuously reduce the cost of its home-improvement products. Sometimes, more fundamental changes in operations, such as redesigning a manufacturing process to reduce costs, may be necessary. To successfully implement their strategies, firms have to do more than analyze their value chains and supply chains and execute key success factors. They also have to have good decision-making processes.

Decision Point

How do companies add value, and what are the dimensions of performance that customers are expecting of companies?

Decision Making, Planning, and Control: The Five-Step Decision-Making Process

We illustrate a five-step decision-making process using the example of the *Daily News*, a newspaper in Boulder, Colorado. Managers use this five-step decision-making process to make many different types of decisions.

The *Daily News* differentiates itself from its competitors by using (1) highly respected journalists who write well-researched news articles, (2) color to enhance attractiveness to readers and advertisers, and (3) a Web site that delivers up-to-the-minute news, interviews, and analyses. The newspaper has the following resources to deliver on this strategy: an automated, computer-integrated, state-of-the-art printing facility; a Web-based information technology infrastructure; and a distribution network that is one of the best in the newspaper industry.

To keep up with steadily increasing production costs, Naomi Crawford, manager of the *Daily News*, needs to increase the company's revenues. To decide what she should do, Naomi works through the five-step decision-making process.

1. **Identify the problem and uncertainties.** Naomi has two main choices:

   a. increase the selling price of the newspaper or
   b. increase the rate per page charged to advertisers.

   The key uncertainty is the effect any increase in prices or rates will have on demand. A decrease in demand could offset the price or rate increases and lead to lower rather than higher revenues.

2. **Obtain information.** Gathering information before making a decision helps managers gain a better understanding of uncertainties. Naomi asks her marketing manager to talk to some representative readers to gauge their reaction to an increase in the newspaper's selling price. She asks her advertising sales manager to talk to current and potential advertisers to assess demand for advertising. She also reviews the effect that past price increases had on readership. Ramon Sandoval, management accountant at the *Daily News*, presents information about the effect of past increases or decreases in advertising rates on advertising revenues. He also collects and analyzes information on advertising rates competing newspapers and other media outlets charge.

3. **Make predictions about the future.** Based on this information, Naomi makes predictions about the future. She concludes that increasing prices would upset readers and decrease readership. She has a different view about advertising rates. She expects a marketwide increase in advertising rates and believes that increasing rates will have little effect on the number of advertising pages sold.

   Naomi recognizes that making predictions requires judgment. She looks for biases in her thinking. Has she correctly judged reader sentiment or is the negative publicity of a price increase overly influencing her decision making? How sure is she that competitors will increase their advertising rates? Is her thinking in this respect biased by how competitors have responded in the past? Have circumstances changed? How confident is she that her sales representatives can convince advertisers to pay higher rates? After retesting her assumptions and reviewing her thinking, Naomi feels comfortable with her predictions and judgments.

4. **Make decisions by choosing among alternatives.** When making decisions, a company's strategy serves as a vital guidepost for the many individuals in different parts of the organization making decisions at different times. Consistent strategies provide a common purpose for these disparate decisions. Only if these decisions can be aligned with its strategy will an organization achieve its goals. Without this alignment, the company's decisions will be uncoordinated, pull the organization in different directions, and produce inconsistent results.

   Consistent with a product differentiation strategy, Naomi decides to increase advertising rates by 4% to $5,200 per page in March 2014, but not increase the selling price of the newspaper. She is confident that the *Daily News*'s distinctive style and Web presence will increase readership, creating value for advertisers. She communicates the new advertising rate schedule to the sales department. Ramon estimates advertising revenues of $4,160,000 ($5,200 per page × 800 pages predicted to be sold in March 2014).

Steps 1 through 4 are collectively referred to as *planning*. **Planning** consists of selecting an organization's goals and strategies, predicting results under various alternative ways of achieving those goals, deciding how to attain the desired goals, and communicating the goals and how to achieve them to the entire organization. Management accountants serve as business partners in these planning activities because they understand the key success factors and what creates value.

The most important planning tool when implementing strategy is a *budget*. A **budget** is the quantitative expression of a proposed plan of action by management and is an aid to coordinating what needs to be done to execute that plan. For March 2014, the budgeted advertising revenue of the *Daily News* equals $4,160,000. The full budget for March 2014 includes budgeted circulation revenue and the production, distribution, and customer-service costs to achieve the company's sales goals; the anticipated cash flows; and the potential financing needs. Because multiple departments help prepare the budget, personnel throughout the organization have to coordinate and communicate with one another as well as with the company's suppliers and customers.

5. **Implement the decision, evaluate performance, and learn.** Managers at the *Daily News* take action to implement the March 2014 budget. The firm's management accountants then collect information on how the company's actual performance compares to planned or budgeted performance (also referred to as scorekeeping). The information on the actual results is different from the *predecision* planning information Naomi collected in Step 2, which enabled her to better understand uncertainties, to make predictions, and to make a decision. Allowing managers to compare actual performance to budgeted performance is the *control* or *postdecision* role of information. **Control** comprises taking actions that implement the planning decisions, evaluating past performance, and providing feedback and learning to help future decision making.

   Measuring actual performance informs managers how well they and their subunits are doing. Linking rewards to performance helps motivate managers. These rewards are both intrinsic (recognition for a job well done) and extrinsic (salary, bonuses, and promotions linked to performance). A budget serves as much as a control tool as a planning tool. Why? Because a budget is a benchmark against which actual performance can be compared.

Consider performance evaluation at the *Daily News*. During March 2014, the newspaper sold advertising, issued invoices, and received payments. The accounting system recorded these invoices and receipts. Exhibit 4 shows the *Daily News*'s advertising revenues for March 2014. This performance report indicates that 760 pages of advertising (40 pages fewer than the budgeted 800 pages) were sold. The average rate per page was $5,080, compared with the budgeted $5,200 rate, yielding actual advertising revenues of $3,860,800. The actual advertising revenues were $299,200 less than the budgeted $4,160,000. Observe how managers use both financial and nonfinancial information, such as pages of advertising, to evaluate performance.

Exhibit 4   Performance Report of Advertising Revenues at the *Daily News* for March 2014

	Actual Result (1)	Budgeted Amount (2)	Difference: (Actual Result – Budgeted Amount) (3) = (1) – (2)	Difference as a Percentage of Budgeted Amount (4) = (3) ÷ (2)
Advertising pages sold	760 pages	800 pages	40 pages Unfavorable	5.0% Unfavorable
Average rate per page	$5,080	$5,200	$120 Unfavorable	2.3% Unfavorable
Advertising revenues	$3,860,800	$4,160,000	$299,200 Unfavorable	7.2% Unfavorable

The performance report in Exhibit 4 spurs investigation and **learning,** which involves examining past performance (the control function) and systematically exploring alternative ways to make better-informed decisions and plans in the future. Learning can lead to changes in goals, strategies, the ways decision alternatives are identified, and the range of information collected when making predictions and sometimes can lead to changes in managers.

The performance report in Exhibit 4 would prompt the management accountant to raise several questions directing the attention of managers to problems and opportunities. Is the strategy of differentiating the *Daily News* from other newspapers attracting more readers? Did the marketing and sales department make sufficient efforts to convince advertisers that, even at the higher rate of $5,200 per page, advertising in the *Daily News* was a good buy? Why was the actual average rate per page ($5,080) less than the budgeted rate ($5,200)? Did some sales representatives offer discounted rates? Did economic conditions cause the decline in advertising revenues? Are revenues falling because editorial and production standards have declined? Are more readers getting their news online?

Answers to these questions could prompt the newspaper's publisher to take subsequent actions, including, for example, adding more sales personnel, making changes in editorial policy, or putting more resources into expanding its presence online and on mobile devices. Good implementation requires the marketing, editorial, and production departments to work together and coordinate their actions.

The management accountant could go further by identifying the specific advertisers that cut back or stopped advertising after the rate increase went into effect. Managers could then decide when and how sales representatives should follow up with these advertisers.

Planning and control activities must be flexible enough so that managers can seize opportunities unforeseen at the time the plan was formulated. In no case should control mean that managers cling to a plan when unfolding events (such as a sensational

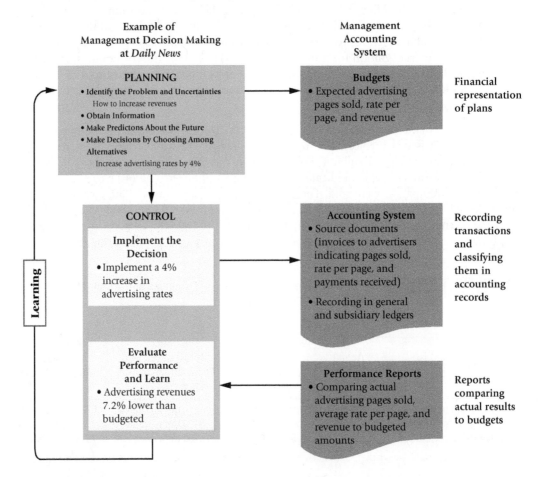

Exhibit 5

How Accounting Aids Decision Making, Planning, and Control at the *Daily News*

news story) indicate that actions not encompassed by that plan (such as spending more money to cover the story) would offer better results for the company (from higher newspaper sales).

The left side of Exhibit 5 provides an overview of the decision-making processes at the *Daily News*. The right side of the exhibit highlights how the management accounting system aids in decision making.

Decision Point

How do managers make decisions to implement strategy?

Key Management Accounting Guidelines

Three guidelines help management accountants provide the most value to the strategic and operational decision making of their companies: (1) employ a cost–benefit approach, (2) give full recognition to behavioral and technical considerations, and (3) use different costs for different purposes.

Cost–Benefit Approach

Managers continually face resource-allocation decisions, such as whether to purchase a new software package or hire a new employee. They use a **cost–benefit approach** when making these decisions. Managers should spend resources if the expected benefits to the company exceed the expected costs. Managers rely on management accounting information to quantify expected benefits and expected costs (although all benefits and costs are not easy to quantify).

Consider the installation of a consulting company's first budgeting system. Previously, the company used historical recordkeeping and little formal planning. A major benefit of installing a budgeting system is that it compels managers to plan ahead, compare actual to budgeted information, learn, and take corrective action. Although the system leads to better decisions and consequently better company performance, the exact benefits are not easy to measure. On the cost side, some costs, such as investments in software and training, are easier to quantify. Others, such as the time spent by managers on the budgeting process, are more difficult to quantify. Regardless, senior managers compare expected benefits and expected costs, exercise judgment, and reach a decision, in this case to install the budgeting system.

Learning Objective 5

Describe three guidelines management accountants follow in supporting managers

... employing a cost–benefit approach, recognizing behavioral as well as technical considerations, and calculating different costs for different purposes

Behavioral and Technical Considerations

When utilizing the cost–benefit approach, managers need to keep in mind a number of technical and behavioral considerations. The technical considerations help managers make wise economic decisions by providing them with the desired information (for example, costs in various value-chain categories) in an appropriate format (for example, actual results versus budgeted amounts) and at the preferred frequency (for example, weekly or quarterly). However, management is not confined to technical matters. Management is primarily a human activity that should focus on encouraging individuals to do their jobs better. Budgets have a behavioral effect by motivating and rewarding employees for achieving an organization's goals. So, when workers underperform, for example, behavioral considerations suggest that managers need to discuss ways to improve their performance with them rather than just sending them a report highlighting their underperformance.

Different Costs for Different Purposes

This text emphasizes that managers use alternative ways to compute costs in different decision-making situations because there are different costs for different purposes. A cost concept used for the purposes of external reporting may not be appropriate for internal, routine reporting.

Consider the advertising costs associated with Microsoft Corporation's launch of a product with a useful life of several years. For external reporting to shareholders, Generally Accepted Accounting Principles (GAAP) require television advertising costs for

Decision Point

What guidelines do management accountants use?

this product to be fully expensed in the income statement in the year they are incurred. However, the television advertising costs could be capitalized and then amortized or written off as expenses over several years if Microsoft's management team believed that doing so would more accurately and fairly measure the performance of the managers that launched the new product.

We now discuss the relationships and reporting responsibilities among managers and management accountants within a company's organization structure.

Learning Objective 6

Understand how management accounting fits into an organization's structure

...for example, the responsibilities of the controller

Organization Structure and the Management Accountant

We focus first on broad management functions and then look at how the management accounting and finance functions support managers.

Line and Staff Relationships

Organizations distinguish between line management and staff management. **Line management,** such as production, marketing, and distribution management, is directly responsible for achieving the goals of the organization. For example, managers of manufacturing divisions are responsible for meeting particular levels of budgeted operating income, product quality and safety, and compliance with environmental laws. Similarly, the pediatrics department in a hospital is responsible for quality of service, costs, and patient billings. **Staff management,** such as management accountants and information technology and human-resources management, provides advice, support, and assistance to line management. A plant manager (a line function) may be responsible for investing in new equipment. A management accountant (a staff function) works as a business partner of the plant manager by preparing detailed operating-cost comparisons of alternative pieces of equipment.

Increasingly, organizations such as Honda and Dell are using teams to achieve their objectives. These teams include both line and staff management so that all inputs into a decision are available simultaneously.

The Chief Financial Officer and the Controller

The **chief financial officer (CFO)**—also called the **finance director** in many countries—is the executive responsible for overseeing the financial operations of an organization. The responsibilities of the CFO vary among organizations, but they usually include the following areas:

- **Controllership**—provides financial information for reports to managers and shareholders and oversees the overall operations of the accounting system.
- **Treasury**—oversees banking and short- and long-term financing, investments, and cash management.
- **Risk management**—manages the financial risk of interest-rate and exchange-rate changes and derivatives management.
- **Taxation**—plans income taxes, sales taxes, and international taxes.
- **Investor relations**—communicates with, responds to, and interacts with shareholders.
- **Strategic planning**—defining strategy and allocating resources to implement strategy.

An independent internal audit function reviews and analyzes financial and other records to attest to the integrity of the organization's financial reports and to adherence to its policies and procedures.

The **controller** (also called the *chief accounting officer*) is the financial executive primarily responsible for management accounting and financial accounting. This text focuses on the controller as the chief management accounting executive. Modern controllers have no line authority except over their own departments. Yet the controller exercises control over the entire organization in a special way. By reporting and interpreting relevant data, the controller influences the behavior of all employees and helps line managers make better decisions.

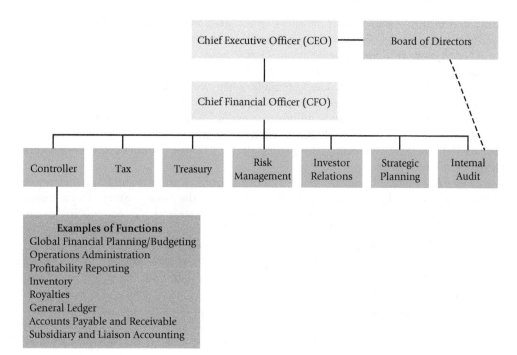

Exhibit 6

Nike: Reporting Relationship for the CFO and the Corporate Controller

Exhibit 6 shows an organization chart of the CFO and the corporate controller at Nike, the leading footwear and sports apparel company. The CFO is a staff manager who reports to and supports the chief executive officer (CEO). As in most organizations, the corporate controller at Nike reports to the CFO. Nike also has regional controllers who support regional managers in the major geographic regions in which the company operates, such as the United States, Asia Pacific, Latin America, and Europe. Because they support the activities of the regional manager, for example, by managing budgets and analyzing costs, regional controllers report to the regional manager rather than the corporate controller. At the same time, to align accounting policies and practices for the whole organization, regional controllers have a functional (often called a dotted-line) responsibility to the corporate controller. Individual countries sometimes have a country controller.

Organization charts such as the one in Exhibit 6 show formal reporting relationships. In most organizations, there also are informal relationships that must be understood when managers attempt to implement their decisions. Examples of informal relationships are friendships among managers (friendships of a professional or personal kind) and the personal preferences of top management about the managers they rely on when making decisions.

Think about what managers do to design and implement strategies and the organization structures within which they operate. Then think about the management accountants' and controllers' roles. It should be clear that the successful management accountant must have technical and analytical competence *as well as* behavioral and interpersonal skills.

Management Accounting Beyond the Numbers[3]

To people outside the profession, it may seem like accountants are just "numbers people." It is true that most accountants are adept financial managers, yet their skills do not stop there. The successful management accountant possesses several skills and characteristics that reach well beyond basic analytical abilities.

Management accountants must work well in cross-functional teams and as a business partner. In addition to being technically competent, the best management accountants

---

[3] United States Senate Permanent Subcommittee on Investigations. *JPMorgan Chase Whale Trades: A Case History of Derivatives Risks and Abuses.* Washington, DC: Government Printing Office, March 15, 2013; Wendy Garling, "Winning the Transformation Battle at the Defense Finance and Accounting Service," Balanced Scorecard Report, May–June 2007; Nixon, Bill, Burns, John, and Mostafa Jazayeri. The role of management accounting in new product design and development decisions. Volume 9, Issue 1. London: Chartered Institute of Management Accountants, November 2011; and Ben Worthen, "H-P Says It Was Duped, Takes $8.8 Billion Charge," The Wall Street Journal (November 12, 2012).

work well in teams, learn about business issues, understand the motivations of different individuals, respect the views of their colleagues, and show empathy and trust.

Management accountants must promote fact-based analysis and make tough-minded, critical judgments without being adversarial. Management accountants must raise tough questions for managers to consider, especially when preparing budgets. They must do so thoughtfully and with the intent of improving plans and decisions. Before the investment bank JP Morgan lost more than $6 billion on "exotic" financial investments (credit-default swaps) in 2012, controllers should have raised questions about these risky investments and the fact that the firm was essentially betting that improving economic conditions abroad would earn it a large profit.

They must lead and motivate people to change and be innovative. Implementing new ideas, however good they may be, is difficult. When the United States Department of Defense (DoD) began consolidating more than 320 finance and accounting systems into a common platform, the accounting services director and his team of management accountants held meetings to make sure everyone in the agency understood the goal for such a change. Ultimately, the DoD aligned each individual's performance with the transformative change and introduced incentive pay to encourage personnel to adopt the platform and drive innovation within this new framework.

They must communicate clearly, openly, and candidly. Communicating information is a large part of a management accountant's job. When premium car companies such as Rolls Royce and Porsche design new models, management accountants work closely with engineers to ensure that each new car supports a carefully defined balance of commercial, engineering, and financial criteria. These efforts are successful because management accountants clearly communicate the information that multi-disciplinary teams need to deliver new innovations profitably.

They must have a strong sense of integrity. Management accountants must never succumb to pressure from managers to manipulate financial information. They must always remember that their primary commitment is to the organization and its shareholders. In 2012, Hewlett-Packard wrote down $8.8 billion on the value of British software maker Autonomy, which it acquired in 2010, due to serious accounting problems. Hewlett-Packard has accused senior managers at Autonomy of "serious accounting improprieties" and "outright misrepresentations" by mischaracterizing some sales of low-margin hardware as software and recognizing some deals with partners as revenue, even when a customer never bought the product. These actions inflated Autonomy's revenue and profitability, which made the company a more attractive acquisition target.

Decision Point ▶

Where does the management accounting function fit into an organization's structure?

Learning Objective 7 ▶

Understand what professional ethics mean to management accountants

…for example, management accountants must maintain integrity and credibility in every aspect of their job

Professional Ethics

At no time has the focus on ethical conduct been sharper than it is today. Corporate scandals at Arthur Andersen, a public accounting firm; Countrywide Financial, a home mortgage company; Enron, an oil and gas company; Lehman Brothers, an investment bank; Olympus, a Japanese optical equipment company; and Bernie Madoff Investment Securities have seriously eroded the public's confidence in corporations. All employees in a company must comply with the organization's—and more broadly, society's—expectations of ethical standards.

Ethics are the foundation of a well-functioning economy. When ethics are weak, suppliers bribe executives to win supply contracts rather than invest in improving quality or lowering costs. Because customers have very little confidence in the quality of products produced, they can become reluctant to buy them, causing markets to fail. Costs are higher because of higher prices paid to suppliers and fewer products being produced and sold. Investors are unsure about the integrity of financial reports, affecting their ability to make investment decisions, resulting in a reluctance to invest and a misallocation of resources. The scandals at Ahold, an international supermarket operator, and Tyco International, a diversified global manufacturing company, and others make clear that value is quickly destroyed by unethical behavior.

Institutional Support

Accountants have special ethical obligations, given that they are responsible for the integrity of the financial information provided to internal and external parties. The Sarbanes–Oxley legislation in the United States was passed in 2002 in response to a series of corporate scandals. The act focused on improving internal control, corporate governance, monitoring of managers, and disclosure practices of public corporations. These regulations impose tough ethical standards and criminal penalties on managers and accountants who don't meet the standards. The regulations also delineate a process for employees to report violations of illegal and unethical acts (these employees are called whistleblowers).

As part of the Sarbanes–Oxley Act, CEOs and CFOs must certify that the financial statements of their firms fairly represent the results of their operations. In order to increase the independence of auditors, the act empowers the audit committee of a company's board of directors (which is composed exclusively of independent directors) to hire, compensate, and terminate the public accounting firm to audit a company. To reduce their financial dependency on their individual clients and increase their independence, the act limits auditing firms from providing consulting, tax, and other advisory services to the companies they are auditing. The act also authorizes the Public Company Accounting Oversight Board to oversee, review, and investigate the work of the auditors.

Professional accounting organizations, which represent management accountants in many countries, offer certification programs indicating that those who have completed them have management accounting and financial management technical knowledge and expertise. These organizations also advocate high ethical standards. In the United States, the Institute of Management Accountants (IMA) has also issued ethical guidelines. Exhibit 7 presents the IMA's guidance on issues relating to competence, confidentiality, integrity, and credibility. To provide support to its members to act ethically at all times, the IMA runs an ethics hotline service. Members can call professional counselors at the IMA's Ethics Counseling Service to discuss their ethical dilemmas. The counselors help identify the key ethical issues and possible alternative ways of resolving them, and confidentiality is guaranteed. The IMA is just one of many institutions that help navigate management accountants through what could be turbulent ethical waters.

Typical Ethical Challenges

Ethical issues can confront management accountants in many ways. Here are two examples:

- **Case A:** A management accountant is concerned about the commercial potential of a software product for which development costs are currently being capitalized as an asset rather than being shown as an expense for internal reporting purposes. The firm's division manager, whose bonus is based, in part, on the division's profits, argues that showing development costs as an asset is justified because the new product will generate profits. However, he presents little evidence to support his argument. The last two products from the division have been unsuccessful. The management accountant wants to make the right decision while avoiding a difficult personal confrontation with his boss, the division manager.
- **Case B:** A packaging supplier, bidding for a new contract, offers a management accountant of the purchasing company an all-expenses-paid weekend to the Super Bowl. The supplier does not mention the new contract when extending the invitation. The management accountant is not a personal friend of the supplier. He knows cost issues are critical when it comes to approving the new contract and is concerned that the supplier will ask for details about the bids placed by competing packaging companies.

In each case, the management accountant is faced with an ethical dilemma. Ethical issues are not always clear-cut. Case A involves competence, credibility, and integrity. The management accountant should request that the division manager provide credible evidence that the new product is commercially viable. If the manager does not provide such evidence, expensing development costs in the current period is appropriate.

Practitioners of management accounting and financial management have an obligation to the public, their profession, the organizations they serve, and themselves to maintain the highest standards of ethical conduct. In recognition of this obligation, the Institute of Management Accountants has promulgated the following standards of ethical professional practice. Adherence to these standards, both domestically and internationally, is integral to achieving the Objectives of Management Accounting. Practitioners of management accounting and financial management shall not commit acts contrary to these standards nor shall they condone the commission of such acts by others within their organizations.

IMA STATEMENT OF ETHICAL PROFESSIONAL PRACTICE

Practitioners of management accounting and financial management shall behave ethically. A commitment to ethical professional practice includes overarching principles that express our values and standards that guide our conduct.

PRINCIPLES

IMA's overarching ethical principles include: Honesty, Fairness, Objectivity, and Responsibility. Practitioners shall act in accordance with these principles and shall encourage others within their organizations to adhere to them.

STANDARDS

A practitioner's failure to comply with the following standards may result in disciplinary action.

COMPETENCE

Each practitioner has a responsibility to:
1. Maintain an appropriate level of professional expertise by continually developing knowledge and skills.
2. Perform professional duties in accordance with relevant laws, regulations, and technical standards.
3. Provide decision support information and recommendations that are accurate, clear, concise, and timely.
4. Recognize and communicate professional limitations or other constraints that would preclude responsible judgment or successful performance of an activity.

CONFIDENTIALITY

Each practitioner has a responsibility to:
1. Keep information confidential except when disclosure is authorized or legally required.
2. Inform all relevant parties regarding appropriate use of confidential information. Monitor subordinates' activities to ensure compliance.
3. Refrain from using confidential information for unethical or illegal advantage.

INTEGRITY

Each practitioner has a responsibility to:
1. Mitigate actual conflicts of interest. Regularly communicate with business associates to avoid apparent conflicts of interest. Advise all parties of any potential conflicts.
2. Refrain from engaging in any conduct that would prejudice carrying out duties ethically.
3. Abstain from engaging in or supporting any activity that might discredit the profession.

CREDIBILITY

Each practitioner has a responsibility to:
1. Communicate information fairly and objectively.
2. Disclose all relevant information that could reasonably be expected to influence an intended user's understanding of the reports, analyses, or recommendations.
3. Disclose delays or deficiencies in information, timeliness, processing, or internal controls in conformance with organization policy and/or applicable law.

Source: IMA Statement of Ethical Professional Practice, 2005. Montvale, NJ: Institute of Management Accountants. Reprinted with permission from the Institute of Management Accountants, Montvale, NJ, www.imanet.org.

Exhibit 8

Resolution of Ethical Conflict

In applying the Standards of Ethical Professional Practice, you may encounter problems identifying unethical behavior or resolving an ethical conflict. When faced with ethical issues, you should follow your organization's established policies on the resolution of such conflict. If these policies do not resolve the ethical conflict, you should consider the following courses of action:

1. Discuss the issue with your immediate supervisor except when it appears that the supervisor is involved. In that case, present the issue to the next level. If you cannot achieve a satisfactory resolution, submit the issue to the next management level. If your immediate superior is the chief executive officer or equivalent, the acceptable reviewing authority may be a group such as the audit committee, executive committee, board of directors, board of trustees, or owners. Contact with levels above the immediate superior should be initiated only with your superior's knowledge, assuming he or she is not involved. Communication of such problems to authorities or individuals not employed or engaged by the organization is not considered appropriate, unless you believe there is a clear violation of the law.
2. Clarify relevant ethical issues by initiating a confidential discussion with an IMA Ethics Counselor or other impartial advisor to obtain a better understanding of possible courses of action.
3. Consult your own attorney as to legal obligations and rights concerning the ethical conflict.

Source: IMA Statement of Ethical Professional Practice, 2005. Montvale, NJ: Institute of Management Accountants. Reprinted with permission from the Institute of Management Accountants, Montvale, NJ, www.imanet.org.

Case B involves confidentiality and integrity. The supplier in Case B may have no intention of asking questions about competitors' bids. However, the appearance of a conflict of interest in Case B is sufficient for many companies to prohibit employees from accepting "favors" from suppliers. Exhibit 8 presents the IMA's guidance on "Resolution of Ethical Conflict." The accountant in Case B should discuss the invitation with his or her immediate supervisor. If the visit is approved, the accountant should inform the supplier that the invitation has been officially approved subject to following corporate policy (which includes not disclosing confidential company information).

Most professional accounting organizations around the globe issue statements about professional ethics. These statements include many of the same issues discussed by the IMA in Exhibits 7 and 8. For example, the Chartered Institute of Management Accountants (CIMA) in the United Kingdom advocates the same four ethical principles shown in Exhibit 7: competency, confidentiality, integrity, and credibility.

Decision Point

What are the ethical responsibilities of management accountants?

Problem for Self-Study

Campbell Soup Company incurs the following costs:

a. Purchase of tomatoes by a canning plant for Campbell's tomato soup products
b. Materials purchased for redesigning Pepperidge Farm biscuit containers to make biscuits stay fresh longer
c. Payment to Backer, Spielvogel, & Bates, the advertising agency, for advertising work on the Healthy Request line of soup products
d. Salaries of food technologists researching feasibility of a Prego pizza sauce that has minimal calories
e. Payment to Safeway for redeeming coupons on Campbell's food products
f. Cost of a toll-free telephone line used for customer inquiries about using Campbell's soup products
g. Cost of gloves used by line operators on the Swanson Fiesta breakfast-food production line
h. Cost of handheld computers used by Pepperidge Farm delivery staff serving major supermarket accounts

Classify each cost item (a–h) as one of the business functions in the value chain in Exhibit 2.

Solution

a. Production
b. Design of products and processes
c. Marketing
d. Research and development
e. Marketing
f. Customer service
g. Production
h. Distribution

▶ Decision Points

The following question-and-answer format summarizes the chapter's learning objectives. Each decision presents a key question related to a learning objective. The guidelines are the answer to that question.

Decision	Guidelines
1. How is financial accounting different from management accounting?	Financial accounting is used to develop reports for external users on past financial performance using GAAP. Management accounting is used to provide future-oriented information to help managers (internal users) make decisions and achieve an organization's goals.
2. How do management accountants support strategic decisions?	Management accountants contribute to strategic decisions by providing information about the sources of competitive advantage.
3. How do companies add value, and what are the dimensions of performance that customers are expecting of companies?	Companies add value through research and development (R&D), design of products and processes, production, marketing, distribution, and customer service. Customers want companies to deliver performance through cost and efficiency, quality, timeliness, and innovation.
4. How do managers make decisions to implement strategy?	Managers use a five-step decision-making process to implement a strategy: (1) identify the problem and uncertainties; (2) obtain information; (3) make predictions about the future; (4) make decisions by choosing among alternatives; and (5) implement the decision, evaluate performance, and learn. The first four steps are planning decisions. They include deciding on an organization's goals, predicting results under various alternative ways of achieving those goals, and deciding how to attain the desired goals. Step 5 is the control decision, which includes taking actions to implement the planning decisions, evaluating past performance, and providing feedback that will help future decision making.
5. What guidelines do management accountants use?	Three guidelines that help management accountants increase their value to managers are (a) employing a cost–benefit approach, (b) recognizing behavioral as well as technical considerations, and (c) identifying different costs for different purposes.
6. Where does the management accounting function fit into an organization's structure?	Management accounting is an integral part of the controller's function. In most organizations, the controller reports to the chief financial officer, who is a key member of the top management team.
7. What are the ethical responsibilities of management accountants?	Management accountants have ethical responsibilities that relate to competence, confidentiality, integrity, and credibility.

Terms to Learn

Like all technical terms, accounting terms have precise meanings. Learn the definitions of new terms when you initially encounter them. The meaning of each of the following terms is given in this chapter.

budget	design of products and processes	research and development (R&D)
chief financial officer (CFO)	distribution	staff management
control	finance director	strategic cost management
controller	financial accounting	strategy
cost accounting	learning	supply chain
cost–benefit approach	line management	sustainability
cost management	management accounting	total quality management (TQM)
customer relationship management (CRM)	marketing	value chain
customer service	planning	
	production	

Assignment Material

Questions

MyAccountingLab

1. How does management accounting differ from financial accounting?
2. "Management accounting should not fit the straitjacket of financial accounting." Explain and give an example.
3. How can a management accountant help formulate strategy?
4. Describe the business functions in the value chain.
5. Explain the term *supply chain* and its importance to cost management.
6. "Management accounting deals only with costs." Do you agree? Explain.
7. How can management accountants help improve quality and achieve timely product deliveries?
8. Describe the five-step decision-making process.
9. Distinguish planning decisions from control decisions.
10. What three guidelines help management accountants provide the most value to managers?
11. "Knowledge of technical issues such as computer technology is a necessary but not sufficient condition to becoming a successful management accountant." Do you agree? Why?
12. As a new controller, reply to this comment by a plant manager: "As I see it, our accountants may be needed to keep records for shareholders and Uncle Sam, but I don't want them sticking their noses in my day-to-day operations. I do the best I know how. No bean counter knows enough about my responsibilities to be of any use to me."
13. Where does the management accounting function fit into an organization's structure?
14. Name the four areas in which standards of ethical conduct exist for management accountants in the United States. What organization sets forth these standards?
15. What steps should a management accountant take if established written policies provide insufficient guidance on how to handle an ethical conflict?

Exercises

MyAccountingLab

16 Value chain and classification of costs, computer company. Compaq Computer incurs the following costs:

a. Electricity costs for the plant assembling the Presario computer line of products
b. Transportation costs for shipping the Presario line of products to a retail chain
c. Payment to David Kelley Designs for design of the Armada Notebook
d. Salary of computer scientist working on the next generation of minicomputers
e. Cost of Compaq employees' visit to a major customer to demonstrate Compaq's ability to interconnect with other computers
f. Purchase of competitors' products for testing against potential Compaq products

g. Payment to television network for running Compaq advertisements
h. Cost of cables purchased from outside supplier to be used with Compaq printers

Classify each of the cost items (a–h) into one of the business functions of the value chain shown in Exhibit 2.

17 Value chain and classification of costs, pharmaceutical company. Pfizer, a pharmaceutical company, incurs the following costs:

a. Payment of booth registration fee at a medical conference to promote new products to physicians
b. Cost of redesigning an insulin syringe to make it less painful
c. Cost of a toll-free telephone line used for customer inquiries about drug usage, side effects of drugs, and so on
d. Equipment purchased to conduct experiments on drugs yet to be approved by the government
e. Sponsorship of a professional golfer
f. Labor costs of workers in the packaging area of a production facility
g. Bonus paid to a salesperson for exceeding a monthly sales quota
h. Cost of FedEx courier service to deliver drugs to hospitals

Classify each of the cost items (a–h) as one of the business functions of the value chain shown in Exhibit 2.

18 Value chain and classification of costs, fast food restaurant. Burger King, a hamburger fast food restaurant, incurs the following costs:

a. Cost of oil for the deep fryer
b. Wages of the counter help who give customers the food they order
c. Cost of the costume for the King on the Burger King television commercials
d. Cost of children's toys given away free with kids' meals
e. Cost of the posters indicating the special "two cheeseburgers for $2.50"
f. Costs of frozen onion rings and French fries
g. Salaries of the food specialists who create new sandwiches for the restaurant chain
h. Cost of "to-go" bags requested by customers who could not finish their meals in the restaurant

Classify each of the cost items (a–h) as one of the business functions of the value chain shown in Exhibit 2 .

19 Key success factors. Dominic Consulting has issued a report recommending changes for its newest manufacturing client, Casper Engines. Casper Engines currently manufactures a single product, which is sold and distributed nationally. The report contains the following suggestions for enhancing business performance:

a. Develop a hybrid engine to stay ahead of competitors
b. Increase training hours of assembly-line personnel to decrease the currently high volumes of scrap and waste.
c. Reduce lead times (time from customer order of product to customer receipt of product) by 20% in order to increase customer retention.
d. Negotiate faster response times with direct material suppliers to allow for lower material inventory levels
e. Benchmark the company's gross margin percentages against its major competitors.

Link each of these changes to the key success factors that are important to managers.

20 Key success factors. Morten Construction Company provides construction services for major projects. Managers at the company believe that construction is a people-management business, and they list the following as factors critical to their success:

a. Provide tools to simplify and complete construction sooner.
b. Foster cooperative relationships with suppliers that allow for more frequent deliveries as and when products are needed.
c. Integrate tools and techniques that reduce errors in construction projects.
d. Provide continuous training for employees on new tools and equipment.
e. Benchmark the company's gross margin percentages against its major competitors.

Match each of the above factors to the key success factors that are important to managers.

21 Planning and control decisions. Conner Company makes and sells brooms and mops. It takes the following actions, not necessarily in the order given. For each action (a–e) state whether it is a planning decision or a control decision.

a. Conner asks its marketing team to consider ways to get back market share from its newest competitor, Swiffer.

b. Conner calculates market share after introducing its newest product.

c. Conner compares costs it actually incurred with costs it expected to incur for the production of the new product.

d. Conner's design team proposes a new product to compete directly with the Swiffer.

e. Conner estimates the costs it will incur to sell 30,000 units of the new product in the first quarter of next fiscal year.

22 Planning and control decisions. Ed Sykes is the president of Valley Tree Service. He takes the following actions, not necessarily in the order given. For each action (**a–e**) state whether it is a planning decision or a control decision.

a. Sykes decides to expand service offerings into an adjacent market.

b. Sykes calculates the profitability of a job recently performed for the state arboretum.

c. Sykes weighs the purchase of an expensive new wood-chipping machine proposed by field managers.

d. Sykes estimates the hourly cost of providing emergency services next year to the local power company.

e. Sykes compares actual fuel costs for operating the company's equipment to budgeted costs.

23 Five-step decision-making process, manufacturing. Tadeski Foods makes frozen dinners that it sells through grocery stores. Typical products include turkey, pot roast, fried chicken, and meatloaf. The managers at Tadeski have recently proposed a line of frozen chicken pies. They take the following actions to help decide whether to launch the line.

a. Tadeski's test kitchen prepares a number of possible recipes for a consumer focus group.

b. Sales managers estimate they will sell more chicken pies in their northern sales territory than in their southern sales territory.

c. Managers discuss the possibility of introducing a new chicken pie.

d. Managers compare actual costs of making chicken pies with their budgeted costs.

e. Costs for making chicken pies are budgeted.

f. The company decides to introduce a new chicken pie.

g. To help decide whether to introduce a new chicken pie, the company researches the costs of potential ingredients.

Classify each of the actions (**a–g**) as a step in the five-step decision-making process (identify the problem and uncertainties; obtain information; make predictions about the future; make decisions by choosing among alternatives; implement the decision, evaluate performance, and learn). The actions are not listed in the order they are performed.

Required

24 Five-step decision-making process, service firm. Brook Exteriors is a firm that provides house-painting services. Richard Brook, the owner, is trying to find new ways to increase revenues. Mr. Brook performs the following actions, not in the order listed.

a. Mr. Brook decides to buy the paint sprayers rather than hire additional painters.

b. Mr. Brook discusses with his employees the possibility of using paint sprayers instead of hand painting to increase productivity and thus profits.

c. Mr. Brook learns of a large potential job that is about to go out for bids.

d. Mr. Brook compares the expected cost of buying sprayers to the expected cost of hiring more workers who paint by hand and estimates profits from both alternatives.

e. Mr. Brook estimates that using sprayers will reduce painting time by 20%.

f. Mr. Brook researches the price of paint sprayers online.

Classify each of the actions (**a–f**) according to its step in the five-step decision-making process (identify the problem and uncertainties; obtain information; make predictions about the future; make decisions by choosing among alternatives; implement the decision, evaluate performance, and learn).

Required

25 Professional ethics and reporting division performance. Maria Mendez is division controller and James Dalton is division manager of the Hestor Shoe Company. Mendez has line responsibility to Dalton, but she also has staff responsibility to the company controller.

Dalton is under severe pressure to achieve the budgeted division income for the year. He has asked Mendez to book $200,000 of revenues on December 31. The customers' orders are firm, but the shoes are still in the production process. They will be shipped on or around January 4. Dalton says to Mendez, "The key event is getting the sales order, not shipping the shoes. You should support me, not obstruct my reaching division goals."

1. Describe Mendez's ethical responsibilities.

2. What should Mendez do if Dalton gives her a direct order to book the sales?

Required

26 Professional ethics and reporting division performance. Joshua Wilson is the controller of Apex Picture Frame Mouldings, a division of Garman Enterprises. As the division is preparing to count year-end inventory, Wilson is approached by Doug Leonard, the division's president. A selection of inventory previously valued at $150,000 had been identified as flawed earlier that month and as a result was determined to be unfit for sale. Leonard tells Wilson that he has decided to count the selected items as regular inventory and that he will "deal with it when things settle down after the first of the year. After all," Leonard adds, "the auditors don't know good picture frame moulding from bad. We've had a rough year, and things are looking up for next year. Our division needs all the profits we can get this year. It's just a matter of timing the write-off." Leonard is Wilson's direct supervisor.

Required

1. Describe Wilson's ethical dilemma.
2. What should Wilson do if Leonard gives him a direct order to include the inventory?

MyAccountingLab

Required

Problems

27 Planning and control decisions, Internet company. PostNews.com offers its subscribers several services, such as an annotated TV guide and local-area information on weather, restaurants, and movie theaters. Its main revenue sources are fees for banner advertisements and fees from subscribers. Recent data are as follows:

Month/Year	Advertising Revenues	Actual Number of Subscribers	Monthly Fee per Subscriber
June 2011	$ 415,972	29,745	$15.50
December 2011	867,246	55,223	20.50
June 2012	892,134	59,641	20.50
December 2012	1,517,950	87,674	20.50
June 2013	2,976,538	147,921	20.50

The following decisions were made from June through October 2013:

a. June 2013: Raised subscription fee to $25.50 per month from July 2013 onward. The budgeted number of subscribers for this monthly fee is shown in the following table.
b. June 2013: Informed existing subscribers that from July onward, monthly fee would be $25.50.
c. July 2013: Offered e-mail service to subscribers and upgraded other online services.
d. October 2013: Dismissed the vice president of marketing after significant slowdown in subscribers and subscription revenues, based on July through September 2013 data in the following table.
e. October 2013: Reduced subscription fee to $22.50 per month from November 2013 onward.

Results for July–September 2013 are as follows:

Month/Year	Budgeted Number of Subscribers	Actual Number of Subscribers	Monthly Fee per Subscriber
July 2013	145,000	129,250	$25.50
August 2013	155,000	142,726	25.50
September 2013	165,000	145,643	25.50

Required

1. Classify each of the decisions (a–e) as a planning or a control decision.
2. Give two examples of other planning decisions and two examples of other control decisions that may be made at PostNews.com.

28 Strategic decisions and management accounting. Consider the following series of independent situations in which a firm is about to make a strategic decision.

Decisions

a. Pedro Phones is about to decide whether to launch production and sale of a cell phone with standard features.
b. Flash Computers is trying to decide whether to produce and sell a new home computer software package that includes the ability to interface with a sewing machine and a vacuum cleaner. There is no such software currently on the market.
c. Celine Cosmetics has been asked to provide a "store brand" lip gloss that will be sold at discount retail stores.
d. Nicholus Meats is considering developing a special line of gourmet bologna made with sun-dried tomatoes, pine nuts, and artichoke hearts.

Required

1. For each decision, state whether the company is following a cost leadership or a product differentiation strategy.
2. For each decision, discuss what information the management accountant can provide about the source of competitive advantage for these firms.

29 Strategic decisions and management accounting. Consider the following series of independent situations in which a firm is about to make a strategic decision.

Decisions

a. A popular restaurant is considering hiring and training inexperienced cooks. The restaurant will no longer hire experienced chefs.

b. An office supply store is considering adding a delivery service that its competitors do not have.

c. A regional airline is deciding whether to install technology that will allow passengers to check themselves in. This technology will reduce the number of desk clerks required inside the airport.

d. A local florist is considering hiring a horticulture specialist to help customers with gardening questions.

Required

1. For each decision, state whether the company is following a cost leadership or a product differentiation strategy.
2. For each decision, discuss what information the managerial accountant can provide about the source of competitive advantage for these firms.

30 Management accounting guidelines. For each of the following items, identify which of the management accounting guidelines applies: cost–benefit approach, behavioral and technical considerations, or different costs for different purposes.

1. Analyzing whether to keep the billing function within an organization or outsource it.
2. Deciding to give bonuses for superior performance to the employees in a Japanese subsidiary and extra vacation time to the employees in a Swedish subsidiary.
3. Including costs of all the value-chain functions before deciding to launch a new product, but including only its manufacturing costs in determining its inventory valuation.
4. Considering the desirability of hiring an additional salesperson.
5. Giving each salesperson the compensation option of choosing either a low salary and a high-percentage sales commission or a high salary and a low-percentage sales commission.
6. Selecting the costlier computer system after considering two systems.
7. Installing a participatory budgeting system in which managers set their own performance targets, instead of top management imposing performance targets on managers.
8. Recording research costs as an expense for financial reporting purposes (as required by U.S. GAAP) but capitalizing and expensing them over a longer period for management performance-evaluation purposes.
9. Introducing a profit-sharing plan for employees.

31 Management accounting guidelines. For each of the following items, identify which of the management accounting guidelines applies: cost–benefit approach, behavioral and technical considerations, or different costs for different purposes.

1. Analyzing whether to produce a component needed for the end product or to outsource it.
2. Deciding whether to compensate the sales force by straight commission or by salary.
3. Including costs related to administrative function to evaluate the financial performance of a division, but including only controllable costs in evaluating the manager's performance.
4. Considering the desirability of purchasing new technology.
5. Basing bonus calculations on financial measures such as return on investment or basing bonus calculations on delivery time to customer.
6. Deciding whether to buy or lease an existing production facility to increase capacity.
7. Determining the loss in future business because of poor quality but including only estimated scrap and waste as potential loss on the budgeted financial statements.

32 Role of controller, role of chief financial officer. George Jimenez is the controller at Balkin Electronics, a manufacturer of devices for the computer industry. The company may promote him to chief financial officer.

Required

1. In this table, indicate which executive is *primarily* responsible for each activity.

Activity	Controller	CFO
Managing the company's long-term investments		
Presenting the financial statements to the board of directors		
Strategic review of different lines of businesses		
Budgeting funds for a plant upgrade		
Managing accounts receivable		
Negotiating fees with auditors		
Assessing profitability of various products		
Evaluating the costs and benefits of a new product design		

2. Based on this table and your understanding of the two roles, what types of training or experience will George find most useful for the CFO position?

33 Budgeting, ethics, pharmaceutical company. Chris Jackson was recently promoted to Controller of Research and Development (R&D) for BrisCor, a *Fortune* 500 pharmaceutical company that manufactures prescription drugs and nutritional supplements. The company's total R&D cost for 2013 was expected (budgeted) to be $5 billion. During the company's midyear budget review, Chris realized that current R&D expenditures were already at $3.5 billion, nearly 40% above the midyear target. At this current rate of expenditure, the R&D division was on track to exceed its total year-end budget by $2 billion!

In a meeting with CFO Ronald Meece later that day, Jackson delivered the bad news. Meece was both shocked and outraged that the R&D spending had gotten out of control. Meece wasn't any more understanding when Jackson revealed that the excess cost was entirely related to research and development of a new drug, Vyacon, which was expected to go to market next year. The new drug would result in large profits for BrisCor, if the product could be approved by year-end.

Meece had already announced his expectations of third-quarter earnings to Wall Street analysts. If the R&D expenditures weren't reduced by the end of the third quarter, Meece was certain that the targets he had announced publicly would be missed and the company's stock price would tumble. Meece instructed Jackson to make up the budget shortfall by the end of the third quarter using "whatever means necessary."

Jackson was new to the controller's position and wanted to make sure that Meece's orders were followed. Jackson came up with the following ideas for making the third-quarter budgeted targets:

a. Stop all research and development efforts on the drug Vyacon until after year-end. This change would delay the drug going to market by at least 6 months. It is possible that in the meantime a BrisCor competitor could make it to market with a similar drug.

b. Sell off rights to the drug Martek. The company had not planned on doing this because, under current market conditions, it would get less than fair value. It would, however, result in a one-time gain that could offset the budget shortfall. Of course, all future profits from Martek would be lost.

c. Capitalize some of the company's R&D expenditures, reducing R&D expense on the income statement. This transaction would not be in accordance with GAAP, but Jackson thought it was justifiable because the Vyacon drug was going to market early next year. Jackson would argue that capitalizing R&D costs this year and expensing them next year would better match revenues and expenses.

Required

1. Referring to the "Standards of Ethical Behavior for Practitioners of Management Accounting and Financial Management," Exhibit 7, which of the preceding items (**a–c**) are acceptable to use? Which are unacceptable?

2. What would you recommend Jackson do?

34 Professional ethics and end-of-year actions. Linda Butler is the new division controller of the snack-foods division of Daniel Foods. Daniel Foods has reported a minimum 15% growth in annual earnings for each of the past 5 years. The snack-foods division has reported annual earnings growth of more than 20% each year in this same period. During the current year, the economy went into a recession. The corporate controller estimates a 10% annual earnings growth rate for Daniel Foods this year. One month before the December 31 fiscal year-end of the current year, Butler estimates the snack-foods division will report an annual earnings growth of only 8%. Rex Ray, the snack-foods division president, is not happy, but he notes that the "end-of-year actions" still need to be taken.

Butler makes some inquiries and is able to compile the following list of end-of-year actions that were more or less accepted by the previous division controller:

a. Deferring December's routine monthly maintenance on packaging equipment by an independent contractor until January of next year.

b. Extending the close of the current fiscal year beyond December 31 so that some sales of next year are included in the current year.

c. Altering dates of shipping documents of next January's sales to record them as sales in December of the current year.

d. Giving salespeople a double bonus to exceed December sales targets.

e. Deferring the current period's advertising by reducing the number of television spots run in December and running more than planned in January of next year.

f. Deferring the current period's reported advertising costs by having Daniel Foods' outside advertising agency delay billing December advertisements until January of next year or by having the agency alter invoices to conceal the December date.

g. Persuading carriers to accept merchandise for shipment in December of the current year even though they normally would not have done so.

1. Why might the snack-foods division president want to take these end-of-year actions?
2. Butler is deeply troubled and reads the "Standards of Ethical Behavior for Practitioners of Management Accounting and Financial Management" in Exhibit 7. Classify each of the end-of-year actions (**a–g**) as acceptable or unacceptable according to that document.
3. What should Butler do if Ray suggests that these end-of-year actions are taken in every division of Daniel Foods and that she will greatly harm the snack-foods division if she does not cooperate and paint the rosiest picture possible of the division's results?

Required

35 Professional ethics and end-of-year actions. Macon Publishing House produces consumer magazines. The house and home division, which sells home-improvement and home-decorating magazines, has seen a 20% reduction in operating income over the past 9 months, primarily due to an economic recession and a depressed consumer housing market. The division's controller, Rhett Gable, has felt pressure from the CFO to improve his division's operating results by the end of the year. Gable is considering the following options for improving the division's performance by year-end:

a. Cancelling two of the division's least profitable magazines, resulting in the layoff of 25 employees.
b. Selling the new printing equipment that was purchased in January and replacing it with discarded equipment from one of the company's other divisions. The previously discarded equipment no longer meets current safety standards.
c. Recognizing unearned subscription revenue (cash received in advance for magazines that will be delivered in the future) as revenue when cash is received in the current month (just before fiscal year-end) instead of showing it as a liability.
d. Reducing the division's Allowance for Bad Debt Expense. This transaction alone would increase operating income by 5%.
e. Recognizing advertising revenues that relate to January in December.
f. Switching from declining balance to straight-line depreciation to reduce depreciation expense in the current year.

1. What are the motivations for Gable to improve the division's year-end operating earnings?
2. From the point of view of the "Standards of Ethical Behavior for Practitioners of Management Accounting and Financial Management," Exhibit 7, which of the preceding items (**a–f**) are acceptable? Which are unacceptable?
3. What should Gable do about the pressure to improve performance?

Required

36 Ethical challenges, global company. Andahl Logistics, a U.S. shipping company, has just begun distributing goods across the Atlantic to Norway. The company began operations in 2011, transporting goods to South America. The company's earnings are currently trailing behind its competitors and Andahl's investors are becoming anxious. Some of the company's largest investors are even talking of selling their interest in the shipping newcomer. Andahl's CEO, Max Chang, calls an emergency meeting with his executive team. Chang needs a plan before his upcoming conference call with uneasy investors. Andahl's executive staff make the following suggestions for salvaging the company's short-term operating results:

a. Stop all transatlantic shipping efforts. The startup costs for the new operations are hurting current profit margins.
b. Make deep cuts in pricing through the end of the year to generate additional revenue.
c. Pressure current customers to take early delivery of goods before the end of the year so that more revenue can be reported in this year's financial statements.
d. Sell off distribution equipment prior to year-end. The sale would result in one-time gains that could offset the company's lagging profits. The owned equipment could be replaced with leased equipment at a lower cost in the current year.
e. Record executive year-end bonus compensation for the current year in the next year when it is paid after the December fiscal year-end.
f. Recognize sales revenues on orders received but not shipped as of the end of the year.
g. Establish corporate headquarters in Ireland before the end of the year, lowering the company's corporate tax rate from 28% to 12.5%.

1. As the management accountant for Andahl, evaluate each of the preceding items (**a–g**) in the context of the "Standards of Ethical Behavior for Practitioners of Management Accounting and Financial Management," Exhibit 7. Which of the items are in violation of these ethics standards and which are acceptable?
2. What should the management accountant do with regard to those items that are in violation of the ethical standards for management accountants?

Required

Glossary

Budget. Quantitative expression of a proposed plan of action by management for a specified period and an aid to coordinating what needs to be done to implement that plan.

Chief financial officer (CFO). Executive responsible for overseeing the financial operations of an organization. Also called *finance director*.

Control. Taking actions that implement the planning decisions, deciding how to evaluate performance, and providing feedback and learning that will help future decision making.

Controller. The financial executive primarily responsible for management accounting and financial accounting. Also called *chief accounting officer*.

Cost accounting. Measures, analyzes, and reports financial and nonfinancial information relating to the costs of acquiring or using resources in an organization. It provides information for both management accounting and financial accounting.

Cost–benefit approach. Approach to decision-making and resource allocation based on a comparison of the expected benefits from attaining company goals and the expected costs.

Cost management. The approaches and activities of managers to use resources to increase value to customers and to achieve organizational goals.

Customer relationship management (CRM). A strategy that integrates people and technology in all business functions to deepen relationships with customers, partners, and distributors.

Customer service. Providing after-sale support to customers.

Design of products and processes. The detailed planning and engineering of products and processes.

Distribution. Delivering products or services to customers.

Finance director. See *chief financial officer (CFO)*.

Financial accounting. Measures and records business transactions and provides financial statements that are based on generally accepted accounting principles. It focuses on reporting to external parties such as investors and banks.

Learning. Involves managers examining past performance and systematically exploring alternative ways to make better-informed decisions and plans in the future.

Line management. Managers (for example, in production, marketing, or distribution) who are directly responsible for attaining the goals of the organization.

Management accounting. Measures, analyzes, and reports financial and nonfinancial information that helps managers make decisions to fulfill the goals of an organization. It focuses on internal reporting.

Marketing. Promoting and selling products or services to customers or prospective customers.

Planning. Selecting organization goals, predicting results under various alternative ways of achieving those goals, deciding how to attain the desired goals, and communicating the goals and how to attain them to the entire organization.

Production. Acquiring, coordinating, and assembling resources to produce a product or deliver a service.

Research and development (R&D). Generating and experimenting with ideas related to new products, services, or processes.

Staff management. Staff (such as management accountants and human resources managers) who provide advice and assistance to line management.

Strategic cost management. Describes cost management that specifically focuses on strategic issues.

Strategy. Specifies how an organization matches its own capabilities with the opportunities in the marketplace to accomplish its objectives.

Supply chain. Describes the flow of goods, services, and information from the initial sources of materials and services to the delivery of products to consumers, regardless of whether those activities occur in the same organization or in other organizations.

Sustainability. The development and implementation of strategies to achieve long-term financial, social, and environmental goals.

Total quality management (TQM). An integrative philosophy of management for continuously improving the quality of products and processes.

Value chain. The sequence of business functions in which customer usefulness is added to products or services of a company.

Photo Credits

Credits are listed in order of appearance.

Chapter 2

An Introduction to Cost Terms and Purposes

From Chapter 2 of *Cost Accounting: A Managerial Emphasis,* Fifteenth Edition. Charles T. Horngren, Srikant M. Datar, Madhav V. Rajan. Copyright © 2015 by Pearson Education, Inc. All rights reserved.

An Introduction to Cost Terms and Purposes

What does the word *cost* mean to you?

Is it the price you pay for something of value, like a cell phone? A cash outflow, like monthly rent? Something that affects profitability, like salaries? Organizations, like individuals, deal with different types of costs. At different times organizations put more or less emphasis on these costs. When times are good, companies often focus on selling as much as they can, with costs taking a backseat. But when times get tough, companies shift their emphasis from selling to cutting costs. Unfortunately, when times are really bad, companies may find that they are unable to cut costs fast enough, leading bankruptcy, as was the case with Hostess Brands.

High Fixed Costs Bankrupt Twinkie Maker[1]

In 2012, Hostess Brands—owner of the iconic Twinkies lunchbox snack—announced it would go out of business and liquidate its assets. Declining sales and trends toward healthier snacking crippled the company given its high fixed costs—costs that did not decrease as the number of Twinkies and Ho Hos sold declined.

After emerging from bankruptcy in 2009, Hostess management tried to turn around the company's fortunes through innovation and workplace efficiency. Despite initial progress reducing its variable costs, the prices of the commodities that Hostess relied on—corn, sugar, and flour—increased during the recession. Unfortunately for Hostess, the remaining large percentage of its operating costs were fixed because union contracts made it difficult to close facilities, consolidate distribution routes, or reduce pensions owed to retired workers.

By the second half of 2011, Hostess was losing $2 million per week. With a stifling debt burden, the company filed for bankruptcy protection again in January 2012. Further cost reductions proved elusive and controversial negotiations with unions resulted in thousands of employees striking that November. Within days, Hostess collapsed under the weight of its fixed costs and filed to liquidate its assets. The wind down resulted in the closure of 33 bakeries, 565 distribution centers, about 5,500 delivery routes, and 570 bakery outlet stores and the loss of 18,500 jobs.

As the story of Hostess Brands illustrates, managers must understand their firms' costs and closely manage them. Organizations as varied as the United Way, the Mayo

---

[1] *Sources:* David A. Kaplan, "Hostess is Bankrupt... Again," *Fortune* (July 26, 2012); Rachel Feintzing, Mike Spector, and Julie Jargon, "Twinkie Maker Hostess to Close," *The Wall Street Journal* (November 16, 2012); "Hostess Brands Obtains Court Authority to Wind Down All Operations, Liquidate Assets, Hostess Brands press release (Irving, TX, November 21, 2012).

Clinic, and Sony generate reports containing a variety of cost concepts and terms managers need to understand to effectively use the reports to run their businesses. This chapter discusses cost concepts and terms that are the basis of accounting information used for internal and external reporting.

Costs and Cost Terminology

Learning Objective 1

Define and illustrate a cost object

...examples of cost objects are products, services, activities, processes, and customers

A **cost** is a resource sacrificed or forgone to achieve a specific objective. A cost (such as the cost of labor or advertising) is usually measured as the monetary amount that must be paid to acquire goods or services. An **actual cost** is the cost incurred (a historical or past cost), as distinguished from a **budgeted cost,** which is a predicted, or forecasted, cost (a future cost).

When you think of a cost, you invariably think of it in the context of putting a price on a particular thing. We call this "thing" a **cost object,** which is anything for which a cost measurement is desired. Suppose you're a manager at BMW's automotive manufacturing plant in Spartanburg, South Carolina. Can you identify some of the plant's cost objects? Now look at Exhibit 1.

You will see that BMW managers not only want to know the cost of various products, such as the BMW X6 sports activity vehicle, but they also want to know the costs of services, projects, customers, activities, and departments. Managers use their knowledge of these costs to guide decisions about, for example, product innovation, quality, and customer service.

Now think about whether a manager at BMW might want to know the *budgeted cost* or the *actual cost* of a cost object. Managers almost always need to know both types of costs when making decisions. For example, comparing budgeted costs to actual costs helps managers evaluate how well they did controlling costs and learn about how they can do better in the future.

How does a cost system determine the costs of various cost objects? Typically in two stages: accumulation followed by assignment. **Cost accumulation** is the collection of cost data in some organized way by means of an accounting system. For example, at its Spartanburg plant, BMW collects (accumulates) in various categories the costs of different types of materials, different classifications of labor, the costs incurred for supervision, and so on. The accumulated costs are then *assigned* to designated cost objects, such as the different models of cars that BMW manufactures at the plant. BMW managers use this cost information in two main ways: (1) when *making* decisions, for instance, about how to price different models of cars or how much to invest in R&D and marketing and (2) for *implementing* decisions, by influencing and motivating employees to act, for example, by providing bonuses to employees for reducing costs.

Now that we know why it is useful for management accountants to assign costs, we turn our attention to some concepts that will help us do it. Again, think of the different types of costs that we just discussed—materials, labor, and supervision. You are probably thinking that some costs, such as the costs of materials, are easier to assign to a cost object than others, such as the costs of supervision. As you will learn, this is indeed the case.

Decision Point

What is the cost object?

Exhibit 1	Examples of Cost Objects at BMW

Cost Object	Illustration
Product	A BMW X6 sports activity vehicle
Service	Telephone hotline providing information and assistance to BMW dealers
Project	R&D project on enhancing the DVD system in BMW cars
Customer	Herb Chambers Motors, the BMW dealer that purchases a broad range of BMW vehicles
Activity	Setting up machines for production or maintaining production equipment
Department	Environmental, health, and safety department

Learning Objective 2

Distinguish between direct costs

...costs that are traced to the cost object

and indirect costs

...costs that are allocated to the cost object

Direct Costs and Indirect Costs

We now describe how costs are classified as direct and indirect costs and the methods used to assign these costs to cost objects.

- **Direct costs of a cost object** are related to the particular cost object and can be traced to it in an economically feasible (cost-effective) way. For example, the cost of steel or tires is a direct cost of BMW X6s. The cost of the steel or tires can be easily traced to or identified with the BMW X6. The workers on the BMW X6 line request materials from the warehouse, and the material requisition document identifies the cost of the materials supplied to the X6. Similarly, individual workers record on their time sheets the hours and minutes they spend working on the X6. The cost of this labor can easily be traced to the X6 and is another example of a direct cost. The term **cost tracing** is used to describe the assignment of direct costs to a particular cost object.

- **Indirect costs of a cost object** are related to the particular cost object but cannot be traced to it in an economically feasible (cost-effective) way. For example, the salaries of plant administrators (including the plant manager) who oversee production of the many different types of cars produced at the Spartanburg plant are an indirect cost of the X6s. Plant administration costs are related to the cost object (X6s) because plant administration is necessary for managing the production of these vehicles. Plant administration costs are indirect costs because plant administrators also oversee the production of other products, such as the Z4 Roadster. Unlike steel or tires, there is no specific request made by supervisors of the X6 production line for plant administration services, and it is virtually impossible to trace plant administration costs to the X6 line.

    The term **cost allocation** is used to describe the assignment of indirect costs to a particular cost object. **Cost assignment** is a general term that encompasses both (1) tracing direct costs to a cost object and (2) allocating indirect costs to a cost object. Exhibit 2 depicts direct costs and indirect costs and both forms of cost assignment—cost tracing and cost allocation—using the BMW X6 as an example.

Exhibit 2
Cost Assignment to a Cost Object

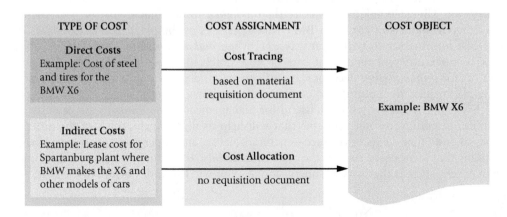

Cost Allocation Challenges

Managers want to assign costs accurately to cost objects because inaccurate product costs will mislead managers about the profitability of different products. This, for example, could result in the managers unknowingly working harder to promote less-profitable products instead of more-profitable products. Generally, managers are more confident about the accuracy of the direct costs of cost objects, such as the cost of steel and tires of the X6.

Consider the cost to lease the Spartanburg plant. This cost is an indirect cost of the X6—there is no separate lease agreement for the area of the plant where the X6 is made. Nonetheless, BMW *allocates* to the X6 a part of the lease cost of the building—for example, on the basis of an estimate of the percentage of the building's floor space occupied for the production of the X6 relative to the total floor space used to produce all models of cars. This approach measures the building resources used by each car model reasonably and accurately. The more floor space a car model occupies, the greater the lease costs assigned to it. Accurately allocating other indirect costs, such as plant administration, to the X6, however, is more difficult. For example, should these costs be allocated on the basis of the number of employees working on each car model or the number of cars produced of each model? Measuring the share of plant administration used by each car model is not clear-cut.

Factors Affecting Direct/Indirect Cost Classifications

Several factors affect whether a cost is classified as direct or indirect:

- **The materiality of the cost in question.** The smaller the amount of a cost—that is, the more immaterial the cost is—the less likely it is economically feasible to trace it to a particular cost object. Consider a mail-order catalog company such as Lands' End. It would be economically feasible to trace the courier charge for delivering a package to an individual customer as a direct cost. In contrast, the cost of the invoice paper included in the package would be classified as an indirect cost. Why? Although the cost of the paper can be traced to each customer, it is not cost-effective to do so. The benefits of knowing that, say, exactly 0.5¢ worth of paper is included in each package do not exceed the data processing and administrative costs of tracing the cost to each package. The time of the sales administrator, who earns a salary of $45,000 a year, is better spent organizing customer information to help with a company's marketing efforts than tracking the cost of paper.

- **Available information-gathering technology.** Improvements in information-gathering technology make it possible to consider more and more costs as direct costs. Bar codes, for example, allow manufacturing plants to treat certain low-cost materials such as clips and screws, which were previously classified as indirect costs, as direct costs of products. At Dell, component parts such as the computer chip and the DVD drive display a bar code that can be scanned at every point in the production process. Bar codes can be read into a manufacturing cost file by waving a "wand" in the same quick and efficient way supermarket checkout clerks enter the cost of each item purchased by a customer.

- **Design of operations.** Classifying a cost as direct is easier if a company's facility (or some part of it) is used exclusively for a specific cost object, such as a specific product or a particular customer. For example, General Chemicals classifies the cost of its facility dedicated to manufacturing soda ash (sodium carbonate) as a direct cost of soda ash.

Be aware that a specific cost may be both a direct cost of one cost object and an indirect cost of another cost object. *That is, the direct/indirect classification depends on the choice of the cost object.* For example, the salary of an assembly department supervisor at BMW is a direct cost if the cost object is the assembly department. However, because the assembly department assembles many different models, the supervisor's salary is an indirect cost if the cost object is a product such as the BMW X6 sports activity vehicle. A useful rule to remember is that the broader the cost object definition is—the assembly department rather than the X6—the higher the proportion direct costs are of total costs and the more confident a manager will be about the accuracy of the resulting cost amounts.

Decision Point

How do managers decide whether a cost is a direct or an indirect cost?

Learning Objective 3

Explain variable costs and fixed costs

...the two basic ways in which costs behave

Cost-Behavior Patterns: Variable Costs and Fixed Costs

Costing systems record the cost of resources acquired, such as materials, labor, and equipment, and track how those resources are used to produce and sell products or services. Recording the costs of resources acquired and used allows managers to see how costs behave. Consider two basic types of cost-behavior patterns found in many accounting systems. A **variable cost** changes *in total* in proportion to changes in the related level of total activity or volume of output produced. A **fixed cost** remains unchanged *in total* for a given time period, despite wide changes in the related level of total activity or volume of output produced. Costs are defined as variable or fixed for *a specific activity* and for *a given time period*. Identifying a cost as variable or fixed provides valuable information for making many management decisions and is an important input when evaluating performance. To illustrate these two basic types of costs, again consider the costs at BMW's Spartanburg, South Carolina, plant.

1. **Variable costs.** If BMW buys a steering wheel at $600 for each of its BMW X6 vehicles, then the total cost of steering wheels is $600 times the number of vehicles produced, as the following table illustrates.

Number of X6s Produced (1)	Variable Cost per Steering Wheel (2)	Total Variable Cost of Steering Wheels (3) = (1) × (2)
1	$600	$ 600
1,000	600	600,000
3,000	600	1,800,000

The steering wheel cost is an example of a variable cost because *total cost* changes in proportion to changes in the number of vehicles produced. However, the cost per unit of a variable cost is constant. For example, the variable cost per steering wheel in column 2 is the same regardless of whether 1,000 or 3,000 X6s are produced. As a result, the total variable cost of steering wheels in column 3 changes proportionately with the number of X6s produced in column 1. So, when considering how variable costs behave, always focus on *total* costs.

Panel A in Exhibit 3 shows a graph of the total variable cost of steering wheels. The cost is represented by a straight line that climbs from left to right. The phrases "strictly variable" and "proportionately variable" are sometimes used to describe the variable cost behavior shown in this panel.

Now consider an example of a variable cost for a different activity—the $20 hourly wage paid each worker to set up machines at the Spartanburg plant. The setup labor cost is a variable cost for setup hours because setup cost changes in total in proportion to the number of setup hours used.

Exhibit 3

Graphs of Variable and Fixed Costs

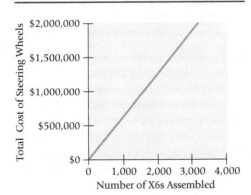

PANEL A: Variable Cost of Steering Wheels at $600 per BMW X6 Assembled

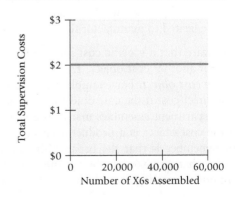

PANEL B: Supervision Costs for the BMW X6 assembly line (in millions)

2. **Fixed costs.** Suppose BMW incurs a total cost of $2,000,000 per year for supervisors who work exclusively on the X6 line. These costs are unchanged in total over a designated range of vehicles produced during a given time span (see Exhibit 3, Panel B). Fixed costs become smaller and smaller on a per-unit basis as the number of vehicles assembled increases, as the following table shows.

Annual Total Fixed Supervision Costs for BMW X6 Assembly Line (1)	Number of X6s Produced (2)	Fixed Supervision Cost per X6 (3) = (1) ÷ (2)
$2,000,000	10,000	$200
$2,000,000	25,000	80
$2,000,000	50,000	40

It is precisely because *total* line supervision costs are fixed at $2,000,000 that fixed supervision cost per X6 decreases as the number of X6s produced increases; the same fixed cost is spread over a larger number of X6s. Do not be misled by the change in fixed cost per unit. Just as in the case of variable costs, when considering fixed costs, always focus on *total costs*. Costs are fixed when total costs remain unchanged despite significant changes in the level of total activity or volume.

Why are some costs variable and other costs fixed? Recall that a cost is usually measured as the amount of money that must be paid to acquire goods and services. The total cost of steering wheels is a variable cost because BMW buys the steering wheels only when they are needed. As more X6s are produced, proportionately more steering wheels are acquired and proportionately more costs are incurred.

Contrast the plant's variable costs with the $2,000,000 of fixed costs per year incurred for the supervision of the X6 assembly line. This level of supervision is acquired and put in place well before BMW uses it to produce X6s and before BMW even knows how many X6s it will produce. Suppose that BMW puts in place supervisors capable of supervising the production of 60,000 X6s each year. If the demand is for only 55,000 X6s, there will be idle capacity. Supervisors on the X6 line could have supervised the production of 60,000 X6s but will supervise only 55,000 X6s because of the lower demand. However, BMW must pay for the unused line supervision capacity because the cost of supervision cannot be reduced in the short run. If demand is even lower—say only 50,000 X6s are demanded—the plant's line supervision costs will still be $2,000,000, and its idle capacity will increase.

Unlike variable costs, fixed costs of resources (such as for line supervision) cannot be quickly and easily changed to match the resources needed or used. Over time, however, managers can take action to reduce a company's fixed costs. For example, if the X6 line needs to be run for fewer hours because the demand for the vehicles falls, BMW may lay off supervisors or move them to another production line. Unlike variable costs that go away automatically if the resources are not used, reducing fixed costs requires active intervention on the part of managers.

Do not assume that individual cost items are inherently variable or fixed. Consider labor costs. Labor costs can be purely variable for units produced when workers are paid on a piece-unit basis (for each unit they make). For example, some companies pay garment workers on a per-shirt-sewed basis, so the firms' labor costs are variable. That is, the costs depend on how many shirts each worker makes. In contrast, other companies negotiate labor union agreements with set annual salaries that contain no-layoff clauses for workers. At a company such as this, the salaries would appropriately be classified as fixed. For decades, Japanese companies provided their workers a lifetime guarantee of employment. Although such a guarantee entails higher fixed labor costs, a firm can benefit from it because workers are more loyal and dedicated, which can improve productivity. However, during an economic downturn, the company risks losing money if its revenues decrease while its fixed costs remain unchanged. The recent global economic crisis has made companies very reluctant to lock in fixed costs. Concepts in Action: Zipcar Helps Twitter Reduce Fixed Costs describes how a car-sharing service offers companies the opportunity to convert the fixed costs of owning corporate cars into variable costs by renting cars on an as-needed basis.

A particular cost item could be variable for one level of activity and fixed for another. Consider annual registration and license costs for a fleet of planes owned by an airline company. Registration and license costs would be a variable cost that would change with the number of planes the company owned. But the registration and license costs for a particular plane are fixed regardless of the miles flown by that plane during a year.

Some costs have both fixed and variable elements and are called *mixed* or *semivariable* costs. For example, a company's telephone costs may consist of a fixed monthly cost as well as a cost per phone-minute used.

Decision Point ▶

How do managers decide whether a cost is a variable or a fixed cost?

Cost Drivers

A **cost driver** is a variable, such as the level of activity or volume, that causally affects costs over a given time span. An *activity* is an event, task, or unit of work with a specified purpose—for example, designing products, setting up machines, or testing products. The level of activity or volume is a cost driver if there is a cause-and-effect relationship between a change in the level of activity or volume and a change in the level of total costs. For example, if product-design costs change with the number of parts in a product, the

Concepts in Action ▶ Zipcar Helps Twitter Reduce Fixed Costs

In many North American and European cities, Avis subsidiary Zipcar has emerged as a way for corporations to reduce the spending on gas, insurance, and parking of corporate cars. Zipcar—which provides an "on-demand" option for urban individuals and businesses to rent a car by the week, the day, or even the hour—has rates beginning around $8 per hour and $75 per day (including gas, insurance, and about 180 miles per day).

Let's think about what Zipcar means for companies. Many small businesses own a company car or two for getting to meetings, making deliveries, and running errands. Similarly, many large companies own a fleet of cars to shuttle visiting executives and clients back and forth from appointments, business lunches, and the airport. Traditionally, owning these cars has involved very high fixed costs, including buying the asset (car), maintenance costs, and insurance for multiple drivers.

Now, however, companies like Twitter can use Zipcar for on-demand mobility while reducing their transportation and overhead costs. Based in downtown San Francisco, Twitter managers use Zipcar to meet venture capitalists and partners in Silicon Valley and when they travel to places like New York and Boston. "We wanted to avoid the cost of taking taxis everywhere or the time delays of mass transit," said Jack Dorsey, the micro-blogging service's co-founder. "Zipcar's the fastest, easiest way to get around town."

From a business perspective, Zipcar allows Twitter and other companies to convert the fixed costs of owning a company car to variable costs. If business slows or a car isn't required to visit a client, Twitter is not saddled with the fixed costs of car ownership. Of course, when business is good, causing Twitter managers to use Zipcar more often, they can end up paying more overall than they would have paid if they purchased and maintained the car themselves.

Along with cutting corporate spending, car sharing services like Zipcar reduce congestion on the road and promote environmental sustainability. Users report reducing their vehicle miles traveled by 44%, and surveys show CO_2 emissions are being cut by up to 50% per user.

Sources: Based on Paul Keegan, "Zipcar–the best new idea in business." *Fortune* (August 27, 2009); Elizabeth Olsen, "Car sharing reinvents the company wheels." *New York Times* (May 7, 2009); John Kell, Avis to Buy Car-Sharing Service Zipcar," *The Wall Street Journal* (Jnauary 2, 2013); Zipcar, Inc., "Zipcar for business case studies"; Zipcar, Inc., "Zipcar rates and plans."

number of parts is a cost driver of product-design costs. Similarly, miles driven is often a cost driver of distribution costs.

The cost driver of a variable cost is the level of activity or volume whose change causes proportionate changes in the variable cost. For example, the number of vehicles assembled is the cost driver of the total cost of steering wheels. If setup workers are paid an hourly wage, the number of setup hours is the cost driver of total (variable) setup costs.

Costs that are fixed in the short run have no cost driver in the short run but may have a cost driver in the long run. Consider the costs of testing, say, 0.1% of the color printers produced at a Hewlett-Packard plant. These costs consist of equipment and staff costs of the testing department, which are difficult to change. Consequently, they are fixed in the short run regardless of changes in the volume of production. In this case, volume of production is not a cost driver of testing costs in the short run. In the long run, however, Hewlett-Packard will increase or decrease the testing department's equipment and staff to the levels needed to support future production volumes. In the long run, volume of production is indeed a cost driver of testing costs. Costing systems that identify the cost of each activity such as testing, design, or setup are called *activity-based costing systems*.

Relevant Range

Relevant range is the band or range of normal activity level or volume in which there is a specific relationship between the level of activity or volume and the cost in question. For example, a fixed cost is fixed only in relation to a given wide range of total activity or volume (at which the company is expected to operate) and only for a given time span (usually a particular budget period). Suppose BMW contracts with Thomas Transport Company (TTC) to transport X6s to BMW dealerships. TTC rents two trucks, and each truck has an annual fixed rental cost of $40,000. The maximum annual usage of each truck is 120,000 miles. In the current year (2014), the predicted combined total hauling of the two trucks is 170,000 miles.

Exhibit 4 shows how annual fixed costs behave at different levels of miles of hauling. Up to 120,000 miles, TTC can operate with one truck; from 120,001 to 240,000 miles, it operates with two trucks; and from 240,001 to 360,000 miles, it operates with three trucks. This pattern will continue as TTC adds trucks to its fleet to provide more miles of hauling. Given the predicted 170,000-mile usage for 2014, the range from 120,001 to 240,000 miles hauled is the range in which TTC expects to operate, resulting in fixed rental costs of $80,000. Within this relevant range, changes in miles hauled will not affect the annual fixed costs.

Fixed costs may change from one year to the next, though. For example, if the total rental fee of the two trucks increases by $2,000 for 2015, the total level of fixed costs will increase to $82,000 (all else remaining the same). If that increase occurs, total rental costs will be fixed at this new level ($82,000) for 2015 for the miles hauled in the 120,001 to 240,000 range.

The relevant range also applies to variable costs. Outside the relevant range, variable costs, such as direct materials costs, may no longer change proportionately with changes in production volumes. For example, above a certain volume, the cost of direct materials may increase at a lower rate because a firm may be able to negotiate price discounts for purchasing greater amounts of materials from its suppliers.

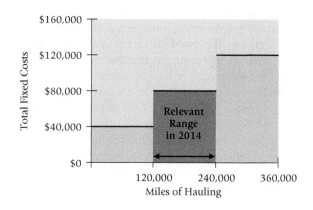

Exhibit 4

Fixed-Cost Behavior at Thomas Transport Company

Assignment of Costs to Cost Object

	Direct Costs	Indirect Costs
Variable Costs	• Cost object: BMW X6s produced Example: Tires used in assembly of automobile	• Cost object: BMW X6s produced Example: Power costs at Spartanburg plant. Power usage is metered only to the plant, where multiple products are assembled.
Fixed Costs	• Cost object: BMW X6s produced Example: Salary of supervisor on BMW X6 assembly line	• Cost object: BMW X6s produced Example: Annual lease costs at Spartanburg plant. Lease is for whole plant, where multiple products are produced.

Cost-Behavior Pattern

Relationships Between Types of Costs

We have introduced two major classifications of costs: direct/indirect and variable/fixed. Costs may simultaneously be as follows:

- Direct and variable
- Direct and fixed
- Indirect and variable
- Indirect and fixed

Exhibit 5 shows examples of costs in each of these four cost classifications for the BMW X6.

Total Costs and Unit Costs

The preceding section concentrated on the behavior patterns of total costs in relation to activity or volume levels. We now consider unit costs.

Unit Costs

A **unit cost**, also called an **average cost**, is calculated by dividing the total cost by the related number of units produced. In many decision contexts, calculating a unit cost is essential. Consider the booking agent who has to make the decision to book Paul McCartney to play at Shea Stadium. She estimates the cost of the event to be $4,000,000. This knowledge is helpful for the decision, but it is not enough.

Before reaching a decision, the booking agent also must predict the number of people who will attend. Without knowing the number of attendees, she cannot make an informed decision about the admission price she needs to charge to recover the cost of the event or even on whether to have the event at all. So she computes the unit cost of the event by dividing the total cost ($4,000,000) by the expected number of people who will attend. If 50,000 people attend, the unit cost is $80 ($4,000,000 ÷ 50,000) per person; if 20,000 attend, the unit cost increases to $200 ($4,000,000 ÷ 20,000). Unless the total cost is "unitized" (that is, averaged by the level of activity or volume), the $4,000,000 cost is difficult to interpret. The unit cost combines the total cost and the number of people in a simple and understandable way.

Accounting systems typically report both total-cost amounts and average-cost-per-unit amounts. The units might be expressed in various ways. Examples are automobiles assembled, packages delivered, or hours worked. Consider Tennessee Products, a manufacturer of speaker systems with a plant in Memphis. Suppose that, in 2014, its first year of operations, the company incurs $40,000,000 of manufacturing costs to produce 500,000 speaker systems. Then the unit cost is $80:

$$\frac{\text{Total manufacturing costs}}{\text{Number of units manufactured}} = \frac{\$40,000,000}{500,000 \text{ units}} = \$80 \text{ per unit}$$

If 480,000 units are sold and 20,000 units remain in ending inventory, the unit-cost concept helps managers determine total costs in the income statement and balance sheet and, therefore, the financial results Tennessee Products reports to shareholders, banks, and the government.

Cost of goods sold in the income statement, 480,000 units × $80 per unit	$38,400,000
Ending inventory in the balance sheet, 20,000 units × $80 per unit	1,600,000
Total manufacturing costs of 500,000 units	$40,000,000

Unit costs are found in all areas of the value chain—for example, the unit cost of a product design, a sales visit, and a customer-service call. By summing unit costs throughout the value chain, managers calculate the unit cost of the different products or services they deliver and determine the profitability of each product or service. Managers use this information, for example, to decide the products in which they should invest more resources, such as R&D and marketing, and the prices they should charge.

Use Unit Costs Cautiously

Although unit costs are regularly used in financial reports and for making product mix and pricing decisions, *managers should think in terms of total costs rather than unit costs for many decisions.* Consider the manager of the Memphis plant of Tennessee Products. Assume the $40,000,000 in costs in 2014 consist of $10,000,000 of fixed costs and $30,000,000 of variable costs (at $60 variable cost per speaker system produced). Suppose the total fixed costs and the variable cost per speaker system in 2015 are expected to be unchanged from 2014. The budgeted costs for 2015 at different production levels, calculated on the basis of total variable costs, total fixed costs, and total costs, are:

Units Produced (1)	Variable Cost per Unit (2)	Total Variable Costs (3) = (1) × (2)	Total Fixed Costs (4)	Total Costs (5) = (3) + (4)	Unit Cost (6) = (5) ÷ (1)
100,000	$60	$ 6,000,000	$10,000,000	$16,000,000	$160.00
200,000	$60	$12,000,000	$10,000,000	$22,000,000	$110.00
500,000	$60	$30,000,000	$10,000,000	$40,000,000	$ 80.00
800,000	$60	$48,000,000	$10,000,000	$58,000,000	$ 72.50
1,000,000	$60	$60,000,000	$10,000,000	$70,000,000	$ 70.00

A plant manager who uses the 2014 unit cost of $80 per unit will underestimate actual total costs if the plant's 2015 output is below the 2014 level of 500,000 units. If the volume produced falls to 200,000 units due to, say, the presence of a new competitor and less demand, actual costs would be $22,000,000. The unit cost of $80 times 200,000 units equals $16,000,000, which underestimates the actual total costs by $6,000,000 ($22,000,000 − $16,000,000). In other words, *the unit cost of $80 applies only when the company produces 500,000 units.*

An overreliance on the unit cost in this situation could lead to insufficient cash being available to pay the company's costs if volume declines to 200,000 units. As the table indicates, for making this decision, managers should think in terms of total variable costs, total fixed costs, and total costs rather than unit cost. As a general rule, first calculate total costs, then compute the unit cost, if it is needed for a particular decision.

◀ Decision Point
How should managers estimate and interpret cost information?

Learning Objective 5

Distinguish inventoriable costs

...assets when incurred, then cost of goods sold

from period costs

...expenses of the period when incurred

Business Sectors, Types of Inventory, Inventoriable Costs, and Period Costs

In this section, we describe the different sectors of the economy, the different types of inventory that companies hold, and some commonly used classifications of manufacturing costs.

Manufacturing-, Merchandising-, and Service-Sector Companies

We define three sectors of the economy and provide examples of companies in each sector.

1. **Manufacturing-sector companies** purchase materials and components and convert them into various finished goods. Examples are automotive companies such as Jaguar, cellular-phone producers such as Nokia, food-processing companies such as Heinz, and computer companies such as Toshiba.

2. **Merchandising-sector companies** purchase and then sell tangible products without changing their basic form. This sector includes companies engaged in retailing (for example, bookstores such as Barnes & Noble and department stores such as Target); distribution (for example, a supplier of hospital products, such as Owens and Minor); or wholesaling (for example, a supplier of electronic components such as Arrow Electronics).

3. **Service-sector companies** provide services (intangible products)—for example, legal advice or audits—to their customers. Examples are law firms such as Wachtell, Lipton, Rosen & Katz; accounting firms such as Ernst & Young; banks such as Barclays; mutual fund companies such as Fidelity; insurance companies such as Aetna; transportation companies such as Singapore Airlines; advertising agencies such as Saatchi & Saatchi; television stations such as Turner Broadcasting; Internet service providers such as Comcast; travel agencies such as American Express; and brokerage firms such as Merrill Lynch.

Types of Inventory

Manufacturing-sector companies purchase materials and components and convert them into finished goods. These companies typically have one or more of the following three types of inventory:

1. **Direct materials inventory.** Direct materials in stock that will be used in the manufacturing process (for example, computer chips and components needed to manufacture cellular phones).

2. **Work-in-process inventory.** Goods partially worked on but not yet completed (for example, cellular phones at various stages of completion in the manufacturing process). This is also called **work in progress**.

3. **Finished goods inventory.** Goods (for example, cellular phones) completed but not yet sold.

Merchandising-sector companies purchase tangible products and then sell them without changing their basic form. These companies hold only one type of inventory, which is products in their original purchased form, called *merchandise inventory*. Service-sector companies provide only services or intangible products and do not hold inventories of tangible products.

Commonly Used Classifications of Manufacturing Costs

Three terms commonly used when describing manufacturing costs are *direct materials costs, direct manufacturing labor costs,* and *indirect manufacturing costs*. These terms build on the direct versus indirect cost distinction we described earlier in the context of manufacturing costs.

1. **Direct materials costs** are the acquisition costs of all materials that eventually become part of the cost object (work in process and then finished goods) and can be traced to the cost object in an economically feasible way. The steel and tires used to make the BMW X6 and the computer chips used to make cellular phones are examples of direct material costs. Note that the costs of direct materials include not only the cost of the materials themselves but the freight-in (inward delivery) charges, sales taxes, and customs duties that must be paid to acquire them.

2. **Direct manufacturing labor costs** include the compensation of all manufacturing labor that can be traced to the cost object (work in process and then finished goods) in an economically feasible way. Examples include wages and fringe benefits paid to machine operators and assembly-line workers who convert direct materials to finished goods.

3. **Indirect manufacturing costs** are all manufacturing costs that are related to the cost object (work in process and then finished goods) but cannot be traced to that cost object in an economically feasible way. Examples include supplies, indirect materials such as lubricants, indirect manufacturing labor such as plant maintenance and cleaning labor, plant rent, plant insurance, property taxes on the plant, plant depreciation, and the compensation of plant managers. This cost category is also referred to as **manufacturing overhead costs** or **factory overhead costs**. We use *indirect manufacturing costs* and *manufacturing overhead costs* interchangeably in this text.

We now describe the distinction between inventoriable costs and period costs.

Inventoriable Costs

Inventoriable costs are all costs of a product that are considered assets in a company's balance sheet when the costs are incurred and that are expensed as cost of goods sold only when the product is sold. For manufacturing-sector companies, all manufacturing costs are inventoriable costs. The costs first accumulate as work-in-process inventory assets (in other words, they are "inventoried") and then as finished goods inventory assets. Consider Cellular Products, a manufacturer of cellular phones. The cost of the company's direct materials, such as computer chips, direct manufacturing labor costs, and manufacturing overhead costs create new assets. They start out as work in process inventory and become finished goods inventory (the cellular phones). When the cellular phones are sold, the costs move from being assets to cost of goods sold expense. This cost is matched against **revenues,** which are inflows of assets (usually cash or accounts receivable) received for products or services customers purchase.

Note that the cost of goods sold includes all manufacturing costs (direct materials, direct manufacturing labor, and manufacturing overhead costs) incurred to produce them. The cellular phones may be sold during a different accounting period than the period in which they were manufactured. Thus, inventorying manufacturing costs in the balance sheet during the accounting period when the phones are manufactured and expensing the manufacturing costs in a later income statement when the phones are sold matches revenues and expenses.

For merchandising-sector companies such as Walmart, inventoriable costs are the costs of purchasing goods that are resold in their same form. These costs are made up of the costs of the goods themselves plus any incoming freight, insurance, and handling costs for those goods. Service-sector companies provide only services or intangible products. The absence of inventories of tangible products for sale means service-sector companies have no inventoriable costs.

Period Costs

Period costs are all costs in the income statement other than cost of goods sold. Period costs, such as marketing, distribution, and customer service costs, are treated as expenses of the accounting period in which they are incurred because managers expect these costs

Exhibit 6

Examples of Period Costs in Combinations of the Direct/Indirect and Variable/Fixed Cost Classifications at a Bank

Assignment of Costs to Cost Object

Cost-Behavior Pattern	Direct Costs	Indirect Costs
Variable Costs	• Cost object: Number of mortgage loans Example: Fees paid to property appraisal company for each mortgage loan	• Cost object: Number of mortgage loans Example: Postage paid to deliver mortgage-loan documents to lawyers/homeowners
Fixed Costs	• Cost object: Number of mortgage loans Example: Salary paid to executives in mortgage loan department to develop new mortgage-loan products	• Cost object: Number of mortgage loans Example: Cost to the bank of sponsoring annual golf tournament

to increase revenues in only that period and not in future periods. Some costs such as R&D costs are treated as period costs because, although these costs may increase revenues in a future period if the R&D efforts are successful, it is highly uncertain if and when these increased revenues will occur. Expensing period costs as they are incurred best matches expenses to revenues.

For manufacturing-sector companies, all nonmanufacturing costs (for example, design costs and costs of shipping products to customers) in the income statement are period costs. For merchandising-sector companies, all costs in the income statement not related to the cost of goods purchased for resale are period costs. Examples of these period costs are labor costs of sales-floor personnel and advertising costs. Because there are no inventoriable costs for service-sector companies, all costs in the income statement are period costs.

Exhibit 5 showed examples of inventoriable costs in direct/indirect and variable/fixed cost classifications for a car manufacturer. Exhibit 6 shows examples of period costs in direct/indirect and variable/fixed cost classifications at a bank.

Decision Point

What are the differences in the accounting for inventoriable versus period costs?

Illustrating the Flow of Inventoriable Costs and Period Costs

Learning Objective 6

Illustrate the flow of inventoriable and period costs

...in manufacturing settings, inventoriable costs flow through work-in-process and finished goods accounts and are expensed when goods are sold; period costs are always expensed as incurred

We illustrate the flow of inventoriable costs and period costs through the income statement of a manufacturing company, where the distinction between inventoriable costs and period costs is most detailed.

Manufacturing-Sector Example

Follow the flow of costs for Cellular Products in Exhibits 7 and 8. Exhibit 7 visually highlights the differences in the flow of inventoriable and period costs for a manufacturing-sector company. Note how, as described in the previous section, inventoriable costs go through the balance sheet accounts of work-in-process inventory and finished goods inventory before entering the cost of goods sold in the income statement. Period costs are expensed directly in the income statement. Exhibit 8 takes the visual presentation in Exhibit 7 and shows how inventoriable costs and period expenses would appear in the income statement and schedule of cost of goods manufactured of a manufacturing company.

We start by tracking the flow of direct materials shown on the left in Exhibit 7 and in Panel B in Exhibit 8. To keep things simple, all numbers are expressed in thousands, except for the per unit amounts.

Step 1: Cost of direct materials used in 2014. Note how the arrows in Exhibit 7 for beginning inventory, $11,000, and direct material purchases, $73,000, "fill up" the direct materials inventory box and how direct materials used, $76,000, "empties out" direct material inventory, leaving an ending inventory of direct materials of $8,000 that becomes the beginning inventory for the next year.

The cost of direct materials used is calculated in Exhibit 8, Panel B (light blue–shaded area), as follows:

Beginning inventory of direct materials, January 1, 2014	$11,000
+ Purchases of direct materials in 2014	73,000
− Ending inventory of direct materials, December 31, 2014	8,000
= Direct materials used in 2014	$76,000

Step 2: Total manufacturing costs incurred in 2014. Total manufacturing costs refers to all direct manufacturing costs and manufacturing overhead costs incurred during 2014 for all goods worked on during the year. Cellular Products classifies its manufacturing costs into the three categories described earlier.

(i) Direct materials used in 2014 (shaded light blue in Exhibit 8, Panel B)	$ 76,000
(ii) Direct manufacturing labor in 2014 (shaded blue in Exhibit 8, Panel B)	9,000
(iii) Manufacturing overhead costs in 2014 (shaded dark blue in Exhibit 8, Panel B)	20,000
Total manufacturing costs incurred in 2014	$105,000

Note how in Exhibit 7 these costs increase work-in-process inventory.

Exhibit 7	Flow of Revenue and Costs for a Manufacturing-Sector Company, Cellular Products (in thousands)

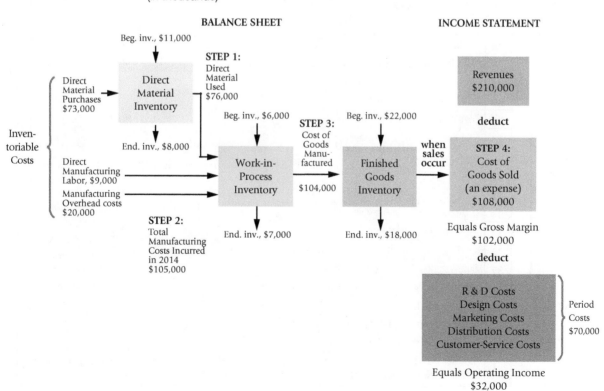

Exhibit 8   Income Statement and Schedule of Cost of Goods Manufactured of a Manufacturing-Sector Company, Cellular Products

	Home	Insert	Page Layout	Formulas	Data	Review	View		
			A				B	C	D
1	**PANEL A: INCOME STATEMENT**								
2			**Cellular Products**						
3			**Income Statement**						
4			**For the Year Ended December 31, 2014 (in thousands)**						
5	Revenues							$210,000	
6	Cost of goods sold:								
7	Beginning finished goods inventory, January 1, 2014						$ 22,000		
8	Cost of goods manufactured (see Panel B)						104,000 ◄		
9	Cost of goods available for sale						126,000		
10	Ending finished goods inventory, December 31, 2014						18,000		
11	Cost of goods sold							108,000	
12	Gross margin (or gross profit)							102,000	
13	Operating costs:								
14	R&D, design, mktg., dist., and cust.-service cost						70,000		
15	Total operating costs							70,000	
16	Operating income							$ 32,000	
17									
18	**PANEL B: COST OF GOODS MANUFACTURED**								
19			**Cellular Products**						
20			**Schedule of Cost of Goods Manufactured[a]**						
21			**For the Year Ended December 31, 2014 (in thousands)**						
22	Direct materials:								
23	Beginning inventory, January 1, 2014						$11,000		
24	Purchases of direct materials						73,000		
25	Cost of direct materials available for use						84,000		
26	Ending inventory, December 31, 2014						8,000		
27	Direct materials used							$ 76,000	
28	Direct manufacturing labor							9,000	
29	Manufacturing overhead costs:								
30	Indirect manufacturing labor						$ 7,000		
31	Supplies						2,000		
32	Heat, light, and power						5,000		
33	Depreciation—plant building						2,000		
34	Depreciation—plant equipment						3,000		
35	Miscellaneous						1,000		
36	Total manufacturing overhead costs							20,000	
37	Manufacturing costs incurred during 2014							105,000	
38	Beginning work-in-process inventory, January 1, 2014							6,000	
39	Total manufacturing costs to account for							111,000	
40	Ending work-in-process inventory, December 31, 2014							7,000	
41	Cost of goods manufactured (to income statement)							$104,000	
42	[a]Note that this schedule can become a schedule of cost of goods manufactured and sold simply by including the beginning and ending finished goods inventory figures in the supporting schedule rather than in the body of the income statement.								

STEP 4 (rows 6–11)
STEP 1 (rows 22–26)
STEP 2 (rows 28–36)
STEP 3 (rows 37–41)

Step 3: Cost of goods manufactured in 2014. **Cost of goods manufactured** refers to the cost of goods brought to completion, whether they were started before or during the current accounting period.

Note how the work-in-process inventory box in Exhibit 7 has a very similar structure to the direct materials inventory box described in Step 1. Beginning work-in-process inventory of $6,000 and total manufacturing costs incurred in 2014 of $105,000 "fill up" the work-in-process inventory box. Some of the manufacturing costs incurred during 2014 are held back as the cost of the ending work-in-process inventory. The ending work-in-process inventory of $7,000 becomes the beginning inventory for the next year, and the $104,000 cost of goods manufactured during 2014 "empties out" the work-in-process inventory while "filling up" the finished goods inventory box.

The cost of goods manufactured in 2014 (shaded green) is calculated in Exhibit 8, Panel B, as follows:

Beginning work-in-process inventory, January 1, 2014	$ 6,000
+ Total manufacturing costs incurred in 2014	105,000
= Total manufacturing costs to account for	111,000
− Ending work-in-process inventory, December 31, 2014	7,000
= Cost of goods manufactured in 2014	$104,000

Step 4: Cost of goods sold in 2014. The cost of goods sold is the cost of finished goods inventory sold to customers during the current accounting period. Looking at the finished goods inventory box in Exhibit 7, we see that the beginning inventory of finished goods of $22,000 and cost of goods manufactured in 2014 of $104,000 "fill up" the finished goods inventory box. The ending inventory of finished goods of $18,000 becomes the beginning inventory for the next year, and the $108,000 cost of goods sold during 2014 "empties out" the finished goods inventory.

This cost of goods sold is an expense that is matched against revenues. The cost of goods sold for Cellular Products (shaded olive green) is computed in Exhibit 8, Panel A, as follows:

Beginning inventory of finished goods, January 1, 2014	$ 22,000
+ Cost of goods manufactured in 2014	104,000
− Ending inventory of finished goods, December 31, 2014	18,000
= Cost of goods sold in 2014	$108,000

Exhibit 9 shows related general ledger T-accounts for Cellular Products' manufacturing cost flow. Note how the cost of goods manufactured ($104,000) is the cost of all goods completed during the accounting period. These costs are all inventoriable costs. Goods completed during the period are transferred to finished goods inventory. These costs become cost of goods sold in the accounting period when the goods are sold. Also note that the direct materials, direct manufacturing labor, and manufacturing overhead costs of the units in work-in-process inventory ($7,000) and finished goods inventory ($18,000) as of December 31, 2014, will appear as an asset in the balance sheet. These costs will become expenses next year when the work-in-process inventory is converted to finished goods and the finished goods are sold.

Exhibit 9	General Ledger T-Accounts for Cellular Products' Manufacturing Cost Flow (in thousands)

Work-in-Process Inventory				Finished Goods Inventory				Cost of Goods Sold	
Bal. Jan. 1, 2014	6,000	Cost of goods		Bal. Jan. 1, 2014	22,000	Cost of		108,000	
Direct materials used	76,000	manufactured	104,000		104,000	goods sold	108,000		
Direct manuf. labor	9,000			Bal. Dec. 31, 2014	18,000				
Indirect manuf. costs	20,000								
Bal. Dec. 31, 2014	7,000								

We can now prepare Cellular Products' income statement for 2014. The income statement of Cellular Products is shown on the right side in Exhibit 7 and in Exhibit 8, Panel A. Revenues of Cellular Products are (in thousands) $210,000. Inventoriable costs expensed during 2014 equal cost of goods sold of $108,000.

$$\text{Gross margin} = \text{Revenues} - \text{Cost of goods sold} = \$210{,}000 - \$108{,}000 = \$102{,}000.$$

The $70,000 of operating costs composed of R&D, design, marketing, distribution, and customer-service costs are period costs of Cellular Products. These period costs include, for example, salaries of salespersons, depreciation on computers and other equipment used in marketing, and the cost of leasing warehouse space for distribution. **Operating income** equals total revenues from operations minus cost of goods sold and operating (period) costs (excluding interest expense and income taxes) or, equivalently, gross margin minus period costs. The operating income of Cellular Products is $32,000 (gross margin, $102,000 – period costs, $70,000). If you are familiar with financial accounting, recall that period costs are typically called selling, general, and administrative expenses in the income statement.

Newcomers to cost accounting frequently assume that indirect costs such as rent, telephone, and depreciation are always costs of the period in which they are incurred and are not associated with inventories. When these costs are incurred in marketing or in corporate headquarters, they are period costs. However, when these costs are incurred in manufacturing, they are manufacturing overhead costs and are inventoriable.

Because costs that are inventoried are not expensed until the units associated with them are sold, a manager can produce more units than are expected to be sold in a period without reducing a firm's net income. In fact, building up inventory in this way defers the expensing of the current period's fixed manufacturing costs as manufacturing costs are inventoried and not expensed until the units are sold in a subsequent period. This in turn actually *increases* the firm's gross margin and operating income even though there is no increase in sales, causing outsiders to believe that the company is more profitable than it actually is.

Recap of Inventoriable Costs and Period Costs

Exhibit 7 highlights the differences between inventoriable costs and period costs for a manufacturing company. The manufacturing costs of finished goods include direct materials, direct manufacturing labor, and manufacturing overhead costs such as supervision, production control, and machine maintenance. All these costs are inventoriable: They are assigned to work-in-process inventory until the goods are completed and then to finished goods inventory until the goods are sold. All nonmanufacturing costs, such as R&D, design, and distribution costs, are period costs.

Decision Point ▶

What is the flow of inventoriable and period costs in manufacturing and merchandising settings?

Inventoriable costs and period costs flow through the income statement at a merchandising company similar to the way costs flow at a manufacturing company. At a merchandising company, however, the flow of costs is much simpler to understand and track. Exhibit 10 shows the inventoriable costs and period costs for a retailer or wholesaler, which buys goods for resale. The only inventoriable cost is the cost of merchandise. (This corresponds to the cost of finished goods manufactured for a manufacturing company.) Purchased goods are held as merchandise inventory, the cost of which is shown as an asset in the balance sheet. As the goods are sold, their costs are shown in the income statement as cost of goods sold. A retailer or wholesaler also has a variety of marketing, distribution, and customer-service costs, which are period costs. In the income statement, period costs are deducted from revenues without ever having been included as part of inventory. Concepts in Action: Cost Structure at Nordstrom Spurs Growth shows the importance of having the right cost structure for period expenses for a retailer.

| Exhibit 10 | Flow of Revenues and Costs for a Merchandising Company (Retailer or Wholesaler) |

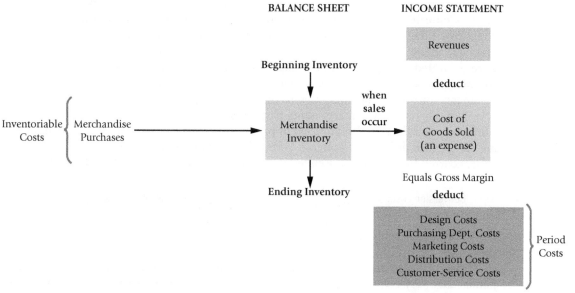

Prime Costs and Conversion Costs

Two terms used to describe cost classifications in manufacturing costing systems are *prime costs* and *conversion costs*. **Prime costs** are all direct manufacturing costs. For Cellular Products,

Prime costs = Direct material costs + Direct manufacturing labor costs = $76,000 + $9,000 = $85,000

Concepts in Action ▸ Cost Structure at Nordstrom Spurs Growth

During the recent global recession, the retail industry was hit hard due to declining economic conditions and changing consumer shopping habits. Since 2009, many long-standing retailers including Circuit City, Blockbuster, and Borders went out of business as their revenues failed to keep pace with the high fixed costs of the retail business, which include high rents and payroll. While some retailers closed their doors, however, other retailers became stronger and were prepared to grow as consumer spending recovered.

While many failed retailers had high fixed costs, Nordstrom, an upscale department store chain, has a more variable cost structure. At Nordstrom, the company's operations are mainly based on a variable cost business model with about 40–45% of its selling, general, and administrative (SGA) costs being variable. These costs include compensation (most salespeople earn a commission), benefits, advertising, and shipping and handling. As consumer spending dropped during the recession, the company reduced costs to mitigate the impact of sluggish sales trends on margins. Similarly, its cost structure enabled Nordstrom to quickly capitalize on the emerging opportunities when market conditions improved.

For example, in 2009 Nordstrom's SGA expenses were 25.5% of its $8.2 billion in revenue. In 2011, its SGA expenses increased to 26.7%, but revenues were $10.5 billion. The company's variable cost flexibility allowed the company to first cut costs and then to aggressively pursue growth while incurring slightly higher SGA costs.

Sources: Based on Nordstrom, Inc., 2012. 2011 Annual Report. Seattle, WA: Nordstrom, Inc.; Zacks Equity Research, "Nordstrom Pinned to Neutral," May 22, 2012.

As we have already discussed, the greater the proportion of prime costs (or direct costs) to total costs, the more confident managers can be about the accuracy of the costs of products. As information-gathering technology improves, companies can add more and more direct-cost categories. For example, power costs might be metered in specific areas of a plant and identified as a direct cost of specific products. Furthermore, if a production line were dedicated to manufacturing a specific product, the depreciation on the production equipment would be a direct manufacturing cost and would be included in prime costs. Computer software companies often have a "purchased technology" direct manufacturing cost item. This item, which represents payments to suppliers who develop software algorithms for a product, is also included in prime costs. **Conversion costs** are all manufacturing costs other than direct material costs. Conversion costs represent all manufacturing costs incurred to convert direct materials into finished goods. For Cellular Products,

$$\text{Conversion costs} = \frac{\text{Direct manufacturing}}{\text{labor costs}} + \frac{\text{Manufacturing}}{\text{overhead costs}} = \$9,000 + \$20,000 = \$29,000$$

Note that direct manufacturing labor costs are a part of both prime costs and conversion costs.

Some manufacturing operations, such as computer-integrated manufacturing (CIM) plants, have very few workers. The workers' roles are to monitor the manufacturing process and to maintain the equipment that produces multiple products. The costing systems in CIM plants do not have a direct manufacturing labor cost category because direct manufacturing labor cost is relatively small and because it is difficult to trace this cost to products. In a CIM plant, the only prime cost is the cost of direct materials. The conversion costs for such a plant are largely manufacturing overhead costs.

Learning Objective 7

Explain why product costs are computed in different ways for different purposes

...examples are pricing and product-mix decisions, government contracts, and financial statements

Measuring Costs Requires Judgment

Measuring costs requires judgment. That's because there are alternative ways for managers to define and classify costs. Different companies or sometimes even different subunits within the same company may define and classify costs differently. Be careful to define and understand the ways costs are measured in a company or situation. We first illustrate this point for labor costs.

Measuring Labor Costs

Consider labor costs for software programming at companies such as Apple, where programmers work on different software applications for products like the iMac, the iPad, and the iPhone. Although labor cost classifications vary among companies, many companies use multiple labor cost categories:

- Direct programming labor costs that can be traced to individual products
- Overhead costs (labor related)
  - Indirect labor compensation for
    Office staff
    Office security
    Rework labor (time spent by direct laborers correcting software errors)
    Overtime premium paid to software programmers (explained next)
    Idle time (explained next)
  - Salaries for managers, department heads, and supervisors
  - Payroll fringe costs, for example, health care premiums and pension costs (explained later)

To retain information on different categories, *indirect labor costs* are commonly divided into many subclassifications, for example, office staff and idle time costs. Note that managers' salaries usually are not classified as indirect labor costs. Instead, the compensation of supervisors, department heads, and all others who are regarded as management is placed in a separate classification of labor-related overhead.

Overtime Premium and Idle Time

Managers need to pay special attention to two classes of indirect labor—overtime premium and idle time. **Overtime premium** is the wage rate paid to workers (for both direct labor and indirect labor) in *excess* of their straight-time wage rates. Overtime premium is usually considered to be a part of indirect costs or overhead. Consider the example of George Flexner, a junior software programmer who writes software for multiple products. He is paid $40 per hour for straight-time and $60 per hour (time and a half) for overtime. His overtime premium is $20 per overtime hour. If he works 44 hours, including 4 overtime hours, in one week, his gross compensation would be classified as follows:

Direct programming labor: 44 hours × $40 per hour	$1,760
Overtime premium: 4 hours × $20 per hour	80
Total compensation for 44 hours	$1,840

In this example, why is the overtime premium of direct programming labor usually considered an overhead cost rather than a direct cost? After all, the premium can be traced to specific products that George worked on while working overtime. Overtime premium is generally not considered a direct cost because the particular job that George worked on during the overtime hours is a matter of chance. For example, assume that George worked on two products for 5 hours each on a specific workday that lasted 10 hours, including 2 overtime hours. Should the product George worked on during hours 9 and 10 be assigned the overtime premium? Or should the premium be prorated over both products? Prorating the overtime premium does not "penalize"—add to the cost of—a particular product solely because it happened to be worked on during the overtime hours. *Instead, the overtime premium is considered to be attributable to the heavy overall volume of work. Its cost is regarded as part of overhead, which is borne by both products.*

Sometimes, though, overtime can definitely be attributed to a single product. For example, the overtime needed to meet the launch deadline for a new product may clearly be the sole source of overtime. In such instances, the overtime premium is regarded as a direct cost of that product.

Another subclassification of indirect labor is the idle time of both direct and indirect labor. **Idle time** refers to the wages paid for unproductive time caused by lack of orders, machine or computer breakdowns, work delays, poor scheduling, and the like. For example, if George had no work for 3 hours during that week while waiting to receive code from another colleague, George's earnings would be classified as follows:

Direct programming labor: 41 hours × $40/hour	$1,640
Idle time (overhead): 3 hours × $40/hour	120
Overtime premium (overhead): 4 hours × $20/hour	80
Total earnings for 44 hours	$1,840

Clearly, in this case, the idle time is not related to a particular product, nor, as we have already discussed, is the overtime premium. Both the overtime premium and the costs of idle time are considered overhead costs.

Benefits of Defining Accounting Terms

Managers, accountants, suppliers, and others will avoid many problems if they thoroughly understand and agree on the classifications and meanings of the cost terms introduced in this chapter. Consider the classification of programming labor *payroll fringe costs,* which include employer payments for employee benefits such as Social Security, life insurance, health insurance, and pensions. Consider, for example, a software programmer who is paid a wage of $40 an hour with fringe benefits totaling, say, $10 per hour. Some companies classify the $40 as a direct programming labor cost of the product for which the software is being written and the $10 as overhead cost. Other companies classify the entire $50 as direct programming labor cost. The latter approach is preferable because the stated wage and the fringe benefit costs together are a fundamental part of acquiring direct software programming labor services.

Caution: In every situation, it is important for managers and management accountants to pinpoint clearly what direct labor includes and what direct labor excludes. This clarity will help prevent disputes regarding cost-reimbursement contracts, income tax payments, and labor union matters, which often can take a substantial amount of time for managers to resolve. Consider that some countries, such as Costa Rica and Mauritius, offer substantial income tax savings to foreign companies that generate employment within their borders. In some cases, to qualify for the tax benefits, the direct labor costs must at least equal a specified percentage of a company's total costs.

When managers do not precisely define direct labor costs, disputes can arise about whether payroll fringe costs should be included as part of direct labor costs when calculating the direct labor percentage for qualifying for such tax benefits. Companies have sought to classify payroll fringe costs as part of direct labor costs to make direct labor costs a higher percentage of total costs. Tax authorities have argued that payroll fringe costs are part of overhead. In addition to payroll fringe costs, other debated items are compensation for training time, idle time, vacations, sick leave, and overtime premium. To prevent disputes, contracts and laws should be as specific as possible about accounting definitions and measurements.

Different Meanings of Product Costs

Many cost terms used by organizations have ambiguous meanings. Consider the term *product cost*. A **product cost** is the sum of the costs assigned to a product for a specific purpose. Different purposes can result in different measures of product cost, as the brackets on the value chain in Exhibit 11 illustrate:

- **Pricing and product-mix decisions.** For the purposes of making decisions about pricing and which products provide the most profits, managers are interested in the overall (total) profitability of different products and, consequently, assign costs incurred in all business functions of the value chain to the different products.

- **Reimbursement under government contracts.** Government contracts often reimburse contractors on the basis of the "cost of a product" plus a prespecified margin of profit. A contract such as this is referred to as a "cost-plus" agreement. Cost-plus agreements are typically used for services and development contracts when it is not easy to predict the amount of money required to design, fabricate, and test items. Because these contracts transfer the risk of cost overruns to the government, agencies such as the Department of Defense and the Department of Energy provide detailed guidelines on the cost items they will allow (and disallow) when calculating the cost of a product. For example, many government agencies explicitly exclude marketing, distribution, and customer-service costs from product costs that qualify for reimbursement, and they may only partially reimburse R&D costs. These agencies want to reimburse contractors for only those costs most closely related to delivering products under the contract. The second bracket in Exhibit 11 shows how the

Exhibit 11

Different Product Costs for Different Purposes

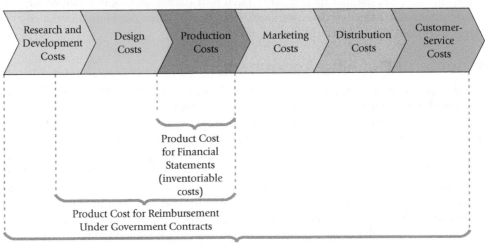

Exhibit 12

Alternative
Classifications of Costs

1. Business function
   a. Research and development
   b. Design of products and processes
   c. Production
   d. Marketing
   e. Distribution
   f. Customer service
2. Assignment to a cost object
   a. Direct cost
   b. Indirect cost
3. Behavior pattern in relation to the level of activity or volume
   a. Variable cost
   b. Fixed cost
4. Aggregate or average
   a. Total cost
   b. Unit cost
5. Assets or expenses
   a. Inventoriable cost
   b Period cost

product-cost calculations for a specific contract may allow for all design and production costs but only part of R&D costs.

- **Preparing financial statements for external reporting under Generally Accepted Accounting Principles (GAAP).** Under GAAP, only manufacturing costs can be assigned to inventories in the financial statements. For the purposes of calculating inventory costs, product costs include only inventoriable (production) costs.

As Exhibit 11 illustrates, product-cost measures range from a narrow set of costs for financial statements—a set that includes only production costs—to a broader set of costs for reimbursement under government contracts to a still broader set of costs for pricing and product-mix decisions.

This section focused on how different purposes result in the inclusion of different cost items of the value chain of business functions when product costs are calculated. The same caution about the need to be clear and precise about cost concepts and their measurement applies to each cost classification introduced in this chapter. Exhibit 12 summarizes the key cost classifications. Using the five-step decision-making process, think about how these different classifications of costs help managers make decisions and evaluate performance.

◀ Decision Point
Why do managers assign different costs to the same cost object?

1. **Identify the problem and uncertainties.** Consider a decision about how much to price a product. This decision often depends on how much it costs to make the product.
2. **Obtain information.** Managers identify the direct and indirect costs of a product in each business function. Managers also gather other information about customers, competitors, and the prices of competing products.
3. **Make predictions about the future.** Managers estimate what it will cost to make the product in the future. This requires managers to predict the quantity of the product they expect the company to sell as well as have an understanding of fixed and variable costs.
4. **Make decisions by choosing among alternatives.** Managers choose a price to charge based on a thorough understanding of costs and other information.
5. **Implement the decision, evaluate performance, and learn.** Managers control costs and learn by comparing the actual total and unit costs against budgeted amounts.

The next section describes how the basic concepts introduced in this chapter lead to a framework for understanding cost accounting and cost management that can then be applied to the study of many topics, such as strategy evaluation, quality, and investment decisions.

A Framework for Cost Accounting and Cost Management

◀ Learning Objective 8
Describe a framework for cost accounting and cost management

. . . three features that help managers make decisions

The following three features of cost accounting and cost management can be used for a wide range of applications:

1. Calculating the cost of products, services, and other cost objects
2. Obtaining information for planning and control and performance evaluation
3. Analyzing the relevant information for making decisions

Calculating the Cost of Products, Services, and Other Cost Objects

You have already learned that costing systems trace direct costs and allocate indirect costs to products. Systems such as job costing and activity-based costing are used to calculate total costs and unit costs of products and services. Managers use this information to formulate strategies and make pricing, product-mix, and cost-management decisions.

Obtaining Information for Planning and Control and Performance Evaluation

Budgeting is the most commonly used tool for planning and control. A budget forces managers to look ahead, to translate a company's strategy into plans, to coordinate and communicate within the organization, and to provide a benchmark for evaluating the company's performance. Managers strive to meet their budget targets, so budgeting often affects the behavior of a company's personnel and the decisions they make.

At the end of a reporting period, managers compare the company's actual results to its planned performance. The manager's tasks are to understand why differences (called variances) between actual and planned performance arise and to use the information provided by these variances as feedback to promote learning and future improvement. Managers also use variances as well as nonfinancial measures, such as defect rates and customer satisfaction ratings, to control and evaluate the performance of various departments, divisions, and managers.

Analyzing the Relevant Information for Making Decisions

When designing strategies and implementing them, managers must understand which revenues and costs to consider and which ones to ignore. Management accountants help managers identify what information is relevant and what information is irrelevant. Consider a decision about whether to buy a product from an outside vendor or make it in-house. The costing system indicates that it costs $25 per unit to make the product in-house. A vendor offers to sell the product for $22 per unit. At first glance, it seems it will cost less for the company to buy the product rather than make it. Suppose, however, that of the $25 to make the product in-house, $5 consists of plant lease costs that the company has already paid under a lease contract. Furthermore, if the product is bought, the plant will remain idle because it is too costly to retool the plant to make another product. That is, there is no opportunity to use the plant in some other profitable way. Under these conditions, it will cost less to make the product than to buy it. That's because making the product costs only an *additional* $20 per unit ($25 – $5), compared with an *additional* $22 per unit if it is bought. The $5 per unit of lease cost is irrelevant to the decision because it is a *past* (or *sunk*) cost that has already been incurred regardless of whether the product is made or bought. Analyzing relevant information is a key aspect of making decisions.

When making strategic decisions about which products and how much to produce, managers must know how revenues and costs vary with changes in output levels. For this purpose, managers need to distinguish fixed costs from variable costs. Operating income changes with changes in units sold and managers use this information to make decisions such as how much to spend on advertising.

Decision Point

What are the three key features of cost accounting and cost management?

Problem for Self-Study

Foxwood Company is a metal- and woodcutting manufacturer, selling products to the home-construction market. Consider the following data for 2014:

Sandpaper	$ 2,000
Materials-handling costs	70,000
Lubricants and coolants	5,000
Miscellaneous indirect manufacturing labor	40,000
Direct manufacturing labor	300,000
Direct materials inventory, Jan. 1, 2014	40,000
Direct materials inventory, Dec. 31, 2014	50,000
Finished goods inventory, Jan. 1, 2014	100,000
Finished goods inventory, Dec. 31, 2014	150,000
Work-in-process inventory, Jan. 1, 2014	10,000
Work-in-process inventory, Dec. 31, 2014	14,000
Plant-leasing costs	54,000
Depreciation—plant equipment	36,000
Property taxes on plant equipment	4,000
Fire insurance on plant equipment	3,000
Direct materials purchased	460,000
Revenues	1,360,000
Marketing promotions	60,000
Marketing salaries	100,000
Distribution costs	70,000
Customer-service costs	100,000

Required

1. Prepare an income statement with a separate supporting schedule of cost of goods manufactured. For all manufacturing items, classify costs as direct costs or indirect costs and indicate by V or F whether each is basically a variable cost or a fixed cost (when the cost object is a product unit). If in doubt, decide on the basis of whether the total cost will change substantially over a wide range of units produced.
2. Suppose that both the direct material costs and the plant-leasing costs are for the production of 900,000 units. What is the direct material cost of each unit produced? What is the plant-leasing cost per unit? Assume that the plant-leasing cost is a fixed cost.
3. Suppose Foxwood Company manufactures 1,000,000 units next year. Repeat the computation in requirement 2 for direct materials and plant-leasing costs. Assume the implied cost-behavior patterns persist.
4. As a management consultant, explain concisely to the company president why the unit cost for direct materials did not change in requirements 2 and 3 but the unit cost for plant-leasing costs did change.

Solution

1.

Foxwood Company
Income Statement
For the Year Ended December 31, 2014

Revenues		$1,360,000
Cost of goods sold		
Beginning finished goods inventory, January 1, 2014	$ 100,000	
Cost of goods manufactured (see the following schedule)	960,000	
Cost of goods available for sale	1,060,000	
Deduct ending finished goods inventory, December 31, 2014	150,000	910,000
Gross margin (or gross profit)		450,000
Operating costs		
Marketing promotions	60,000	
Marketing salaries	100,000	
Distribution costs	70,000	
Customer-service costs	100,000	330,000
Operating income		$ 120,000

Foxwood Company
Schedule of Cost of Goods Manufactured
For the Year Ended December 31, 2014

Direct materials		
Beginning inventory, January 1, 2014		$ 40,000
Purchases of direct materials		460,000
Cost of direct materials available for use		500,000
Ending inventory, December 31, 2014		50,000
Direct materials used		450,000 (V)
Direct manufacturing labor		300,000 (V)
Indirect manufacturing costs		
Sandpaper	$ 2,000 (V)	
Materials-handling costs	70,000 (V)	
Lubricants and coolants	5,000 (V)	
Miscellaneous indirect manufacturing labor	40,000 (V)	
Plant-leasing costs	54,000 (F)	
Depreciation—plant equipment	36,000 (F)	
Property taxes on plant equipment	4,000 (F)	
Fire insurance on plant equipment	3,000 (F)	214,000
Manufacturing costs incurred during 2014		964,000
Beginning work-in-process inventory, January 1, 2014		10,000
Total manufacturing costs to account for		974,000
Ending work-in-process inventory, December 31, 2014		14,000
Cost of goods manufactured (to income statement)		$ 960,000

2. Direct material unit cost = Direct materials used ÷ Units produced
   $$= \$450{,}000 \div 900{,}000 \text{ units} = \$0.50 \text{ per unit}$$
   Plant-leasing unit cost = Plant-leasing costs ÷ Units produced
   $$= \$54{,}000 \div 900{,}000 \text{ units} = \$0.06 \text{ per unit}$$

3. The direct material costs are variable, so they would increase in total from \$450,000 to \$500,000 (1,000,000 units × \$0.50 per unit). However, their unit cost would be unaffected: \$500,000 ÷ 1,000,000 units = \$0.50 per unit.

   In contrast, the plant-leasing costs of \$54,000 are fixed, so they would not increase in total. However, the plant-leasing cost per unit would decline from \$0.060 to \$0.054: \$54,000 ÷ 1,000,000 units = \$0.054 per unit.

4. The explanation would begin with the answer to requirement 3. As a consultant, you should stress that the unitizing (averaging) of costs that have different behavior patterns can be misleading. A common error is to assume that a total unit cost, which is often a sum of variable unit cost and fixed unit cost, is an indicator that total costs change in proportion to changes in production levels. You must be wary, especially about average fixed cost per unit. Too often, unit fixed cost is erroneously regarded as being indistinguishable from unit variable cost.

▶ Decision Points

The following question-and-answer format summarizes the chapter's learning objectives. Each decision presents a key question related to a learning objective. The guidelines are the answer to that question.

Decision	Guidelines
1. What is a cost object?	A cost object is anything for which a manager needs a separate measurement of cost. Examples include a product, a service, a project, a customer, a brand category, an activity, and a department.
2. How do managers decide whether a cost is a direct or an indirect cost?	A direct cost is any cost that is related to a particular cost object and can be traced to that cost object in an economically feasible way. Indirect costs are related to a particular cost object but cannot be traced to it in an economically feasible way. The same cost can be direct for one cost object and indirect for another cost object. This text uses *cost tracing* to describe the assignment of direct costs to a cost object and *cost allocation* to describe the assignment of indirect costs to a cost object.
3. How do managers decide whether a cost is a variable or a fixed cost?	A variable cost changes *in total* in proportion to changes in the related level of total activity or volume of output produced. A fixed cost remains unchanged *in total* for a given time period despite wide changes in the related level of total activity or volume of output produced.
4. How should managers estimate and interpret cost information?	In general, focus on total costs, not unit costs. When making total cost estimates, think of variable costs as an amount per unit and fixed costs as a total amount. Interpret the unit cost of a cost object cautiously when it includes a fixed-cost component.
5. What are the differences in the accounting for inventoriable versus period costs?	Inventoriable costs are all costs of a product that a company regards as an asset in the accounting period in which they are incurred and which become cost of goods sold in the accounting period in which the product is sold. Period costs are expensed in the accounting period in which they are incurred and are all of the costs in an income statement other than cost of goods sold.

Decision	Guidelines
6. What is the flow of inventoriable and period costs in manufacturing and merchandising settings?	In manufacturing settings, inventoriable costs flow through work-in-process and finished goods accounts, and are expensed as cost of goods sold. Period costs are expensed as they are incurred. In merchandising settings, only the cost of merchandise is treated as inventoriable.
7. Why do managers assign different costs to the same cost objects?	Managers can assign different costs to the same cost object depending on the purpose. For example, for the external reporting purpose in a manufacturing company, the inventoriable cost of a product includes only manufacturing costs. In contrast, costs from all business functions of the value chain often are assigned to a product for pricing and product-mix decisions.
8. What are the three key features of cost accounting and cost management?	Three features of cost accounting and cost management are (1) calculating the cost of products, services, and other cost objects; (2) obtaining information for planning and control and performance evaluation; and (3) analyzing relevant information for making decisions.

Terms to Learn

Do not proceed before you check your understanding of the following terms. The chapter contains definitions of the following important terms:

actual cost	direct manufacturing labor costs	operating income
average cost	direct material costs	overtime premium
budgeted cost	direct materials inventory	period costs
conversion costs	factory overhead costs	prime costs
cost	finished goods inventory	product cost
cost accumulation	fixed cost	relevant range
cost allocation	idle time	revenues
cost assignment	indirect costs of a cost object	service-sector companies
cost driver	indirect manufacturing costs	unit cost
cost object	inventoriable costs	variable cost
cost of goods manufactured	manufacturing overhead costs	work-in-process inventory
cost tracing	manufacturing-sector companies	work in progress
direct costs of a cost object	merchandising-sector companies	

Assignment Material

MyAccountingLab

Questions

1 Define cost object and give three examples.
2 Define direct costs and indirect costs.
3 Why do managers consider direct costs to be more accurate than indirect costs?
4 Name three factors that will affect the classification of a cost as direct or indirect.
5 Define variable cost and fixed cost. Give an example of each.
6 What is a cost driver? Give one example.
7 What is the relevant range? What role does the relevant-range concept play in explaining how costs behave?
8 Explain why unit costs must often be interpreted with caution.
9 Describe how manufacturing-, merchandising-, and service-sector companies differ from one another.
10 What are three different types of inventory that manufacturing companies hold?
11 Distinguish between inventoriable costs and period costs.

12 Define the following: direct material costs, direct manufacturing-labor costs, manufacturing over-head costs, prime costs, and conversion costs.

13 Describe the overtime-premium and idle-time categories of indirect labor.

14 Define product cost. Describe three different purposes for computing product costs.

15 What are three common features of cost accounting and cost management?

Exercises

MyAccountingLab

16 **Computing and interpreting manufacturing unit costs.** Minnesota Office Products (MOP) produces three different paper products at its Vaasa lumber plant: Supreme, Deluxe, and Regular. Each product has its own dedicated production line at the plant. It currently uses the following three-part classification for its manufacturing costs: direct materials, direct manufacturing labor, and manufacturing overhead costs. Total manufacturing overhead costs of the plant in July 2014 are $150 million ($15 million of which are fixed). This total amount is allocated to each product line on the basis of the direct manufacturing labor costs of each line. Summary data (in millions) for July 2014 are as follows:

	Supreme	Deluxe	Regular
Direct material costs	$ 89	$ 57	$ 60
Direct manufacturing labor costs	$ 16	$ 26	$ 8
Manufacturing overhead costs	$ 48	$ 78	$ 24
Units produced	125	150	140

Required

1. Compute the manufacturing cost per unit for each product produced in July 2014.
2. Suppose that, in August 2014, production was 150 million units of Supreme, 190 million units of Deluxe, and 220 million units of Regular. Why might the July 2014 information on manufacturing cost per unit be misleading when predicting total manufacturing costs in August 2014?

17 **Direct, indirect, fixed, and variable costs.** Wonder Bakery manufactures two types of bread, which it sells as wholesale products to various specialty retail bakeries. Each loaf of bread requires a three-step process. The first step is mixing. The mixing department combines all of the necessary ingredients to create the dough and processes it through high-speed mixers. The dough is then left to rise before baking. The second step is baking, which is an entirely automated process. The baking department molds the dough into its final shape and bakes each loaf of bread in a high-temperature oven. The final step is finishing, which is an entirely manual process. The finishing department coats each loaf of bread with a special glaze, allows the bread to cool, and then carefully packages each loaf in a specialty carton for sale in retail bakeries.

Required

1. Costs involved in the process are listed next. For each cost, indicate whether it is a direct variable, direct fixed, indirect variable, or indirect fixed cost, assuming "units of production of each kind of bread" is the cost object.

Costs:

Yeast	Mixing department manager
Flour	Materials handlers in each department
Packaging materials	Custodian in factory
Depreciation on ovens	Night guard in factory
Depreciation on mixing machines	Machinist (running the mixing machine)
Rent on factory building	Machine maintenance personnel in each department
Fire insurance on factory building	Maintenance supplies for factory
Factory utilities	Cleaning supplies for factory
Finishing department hourly laborers	

2. If the cost object were the "mixing department" rather than units of production of each kind of bread, which preceding costs would now be direct instead of indirect costs?

18 **Classification of costs, service sector.** Market Focus is a marketing research firm that organizes focus groups for consumer-product companies. Each focus group has eight individuals who are paid $60 per session to provide comments on new products. These focus groups meet in hotels and are led by a trained, independent marketing specialist hired by Market Focus. Each specialist is paid a fixed retainer to conduct a minimum number of sessions and a per session fee of $2,200. A Market Focus staff member attends each session to ensure that all the logistical aspects run smoothly.

Required

Classify each cost item (**A–H**) as follows:

   a. Direct or indirect (D or I) costs of each individual focus group.
   b. Variable or fixed (V or F) costs of how the total costs of Market Focus change as the number of focus groups conducted changes. (If in doubt, select on the basis of whether the total costs will change substantially if there is a large change in the number of groups conducted.)

You will have two answers (D or I; V or F) for each of the following items:

Cost Item	D or I	V or F
A. Payment to individuals in each focus group to provide comments on new products		
B. Annual subscription of Market Focus to *Consumer Reports* magazine		
C. Phone calls made by Market Focus staff member to confirm individuals will attend a focus group session (Records of individual calls are not kept.)		
D. Retainer paid to focus group leader to conduct 18 focus groups per year on new medical products		
E. Recruiting cost to hire marketing specialists		
F. Lease payment by Market Focus for corporate office		
G. Cost of tapes used to record comments made by individuals in a focus group session (These tapes are sent to the company whose products are being tested.)		
H. Gasoline costs of Market Focus staff for company-owned vehicles (Staff members submit monthly bills with no mileage breakdowns.)		
I. Costs incurred to improve the design of focus groups to make them more effective		

19 Classification of costs, merchandising sector. Band Box Entertainment (BBE) operates a large store in Atlanta, Georgia. The store has both a movie (DVD) section and a music (CD) section. BBE reports revenues for the movie section separately from the music section.

Required

Classify each cost item (**A–H**) as follows:

   a. Direct or indirect (D or I) costs of the total number of DVDs sold.
   b. Variable or fixed (V or F) costs of how the total costs of the movie section change as the total number of DVDs sold changes. (If in doubt, select on the basis of whether the total costs will change substantially if there is a large change in the total number of DVDs sold.)

You will have two answers (D or I; V or F) for each of the following items:

Cost Item	D or I	V or F
A . Annual retainer paid to a video distributor		
B. Cost of store manager's salary		
C. Costs of DVDs purchased for sale to customers		
D. Subscription to *DVD Trends* magazine		
E. Leasing of computer software used for financial budgeting at the BBE store		
F. Cost of popcorn provided free to all customers of the BBE store		
G. Cost of cleaning the store every night after closing		
H. Freight-in costs of DVDs purchased by BBE		

20 Classification of costs, manufacturing sector. The Kitakyushu, Japan, plant of Nissan Motor Corporation assembles two types of cars (Teanas and Muranos). Separate assembly lines are used for each type of car.

Required

Classify each cost item (**A–H**) as follows:

   a. Direct or indirect (D or I) costs for the total number of Teanas assembled.
   b. Variable or fixed (V or F) costs depending on how total costs change as the total number of Teanas assembled changes. (If in doubt, select on the basis of whether the total costs will change substantially if there is a large change in the total number of Teanas assembled.)

You will have two answers (D or I; V or F) for each of the following items:

Cost Item	D or I	V or F
A. Cost of tires used on Teanas		
B. Salary of public relations manager for Kitakyushu plant		
C. Annual awards dinner for Teana suppliers		
D. Cost of lubricant used on the Teana assembly line		

E. Freight costs of Teana engines shipped from Yokohama to Kitakyushu

F. Electricity costs for Teana assembly line (single bill covers entire plant)

G. Wages paid to temporary assembly-line workers hired in periods of high Teana production (paid on hourly basis)

H. Annual fire-insurance policy cost for Kitakyushu plant

21 Variable costs, fixed costs, total costs. Bridget Ashton is getting ready to open a small restaurant. She is on a tight budget and must choose between the following long-distance phone plans:

Plan A: Pay 10 cents per minute of long-distance calling.

Plan B: Pay a fixed monthly fee of $15 for up to 240 long-distance minutes and 8 cents per minute thereafter (if she uses fewer than 240 minutes in any month, she still pays $15 for the month).

Plan C: Pay a fixed monthly fee of $22 for up to 510 long-distance minutes and 5 cents per minute thereafter (if she uses fewer than 510 minutes, she still pays $22 for the month).

1. Draw a graph of the total monthly costs of the three plans for different levels of monthly long-distance calling.

2. Which plan should Ashton choose if she expects to make 100 minutes of long-distance calls? 240 minutes? 540 minutes?

Required

22 Variable and Fixed Costs. Beacher Motors specializes in producing one specialty vehicle. It is called Surfer and is styled to easily fit multiple surfboards in its back area and top-mounted storage racks. Beacher has the following manufacturing costs:

Plant management costs, $1,200,000 per year

Cost of leasing equipment, $1,800,000 per year

Workers' wages, $700 per Surfer vehicle produced

Direct materials costs: Steel, $1,500 per Surfer; Tires, $125 per tire, each Surfer takes 5 tires (one spare).

City license, which is charged monthly based on the number of tires used in production:

0–500 tires	$ 50,000
501–1,000 tires	$ 74,500
more than 1,000 tires	$200,000

Beacher currently produces 110 vehicles per month.

1. What is the variable manufacturing cost per vehicle? What is the fixed manufacturing cost per month?

2. Plot a graph for the variable manufacturing costs and a second for the fixed manufacturing costs per month. How does the concept of relevant range relate to your graphs? Explain.

3. What is the total manufacturing cost of each vehicle if 100 vehicles are produced each month? 225 vehicles? How do you explain the difference in the manufacturing cost per unit?

Required

23 Variable costs, fixed costs, relevant range. Dotball Candies manufactures jaw-breaker candies in a fully automated process. The machine that produces candies was purchased recently and can make 4,400 per month. The machine costs $9,500 and is depreciated using straight-line depreciation over 10 years assuming zero residual value. Rent for the factory space and warehouse and other fixed manufacturing overhead costs total $1,300 per month.

Dotball currently makes and sells 3,100 jaw-breakers per month. Dotball buys just enough materials each month to make the jaw-breakers it needs to sell. Materials cost 10 cents per jawbreaker.

Next year Dotball expects demand to increase by 100%. At this volume of materials purchased, it will get a 10% discount on price. Rent and other fixed manufacturing overhead costs will remain the same.

1. What is Dotball's current annual relevant range of output?

2. What is Dotball's current annual fixed manufacturing cost within the relevant range? What is the annual variable manufacturing cost?

3. What will Dotball's relevant range of output be next year? How, if at all, will total annual fixed and variable manufacturing costs change next year? Assume that if it needs to Dotball could buy an identical machine at the same cost as the one it already has.

Required

24 Cost drivers and value chain. Roxbury Mobile Company (RMC) is developing a new touch-screen smartphone to compete in the cellular phone industry. The company will sell the phones at wholesale prices to cell phone companies, which will in turn sell them in retail stores to the final customer. RMC has undertaken the following activities in its value chain to bring its product to market:

Identify customer needs (What do smartphone users want?)

Perform market research on competing brands

An Introduction to Cost Terms and Purposes

Design a prototype of the RMC smartphone

Market the new design to cell phone companies

Manufacture the RMC smartphone

Process orders from cell phone companies

Package the RMC smartphones

Deliver the RMC smartphones to the cell phone companies

Provide online assistance to cell phone users for use of the RMC smartphone

Make design changes to the smartphone based on customer feedback

During the process of product development, production, marketing, distribution, and customer service, RMC has kept track of the following cost drivers:

Number of smartphones shipped by RMC

Number of design changes

Number of deliveries made to cell phone companies

Engineering hours spent on initial product design

Hours spent researching competing market brands

Customer-service hours

Number of smartphone orders processed

Number of cell phone companies purchasing the RMC smartphone

Machine hours required to run the production equipment

Number of surveys returned and processed from competing smartphone users

Required

1. Identify each value chain activity listed at the beginning of the exercise with one of the following value-chain categories:
   a. Design of products and processes
   b. Production
   c. Marketing
   d. Distribution
   e. Customer service

2. Use the list of preceding cost drivers to find one or more reasonable cost drivers for each of the activities in RMC's value chain.

25 Cost drivers and functions. The representative cost drivers in the right column of this table are randomized so they do not match the list of functions in the left column.

Function	Representative Cost Driver
1. Accounts payable	A. Number of invoices sent
2. Recruiting	B. Number of purchase orders
3. Data processing	C. Number of research scientists
4. Research and development	D. Hours of computer processing unit (CPU)
5. Purchasing	E. Number of employees hired
6. Warehousing	F. Number of payments processed
7. Billing	G. Number of pallets moved

Required

1. Match each function with its representative cost driver.
2. Give a second example of a cost driver for each function.

26 Total costs and unit costs, service setting. The Big Event (TBE) recently started a business organizing food and music at weddings and other large events. In order to better understand the profitability of the business, the owner has asked you for an analysis of costs—what costs are fixed, what costs are variable, and so on, for each event. You have the following cost information:

Music costs: $10,000 per event

Catering costs:

Food: $65 per guest

Setup/cleanup: $15 per guest

Fixed fee: $4,000 per event

The Big Event has allowed the caterer, who is also new in business, to place business cards on each table as a form of advertising. This has proved quite effective, and the caterer gives TBE a discount of $5 per guest in exchange for allowing the caterer to advertise.

1. Draw a graph depicting fixed costs, variable costs, and total costs for each event versus the number of guests.
2. Suppose 150 persons attend the next event. What is TBE's total net cost and the cost per attendee?
3. Suppose instead that 200 persons attend. What is TBE's total net cost and the cost per attendee.
4. How should TBE charge customers for its services? Explain briefly.

Required

27 **Total and unit cost, decision making.** Gayle's Glassworks makes glass flanges for scientific use. Materials cost $1 per flange, and the glass blowers are paid a wage rate of $28 per hour. A glass blower blows 10 flanges per hour. Fixed manufacturing costs for flanges are $28,000 per period. Period (nonmanufacturing) costs associated with flanges are $10,000 per period and are fixed.

1. Graph the fixed, variable, and total manufacturing cost for flanges, using units (number of flanges) on the x-axis.
2. Assume Gayle's Glassworks manufactures and sells 5,000 flanges this period. Its competitor, Flora's Flasks, sells flanges for $10 each. Can Gayle sell below Flora's price and still make a profit on the flanges?
3. How would your answer to requirement 2 differ if Gayle's Glassworks made and sold 10,000 flanges this period? Why? What does this indicate about the use of unit cost in decision making?

Required

28 **Inventoriable costs versus period costs.** Each of the following cost items pertains to one of these companies: Star Market (a merchandising-sector company), Maytag (a manufacturing-sector company), and Yahoo! (a service-sector company):

a. Cost of lettuce and tomatoes on sale in Star Market's produce department
b. Electricity used to provide lighting for assembly-line workers at a Maytag refrigerator-assembly plant
c. Depreciation on Yahoo!'s computer equipment used to update its Web site
d. Electricity used to provide lighting for Star Market's store aisles
e. Depreciation on Maytag's computer equipment used for quality testing of refrigerator components during the assembly process
f. Salaries of Star Market's marketing personnel planning local-newspaper advertising campaigns
g. Perrier mineral water purchased by Yahoo! for consumption by its software engineers
h. Salaries of Yahoo!'s marketing personnel selling advertising
i. Depreciation on vehicles used to transport Maytag refrigerators to retail stores

1. Distinguish between manufacturing-, merchandising-, and service-sector companies.
2. Distinguish between inventoriable costs and period costs.
3. Classify each of the cost items (**a–h**) as an inventoriable cost or a period cost. Explain your answers.

Required

Problems

MyAccountingLab

29 **Computing cost of goods purchased and cost of goods sold.** The following data are for Marvin Department Store. The account balances (in thousands) are for 2014.

Marketing, distribution, and customer-service costs	$ 37,000
Merchandise inventory, January 1, 2014	27,000
Utilities	17,000
General and administrative costs	43,000
Merchandise inventory, December 31, 2014	34,000
Purchases	155,000
Miscellaneous costs	4,000
Transportation-in	7,000
Purchase returns and allowances	4,000
Purchase discounts	6,000
Revenues	280,000

1. Compute (**a**) the cost of goods purchased and (**b**) the cost of goods sold.
2. Prepare the income statement for 2014.

Required

30 Cost of goods purchased, cost of goods sold, and income statement. The following data are for Montgomery Retail Outlet Stores. The account balances (in thousands) are for 2014.

Marketing and advertising costs	$ 48,000
Merchandise inventory, January 1, 2014	90,000
Shipping of merchandise to customers	4,000
Building depreciation	8,400
Purchases	520,000
General and administrative costs	64,000
Merchandise inventory, December 31, 2014	104,000
Merchandise freight-in	20,000
Purchase returns and allowances	22,000
Purchase discounts	18,000
Revenues	640,000

Required

1. Compute **(a)** the cost of goods purchased and **(b)** the cost of goods sold.
2. Prepare the income statement for 2014.

31 Flow of Inventoriable Costs. Renka's Heaters selected data for October 2014 are presented here (in millions):

Direct materials inventory 10/1/2014	$ 105
Direct materials purchased	365
Direct materials used	385
Total manufacturing overhead costs	450
Variable manufacturing overhead costs	265
Total manufacturing costs incurred during October 2014	1,610
Work-in-process inventory 10/1/2014	230
Cost of goods manufactured	1,660
Finished goods inventory 10/1/2014	130
Cost of goods sold	1,770

Required

Calculate the following costs:

1. Direct materials inventory 10/31/2014
2. Fixed manufacturing overhead costs for October 2014
3. Direct manufacturing labor costs for October 2014
4. Work-in-process inventory 10/31/2014
5. Cost of finished goods available for sale in October 2014
6. Finished goods inventory 10/31/2014

32 Cost of goods manufactured, income statement, manufacturing company. Consider the following account balances (in thousands) for the Peterson Company:

Peterson Company	Beginning of 2014	End of 2014
Direct materials inventory	21,000	23,000
Work-in-process inventory	26,000	25,000
Finished goods inventory	13,000	20,000
Purchases of direct materials		74,000
Direct manufacturing labor		22,000
Indirect manufacturing labor		17,000
Plant insurance		7,000
Depreciation—plant, building, and equipment		11,000
Repairs and maintenance—plant		3,000
Marketing, distribution, and customer-service costs		91,000
General and administrative costs		24,000

Required

1. Prepare a schedule for the cost of goods manufactured for 2014.
2. Revenues for 2014 were $310 million. Prepare the income statement for 2014.

33 Cost of goods manufactured, income statement, manufacturing company. Consider the following account balances (in thousands) for the Shaler Corporation:

Shaler Corporation	Beginning of 2014	End of 2014
Direct materials inventory	130,000	68,000
Work-in-process inventory	166,000	144,000
Finished goods inventory	246,000	204,000
Purchases of direct materials		256,000
Direct manufacturing labor		212,000
Indirect manufacturing labor		96,000
Indirect materials		28,000
Plant insurance		4,000
Depreciation—plant, building, and equipment		42,000
Plant utilities		24,000
Repairs and maintenance—plant		16,000
Equipment leasing costs		64,000
Marketing, distribution, and customer-service costs		124,000
General and administrative costs		68,000

Required

1. Prepare a schedule for the cost of goods manufactured for 2014.
2. Revenues (in thousands) for 2014 were $1,200,000. Prepare the income statement for 2014.

34 Income statement and schedule of cost of goods manufactured. The Howell Corporation has the following account balances (in millions):

For Specific Date		For Year 2014	
Direct materials inventory, Jan. 1, 2014	$15	Purchases of direct materials	$325
Work-in-process inventory, Jan. 1, 2014	10	Direct manufacturing labor	100
Finished goods inventory, Jan. 1, 2014	70	Depreciation—plant and equipment	80
Direct materials inventory, Dec. 31, 2014	20	Plant supervisory salaries	5
Work-in-process inventory, Dec. 31, 2014	5	Miscellaneous plant overhead	35
Finished goods inventory, Dec. 31, 2014	55	Revenues	950
		Marketing, distribution, and customer-service costs	240
		Plant supplies used	10
		Plant utilities	30
		Indirect manufacturing labor	60

Required

Prepare an income statement and a supporting schedule of cost of goods manufactured for the year ended December 31, 2014. (For additional questions regarding these facts, see the next problem.)

35 Interpretation of statements (continuation of 34).

Required

1. How would the answer to Problem 34 be modified if you were asked for a schedule of cost of goods manufactured and sold instead of a schedule of cost of goods manufactured? Be specific.
2. Would the sales manager's salary (included in marketing, distribution, and customer-service costs) be accounted for any differently if the Howell Corporation were a merchandising-sector company instead of a manufacturing-sector company? Using the flow of manufacturing costs outlined in Exhibit 9, describe how the wages of an assembler in the plant would be accounted for in this manufacturing company.
3. Plant supervisory salaries are usually regarded as manufacturing overhead costs. When might some of these costs be regarded as direct manufacturing costs? Give an example.

4. Suppose that both the direct materials used and the plant and equipment depreciation are related to the manufacture of 1 million units of product. What is the unit cost for the direct materials assigned to those units? What is the unit cost for plant and equipment depreciation? Assume that yearly plant and equipment depreciation is computed on a straight-line basis.

5. Assume that the implied cost-behavior patterns in requirement 4 persist. That is, direct material costs behave as a variable cost and plant and equipment depreciation behaves as a fixed cost. Repeat the computations in requirement 4, assuming that the costs are being predicted for the manufacture of 1.2 million units of product. How would the total costs be affected?

6. As a management accountant, explain concisely to the president why the unit costs differed in requirements 4 and 5.

36 Income statement and schedule of cost of goods manufactured. The following items (in millions) pertain to Chester Corporation:

Chester's manufacturing costing system uses a three-part classification of direct materials, direct manufacturing labor, and manufacturing overhead costs.

For Specific Date		For Year 2014	
Work-in-process inventory, Jan. 1, 2014	$15	Plant utilities	$ 6
Direct materials inventory, Dec. 31, 2014	9	Indirect manufacturing labor	25
Finished goods inventory, Dec. 31, 2014	19	Depreciation—plant and equipment	8
Accounts payable, Dec. 31, 2014	28	Revenues	354
Accounts receivable, Jan. 1, 2014	57	Miscellaneous manufacturing overhead	17
Work-in-process inventory, Dec. 31, 2014	7	Marketing, distribution, and customer-service costs	91
Finished goods inventory, Jan 1, 2014	43	Direct materials purchased	82
Accounts receivable, Dec. 31, 2014	30	Direct manufacturing labor	41
Accounts payable, Jan. 1, 2014	40	Plant supplies used	5
Direct materials inventory, Jan. 1, 2014	39	Property taxes on plant	3

Required

Prepare an income statement and a supporting schedule of cost of goods manufactured. (For additional questions regarding these facts, see the next problem.)

37 Terminology, interpretation of statements (continuation of 36).

Required

1. Calculate total prime costs and total conversion costs.
2. Calculate total inventoriable costs and period costs.
3. Design costs and R&D costs are not considered product costs for financial statement purposes. When might some of these costs be regarded as product costs? Give an example.
4. Suppose that both the direct materials used and the depreciation on plant and equipment are related to the manufacture of 1 million units of product. Determine the unit cost for the direct materials assigned to those units and the unit cost for depreciation on plant and equipment. Assume that yearly depreciation is computed on a straight-line basis.
5. Assume that the implied cost-behavior patterns in requirement 4 persist. That is, direct material costs behave as a variable cost and depreciation on plant and equipment behaves as a fixed cost. Repeat the computations in requirement 4, assuming that the costs are being predicted for the manufacture of 2 million units of product. Determine the effect on total costs.
6. Assume that depreciation on the equipment (but not the plant) is computed based on the number of units produced because the equipment deteriorates with units produced. The depreciation rate on equipment is $1 per unit. Calculate the depreciation on equipment assuming (a) 1 million units of product are produced and (b) 2 million units of product are produced.

38 Labor cost, overtime, and idle time. Louie Anderson works in the production department of Southwest Plasticworks as a machine operator. Louie, a long-time employee of Southwest, is paid on an hourly basis at a rate of $20 per hour. Louie works five 8-hour shifts per week Monday–Friday (40 hours). Any time Louie works over and above these 40 hours is considered overtime for which he is paid at a rate of time and a half ($30 per hour). If the overtime falls on weekends, Louie is paid at a rate of double time ($40 per hour). Louie is also paid an additional $20 per hour for any holidays worked, even if it is part of his regular 40 hours. Louie is paid his regular wages even if the machines are down (not operating) due to regular machine maintenance, slow order periods, or unexpected mechanical problems. These hours are considered "idle time."

During December Louie worked the following hours:

	Hours worked including machine downtime	Machine downtime
Week 1	48	6.4
Week 2	44	2.0
Week 3	43	5.8
Week 4	46	3.5

Included in the total hours worked are two company holidays (Christmas Eve and Christmas Day) during Week 4. All overtime worked by Louie was Monday–Friday, except for the hours worked in Week 3; all of the Week 3 overtime hours were worked on a Saturday.

Required

1. Calculate (a) direct manufacturing labor, (b) idle time, (c) overtime and holiday premium, and (d) total earnings for Louie in December.
2. Is idle time and overtime premium a direct or indirect cost of the products that Louie worked on in December? Explain.

39 Missing records, computing inventory costs. Ron Howard recently took over as the controller of Johnson Brothers Manufacturing. Last month, the previous controller left the company with little notice and left the accounting records in disarray. Ron needs the ending inventory balances to report first-quarter numbers.

For the previous month (March 2014) Ron was able to piece together the following information:

Direct materials purchased	$120,000
Work-in-process inventory, 3/1/2014	$ 35,000
Direct materials inventory, 3/1/2014	$ 12, 500
Finished goods inventory, 3/1/2014	$160,000
Conversion costs	$330,000
Total manufacturing costs added during the period	$420,000
Cost of goods manufactured	4 times direct materials used
Gross margin as a percentage of revenues	20%
Revenues	$518,750

Calculate the cost of:

Required

1. Finished goods inventory, 3/31/2014
2. Work-in-process inventory, 3/31/2014
3. Direct materials inventory, 3/31/2014

40 Comprehensive problem on unit costs, product costs. Atlanta Office Equipment manufactures and sells metal shelving. It began operations on January 1, 2014. Costs incurred for 2014 are as follows (V stands for variable; F stands for fixed):

Direct materials used	$149,500 V
Direct manufacturing labor costs	34,500 V
Plant energy costs	6,000 V
Indirect manufacturing labor costs	12,000 V
Indirect manufacturing labor costs	17,000 F
Other indirect manufacturing costs	7,000 V
Other indirect manufacturing costs	27,000 F
Marketing, distribution, and customer-service costs	126,000 V
Marketing, distribution, and customer-service costs	47,000 F
Administrative costs	58,000 F

Variable manufacturing costs are variable with respect to units produced. Variable marketing, distribution, and customer-service costs are variable with respect to units sold.
Inventory data are as follows:

	Beginning: January 1, 2014	Ending: December 31, 2014
Direct materials	0 lb	2,300 lbs
Work in process	0 units	0 units
Finished goods	0 units	? units

Production in 2014 was 115,000 units. Two pounds of direct materials are used to make one unit of finished product.

Revenues in 2014 were $540,000. The selling price per unit and the purchase price per pound of direct materials were stable throughout the year. The company's ending inventory of finished goods is carried at the average unit manufacturing cost for 2014. Finished-goods inventory at December 31, 2014, was $15,400.

Required

1. Calculate direct materials inventory, total cost, December 31, 2014.
2. Calculate finished-goods inventory, total units, December 31, 2014.
3. Calculate selling price in 2014.
4. Calculate operating income for 2014.

41 Cost classification; ethics. Jason Hand, the new plant manager of Old Tree Manufacturing Plant Number 7, has just reviewed a draft of his year-end financial statements. Hand receives a year-end bonus of 8% of the plant's operating income before tax. The year-end income statement provided by the plant's controller was disappointing to say the least. After reviewing the numbers, Hand demanded that his controller go back and "work the numbers" again. Hand insisted that if he didn't see a better operating income number the next time around he would be forced to look for a new controller.

Old Tree Manufacturing classifies all costs directly related to the manufacturing of its product as product costs. These costs are inventoried and later expensed as costs of goods sold when the product is sold. All other expenses, including finished goods warehousing costs of $3,570,000, are classified as period expenses. Hand had suggested that warehousing costs be included as product costs because they are "definitely related to our product." The company produced 210,000 units during the period and sold 190,000 units.

As the controller reworked the numbers, he discovered that if he included warehousing costs as product costs, he could improve operating income by $340,000. He was also sure these new numbers would make Hand happy.

Required

1. Show numerically how operating income would improve by $340,000 just by classifying the preceding costs as product costs instead of period expenses.
2. Is Hand correct in his justification that these costs are "definitely related to our product"?
3. By how much will Hand profit personally if the controller makes the adjustments in requirement 1?
4. What should the plant controller do?

42 Finding unknown amounts. An auditor for the Internal Revenue Service is trying to reconstruct some partially destroyed records of two taxpayers. For each of the cases in the accompanying list, find the unknowns designated by the letters A through D.

	Case 1	Case 2
	(in thousands)	
Accounts receivable, 12/31	$ 9,000	$ 3,150
Cost of goods sold	A	30,000
Accounts payable, 1/1	4, 500	2,550
Accounts payable, 12/31	2,700	2,250
Finished goods inventory, 12/31	B	7,950
Gross margin	16,950	C
Work-in-process inventory, 1/1	0	1,200
Work-in-process inventory, 12/31	0	4,500
Finished goods inventory, 1/1	6,000	6,000
Direct materials used	12,000	18,000
Direct manufacturing labor	4,500	7,500
Manufacturing overhead costs	10,500	D
Purchases of direct materials	13,500	10,500
Revenues	48,000	47,700
Accounts receivable, 1/1	3,000	2,100

Glossary

Actual cost.   Cost incurred (a historical or past cost), as distinguished from a budgeted or forecasted cost.

Average cost.   See *unit cost*.

Budgeted cost.   Predicted or forecasted cost (future cost) as distinguished from an actual or historical cost.

Conversion costs.   All manufacturing costs other than direct material costs.

Cost.   Resource sacrificed or forgone to achieve a specific objective.

Cost accumulation.   Collection of cost data in some organized way by means of an accounting system.

Cost allocation.   Assignment of indirect costs to a particular cost object.

Cost assignment.   General term that encompasses both (1) tracing accumulated costs that have a direct relationship to a cost object and (2) allocating accumulated costs that have an indirect relationship to a cost object.

Cost driver.   A variable, such as the level of activity or volume, that causally affects costs over a given time span.

Cost object.   Anything for which a measurement of costs is desired.

Cost of goods manufactured.   Cost of goods brought to completion, whether they were started before or during the current accounting period.

Cost tracing.   Describes the assignment of direct costs to a particular cost object.

Direct costs of a cost object.   Costs related to the particular cost object that can be traced to that object in an economically feasible (cost-effective) way.

Direct manufacturing labor costs.   Include the compensation of all manufacturing labor that can be traced to the cost object (work in process and then finished goods) in an economically feasible way.

Direct materials costs.   Acquisition costs of all materials that eventually become part of the cost object (work in process and then finished goods), and that can be traced to the cost object in an economically feasible way.

Direct materials inventory.   Direct materials in stock and awaiting use in the manufacturing process.

Factory overhead costs.   See *indirect manufacturing costs.*

Finished goods inventory.   Goods completed but not yet sold.

Fixed cost.   Cost that remains unchanged in total for a given time period, despite wide changes in the related level of total activity or volume.

Idle time.   Wages paid for unproductive time caused by lack of orders, machine breakdowns, material shortages, poor scheduling, and the like.

Indirect costs of a cost object.   Costs related to the particular cost object that cannot be traced to that object in an economically feasible (cost-effective) way.

Indirect manufacturing costs.   All manufacturing costs that are related to the cost object (work in process and then finished goods) but that cannot be traced to that cost object in an economically feasible way. Also called *manufacturing overhead costs* and *factory overhead costs.*

Inventoriable costs.   All costs of a product that are considered as assets in the balance sheet when they are incurred and that become cost of goods sold only when the product is sold.

Manufacturing overhead costs.   See *indirect manufacturing costs.*

Manufacturing-sector companies.   Companies that purchase materials and components and convert them into various finished goods.

Merchandising-sector companies.   Companies that purchase and then sell tangible products without changing their basic form.

Operating income.   Total revenues from operations minus cost of goods sold and operating costs (excluding interest expense and income taxes).

Overtime premium.   Wage rate paid to workers (for both direct labor and indirect labor) in excess of their straight-time wage rates.

Period costs.   All costs in the income statement other than cost of goods sold.

Prime costs.   All direct manufacturing costs.

Product cost.   Sum of the costs assigned to a product for a specific purpose.

Relevant range.   Band of normal activity level or volume in which there is a specific relationship between the level of activity or volume and the cost in question.

Revenues.   Inflows of assets (usually cash or accounts receivable) received for products or services provided to customers.

Service-sector companies.   Companies that provide services or intangible products to their customers.

Unit cost.   Cost computed by dividing total cost by the number of units. Also called *average cost.*

Variable cost.   Cost that changes in total in proportion to changes in the related level of total activity or volume.

Work-in-process inventory.   Goods partially worked on but not yet completed. Also called *work in progress.*

Work in progress.   See *work-in-process inventory.*

Photo Credits

Credits are listed in order of appearance.

Photo 1: Rachel Youdelman/Pearson Education, Inc.
Photo 2: Jim Wilson/The New York Times/Redux Pictures
Photo 3: Kristoffer Tripplaar/Alamy

Chapter 3

Chapter 3

Cost–Volume–Profit Analysis

From Chapter 3 of *Cost Accounting: A Managerial Emphasis,* Fifteenth Edition. Charles T. Horngren, Srikant M. Datar, Madhav V. Rajan. Copyright © 2015 by Pearson Education, Inc. All rights reserved.

Cost–Volume–Profit Analysis

All managers want to know how profits will change as the units sold of a product or service change.

Home Depot managers, for example, might wonder how many units of a new power drill must be sold to break even or make a certain amount of profit. Procter & Gamble managers might ask themselves how expanding their business in Nigeria would affect costs, revenues, and profits. These questions have a common "what-if" theme: What if we sold more power drills? What if we started selling in Nigeria? Examining the results of these what-if possibilities and alternatives helps managers make better decisions.

Managers must also decide how to price their products and understand the effect of their pricing decisions on revenues and profits. The following article explains how the Irish rock band U2 decided whether it should decrease the prices of some of its tickets during a recent world tour. Does lowering ticket prices sound like a wise strategy to you?

How "The Biggest Rock Show Ever" Turned a Big Profit[1]

On its recent world tour across North America, Europe, and Asia, the rock bank U2 performed on an imposing 164-foot-high stage that resembled a spaceship, complete with a massive video screen and footbridges leading to ringed catwalks. U2 used three separate stages—each one costing nearly $40 million dollars. Additional expenses for the tour were $750,000 daily. As a result, the tour's success depended not only on the quality of each night's concert but also on recouping its tremendous fixed costs—costs that did not change with the number of fans in the audience.

To cover its high fixed costs and make a profit, U2 needed to sell a lot of tickets. To maximize the tour's revenue, tickets were sold for as little as $30, and a unique in-the-round stage configuration boosted stadium capacities by roughly 20%. The plan worked. U2 shattered attendance records in most of the venues it played. By the end of the tour, the band played to more than 7 million fans, racking up almost $736 million in ticket and merchandise sales... and went in to the history books as the biggest tour ever. As you read this chapter, you will begin to understand how and why U2 made the decision to lower prices.

Businesses that have high fixed costs have to pay particular attention to the "what-ifs" behind decisions because making the wrong choices can be disastrous. Examples of well-known companies that have high fixed costs are American Airlines

---

[1] *Sources:* Gundersen, Edna. 2009. U2 turns 360 stadium tour into attendance-shattering sellouts. *USA Today*, October 4; and Waddell, Ray. 2011. U2's "360" Tour Gross: $736,137,344! *Billboard*, July 29.

and General Motors. When companies have high fixed costs, they need significant revenues just to break even. In the airline industry, for example, companies' fixed costs are so high the profits most airlines make come from the last two to five passengers who board each flight! Consequently, when revenues at American Airlines dropped, it was forced to declare bankruptcy. In this chapter, you will see how cost–volume–profit (CVP) analysis helps managers minimize such risks.

Essentials of CVP Analysis

Managers use **cost–volume–profit (CVP) analysis** to study the behavior of and relationship among these elements as changes occur in the number of units sold, the selling price, the variable cost per unit, or the fixed costs of a product. Consider this example:

> Example: Emma Jones is a young entrepreneur who recently used *GMAT Success*, a test-prep book and software package for the business school admission test. Emma loved the book and program so much that after graduating she signed a contract with *GMAT Success's* publisher to sell the learning materials. She recently sold them at a college fair in Boston and is now thinking of selling them at a college fair in Chicago. Emma knows she can purchase each package (book and software) from the publisher for $120 per package, with the privilege of returning all unsold packages and receiving a full $120 refund per package. She also knows that she must pay $2,000 to rent a booth at the fair. She will incur no other costs. Should she rent the booth or not?

Emma, like most managers who face such a situation, will need to work through the series of steps introduced to make the most profitable decisions.

1. **Identify the problem and uncertainties.** Every managerial decision involves selecting a course of action. The decision to rent the booth hinges on how Emma resolves two important uncertainties: the price she can charge and the number of packages she can sell at that price. Emma must decide knowing that the outcome of the action she chooses is uncertain. The more confident she is about selling a large number of packages at a high price, the more willing she will be to rent the booth.

2. **Obtain information.** When faced with uncertainty, managers obtain information that might help them understand the uncertainties more clearly. For example, Emma gathers information about the type of individuals likely to attend the fair and other test-prep packages that might be sold at the fair. She also gathers data from her experience selling the packages at the Boston fair.

3. **Make predictions about the future.** Managers make predictions using all the information available to them. Emma predicts she can charge $200 for the *GMAT Success* package. At that price, she is reasonably confident that she will be able to sell at least 30 packages and possibly as many as 60. Emma must be realistic and exercise judgment when making these predictions. If they are too optimistic, she will rent the booth when she should not. If they are too pessimistic, she will not rent the booth when she should.

Emma's predictions rest on the belief that her experience at the Chicago fair will be similar to her experience at the Boston fair 4 months earlier. Yet Emma is uncertain about several aspects of her prediction. Are the fairs truly comparable? For example, will attendance at the two fairs be the same? Have market conditions changed over the past 4 months? Are there any biases creeping into her thinking? She is keen on selling at the Chicago fair because sales in the last couple of months have been lower than expected. Is this experience making her predictions overly optimistic? Has she ignored some of the competitive risks? Will the other test-prep vendors at the fair reduce their prices? If they do, should she? How many packages can she expect to sell if she does?

Emma rethinks her plan and retests her assumptions. She obtains data about student attendance and total sales in past years from the organizers of the fair. In the end, she feels quite confident that her predictions are reasonable, accurate, and carefully thought through.

4. **Make decisions by choosing among alternatives.** Emma uses the CVP analysis that follows and decides to rent the booth at the Chicago fair.

5. **Implement the decision, evaluate performance, and learn.** Thoughtful managers never stop learning. They compare their actual performance to predicted performance to understand why things worked out the way they did and what they might learn. At the end of the Chicago fair, for example, Emma would want to evaluate whether her predictions about price and the number of packages she could sell were correct. This will help her make better decisions about renting booths at future fairs.

How does Emma use CVP analysis in Step 4 to make her decision? She begins by identifying which costs are fixed and which costs are variable and then calculates *contribution margin*.

Contribution Margin

The booth-rental cost of $2,000 is a fixed cost because it will not change no matter how many packages Emma sells. The total cost of the packages is a variable cost because it increases in proportion to the number of packages sold and she can return whatever she doesn't sell for a full refund.

To understand how her operating income will change by selling different quantities of packages, Emma calculates operating income if sales are 5 packages and if sales are 40 packages.

	5 packages sold	**40 packages sold**
Revenues	$ 1,000 ($200 per package × 5 packages)	$8,000 ($200 per package × 40 packages)
Variable purchase costs	600 ($120 per package × 5 packages)	4,800 ($120 per package × 40 packages)
Fixed costs	2,000	2,000
Operating income	$(1,600)	$1,200

The only numbers that change from selling different quantities of packages are *total revenues* and *total variable costs*. The difference between total revenues and total variable costs is called **contribution margin**. That is,

$$\text{Contribution margin} = \text{Total revenues} - \text{Total variable costs}$$

Contribution margin indicates why operating income changes as the number of units sold changes. The contribution margin when Emma sells 5 packages is $400 ($1,000 in total revenues minus $600 in total variable costs); the contribution margin when Emma sells 40 packages is $3,200 ($8,000 in total revenues minus $4,800 in total variable costs). When calculating the contribution margin, be sure to subtract all variable costs. For example, if Emma incurred some variable selling costs because she paid a commission to salespeople for each package they sold at the fair, variable costs would include the cost of each package plus the sales commission paid on it.

Contribution margin per unit is a useful tool for calculating contribution margin and operating income. It is defined as:

$$\text{Contribution margin per unit} = \text{Selling price} - \text{Variable cost per unit}$$

In the *GMAT Success* example, the contribution margin per package, or per unit, is $200 − $120 = $80. Contribution margin per unit recognizes the tight coupling of selling price and variable cost per unit. Unlike fixed costs, Emma will only incur the variable cost per unit of $120 when she sells a unit of *GMAT Success*.

Contribution margin per unit provides a second way to calculate contribution margin:

$$\text{Contribution margin} = \text{Contribution margin per unit} \times \text{Number of units sold}$$

For example, when Emma sells 40 packages, contribution margin = $80 per unit × 40 units = $3,200.

Even before she gets to the fair, Emma incurs $2,000 in fixed costs. Because the contribution margin per unit is $80, Emma will recover $80 for each package that she sells at the fair. Emma hopes to sell enough packages to fully recover the $2,000 she spent renting the booth and to then make a profit.

Exhibit 1 shows contribution margins for different quantities of packages sold. The income statement in Exhibit 1 is called a **contribution income statement** because it groups costs into variable costs and fixed costs to highlight contribution margin.

$$\text{Operating income} = \text{Contribution margin} - \text{Fixed costs}$$

Each additional package sold from 0 to 1 to 5 increases contribution margin by $80 per package and helps Emma recover more and more of her fixed costs and reduce her operating loss. If Emma sells 25 packages, contribution margin equals $2,000 ($80 per package × 25 packages). This quantity exactly recovers her fixed costs and results in $0 operating income. If Emma sells 40 packages, contribution margin increases by another $1,200 ($3,200 − $2,000), all of which becomes operating income. As you look across Exhibit 1 from left to right, you see that the increase in contribution margin exactly equals the increase in operating income (or the decrease in operating loss).

When companies, such as Samsung and Prada, sell multiple products, calculating contribution margin per unit is cumbersome. Instead of expressing contribution margin in dollars per unit, these companies express it as a percentage called **contribution margin percentage** (or **contribution margin ratio**):

$$\text{Contribution margin percentage (or contribution margin ratio)} = \frac{\text{Contribution margin}}{\text{Revenues}}$$

Consider a sales level such as the 40 units sold in Exhibit 1:

$$\text{Contribution margin percentage} = \frac{\$3,200}{\$8,000} = 0.40, \text{ or } 40\%$$

	Home	Insert	Page Layout	Formulas	Data	Review	View	
	A	B	C	D	E	F	G	H
1				Number of Packages Sold				
2				0	1	5	25	40
3	Revenues	$ 200	per package	$ 0	$ 200	$ 1,000	$5,000	$8,000
4	Variable costs	$ 120	per package	0	120	600	3,000	4,800
5	Contribution margin	$ 80	per package	0	80	400	2,000	3,200
6	Fixed costs	$2,000		2,000	2,000	2,000	2,000	2,000
7	Operating income			$(2,000)	$(1,920)	$(1,600)	$ 0	$1,200

Contribution margin percentage is the contribution margin per dollar of revenue. Emma earns 40% for each dollar of revenue (40 cents) she takes in. Contribution margin percentage is a handy way to calculate contribution margin for different dollar amounts of revenue. Rearranging terms in the equation defining contribution margin percentage, we get:

$$\text{Contribution margin} = \text{Contribution margin percentage} \times \text{Revenues (in dollars)}$$

To derive the relationship between operating income and contribution margin percentage, recall that:

$$\text{Operating income} = \text{Contribution margin} - \text{Fixed costs}$$

Substituting for contribution margin in the above equation:

$$\text{Operating income} = \text{Contribution margin percentage} \times \text{Revenues} - \text{Fixed costs}$$

For example, in Exhibit 1, if Emma sells 40 packages:

Revenues	$8,000
Contribution margin percentage	40%
Contribution margin, 40% × $8,000	$3,200
Fixed costs	2,000
Operating income	$1,200

When there is only one product, as in our example, we can divide both the numerator and denominator of the contribution margin percentage equation by the quantity of units sold and calculate contribution margin percentage as follows:

$$\text{Contribution margin percentage} = \frac{\text{Contribution margin/Quantity of units sold}}{\text{Revenues/Quantity of units sold}}$$
$$= \frac{\text{Contribution margin per unit}}{\text{Selling price}}$$

In our example,

$$\text{Contribution margin percentage} = \frac{\$80}{\$200} = 0.40, \text{ or } 40\%$$

Contribution margin percentage is a useful tool for calculating how a change in revenues changes contribution margin. As Emma's revenues increase by $3,000 from $5,000 to $8,000, her contribution margin increases from $2,000 to $3,200 (by $1,200):

Contribution margin at revenue of $8,000, 0.40 × $8,000	$3,200
Contribution margin at revenue of $5,000, 0.40 × $5,000	2,000
Change in contribution margin when revenue increases by $3,000, 0.40 × $3,000	$1,200

$$\text{Change in contribution margin} = \text{Contribution margin percentage} \times \text{Change in revenues}$$

Contribution margin analysis is a widely used technique. For example, managers at Home Depot use contribution margin analysis to evaluate how sales fluctuations during a recession will affect the company's profitability.

Expressing CVP Relationships

How was the Excel spreadsheet in Exhibit 1 constructed? Underlying the exhibit are some equations that express the CVP relationships. To make good decisions using CVP analysis, we must understand these relationships and the structure of the contribution income statement in Exhibit 1. There are three related ways (we will call them "methods") to think more deeply about and model CVP relationships:

1. The equation method
2. The contribution margin method
3. The graph method

As you will learn later in the chapter, different methods are useful for different decisions.

The equation method and the contribution margin method are most useful when managers want to determine operating income at a few specific sales levels (for example, 5, 15, 25, and 40 units sold). The graph method helps managers visualize the relationship between units sold and operating income over a wide range of quantities.

Equation Method

Each column in Exhibit 1 is expressed as an equation.

$$\text{Revenues} - \text{Variable costs} - \text{Fixed costs} = \text{Operating income}$$

How are revenues in each column calculated?

$$\text{Revenues} = \text{Selling price } (SP) \times \text{Quantity of units sold } (Q)$$

How are variable costs in each column calculated?

$$\text{Variable costs} = \text{Variable cost per unit } (VCU) \times \text{Quantity of units sold } (Q)$$

So,

$$\left[\left(\begin{array}{c} \text{Selling} \\ \text{price} \end{array} \right) \times \left(\begin{array}{c} \text{Quantity of} \\ \text{units sold} \end{array} \right) - \left(\begin{array}{c} \text{Variable cost} \\ \text{per unit} \end{array} \right) \times \left(\begin{array}{c} \text{Quantity of} \\ \text{units sold} \end{array} \right) \right] - \begin{array}{c} \text{Fixed} \\ \text{costs} \end{array} = \begin{array}{c} \text{Operating} \\ \text{income} \end{array} \quad \text{(Equation 1)}$$

Equation 1 becomes the basis for calculating operating income for different quantities of units sold. For example, if you go to cell F7 in Exhibit 1, the calculation of operating income when Emma sells 5 packages is

$$(\$200 \times 5) - (\$120 \times 5) - \$2,000 = \$1,000 - \$600 - \$2,000 = -\$1,600$$

Contribution Margin Method

Rearranging equation 1,

$$\left[\left(\begin{array}{c} \text{Selling} \\ \text{price} \end{array} - \begin{array}{c} \text{Variable cost} \\ \text{per unit} \end{array} \right) \times \left(\begin{array}{c} \text{Quantity of} \\ \text{units sold} \end{array} \right) \right] - \begin{array}{c} \text{Fixed} \\ \text{costs} \end{array} = \begin{array}{c} \text{Operating} \\ \text{income} \end{array}$$

$$\left(\begin{array}{c} \text{Contribution margin} \\ \text{per unit} \end{array} \times \begin{array}{c} \text{Quantity of} \\ \text{units sold} \end{array} \right) - \begin{array}{c} \text{Fixed} \\ \text{costs} \end{array} = \begin{array}{c} \text{Operating} \\ \text{income} \end{array} \quad \text{(Equation 2)}$$

In our *GMAT Success* example, contribution margin per unit is \$80 (\$200 − \$120), so when Emma sells 5 packages,

$$\text{Operating income} = (\$80 \times 5) - \$2,000 = -\$1,600$$

Equation 2 expresses the basic idea we described earlier—each unit sold helps Emma recover \$80 (in contribution margin) of the \$2,000 in fixed costs.

Graph Method

The graph method helps managers visualize the relationships between total revenues and total costs. The graph shows each relationship as a line. Exhibit 2 illustrates the graph method for selling *GMAT Success*. Because we have assumed that total costs and total revenues behave in a linear way, we need only two points to plot the line representing each of them.

1. **Total costs line.** The total costs line is the sum of fixed costs and variable costs. Fixed costs are \$2,000 for all quantities of units sold within the relevant range. To plot the

Exhibit 2

Cost–Volume Graph for *GMAT Success*

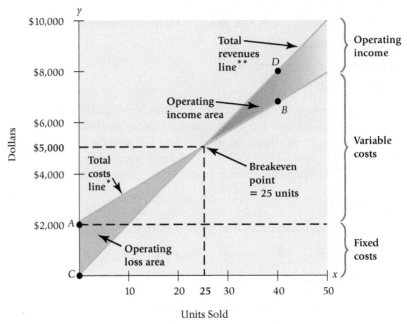

*Slope of the total costs line is the variable cost per unit = $120
**Slope of the total revenues line is the selling price = $200

total costs line, use as one point the $2,000 fixed costs at zero units sold (point A) because variable costs are $0 when no units are sold. Select a second point by choosing any other output level (say, 40 units sold) and determine the corresponding total costs. Total variable costs at this output level are $4,800 (40 units × $120 per unit). Remember, fixed costs are $2,000 at all quantities of units sold within the relevant range, so total costs at 40 units sold equal $6,800 ($2,000 + $4,800), which is point B in Exhibit 2. The total costs line is the straight line from point A through point B.

2. **Total revenues line.** One convenient starting point is $0 revenues at 0 units sold, which is point C in Exhibit 2. Select a second point by choosing any other convenient output level and determining the corresponding total revenues. At 40 units sold, total revenues are $8,000 ($200 per unit × 40 units), which is point D in Exhibit 2. The total revenues line is the straight line from point C through point D.

   The profit or loss at any sales level can be determined by the vertical distance between the two lines at that level in Exhibit 2. For quantities fewer than 25 units sold, total costs exceed total revenues, and the purple area indicates operating losses. For quantities greater than 25 units sold, total revenues exceed total costs, and the blue-green area indicates operating incomes. At 25 units sold, total revenues equal total costs. Emma will break even by selling 25 packages.

Decision Point

How can CVP analysis help managers?

Like Emma, many companies, particularly small- and medium-sized companies, use the graph method to see how their revenues and costs will change as the quantity of units sold changes. The graph helps them understand their regions of profitability and unprofitability.

Cost-Volume-Profit Assumptions

Now that you know how CVP analysis works, think about the following assumptions we made during the analysis:

1. Changes in revenues and costs arise only because of changes in the number of product (or service) units sold. The number of units sold is the only revenue driver and the only cost driver. Just as a cost driver is any factor that affects costs, a **revenue driver** is a variable, such as volume, that causally affects revenues.

2. Total costs can be separated into two components: a fixed component that does not vary with units sold (such as Emma's $2,000 booth fee) and a variable component that changes based on units sold (such as the $120 cost per *GMAT Success* package).

3. When represented graphically, the behaviors of total revenues and total costs are linear (meaning they can be represented as a straight line) in relation to units sold within a relevant range (and time period).

4. Selling price, variable cost per unit, and total fixed costs (within a relevant range and time period) are known and constant.

As you can tell from these assumptions, to conduct a CVP analysis, you need to correctly distinguish fixed from variable costs. Always keep in mind, however, that whether a cost is variable or fixed depends on the time period for a decision.

The shorter the time horizon, the higher the percentage of total costs considered fixed. For example, suppose an American Airlines plane will depart from its gate in the next hour and currently has 20 seats unsold. A potential passenger arrives with a transferable ticket from a competing airline. American's variable costs of placing one more passenger in an otherwise empty seat (such as the cost of providing the passenger with a free beverage) is negligible. With only an hour to go before the flight departs, virtually all costs (such as crew costs and baggage-handling costs) are fixed.

Alternatively, suppose American Airlines must decide whether to continue to offer this particular flight next year. If American Airlines decides to cancel this flight because very few passengers during the last year have taken it, many more of its costs, including crew costs, baggage-handling costs, and airport fees for the flight, would be considered variable: Over this longer 1-year time period, American Airlines would not have to incur these costs if the flight were no longer operating. Always consider the relevant range, the length of the time horizon, and the specific decision situation when classifying costs as variable or fixed.

Breakeven Point and Target Operating Income

◀ Learning Objective **2**

Determine the breakeven point and output level needed to achieve a target operating income

...compare contribution margin and fixed costs

Managers and entrepreneurs like Emma always want to know how much they must sell to earn a given amount of income. Equally important, they want to know how much they must sell to avoid a loss.

Breakeven Point

The **breakeven point** (**BEP**) is that quantity of output sold at which total revenues equal total costs—that is, the quantity of output sold that results in $0 of operating income. You have already learned how to use the graph method to calculate the breakeven point. Recall from Exhibit 1 that operating income was $0 when Emma sold 25 units; this is the breakeven point. But by understanding the equations underlying the calculations in Exhibit 1, we can calculate the breakeven point directly for selling *GMAT Success* rather than trying out different quantities and checking when operating income equals $0.

Recall the equation method (equation 1):

$$\left[\left(\begin{array}{c}\text{Selling}\\\text{price}\end{array} \times \begin{array}{c}\text{Quantity of}\\\text{units sold}\end{array}\right) - \left(\begin{array}{c}\text{Variable cost}\\\text{per unit}\end{array} \times \begin{array}{c}\text{Quantity of}\\\text{units sold}\end{array}\right)\right] - \begin{array}{c}\text{Fixed}\\\text{costs}\end{array} = \begin{array}{c}\text{Operating}\\\text{income}\end{array}$$

Setting operating income equal to $0 and denoting quantity of output units that must be sold by Q,

$$(\$200 \times Q) - (\$120 \times Q) - \$2,000 = \$0$$
$$\$80 \times Q = \$2,000$$
$$Q = \$2,000 \div \$80 \text{ per unit} = 25 \text{ units}$$

If Emma sells fewer than 25 units, she will incur a loss; if she sells 25 units, she will break even; and if she sells more than 25 units, she will make a profit. Although this breakeven point is expressed in units, it can also be expressed in revenues: 25 units × $200 selling price = $5,000.

Recall the contribution margin method (equation 2):

$$\left(\begin{array}{c} \text{Contribution} \\ \text{margin per unit} \end{array} \times \begin{array}{c} \text{Quantity of} \\ \text{units sold} \end{array} \right) - \text{Fixed costs} = \text{Operating income}$$

At the breakeven point, operating income is by definition $0, and so,

$$\text{Contribution margin per unit} \times \text{Breakeven quantity of units} = \text{Fixed costs} \qquad \text{(Equation 3)}$$

Rearranging equation 3 and entering the data,

$$\begin{array}{c} \text{Breakeven} \\ \text{number of units} \end{array} = \frac{\text{Fixed costs}}{\text{Contribution margin per unit}} = \frac{\$2,000}{\$80 \text{ per unit}} = 25 \text{ units}$$

$$\text{Breakeven revenues} = \text{Breakeven number of units} \times \text{Selling price}$$
$$= 25 \text{ units} \times \$200 \text{ per unit} = \$5,000$$

In practice (because companies have multiple products), management accountants usually calculate the breakeven point directly in terms of revenues using contribution margin percentages. Recall that in the *GMAT Success* example, at revenues of $8,000, contribution margin is $3,200:

$$\begin{array}{c} \text{Contribution margin} \\ \text{percentage} \end{array} = \frac{\text{Contribution margin}}{\text{Revenues}} = \frac{\$3,200}{\$8,000} = 0.40, \text{ or } 40\%$$

That is, 40% of each dollar of revenue, or 40 cents, is the contribution margin. To break even, contribution margin must equal Emma's fixed costs, which are $2,000. To earn $2,000 of contribution margin, when $1 of revenue results in a $0.40 contribution margin, revenues must equal $2,000 ÷ 0.40 = $5,000.

$$\begin{array}{c} \text{Breakeven} \\ \text{revenues} \end{array} = \frac{\text{Fixed costs}}{\text{Contribution margin \%}} = \frac{\$2,000}{0.40} = \$5,000$$

While the breakeven point tells managers how much they must sell to avoid a loss, managers are equally interested in how they will achieve the operating income targets underlying their strategies and plans. In our example, selling 25 units at a price of $200 (equal to revenue of $5,000) assures Emma that she will not lose money if she rents the booth. While this news is comforting, how does Emma determine how much she needs to sell to achieve a targeted amount of operating income?

Target Operating Income

Suppose Emma wants to earn an operating income of $1,200? How many units must she sell? One approach is to keep plugging in different quantities into Exhibit 1 and check when operating income equals $1,200. Exhibit 1 shows that operating income is $1,200 when 40 packages are sold. A more convenient approach is to use equation 1.

$$\left[\left(\begin{array}{c} \text{Selling} \\ \text{price} \end{array} \times \begin{array}{c} \text{Quantity of} \\ \text{units sold} \end{array} \right) - \left(\begin{array}{c} \text{Variable cost} \\ \text{per unit} \end{array} \times \begin{array}{c} \text{Quantity of} \\ \text{units sold} \end{array} \right) \right] - \begin{array}{c} \text{Fixed} \\ \text{costs} \end{array} = \begin{array}{c} \text{Operating} \\ \text{income} \end{array} \qquad \text{(Equation 1)}$$

We denote by Q the unknown quantity of units Emma must sell to earn an operating income of $1,200. Selling price is $200, variable cost per package is $120, fixed costs are $2,000, and target operating income is $1,200. Substituting these values into equation 1, we have

$$(\$200 \times Q) - (\$120 \times Q) - \$2,000 = \$1,200$$
$$\$80 \times Q = \$2,000 + \$1,200 = \$3,200$$
$$Q = \$3,200 \div \$80 \text{ per unit} = 40 \text{ units}$$

Alternatively, we could use equation 2,

$$\left(\begin{array}{c}\text{Contribution margin} \\ \text{per unit}\end{array} \times \begin{array}{c}\text{Quantity of} \\ \text{units sold}\end{array}\right) - \begin{array}{c}\text{Fixed} \\ \text{costs}\end{array} = \begin{array}{c}\text{Operating} \\ \text{income}\end{array} \qquad \text{(Equation 2)}$$

Given a target operating income ($1,200 in this case), we can rearrange terms to get equation 4.

$$\begin{array}{c}\text{Quantity of units} \\ \text{required to be sold}\end{array} = \frac{\text{Fixed costs} + \text{Target operating income}}{\text{Contribution margin per unit}} \qquad \text{(Equation 4)}$$

$$\begin{array}{c}\text{Quantity of units} \\ \text{required to be sold}\end{array} = \frac{\$2,000 + \$1,200}{\$80 \text{ per unit}} = 40 \text{ units}$$

Proof:

Revenues, $200 per unit × 40 units	$8,000
Variable costs, $120 per unit × 40 units	4,800
Contribution margin, $80 per unit × 40 units	3,200
Fixed costs	2,000
Operating income	$1,200

The revenues needed to earn an operating income of $1,200 can also be calculated directly by recognizing (1) that $3,200 of contribution margin must be earned (to cover the fixed costs of $2,000 plus earn an operating income of $1,200) and (2) that $1 of revenue earns $0.40 (40 cents) of contribution margin (the contribution margin percentage is 40%). To earn a contribution margin of $3,200, revenues must equal $3,200 ÷ 0.40 = $8,000. That is,

$$\begin{array}{c}\text{Revenues needed to earn} \\ \text{target operating income}\end{array} = \frac{\text{Fixed costs} + \text{Target operating income}}{\text{Contribution margin percentage}}$$

$$\text{Revenues needed to earn operating income of } \$1,200 = \frac{\$2,000 + \$1,200}{0.40} = \frac{\$3,200}{0.40} = \$8,000$$

Could we use the graph method and the graph in Exhibit 2 to figure out how many units Emma must sell to earn an operating income of $1,200? Yes, but it is not as easy to determine the precise point at which the difference between the total revenues line and the total costs line equals $1,200. Recasting Exhibit 2 in the form of a profit–volume (PV) graph, however, makes it easier to answer this question.

A **PV graph** shows how changes in the quantity of units sold affect operating income. Exhibit 3 is the PV graph for *GMAT Success* (fixed costs, $2,000; selling price, $200; and variable cost per unit, $120). The PV line can be drawn using two points. One convenient

Exhibit 3

Profit–Volume Graph for *GMAT Success*

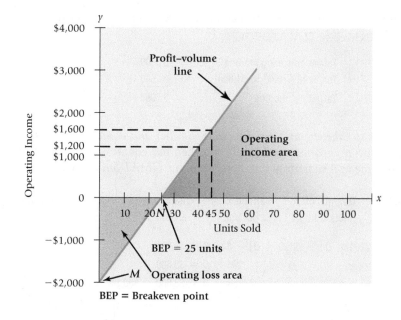

Decision Point

How can managers determine the breakeven point or the output needed to achieve a target operating income?

point (M) is the operating loss at 0 units sold, which is equal to the fixed costs of $2,000 and is shown at −$2,000 on the vertical axis. A second convenient point (N) is the breakeven point, which is 25 units in our example. The PV line is the straight line from point M through point N. To find the number of units Emma must sell to earn an operating income of $1,200, draw a horizontal line parallel to the x-axis corresponding to $1,200 on the vertical axis (the y-axis). At the point where this line intersects the PV line, draw a vertical line down to the horizontal axis (the x-axis). The vertical line intersects the x-axis at 40 units, indicating that by selling 40 units Emma will earn an operating income of $1,200.

Just like Emma, managers at larger companies such as California Pizza Kitchen use profit–volume analyses to understand how profits change with sales volumes. They use this understanding to target the sales levels they need to achieve to meet their profit plans.

Learning Objective 3

Understand how income taxes affect CVP analysis

...focus on net income

Target Net Income and Income Taxes

Net income is operating income plus nonoperating revenues (such as interest revenue) minus nonoperating costs (such as interest cost) minus income taxes. For simplicity, throughout this chapter we assume nonoperating revenues and nonoperating costs are zero. So, our net income equation will simply be:

$$\text{Net income} = \text{Operating income} - \text{Income taxes}$$

Until now, we have ignored the effect of income taxes in our CVP analysis. In many companies, managers' income targets are expressed in terms of net income because the company's top executives want them to consider the effect their decisions have on the firm's operating income *after* income taxes. Some decisions might not result in a large operating income, but their tax consequences make them attractive because they have a positive effect on net income—the measure that drives shareholders' dividends and returns.

To make net income evaluations, CVP calculations for target income must be stated in terms of target net income instead of target operating income. For example, Emma may be interested in knowing the quantity of units of *GMAT Success* she must sell to earn a net income of $960, assuming an income tax rate of 40%.

$$\text{Target net income} = \left(\begin{array}{c}\text{Target} \\ \text{operating income}\end{array}\right) - \left(\begin{array}{c}\text{Target} \\ \text{operating income}\end{array} \times \text{Tax rate}\right)$$

$$\text{Target net income} = (\text{Target operating income}) \times (1 - \text{Tax rate})$$

$$\text{Target operating income} = \frac{\text{Target net income}}{1 - \text{Tax rate}} = \frac{\$960}{1 - 0.40} = \$1,600$$

In other words, to earn a target net income of $960, Emma's target operating income is $1,600.

Proof:

Target operating income	$1,600
Tax at 40% (0.40 × $1,600)	640
Target net income	$ 960

The key step is to take the target net income number and convert it into the corresponding target operating income number. We can then use equation 1 to determine the target operating income and substitute numbers from our *GMAT Success* example.

$$\left[\left(\begin{array}{c}\text{Selling} \\ \text{price}\end{array} \times \begin{array}{c}\text{Quantity of} \\ \text{units sold}\end{array}\right) - \left(\begin{array}{c}\text{Variable cost} \\ \text{per unit}\end{array} \times \begin{array}{c}\text{Quantity of} \\ \text{unit sold}\end{array}\right)\right] - \begin{array}{c}\text{Fixed} \\ \text{costs}\end{array} = \begin{array}{c}\text{Operating} \\ \text{income}\end{array} \quad \text{(Equation 1)}$$

$$(\$200 \times Q) - (\$120 \times Q) - \$2,000 = \$1,600$$

$$\$80 \times Q = \$3,600$$

$$Q = \$3,600 \div \$80 \text{ per unit} = 45 \text{ units}$$

Alternatively, we can calculate the number of units Emma must sell by using the contribution margin method and equation 4:

$$\frac{\text{Quantity of units}}{\text{required to be sold}} = \frac{\text{Fixed costs } + \text{ Target operating income}}{\text{Contribution margin per unit}} \quad \text{(Equation 4)}$$

$$= \frac{\$2{,}000 + \$1{,}600}{\$80 \text{ per unit}} = 45 \text{ units}$$

Proof:

Revenues, $200 per unit $\times$ 45 units	$9,000
Variable costs, $120 per unit $\times$ 45 units	5,400
Contribution margin	3,600
Fixed costs	2,000
Operating income	1,600
Income taxes, $1,600 $\times$ 0.40	640
Net income	$ 960

Emma can also use the PV graph in Exhibit 3. To earn the target operating income of $1,600, Emma needs to sell 45 units.

Focusing the analysis on target net income instead of target operating income will not change the breakeven point because, by definition, operating income at the breakeven point is $0 and no income taxes are paid when there is no operating income.

Decision Point

How can managers incorporate income taxes into CVP analysis?

Using CVP Analysis for Decision Making

You have learned how CVP analysis is useful for calculating the units that need to be sold to break even or to achieve a target operating income or target net income. A manager can also use CVP analysis to make other strategic decisions. Consider a decision about choosing the features for a product, such as the engine size, transmission system, or steering system for a new car model. Different choices will affect the vehicle's selling price, variable cost per unit, fixed costs, units sold, and operating income. CVP analysis helps managers make product decisions by estimating the expected profitability of these choices. We return to our *GMAT Success* example to show how Emma can use a CVP analysis to make decisions about advertising and selling price.

Learning Objective 4

Explain how managers use CVP analysis to make decisions

...choose the alternative that maximizes operating income

Decision to Advertise

Suppose Emma anticipates selling 40 units of the *GMAT Success* package at the fair. Exhibit 3 indicates that Emma's operating income will be $1,200. Emma is considering advertising the product and its features in the fair brochure. The advertisement will be a fixed cost of $500. Emma thinks that advertising will increase sales by 10% to 44 packages. Should Emma advertise? The following table presents the CVP analysis.

	40 Packages Sold with No Advertising (1)	44 Packages Sold with Advertising (2)	Difference (3) = (2) − (1)
Revenues ($200 $\times$ 40; $200 $\times$ 44)	$8,000	$8,800	$ 800
Variable costs ($120 $\times$ 40; $120 $\times$ 44)	4,800	5,280	480
Contribution margin ($80 $\times$ 40; $80 $\times$ 44)	3,200	3,520	320
Fixed costs	2,000	2,500	500
Operating income	$1,200	$1,020	$ (180)

Operating income will decrease from $1,200 to $1,020, so Emma should not advertise. Note that Emma could focus only on the difference column and come to the same conclusion: If Emma advertises, contribution margin will increase by $320 (revenues,

$800 − variable costs, $480) and fixed costs will increase by $500, resulting in a $180 decrease in operating income.

When using CVP analysis, try evaluating your decisions based on differences rather than mechanically working through the contribution income statement. What if advertising costs were $400 or $600 instead of $500? Analyzing differences allows managers to get to the heart of CVP analysis and sharpens their intuition by focusing only on the revenues and costs that will change as a result of a decision.

Decision to Reduce the Selling Price

Having decided not to advertise, Emma is contemplating whether to reduce the selling price to $175. At this price, she thinks she will sell 50 units. At this quantity, the test-prep package company that supplies *GMAT Success* will sell the packages to Emma for $115 per unit instead of $120. Should Emma reduce the selling price?

Contribution margin from lowering price to $175: ($175 − $115) per unit × 50 units	$3,000
Contribution margin from maintaining price at $200: ($200 − $120) per unit × 40 units	3,200
Change in contribution margin from lowering price	$ (200)

Decreasing the price will reduce contribution margin by $200 and, because the fixed costs of $2,000 will not change, will also reduce Emma's operating income by $200. Emma should not reduce the selling price.

Determining Target Prices

Emma could also ask, "At what price can I sell 50 units (purchased at $115 per unit) and continue to earn an operating income of $1,200?" The answer is $179, as the following calculations show.

Target operating income	$1,200
Add fixed costs	2,000
Target contribution margin	$3,200
Divided by number of units sold	÷ 50 units
Target contribution margin per unit	$ 64
Add variable cost per unit	115
Target selling price	$ 179

Proof:		
	Revenues, $179 per unit × 50 units	$8,950
	Variable costs, $115 per unit × 50 units	5,750
	Contribution margin	3,200
	Fixed costs	2,000
	Operating income	$1,200

Decision Point

How do managers use CVP analysis to make decisions?

Emma should also examine the effects of other decisions, such as simultaneously increasing her advertising costs and raising or lowering the price of *GMAT Success* packages. In each case, Emma will estimate the effects these actions are likely to have on the demand for *GMAT Success*. She will then compare the changes in contribution margin (through the effects on selling prices, variable costs, and quantities of units sold) to the changes in fixed costs and choose the alternative that provides the highest operating income.

Strategic decisions invariably entail risk. Managers can use CVP analysis to evaluate how the operating income of their companies will be affected if the outcomes they predict are not achieved—say, if sales are 10% lower than they estimated. Evaluating this risk affects other strategic decisions a manager might make. For example, if the probability of a decline in sales seems high, a manager may take actions to change the cost structure to have more variable costs and fewer fixed costs.

Sensitivity Analysis and Margin of Safety

Sensitivity analysis is a "what-if" technique managers use to examine how an outcome will change if the original predicted data are not achieved or if an underlying assumption changes. The analysis answers questions such as "What will operating income be if the quantity of units sold decreases by 5% from the original prediction?" and "What will operating income be if variable cost per unit increases by 10%?" This helps visualize the possible outcomes that might occur *before* the company commits to funding a project. For example, companies such as Boeing and Airbus use CVP analysis to evaluate how many airplanes they need to sell in order to recover the multibillion-dollar costs of designing and developing new ones. The managers then do a sensitivity analysis to test how sensitive their conclusions are to different assumptions, such as the size of the market for the airplane, its selling price, and the market share they think it can capture.

Electronic spreadsheets, such as Excel, enable managers to systematically and efficiently conduct CVP-based sensitivity analyses and to examine the effect and interaction of changes in selling price, variable cost per unit, and fixed costs on target operating income. Exhibit 4 displays a spreadsheet for the *GMAT Success* example.

Using the spreadsheet, Emma can immediately see how many units she needs to sell to achieve particular operating-income levels, given alternative levels of fixed costs and variable cost per unit that she may face. For example, she must sell 32 units to earn an operating income of $1,200 if fixed costs are $2,000 and variable cost per unit is $100. Emma can also use Exhibit 4 to determine that she needs to sell 56 units to break even if the fixed cost of the booth rental at the Chicago fair is raised to $2,800 and if the variable cost per unit charged by the test-prep package supplier increases to $150. Emma can use this information along with sensitivity analysis and her predictions about how much she can sell to decide if she should rent the booth.

Another aspect of sensitivity analysis is **margin of safety:**

$$\text{Margin of safety} = \text{Budgeted (or actual) revenues} - \text{Breakeven revenues}$$

$$\text{Margin of safety (in units)} = \text{Budgeted (or actual) sales quantity} - \text{Breakeven quantity}$$

The margin of safety answers the "what-if" question: If budgeted revenues are above the breakeven point and drop, how far can they fall below budget before the breakeven point is reached? Sales might decrease as a result of factors such as a poorly executed

Exhibit 4

Spreadsheet Analysis of CVP Relationships for *GMAT Success*

	Home	Insert	Page Layout	Formulas	Data	Review	View
	D5	▼	*fx*	=($A5+D$3)/(F1-$B5)			
	A	B	C	D	E	F
1			Number of units required to be sold at $200			
2			Selling Price to Earn Target Operating Income of			
3		Variable Costs	$0	$1,200	$1,600	$2,000
4	Fixed Costs	per Unit	(Breakeven point)			
5	$2,000	$100	20	32[a]	36	40
6	$2,000	$120	25	40	45	50
7	$2,000	$150	40	64	72	80
8	$2,400	$100	24	36	40	44
9	$2,400	$120	30	45	50	55
10	$2,400	$150	48	72	80	88
11	$2,800	$100	28	40	44	48
12	$2,800	$120	35	50	55	60
13	$2,800	$150	56	80	88	96
14						
15	[a]Number of units					
16	required to be sold					

$$^{a}\text{Number of units required to be sold} = \frac{\text{Fixed costs} + \text{Target operating income}}{\text{Contribution margin per unit}} = \frac{\$2,000 + \$1,200}{\$200 - \$100} = 32$$

marketing program or a competitor introducing a better product. Assume that Emma has fixed costs of $2,000, a selling price of $200, and variable cost per unit of $120. From Exhibit 1, if Emma sells 40 units, budgeted revenues are $8,000 and budgeted operating income is $1,200. The breakeven point is 25 units or $5,000 in total revenues.

$$\text{Margin of safety} = \frac{\text{Budgeted}}{\text{revenues}} - \frac{\text{Breakeven}}{\text{revenues}} = \$8,000 - \$5,000 = \$3,000$$

$$\frac{\text{Margin of}}{\text{safety (in units)}} = \frac{\text{Budgeted}}{\text{sales (units)}} - \frac{\text{Breakeven}}{\text{sales (units)}} = 40 - 25 = 15 \text{ units}$$

Sometimes margin of safety is expressed as a percentage:

$$\text{Margin of safety percentage} = \frac{\text{Margin of safety in dollars}}{\text{Budgeted (or actual) revenues}}$$

In our example, margin of safety percentage $= \dfrac{\$3,000}{\$8,000} = 37.5\%$

This result means that revenues would have to decrease substantially, by 37.5%, to reach the breakeven revenues. The high margin of safety gives Emma confidence that she is unlikely to suffer a loss.

If, however, Emma expects to sell only 30 units, budgeted revenues would be $6,000 ($200 per unit × 30 units) and the margin of safety would equal:

$$\text{Budgeted revenues} - \text{Breakeven revenues} = \$6,000 - \$5,000 = \$1,000$$

$$\frac{\text{Margin of}}{\text{safety percentage}} = \frac{\text{Margin of safety in dollars}}{\text{Budgeted (or actual) revenues}} = \frac{\$1,000}{\$6,000} = 16.67\%$$

The analysis implies that if revenues fall by more than 16.67%, Emma would suffer a loss. A low margin of safety increases the risk of a loss, which means Emma would need to look for ways to lower the breakeven point by reducing fixed costs or increasing contribution margin. For example, she would need to evaluate if her product is attractive enough to customers to allow her to charge a higher price without reducing the demand for it or if she could purchase the software at a lower cost. If Emma can neither reduce her fixed costs nor increase contribution margin and if she does not have the tolerance for this level of risk, she will prefer not to rent a booth at the fair.

Sensitivity analysis gives managers a good feel for a decision's risks. It is a simple approach to recognizing **uncertainty**, which is the possibility that an actual amount will deviate from an expected amount. A more comprehensive approach to recognizing uncertainty is to compute expected values using probability distributions. This approach is illustrated in the appendix to this chapter.

Decision Point

What can managers do to cope with uncertainty or changes in underlying assumptions?

Learning Objective 6

Use CVP analysis to plan variable and fixed costs

...compare risk of losses versus higher returns

Cost Planning and CVP

Managers have the ability to choose the levels of fixed and variable costs in their cost structures. This is a strategic decision. In this section, we describe various factors that managers and management accountants consider as they make this decision.

Alternative Fixed-Cost/Variable-Cost Structures

CVP-based sensitivity analysis highlights the risks and returns as fixed costs are substituted for variable costs in a company's cost structure. In Exhibit 4, compare line 6 and line 11.

| | | | Number of units required to be sold at $200 selling price to earn target operating income of | |
	Fixed Cost	**Variable Cost**	**$0 (Breakeven point)**	**$2,000**
Line 6	$2,000	$120	25	50
Line 11	$2,800	$100	28	48

Exhibit 5

Profit–Volume Graph
for Alternative Rental
Options for *GMAT
Success*

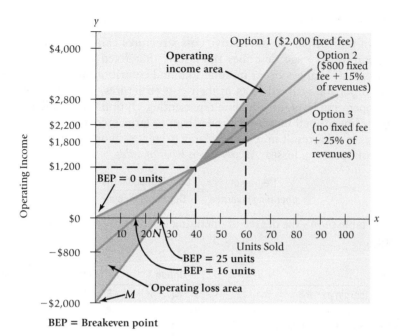

BEP = Breakeven point

Line 11, which has higher fixed costs and lower variable costs than line 6, has a higher breakeven point but requires fewer units to be sold (48 vs. 50) to earn an operating income of $2,000. CVP analysis can help managers evaluate various fixed-cost/variable-cost structures. We next consider the effects of these choices in more detail. Suppose the Chicago fair organizers offer Emma three rental alternatives:

Option 1: $2,000 fixed fee

Option 2: $800 fixed fee plus 15% of *GMAT Success* revenues

Option 3: 25% of *GMAT Success* revenues with no fixed fee

Emma is interested in how her choice of a rental agreement will affect the income she earns and the risks she faces. Exhibit 5 graphically depicts the profit–volume relationship for each option.

- The line representing the relationship between units sold and operating income for Option 1 is the same as the line in the PV graph shown in Exhibit 3 (fixed costs of $2,000 and contribution margin per unit of $80).
- The line representing Option 2 shows fixed costs of $800 and a contribution margin per unit of $50 [selling price, $200, minus variable cost per unit, $120, minus variable rental fees per unit, $30 (0.15 × $200)].
- The line representing Option 3 shows fixed costs of $0 and a contribution margin per unit of $30 [$200 − $120 − $50 (0.25 × $200)].

Option 3 has the lowest breakeven point (0 units), and Option 1 has the highest breakeven point (25 units). Option 1 is associated with the highest risk of loss if sales are low, but it also has the highest contribution margin per unit ($80) and therefore the highest operating income when sales are high (greater than 40 units).

The choice among Options 1, 2, and 3 is a strategic decision. As with most strategic decisions, what Emma decides will significantly affect her operating income (or loss), depending on the demand for the product. Faced with this uncertainty, Emma's choice will be influenced by her confidence in the level of demand for *GMAT Success* packages and her willingness to risk losses if demand is low. For example, if Emma's tolerance for risk is high, she will choose Option 1 with its high potential rewards. If, however, Emma is risk averse, she will prefer Option 3, where the rewards are smaller if sales are high but where she never suffers a loss if sales are low.

Operating Leverage

The risk-return tradeoff across alternative cost structures can be measured as *operating leverage*. **Operating leverage** describes the effects that fixed costs have on changes in operating income as changes occur in units sold and contribution margin. Organizations with a high proportion of fixed costs in their cost structures, as is the case with Option 1, have high operating leverage. The line representing Option 1 in Exhibit 5 is the steepest of the three lines. Small increases in sales lead to large increases in operating income. Small decreases in sales result in relatively large decreases in operating income, leading to a greater risk of operating losses. *At any given level of sales,*

$$\frac{\text{Degree of}}{\text{operating leverage}} = \frac{\text{Contribution margin}}{\text{Operating income}}$$

The following table shows the **degree of operating leverage** at sales of 40 units for the three rental options.

	Option 1	Option 2	Option 3
1. Contribution margin per unit	$ 80	$ 50	$ 30
2. Contribution margin (row 1 × 40 units)	$3,200	$2,000	$1,200
3. Operating income (from Exhibit 5)	$1,200	$1,200	$1,200
4. Degree of operating leverage (row 2 ÷ row 3)	$\frac{\$3,200}{\$1,200}=2.67$	$\frac{\$2,000}{\$1,200}=1.67$	$\frac{\$1,200}{\$1,200}=1.00$

These results indicate that, when sales are 40 units, a 1% change in sales and contribution margin will result in 2.67% change in operating income for Option 1. For Option 3, a 1% change in sales and contribution margin will result in only a 1% change in operating income. Consider, for example, a sales increase of 50% from 40 to 60 units. Contribution margin will increase by 50% under each option. Operating income, however, will increase by 2.67 × 50% = 133% from $1,200 to $2,800 in Option 1, but it will increase by only 1.00 × 50% = 50% from $1,200 to $1,800 in Option 3 (see Exhibit 5). The degree of operating leverage at a given level of sales helps managers calculate the effect of sales fluctuations on operating income.

Keep in mind that, in the presence of fixed costs, the degree of operating leverage is different at different levels of sales. For example, at sales of 60 units, the degree of operating leverage under each of the three options is as follows:

	Option 1	Option 2	Option 3
1. Contribution margin per unit	$ 80	$ 50	$ 30
2. Contribution margin (row 1 × 60 units)	$4,800	$3,000	$1,800
3. Operating income (from Exhibit 5)	$2,800	$2,200	$1,800
4. Degree of operating leverage (row 2 ÷ row 3)	$\frac{\$4,800}{\$2,800}=1.71$	$\frac{\$3,000}{\$2,200}=1.36$	$\frac{\$1,800}{\$1,800}=1.00$

The degree of operating leverage decreases from 2.67 (at sales of 40 units) to 1.71 (at sales of 60 units) under Option 1 and from 1.67 to 1.36 under Option 2. In general, whenever there are fixed costs, the degree of operating leverage decreases as the level of sales increases beyond the breakeven point. If fixed costs are $0 as they are in Option 3, contribution margin equals operating income and the degree of operating leverage equals 1.00 at all sales levels.

It is important for managers to monitor operating leverage carefully. Consider companies such as General Motors and American Airlines. Their high operating leverage was a major reason for their financial problems. Anticipating high demand for their services, these companies borrowed money to acquire assets, resulting in high fixed costs. As their sales declined, these companies suffered losses and could not generate enough cash to service their interest and debt, causing them to seek bankruptcy protection.

Managers and management accountants should distinguish fixed from variable costs and then evaluate how the level of fixed costs and variable costs they choose will affect the risk-return tradeoffs of their firms. Distinguishing fixed from variable costs is fairly straightforward in some cases. In others it's more challenging because costs do not vary only with the number of units sold but with the number of different types of products or services offered, the number of batches in which products are produced, or the complexity of operations. Differentiating fixed from variable costs requires careful judgment.

What actions can managers take to reduce fixed costs? Nike, the shoe and apparel company, does no manufacturing and incurs no fixed costs of operating and maintaining manufacturing plants. Instead, it buys its products from various suppliers. As a result, all of Nike's costs of producing products are variable costs. Nike reduces its risk of loss by increasing variable costs and reducing fixed costs. Concepts in Action: Cost–Volume–Profit Analysis Makes Megabus a Mega-Success describes how Megabus, an intercity bus operator, developed an innovative business model to reduce its fixed costs.

To reduce both fixed costs and variable costs, many companies are moving their manufacturing facilities from the United States to lower-cost countries, such as Mexico and China. Other companies, such as General Electric and Hewlett-Packard, have shifted service functions, such as after-sales customer service, to their customer call centers in countries such as India. These decisions by companies are often controversial. Some economists argue that outsourcing helps keep costs, and therefore prices, low and enables U.S. companies to remain globally competitive. Others argue that outsourcing reduces job opportunities in the United States and hurts working-class families.

Decision Point

How should managers choose among different variable-cost/fixed-cost structures?

Concepts in Action

Cost–Volume–Profit Analysis Makes Megabus a Mega-Success

Many travelers are shunning airlines and leaving their cars at home to take the low-fare Megabus between major U.S. cities. Megabus, one of a growing number of express bus services, has a simple business model. Most tickets are sold online and are paperless. The first passengers to reserve seats on each bus get the cheapest prices, often starting at $1, and fares vary based on demand. Buses outfitted with free Wi-Fi connections and other perks link city centers such as Boston, New York, and Washington, D.C. The buses make few if any stops, so travel times are often the same as driving and only slightly longer than taking the train, at a fraction of the price.

To offer rock-bottom prices and good service, Megabus is fanatical about keeping costs down. Aside from buses and a barebones back-office staff, Megabus has virtually no fixed costs. The company has drastically reduced rent and labor expenses, eschewing bus terminals for city-center curbside pickup, and customers pay extra to order tickets from an agent. The bus fleet is also in constant use. As chief executive Dale Moser stated, "You cut all that overhead out of your business, you find you can pass that savings on to customers, thus driving volume." Without high fixed costs, Megabus can also easily add and subtract departures profitably. During the Thanksgiving and Christmas holiday seasons, Megabus sells as many tickets as are requested on its Web site, adding buses as needed.

Since hitting the road in 2006, Megabus has changed the way many Americans—especially those in their 20s and 30s—travel. In 2012, Megabus did $152.8 million in business with profits of $21 million, and the company served its 25 millionth customer.

Sources: Ben Austen, "The Megabus Effect," *Bloomberg Businessweek* (April 7, 2011); Ken Belson, "Thinking Outside Rails and Runways, and Taking the Bus," *The New York Times* (May 5, 2010); Josh Sanburn, "Reinventing The Wheels," *Time* (November 15, 2012); No author, "Stagecoach gets on the buses for improved profits," *Yorkshire Post* (June 27, 2013); Stagecoach Group plc, Preliminary results for the year ended 30 April 2013 (Perth, Scotland: Stagecoach Group plc, 2013).

Learning
Objective 7

Apply CVP analysis to
a company producing
multiple products

...assume sales mix
of products remains
constant as total units
sold changes

Effects of Sales Mix on Income

Sales mix is the quantities (or proportion) of various products (or services) that constitute a company's total unit sales. Suppose Emma is now budgeting for a subsequent college fair in New York. She plans to sell two different test-prep packages—*GMAT Success* and *GRE Guarantee*—and budgets the following:

	GMAT Success	*GRE Guarantee*	Total
Expected sales	60	40	100
Revenues, $200 and $100 per unit	$12,000	$4,000	$16,000
Variable costs, $120 and $70 per unit	7,200	2,800	10,000
Contribution margin, $80 and $30 per unit	$ 4,800	$1,200	6,000
Fixed costs			4,500
Operating income			$ 1,500

What is the breakeven point for Emma's business now? The total number of units that must be sold to break even in a multiproduct company depends on the sales mix. For Emma, this is the combination of the number of units of *GMAT Success* sold and the number of units of *GRE Guarantee* sold. We assume that the budgeted sales mix (60 units of *GMAT Success* sold for every 40 units of *GRE Guarantee* sold, that is, a ratio of 3:2) will not change at different levels of total unit sales. That is, we think of Emma selling a bundle of 3 units of *GMAT Success* and 2 units of *GRE Guarantee*. (Note that this does not mean that Emma physically bundles the two products together into one big package.)

Each bundle yields a contribution margin of $300, calculated as follows:

	Number of Units of *GMAT Success* and *GRE Guarantee* in Each Bundle	Contribution Margin per Unit for *GMAT Success* and *GRE Guarantee*	Contribution Margin of the Bundle
GMAT *Success*	3	$80	$240
GRE *Guarantee*	2	30	60
Total			$300

To compute the breakeven point, we calculate the number of bundles Emma needs to sell.

$$\text{Breakeven point in bundles} = \frac{\text{Fixed costs}}{\text{Contribution margin per bundle}} = \frac{\$4,500}{\$300 \text{ per bundle}} = 15 \text{ bundles}$$

The breakeven point in units of *GMAT Success* and *GRE Guarantee* is as follows:

GMAT Success: 15 bundles × 3 units per bundle	45 units
GRE Guarantee: 15 bundles × 2 units per bundle	30 units
Total number of units to break even	75 units

The breakeven point in dollars for *GMAT Success* and *GRE Guarantee* is as follows:

GMAT Success: 45 units × $200 per unit	$ 9,000
GRE Guarantee: 30 units × $100 per unit	3,000
Breakeven revenues	$12,000

When there are multiple products, it is often convenient to use the contribution margin percentage. Under this approach, Emma also calculates the revenues from selling a bundle of 3 units of *GMAT Success* and 2 units of *GRE Guarantee*:

	Number of Units of GMAT Success and GRE Guarantee in Each Bundle	Selling Price for GMAT Success and GRE Guarantee	Revenue of the Bundle
GMAT *Success*	3	$200	$600
GRE *Guarantee*	2	100	200
Total			$800

$$\text{Contribution margin percentage for the bundle} = \frac{\text{Contribution margin of the bundle}}{\text{Revenue of the bundle}} = \frac{\$300}{\$800} = 0.375, \text{ or } 37.5\%$$

$$\text{Breakeven revenues} = \frac{\text{Fixed costs}}{\text{Contribution margin \% for the bundle}} = \frac{\$4,500}{0.375} = \$12,000$$

$$\text{Number of bundles required to be sold to break even} = \frac{\text{Breakeven revenues}}{\text{Revenue per bundle}} = \frac{\$12,000}{\$800 \text{ per bundle}} = 15 \text{ bundles}$$

The breakeven point in units and dollars for *GMAT Success* and *GRE Guarantee* are as follows:

GMAT *Success*: 15 bundles × 3 units per bundle = 45 units × $200 per unit = $9,000

GRE *Guarantee*: 15 bundles × 2 units per bundle = 30 units × $100 per unit = $3,000

Recall that in all our calculations we have assumed that the budgeted sales mix (3 units of *GMAT Success* for every 2 units of *GRE Guarantee*) will not change at different levels of total unit sales.

Of course, there are many different sales mixes (in units) that can result in a contribution margin of $4,500 and cause Emma to break even, as the following table shows:

Sales Mix (Units)		Contribution Margin from		
GMAT Success (1)	GRE Guarantee (2)	GMAT Success (3) = $80 × (1)	GRE Guarantee (4) = $30 × (2)	Total Contribution Margin (5) = (3) + (4)
48	22	$3,840	$ 660	$4,500
36	54	2,880	1,620	4,500
30	70	2,400	2,100	4,500

If, for example, the sales mix changes to 3 units of *GMAT Success* for every 7 units of *GRE Guarantee*, the breakeven point increases from 75 units to 100 units, composed of 30 units of *GMAT Success* and 70 units of *GRE Guarantee*. The breakeven quantity increases because the sales mix has shifted toward the lower-contribution-margin product, *GRE Guarantee* (which is $30 per unit compared to *GMAT Success*'s $80 per unit). In general, for any given total quantity of units sold, as the sales mix shifts toward units with lower contribution margins (more units of *GRE Guarantee* compared to *GMAT Success*), the lower operating income will be.

How do companies choose their sales mix? They adjust their mix to respond to demand changes. For example, as gasoline prices increase and customers want smaller cars, auto companies, such as Ford, Volkswagen, and Toyota, shift their production mix to produce smaller cars. This shift to smaller cars might result in an increase in the breakeven point because the sales mix has shifted toward lower-contribution-margin products. Despite this increase in the breakeven point, shifting the sales mix to smaller cars is the correct decision because the demand for larger cars has fallen. At no point should a manager focus on changing the sales mix to lower the breakeven point without taking into account customer preferences and demand. Of course, the shift in sales mix to smaller cars prompts managers at Ford, Volkswagen, and Toyota to take other actions such as reducing fixed costs and increasing contribution margins on smaller cars by charging higher prices for features that customers are willing to pay for or lowering variable costs.

The multiproduct case has two cost drivers, *GMAT Success* and *GRE Guarantee*, It shows how CVP and breakeven analyses can be adapted when there are multiple cost drivers. The key point is that many different combinations of cost drivers can result in a given contribution margin.

Decision Point

How can managers apply CVP analysis to a company producing multiple products?

Learning Objective 8

Apply CVP analysis in service and not-for-profit organizations

...define appropriate output measures

CVP Analysis in Service and Not-for-Profit Organizations

So far, our CVP analysis has focused on Emma's merchandising company. Of course, managers at manufacturing companies such as BMW, service companies such as Bank of America, and not-for-profit organizations such as the United Way also use CVP analysis to make decisions. To apply CVP analysis in service and not-for-profit organizations, we need to focus on measuring their output, which is different from the tangible units sold by manufacturing and merchandising companies. Examples of output measures in various service industries (for example, airlines, hotels/motels, and hospitals) and not-for-profit organizations (for example, universities) are as follows:

Industry	Measure of Output
Airlines	Passenger miles
Hotels/motels	Room-nights occupied
Hospitals	Patient days
Universities	Student credit-hours

Consider the Oregon Department of Social Services, a not-for-profit agency that helps disabled people seeking employment. The agency has a $900,000 budget appropriation from the State of Oregon (its revenue) for 2014. On average, the agency supplements each person's income by $5,000 annually. The agency's only other costs are fixed costs of rent and administrative salaries equal to $270,000. The agency manager wants to know how many people could be assisted in 2014. We can use CVP analysis here by setting the agency's operating income to $0. Let Q be the number of disabled people to be assisted:

$$\text{Revenues} - \text{Variable costs} - \text{Fixed costs} = 0$$
$$\$900{,}000 - \$5{,}000\,Q - \$270{,}000 = 0$$
$$\$5{,}000\,Q = \$900{,}000 - \$270{,}000 = \$630{,}000$$
$$Q = \$630{,}000 \div \$5{,}000 \text{ per person} = 126 \text{ people}$$

Suppose the nonprofit's budget appropriation for 2015 will be reduced by 15% to $900,000 × (1 − 0.15) = $765,000. The manager wants to know how many people with disabilities could be assisted with this reduced budget. Assume the monetary assistance per person and the agency's fixed costs don't change:

$$\$765{,}000 - \$5{,}000\,Q - \$270{,}000 = 0$$
$$\$5{,}000\,Q = \$765{,}000 - \$270{,}000 = \$495{,}000$$
$$Q = \$495{,}000 \div \$5{,}000 \text{ per person} = 99 \text{ people}$$

So, in 2015, instead of assisting 126 people, the agency can assist only 99. Note the following two characteristics of the CVP relationships in this nonprofit situation:

1. The percentage drop in the number of people assisted, (126 − 99) ÷ 126, or 21.4%, is greater than the 15% reduction in the budget appropriation. It is greater because

the $270,000 in fixed costs still must be paid, leaving a proportionately lower budget to assist people. In other words, the percentage drop in people assisted exceeds the percentage drop in budget appropriation.

2. Given the reduced budget appropriation (revenues) of $765,000 in 2015, the manager can adjust the agency's operations to stay within this appropriation in one or more of three ways: (a) by reducing the number of people assisted from the current 126, (b) by reducing the variable cost per person (the extent of assistance given a person) from the current $5,000 per person, or (c) by reducing the agency's total fixed costs from the current $270,000.

Decision Point

How do managers apply CVP analysis in service and not-for-profit organizations?

Contribution Margin Versus Gross Margin

Learning Objective 9

Distinguish contribution margin

…revenues minus all variable costs

from gross margin

…revenues minus cost of goods sold

We can consider two important concepts relating to profit margin—contribution margin, which was introduced in this chapter, and gross margin. Is there a relationship between these two concepts? In the following equations, we clearly distinguish contribution margin, which provides information for CVP analysis, from gross margin, a measure of competitiveness.

$$\text{Gross margin} = \text{Revenues} - \text{Cost of goods sold}$$
$$\text{Contribution margin} = \text{Revenues} - \text{All variable costs}$$

The gross margin measures how much a company can charge for its products over and above the cost of acquiring or producing them. Companies, such as brand-name pharmaceuticals producers, have high gross margins because their products are often patented and provide unique and distinctive benefits to consumers. In contrast, manufacturers of generic medicines and basic chemicals have low gross margins because the market for these products is highly competitive. Contribution margin indicates how much of a company's revenues are available to cover fixed costs. It helps in assessing the risk of losses. For example, the risk of loss is low if the contribution margin exceeds a company's fixed costs even when sales are low. Gross margin and contribution margin are related but give different insights. For example, a company operating in a competitive market with a low gross margin will have a low risk of loss if its fixed costs are small.

Consider the distinction between gross margin and contribution margin in the manufacturing sector. The concepts differ in two ways: fixed manufacturing costs and variable nonmanufacturing costs. The following example (figures assumed) illustrates this difference:

Contribution Income Statement Emphasizing Contribution Margin (in thousands)			Financial Accounting Income Statement Emphasizing Gross Margin (in thousands)	
Revenues		$1,000	Revenues	$1,000
Variable manufacturing costs	$250		Cost of goods sold (variable manufacturing costs, $250 + fixed manufacturing costs, $160)	410
Variable nonmanufacturing costs	270	520		
Contribution margin		480	Gross margin	590
Fixed manufacturing costs	160			
Fixed nonmanufacturing costs	138	298	Nonmanufacturing costs (variable, $270 + fixed $138)	408
Operating income		$ 182	Operating income	$ 182

Fixed manufacturing costs of $160,000 are not deducted from revenues when computing the contribution margin but are deducted when computing the gross margin. The cost of goods sold in a manufacturing company includes all variable manufacturing costs and all fixed manufacturing costs ($250,000 + $160,000). The company's variable nonmanufacturing costs (such as commissions paid to salespersons) of $270,000 are deducted from revenues when computing the contribution margin but are not deducted when computing gross margin.

Decision Point ▶

What is the difference between contribution margin and gross margin?

Like contribution margin, gross margin can be expressed as a total, as an amount per unit, or as a percentage. For example, the **gross margin percentage** is the gross margin divided by revenues—59% ($590 ÷ $1,000) in our manufacturing-sector example.

One reason why managers sometimes confuse gross margin and contribution margin with each other is that the two are often identical in the case of merchandising companies because the cost of goods sold equals the variable cost of goods purchased (and subsequently sold).

Problem for Self-Study

Wembley Travel Agency specializes in flights between Los Angeles and London. It books passengers on United Airlines at $900 per round-trip ticket. Until last month, United paid Wembley a commission of 10% of the ticket price paid by each passenger. This commission was Wembley's only source of revenues. Wembley's fixed costs are $14,000 per month (for salaries, rent, and so on), and its variable costs, such as sales commissions and bonuses, are $20 per ticket purchased for a passenger.

United Airlines has just announced a revised payment schedule for all travel agents. It will now pay travel agents a 10% commission per ticket up to a maximum of $50. Any ticket costing more than $500 generates only a $50 commission, regardless of the ticket price. Wembley's managers are concerned about how United's new payment schedule will affect its breakeven point and profitability.

1. Under the old 10% commission structure, how many round-trip tickets must Wembley sell each month (a) to break even and (b) to earn an operating income of $7,000?
2. How does United's revised payment schedule affect your answers to (a) and (b) in requirement 1?

Solution

1. Wembley receives a 10% commission on each ticket: 10% × $900 = $90. Thus,

$$\text{Selling price} = \$90 \text{ per ticket}$$
$$\text{Variable cost per unit} = \$20 \text{ per ticket}$$
$$\text{Contribution margin per unit} = \$90 - \$20 = \$70 \text{ per ticket}$$
$$\text{Fixed costs} = \$14,000 \text{ per month}$$

a. $$\frac{\text{Breakeven number}}{\text{of tickets}} = \frac{\text{Fixed costs}}{\text{Contribution margin per unit}} = \frac{\$14,000}{\$70 \text{ per ticket}} = 200 \text{ tickets}$$

b. When target operating income = $7,000 per month,

$$\frac{\text{Quantity of tickets}}{\text{required to be sold}} = \frac{\text{Fixed costs} + \text{Target operating income}}{\text{Contribution margin per unit}}$$

$$= \frac{\$14,000 + \$7,000}{\$70 \text{ per ticket}} = \frac{\$21,000}{\$70 \text{ per ticket}} = 300 \text{ tickets}$$

2. Under the new system, Wembley would receive only $50 on the $900 ticket. Thus,

$$\text{Selling price} = \$50 \text{ per ticket}$$
$$\text{Variable cost per unit} = \$20 \text{ per ticket}$$
$$\text{Contribution margin per unit} = \$50 - \$20 = \$30 \text{ per ticket}$$
$$\text{Fixed costs} = \$14,000 \text{ per month}$$

a. $$\frac{\text{Breakeven number}}{\text{of tickets}} = \frac{\$14,000}{\$30 \text{ per ticket}} = 467 \text{ tickets (rounded up)}$$

b. $$\frac{\text{Quantity of tickets}}{\text{required to be sold}} = \frac{\$21,000}{\$30 \text{ per ticket}} = 700 \text{ tickets}$$

The $50 cap on the commission paid per ticket causes the breakeven point to more than double (from 200 to 467 tickets) and the tickets required to be sold to earn $7,000 per month to also more than double (from 300 to 700 tickets). As would be expected, managers at Wembley reacted very negatively to the United Airlines announcement to change commission payments. Unfortunately for Wembley, other airlines also changed their commission structure in similar ways.

▶ Decision Points

The following question-and-answer format summarizes the chapter's learning objectives. Each decision presents a key question related to a learning objective. The guidelines are the answer to that question.

Decision	Guidelines
1. How can CVP analysis help managers?	CVP analysis assists managers in understanding the behavior of a product's or service's total costs, total revenues, and operating income as changes occur in the output level, selling price, variable costs, or fixed costs.
2. How can managers determine the breakeven point or the output needed to achieve a target operating income?	The breakeven point is the quantity of output at which total revenues equal total costs. The three methods for computing the breakeven point and the quantity of output to achieve target operating income are the equation method, the contribution margin method, and the graph method. Each method is merely a restatement of the others. Managers often select the method they find easiest to use in a specific decision situation.
3. How can managers incorporate income taxes into CVP analysis?	Income taxes can be incorporated into CVP analysis by using the target net income to calculate the target operating income. The breakeven point is unaffected by income taxes because no income taxes are paid when operating income equals zero.
4. How do managers use CVP analysis to make decisions?	Managers compare how revenues, costs, and contribution margins change across various alternatives. They then choose the alternative that maximizes operating income.
5. What can managers do to cope with uncertainty or changes in underlying assumptions?	Sensitivity analysis is a "what-if" technique that examines how an outcome will change if the original predicted data are not achieved or if an underlying assumption changes. When making decisions, managers use CVP analysis to compare contribution margins and fixed costs under different assumptions. Managers also calculate the margin of safety equal to budgeted revenues minus breakeven revenues.
6. How should managers choose among different variable-cost/fixed-cost structures?	Choosing the variable-cost/fixed-cost structure is a strategic decision for companies. CVP analysis helps managers compare the risk of losses when revenues are low and the upside profits when revenues are high for different proportions of variable and fixed costs in a company's cost structure.
7. How can managers apply CVP analysis to a company producing multiple products?	Managers apply CVP analysis in a company producing multiple products by assuming the sales mix of products sold remains constant as the total quantity of units sold changes.
8. How do managers apply CVP analysis in service and not-for-profit organizations?	Managers define output measures such as passenger-miles in the case of airlines or patient-days in the context of hospitals and identify costs that are fixed and those that vary with these measures of output.
9. What is the difference between contribution margin and gross margin?	Contribution margin is revenues minus all variable costs whereas gross margin is revenues minus cost of goods sold. Contribution margin measures the risk of a loss, whereas gross margin measures the competitiveness of a product.

Appendix

Decision Models and Uncertainty[2]

This appendix explores the characteristics of uncertainty, describes an approach managers can use to make decisions in a world of uncertainty, and illustrates the insights gained when uncertainty is recognized in CVP analysis. In the face of uncertainty, managers rely on decision models to help them make the right choices.

Role of a Decision Model

Uncertainty is the possibility that an actual amount will deviate from an expected amount. In the *GMAT Success* example, Emma might forecast sales at 42 units, but actual sales might turn out to be 30 units or 60 units. A decision model helps managers deal with such uncertainty. It is a formal method for making a choice, commonly involving both quantitative and qualitative analyses. The quantitative analysis usually includes the following steps:

Step 1:   Identify a choice criterion. A **choice criterion** is an objective that can be quantified, such as maximize income or minimize costs. Managers use the choice criterion to choose the best alternative action. Emma's choice criterion is to maximize expected operating income at the Chicago college fair.

Step 2:   Identify the set of alternative actions that can be taken. We use the letter a with subscripts $_1, _2,$ and $_3$ to distinguish each of Emma's three possible actions:

$a_1 =$ Pay \$2,000 fixed fee

$a_2 =$ Pay \$800 fixed fee plus 15% of *GMAT Success* revenues

$a_3 =$ Pay 25% of *GMAT Success* revenues with no fixed fee

Step 3:   Identify the set of events that can occur. An **event** is a possible relevant occurrence, such as the actual number of *GMAT Success* packages Emma might sell at the fair. The set of events should be mutually exclusive and collectively exhaustive. Events are mutually exclusive if they cannot occur at the same time. Events are collectively exhaustive if, taken together, they make up the entire set of possible relevant occurrences (no other event can occur). Examples of mutually exclusive and collectively exhaustive events are growth, decline, or no change in industry demand and increase, decrease, or no change in interest rates. Only one event out of the entire set of mutually exclusive and collectively exhaustive events will actually occur.

Suppose Emma's only uncertainty is the number of units of *GMAT Success* that she can sell. For simplicity, suppose Emma estimates that sales will be either 30 or 60 units. This set of events is mutually exclusive because clearly sales of 30 units and 60 units cannot both occur at the same time. It is collectively exhaustive because under our assumptions sales cannot be anything other than 30 or 60 units. We use the letter x with subscripts $_1$ and $_2$ to distinguish the set of mutually exclusive and collectively exhaustive events:

$x_1 =$ 30 units

$x_2 =$ 60 units

Step 4:   Assign a probability to each event that can occur. A **probability** is the likelihood or chance that an event will occur. The decision model approach to coping with uncertainty assigns probabilities to events. A **probability distribution** describes the likelihood, or the probability, that each of the mutually exclusive and collectively exhaustive set of events will occur. In some cases, there will be much evidence to guide the assignment of probabilities. For example, the probability of obtaining heads in the toss of a coin is 1/2 and that of drawing a particular playing card from a standard, well-shuffled deck is 1/52. In business, the probability of having a specified percentage of defective units may be

---

[2] *Source:* Based on teaching notes prepared by R. Williamson.

assigned with great confidence on the basis of production experience with thousands of units. In other cases, there will be little evidence supporting estimated probabilities—for example, expected sales of a new pharmaceutical product next year. Suppose that Emma, on the basis of past experience, assesses a 60% chance, or a 6/10 probability, that she will sell 30 units and a 40% chance, or a 4/10 probability, that she will sell 60 units. Using $P(x)$ as the notation for the probability of an event, the probabilities are as follows:

$$P(x_1) = 6/10 = 0.60$$
$$P(x_2) = 4/10 = 0.40$$

The sum of these probabilities must equal 1.00 because these events are mutually exclusive and collectively exhaustive.

Step 5: Identify the set of possible outcomes. **Outcomes** specify, in terms of the choice criterion, the predicted economic results of the various possible combinations of actions and events. In the *GMAT Success* example, the outcomes are the six possible operating incomes displayed in the decision table in Exhibit 6. A **decision table** is a summary of the alternative actions, events, outcomes, and probabilities of events.

Distinguish among actions, events, and outcomes. Actions are decision choices available to managers—for example, the particular rental alternatives that Emma can choose. Events are the set of all relevant occurrences that can happen—for example, the different quantities of *GMAT Success* packages that may be sold at the fair. The outcome is operating income, which depends both on the action the manager selects (rental alternative chosen) and the event that occurs (the quantity of packages sold).

Exhibit 7 presents an overview of relationships among a decision model, the implementation of a chosen action, its outcome, and subsequent performance evaluation. Thoughtful managers step back and evaluate what happened and learn from their experiences. This learning serves as feedback for adapting the decision model for future actions.

Expected Value

An **expected value** is the weighted average of the outcomes, with the probability of each outcome serving as the weight. When the outcomes are measured in monetary terms, expected value is often called **expected monetary value**. Using information in Exhibit 6,

Exhibit 6 Decision Table for *GMAT Success*

	A	B	C	D	E	F	G	H	I
1	Selling price = $200					Operating Income			
2	Package cost = $120					Under Each Possible Event			
3			Percentage						
4		Fixed	of Fair	Event x_1: Units Sold = 30			Event x_2: Units Sold = 60		
5	**Actions**	Fee	Revenues	Probability(x_1) = 0.60			Probability(x_2) = 0.40		
6	a_1: Pay $2,000 fixed fee	$2,000	0%	$400[l]			$2,800[m]		
7	a_2: Pay $800 fixed fee plus 15% of revenues	$ 800	15%	$700[n]			$2,200[p]		
8	a_3: Pay 25% of revenues with no fixed fee	$ 0	25%	$900[q]			$1,800[r]		
9									
10	[l]Operating income = ($200 – $120)(30) – $2,000	=	$ 400						
11	[m]Operating income = ($200 – $120)(60) – $2,000	=	$2,800						
12	[n]Operating income = ($200 – $120 – 15% × $200)(30) – $800	=	$ 700						
13	[p]Operating income = ($200 – $120 – 15% × $200)(60) – $800	=	$2,200						
14	[q]Operating income = ($200 – $120 – 25% × $200)(30)	=	$ 900						
15	[r]Operating income = ($200 – $120 – 25% × $200)(60)	=	$1,800						

Exhibit 7 A Decision Model and Its Link to Performance Evaluation

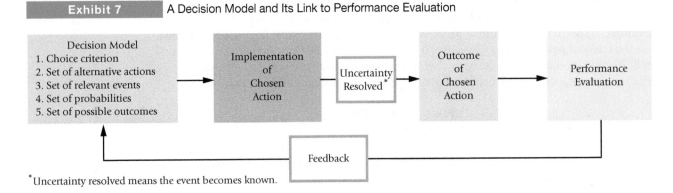

*Uncertainty resolved means the event becomes known.

the expected monetary value of each booth-rental alternative denoted by $E(a_1)$, $E(a_2)$, and $E(a_3)$ is as follows:

Pay $2,000 fixed fee:	$E(a_1) = (0.60 \times \$400) + (0.40 \times \$2,800) = \$1,360$
Pay $800 fixed fee plus 15% of revenues:	$E(a_2) = (0.60 \times \$700) + (0.40 \times \$2,200) = \$1,300$
Pay 25% of revenues with no fixed fee:	$E(a_3) = (0.60 \times \$900) + (0.40 \times \$1,800) = \$1,260$

To maximize expected operating income, Emma should select action a_1—*pay* the fair organizers a $2,000 fixed fee.

To interpret the expected value of selecting action a_1, imagine that Emma attends many fairs, each with the probability distribution of operating incomes given in Exhibit 6. For a specific fair, Emma will earn operating income of either $400, if she sells 30 units, or $2,800, if she sells 60 units. But if Emma attends 100 fairs, she will expect to earn $400 operating income 60% of the time (at 60 fairs) and $2,800 operating income 40% of the time (at 40 fairs), for a total operating income of $136,000 ($400 × 60 + $2,800 × 40). The expected value of $1,360 is the operating income per fair that Emma will earn when averaged across all fairs ($136,000 ÷ 100). Of course, in many real-world situations, managers must make one-time decisions under uncertainty. Even in these cases, expected value is a useful tool for choosing among alternatives.

Consider the effect of uncertainty on the preferred action choice. If Emma were certain she would sell only 30 units (that is, $P(x_1) = 1$), she would prefer alternative a_3—pay 25% of revenues with no fixed fee. To follow this reasoning, examine Exhibit 6. When 30 units are sold, alternative a_3 yields the maximum operating income of $900. Because fixed costs are $0, booth-rental costs are lower, equal to $1,500 (25% of revenues = 0.25 × $200 per unit × 30 units), when sales are low.

However, if Emma were certain she would sell 60 packages (that is, $P(x_2) = 1$), she would prefer alternative a_1—pay a $2,000 fixed fee. Exhibit 6 indicates that when 60 units are sold, alternative a_1 yields the maximum operating income of $2,800. That's because, when 60 units are sold, rental payments under a_2 ($800 + 0.15 × $200 per unit × 60 units = $2,600) and a_3 (0.25 × $200 per unit × 60 units = $3,000) are more than the fixed $2,000 fee under a_1.

Despite the high probability of selling only 30 units, Emma still prefers to take action a_1, which is to pay a fixed fee of $2,000. That's because the high risk of low operating income (the 60% probability of selling only 30 units) is more than offset by the high return from selling 60 units, which has a 40% probability. If Emma were more averse to risk (measured in our example by the difference between operating incomes when 30 vs. 60 units are sold), she might have preferred action a_2 or a_3. For example, action a_2 ensures an operating income of at least $700, greater than the operating income of $400 that she would earn under action a_1 if only 30 units were sold. Of course, choosing a_2 limits the upside potential to $2,200 relative to $2,800 under a_1, if 60 units are sold. If Emma is very concerned about downside risk, however, she may be willing to forgo some upside benefits to protect against a $400 outcome by choosing a_2.[3]

[3] For more formal approaches, refer to Moore, J., and L. Weatherford, *Decision modeling with Microsoft Excel*, 6th ed. (Upper Saddle River, NJ: Prentice Hall, 2001).

Good Decisions and Good Outcomes

Always distinguish between a good decision and a good outcome. One can exist without the other. Suppose you are offered a one-time-only gamble tossing a coin. You will win $20 if the outcome is heads, but you will lose $1 if the outcome is tails. As a decision maker, you proceed through the logical phases: gathering information, assessing outcomes, and making a choice. You accept the bet. Why? Because the expected value is $9.50 [0.5($20) + 0.5(− $1)]. The coin is tossed and the outcome is tails. You lose. From your viewpoint, this was a good decision but a bad outcome.

A decision can be made only on the basis of information that is available at the time of evaluating and making the decision. By definition, uncertainty rules out guaranteeing that the best outcome will always be obtained. As in our example, it is possible that bad luck will produce bad outcomes even when good decisions have been made. A bad outcome does not mean a bad decision was made. The best protection against a bad outcome is a good decision.

Terms to Learn

This chapter contains definitions of the following important terms:

breakeven point (BEP)	decision table	outcomes
choice criterion	degree of operating leverage	probability
contribution income statement	event	probability distribution
contribution margin	expected monetary value	PV graph
contribution margin per unit	expected value	revenue driver
contribution margin percentage	gross margin percentage	sales mix
contribution margin ratio	margin of safety	sensitivity analysis
cost–volume–profit (CVP)	net income	uncertainty
analysis	operating leverage	

Assignment Material

Note: To underscore the basic CVP relationships, the assignment material ignores income taxes unless stated otherwise.

Questions

MyAccountingLab

1 Define cost–volume–profit analysis.
2 Describe the assumptions underlying CVP analysis.
3 Distinguish between operating income and net income.
4 Define contribution margin, contribution margin per unit, and contribution margin percentage.
5 Describe three methods that managers can use to express CVP relationships.
6 Why is it more accurate to describe the subject matter of this chapter as CVP analysis rather than as breakeven analysis?
7 "CVP analysis is both simple and simplistic. If you want realistic analysis to underpin your decisions, look beyond CVP analysis." Do you agree? Explain.
8 How does an increase in the income tax rate affect the breakeven point?
9 Describe sensitivity analysis. How has the advent of the electronic spreadsheet affected the use of sensitivity analysis?
10 Give an example of how a manager can decrease variable costs while increasing fixed costs.
11 Give an example of how a manager can increase variable costs while decreasing fixed costs.
12 What is operating leverage? How is knowing the degree of operating leverage helpful to managers?
13 "There is no such thing as a fixed cost. All costs can be 'unfixed' given sufficient time." Do you agree? What is the implication of your answer for CVP analysis?
14 How can a company with multiple products compute its breakeven point?
15 "In CVP analysis, gross margin is a less-useful concept than contribution margin." Do you agree? Explain briefly.

Exercises

16 **CVP computations.** Fill in the blanks for each of the following independent cases.

Case	Revenues	Variable Costs	Fixed Costs	Total Costs	Operating Income	Contribution Margin Percentage
a.		$800		$1,200	$1,000	
b.	$2,400		$400		$ 700	
c.	$ 900	$500		$ 900		
d.	$1,800		$400			50%

17 **CVP computations.** Garrett Manufacturing sold 410,000 units of its product for $68 per unit in 2014. Variable cost per unit is $60, and total fixed costs are $1,640,000.

1. Calculate (a) contribution margin and (b) operating income.
2. Garrett's current manufacturing process is labor intensive. Kate Schoenen, Garrett's production manager, has proposed investing in state-of-the-art manufacturing equipment, which will increase the annual fixed costs to $5,330,000. The variable costs are expected to decrease to $54 per unit. Garrett expects to maintain the same sales volume and selling price next year. How would acceptance of Schoenen's proposal affect your answers to (a) and (b) in requirement 1?
3. Should Garrett accept Schoenen's proposal? Explain.

18 **CVP analysis, changing revenues and costs.** Brilliant Travel Agency specializes in flights between Toronto and Jamaica. It books passengers on Ontario Air. Brilliant's fixed costs are $36,000 per month. Ontario Air charges passengers $1,300 per round-trip ticket.

Calculate the number of tickets Brilliant must sell each month to (a) break even and (b) make a target operating income of $12,000 per month in each of the following independent cases.

1. Brilliant's variable costs are $34 per ticket. Ontario Air pays Brilliant 10% commission on ticket price.
2. Brilliant's variable costs are $30 per ticket. Ontario Air pays Brilliant 10% commission on ticket price.
3. Brilliant's variable costs are $30 per ticket. Ontario Air pays $46 fixed commission per ticket to Brilliant. Comment on the results.
4. Brilliant's variable costs are $30 per ticket. It receives $46 commission per ticket from Ontario Air. It charges its customers a delivery fee of $8 per ticket. Comment on the results.

19 **CVP exercises.** The Incredible Donut owns and operates six doughnut outlets in and around Kansas City. You are given the following corporate budget data for next year:

Revenues	$10,400,000
Fixed costs	$ 2,100,000
Variable costs	$ 7,900,000

Variable costs change based on the number of doughnuts sold.

Compute the budgeted operating income for each of the following deviations from the original budget data. (Consider each case independently.)

1. An 11% increase in contribution margin, holding revenues constant
2. An 11% decrease in contribution margin, holding revenues constant
3. A 4% increase in fixed costs
4. A 4% decrease in fixed costs
5. A 7% increase in units sold
6. A 7% decrease in units sold
7. An 11% increase in fixed costs and a 11% increase in units sold
8. A 4% increase in fixed costs and a 4% decrease in variable costs
9. Which of these alternatives yields the highest budgeted operating income? Explain why this is the case.

20 CVP exercises. The Doral Company manufactures and sells pens. Currently, 5,000,000 units are sold per year at $0.50 per unit. Fixed costs are $900,000 per year. Variable costs are $0.30 per unit.

Consider each case separately:

1. **a.** What is the current annual operating income?
   b. What is the present breakeven point in revenues?

Compute the new operating income for each of the following changes:

2. A $0.04 per unit increase in variable costs
3. A 10% increase in fixed costs and a 10% increase in units sold
4. A 20% decrease in fixed costs, a 20% decrease in selling price, a 10% decrease in variable cost per unit, and a 40% increase in units sold

Compute the new breakeven point in units for each of the following changes:

5. A 10% increase in fixed costs
6. A 10% increase in selling price and a $20,000 increase in fixed costs

Required

21 CVP analysis, income taxes. Brooke Motors is a small car dealership. On average, it sells a car for $27,000, which it purchases from the manufacturer for $23,000. Each month, Brooke Motors pays $48,200 in rent and utilities and $68,000 for salespeople's salaries. In addition to their salaries, salespeople are paid a commission of $600 for each car they sell. Brooke Motors also spends $13,000 each month for local advertisements. Its tax rate is 40%.

1. How many cars must Brooke Motors sell each month to break even?
2. Brooke Motors has a target monthly net income of $51,000. What is its target monthly operating income? How many cars must be sold each month to reach the target monthly net income of $51,000?

Required

22 CVP analysis, income taxes. The Swift Meal has two restaurants that are open 24 hours a day. Fixed costs for the two restaurants together total $456,000 per year. Service varies from a cup of coffee to full meals. The average sales check per customer is $9.50. The average cost of food and other variable costs for each customer is $3.80. The income tax rate is 30%. Target net income is $159,600.

1. Compute the revenues needed to earn the target net income.
2. How many customers are needed to break even? To earn net income of $159,600?
3. Compute net income if the number of customers is 145,000.

Required

23 CVP analysis, sensitivity analysis. Tuff Kids Jeans Co. sells blue jeans wholesale to major retailers across the country. Each pair of jeans has a selling price of $30 with $21 in variable costs of goods sold. The company has fixed manufacturing costs of $1,200,000 and fixed marketing costs of $300,000. Sales commissions are paid to the wholesale sales reps at 5% of revenues. The company has an income tax rate of 25%.

1. How many jeans must Tuff Kids sell in order to break even?
2. How many jeans must the company sell in order to reach:
   a. a target operating income of $450,000?
   b. a net income of $450,000?
3. How many jeans would TuffKids have to sell to earn the net income in part 2b if (consider each requirement independently).
   a. The contribution margin per unit increases by 10%
   b. The selling price is increased to $32.50
   c. The company outsources manufacturing to an overseas company increasing variable costs per unit by $2.00 and saving 60% of fixed manufacturing costs.

Required

24 CVP analysis, margin of safety. Suppose Lattin Corp.'s breakeven point is revenues of $1,500,000. Fixed costs are $720,000.

1. Compute the contribution margin percentage.
2. Compute the selling price if variable costs are $13 per unit.
3. Suppose 90,000 units are sold. Compute the margin of safety in units and dollars.
4. What does this tell you about the risk of Lattin making a loss? What are the most likely reasons for this risk to increase?

Required

25 Operating leverage. Carmel Rugs is holding a 2-week carpet sale at Jean's Club, a local warehouse store. Carmel Rugs plans to sell carpets for $1,000 each. The company will purchase the carpets from a local distributor for $400 each, with the privilege of returning any unsold units for a full refund. Jean's Club has offered Carmel Rugs two payment alternatives for the use of space.

- Option 1: A fixed payment of $17,400 for the sale period
- Option 2: 20% of total revenues earned during the sale period

Assume Carmel Rugs will incur no other costs.

Required

1. Calculate the breakeven point in units for (a) option 1 and (b) option 2.
2. At what level of revenues will Carmel Rugs earn the same operating income under either option?
   a. For what range of unit sales will Carmel Rugs prefer option 1?
   b. For what range of unit sales will Carmel Rugs prefer option 2?
3. Calculate the degree of operating leverage at sales of 87 units for the two rental options.
4. Briefly explain and interpret your answer to requirement 3.

26 CVP analysis, international cost structure differences. Plush Decor, Inc., is considering three possible countries for the sole manufacturing site of its newest area rug: Italy, Spain, and Singapore. All area rugs are to be sold to retail outlets in the United States for $200 per unit. These retail outlets add their own markup when selling to final customers. Fixed costs and variable cost per unit (area rug) differ in the three countries.

Country	Sales Price to Retail Outlets	Annual Fixed Costs	Variable Manufacturing Cost per Area Rug	Variable Marketing & Distribution Cost per Area Rug
Italy	$200.00	$ 6,386,000	$70.00	$27.00
Spain	200.00	5,043,000	61.00	16.00
Singapore	200.00	12,240,000	84.00	14.00

Required

1. Compute the breakeven point for Plush Decor, Inc., in each country in (a) units sold and (b) revenues.
2. If Plush Decor, Inc., plans to produce and sell 80,000 rugs in 2014, what is the budgeted operating income for each of the three manufacturing locations? Comment on the results.

27 Sales mix, new and upgrade customers. Chartz 1-2-3 is a top-selling electronic spreadsheet product. Chartz is about to release version 5.0. It divides its customers into two groups: new customers and upgrade customers (those who previously purchased Chartz 1-2-3 4.0 or earlier versions). Although the same physical product is provided to each customer group, sizable differences exist in selling prices and variable marketing costs:

	New Customers		Upgrade Customers	
Selling price		$195		$115
Variable costs				
Manufacturing	$15		$15	
Marketing	50	65	20	35
Contribution margin		$130		$ 80

The fixed costs of Chartz 1-2-3 5.0 are $16,500,000. The planned sales mix in units is 60% new customers and 40% upgrade customers.

Required

1. What is the Chartz 1-2-3 5.0 breakeven point in units, assuming that the planned 60%/40% sales mix is attained?
2. If the sales mix is attained, what is the operating income when 170,000 total units are sold?
3. Show how the breakeven point in units changes with the following customer mixes:
   a. New 40% and upgrade 60%
   b. New 80% and upgrade 20%
   c. Comment on the results.

28 Sales mix, three products. The Janowski Company has three product lines of mugs—A, B, and C—with contribution margins of $5, $4, and $3, respectively. The president foresees sales of 168,000 units in the coming period, consisting of 24,000 units of A, 96,000 units of B, and 48,000 units of C. The company's fixed costs for the period are $405,000.

Required

1. What is the company's breakeven point in units, assuming that the given sales mix is maintained?
2. If the sales mix is maintained, what is the total contribution margin when 168,000 units are sold? What is the operating income?
3. What would operating income be if the company sold 24,000 units of A, 48,000 units of B, and 96,000 units of C? What is the new breakeven point in units if these relationships persist in the next period?
4. Comparing the breakeven points in requirements 1 and 3, is it always better for a company to choose the sales mix that yields the lower breakeven point? Explain.

29 CVP, not-for-profit. Genesee Music Society is a not-for-profit organization that brings guest artists to the community's greater metropolitan area. The music society just bought a small concert hall in the center of town to house its performances. The lease payments on the concert hall are expected to be $4,000 per month. The organization pays its guest performers $1,800 per concert and anticipates corresponding ticket sales to be $4,500 per concert. The music society also incurs costs of approximately $1,000 per concert for marketing and advertising. The organization pays its artistic director $33,000 per year and expects to receive $30,000 in donations in addition to its ticket sales.

Required

1. If the Genesee Music Society just breaks even, how many concerts does it hold?
2. In addition to the organization's artistic director, the music society would like to hire a marketing director for $25,500 per year. What is the breakeven point? The music society anticipates that the addition of a marketing director would allow the organization to increase the number of concerts to 41 per year. What is the music society's operating income/(loss) if it hires the new marketing director?
3. The music society expects to receive a grant that would provide the organization with an additional $17,000 toward the payment of the marketing director's salary. What is the breakeven point if the music society hires the marketing director and receives the grant?

30 Contribution margin, decision making. McCarthy Men's Clothing's revenues and cost data for 2014 are as follows:

Revenues		$500,000
Cost of goods sold		250,000
Gross margin		250,000
Operating costs:		
Salaries fixed	$160,000	
Sales commissions (11% of sales)	55,000	
Depreciation of equipment and fixtures	15,000	
Store rent ($4,000 per month)	48,000	
Other operating costs	40,000	318,000
Operating income (loss)		$ (68,000)

Mr. McCarthy, the owner of the store, is unhappy with the operating results. An analysis of other operating costs reveals that it includes $35,000 variable costs, which vary with sales volume, and $5,000 (fixed) costs.

Required

1. Compute the contribution margin of McCarthy Men's Clothing.
2. Compute the contribution margin percentage.
3. Mr. McCarthy estimates that he can increase units sold, and hence revenues by 20% by incurring additional advertising costs of $12,000. Calculate the impact of the additional advertising costs on operating income.
4. What other actions can Mr. McCarthy take to improve operating income?

31 Contribution margin, gross margin, and margin of safety. Mirabella Cosmetics manufactures and sells a face cream to small ethnic stores in the greater New York area. It presents the monthly operating income statement shown here to George Lopez, a potential investor in the business. Help Mr. Lopez understand Mirabella's cost structure.

Cost–Volume–Profit Analysis

	A	B	C	D
1	Mirabella Cosmetics			
2	Operating Income Statement, June 2014			
3	Units sold			10,000
4	Revenues			$100,000
5	Cost of goods sold			
6	Variable manufacturing costs		$55,000	
7	Fixed manufacturing costs		20,000	
8	Total			75,000
9	Gross margin			25,000
10	Operating costs			
11	Variable marketing costs		$ 5,000	
12	Fixed marketing & administration costs		10,000	
13	Total operating costs			15,000
14	Operating income			$ 10,000

Required

1. Recast the income statement to emphasize contribution margin.
2. Calculate the contribution margin percentage and breakeven point in units and revenues for June 2014.
3. What is the margin of safety (in units) for June 2014?
4. If sales in June were only 8,000 units and Mirabella's tax rate is 30%, calculate its net income.

32 Uncertainty and expected costs. Hillmart Corp., an international retail giant, is considering implementing a new business-to-business (B2B) information system for processing merchandise orders. The current system costs Hillmart $1,000,000 per month and $45 per order. Hillmart has two options, a partially automated B2B and a fully automated B2B system. The partially automated B2B system will have a fixed cost of $5,000,000 per month and a variable cost of $35 per order. The fully automated B2B system has a fixed cost of $11,000,000 per month and $20 per order.

Based on data from the past two years, Hillmart has determined the following distribution on monthly orders:

Monthly Number of Orders	Probability
300,000	0.15
400,000	0.20
500,000	0.40
600,000	0.15
700,000	0.10

Required

1. Prepare a table showing the cost of each plan for each quantity of monthly orders.
2. What is the expected cost of each plan?
3. In addition to the information systems costs, what other factors should Hillmart consider before deciding to implement a new B2B system?

MyAccountingLab   Problems

33 CVP analysis, service firm. Lifetime Escapes generates average revenue of $7,500 per person on its 5-day package tours to wildlife parks in Kenya. The variable costs per person are as follows:

Airfare	$1,600
Hotel accommodations	3,100
Meals	600
Ground transportation	300
Park tickets and other costs	700
Total	$6,300

Annual fixed costs total $570,000.

Required

1. Calculate the number of package tours that must be sold to break even.
2. Calculate the revenue needed to earn a target operating income of $102,000.

3. If fixed costs increase by $19,000, what decrease in variable cost per person must be achieved to maintain the breakeven point calculated in requirement 1?

4. The general manager at Lifetime Escapes proposes to increase the price of the package tour to $8,200 to decrease the breakeven point in units. Using information in the original problem, calculate the new breakeven point in units. What factors should the general manager consider before deciding to increase the price of the package tour?

34 CVP, target operating income, service firm. KinderKids provides daycare for children Mondays through Fridays. Its monthly variable costs per child are as follows:

Lunch and snacks	$100
Educational supplies	30
Other supplies (paper products, toiletries, etc.)	20
Total	$150

Monthly fixed costs consist of the following:

Rent	$1,500
Utilities	150
Insurance	200
Salaries	1,700
Miscellaneous	450
Total	$4,000

KinderKids charges each parent $400 per child per month.

Required

1. Calculate the breakeven point.
2. KinderKids' target operating income is $5,000 per month. Compute the number of children who must be enrolled to achieve the target operating income.
3. KinderKids lost its lease and had to move to another building. Monthly rent for the new building is $2,200. At the suggestion of parents, KinderKids plans to take children on field trips. Monthly costs of the field trips are $1,100. By how much should KinderKids increase fees per child to meet the target operating income of $5,000 per month, assuming the same number of children as in requirement 2?

35 CVP analysis, margin of safety. (CMA, adapted) Arvin Tax Preparation Services has total budgeted revenues for 2014 of $618,000, based on an average price of $206 per tax return prepared. The company would like to achieve a margin of safety percentage of at least 45%. The company's current fixed costs are $327,600, and variable costs average $24 per customer. (Consider each of the following separately).

Required

1. Calculate Arvin's breakeven point and margin of safety in units.
2. Which of the following changes would help Arvin achieve its desired margin of safety?
  a. Average revenue per customer increases to $224.
  b. Planned number of tax returns prepared increases by 15%.
  c. Arvin purchases new tax software that results in a 5% increase to fixed costs but e-files all tax returns, which reduces mailing costs an average $2 per customer.

36 CVP analysis, income taxes. (CMA, adapted) J.T.Brooks and Company, a manufacturer of quality handmade walnut bowls, has had a steady growth in sales for the past 5 years. However, increased competition has led Mr. Brooks, the president, to believe that an aggressive marketing campaign will be necessary next year to maintain the company's present growth. To prepare for next year's marketing campaign, the company's controller has prepared and presented Mr. Brooks with the following data for the current year, 2014:

Variable cost (per bowl)	
Direct materials	$ 3.00
Direct manufacturing labor	8.00
Variable overhead (manufacturing, marketing, distribution, and customer service)	7.50
Total variable cost per bowl	$ 18.50
Fixed costs	
Manufacturing	$ 20,000
Marketing, distribution, and customer service	194,500
Total fixed costs	$214,500
Selling price	$ 35.00
Expected sales, 22,000 units	$770,000
Income tax rate	40%

1. What is the projected net income for 2014?
2. What is the breakeven point in units for 2014?
3. Mr. Brooks has set the revenue target for 2015 at a level of $875,000 (or 25,000 bowls). He believes an additional marketing cost of $16,500 for advertising in 2015, with all other costs remaining constant, will be necessary to attain the revenue target. What is the net income for 2015 if the additional $16,500 is spent and the revenue target is met?
4. What is the breakeven point in revenues for 2015 if the additional $16,500 is spent for advertising?
5. If the additional $16,500 is spent, what are the required 2015 revenues for 2015 net income to equal 2014 net income?
6. At a sales level of 25,000 units, what maximum amount can be spent on advertising if a 2015 net income of $108,450 is desired?

37 CVP, sensitivity analysis. The Derby Shoe Company produces its famous shoe, the Divine Loafer that sells for $70 per pair. Operating income for 2013 is as follows:

Sales revenue ($70 per pair)	$350,000
Variable cost ($30 per pair)	150,000
Contribution margin	200,000
Fixed cost	100,000
Operating income	$100,000

Derby Shoe Company would like to increase its profitability over the next year by at least 25%. To do so, the company is considering the following options:

1. Replace a portion of its variable labor with an automated machining process. This would result in a 20% decrease in variable cost per unit but a 15% increase in fixed costs. Sales would remain the same.
2. Spend $25,000 on a new advertising campaign, which would increase sales by 10%.
3. Increase both selling price by $10 per unit and variable costs by $8 per unit by using a higher-quality leather material in the production of its shoes. The higher-priced shoe would cause demand to drop by approximately 20%.
4. Add a second manufacturing facility that would double Derby's fixed costs but would increase sales by 60%.

Evaluate each of the alternatives considered by Derby Shoes. Do any of the options meet or exceed Derby's targeted increase in income of 25%? What should Derby do?

38 CVP analysis, shoe stores. The HighStep Shoe Company operates a chain of shoe stores that sell 10 different styles of inexpensive men's shoes with identical unit costs and selling prices. A unit is defined as a pair of shoes. Each store has a store manager who is paid a fixed salary. Individual salespeople receive a fixed salary and a sales commission. HighStep is considering opening another store that is expected to have the revenue and cost relationships shown here.

	Home	Insert	Page Layout	Formulas	Data	Review	View	
	A		B		C	D		E
1	Unit Variable Data (per pair of shoes)					Annual Fixed Costs		
2	Selling price		$60.00			Rent		$ 30,000
3	Cost of shoes		$37.00			Salaries		100,000
4	Sales commission		3.00			Advertising		40,000
5	Variable cost per unit		$40.00			Other fixed costs		10,000
6						Total fixed costs		$180,000

Consider each question independently:

1. What is the annual breakeven point in (a) units sold and (b) revenues?
2. If 8,000 units are sold, what will be the store's operating income (loss)?

3. If sales commissions are discontinued and fixed salaries are raised by a total of $15,500, what would be the annual breakeven point in (a) units sold and (b) revenues?

4. Refer to the original data. If, in addition to his fixed salary, the store manager is paid a commission of $2.00 per unit sold, what would be the annual breakeven point in (a) units sold and (b) revenues?

5. Refer to the original data. If, in addition to his fixed salary, the store manager is paid a commission of $2.00 *per unit in excess of the breakeven point*, what would be the store's operating income if 12,000 units were sold?

39 CVP analysis, shoe stores (continuation of 38). Refer to requirement 3 of Problem 38. In this problem, assume the role of the owner of HighStep.

Required

1. As owner, which sales compensation plan would you choose if forecasted annual sales of the new store were at least 10,000 units? What do you think of the motivational aspect of your chosen compensation plan?

2. Suppose the target operating income is $69,000. How many units must be sold to reach the target operating income under (a) the original salary-plus-commissions plan and (b) the higher-fixed-salaries-only plan? Which method would you prefer? Explain briefly.

3. You open the new store on January 1, 2014, with the original salary-plus-commission compensation plan in place. Because you expect the cost of the shoes to rise due to inflation, you place a firm bulk order for 11,000 shoes and lock in the $37 price per unit. But toward the end of the year, only 9,500 shoes are sold, and you authorize a markdown of the remaining inventory to $50 per unit. Finally, all units are sold. Salespeople, as usual, get paid a commission of 5% of revenues. What is the annual operating income for the store?

40 Alternate cost structures, uncertainty, and sensitivity analysis. Deckle Printing Company currently leases its only copy machine for $1,200 a month. The company is considering replacing this leasing agreement with a new contract that is entirely commission based. Under the new agreement, Deckle would pay a commission for its printing at a rate of $20 for every 500 pages printed. The company currently charges $0.15 per page to its customers. The paper used in printing costs the company $0.04 per page and other variable costs, including hourly labor amounting to $0.05 per page.

Required

1. What is the company's breakeven point under the current leasing agreement? What is it under the new commission-based agreement?

2. For what range of sales levels will Deckle prefer (a) the fixed lease agreement (b) the commission agreement?

3. Do this question only if you have covered the chapter appendix in your class. Deckle estimates that the company is equally likely to sell 20,000, 30,000, 40,000, 50,000, or 60,000 pages of print. Using information from the original problem, prepare a table that shows the expected profit at each sales level under the fixed leasing agreement and under the commission-based agreement. What is the expected value of each agreement? Which agreement should Deckle choose?

41 CVP, alternative cost structures. SuperShades operates a kiosk at the local mall, selling sunglasses for $20 each. SuperShades currently pays $800 a month to rent the space and pays two full-time employees to each work 160 hours a month at $10 per hour. The store shares a manager with a neighboring mall and pays 50% of the manager's annual salary of $40,000 and benefits equal to 20% of salary. The wholesale cost of the sunglasses to the company is $5 a pair.

Required

1. How many sunglasses does SuperShades need to sell each month to break even?

2. If SuperShades wants to earn an operating income of $4,500 per month, how many sunglasses does the store need to sell?

3. If the store's hourly employees agreed to a 15% sales-commission-only pay structure, instead of their hourly pay, how many sunglasses would SuperShades need to sell to earn an operating income of $4,500?

4. Assume SuperShades pays its employees hourly under the original pay structure, but is able to pay the mall 8% of its monthly revenue instead of monthly rent. At what sales levels would SuperShades prefer to pay a fixed amount of monthly rent, and at what sales levels would it prefer to pay 8% of its monthly revenue as rent?

42 CVP analysis, income taxes, sensitivity. (CMA, adapted) Carlisle Engine Company manufactures and sells diesel engines for use in small farming equipment. For its 2014 budget, Carlisle Engine Company estimates the following:

Selling price	$ 4,000
Variable cost per engine	$ 1,000
Annual fixed costs	$4,800,000
Net income	$1,200,000
Income tax rate	20%

The first-quarter income statement, as of March 31, reported that sales were not meeting expectations. During the first quarter, only 400 units had been sold at the current price of $4,000. The income statement showed that variable and fixed costs were as planned, which meant that the 2014 annual net income projection would not be met unless management took action. A management committee was formed and presented the following mutually exclusive alternatives to the president:

a. Reduce the selling price by 15%. The sales organization forecasts that at this significantly reduced price, 2,100 units can be sold during the remainder of the year. Total fixed costs and variable cost per unit will stay as budgeted.

b. Lower variable cost per unit by $300 through the use of less-expensive direct materials. The selling price will also be reduced by $400, and sales of 1,750 units are expected for the remainder of the year.

c. Reduce fixed costs by 10% and lower the selling price by 30%. Variable cost per unit will be unchanged. Sales of 2,200 units are expected for the remainder of the year.

1. If no changes are made to the selling price or cost structure, determine the number of units that Carlisle Engine Company must sell (a) to break even and (b) to achieve its net income objective.
2. Determine which alternative Carlisle Engine should select to achieve its net income objective. Show your calculations.

43 Choosing between compensation plans, operating leverage. (CMA, adapted) BioPharm Corporation manufactures pharmaceutical products that are sold through a network of external sales agents. The agents are paid a commission of 20% of revenues. BioPharm is considering replacing the sales agents with its own salespeople, who would be paid a commission of 13% of revenues and total salaries of $2,240,000. The income statement for the year ending December 31, 2013, under the two scenarios is shown here.

	A	B	C	D	E
1			BioPharm Corporation		
2			Income Statement		
3			For theYear Ended December 31, 2013		
4			Using Sales Agents		Using Own Sales Force
5	Revenues		$32,000,000		$32,000,000
6	Cost of goods sold				
7	Variable	$12,160,000		$12,160,000	
8	Fixed	3,750,000	15,910,000	3,750,000	15,910,000
9	Gross margin		16,090,000		16,090,000
10	Marketing costs				
11	Commissions	$ 6,400,000		$ 4,160,000	
12	Fixed costs	3,660,000	10,060,000	5,900,000	10,060,000
13	Operating income		$ 6,030,000		$ 6,030,000

1. Calculate BioPharm's 2013 contribution margin percentage, breakeven revenues, and degree of operating leverage under the two scenarios.
2. Describe the advantages and disadvantages of each type of sales alternative.
3. In 2014, BioPharm uses its own salespeople, who demand a 16% commission. If all other cost-behavior patterns are unchanged, how much revenue must the salespeople generate in order to earn the same operating income as in 2013?

44 Sales mix, three products. The Ronowski Company has three product lines of belts—A, B, and C—with contribution margins of $3, $2, and $1, respectively. The president foresees sales of 200,000 units in the coming period, consisting of 20,000 units of A, 100,000 units of B, and 80,000 units of C. The company's fixed costs for the period are $255,000.

Required

1. What is the company's breakeven point in units, assuming that the given sales mix is maintained?
2. If the sales mix is maintained, what is the total contribution margin when 200,000 units are sold? What is the operating income?
3. What would operating income be if 20,000 units of A, 80,000 units of B, and 100,000 units of C were sold? What is the new breakeven point in units if these relationships persist in the next period?

45 Multiproduct CVP and decision making. Crystal Clear Products produces two types of water filters. One attaches to the faucet and cleans all water that passes through the faucet. The other is a pitcher-cum-filter that only purifies water meant for drinking.

The unit that attaches to the faucet is sold for $100 and has variable costs of $35.
The pitcher-cum-filter sells for $120 and has variable costs of $30.

Crystal Clear sells two faucet models for every three pitchers sold. Fixed costs equal $1,200,000.

Required

1. What is the breakeven point in unit sales and dollars for each type of filter at the current sales mix?
2. Crystal Clear is considering buying new production equipment. The new equipment will increase fixed cost by $208,000 per year and will decrease the variable cost of the faucet and the pitcher units by $5 and $10, respectively. Assuming the same sales mix, how many of each type of filter does Crystal Clear need to sell to break even?
3. Assuming the same sales mix, at what total sales level would Crystal Clear be indifferent between using the old equipment and buying the new production equipment? If total sales are expected to be 24,000 units, should Crystal Clear buy the new production equipment?

46 Sales mix, two products. The Stackpole Company retails two products: a standard and a deluxe version of a luggage carrier. The budgeted income statement for next period is as follows:

	Standard Carrier	Deluxe Carrier	Total
Units sold	187,500	62,500	250,000
Revenues at $28 and $50 per unit	$5,250,000	$3,125,000	$8,375,000
Variable costs at $18 and $30 per unit	3,375,000	1,875,000	5,250,000
Contribution margins at $10 and $20 per unit	$1,875,000	$1,250,000	3,125,000
Fixed costs			2,250,000
Operating income			$ 875,000

Required

1. Compute the breakeven point in units, assuming that the company achieves its planned sales mix.
2. Compute the breakeven point in units (a) if only standard carriers are sold and (b) if only deluxe carriers are sold.
3. Suppose 250,000 units are sold but only 50,000 of them are deluxe. Compute the operating income. Compute the breakeven point in units. Compare your answer with the answer to requirement 1. What is the major lesson of this problem?

47 Gross margin and contribution margin. The Museum of America is preparing for its annual appreciation dinner for contributing members. Last year, 525 members attended the dinner. Tickets for the dinner were $24 per attendee. The profit report for last year's dinner follows.

Ticket sales	$12,600
Cost of dinner	15,300
Gross margin	(2,700)
Invitations and paperwork	2,500
Profit (loss)	$(5,200)

This year the dinner committee does not want to lose money on the dinner. To help achieve its goal, the committee analyzed last year's costs. Of the $15,300 cost of the dinner, $9,000 were fixed costs and $6,300 were variable costs. Of the $2,500 cost of invitations and paperwork, $1,975 were fixed and $525 were variable.

1. Prepare last year's profit report using the contribution margin format.
2. The committee is considering expanding this year's dinner invitation list to include volunteer members (in addition to contributing members). If the committee expands the dinner invitation list, it expects attendance to double. Calculate the effect this will have on the profitability of the dinner assuming fixed costs will be the same as last year.

48 Ethics, CVP analysis. Kirk Corporation produces a molded plastic casing, LX201, for desktop computers. Summary data from its 2013 income statement are as follows:

Revenues	$4,000,000
Variable costs	2,400,000
Fixed costs	1,728,000
Operating income	$ (128,000)

Bridgett Hewitt, Kirk's president, is very concerned about Kirk Corporation's poor profitability. She asks Julian Buckner, production manager, and Seth Madden, controller, to see if there are ways to reduce costs.

After 2 weeks, Julian returns with a proposal to reduce variable costs to 52% of revenues by reducing the costs Kirk currently incurs for safe disposal of wasted plastic. Seth is concerned that this would expose the company to potential environmental liabilities. He tells Julian, "We would need to estimate some of these potential environmental costs and include them in our analysis." "You can't do that," Julian replies. "We are not violating any laws. There is some possibility that we may have to incur environmental costs in the future, but if we bring it up now, this proposal will not go through because our senior management always assumes these costs to be larger than they turn out to be. The market is very tough, and we are in danger of shutting down the company and costing all of us our jobs. The only reason our competitors are making money is because they are doing exactly what I am proposing."

1. Calculate Kirk Corporation's breakeven revenues for 2013.
2. Calculate Kirk Corporation's breakeven revenues if variable costs are 52% of revenues.
3. Calculate Kirk Corporation's operating income for 2013 if variable costs had been 52% of revenues.
4. Given Julian Buckner's comments, what should Seth Madden do?

49 Deciding where to produce. (CMA, adapted) Portal Corporation produces the same power generator in two Illinois plants, a new plant in Peoria and an older plant in Moline. The following data are available for the two plants.

	A	B	C	D	E
1		**Peoria**		**Moline**	
2	Selling price		$150.00		$150.00
3	Variable manufacturing cost per unit	$72.00		$88.00	
4	Fixed manufacturing cost per unit	30.00		15.00	
5	Variable marketing and distribution cost per unit	14.00		14.00	
6	Fixed marketing and distribution cost per unit	19.00		14.50	
7	Total cost per unit		135.00		131.50
8	Operating income per unit		$ 15.00		$ 18.50
9	Production rate per day	400	units	320	units
10	Normal annual capacity usage	240	days	240	days
11	Maximum annual capacity	300	days	300	days

All fixed costs per unit are calculated based on a normal capacity usage consisting of 240 working days. When the number of working days exceeds 240, overtime charges raise the variable manufacturing costs of additional units by $3.00 per unit in Peoria and $8.00 per unit in Moline.

Portal Corporation is expected to produce and sell 192,000 power generators during the coming year. Wanting to take advantage of the higher operating income per unit at Moline, the company's production manager has decided to manufacture 96,000 units at each plant, resulting in a plan in which Moline operates at maximum capacity (320 units per day × 300 days) and Peoria operates at its normal volume (400 units per day × 240 days).

Required

1. Calculate the breakeven point in units for the Peoria plant and for the Moline plant.
2. Calculate the operating income that would result from the production manager's plan to produce 96,000 units at each plant.
3. Determine how the production of 192,000 units should be allocated between the Peoria and Moline plants to maximize operating income for Portal Corporation. Show your calculations.

Glossary

Breakeven point (BEP).   Quantity of output sold at which total revenues equal total costs, that is where the operating income is zero.

Choice criterion.   Objective that can be quantified in a decision model.

Contribution income statement.   Income statement that groups costs into variable costs and fixed costs to highlight the contribution margin.

Contribution margin.   Total revenues minus total variable costs.

Contribution margin per unit.   Selling price minus the variable cost per unit.

Contribution margin percentage.   Contribution margin per unit divided by selling price. Also called *contribution margin ratio*.

Contribution margin ratio.   See *contribution margin percentage*.

Cost–volume–profit (CVP) analysis.   Examines the behavior of total revenues, total costs, and operating income as changes occur in the units sold, the selling price, the variable cost per unit, or the fixed costs of a product.

Decision table.   Summary of the alternative actions, events, outcomes, and probabilities of events in a decision model.

Degree of operating leverage.   Contribution margin divided by operating income at any given level of sales.

Event.   A possible relevant occurrence in a decision model.

Expected monetary value.   See *expected value*.

Expected value.   Weighted average of the outcomes of a decision with the probability of each outcome serving as the weight. Also called *expected monetary value*.

Gross margin percentage.   Gross margin divided by revenues.

Margin of safety.   Amount by which budgeted (or actual) revenues exceed breakeven revenues.

Net income.   Operating income plus nonoperating revenues (such as interest revenue) minus nonoperating costs (such as interest cost) minus income taxes.

Operating leverage.   Effects that fixed costs have on changes in operating income as changes occur in units sold and hence in contribution margin.

Outcomes.   Predicted economic results of the various possible combinations of actions and events in a decision model.

Probability.   Likelihood or chance that an event will occur.

Probability distribution.   Describes the likelihood (or the probability) that each of the mutually exclusive and collectively exhaustive set of events will occur.

PV graph.   Shows how changes in the quantity of units sold affect operating income.

Revenue driver.   A variable, such as volume, that causally affects revenues.

Sales mix.   Quantities of various products or services that constitute total unit sales.

Sensitivity analysis.   A what-if technique that managers use to calculate how an outcome will change if the original predicted data are not achieved or if an underlying assumption changes.

Uncertainty.   The possibility that an actual amount will deviate from an expected amount.

Photo Credits

Credits are listed in order of appearance.

Photo 1: Lyle A. Waisman/Getty Images
Photo 2: Steve Skjold/Alamy

Chapter 4

Chapter 4

Job Costing

From Chapter 4 of *Cost Accounting: A Managerial Emphasis,* Fifteenth Edition. Charles T. Horngren, Srikant M. Datar, Madhav V. Rajan. Copyright © 2015 by Pearson Education, Inc. All rights reserved.

Job Costing

No one likes to lose money.

Whether a company is a new startup venture providing marketing consulting services or an established manufacturer of custom-built motorcycles, knowing how to job cost—that is, knowing how much it costs to produce an individual product—is critical if a company is to generate a profit. As the following article shows, KB Home, a leading U.S. homebuilder, knows this all too well.

Job Costing and "Green" Home Construction[1]

Making a profit on a project depends on pricing it correctly. At KB Home, a leading U.S. homebuilder, managers and employees are responsible for the costing and pricing of the company's new "green" ZeroHouse 2.0 homes. These environmentally friendly homes include solar power systems, solar thermal water heaters, LED lights, and even electric-vehicle charging stations to help homeowners enhance their energy efficiency.

For each custom ZeroHouse 2.0 home that KB Home builds, company managers use historical data and marketplace information to carefully estimate all costs associated with the project: direct costs, indirect costs, and general administrative costs. Direct costs include environmentally responsible building materials, solar panels, and direct labor. Indirect costs include the cost of supervisory labor, company-owned equipment, and safety equipment. Finally, general administrative costs allocated to each project include office rent, utilities, and insurance.

Throughout the homebuilding process, on-site managers report on the status of each ZeroHouse 2.0 under construction. These managers are also responsible for identifying any potential problems with a project and determining the alterations necessary to ensure high-quality, on-time delivery within the original project budget.

For KB Home and other "green" homebuilders, job costing is critical ... and will be even more important in the years ahead. In 2011, "green" homes comprised 17% of the home-construction market, and that number is expected to increase 29–38% by 2016, as more homebuyers request environmentally friendly homes that lower their energy use while saving them money.

Just like at KB Home, managers at Nissan want to know how much it costs to manufacture its new Leaf electric car, and managers at Ernst & Young want to know what it costs to audit Whole Foods, the organic grocer. Knowing the costs and profitability of jobs helps managers pursue their business strategies, develop pricing

---

[1] *Sources*: McGraw-Hill Construction/National Association of Home Builders, *New and Remodeled Green Homes: Transforming the Residential Market*, May 2012; KB Home, *Sustainability Report 2012*, Los Angeles: KB Home, 2013; Robbie Whelan, "Martha Stewart Green Homes—Who Will Buy Them?," Developments blog, *The Wall Street Journal*, January 12, 2011, http://blogs.wsj.com/; and multiple conversations with KB Home managers, 2013 (various dates).

plans, and meet external reporting requirements. Of course, when making decisions, managers combine cost information with noncost information, such as their personal observations about operations, and nonfinancial performance measures, like quality and customer satisfaction.

Building-Block Concepts of Costing Systems

◀ **Learning Objective** 1

Describe the building-block concepts of costing systems

…the building blocks are cost object, direct costs, indirect costs, cost pools, and cost-allocation bases

Before we begin our discussion of costing systems, let's discuss cost-related terms and introduce the new terms we will need to discuss the topics in this chapter.

1. A *cost object* is anything for which a measurement of costs is desired—for example, a product, such as an iMac computer, or a service, such as the cost of repairing an iMac computer.

2. The *direct costs of a cost object* are costs related to a particular cost object that can be traced to that cost object in an economically feasible (cost-effective) way—for example, the cost of purchasing the main computer board or the cost of parts used to make an iMac computer.

3. The *indirect costs of a cost object* are costs related to a particular cost object that cannot be traced to that cost object in an economically feasible (cost-effective) way—for example, the salaries of supervisors who oversee multiple products, only one of which is the iMac, or the rent paid for the repair facility that repairs many different Apple computer products besides the iMac. Indirect costs are allocated to the cost object using a cost-allocation method. *Cost assignment* is a general term for assigning costs, whether direct or indirect, to a cost object. *Cost tracing* is the process of assigning direct costs. *Cost allocation* is the process of assigning indirect costs. The relationship among these three concepts can be graphically represented as

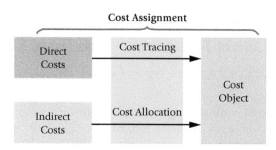

Throughout this chapter, the costs assigned to a cost object, such as a BMW Mini Cooper car, or a service, such as an audit of the MTV network, include both variable costs and costs that are fixed in the short run. Managers cost products and services to guide their long-run strategic decisions (for example, about the mix of products and services to produce and sell or the prices to charge for various products). In the long run, managers want revenues to exceed total (variable plus fixed) costs.

We also need to introduce and explain two more terms before discussing costing systems:

4. **Cost pool.** A **cost pool** is a grouping of individual indirect cost items. Cost pools can range from broad, such as all manufacturing-plant costs, to narrow, such as the costs of operating metal-cutting machines. Cost pools are often organized in conjunction with cost-allocation bases.

5. **Cost-allocation base.** How should a company allocate the costs of operating metal-cutting machines among different products? One way is based on the number of machine-hours used to produce different products. The **cost-allocation base** (number of machine-hours) is a systematic way to link an indirect cost or group of indirect costs (operating costs of all metal-cutting machines) to cost objects (different products). For example, if the indirect costs of operating metal-cutting machines is $500,000 based on running these machines for 10,000 hours, the cost-allocation rate is $500,000 ÷ 10,000 hours = $50 per machine-hour, where machine-hours is the cost-allocation base. If a product uses 800 machine-hours, it will be allocated $40,000, $50 per machine-hour × 800 machine-hours. The ideal cost-allocation base is the cost driver of the indirect costs because there is a cause-and-effect relationship between the cost-allocation base and the indirect costs. A cost-allocation base can be either financial (such as direct labor costs) or nonfinancial (such as the number of machine-hours). When the cost object is a job, product, or customer, the cost-allocation base is also called a **cost-application base.** For example, when the cost object is a department or another cost pool, the cost-allocation base is not called a cost-application base.

Sometimes a cost may need to be allocated when the cause-and-effect relationship is not clear-cut. Consider a corporatewide advertising program that promotes the general image of a company and its various divisions, rather than the image of an individual product. Many companies, such as PepsiCo, allocate costs like these to their individual divisions on the basis of revenues: The higher a division's revenue, the higher the business's allocated cost of the advertising program. Allocating costs this way is based on the criterion of *benefits received* rather than cause-and-effect. Divisions with higher revenues benefit from the advertising more than divisions with lower revenues and therefore ought to be allocated more of the advertising costs.

Another criterion for allocating some costs is the cost object's *ability to bear* the costs allocated to it. The city government of Houston, Texas, for example, distributes the costs of the city manager's office to other city departments—including the police department, fire department, library system, and others—based on the size of their budgets. The city's rationale is that larger departments should absorb a larger share of the costs. Organizations generally use the cause-and-effect criterion to allocate costs, followed by benefits received, and finally, and more rarely, by ability to bear.

The concepts represented by these five terms constitute the building blocks we will use to design the costing systems described in this chapter.

Decision Point ▶

What are the building block concepts of a costing system?

Learning Objective 2 ▶

Distinguish job costing

...job costing is used to cost a distinct product

from process costing

...process costing is used to cost masses of identical or similar units

Job-Costing and Process-Costing Systems

Management accountants use two basic types of costing systems to assign costs to products or services.

1. **Job-costing system.** In a job-costing system, the cost object is a unit or multiple units of a distinct product or service called a **job.** Each job generally uses different amounts of resources. The product or service is often a single unit, such as a specialized machine made at Hitachi, a construction project managed by Bechtel Corporation, a repair job done at an Audi Service Center, or an advertising campaign produced by Saatchi & Saatchi. Each special machine made by Hitachi is unique and distinct from the other machines made at the plant. An advertising campaign for one client

at Saatchi & Saatchi is unique and distinct from advertising campaigns for other clients. Job costing is also used by companies such as Ethan Allen to cost multiple identical units of distinct furniture products. Because the products and services are distinct, job-costing systems are used to accumulate costs separately for each product or service.

2. **Process-costing system.** In a process-costing system, the cost object is masses of identical or similar units of a product or service. For example, Citibank provides the same service to all its customers when processing customer deposits. Intel provides the same product (say, a Pentium 6 chip) to each of its customers. All Minute Maid consumers receive the same frozen orange juice product. In each period, process-costing systems divide the total costs of producing an identical or similar product or service by the total number of units produced to obtain a per-unit cost. This per-unit cost is the average unit cost that applies to each of the identical or similar units produced in that period.

Exhibit 1 presents examples of job costing and process costing in the service, merchandising, and manufacturing sectors. These two types of costing systems lie at opposite ends of a continuum; in between, one type of system can blur into the other to some degree.

Many companies have costing systems that are neither pure job-costing systems nor pure process-costing systems but have elements of both, tailored to the underlying operations. For example, Kellogg Corporation uses job costing to calculate the total cost to manufacture each of its different and distinct types of products—such as Corn Flakes,

Decision Point

How do you distinguish job costing from process costing?

Exhibit 1

Examples of Job Costing and Process Costing in the Service, Merchandising, and Manufacturing Sectors

	Service Sector	Merchandising Sector	Manufacturing Sector
Job Costing Used	• Audit engagements done by PricewaterhouseCoopers • Consulting engagements done by McKinsey & Co. • Advertising-agency campaigns run by Ogilvy & Mather • Individual legal cases argued by Hale & Dorr • Computer-repair jobs done by CompUSA • Movies produced by Universal Studios	• L. L. Bean sending individual items by mail order • Special promotion of new products by Walmart	• Assembly of individual aircrafts at Boeing • Construction of ships at Litton Industries
Process Costing Used	• Bank-check clearing at Bank of America • Postal delivery (standard items) by U.S. Postal Service	• Grain dealing by Arthur Daniel Midlands • Lumber dealing by Weyerhauser	• Oil refining by Shell Oil • Beverage production by PepsiCo

Crispix, and Froot Loops—and process costing to calculate the per-unit cost of producing each identical box of Corn Flakes, each identical box of Crispix, and so on. In this chapter, we focus on job-costing systems.

Job Costing: Evaluation and Implementation

Learning Objective 3

Describe the approaches to evaluating and implementing job-costing systems

...to determine costs of jobs in a timely manner

We illustrate job costing using the example of Robinson Company, which manufactures and installs specialized machinery for the paper-making industry. In early 2013, Robinson receives a request to bid on the manufacturing and installation of a new paper-making machine for the Western Pulp and Paper Company (WPP). Robinson had never made a machine quite like this one, and its managers wonder what to bid for the job. In order to make decisions about the job, Robinson's management team works through the five-step decision-making process.

1. **Identify the problems and uncertainties.** The decision of whether and how much to bid for the WPP job depends on how management resolves two critical uncertainties: (1) what it will cost to complete the job; and (2) the prices Robinson's competitors are likely to bid.

2. **Obtain information.** Robinson's managers first evaluate whether doing the WPP job is consistent with the company's strategy. Do they want to do more of these kinds of jobs? Is this an attractive segment of the market? Will Robinson be able to develop a competitive advantage over its competitors and satisfy customers such as WPP? After completing their research, Robinson's managers conclude that the WPP job fits well with the company's strategy.

   Robinson's managers study the drawings and engineering specifications provided by WPP and decide on the technical details of the machine. They compare the specifications of this machine to similar machines they have made in the past, identify competitors that might bid on the job, and gather information on what these bids might be.

3. **Make predictions about the future.** Robinson's managers estimate the cost of direct materials, direct manufacturing labor, and overhead for the WPP job. They also consider qualitative factors and risk factors and evaluate any biases they might have. For example, do engineers and employees working on the WPP job have the necessary skills and technical competence? Would they find the experience valuable and challenging? How accurate are the cost estimates, and what is the likelihood of cost overruns? What biases do Robinson's managers have to be careful about?

4. **Make decisions by choosing among alternatives.** Robinson's managers consider several alternative bids based on what they believe competing firms will bid, the technical expertise needed for the job, business risks, and other qualitative factors. Ultimately Robinson decides to bid $15,000. The manufacturing cost estimate is $9,705 (as described later in the chapter), which yields a markup of more than 50% on manufacturing cost.

5. **Implement the decision, evaluate performance, and learn.** Robinson wins the bid for the WPP job. As Robinson works on the job, management accountants carefully track all of the costs incurred (which are detailed later in this chapter). Ultimately, Robinson's managers will compare the predicted amounts against actual costs to evaluate how well the company did on the WPP job.

In its job-costing system, Robinson accumulates the costs incurred for a job in different parts of the value chain, such as manufacturing, marketing, and customer service. We focus here on Robinson's manufacturing function (which also includes the product's installation). To make a machine, Robinson purchases some components from outside suppliers and makes other components itself. Each of Robinson's jobs also has a service element: installing a machine at a customer's site, integrating it with the customer's other machines and processes, and ensuring the machine meets the customer's expectations.

One form of a job-costing system Robinson can use is **actual costing**, which is a costing system that traces direct costs to a cost object based on the *actual direct-cost rate*s times the actual quantities of the direct-cost inputs used. Indirect costs are allocated based on the *actual indirect-cost rates* times the actual quantities of the cost-allocation bases. An actual indirect-cost rate is calculated by dividing actual annual indirect costs by the actual annual quantity of the cost-allocation base.

$$\frac{\text{Actual indirect}}{\text{cost rate}} = \frac{\text{Actual annual indirect costs}}{\text{Actual annual quantity of the cost-allocation base}}$$

As its name suggests, actual costing systems calculate the actual costs of jobs. Yet actual costing systems are not commonly found in practice because actual costs cannot be computed in a *timely* manner.[2] The problem is not with computing direct-cost rates for direct materials and direct manufacturing labor. For example, Robinson records the actual prices paid for materials. As it uses these materials, the prices paid serve as actual direct-cost rates for charging material costs to jobs. As we discuss next, calculating actual indirect-cost rates on a timely basis each week or each month is, however, a problem. Robinson can only calculate actual indirect-cost rates at the end of the fiscal year. However, the firm's managers are unwilling to wait that long to learn the costs of various jobs because they need cost information to monitor and manage the cost of jobs while they are in progress. Ongoing cost information about jobs also helps managers bid on new jobs while old jobs are in progress.

Time Period Used to Compute Indirect-Cost Rates

There are two reasons for using longer periods, such as a year, to calculate indirect-cost rates.

1. **The numerator reason (indirect-cost pool).** The shorter the period, the greater is the influence of seasonal patterns on the amount of costs. For example, if indirect-cost rates were calculated each month, the costs of heating (included in the numerator) would be charged to production only during the winter months. An annual period incorporates the effects of all four seasons into a single, annual indirect-cost rate.

   Levels of total indirect costs are also affected by nonseasonal erratic costs. Nonseasonal erratic costs are the costs incurred in a particular month that benefit operations during future months, such as equipment-repair costs and the costs of vacation and holiday pay for employees. If monthly indirect-cost rates were calculated, the jobs done in a month in which there were high, nonseasonal erratic costs would be charged with these higher costs. Pooling all indirect costs together over the course of a full year and calculating a single annual indirect-cost rate helps smooth some of the erratic bumps in costs associated with shorter periods.

2. **The denominator reason (quantity of the cost-allocation base).** Another reason for longer periods is to avoid spreading monthly fixed indirect costs over fluctuating levels of monthly output and fluctuating quantities of the cost-allocation base. Consider the following example.

Reardon and Pane is a firm of tax accountants whose work follows a highly seasonal pattern. Tax season (January–April) is very busy. Other times of the year are less busy. The firm has both variable indirect costs and fixed indirect costs. Variable indirect costs (such as supplies, power, and indirect support labor) vary with the quantity of the cost-allocation base (direct professional labor-hours). Fixed indirect costs (depreciation and general administrative support) do not vary with short-run fluctuations in the quantity of the cost-allocation base:

	Indirect Costs			Direct Professional Labor-Hours (4)	Variable Indirect Cost Rate per Direct Professional Labor-Hour (5) = (1) ÷ (4)	Fixed Indirect Cost Rate per Direct Professional Labor-Hour (6) = (2) ÷ (4)	Total Allocation Rate per Direct Professional Labor-Hour (7) = (3) ÷ (4)
	Variable (1)	Fixed (2)	Total (3)				
High-output month	$40,000	$60,000	$100,000	3,200	$12.50	$18.75	$31.25
Low-output month	10,000	60,000	70,000	800	$12.50	$75.00	87.50

---

[2] Actual costing is presented in more detail later in the chapter.

Variable indirect costs change in proportion to changes in the number of direct professional labor-hours worked. Therefore, the variable indirect-cost rate is the same in both the high-output months and the low-output months ($12.50 in both as the table shows). Sometimes overtime payments can cause the variable indirect-cost rate to be higher in high-output months. In such cases, variable indirect costs will be allocated at a higher rate to production in high-output months relative to production in low-output months.

Now consider the fixed costs of $60,000. The fixed costs cause monthly total indirect-cost rates to vary considerably—from $31.25 per hour to $87.50 per hour. Few managers believe that identical jobs done in different months should be allocated such significantly different indirect-cost charges per hour ($87.50 ÷ $31.25 = 2.80, or 280%) because of fixed costs. Furthermore, if fees for preparing tax returns are based on costs, fees would be high in low-output months leading to lost business, when in fact management wants to accept more bids to use the idle capacity during these months.

Reardon and Pane chose a specific level of capacity based on a time horizon far beyond a mere month. An average, annualized rate based on the relationship between total annual indirect costs and the total annual level of output smoothes the effect of monthly variations in output levels. This rate is more representative of the total costs and total output the company's managers considered when choosing the level of capacity and, therefore, fixed costs. Another denominator reason for using annual overhead rates is because the number of Monday-to-Friday workdays in a month affects the calculation of monthly indirect-cost rates. The number of workdays per month varies from 20 to 23 during a year. Because February has the fewest workdays (and consequently labor-hours), if separate rates are computed each month, jobs done in February would bear a greater share of the firm's indirect costs (such as depreciation and property taxes) than identical jobs in other months. An annual period reduces the effect that the number of working days per month has on unit costs.

Decision Point

What is the main challenge of implementing job-costing systems?

Normal Costing

As we indicated, because it's hard to calculate actual indirect-cost rates on a weekly or monthly basis, managers cannot calculate the actual costs of jobs as they are completed. Nonetheless, managers want a close approximation of the costs of various jobs regularly during the year, not just at the end of the fiscal year. They want to know manufacturing costs (and other costs, such as marketing costs) to price jobs, monitor and manage costs, evaluate the success of jobs, learn about what did and did not work, bid on new jobs, and prepare interim financial statements. Because companies need immediate access to job costs, few wait to allocate overhead costs until the end of the accounting year. Instead, a *predetermined* or *budgeted* indirect-cost rate is calculated for each cost pool at the beginning of a fiscal year, and overhead costs are allocated to jobs as work progresses. For the numerator and denominator reasons already described, the **budgeted indirect-cost rate** for each cost pool is computed as follows:

$$\frac{\text{Budgeted indirect}}{\text{cost rate}} = \frac{\text{Budgeted annual indirect costs}}{\text{Budgeted annual quantity of the cost-allocation base}}$$

Using budgeted indirect-cost rates gives rise to normal costing.

Normal costing is a costing system that (1) traces direct costs to a cost object by using the actual direct-cost rates times the actual quantities of the direct-cost inputs and (2) allocates indirect costs based on the *budgeted* indirect-cost rates times the actual quantities of the cost-allocation bases.

Learning Objective 4

Outline the seven-step approach to normal costing

...the seven-step approach is used to compute direct and indirect costs of a job

General Approach to Job Costing Using Normal Costing

We illustrate normal costing for the Robinson Company example using the following seven steps to assign costs to an individual job. This approach is commonly used by companies in the manufacturing, merchandising, and service sectors.

Step 1: Identify the Job That Is the Chosen Cost Object. The cost object in the Robinson Company example is Job WPP 298, manufacturing a paper-making machine for Western Pulp and Paper (WPP) in 2013. Robinson's managers and management accountants gather information to cost jobs through source documents. A **source document** is an original record (such as a labor time card on which an employee's work hours are recorded) that supports journal entries in an accounting system. The main source document for Job WPP 298 is a job-cost record. A **job-cost record**, also called a **job-cost sheet**, is used to record and accumulate all the costs assigned to a specific job, starting when work begins. Exhibit 2 shows the job-cost record for the paper-making machine ordered by WPP. Follow the various steps in costing Job WPP 298 on the job-cost record in Exhibit 2.

Exhibit 2   Source Documents at Robinson Company: Job-Cost Record

	A	B	C	D	E	F
1			JOB-COST RECORD			
2	JOB NO:	WPP 298		CUSTOMER:	Western Pulp and Paper	
3	Date Started:	Feb. 4, 2013		Date Completed	Feb. 28, 2013	
4						
5						
6	DIRECT MATERIALS					
7	Date	Materials		Quantity	Unit	Total
8	Received	Requisition No.	Part No.	Used	Cost	Costs
9	Feb. 4, 2013	2013: 198	MB 468-A	8	$14	$ 112
10	Feb. 4, 2013	2013: 199	TB 267-F	12	63	756
11						•
12						•
13	Total					$ 4,606
14						
15	DIRECT MANUFACTURING LABOR					
16	Period	Labor Time	Employee	Hours	Hourly	Total
17	Covered	Record No.	No.	Used	Rate	Costs
18	Feb. 4-10, 2013	LT 232	551-87-3076	25	$18	$ 450
19	Feb. 4-10, 2013	LT 247	287-31-4671	5	19	95
20	•	•	•	•	•	•
21	•	•	•	•	•	•
22	Total			88		$ 1,579
23						
24	MANUFACTURING OVERHEAD*					
25		Cost Pool		Allocation Base	Allocation-	Total
26	Date	Category	Allocation Base	Quantity Used	Base Rate	Costs
27	Dec. 31, 2013	Manufacturing	Direct Manufacturing	88 hours	$40	$ 3,520
28			Labor-Hours			
29						
30	Total					$ 3,520
31	TOTAL MANUFACTURING COST OF JOB					$ 9,705
32						
33						
34	*The Robinson Company uses a single manufacturing-overhead cost pool. The use of multiple overhead cost pools					
35	would mean multiple entries in the "Manufacturing Overhead" section of the job-cost record.					
36						

| Exhibit 3 | Source Documents at Robinson Company: Materials-Requisition Record and Labor-Time Sheet |

PANEL A:

MATERIALS-REQUISITION RECORD				
Materials-Requisition Record No.				2013: 198
Job No. __WPP 298__		Date:		FEB. 4, 2013
Part No.	Part Description	Quantity	Unit Cost	Total Cost
MB 468-A	Metal Brackets	8	$14	$112
Issued By: B. Clyde		Date:		Feb. 4, 2013
Received By: L. Daley		Date:		Feb. 4, 2013

PANEL B:

LABOR-TIME SHEET								
Labor-Time Record No:				LT 232				
Employee Name: _G. L. Cook_			Employee No: _551-87-3076_					
Employee Classification Code:			Grade 3 Machinist					
Hourly Rate: $18								
Week Start: _Feb. 4, 2013_			Week End: _Feb. 10, 2013_					
Job. No.	M	T	W	Th	F	S	Su	Total
WPP 298	4	8	3	6	4	0	0	25
JL 256	3	0	4	2	3	0	0	12
Maintenance	1	0	1	0	1	0	0	3
Total	8	8	8	8	8	0	0	40
Supervisor: R. Stuart	Date: Feb. 10, 2013							

Step 2: Identify the Direct Costs of the Job. Robinson identifies two direct-manufacturing cost categories: direct materials and direct manufacturing labor.

- **Direct materials:** On the basis of the engineering specifications and drawings provided by WPP, a manufacturing engineer orders materials from the storeroom using a basic source document called a **materials-requisition record,** which contains information about the cost of direct materials used on a specific job and in a specific department. Exhibit 3, Panel A, shows a materials-requisition record for the Robinson Company. See how the record specifies the job for which the material is requested (WPP 298) and describes the material (Part Number MB 468-A, metal brackets), the actual quantity (8), the actual unit cost ($14), and the actual total cost ($112). The $112 actual total cost also appears on the job-cost record in Exhibit 2. If we add the cost of all materials requisitions, the total actual direct materials cost is $4,606, which is shown in the Direct Materials panel of the job-cost record in Exhibit 2.

- **Direct manufacturing labor:** Accounting for direct manufacturing labor is similar to accounting for direct materials. The source document for direct manufacturing labor is a **labor-time sheet,** which contains information about the amount of labor time used for a specific job in a specific department. Exhibit 3, Panel B, shows a typical weekly labor-time sheet for a particular employee (G. L. Cook). Each day Cook records the time spent on individual jobs (in this case WPP 298 and JL 256), as well as the time spent on other tasks, such as the maintenance of machines or cleaning, that are not related to a specific job.

  The 25 hours that Cook spent on Job WPP 298 appears on the job-cost record in Exhibit 2 at a cost of $450 (25 hours × $18 per hour). Similarly, the job-cost record for Job JL 256 will show a cost of $216 (12 hours × $18 per hour). The three hours of time spent on maintenance and cleaning at $18 per hour equals $54. This cost is part of indirect manufacturing costs because it is not traceable to any particular job. This indirect cost is included as part of the manufacturing-overhead cost pool allocated to jobs. The total direct manufacturing labor costs of $1,579 for the paper-making machine that appears in the Direct Manufacturing Labor panel of the job-cost record in Exhibit 2 is the sum of all the direct manufacturing labor costs charged to Job WPP 298 by different employees.

  All costs other than direct materials and direct manufacturing labor are classified as indirect costs.

Step 3: Select the Cost-Allocation Bases to Use for Allocating Indirect Costs to the Job. Recall that indirect manufacturing costs are costs that are necessary to do a job but that cannot be traced to a specific job. It would be impossible to complete a job without incurring indirect costs such as supervision, manufacturing engineering, utilities, and repairs. Moreover, different jobs require different quantities of indirect resources. Because these costs cannot be traced to a specific job, managers must allocate them to jobs in a systematic way.

Companies often use multiple cost-allocation bases to allocate indirect costs because different indirect costs have different cost drivers. For example, some indirect costs such as depreciation and repairs of machines are more closely related to machine-hours. Other indirect costs such as supervision and production support are more closely related to direct manufacturing labor-hours. Robinson, however, chooses direct manufacturing labor-hours as the sole allocation base for linking all indirect manufacturing costs to jobs. The managers do so because, in Robinson's labor-intensive environment, they believe the number of direct manufacturing labor-hours drives the manufacturing overhead resources required by individual jobs. (Managers in many manufacturing environments often need to broaden the set of cost drivers.) In 2013, Robinson budgets 28,000 direct manufacturing labor-hours.

Step 4: Identify the Indirect Costs Associated with Each Cost-Allocation Base. Because Robinson believes that a single cost-allocation base—direct manufacturing labor-hours— can be used to allocate indirect manufacturing costs to jobs, Robinson creates a single cost pool called manufacturing overhead costs. This pool represents all indirect costs of the Manufacturing Department that are difficult to trace directly to individual jobs. In 2013, budgeted manufacturing overhead costs total $1,120,000.

As we saw in Steps 3 and 4, managers first identify cost-allocation bases and then identify the costs related to each cost-allocation base, not the other way around. They choose this order because managers must first understand their companies' cost drivers (the reasons why costs are being incurred) before they can determine the costs associated with each cost driver. Otherwise, there is nothing to guide the creation of cost pools. Of course, Steps 3 and 4 are often done almost simultaneously.

Step 5: Compute the Rate per Unit of Each Cost-Allocation Base Used to Allocate Indirect Costs to the Job. For each cost pool, the budgeted indirect-cost rate is calculated by dividing the budgeted total indirect costs in the pool (determined in Step 4) by the budgeted total quantity of the cost-allocation base (determined in Step 3). Robinson calculates the allocation rate for its single manufacturing overhead cost pool as follows:

$$\text{Budgeted manufacturing overhead rate} = \frac{\text{Budgeted manufacturing overhead costs}}{\text{Budgeted total quantity of cost-allocation base}}$$

$$= \frac{\$1,120,000}{28,000 \text{ direct manufacturing labor-hours}}$$

$$= \$40 \text{ per direct manufacturing labor-hour}$$

Step 6: Compute the Indirect Costs Allocated to the Job. The indirect costs of a job are calculated by multiplying the *actual* quantity of each different allocation base (one allocation base for each cost pool) associated with the job by the *budgeted* indirect cost rate of each allocation base (computed in Step 5). Recall that Robinson's managers selected direct manufacturing labor-hours as the only cost-allocation base. Robinson uses 88 direct manufacturing labor-hours on the WPP 298 job. Consequently, the manufacturing overhead costs allocated to WPP 298 equal $3,520 ($40 per direct manufacturing labor-hour × 88 hours) and appear in the Manufacturing Overhead panel of the WPP 298 job-cost record in Exhibit 2.

Step 7: Compute the Total Cost of the Job by Adding All Direct and Indirect Costs Assigned to the Job. Exhibit 2 shows that the total manufacturing costs of the WPP job are $9,705.

Direct manufacturing costs		
Direct materials	$4,606	
Direct manufacturing labor	1,579	$ 6,185
Manufacturing overhead costs		
($40 per direct manufacturing labor-hour × 88 hours)		3,520
Total manufacturing costs of job WPP 298		$9,705

Concepts in Action

The Job Costing "Game Plan" at the New Cowboys Stadium

Although the Dallas Cowboys have won five Super Bowls, many football fans recognize the team for its futuristic home, Cowboys Stadium in Arlington, Texas. The 80,000-seat stadium, built in 3 years, features two arches spanning a quarter-mile in length over the dome, a retractable roof, the largest retractable glass doors in the world (in each end zone), canted glass exterior walls, and a 600-ton video screen. For Manhattan Construction, the company that managed the $1.2 billion Cowboys Stadium project, understanding the costs of these features was critical for making successful pricing decisions and ensuring that the project was profitable.

The Cowboys Stadium project had five stages: (1) conceptualization, (2) design and planning, (3) preconstruction, (4) construction, and (5) finalization and delivery. During this process, Manhattan Construction hired architects and subcontractors, created blueprints, purchased and cleared land, constructed the stadium, built out and finished interiors, and completed last-minute changes before the stadium's 2009 opening. To ensure proper allocation and accounting of resources, project managers used a job-costing system. They then allocated estimated overhead costs (supervisor salaries, rent, materials handling, and so on). Manhattan Construction was able to estimate the project's profitability based on the percentage of work completed and revenue earned, while providing the Dallas Cowboys with clear, concise, and transparent costing data.

Just like quarterback Tony Romo navigating opposing defenses, Manhattan Construction was able to leverage its job-costing system to ensure the successful construction of a stadium as iconic as the blue star on the Cowboys' helmets.

Sources: Based on interview with Mark Penny, Project Manager, Manhattan Construction Co., 2010; David Dillon, "New Cowboys Stadium Has Grand Design, but Discipline Isn't Compromised," *The Dallas Morning News* (June 3, 2009); Brooke Knudson, "Profile: Dallas Cowboys Stadium," *Construction Today* (December 22, 2008); and Dallas Cowboys, "Cowboys Stadium: Architecture Fact Sheet."

Recall that Robinson bid a price of $15,000 for the job. At that revenue, the normal-costing system shows the job's gross margin is $5,295 ($15,000 − $9,705) and its gross-margin percentage is 35.3% ($5,295 ÷ $15,000 = 0.353).

Robinson's manufacturing managers and sales managers can use the gross margin and gross-margin percentage calculations to compare the different jobs to try to understand why some jobs aren't as profitable as others. Were direct materials wasted? Was the direct manufacturing labor cost of the jobs too high? Were the jobs simply underpriced? A job-cost analysis provides the information managers needed to gauge the manufacturing and sales performance of their firms (see Concepts in Action: The Job Costing "Game Plan" at the New Cowboys Stadium).

Exhibit 4 is an overview of Robinson Company's job-costing system. This exhibit represents the concepts comprising the five building blocks of job-costing systems introduced at the beginning of this chapter: (1) cost objects, (2) the direct costs of a cost object, (3) the indirect (overhead) costs of a cost object, (4) the indirect-cost pool, and (5) the cost-allocation base. (The symbols in the exhibit are used consistently in the costing-system overviews presented in this text. A triangle always identifies a direct cost, a rectangle represents the indirect-cost pool, and an octagon describes the cost-allocation base.) Costing-system overviews such as Exhibit 4 are important learning tools. We urge you to sketch one when you need to understand a costing system.

Note the similarities between Exhibit 4 and the cost of the WPP 298 job described in Step 7. Exhibit 4 shows two direct-cost categories (direct materials and direct

Decision Point

How do you implement a normal-costing system?

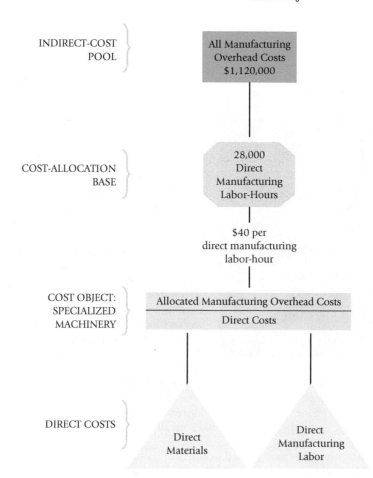

Exhibit 4

Job-Costing Overview for Determining Manufacturing Costs of Jobs at Robinson Company.

manufacturing labor) and one indirect-cost category (manufacturing overhead) used to allocate indirect costs. The costs in Step 7 also have three dollar amounts, each corresponding respectively to the two direct-cost and one indirect-cost categories.

The Role of Technology

Information technology gives managers quick and accurate job-costing information, making it easier for them to manage and control jobs. Consider, for example, the direct materials charged to jobs. Managers control these costs as materials are purchased and used. Using Electronic Data Interchange (EDI) technology, companies like Robinson order materials from their suppliers by clicking a few keys on a computer keyboard. EDI, an electronic computer link between a company and its suppliers, ensures that the order is transmitted quickly and accurately with minimal paperwork and costs. A bar code scanner records the receipt of incoming materials, and a computer matches the receipt with the order, prints out a check to the supplier, and records the materials received. When an operator on the production floor transmits a request for materials via a computer terminal, the computer prepares a materials-requisition record, instantly recording the issue of materials in the materials and job-cost records. Each day, the computer sums the materials-requisition records charged to a particular job or manufacturing department. A performance report is then prepared monitoring the actual costs of direct materials. The use of direct materials can be reported hourly if managers believe the benefits exceed the cost of such frequent reporting. The Concepts in Action: Home Depot Undergoes an Inventory Management "Fix-It" describes Home Depot's use of technology to manage its inventory.

Similarly, information about direct manufacturing labor is obtained as employees log into computer terminals and key in job numbers, their employee numbers, and start and end times of their work on different jobs. The computer automatically prints the labor time record and, using hourly rates stored for each employee, calculates the direct manufacturing

Concepts in Action ▶ Home Depot Undergoes an Inventory Management "Fix-It"

At the end of 2012, Home Depot had $10.7 billion worth of inventory. For many years, however, the world's largest home-improvement retailer struggled to know where that entire inventory was at any given time due to dated technology. As a result, Home Depot performed its own renovation to transform its inventory management using state-of-the-art technology across more than 2,200 stores in the United States, Canada, and Mexico.

Today, Home Depot uses advanced databases and mobile devices that help workers locate and manage inventory on the spot. When merchandise is scanned at the checkout, computer systems are automatically alerted when additional inventory is needed on store shelves. While Home Depot previously sent half-empty trucks to individual stores, new "rapid deployment" distribution centers now combine shipments to area stores, which trims costs and cuts truck trips by 50%. The company has deployed 59,000 "First Phone" mobile wireless devices that give store workers instant access to product information, check inventory levels, speed checkout times, and even allow customers to purchase their items through a PayPal account.

Home Depot's inventory management fix-it efforts have yielded significant benefits for the company. The new technology has helped more effectively manage inventory volume, reduce stockouts, reduce the need to sell overstocked items at clearance prices, and churn through inventory at a faster pace. Additionally, Home Depot employees now spend only 45% of their workday on stocking and inventory, down from 60% in 2008. This allows for more time helping customers, which increases sales.

Sources: Based on Miguel Bustillo, "Home Depot Undergoes Renovation," *The Wall Street Journal* (February 24, 2010); Meridith Levinson Sun, "Home Improvement," CIO (August 2004); Rachel Tobin Ramos, "Home Depot Getting Better Handle on Products," *The Atlanta Journal-Constitution* (March 29, 2010); Joel Schectman, "Home Depot Rolls Out New Mobile Devices for Workers," CIO Journal blog, *The Wall Street Journal*, June 21, 2012, http://blogs.wsj.com/; The Home Depot, Inc., 2013 Form 10-K (March 28, 2011).

labor costs of individual jobs. Information technology can also give managers instant feedback to help them control manufacturing overhead costs, jobs in process, jobs completed, and jobs shipped and installed at customer sites.

Learning Objective 5 ▶

Distinguish actual costing

...actual costing uses actual indirect-cost rates

from normal costing

...normal costing uses budgeted indirect-cost rates

Actual Costing

How would the cost of Job WPP 298 change if Robinson had used actual costing rather than normal costing? Both actual costing and normal costing trace direct costs to jobs in the same way because source documents identify the actual quantities and actual rates of direct materials and direct manufacturing labor for a job as the work is being done. The only difference between costing a job with normal costing and actual costing is that normal costing uses *budgeted* indirect-cost rates, whereas actual costing uses *actual* indirect-cost rates calculated annually at the end of the year. Exhibit 5 distinguishes actual costing from normal costing.

The following actual data for 2013 are for Robinson's manufacturing operations:

	Actual
Total manufacturing overhead costs	$1,215,000
Total direct manufacturing labor-hours	27,000

	Actual Costing	Normal Costing
Direct Costs	*Actual direct-cost rates* × *actual quantities of direct-cost inputs*	*Actual direct-cost rates* × *actual quantities of direct-cost inputs*
Indirect Costs	*Actual indirect-cost rates* × *actual quantities of cost-allocation bases*	*Budgeted indirect-cost rates* × *actual quantities of cost-allocation bases*

Exhibit 5

Actual Costing and
Normal Costing
Methods

Steps 1 and 2 are the same in both normal and actual costing: Step 1 identifies WPP 298 as the cost object; Step 2 calculates actual direct materials costs of $4,606 and actual direct manufacturing labor costs of $1,579. Recall from Step 3 that Robinson uses a single cost-allocation base, direct manufacturing labor-hours, to allocate all manufacturing overhead costs to jobs. The actual quantity of direct manufacturing labor-hours for 2013 is 27,000 hours. In Step 4, Robinson groups all actual indirect manufacturing costs of $1,215,000 into a single manufacturing overhead cost pool. In Step 5, the **actual indirect-cost rate** is calculated by dividing actual total indirect costs in the pool (determined in Step 4) by the actual total quantity of the cost-allocation base (determined in Step 3). Robinson calculates the actual manufacturing overhead rate in 2013 for its single manufacturing overhead cost pool as follows:

$$\frac{\text{Actual manufacturing}}{\text{overhead rate}} = \frac{\text{Actual annual manufacturing overhead costs}}{\text{Actual annual quantity of the cost-allocation base}}$$

$$= \frac{\$1,215,000}{27,000 \text{ direct manufacturing labor-hours}}$$

$$= \$45 \text{ per direct manufacturing labor-hour}$$

In Step 6, under an actual-costing system,

$$\frac{\text{Manufacturing overhead costs}}{\text{allocated to WPP 298}} = \frac{\text{Actual manufacturing}}{\text{overhead rate}} \times \frac{\text{Actual quantity of direct}}{\text{manufacturing labor-hours}}$$

$$= \frac{\$45 \text{ per direct manuf.}}{\text{labor-hour}} \times \frac{88 \text{ direct manufacturing}}{\text{labor-hours}}$$

$$= \$3,960$$

In Step 7, the cost of the job under actual costing is $10,145, calculated as follows:

Direct manufacturing costs		
Direct materials	$4,606	
Direct manufacturing labor	1,579	$ 6,185
Manufacturing overhead costs		
($45 per direct manufacturing labor-hour × 88 actual direct manufacturing labor-hours)		3,960
Total manufacturing costs of job		$10,145

The manufacturing cost of the WPP 298 job is higher by $440 under actual costing ($10,145) than it is under normal costing ($9,705) because the actual indirect-cost rate is $45 per hour, whereas the budgeted indirect-cost rate is $40 per hour. That is, ($45 − $40) × 88 actual direct manufacturing labor-hours = $440.

As we discussed previously, the manufacturing costs of a job are available much earlier in a normal-costing system. Consequently, Robinson's manufacturing and sales managers can evaluate the profitability of different jobs, the efficiency with which the jobs are done, and the pricing of different jobs as soon as they are completed, while the experience is still fresh in everyone's mind. Another advantage of normal costing is that it provides managers with information earlier—while there is still time to take corrective actions, such as improving the company's labor efficiency or reducing the company's

Decision Point

How do you distinguish actual costing from normal costing?

overhead costs. At the end of the year, though, costs allocated using normal costing will not, in general, equal actual costs incurred. If the differences are significant, adjustments will need to be made so that the cost of jobs and the costs in various inventory accounts are based on actual rather than normal costing. We describe these adjustments later in the chapter.

The next section explains how a normal job-costing system aggregates the costs and revenues for all jobs worked on during a particular month. *Instructors and students who do not wish to explore these details can go directly to the section "Budgeted Indirect Costs and End-of-Accounting-Year Adjustments."*

Learning Objective **6** ▶

Track the flow of costs in a job-costing system

...from purchase of materials to sale of finished goods

A Normal Job-Costing System in Manufacturing

The following example looks at events that occurred at Robinson Company in February 2013. Before getting into the details of normal costing, study Exhibit 6, which provides a broad framework for understanding the flow of costs in job costing.

The upper part of Exhibit 6 shows the flow of inventoriable costs from the purchase of materials and other manufacturing inputs to their conversion into work-in-process and finished goods, to the sale of finished goods.

Direct materials used and direct manufacturing labor can be easily traced to jobs. They become part of work-in-process inventory on the balance sheet because direct manufacturing labor transforms direct materials into another asset, work-in-process inventory. Robinson also incurs manufacturing overhead costs (including indirect materials and indirect manufacturing labor) to convert direct materials into work-in-process inventory. The overhead (indirect) costs, however, cannot be easily traced to individual jobs. Manufacturing overhead costs, therefore, are first accumulated in a manufacturing overhead account and then allocated to individual jobs. As manufacturing overhead costs are allocated, they become part of work-in-process inventory.

As individual jobs are completed, work-in-process inventory becomes another balance sheet asset, finished goods inventory. Only when finished goods are sold is the expense of cost of goods sold recognized in the income statement and matched against revenues earned.

The lower part of Exhibit 6 shows the period costs—marketing and customer-service costs. These costs do not create any assets on the balance sheet because they are not incurred to transform materials into a finished product. Instead, they are expensed in the income statement as they are incurred to best match revenues.

We next describe the entries made in the general ledger.

| Exhibit 6 | Flow of Costs in Job Costing |

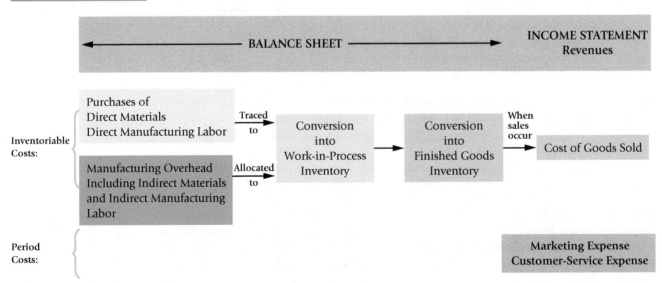

General Ledger

You know by this point that a job-costing system has a separate job-cost record for each job. A summary of the job-cost record is typically found in a subsidiary ledger. The general ledger account Work-in-Process Control presents the total of these separate job-cost records pertaining to all unfinished jobs. The job-cost records and Work-in-Process Control account track job costs from when jobs start until they are complete. When jobs are completed or sold, they are recorded in the finished goods inventory records of jobs in the subsidiary ledger. The general ledger account Finished Goods Control records the total of these separate job-cost records for all jobs completed and subsequently for all jobs sold.

Exhibit 7 shows T-account relationships for Robinson Company's general ledger. The general ledger gives a "bird's-eye view" of the costing system. The amounts shown in Exhibit 7 are based on the monthly transactions and journal entries that follow. As you go through each journal entry, use Exhibit 7 to see how the various entries being made come together. General ledger accounts with "Control" in their titles (for example, Materials Control and Accounts Payable Control) have underlying subsidiary ledgers that contain additional details, such as each type of material in inventory and individual suppliers Robinson must pay.

Some companies simultaneously make entries in the general ledger and subsidiary ledger accounts. Others, such as Robinson, make entries in the subsidiary ledger when transactions occur and entries in the general ledger less frequently, often on a monthly basis.

| Exhibit 7 | Manufacturing Job-Costing System Using Normal Costing: Diagram of General Ledger Relationships for February 2013 |

GENERAL LEDGER

① Purchase of direct and indirect materials, $89,000
② Usage of direct materials, $81,000, and indirect materials, $4,000

③ Cash paid for direct manufacturing labor, $39,000, and indirect manufacturing labor, $15,000

④ Incurrence of other manufacturing dept. overhead, $75,000
⑤ Allocation of manufacturing overhead, $80,000

⑥ Completion and transfer to finished goods, $188,800
⑦ Cost of goods sold, $180,000

⑧ Incurrence of marketing and customer-service costs, $60,000
⑨ Sales, $270,000

MATERIALS CONTROL
① 89,000 | ② 85,000

MANUFACTURING OVERHEAD CONTROL
② 4,000
③ 15,000
④ 75,000

CASH CONTROL
③ 54,000
④ 57,000
⑧ 60,000

MANUFACTURING OVERHEAD ALLOCATED
⑤ 80,000

ACCOUNTS PAYABLE CONTROL
① 89,000

ACCUMULATED DEPRECIATION CONTROL
④ 18,000

WORK-IN-PROCESS CONTROL
② 81,000 | ⑥ 188,800
③ 39,000
⑤ 80,000
Bal. 11,200

FINISHED GOODS CONTROL
⑥ 188,800 | ⑦ 180,000
Bal. 8,800

ACCOUNTS RECEIVABLE CONTROL
⑨ 270,000

REVENUES
⑨ 270,000

COST OF GOODS SOLD
⑦ 180,000

MARKETING EXPENSES
⑧ 45,000

CUSTOMER-SERVICE EXPENSES
⑧ 15,000

The debit balance of $11,200 in the Work-in-Process Control account represents the total cost of all jobs that have not been completed as of the end of February 2013. There were no incomplete jobs as of the beginning of February 2013.

The debit balance of $8,800 in the Finished Goods Control account represents the cost of all jobs that have been completed but not sold as of the end of February 2013. There were no jobs completed but not sold as of the beginning of February 2013.

A general ledger should be viewed as only one of many tools managers can use for planning and control. To control operations, managers rely on not only the source documents used to record amounts in the subsidiary ledgers, but also on nonfinancial information such as the percentage of jobs requiring rework.

Explanations of Transactions

We next look at a summary of Robinson Company's transactions for February 2013 and the corresponding journal entries for those transactions.

1. Purchases of materials (direct and indirect) on credit, $89,000

Materials Control	89,000	
Accounts Payable Control		89,000

2. Usage of direct materials, $81,000, and indirect materials, $4,000

Work-in-Process Control	81,000	
Manufacturing Overhead Control	4,000	
Materials Control		85,000

3. Manufacturing payroll for February: direct labor, $39,000, and indirect labor, $15,000, paid in cash

Work-in-Process Control	39,000	
Manufacturing Overhead Control	15,000	
Cash Control		54,000

4. Other manufacturing overhead costs incurred during February, $75,000, consisting of
   - supervision and engineering salaries, $44,000 (paid in cash);
   - plant utilities, repairs, and insurance, $13,000 (paid in cash); and
   - plant depreciation, $18,000

Manufacturing Overhead Control	75,000	
Cash Control		57,000
Accumulated Depreciation Control		18,000

5. Allocation of manufacturing overhead to jobs, $80,000

Work-in-Process Control	80,000	
Manufacturing Overhead Allocated		80,000

Under normal costing, **manufacturing overhead allocated**—or **manufacturing overhead applied**—is the amount of manufacturing overhead costs allocated to individual jobs based on the budgeted rate multiplied by the actual quantity of the allocation base used for each job. Manufacturing overhead allocated contains all manufacturing overhead costs assigned to jobs using a cost-allocation base because overhead costs cannot be traced specifically to jobs in an economically feasible way.

Keep in mind the distinct difference between transactions 4 and 5. In transaction 4, actual overhead costs incurred throughout the month are added (debited) to the Manufacturing Overhead Control account. These costs are not debited to Work-in-Process Control because unlike direct costs, they cannot be traced to individual jobs. Manufacturing overhead costs are added (debited) to individual jobs and to Work-in-Process Control *only when* manufacturing overhead costs are allocated in transaction 5. At the time these costs are allocated, Manufacturing Overhead Control is, *in effect,* decreased (credited) via its contra account, Manufacturing Overhead Allocated. Manufacturing Overhead Allocated is referred to as a *contra account* because the amounts debited to it represent the amounts credited to the Manufacturing

Overhead Control account. Having Manufacturing Overhead Allocated as a contra account allows the job-costing system to separately retain information about the manufacturing overhead costs the company has *incurred* (in the Manufacturing Overhead Control account) as well as the amount of manufacturing overhead costs it has *allocated* (in the Manufacturing Overhead Allocated account). If the allocated manufacturing overhead had been credited to manufacturing overhead control, the company would lose information about the actual manufacturing overhead costs it is incurring.

Under the normal-costing system described in our Robinson Company example, at the beginning of the year, the company calculated the budgeted manufacturing overhead rate of $40 per direct manufacturing labor-hour by predicting the company's annual manufacturing overhead costs and annual quantity of the cost-allocation base. Almost certainly, the actual amounts allocated will differ from the predictions. We discuss what to do with this difference later in the chapter.

6. The sum of all individual jobs completed and transferred to finished goods in February 2013 is $188,800

Finished Goods Control	188,800	
Work-in-Process Control		188,800

7. Cost of goods sold, $180,000

Cost of Goods Sold	180,000	
Finished Goods Control		180,000

8. Marketing costs for February 2013, $45,000, and customer-service costs for February 2013, $15,000, paid in cash

Marketing Expenses	45,000	
Customer-Service Expenses	15,000	
Cash Control		60,000

9. Sales revenues from all jobs sold and delivered in February 2013, all on credit, $270,000

Accounts Receivable Control	270,000	
Revenues		270,000

Subsidiary Ledgers

Exhibits 8 and 9 present subsidiary ledgers that contain the underlying details—the "worm's-eye view"—that help Robinson's managers keep track of the WPP 298 job, as opposed to the "bird's-eye view" of the general ledger. The sum of all entries in underlying subsidiary ledgers equals the total amount in the corresponding general ledger control accounts.

Materials Records by Type of Material

The subsidiary ledger for materials at Robinson Company—called *Materials Records*—is used to continuously record the quantity of materials received, issued to jobs, and the inventory balances for each type of material. Panel A of Exhibit 8 shows the Materials Record for Metal Brackets (Part No. MB 468-A). In many companies, the source documents supporting the receipt and issue of materials (the material requisition record in Exhibit 3, Panel A) are scanned into a computer. Software programs then automatically update the Materials Records and make all the necessary accounting entries in the subsidiary and general ledgers. The cost of materials received across all types of direct and indirect material records for February 2013 is $89,000 (Exhibit 8, Panel A). The cost of materials issued across all types of direct and indirect material records for February 2013 is $85,000 (Exhibit 8, Panel A).

| Exhibit 8 | Subsidiary Ledgers for Materials, Labor, and Manufacturing Department Overhead[1] |

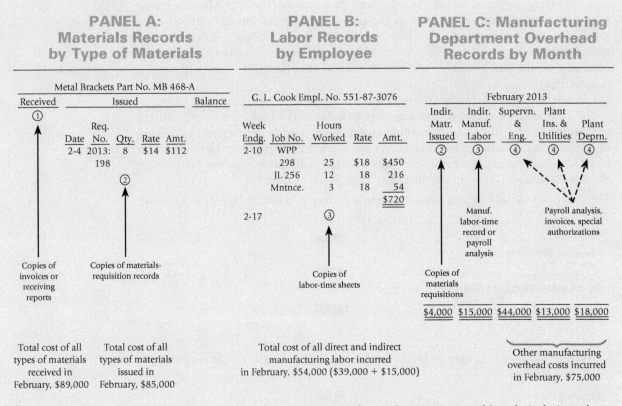

As direct materials are used, they are recorded as issued in the Materials Records (see Exhibit 8, Panel A, for a record of the Metal Brackets issued for the WPP machine job). Direct materials are also charged to Work-in-Process Inventory Records for Jobs, which are the subsidiary ledger accounts for the Work-in-Process Control account in the general ledger. For example, the metal brackets used in the WPP machine job appear as direct material costs of $112 in the subsidiary ledger under the work-in-process inventory record for WPP 298 [Exhibit 9, Panel A, which is based on the job-cost record source document in Exhibit 2]. The cost of direct materials used across all job-cost records for February 2013 is $81,000 (Exhibit 9, Panel A).

As indirect materials (for example, lubricants) are used, they are charged to the Manufacturing Department overhead records (Exhibit 8, Panel C), which comprise the subsidiary ledger for the Manufacturing Overhead Control account. The Manufacturing Department overhead records are used to accumulate actual costs in individual overhead categories by each indirect-cost-pool account in the general ledger. Recall that Robinson has only one indirect-cost pool: Manufacturing Overhead. The cost of indirect materials used is not added directly to individual job records. Instead, this cost is allocated to individual job records as a part of manufacturing overhead.

Labor Records by Employee

Labor records by employee (see Exhibit 8, Panel B, for G. L. Cook) are used to trace the costs of direct manufacturing labor to individual jobs and to accumulate the costs of indirect manufacturing labor in the Manufacturing Department overhead records (Exhibit 8, Panel C). The labor records are based on the labor-time sheet source documents (see Exhibit 3, Panel B). The subsidiary ledger for employee

| Exhibit 9 | Subsidiary Ledgers for Individual Jobs[1] |

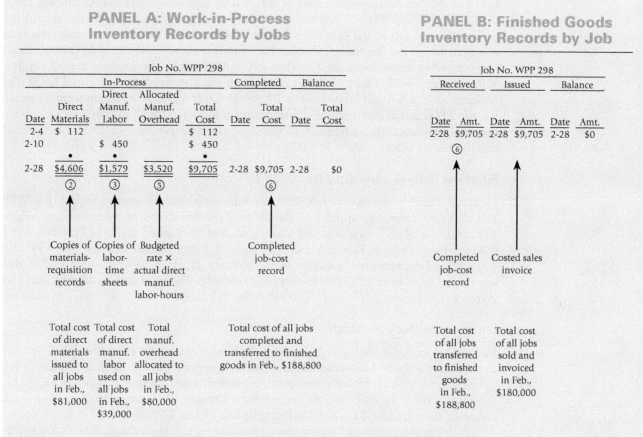

PANEL A: Work-in-Process Inventory Records by Jobs

Job No. WPP 298

| | In-Process | | | | Completed | | Balance | |
| | Direct Manuf. | Allocated Manuf. | | | | | | |
Date	Direct Materials	Direct Manuf. Labor	Allocated Manuf. Overhead	Total Cost	Date	Total Cost	Date	Total Cost
2-4	$ 112			$ 112				
2-10		$ 450		$ 450				
	•	•		•				
2-28	$4,606	$1,579	$3,520	$9,705	2-28	$9,705	2-28	$0
	②	③	⑤			⑥		

Copies of materials-requisition records

Copies of labor-time sheets

Budgeted rate × actual direct manuf. labor-hours

Completed job-cost record

Total cost of direct materials issued to all jobs in Feb., $81,000

Total cost of direct manuf. labor used on all jobs in Feb., $39,000

Total manuf. overhead allocated to all jobs in Feb., $80,000

Total cost of all jobs completed and transferred to finished goods in Feb., $188,800

PANEL B: Finished Goods Inventory Records by Job

Job No. WPP 298

| Received | | Issued | | Balance | |
Date	Amt.	Date	Amt.	Date	Amt.
2-28	$9,705	2-28	$9,705	2-28	$0
⑥					

Completed job-cost record

Costed sales invoice

Total cost of all jobs transferred to finished goods in Feb., $188,800

Total cost of all jobs sold and invoiced in Feb., $180,000

[1]The arrows show how the supporting documentation (for example, copies of materials requisition records) results in the journal entry number shown in circles (for example, journal entry number 2) that corresponds to the entries in Exhibit 7.

labor records (Exhibit 8, Panel B) shows the different jobs that G. L. Cook, Employee No. 551-87-3076, worked on and the $720 of wages owed to Cook, for the week ending February 10. The sum of total wages owed to all employees for February 2013 is $54,000. The job-cost record for WPP 298 shows direct manufacturing labor costs of $450 for the time Cook spent on the WPP machine job during that week (Exhibit 9, Panel A). Total direct manufacturing labor costs recorded in all job-cost records (the subsidiary ledger for Work-in-Process Control) for February 2013 is $39,000.

G. L. Cook's employee record shows $54 for maintenance, which is an indirect manufacturing labor cost. The total indirect manufacturing labor costs of $15,000 for February 2013 appear in the Manufacturing Department overhead records in the subsidiary ledger (Exhibit 8, Panel C). These costs, by definition, cannot be traced to an individual job. Instead, they are allocated to individual jobs as a part of manufacturing overhead.

Manufacturing Department Overhead Records by Month

The Manufacturing Department overhead records (see Exhibit 8, Panel C) that make up the subsidiary ledger for the Manufacturing Overhead Control account show details of different categories of overhead costs such as indirect materials, indirect manufacturing labor, supervision and engineering, plant insurance and utilities, and plant depreciation. The source documents for these entries include invoices (for example, a utility bill) and special schedules (for example, a depreciation schedule) from the responsible accounting officer. Manufacturing department overhead for February 2013 is indirect materials, $4,000; indirect manufacturing labor, $15,000; and other manufacturing overhead, $75,000 (Exhibit 8, Panel C).

Work-in-Process Inventory Records by Jobs

As we have already discussed, the job-cost record for each individual job in the subsidiary ledger is debited by the actual cost of direct materials and direct manufacturing labor used by individual jobs. In Robinson's normal-costing system, the job-cost record for each individual job in the subsidiary ledger is also debited for manufacturing overhead allocated based on the budgeted manufacturing overhead rate times the actual direct manufacturing labor-hours used in that job. For example, the job-cost record for Job WPP 298 (Exhibit 9, Panel A) shows Manufacturing Overhead Allocated of $3,520 (the budgeted rate of $40 per labor-hour $\times$ 88 actual direct manufacturing labor-hours used). For the 2,000 actual direct manufacturing labor-hours used for all jobs in February 2013, the total manufacturing overhead allocated equals $40 per labor-hour $\times$ 2,000 direct manufacturing labor-hours = $80,000.

Finished Goods Inventory Records by Jobs

Exhibit 9, Panel A, shows that Job WPP 298 was completed at a cost of $9,705. Job WPP 298 also simultaneously appears in the finished goods records of the subsidiary ledger. The total cost of all jobs completed and transferred to finished goods in February 2013 is $188,800 (Exhibit 9, Panels A and B). Exhibit 9, Panel B, indicates that Job WPP 298 was sold and delivered to the customer on February 28, 2013, at which time $9,705 was transferred from finished goods to cost of goods sold. The total cost of all jobs sold and invoiced in February 2013 is $180,000 (Exhibit 9, Panel B).

Other Subsidiary Records

Just as it does for manufacturing payroll, Robinson maintains employee labor records in subsidiary ledgers for marketing and customer-service payroll as well as records for different types of advertising costs (print, television, and radio). An accounts receivable subsidiary ledger is also used to record the February 2013 amounts due from each customer, including the $15,000 due from the sale of Job WPP 298.

At this point, pause and review the nine entries in this example. Exhibit 7 is a handy summary of all nine general-ledger entries presented in the form of T-accounts. Be sure to trace each journal entry, step by step, to T-accounts in the general ledger presented in Exhibit 7. Robinson's managers will use this information to evaluate how Robinson has performed on the WPP job.

Exhibit 10 provides Robinson's income statement for February 2013 using information from entries 7, 8, and 9. Managers could further subdivide the cost of goods sold calculations. The benefit of using the subdivided format is that it allows managers to discern detailed performance trends that can help them improve the efficiency on future jobs.

Revenues		$270,000
Cost of goods sold ($180,000 + $14,000[1])		194,000
Gross margin		76,000
Operating costs		
Marketing costs	$45,000	
Customer-service costs	15,000	
Total operating costs		60,000
Operating income		$ 16,000

[1]Cost of goods sold has been increased by $14,000, the difference between the Manufacturing overhead control account ($94,000) and the Manufacturing overhead allocated ($80,000). In a later section of this chapter, we discuss this adjustment, which represents the amount by which actual manufacturing overhead cost exceeds the manufacturing overhead allocated to jobs during February 2013.

Nonmanufacturing Costs and Job Costing

Companies use product costs for different purposes. The product costs reported as inventoriable costs to shareholders may differ from the product costs reported to managers to guide their pricing and product-mix decisions. Managers must keep in mind that even though marketing and customer-service costs are expensed when incurred for financial accounting purposes, companies often trace or allocate these costs to individual jobs for pricing, product-mix, and cost-management decisions.

Robinson can trace direct marketing costs and customer-service costs to jobs the same way in which it traces direct manufacturing costs to jobs. Assume these costs have the same cost-allocation base, revenues, and are included in a single cost pool. Robinson can then calculate a budgeted indirect-cost rate by dividing budgeted indirect marketing costs plus budgeted indirect customer-service costs by budgeted revenues. Robinson can use this rate to allocate these indirect costs to jobs. For example, if this rate were 15% of revenues, Robinson would allocate $2,250 to Job WPP 298 (0.15 × $15,000, the revenue from the job). By assigning both manufacturing costs and nonmanufacturing costs to jobs, Robinson can compare all costs against the revenues that different jobs generate.

Decision Point

How are transactions recorded in a manufacturing job-costing system?

Budgeted Indirect Costs and End-of-Accounting-Year Adjustments

Managers try to closely approximate actual manufacturing overhead costs and actual direct manufacturing labor-hours when calculating the budgeted indirect cost rate. However, for the numerator and denominator reasons explained earlier in the chapter, under normal costing, a company's actual overhead costs incurred each month are not likely to equal its overhead costs allocated each month. Even at the end of the year, allocated costs are unlikely to equal actual costs because they are based on estimates made up to 12 months before actual costs are incurred. We now describe adjustments that management accountants need to make when, at the end of the fiscal year, indirect costs allocated differ from actual indirect costs incurred. These adjustments affect the reported income numbers used to evaluate managerial performance.

Learning Objective 7

Dispose of under- or overallocated manufacturing overhead costs at the end of the fiscal year using alternative methods

...for example, writing off this amount to the Cost of Goods Sold account

Underallocated and Overallocated Indirect Costs

Underallocated indirect costs occur when the allocated amount of indirect costs in an accounting period is less than the actual (incurred) amount. **Overallocated indirect costs** occur when the allocated amount of indirect costs in an accounting period is greater than the actual (incurred) amount.

Underallocated (overallocated) indirect costs = Actual indirect costs incurred − Indirect costs allocated

Underallocated (overallocated) indirect costs are also called **underapplied (overapplied) indirect costs** and **underabsorbed (overabsorbed) indirect costs**.

Consider the manufacturing overhead cost pool at Robinson Company. There are two indirect-cost accounts in the general ledger that have to do with manufacturing overhead:

1. Manufacturing Overhead Control, the record of the actual costs in all the individual overhead categories (such as indirect materials, indirect manufacturing labor, supervision, engineering, utilities, and plant depreciation)

2. Manufacturing Overhead Allocated, the record of the manufacturing overhead allocated to individual jobs on the basis of the budgeted rate multiplied by actual direct manufacturing labor-hours

At the end of the year, the overhead accounts show the following amounts.

Manufacturing Overhead Control		Manufacturing Overhead Allocated	
Bal. Dec. 31, 2013	1,215,000	Bal. Dec. 31, 2013	1,080,000

The $1,080,000 credit balance in Manufacturing Overhead Allocated results from multiplying the 27,000 actual direct manufacturing labor-hours worked on all jobs in 2013 by the budgeted rate of $40 per direct manufacturing labor-hour.

The $135,000 ($1,215,000 − $1,080,000) difference (a net debit) is an underallocated amount because actual manufacturing overhead costs are greater than the allocated amount. This difference arises for two reasons related to the computation of the $40 budgeted hourly rate:

1. **Numerator reason (indirect-cost pool).** Actual manufacturing overhead costs of $1,215,000 are greater than the budgeted amount of $1,120,000.
2. **Denominator reason (quantity of allocation base).** Actual direct manufacturing labor-hours of 27,000 are fewer than the budgeted 28,000 hours.

There are three main approaches to accounting for the $135,000 underallocated manufacturing overhead caused by Robinson underestimating manufacturing overhead costs and overestimating the quantity of the cost-allocation base: (1) adjusted allocation-rate approach, (2) proration approach, and (3) writeoff to cost of goods sold approach.

Adjusted Allocation-Rate Approach

The **adjusted allocation-rate approach** restates all overhead entries in the general ledger and subsidiary ledgers using actual cost rates rather than budgeted cost rates. First, the actual manufacturing overhead rate is computed at the end of the fiscal year. Then the manufacturing overhead costs allocated to every job during the year are recomputed using the actual manufacturing overhead rate (rather than the budgeted manufacturing overhead rate). Finally, end-of-year closing entries are made. The result is that at year-end, every job-cost record and finished goods record—as well as the ending Work-in-Process Control, Finished Goods Control, and Cost of Goods Sold accounts—represent actual manufacturing overhead costs incurred.

The widespread adoption of computerized accounting systems has greatly reduced the cost of using the adjusted allocation-rate approach. In our Robinson example, the actual manufacturing overhead ($1,215,000) exceeds the manufacturing overhead allocated ($1,080,000) by 12.5% [($1,215,000 − $1,080,000) ÷ $1,080,000]. At year-end, Robinson could increase the manufacturing overhead allocated to each job in 2013 by 12.5% using a single software command. The command would adjust both the subsidiary ledgers and the general ledger.

Consider the Western Pulp and Paper machine job, WPP 298. Under normal costing, the manufacturing overhead allocated to the job is $3,520 (the budgeted rate of $40 per direct manufacturing labor-hour × 88 hours). Increasing the manufacturing overhead allocated by 12.5%, or $440 ($3,520 × 0.125), means the adjusted amount of manufacturing overhead allocated to Job WPP 298 equals $3,960 ($3,520 + $440). Note that using actual costing, manufacturing overhead allocated to this job is $3,960 (the actual rate of $45 per direct manufacturing labor-hour × 88 hours). Making this adjustment under normal costing for each job in the subsidiary ledgers ensures that actual manufacturing overhead costs of $1,215,000 are allocated to jobs.

The adjusted allocation-rate approach yields the benefits of both the *timeliness and convenience of normal costing during the year and the allocation of actual manufacturing overhead costs at year-end.* Each individual job-cost record and the end-of-year account balances for inventories and cost of goods sold are adjusted to actual costs. These adjustments, in turn, will affect the income Robinson reports. Knowing the actual profitability of individual jobs after they are completed provides managers with accurate and useful insights for future decisions about which jobs to undertake, how to price them, and how to manage their costs.

Proration Approach

The **proration** approach spreads underallocated overhead or overallocated overhead among ending work-in-process inventory, finished goods inventory, and cost of goods sold. Materials inventory is not included in this proration because no manufacturing overhead costs have been allocated to it. We illustrate end-of-year proration in the Robinson Company example. Assume the following actual results for Robinson Company in 2013:

	A	B	C
1	Account	Account Balance (Before Proration)	Allocated Manufacturing Overhead Included in Each Account Balance (Before Proration)
2	Work-in-process control	$ 50,000	$ 16,200
3	Finished goods control	75,000	31,320
4	Cost of goods sold	2,375,000	1,032,480
5		$2,500,000	$1,080,000

How should Robinson prorate the underallocated $135,000 of manufacturing overhead at the end of 2013?

Robinson prorates underallocated or overallocated amounts on the basis of the total amount of manufacturing overhead allocated in 2013 (before proration) in the ending balances of Work-in-Process Control, Finished Goods Control, and Cost of Goods Sold accounts. The $135,000 underallocated overhead is prorated over the three accounts in proportion to the total amount of manufacturing overhead allocated (before proration) in column 2 of the following table, resulting in the ending balances (after proration) in column 5 at actual costs.

	A	B	C	D	E	F	G
10		Account Balance (Before Proration)	Allocated Manufacturing Overhead Included in Each Account Balance (Before Proration)	Allocated Manufacturing Overhead Included in Each Account Balance as a Percent of Total	Proration of $135,000 of Underallocated Manufacturing Overhead		Account Balance (After Proration)
11	Account	(1)	(2)	(3) = (2) / $1,080,000	(4) = (3) x $135,000		(5) = (1) + (4)
12	Work-in-process control	$ 50,000	$ 16,200	1.5%	0.015 x $135,000 =	$ 2,025	$ 52,025
13	Finished goods control	75,000	31,320	2.9%	0.029 x 135,000 =	3,915	78,915
14	Cost of goods sold	2,375,000	1,032,480	95.6%	0.956 x 135,000 =	129,060	2,504,060
15	Total	$2,500,000	$1,080,000	100.0%		$135,000	$2,635,000

Prorating on the basis of the manufacturing overhead allocated (before proration) results in Robinson allocating manufacturing overhead based on actual manufacturing overhead costs. Recall that Robinson's actual manufacturing overhead ($1,215,000) in 2013 exceeds its manufacturing overhead allocated ($1,080,000) in 2013 by 12.5%. The proration amounts in column 4 can also be derived by multiplying the balances in column 2 by 0.125. For example, the $3,915 proration to Finished Goods is 0.125 × $31,320. Adding these amounts effectively means allocating manufacturing overhead at 112.5% of what had been allocated before. The journal entry to record this proration is as follows:

Work-in-Process Control	2,025	
Finished Goods Control	3,915	
Cost of Goods Sold	129,060	
Manufacturing Overhead Allocated	1,080,000	
Manufacturing Overhead Control		1,215,000

If manufacturing overhead had been overallocated, the Work-in-Process Control, Finished Goods Control, and Cost of Goods Sold accounts would be decreased (credited) instead of increased (debited).

This journal entry closes (brings to zero) the manufacturing overhead-related accounts and restates the 2013 ending balances for Work-in-Process Control, Finished Goods Control, and Cost of Goods Sold to what they would have been if actual manufacturing overhead rates had been used rather than budgeted manufacturing overhead rates. This method reports the same 2013 ending balances in the general ledger as the adjusted allocation-rate approach does. However, unlike the adjusted allocation-rate approach, the sum of the amounts shown in the subsidiary ledgers will not match the amounts shown in the general ledger after proration because no adjustments from budgeted to actual manufacturing overhead rates are made in the individual job-cost records. The objective of the proration approach is to only adjust the general ledger to actual manufacturing overhead rates for purposes of financial reporting. The increase in cost of goods sold expense by $129,060 as a result of the proration causes Robinson's reported operating income to decrease by the same amount.

Some companies use the proration approach but base it on the ending balances of Work-in-Process Control, Finished Goods Control, and Cost of Goods Sold accounts prior to proration (see column 1 of the preceding table). The following table shows that prorations based on ending account balances are not the same as the more accurate prorations calculated earlier based on the amount of manufacturing overhead allocated to the accounts because the proportions of manufacturing overhead costs to total costs in these accounts are not the same.

	Home	Insert	Page Layout	Formulas	Data	Review	View	
	A	B	C	D	E	F		
1		Account Balance (Before Proration)	Account Balance as a Percent of Total	Proration of $135,000 of Underallocated Manufacturing Overhead		Account Balance (After Proration)		
2	Account	(1)	(2) = (1) / $2,500,000	(3) = (2) x $135,000		(4) = (1) + (3)		
3	Work-in-process control	$ 50,000	2.0%	0.02 x $135,000 =	$ 2,700	$ 52,700		
4	Finished goods control	75,000	3.0%	0.03 x 135,000 =	4,050	79,050		
5	Cost of goods sold	2,375,000	95.0%	0.95 x 135,000 =	128,250	2,503,250		
6	Total	$2,500,000	100.0%		$135,000	$2,635,000		

However, proration based on ending balances is frequently justified as being an expedient way of approximating the more accurate results from using manufacturing overhead costs allocated.

Writeoff to Cost of Goods Sold Approach

Under the writeoff approach, the total under- or overallocated manufacturing overhead is included in this year's Cost of Goods Sold. For Robinson, the journal entry would be as follows:

Cost of Goods Sold	135,000	
Manufacturing Overhead Allocated	1,080,000	
Manufacturing Overhead Control		1,215,000

Robinson's two Manufacturing Overhead accounts—Manufacturing Overhead Control and Manufacturing Overhead Allocated—are closed with the difference between them included in cost of goods sold. The Cost of Goods Sold account after the writeoff equals $2,510,000, the balance before the writeoff of $2,375,000 *plus the underallocated* manufacturing overhead amount of $135,000. This results in operating income decreasing by $135,000.

Choosing Among Approaches

Which of the three approaches of dealing with underallocated overhead and overallocated overhead is the best one to use? When making this decision, managers should consider the amount of underallocated or overallocated overhead and the purpose of the adjustment, as the following table indicates.

If the purpose of the adjustment is to . . .	and the total amount of underallocation or overallocation is . . .	then managers prefer to use the . . .
state the balance sheet and income statements based on actual rather than budgeted manufacturing overhead rates	big, relative to total operating income, and inventory levels are high	proration method because it is the most accurate method of allocating actual manufacturing overhead costs to the general ledger accounts.
state the balance sheet and income statements based on actual rather than budgeted manufacturing overhead rates	small, relative to total operating income, or inventory levels are low	writeoff to cost of goods sold approach because it is a good approximation of the more accurate proration method.
provide an accurate record of actual individual job costs in order to conduct a profitability analysis, learn how to better manage the costs of jobs, and bid on future jobs	big, relative to total operating income,	adjusted-allocation rate method because it makes adjustments in individual job records in addition to the general ledger accounts.

Many management accountants and managers argue that to the extent that the underallocated overhead cost measures inefficiency during the period, it should be written off to the Cost of Goods Sold account instead of being prorated to the Work-in-Process or Finished Goods inventory accounts. This line of reasoning favors applying a combination of the writeoff and proration methods. For example, the portion of the underallocated overhead cost that is due to inefficiency (say, because of excessive spending or idle capacity) and that could have been avoided should be written off to the Cost of Goods Sold account, whereas the portion that is unavoidable should be prorated. Unlike full proration, this approach avoids making the costs of inefficiency part of inventory assets.

As our discussion suggests, choosing which method to use and determining the amount to be written off is often a matter of judgment. The method managers choose affects the operating income a company reports. In the case of underallocated overhead, the method of writing it off to cost of goods sold results in lower operating income compared to proration. In the case of overallocated overhead, proration results in lower operating income compared to writing the overhead off to cost of goods sold. Reporting lower operating income lowers the company's taxes, saving the company cash and increasing the company's value. Reporting higher operating income, however, can increase the compensation managers earn even though it results in higher taxes for the company. Top managers design compensation plans to encourage managers to take actions that increase a company's value. For example, the compensation plan might reward the managers for after-tax cash flow metrics, in addition to achieving various levels of operating income, to align decision making and performance evaluation. Occasionally, if a company is experiencing financial difficulty, its managers may prefer to report higher operating income to avoid showing losses that could affect the firm's credit rating and result in its loans being called. In general, however, managers should choose the method that increases the company's value and best represents its performance, while consistently applying the same method year after year. At no time should managers make choices that are illegal or unethical.

Robinson's managers believed that a single manufacturing overhead cost pool with direct manufacturing labor-hours as the cost-allocation base was appropriate for allocating all manufacturing overhead costs to jobs. Had Robinson's managers felt that

Decision Point

How should managers dispose of under- or overallocated manufacturing overhead costs at the end of the accounting year?

139

different manufacturing departments (for example, machining and assembly) used overhead resources differently, they would have assigned overhead costs to each department and calculated a separate overhead allocation rate for each department based on the cost driver of the overhead costs in each department. The general ledger would contain Manufacturing Overhead Control and Manufacturing Overhead Allocated accounts for each department, resulting in end-of-year adjustments for underallocated or overallocated overhead costs for each department.

Learning Objective 8 ▶

Understand variations from normal costing

…some variations from normal costing use budgeted direct-cost rates

Variations from Normal Costing: A Service-Sector Example

Job costing is also very useful in service organizations such as accounting and consulting firms, advertising agencies, auto repair shops, and hospitals. In an accounting firm, each audit is a job. The costs of each audit are accumulated in a job-cost record, much like the document used by Robinson Company, based on the seven-step approach described earlier. On the basis of labor-time sheets, direct labor costs of the professional staff—audit partners, audit managers, and audit staff—are traced to individual jobs. Other direct costs, such as travel, out-of-town meals and lodging, phone, fax, and copying, are also traced to jobs. The costs of secretarial support, office staff, rent, and depreciation of furniture and equipment are indirect costs because these costs cannot be traced to jobs in an economically feasible way. Indirect costs are allocated to jobs, for example, using a cost-allocation base such as number of professional labor-hours.

In some service organizations, a variation from normal costing is helpful because actual direct-labor costs, the largest component of total costs, can be difficult to trace to jobs as they are completed. For example, the actual direct-labor costs of an audit may include bonuses that become known only at the end of the year (a numerator reason). Also, the hours worked each period might vary significantly depending on the number of working days each month and the demand for services (a denominator reason) while the direct-labor costs remain largely fixed. It would be inappropriate to charge a job with higher actual direct labor costs simply because a month had fewer working days or demand for services was low in that month. Using budgeted rates gives a better picture of the direct labor cost per hour that the company had planned when it hired the workers. In situations like these, a company needing timely information during the progress of an audit will use budgeted rates for some direct costs and budgeted rates for other indirect costs. All budgeted rates are calculated at the start of the fiscal year. In contrast, normal costing uses actual cost rates for all direct costs and budgeted cost rates only for indirect costs.

The mechanics of using budgeted rates for direct costs are similar to the methods employed when using budgeted rates for indirect costs in normal costing. We illustrate this for Donahue and Associates, a public accounting firm. For 2013, Donahue budgets total direct-labor costs of $14,400,000, total indirect costs of $12,960,000, and total direct (professional) labor-hours of 288,000. In this case,

$$\text{Budgeted direct-labor cost rate} = \frac{\text{Budgeted total direct-labor costs}}{\text{Budgeted total direct-labor hours}}$$

$$= \frac{\$14,400,000}{288,000 \text{ direct labor-hours}} = \$50 \text{ per direct labor-hour}$$

Assuming only one indirect-cost pool and total direct-labor costs as the cost-allocation base,

$$\text{Budgeted indirect cost rate} = \frac{\text{Budgeted total costs in indirect cost pool}}{\text{Budgeted total quantity of cost-allocation base (direct-labor costs)}}$$

$$= \frac{\$12,960,000}{\$14,400,000} = 0.90, \text{ or } 90\% \text{ of direct-labor costs}$$

Suppose that in March 2013, an audit of Hanley Transport, a client of Donahue, uses 800 direct labor-hours. Donahue calculates the direct-labor costs of the audit by multiplying the budgeted direct-labor cost rate, $50 per direct labor-hour, by 800, the actual quantity of direct labor-hours. The indirect costs allocated to the Hanley Transport audit are determined by multiplying the budgeted indirect-cost rate (90%) by the direct-labor costs assigned to the job ($40,000). Assuming no other direct costs for travel and the like, the cost of the Hanley Transport audit is as follows:

Direct-labor costs, $50 × 800	$ 40,000
Indirect costs allocated, 90% × $40,000	36,000
Total	$76,000

At the end of the fiscal year, the direct costs traced to jobs using budgeted rates will generally not equal actual direct costs because the actual rate and the budgeted rate are developed at different times using different information. End-of-year adjustments for underallocated or overallocated direct costs would need to be made in the same way that adjustments are made for underallocated or overallocated indirect costs.

The Donahue and Associates example illustrates that all costing systems do not exactly match either the actual-costing system or the normal-costing system described earlier in the chapter. As another example, engineering consulting firms, such as Tata Consulting Engineers in India and Terracon Consulting Engineers in the United States, often use budgeted rates to allocate indirect costs (such as engineering and office-support costs) as well as some direct costs (such as professional labor-hours) and trace some actual direct costs (such as the cost of making blueprints and fees paid to outside experts). Users of costing systems should be aware of the different systems that they may encounter.

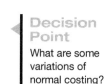

Decision Point

What are some variations of normal costing?

Problem for Self-Study

Your manager asks you to bring the following incomplete accounts of Endeavor Printing, Inc., up to date through January 31, 2014. Consider the data that appear in the T-accounts as well as the following information in items (a) through (j).

Endeavor's normal-costing system has two direct-cost categories (direct material costs and direct manufacturing labor costs) and one indirect-cost pool (manufacturing overhead costs, which are allocated using direct manufacturing labor costs).

Materials Control		Wages Payable Control	
12-31-2013 Bal. 15,000			1-31-2014 Bal. 3,000

Work-in-Process Control		Manufacturing Overhead Control	
		1-31-2014 Bal. 57,000	

Finished Goods Control		Costs of Goods Sold	
12-31-2013 Bal. 20,000			

Additional information follows:

a. Manufacturing overhead is allocated using a budgeted rate that is set every December. You forecast next year's manufacturing overhead costs and next year's direct manufacturing labor costs. The budget for 2014 is $600,000 for manufacturing overhead costs and $400,000 for direct manufacturing labor costs.

b. The only job unfinished on January 31, 2014, is No. 419, on which direct manufacturing labor costs are $2,000 (125 direct manufacturing labor-hours) and direct material costs are $8,000.

c. Total direct materials issued to production during January 2014 are $90,000.

d. Cost of goods completed during January is $180,000.

e. Materials inventory as of January 31, 2014, is $20,000.

f. Finished goods inventory as of January 31, 2014, is $15,000.

g. All plant workers earn the same wage rate. Direct manufacturing labor-hours used for January total 2,500 hours. Other labor costs total $10,000.

h. The gross plant payroll paid in January equals $52,000. Ignore withholdings.

i. All "actual" manufacturing overhead cost incurred during January has already been posted.

j. All materials are direct materials.

Required

Calculate the following:

1. Materials purchased during January
2. Cost of Goods Sold during January
3. Direct manufacturing labor costs incurred during January
4. Manufacturing Overhead Allocated during January
5. Balance, Wages Payable Control, December 31, 2013
6. Balance, Work-in-Process Control, January 31, 2014
7. Balance, Work-in-Process Control, December 31, 2013
8. Manufacturing Overhead Underallocated or Overallocated for January 2014

Solution

Amounts from the T-accounts are labeled "(T)."

1. From Materials Control T-account, Materials purchased: $90,000 (c) + $20,000 (e) – $15,000 (T) = $95,000

2. From Finished Goods Control T-account, Cost of Goods Sold: $20,000 (T) + $180,000 (d) – $15,000 (f) = $185,000

3. Direct manufacturing wage rate: $2,000 (b) ÷ 125 direct manufacturing labor-hours (b) = $16 per direct manufacturing labor-hour

   Direct manufacturing labor costs: 2,500 direct manufacturing labor-hours (g) × $16 per direct manufacturing labor-hour = $40,000

4. Manufacturing overhead rate: $600,000 (a) ÷ $400,000 (a) = 150%

   Manufacturing Overhead Allocated: 150% of $40,000 (see 3) = 1.50 × $40,000 = $60,000

5. From Wages Payable Control T-account, Wages Payable Control, December 31, 2013: $52,000 (h) + $3,000 (T) – $40,000 (see 3) – $10,000 (g) = $5,000

6. Work-in-Process Control, January 31, 2014: $8,000 (b) + $2,000 (b) + 150% of $2,000 (b) = $13,000 (This answer is used in item 7.)

7. From Work-in-Process Control T-account, Work-in-Process Control, December 31, 2013: $180,000 (d) + $13,000 (see 6) – $90,000 (c) – $40,000 (see 3) – $60,000 (see 4) = $3,000

8. Manufacturing overhead overallocated: $60,000 (see 4) – $57,000 (T) = $3,000.

Letters alongside entries in T-accounts correspond to letters in the preceding additional information. Numbers alongside entries in T-accounts correspond to numbers in the preceding requirements.

Materials Control

December 31, 2013, Bal.	(given)	15,000			
	(1)	95,000*		(c)	90,000
January 31, 2014, Bal.	(e)	20,000			

Work-in-Process Control

December 31, 2013, Bal.	(7)	3,000		(d)	180,000
Direct materials	(c)	90,000			
Direct manufacturing labor	(b) (g) (3)	40,000			
Manufacturing overhead allocated	(3) (a) (4)	60,000			
January 31, 2014, Bal.	(b) (6)	13,000			

*Can be computed only after all other postings in the account have been made.

Finished Goods Control

December 31, 2013, Bal.	(given)	20,000		(2)	185,000
	(d)	180,000			
January 31, 2014, Bal.	(f)	15,000			

Wages Payable Control

	(h)	52,000	December 31, 2013, Bal.	(5)	5,000
				(g) (3)	40,000
				(g)	10,000
			January 31, 2014	(given)	3,000

Manufacturing Overhead Control

Total January charges	(given)	57,000

Manufacturing Overhead Allocated

	(3) (a) (4)	60,000

Cost of Goods Sold

(d) (f) (2)	185,000

▶ Decision Points

The following question-and-answer format summarizes the chapter's learning objectives. Each decision presents a key question related to a learning objective. The guidelines are the answer to that question.

Decision	Guidelines
1. What are the building-block concepts of a costing system?	The building-block concepts of a costing system are a cost object, direct costs of a cost object, indirect costs of a cost object, cost pool, and cost-allocation base. Costing-system overview diagrams represent these concepts in a systematic way. Costing systems aim to report cost numbers that reflect the way cost objects (such as products or services) use the resources of an organization.
2. How do you distinguish job costing from process costing?	Job-costing systems assign costs to distinct units of a product or service. Process-costing systems assign costs to masses of identical or similar units and compute unit costs on an average basis. These two costing systems represent opposite ends of a continuum. The costing systems of many companies combine some elements of both job costing and process costing.
3. What is the main challenge of implementing job-costing systems?	The main challenge of implementing job-costing systems is estimating actual costs of jobs in a timely manner.
4. How do you implement a normal-costing system?	A general seven-step approach to normal costing requires identifying (1) the job, (2) the actual direct costs, (3) the budgeted cost-allocation bases, (4) the budgeted indirect-cost pools, (5) the budgeted cost-allocation rates, (6) the allocated indirect costs (budgeted rates times actual quantities of the cost-allocation bases), and (7) the total direct and indirect costs of a job.
5. How do you distinguish actual costing from normal costing?	Actual costing and normal costing differ in the type of indirect-cost rates used:

	Actual Costing	Normal Costing
Direct-cost rates	Actual rates	Actual rates
Indirect-cost rates	Actual rates	Budgeted rates

Both systems use actual quantities of inputs for tracing direct costs and actual quantities of the cost-allocation bases for allocating indirect costs.

Decision	Guidelines
6. How are transactions recorded in a manufacturing job-costing system?	A job-costing system in manufacturing records the flow of inventoriable costs in the general and subsidiary ledgers for (a) acquisition of materials and other manufacturing inputs, (b) their conversion into work in process, (c) their conversion into finished goods, and (d) the sale of finished goods. The job-costing system expenses period costs, such as marketing costs, as they are incurred.
7. How should managers dispose of under- or overallocated manufacturing overhead costs at the end of the accounting year?	The two standard approaches to disposing of under- or overallocated manufacturing overhead costs at the end of the accounting year for the purposes of stating balance sheet and income statement amounts at actual costs are (1) to adjust the allocation rate and (2) to prorate on the basis of the total amount of the allocated manufacturing overhead cost in the ending balances of Work-in-Process Control, Finished Goods Control, and Cost of Goods Sold accounts. Many companies write off amounts of under- or overallocated manufacturing overhead to Cost of Goods Sold when amounts are immaterial or underallocated overhead costs are the result of inefficiencies.
8. What are some variations of normal costing?	In some variations from normal costing, organizations use budgeted rates to assign direct costs, as well as indirect costs, to jobs.

Terms to Learn

This chapter contains definitions of the following important terms:

actual costing	job-cost sheet	overapplied indirect costs
actual indirect-cost rate	job-costing system	process-costing system
adjusted allocation-rate approach	labor-time sheet	proration
budgeted indirect-cost rate	manufacturing overhead allocated	source document
cost-allocation base	manufacturing overhead applied	underabsorbed indirect costs
cost-application base	materials-requisition record	underallocated indirect costs
cost pool	normal costing	underapplied indirect costs
job	overabsorbed indirect costs	
job-cost record	overallocated indirect costs	

Assignment Material

MyAccountingLab

Questions

1 Define cost pool, cost tracing, cost allocation, and cost-allocation base.
2 How does a job-costing system differ from a process-costing system?
3 Why might an advertising agency use job costing for an advertising campaign by PepsiCo, whereas a bank might use process costing to determine the cost of checking account deposits?
4 Describe the seven steps in job costing.
5 Give examples of two cost objects in companies using job costing.
6 Describe three major source documents used in job-costing systems.
7 What is the advantage of using computerized source documents to prepare job-cost records?
8 Give two reasons why most organizations use an annual period rather than a weekly or monthly period to compute budgeted indirect-cost rates.
9 Distinguish between actual costing and normal costing.
10 Describe two ways in which a house-construction company may use job-cost information.
11 Comment on the following statement: "In a normal-costing system, the amounts in the Manufacturing Overhead Control account will always equal the amounts in the Manufacturing Overhead Allocated account."

12 Describe three different debit entries to the Work-in-Process Control T-account under normal costing.

13 Describe three alternative ways to dispose of under- or overallocated overhead costs.

14 When might a company use budgeted costs rather than actual costs to compute direct-labor rates?

15 Describe briefly why Electronic Data Interchange (EDI) is helpful to managers.

Exercises

16 **Job costing, process costing.** In each of the following situations, determine whether job costing or process costing would be more appropriate.

a. A CPA firm
b. An oil refinery
c. A custom furniture manufacturer
d. A tire manufacturer
e. A textbook publisher
f. A pharmaceutical company
g. An advertising agency
h. An architecture firm
i. A flour mill
j. A paint manufacturer
k. A nursing home

l. A landscaping company
m. A cola-drink-concentrate producer
n. A movie studio
o. A law firm
p. A commercial aircraft manufacturer
q. A management consulting firm
r. A plumbing contractor
s. A catering service
t. A paper mill
u. An auto repair shop

17 **Actual costing, normal costing, accounting for manufacturing overhead.** Destin Products uses a job-costing system with two direct-cost categories (direct materials and direct manufacturing labor) and one manufacturing overhead cost pool. Destin allocates manufacturing overhead costs using direct manufacturing labor costs. Destin provides the following information:

	Budget for 2014	Actual Results for 2014
Direct material costs	$2,000,000	$1,900,000
Direct manufacturing labor costs	1,500,000	1,450,000
Manufacturing overhead costs	2,700,000	2,755,000

1. Compute the actual and budgeted manufacturing overhead rates for 2014.
2. During March, the job-cost record for Job 626 contained the following information:

Direct materials used	$40,000
Direct manufacturing labor costs	$30,000

Compute the cost of Job 626 using (a) actual costing and (b) normal costing.
3. At the end of 2014, compute the under- or overallocated manufacturing overhead under normal costing. Why is there no under- or overallocated overhead under actual costing?
4. Why might managers at Destin Products prefer to use normal costing?

18 **Job costing, normal and actual costing.** Anderson Construction assembles residential houses. It uses a job-costing system with two direct-cost categories (direct materials and direct labor) and one indirect-cost pool (assembly support). Direct labor-hours is the allocation base for assembly support costs. In December 2013, Anderson budgets 2014 assembly-support costs to be $8,000,000 and 2014 direct labor-hours to be 160,000.

At the end of 2014, Anderson is comparing the costs of several jobs that were started and completed in 2014.

	Laguna Model	Mission Model
Construction period	Feb–June 2014	May–Oct 2014
Direct material costs	$106,650	$127,970
Direct labor costs	$ 36,276	$ 41,750
Direct labor-hours	920	1,040

Direct materials and direct labor are paid for on a contract basis. The costs of each are known when direct materials are used or when direct labor-hours are worked. The 2014 actual assembly-support costs were $7,614,000, and the actual direct labor-hours were 162,000.

1. Compute the (a) budgeted indirect-cost rate and (b) actual indirect-cost rate. Why do they differ?
2. What are the job costs of the Laguna Model and the Mission Model using (a) normal costing and (b) actual costing?
3. Why might Anderson Construction prefer normal costing over actual costing?

19 Budgeted manufacturing overhead rate, allocated manufacturing overhead. Gammaro Company uses normal costing. It allocates manufacturing overhead costs using a budgeted rate per machine-hour. The following data are available for 2014:

Budgeted manufacturing overhead costs	$4,200,000
Budgeted machine-hours	175,000
Actual manufacturing overhead costs	$4,050,000
Actual machine-hours	170,000

1. Calculate the budgeted manufacturing overhead rate.
2. Calculate the manufacturing overhead allocated during 2014.
3. Calculate the amount of under- or overallocated manufacturing overhead. Why do Gammaro's managers need to calculate this amount?

20 Job costing, accounting for manufacturing overhead, budgeted rates. The Lynn Company uses a normal job-costing system at its Minneapolis plant. The plant has a machining department and an assembly department. Its job-costing system has two direct-cost categories (direct materials and direct manufacturing labor) and two manufacturing overhead cost pools (the machining department overhead, allocated to jobs based on actual machine-hours, and the assembly department overhead, allocated to jobs based on actual direct manufacturing labor costs). The 2014 budget for the plant is as follows:

	Machining Department	Assembly Department
Manufacturing overhead	$1,800,000	$3,600,000
Direct manufacturing labor costs	$1,400,000	$2,000,000
Direct manufacturing labor-hours	100,000	200,000
Machine-hours	50,000	200,000

1. Present an overview diagram of Lynn's job-costing system. Compute the budgeted manufacturing overhead rate for each department.
2. During February, the job-cost record for Job 494 contained the following:

	Machining Department	Assembly Department
Direct materials used	$45,000	$70,000
Direct manufacturing labor costs	$14,000	$15,000
Direct manufacturing labor-hours	1,000	1,500
Machine-hours	2,000	1,000

Compute the total manufacturing overhead costs allocated to Job 494.
3. At the end of 2014, the actual manufacturing overhead costs were $2,100,000 in machining and $3,700,000 in assembly. Assume that 55,000 actual machine-hours were used in machining and that actual direct manufacturing labor costs in assembly were $2,200,000. Compute the over- or underallocated manufacturing overhead for each department.

21 Job costing, consulting firm. Taylor & Associates, a consulting firm, has the following condensed budget for 2014:

Revenues		$20,000,000
Total costs:		
Direct costs		
Professional Labor	$5,000,000	
Indirect costs		
Client support	13,000,000	18,000,000
Operating income		$ 2,000,000

Taylor has a single direct-cost category (professional labor) and a single indirect-cost pool (client support). Indirect costs are allocated to jobs on the basis of professional labor costs.

1. Prepare an overview diagram of the job-costing system. Calculate the 2014 budgeted indirect-cost rate for Taylor & Associates.
2. The markup rate for pricing jobs is intended to produce operating income equal to 10% of revenues. Calculate the markup rate as a percentage of professional labor costs.
3. Taylor is bidding on a consulting job for Tasty Chicken, a fast food chain specializing in poultry meats. The budgeted breakdown of professional labor on the job is as follows:

Required

Professional Labor Category	Budgeted Rate per Hour	Budgeted Hours
Director	$200	3
Partner	100	16
Associate	50	40
Assistant	30	160

Calculate the budgeted cost of the Tasty Chicken job. How much will Taylor bid for the job if it is to earn its target operating income of 10% of revenues?

22 Time period used to compute indirect cost rates. Plunge Manufacturing produces outdoor wading and slide pools. The company uses a normal-costing system and allocates manufacturing overhead on the basis of direct manufacturing labor-hours. Most of the company's production and sales occur in the first and second quarters of the year. The company is in danger of losing one of its larger customers, Socha Wholesale, due to large fluctuations in price. The owner of Plunge has requested an analysis of the manufacturing cost per unit in the second and third quarters. You have been provided the following budgeted information for the coming year:

	Quarter			
	1	2	3	4
Pools manufactured and sold	565	490	245	100

It takes 1 direct manufacturing labor-hour to make each pool. The actual direct material cost is $14.00 per pool. The actual direct manufacturing labor rate is $20 per hour. The budgeted variable manufacturing overhead rate is $15 per direct manufacturing labor-hour. Budgeted fixed manufacturing overhead costs are $12,250 each quarter.

1. Calculate the total manufacturing cost per unit for the second and third quarter assuming the company allocates manufacturing overhead costs based on the budgeted manufacturing overhead rate determined for each quarter.
2. Calculate the total manufacturing cost per unit for the second and third quarter assuming the company allocates manufacturing overhead costs based on an annual budgeted manufacturing overhead rate.
3. Plunge Manufacturing prices its pools at manufacturing cost plus 30%. Why might Socha Wholesale be seeing large fluctuations in the prices of pools? Which of the methods described in requirements 1 and 2 would you recommend Plunge use? Explain.

Required

23 Accounting for manufacturing overhead. Jamison Woodworking uses normal costing and allocates manufacturing overhead to jobs based on a budgeted labor-hour rate and actual direct labor-hours. Under- or overallocated overhead, if immaterial, is written off to Cost of Goods Sold. During 2014, Jamison recorded the following:

Budgeted manufacturing overhead costs	$4,400,000
Budgeted direct labor-hours	200,000
Actual manufacturing overhead costs	$4,650,000
Actual direct labor-hours	212,000

1. Compute the budgeted manufacturing overhead rate.
2. Prepare the summary journal entry to record the allocation of manufacturing overhead.
3. Compute the amount of under- or overallocated manufacturing overhead. Is the amount significant enough to warrant proration of overhead costs, or would it be permissible to write it off to cost of goods sold? Prepare the journal entry to dispose of the under- or overallocated overhead.

Required

24 Job costing, journal entries. The University of Chicago Press is wholly owned by the university. It performs the bulk of its work for other university departments, which pay as though the press were an outside business enterprise. The press also publishes and maintains a stock of books for general sale. The press uses normal costing to cost each job. Its job-costing system has two direct-cost categories (direct materials and direct manufacturing labor) and one indirect-cost pool (manufacturing overhead, allocated on the basis of direct manufacturing labor costs).

The following data (in thousands) pertain to 2014:

Direct materials and supplies purchased on credit	$ 800
Direct materials used	710
Indirect materials issued to various production departments	100
Direct manufacturing labor	1,300
Indirect manufacturing labor incurred by various production departments	900
Depreciation on building and manufacturing equipment	400
Miscellaneous manufacturing overhead* incurred by various production departments (ordinarily would be detailed as repairs, photocopying, utilities, etc.)	550
Manufacturing overhead allocated at 160% of direct manufacturing labor costs	?
Cost of goods manufactured	4,120
Revenues	8,000
Cost of goods sold (before adjustment for under- or overallocated manufacturing overhead)	4,020
Inventories, December 31, 2013 (not 2014):	
Materials Control	100
Work-in-Process Control	60
Finished Goods Control	500

1. Prepare an overview diagram of the job-costing system at the University of Chicago Press.
2. Prepare journal entries to summarize the 2014 transactions. As your final entry, dispose of the year-end under- or overallocated manufacturing overhead as a writeoff to Cost of Goods Sold. Number your entries. Explanations for each entry may be omitted.
3. Show posted T-accounts for all inventories, Cost of Goods Sold, Manufacturing Overhead Control, and Manufacturing Overhead Allocated.
4. How did the University of Chicago Press perform in 2014?

25 Journal entries, T-accounts, and source documents. Creation Company produces gadgets for the coveted small appliance market. The following data reflect activity for the year 2014:

Costs incurred:	
Purchases of direct materials (net) on credit	$122,000
Direct manufacturing labor cost	83,000
Indirect labor	54,000
Depreciation, factory equipment	32,000
Depreciation, office equipment	7,900
Maintenance, factory equipment	29,000
Miscellaneous factory overhead	9,900
Rent, factory building	78,000
Advertising expense	94,000
Sales commissions	33,000
Inventories:	

	January 1, 2014	December 31, 2014
Direct materials	$ 9,800	$13,000
Work in process	6,300	23,000
Finished goods	68,000	27,000

---

*The term *manufacturing overhead* is not used uniformly. Other terms that are often encountered in printing companies include *job overhead* and *shop overhead*.

Creation Co. uses a normal-costing system and allocates overhead to work in process at a rate of $2.60 per direct manufacturing labor dollar. Indirect materials are insignificant so there is no inventory account for indirect materials.

Required

1. Prepare journal entries to record the transactions for 2014 including an entry to close out over- or underallocated overhead to cost of goods sold. For each journal entry indicate the source document that would be used to authorize each entry. Also note which subsidiary ledger, if any, should be referenced as backup for the entry.
2. Post the journal entries to T-accounts for all of the inventories, Cost of Goods Sold, the Manufacturing Overhead Control Account, and the Manufacturing Overhead Allocated Account.

26 Job costing, journal entries. Donald Transport assembles prestige manufactured homes. Its job-costing system has two direct-cost categories (direct materials and direct manufacturing labor) and one indirect-cost pool (manufacturing overhead allocated at a budgeted $31 per machine-hour in 2014). The following data (in millions) show operation costs for 2014:

Materials Control, beginning balance, January 1, 2014	$ 18
Work-in-Process Control, beginning balance, January 1, 2014	9
Finished Goods Control, beginning balance, January 1, 2014	10
Materials and supplies purchased on credit	154
Direct materials used	152
Indirect materials (supplies) issued to various production departments	19
Direct manufacturing labor	96
Indirect manufacturing labor incurred by various production departments	34
Depreciation on plant and manufacturing equipment	28
Miscellaneous manufacturing overhead incurred (ordinarily would be detailed as repairs, utilities, etc., with a corresponding credit to various liability accounts)	13
Manufacturing overhead allocated, 3,000,000 actual machine-hours	?
Cost of goods manufactured	298
Revenues	410
Cost of goods sold	294

Required

1. Prepare an overview diagram of Donald Transport's job-costing system.
2. Prepare journal entries. Number your entries. Explanations for each entry may be omitted. Post to T-accounts. What is the ending balance of Work-in-Process Control?
3. Show the journal entry for disposing of under- or overallocated manufacturing overhead directly as a year-end writeoff to Cost of Goods Sold. Post the entry to T-accounts.
4. How did Donald Transport perform in 2014?

27 Job costing, unit cost, ending work in process. Rafael Company produces pipes for concert-quality organs. Each job is unique. In April 2013, it completed all outstanding orders, and then, in May 2013, it worked on only two jobs, M1 and M2:

Rafael Company, May 2013	Job M1	Job M2
Direct materials	$ 78,000	$ 51,000
Direct manufacturing labor	273,000	208,000

Direct manufacturing labor is paid at the rate of $26 per hour. Manufacturing overhead costs are allocated at a budgeted rate of $20 per direct manufacturing labor-hour. Only Job M1 was completed in May.

Required

1. Calculate the total cost for Job M1.
2. 1,100 pipes were produced for Job M1. Calculate the cost per pipe.
3. Prepare the journal entry transferring Job M1 to finished goods.
4. What is the ending balance in the Work-in-Process Control account?

28 Job costing; actual, normal, and variation from normal costing. Cheney & Partners, a Quebec-based public accounting partnership, specializes in audit services. Its job-costing system has a single direct-cost category (professional labor) and a single indirect-cost pool (audit support, which contains all costs of the

Job Costing

Audit Support Department). Audit support costs are allocated to individual jobs using actual professional labor-hours. Cheney & Partners employs 10 professionals to perform audit services.

Budgeted and actual amounts for 2014 are as follows:

	A	B	C
1	**Cheney & Partners**		
2	**Budget for 2014**		
3	Professional labor compensation	$960,000	
4	Audit support department costs	$720,000	
5	Professional labor-hours billed to clients	16,000	hours
6			
7	**Actual results for 2014**		
8	Audit support department costs	$744,000	
9	Professional labor-hours billed to clients	15,500	hours
10	Actual professional labor cost rate	$ 53	per hour

Required

1. Compute the direct-cost rate and the indirect-cost rate per professional labor-hour for 2014 under (a) actual costing, (b) normal costing, and (c) the variation from normal costing that uses budgeted rates for direct costs.
2. Which job-costing system would you recommend Cheney & Partners use? Explain.
3. Cheney's 2014 audit of Pierre & Co. was budgeted to take 170 hours of professional labor time. The actual professional labor time spent on the audit was 185 hours. Compute the cost of the Pierre & Co. audit using (a) actual costing, (b) normal costing, and (c) the variation from normal costing that uses budgeted rates for direct costs. Explain any differences in the job cost.

29 Job costing; variation on actual, normal, and variation from normal costing. Creative Solutions designs Web pages for clients in the education sector. The company's job-costing system has a single direct cost category (Web-designing labor) and a single indirect cost pool composed of all overhead costs. Overhead costs are allocated to individual jobs based on direct labor-hours. The company employs six Web designers. Budgeted and actual information regarding Creative Solutions follows:

Budget for 2014:

Direct labor costs	$273,000
Direct labor-hours	10,500
Overhead costs	$157,500

Actual results for 2014:

Direct labor costs	$285,000
Direct labor-hours	11,400
Overhead costs	$159,600

Required

1. Compute the direct cost rate and the indirect cost rate per Web-designing labor-hour for 2014 under (a) actual costing, (b) normal costing, and (c) the variation from normal costing that uses budgeted rates for direct costs.
2. Which method would you suggest Creative Solutions use? Explain.
3. Creative Solutions' Web design for Greenville Day School was budgeted to take 86 direct labor-hours. The actual time spent on the project was 79 hours. Compute the cost of the Greenville Day School job using (a) actual costing, (b) normal costing, and (c) the variation from normal costing that uses budgeted rates for direct cost.

30 Proration of overhead. The Ride-On-Wave Company (ROW) produces a line of non-motorized boats. ROW uses a normal-costing system and allocates manufacturing overhead using direct manufacturing labor cost. The following data are for 2014:

Budgeted manufacturing overhead cost	$125,000
Budgeted direct manufacturing labor cost	$250,000
Actual manufacturing overhead cost	$117,000
Actual direct manufacturing labor cost	$228,000

Inventory balances on December 31, 2014, were as follows:

Account	Ending balance	2014 direct manufacturing labor cost in ending balance
Work in process	$ 50,700	$ 20,520
Finished goods	245,050	59,280
Cost of goods sold	549,250	148,200

Required

1. Calculate the manufacturing overhead allocation rate.
2. Compute the amount of under- or overallocated manufacturing overhead.
3. Calculate the ending balances in work in process, finished goods, and cost of goods sold if under- or overallocated manufacturing overhead is as follows:
   a. Written off to cost of goods sold
   b. Prorated based on ending balances (before proration) in each of the three accounts
   c. Prorated based on the overhead allocated in 2014 in the ending balances (before proration) in each of the three accounts
4. Which method would you choose? Justify your answer.

Problems

MyAccountingLab

31 Job costing, accounting for manufacturing overhead, budgeted rates. The Pisano Company uses a job-costing system at its Dover, Delaware, plant. The plant has a machining department and a finishing department. Pisano uses normal costing with two direct-cost categories (direct materials and direct manufacturing labor) and two manufacturing overhead cost pools (the machining department with machine-hours as the allocation base and the finishing department with direct manufacturing labor costs as the allocation base). The 2014 budget for the plant is as follows:

	Machining Department	Finishing Department
Manufacturing overhead costs	$9,065,000	$8,181,000
Direct manufacturing labor costs	$ 970,000	$4,050,000
Direct manufacturing labor-hours	36,000	155,000
Machine-hours	185,000	37,000

Required

1. Prepare an overview diagram of Pisano's job-costing system.
2. What is the budgeted manufacturing overhead rate in the machining department? In the finishing department?
3. During the month of January, the job-cost record for Job 431 shows the following:

	Machining Department	Finishing Department
Direct materials used	$13,000	$ 5,000
Direct manufacturing labor costs	$ 900	$1,250
Direct manufacturing labor-hours	20	70
Machine-hours	140	20

Compute the total manufacturing overhead cost allocated to Job 431.
4. Assuming that Job 431 consisted of 300 units of product, what is the cost per unit?
5. Amounts at the end of 2014 are as follows:

	Machining Department	Finishing Department
Manufacturing overhead incurred	$10,000,000	$7,982,000
Direct manufacturing labor costs	$ 1,030,000	$4,100,000
Machine-hours	200,000	34,000

Compute the under- or overallocated manufacturing overhead for each department and for the Dover plant as a whole.
6. Why might Pisano use two different manufacturing overhead cost pools in its job-costing system?

32 Service industry, job costing, law firm. Kidman & Associates is a law firm specializing in labor relations and employee-related work. It employs 30 professionals (5 partners and 25 associates) who work directly with its clients. The average budgeted total compensation per professional for 2014 is $97,500. Each professional is budgeted to have 1,500 billable hours to clients in 2014. All professionals work for clients to their maximum 1,500 billable hours available. All professional labor costs are included in a single direct-cost category and are traced to jobs on a per-hour basis. All costs of Kidman & Associates other than professional labor costs are included in a single indirect-cost pool (legal support) and are allocated to jobs using professional labor-hours as the allocation base. The budgeted level of indirect costs in 2014 is $2,475,000.

Required

1. Prepare an overview diagram of Kidman's job-costing system.
2. Compute the 2014 budgeted direct-cost rate per hour of professional labor.
3. Compute the 2014 budgeted indirect-cost rate per hour of professional labor.
4. Kidman & Associates is considering bidding on two jobs:
   a. Litigation work for Richardson, Inc., which requires 120 budgeted hours of professional labor
   b. Labor contract work for Punch, Inc., which requires 160 budgeted hours of professional labor
   Prepare a cost estimate for each job.

33 Service industry, job costing, two direct- and two indirect-cost categories, law firm (continuation of 32). Kidman has just completed a review of its job-costing system. This review included a detailed analysis of how past jobs used the firm's resources and interviews with personnel about what factors drive the level of indirect costs. Management concluded that a system with two direct-cost categories (professional partner labor and professional associate labor) and two indirect-cost categories (general support and secretarial support) would yield more accurate job costs. Budgeted information for 2014 related to the two direct-cost categories is as follows:

	Professional Partner Labor	Professional Associate Labor
Number of professionals	5	25
Hours of billable time per professional	1,500 per year	1,500 per year
Total compensation (average per professional)	$210,000	$75,000

Budgeted information for 2014 relating to the two indirect-cost categories is as follows:

	General Support	Secretarial Support
Total costs	$2,025,000	$450,000
Cost-allocation base	Professional labor-hours	Partner labor-hours

Required

1. Compute the 2014 budgeted direct-cost rates for (a) professional partners and (b) professional associates.
2. Compute the 2014 budgeted indirect-cost rates for (a) general support and (b) secretarial support.
3. Compute the budgeted costs for the Richardson and Punch jobs, given the following information:

	Richardson, Inc.	Punch, Inc.
Professional partners	48 hours	32 hours
Professional associates	72 hours	128 hours

4. Comment on the results in requirement 3. Why are the job costs different from those computed in Problem 32?
5. Would you recommend Kidman & Associates use the job-costing system in Problem 32 or the job-costing system in this problem? Explain.

34 Proration of overhead. (Z. Iqbal, adapted) The Zaf Radiator Company uses a normal-costing system with a single manufacturing overhead cost pool and machine-hours as the cost-allocation base. The following data are for 2014:

Budgeted manufacturing overhead costs	$4,800,000
Overhead allocation base	Machine-hours
Budgeted machine-hours	80,000
Manufacturing overhead costs incurred	$4,900,000
Actual machine-hours	75,000

Machine-hours data and the ending balances (before proration of under- or overallocated overhead) are as follows:

	Actual Machine-Hours	**2014 End-of-Year Balance**
Cost of Goods Sold	60,000	$8,000,000
Finished Goods Control	11,000	1,250,000
Work-in-Process Control	4,000	750,000

Required

1. Compute the budgeted manufacturing overhead rate for 2014.
2. Compute the under- or overallocated manufacturing overhead of Zaf Radiator in 2014. Dispose of this amount using the following:
   a. Writeoff to Cost of Goods Sold
   b. Proration based on ending balances (before proration) in Work-in-Process Control, Finished Goods Control, and Cost of Goods Sold
   c. Proration based on the overhead allocated in 2014 (before proration) in the ending balances of Work-in-Process Control, Finished Goods Control, and Cost of Goods Sold
3. Which method do you prefer in requirement 2? Explain.

35 Normal costing, overhead allocation, working backward. Gardi Manufacturing uses normal costing for its job-costing system, which has two direct-cost categories (direct materials and direct manufacturing labor) and one indirect-cost category (manufacturing overhead). The following information is obtained for 2014:

- Total manufacturing costs, $8,300,000
- Manufacturing overhead allocated, $4,100,000 (allocated at a rate of 250% of direct manufacturing labor costs)
- Work-in-process inventory on January 1, 2014, $420,000
- Cost of finished goods manufactured, $8,100,000

Required

1. Use information in the first two bullet points to calculate (a) direct manufacturing labor costs in 2014 and (b) cost of direct materials used in 2014.
2. Calculate the ending work-in-process inventory on December 31, 2014.

36 Proration of overhead with two indirect cost pools. Premier Golf Carts makes custom golf carts that it sells to dealers across the Southeast. The carts are produced in two departments, fabrication (a mostly automated department) and custom finishing (a mostly manual department). The company uses a normal-costing system in which overhead in the fabrication department is allocated to jobs on the basis of machine-hours and overhead in the finishing department is allocated to jobs based on direct labor-hours. During May, Premier Golf Carts reported actual overhead of $49,500 in the fabrication department and $22,200 in the finishing department. Additional information follows:

Manufacturing overhead rate (fabrication department)	$20 per machine-hour
Manufacturing overhead rate (finishing department)	$16 per direct labor-hour
Machine-hours (fabrication department) for May	2,000 machine-hours
Direct labor-hours (finishing department) for May	1,200 labor-hours
Work in process inventory, May 31	$50,000
Finished goods inventory, May 31	$150,000
Cost of goods sold, May	$300,000

Premier Golf Carts prorates under- and overallocated overhead monthly to work in process, finished goods, and cost of goods sold based on the ending balance in each account.

1. Calculate the amount of overhead allocated in the fabrication department and the finishing department in May.
2. Calculate the amount of under- or overallocated overhead in each department and in total.
3. How much of the under- or overallocated overhead will be prorated to (a) work in process inventory, (b) finished goods inventory, and (c) cost of goods sold based on the ending balance (before proration) in each of the three accounts? What will be the balance in work in process, finished goods, and cost of goods sold after proration?
4. What would be the effect of writing off under- and overallocated overhead to cost of goods sold? Would it be reasonable for Premier Golf Carts to change to this simpler method?

37 General ledger relationships, under- and overallocation. (S. Sridhar, adapted) Southwick Company uses normal costing in its job-costing system. Partially completed T-accounts and additional information for Southwick for 2014 are as follows:

Direct Materials Control			Work-in-Process Control			Finished Goods Control		
1-1-2014	25,000	234,000	1-1-2014	44,000		1-1-2014	10,000	880,000
	240,000		Dir. manuf.				925,000	
			labor	348,000				

Manufacturing Overhead Control		Manufacturing Overhead Allocated		Cost of Goods Sold	
514,000					

Additional information follows:

a. Direct manufacturing labor wage rate was $12 per hour.
b. Manufacturing overhead was allocated at $16 per direct manufacturing labor-hour.
c. During the year, sales revenues were $1,050,000, and marketing and distribution costs were $125,000.

1. What was the amount of direct materials issued to production during 2014?
2. What was the amount of manufacturing overhead allocated to jobs during 2014?
3. What was the total cost of jobs completed during 2014?
4. What was the balance of work-in-process inventory on December 31, 2014?
5. What was the cost of goods sold before proration of under- or overallocated overhead?
6. What was the under- or overallocated manufacturing overhead in 2014?
7. Dispose of the under- or overallocated manufacturing overhead using the following:
   a. Writeoff to Cost of Goods Sold
   b. Proration based on ending balances (before proration) in Work-in-Process Control, Finished Goods Control, and Cost of Goods Sold
8. Using each of the approaches in requirement 7, calculate Southwick's operating income for 2014.
9. Which approach in requirement 7 do you recommend Southwick use? Explain your answer briefly.

38 Overview of general ledger relationships. Brandon Company uses normal costing in its job-costing system. The company produces custom bikes for toddlers. The beginning balances (December 1) and ending balances (as of December 30) in their inventory accounts are as follows:

	Beginning Balance 12/1	Ending Balance 12/31
Materials Control	$2,100	$ 8,500
Work-in-Process Control	6,700	9,000
Manufacturing Department Overhead Control	—	94,000
Finished Goods Control	4,400	19,400

Additional information follows:

a. Direct materials purchased during December were $66,300.
b. Cost of goods manufactured for December was $234,000.
c. No direct materials were returned to suppliers.
d. No units were started or completed on December 31 and no direct materials were requisitioned on December 31.
e. The manufacturing labor costs for the December 31 working day: direct manufacturing labor, $4,300, and indirect manufacturing labor, $1,400.
f. Manufacturing overhead has been allocated at 110% of direct manufacturing labor costs through December 31.

1. Prepare journal entries for the December 31 payroll.
2. Use T-accounts to compute the following:
   a. The total amount of materials requisitioned into work in process during December
   b. The total amount of direct manufacturing labor recorded in work in process during December (Hint: You have to solve requirements **2b** and **2c** simultaneously)
   c. The total amount of manufacturing overhead recorded in work in process during December
   d. Ending balance in work in process, December 31
   e. Cost of goods sold for December before adjustments for under- or overallocated manufacturing overhead
3. Prepare closing journal entries related to manufacturing overhead. Assume that all under- or overallocated manufacturing overhead is closed directly to Cost of Goods Sold.

39 Allocation and proration of overhead. InStep Company prints custom training material for corporations. The business was started January 1, 2014. The company uses a normal-costing system. It has two direct cost pools, materials and labor, and one indirect cost pool, overhead. Overhead is charged to printing jobs on the basis of direct labor cost. The following information is available for 2014.

Budgeted direct labor costs	$225,000
Budgeted overhead costs	$315,000
Costs of actual material used	$148,500
Actual direct labor costs	$213,500
Actual overhead costs	$302,100

There were two jobs in process on December 31, 2014: Job 11 and Job 12. Costs added to each job as of December 31 are as follows:

	Direct materials	Direct labor
Job 11	$4,870	$5,100
Job 12	$5,910	$6,800

InStep Company has no finished goods inventories because all printing jobs are transferred to cost of goods sold when completed.

1. Compute the overhead allocation rate.
2. Calculate the balance in ending work in process and cost of goods sold before any adjustments for under- or overallocated overhead.
3. Calculate under- or overallocated overhead.
4. Calculate the ending balances in work in process and cost of goods sold if the under- or overallocated overhead amount is as follows:
   a. Written off to cost of goods sold
   b. Prorated using the overhead allocated in 2014 (before proration) in the ending balances of cost of goods sold and work-in-process control accounts
5. Which of the methods in requirement 4 would you choose? Explain.

40 Job costing, contracting, ethics. Rand Company manufactures modular homes. The company has two main products that it sells commercially: a 1,000-square-foot, one-bedroom model and a 1,500-square-foot, two-bedroom model. The company recently began providing emergency housing (huts) to the Federal Emergency Management Agency (FEMA). The emergency housing is similar to the 1,000-square-foot model.

FEMA has requested Rand to create a bid for 150 emergency huts to be sent for wildfire victims in the West. Your manager has asked that you prepare this bid. In preparing the bid, you find a recent invoice to FEMA for 200 huts provided during the most recent hurricane season in the South. You also have a standard cost sheet for the 1,000-square-foot model sold commercially. Both are provided as follows:

Standard cost sheet: 1,000-sq.-ft., one-bedroom model

Direct materials		$9,500
Direct manufacturing labor	32 hours	704
Manufacturing overhead*	$3.50 per direct labor dollar	2,464
Total cost		$12,668
Retail markup on total cost		25%
Retail price		$15,835

INVOICE

DATE: September 15, 2014

BILL TO: FEMA

FOR: 200 Emergency Huts

SHIP TO: Sarasota, Florida

Direct materials	$2,090,000
Direct manufacturing labor**	164,400
Manufacturing overhead	575,400
Total cost	2,829,800
Government contract markup on total cost	20%
Total due	$3,395,760

Required

1. Calculate the total bid if you base your calculations on the standard cost sheet assuming a cost plus 20% government contract.
2. Calculate the total bid if you base your calculations on the September 15, 2014, invoice assuming a cost plus 20% government contract.
3. What are the main discrepancies between the bids you calculated in requirements 1 and 2?
4. What bid should you present to your manager? What principles from the IMA "Standards of Ethical Conduct for Practitioners of Management Accounting and Financial Management" should guide your decision? As the manager, what would you do?

41 Job costing—service industry. Jordan Brady schedules gigs for local bands and creates CDs and T-shirts to sell at each gig. Brady uses a normal-costing system with two direct-cost pools, labor and materials, and one indirect-cost pool, general overhead. General overhead is allocated to each gig based on 120% of direct labor cost. Actual overhead equaled allocated overhead as of March 2014. Actual overhead in April was $1,980. All costs incurred during the planning stage for a gig and during the gig are gathered in a balance sheet account called "Gigs in Progress (GIP)." When a gig is completed, the costs are transferred to an income statement account called "Cost of Completed Gigs (CCG)." Following is cost information for April 2014:

	From Beginning GIP		Incurred in April	
Band	Materials	Labor	Materials	Labor
Irok	$570	$750	$110	$200
Freke Out	700	550	140	100
Bottom Rung	250	475	310	250
Dish Towel	—	—	540	450
Rail Ride	—	—	225	250

---

*Overhead cost pool includes inspection labor ($15 per hour), setup labor ($12 per hour), and other indirect costs associated with production.
**Direct manufacturing labor includes 30 production hours per unit, 4 inspection hours per unit, and 6 setup hours per unit.

As of April 1, there were three gigs in progress: *Irok, Freke Out,* and *Bottom Rung.* The gigs for *Dish Towel* and *Rail Ride* were started during April. The gigs for *Freke Out* and *Dish Towel* were completed during April.

Required

1. Calculate GIP at the end of April.
2. Calculate CCG for April.
3. Calculate under- or overallocated overhead at the end of April.
4. Calculate the ending balances in GIP and CCG if the under- or overallocated overhead amount is as follows:
   a. Written off to CCG
   b. Prorated based on the ending balances (before proration) in GIP and CCG
   c. Prorated based on the overhead allocated in April in the ending balances of GIP and CCG (before proration)
5. Which method would you choose? Explain. Would your choice depend on whether overhead cost is underallocated or overallocated? Explain.

Glossary

Actual costing. A costing system that traces direct costs to a cost object by using the actual direct-cost rates times the actual quantities of the direct-cost inputs and allocates indirect costs based on the actual indirect-cost rates times the actual quantities of the cost allocation bases.

Actual indirect-cost rate. Actual total indirect costs in a cost pool divided by the actual total quantity of the cost-allocation base for that cost pool.

Adjusted allocation-rate approach. Restates all overhead entries in the general ledger and subsidiary ledgers using actual cost rates rather than budgeted cost rates.

Budgeted indirect-cost rate. Budgeted annual indirect costs in a cost pool divided by the budgeted annual quantity of the cost allocation base.

Cost-allocation base. A factor that links in a systematic way an indirect cost or group of indirect costs to a cost object.

Cost-application base. Cost-allocation base when the cost object is a job, product, or customer.

Cost pool. A grouping of individual cost items.

Job. A unit or multiple units of a distinct product or service.

Job-cost record. Source document that records and accumulates all the costs assigned to a specific job, starting when work begins. Also called *job-cost sheet.*

Job-cost sheet. See *job-cost record.*

Job-costing system. Costing system in which the cost object is a unit or multiple units of a distinct product or service called a job.

Labor-time sheet. Source document that contains information about the amount of labor time used for a specific job in a specific department.

Manufacturing overhead allocated. Amount of manufacturing overhead costs allocated to individual jobs, products, or services based on the budgeted rate multiplied by the actual quantity used of the cost-allocation base. Also called *manufacturing overhead applied.*

Manufacturing overhead applied. See *manufacturing overhead allocated.*

Materials-requisition record. Source document that contains information about the cost of direct materials used on a specific job and in a specific department.

Normal costing. A costing system that traces direct costs to a cost object by using the actual direct-cost rates times the actual quantities of the direct-cost inputs and that allocates indirect costs based on the budgeted indirect-cost rates times the actual quantities of the cost-allocation bases.

Overabsorbed indirect costs. See *overallocated indirect costs.*

Overallocated indirect costs. Allocated amount of indirect costs in an accounting period is greater than the actual (incurred) amount in that period. Also called *overapplied indirect costs* and *overabsorbed indirect costs.*

Overapplied indirect costs. See *overallocated indirect costs.*

Process-costing system. Costing system in which the cost object is masses of identical or similar units of a product or service.

Proration. The spreading of underallocated manufacturing overhead or overallocated manufacturing overhead among ending work in process, finished goods, and cost of goods sold.

Source document. An original record that supports journal entries in an accounting system.

Underabsorbed indirect costs. See *underallocated indirect costs*.

Underallocated indirect costs. Allocated amount of indirect costs in an accounting period is less than the actual (incurred) amount in that period. Also called *underapplied indirect costs* or *underabsorbed indirect costs*.

Underapplied indirect costs. See *underallocated indirect costs*.

Photo Credits

Credits are listed in order of appearance.

Photo 1: Ludinko/Shutterstock
Photo 2: Tony Gutierrez/AP Images
Photo 3: Joe Raedle/Staff/Getty Images

Chapter 5

Activity-Based Costing and Activity-Based Management

From Chapter 5 of *Cost Accounting: A Managerial Emphasis,* Fifteenth Edition. Charles T. Horngren, Srikant M. Datar, Madhav V. Rajan. Copyright © 2015 by Pearson Education, Inc. All rights reserved.

Activity-Based Costing and Activity-Based Management

A good mystery never fails to capture the imagination.

Money is stolen or lost, property disappears, or someone meets with foul play. On the surface, many people may view these cases as typical. Someone with a trained eye, however, may uncover hidden facts, details, and patterns. Getting to the bottom of the case, understanding what happened and why, and taking action can make the difference between a solved case and an unsolved one. Business and organizations face similar cases. Their costing systems are often mysteries with unresolved questions: Why are we bleeding red ink? Are we pricing our products accurately? Activity-based costing can help unravel the mystery and result in improved operations, as LG Electronics discovered.

LG Electronics Reduces Costs and Inefficiencies Through Activity-Based Costing[1]

Based in Seoul, South Korea, LG Electronics is one of the world's largest manufacturers of flat-screen televisions and mobile phones. In 2012, the company spent $35.9 billion to purchase the semiconductors, metals, connectors, and other materials to manufacture its many electronic devices.

Until recently, however, LG Electronics did not have a centralized procurement system to leverage its scale and control rising supply costs. When LG Electronics hired its first chief procurement officer in 2009, he turned to activity-based costing (ABC) to identify opportunities for improvement. ABC analysis of the company's procurement system revealed that most company resources were applied to administrative tasks that were done manually and at a very high cost rather than to strategic tasks such as lowering supply costs.

The ABC analysis led LG Electronics to change many of its procurement practices and processes, improve efficiency, and focus on the highest-value tasks such as managing costs of commodity products and negotiating with suppliers. In 2012, LG Electronics saved $4.7 billion in direct material costs. Furthermore, the company

---

[1] *Sources:* Based on J. Carbone, "LG Electronics centralizes purchasing to save," *Purchasing* (April 2009); K. Yoou-chul, "CPO expects to save $1 billion in procurement," *The Korea Times* (April 1, 2009); "Linton's goals" (May 12, 2009); M. Ihlwan, "Innovation Close-up: LG Electronics," *Bloomberg Businessweek* (April 15, 2010); T. Linton and J. Choi, Global Procurement Transformation: New Frontiers for Global Innovation, in Proceedings of 95th Annual International Supply Management Conference, April 2012; and LG Corp., "Business Partners for Win-Win Growth, http://www.lg.com/global/sustainability/business-partner/win-win-growth, accessed May 2013.

developed an innovative global procurement strategy for its televisions, mobile phones, computers, and home-theater systems by implementing competitive bidding among suppliers, standardizing parts across product lines, and developing the capability to purchase more goods in China. As a result, today 44% of LG Electronics' global purchasing is sourced from outside of South Korea.

Most companies, such as Dell, Oracle, JP Morgan Chase, and Honda, offer more than one product (or service). Dell Computer, for example, produces desktops, laptops, and servers. Manufacturing these products entails three basic activities: (1) designing computers, (2) ordering component parts, and (3) assembling the product. Different products require different quantities of the three activities. A server, for example, has a more complex design, many more parts, and a more complex assembly than a desktop computer.

Dell separately tracks activity costs by product in its activity-based costing (ABC) system. In this chapter, we describe these types of systems and how they help companies make better decisions about pricing and product mix. And, just as in the case of LG Electronics, we show how ABC systems help managers make cost management decisions by improving product designs, processes, and efficiency.

Broad Averaging and Its Consequences

Learning Objective 1

Explain how broad averaging undercosts and overcosts products or services

…it does not measure the different resources consumed by different products and services

Historically, companies (such as television and automobile manufacturers) produced a limited variety of products. These companies used few overhead resources to support these simple operations, so indirect (or overhead) costs were a relatively small percentage of total costs. Managers used simple costing systems to allocate overhead costs broadly in an easy, inexpensive, and reasonably accurate way. But as product diversity and indirect costs increased, broad averaging led to inaccurate product costs. That's because simple *peanut-butter costing* (yes, that's what it's called) broadly averages or spreads the cost of resources uniformly to cost objects (such as products or services) when, in fact, the individual products or services use those resources in nonuniform ways.

Undercosting and Overcosting

The following example illustrates how averaging can result in inaccurate and misleading cost data. Consider the cost of a restaurant bill for four colleagues who meet monthly to discuss business developments. Each diner orders separate entrees, desserts, and drinks. The restaurant bill for the most recent meeting is as follows.

	Emma	James	Jessica	Matthew	Total	Average
Entree	$11	$20	$15	$14	$ 60	$15
Dessert	0	8	4	4	16	4
Drinks	4	14	8	6	32	8
Total	$15	$42	$27	$24	$108	$27

If the $108 total restaurant bill is divided evenly, $27 is the average cost per diner. This cost-averaging approach treats each diner the same. When costs are averaged across all four diners, both Emma and Matthew are overcosted, James is undercosted, and Jessica is (by coincidence) accurately costed. Emma, especially, may object to paying the average bill of $27 because her individual bill is only $15.

Broad averaging often leads to undercosting or overcosting of products or services:

- **Product undercosting**—a product consumes a high level of resources per unit but is reported to have a low cost per unit (James's dinner).

- **Product overcosting**—a product consumes a low level of resources per unit but is reported to have a high cost per unit (Emma's dinner).

What are the strategic consequences of product undercosting and overcosting? Suppose a manager uses cost information about products to guide pricing decisions. Undercosted products will be underpriced and may even lead to sales that actually result in losses because the sales may bring in less revenue than the cost of resources they use. Overcosted products will lead to overpricing, causing those products to lose market share to competitors producing similar products. But what if prices are determined by the market based on consumer demand and competition among companies? In this case, product undercosting and overcosting cause managers to focus on the wrong products. Managers give greater attention to overcosted products that show low profits when in fact costs and profits from these products are perfectly reasonable. They give less attention to undercosted products thinking they are highly profitable, when in fact these products consume large amounts of resources and are far less profitable than they appear.

Product-Cost Cross-Subsidization

Product-cost cross-subsidization means that if a company undercosts one of its products, it will overcost at least one of its other products. Similarly, if a company overcosts one of its products, it will undercost at least one of its other products. Product-cost cross-subsidization is very common when a cost is uniformly spread—meaning it is broadly averaged—across multiple products without managers recognizing the amount of resources each product consumes.

In the restaurant-bill example, the amount of cost cross-subsidization of each diner can be readily computed *because all cost items can be traced as direct costs to each diner.* If all diners pay $27, Emma is paying $12 more than her actual cost of $15. She is cross-subsidizing James who is paying $15 less than his actual cost of $42. Calculating the amount of cost cross-subsidization takes more work when there are indirect costs to be considered. Why? Because when two or more diners use the resources represented by indirect costs, we need to find a way to allocate costs to each diner. Consider, for example, a $40 bottle of wine whose cost is shared equally. Each diner would pay $10 ($40 ÷ 4). Suppose Matthew drinks two glasses of wine, while Emma, James, and Jessica drink one glass each for a total of five glasses. Allocating the cost of the bottle of wine on the basis of the glasses of wine that each diner drinks would result in Matthew paying $16 ($40 × 2/5) and each of the others paying $8 ($40 × 1/5). In this case, by sharing the cost equally, Emma, James, and Jessica are each paying $2 ($10 − $8) more and are cross-subsidizing Matthew who is paying $6 ($16 − $10) less for his wine for the night.

To see the effects of broad averaging on direct and indirect costs, we next consider Plastim Corporation's costing system.

Decision Point ▶
When does product undercosting or overcosting occur?

Simple Costing System at Plastim Corporation

Plastim Corporation manufactures lenses for the rear taillights of automobiles. A lens, made from black, red, orange, or white plastic, is the part of the taillight visible on the automobile's exterior. Lenses are made by injecting molten plastic into a mold, which gives the lens its desired shape. The mold is cooled to allow the molten plastic to solidify, and the lens is removed.

Plastim has a contract with Giovanni Motors, a major automobile manufacturer, to make two types of lenses: a complex lens called C5 and a simple lens called S3. The complex lens is large and has special features, such as multicolor molding (when more than one color is injected into the mold) and a complex shape that wraps around the corner of the car. Manufacturing C5 lenses is complicated because various parts in the mold must align and fit precisely. The S3 lens is simpler to make because it has a single color and few special features.

Design, Manufacturing, and Distribution Processes

Whether lenses are simple or complex, Plastim follows this sequence of steps to design, produce, and distribute them:

- **Design products and processes.** Each year Giovanni Motors specifies details of the simple and complex lenses it needs for its new models of cars. Plastim's design department designs the new molds and specifies the manufacturing process to make the lenses.
- **Manufacture lenses.** The lenses are molded, finished, cleaned, and inspected.
- **Distribute lenses.** Finished lenses are packed and sent to Giovanni Motors.

Plastim is operating at capacity and incurs very low marketing costs. Because of its high-quality products, Plastim has minimal customer-service costs. Plastim competes with several other companies who also manufacture simple lenses. At a recent meeting, Giovanni's purchasing manager informed Plastim's sales manager that Bandix, which makes only simple lenses, is offering to supply the S3 lens to Giovanni at a price of $53, well below the $63 price that Plastim is currently projecting and budgeting for 2014. Unless Plastim can lower its selling price, it will lose the Giovanni business for the simple lens for the upcoming model year. Fortunately, the same competitive pressures do not exist for the complex lens, which Plastim currently sells to Giovanni at $137 per lens.

Plastim's managers have two primary options:

- Give up the Giovanni business in simple lenses if selling them is unprofitable. Bandix makes only simple lenses and perhaps, therefore, uses simpler technology and processes than Plastim. The simpler operations may give Bandix a cost advantage that Plastim cannot match. If so, it is better for Plastim to not supply the S3 lens to Giovanni.
- Reduce the price of the simple lens and either accept a lower margin or aggressively seek to reduce costs.

To make these long-run strategic decisions, managers first need to understand the costs to design, make, and distribute the S3 and C5 lenses.

Bandix makes only simple lenses and can fairly accurately calculate the cost of a lens by dividing total costs by the number of simple lenses produced. Plastim's costing environment is more challenging because the manufacturing overhead costs support the production of both simple and complex lenses. Plastim's managers and management accountants need to find a way to allocate overhead costs to each type of lens.

In computing costs, Plastim assigns both variable costs and costs that are fixed in the short run to the S3 and C5 lenses. Managers cost products and services to guide long-run strategic decisions, such as what mix of products and services to produce and sell and what prices to charge for them. In the long run, managers have the ability to influence all costs. The firm will only survive in the long run if revenues exceed total costs, regardless of whether these costs are variable or fixed in the short run.

To guide pricing and cost-management decisions, Plastim's managers assign both manufacturing and nonmanufacturing costs to the S3 and C5 lenses. If managers had wanted to calculate the cost of inventory, Plastim's management accountants would have assigned only manufacturing costs to the lenses, as required by Generally Accepted Accounting Principles. Surveys of company practice across the globe indicate that the vast majority of companies use costing systems not just for inventory costing but also for strategic purposes, such as pricing and product-mix decisions and decisions about cost reduction, process improvement, design, and planning and budgeting. Managers of these companies assign all costs to products and services. Even merchandising-sector companies (for whom inventory costing is straightforward) and service-sector companies (who have no inventory) expend considerable resources in designing and operating their costing systems to allocate costs for strategic purposes.

Simple Costing System Using a Single Indirect-Cost Pool

Plastim currently has a simple costing system that allocates indirect costs using a single indirect-cost rate. Exhibit 1 shows an overview of Plastim's simple costing system. Use this exhibit as a guide as you study the following steps, each of which is marked in Exhibit 1.

Step 1: Identify the Products That Are the Chosen Cost Objects. The cost objects are the 60,000 simple S3 lenses and the 15,000 complex C5 lenses that Plastim will produce in 2014. Plastim's management accountants first calculate the total costs and then the unit cost of designing, manufacturing, and distributing lenses.

Step 2: Identify the Direct Costs of the Products. The direct costs are direct materials and direct manufacturing labor. Exhibit 2 shows the direct and indirect costs for the S3 and the C5 lenses using the simple costing system. The direct cost calculations appear on lines 5, 6, and 7 in Exhibit 2. Plastim's simple costing system classifies all costs other than direct materials and direct manufacturing labor as indirect costs.

Step 3: Select the Cost-Allocation Bases to Use for Allocating Indirect (or Overhead) Costs to the Products. A majority of the indirect costs consist of salaries paid to supervisors, engineers, manufacturing support, and maintenance staff that support direct manufacturing labor. Plastim's managers use direct manufacturing labor-hours as the only allocation base to allocate all manufacturing and nonmanufacturing indirect costs to S3 and C5. In 2014, Plastim's managers budget 39,750 direct manufacturing labor-hours.

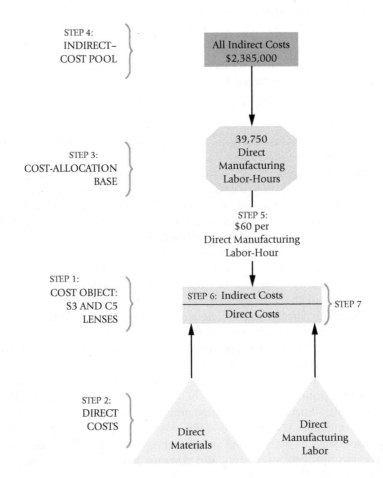

Exhibit 1

Overview of Plastim's
Simple Costing System

| Exhibit 2 | Plastim's Product Costs Using the Simple Costing System |

	A	B	C	D	E	F	G
1		60,000			15,000		
2		Simple Lenses (S3)			Complex Lenses (C5)		
3		Total	per Unit		Total	per Unit	Total
4		(1)	(2) = (1) ÷ 60,000		(3)	(4) = (3) ÷ 15,000	(5) = (1) + (3)
5	Direct materials	$1,125,000	$18.75		$ 675,000	$45.00	$1,800,000
6	Direct manufacturing labor	600,000	10.00		195,000	13.00	795,000
7	Total direct costs (Step 2)	1,725,000	28.75		870,000	58.00	2,595,000
8	Indirect costs allocated (Step 6)	1,800,000	30.00		585,000	39.00	2,385,000
9	Total costs (Step 7)	$3,525,000	$58.75		$1,455,000	$97.00	$4,980,000
10							

Step 4: Identify the Indirect Costs Associated with Each Cost-Allocation Base. Because Plastim uses only a single cost-allocation base, Plastim's management accountants group all budgeted indirect costs of $2,385,000 for 2014 into a single overhead cost pool.

Step 5: Compute the Rate per Unit of Each Cost-Allocation Base.

$$\text{Budgeted indirect-cost rate} = \frac{\text{Budgeted total costs in indirect-cost pool}}{\text{Budgeted total quantity of cost-allocation base}}$$

$$= \frac{\$2,385,000}{39,750 \text{ direct manufacturing labor-hours}}$$

$$= \$60 \text{ per direct manufacturing labor-hour}$$

Step 6: Compute the Indirect Costs Allocated to the Products. Plastim's managers budget 30,000 total direct manufacturing labor-hours to make the 60,000 S3 lenses and 9,750 total direct manufacturing labor-hours to make the 15,000 C5 lenses. Exhibit 2 shows indirect costs of $1,800,000 ($60 per direct manufacturing labor-hour × 30,000 direct manufacturing labor-hours) allocated to the simple lens and $585,000 ($60 per direct manufacturing labor-hour × 9,750 direct manufacturing labor-hours) allocated to the complex lens.

Step 7: Compute the Total Cost of the Products by Adding All Direct and Indirect Costs Assigned to the Products. Exhibit 2 presents the product costs for the simple and complex lenses. The direct costs are calculated in Step 2 and the indirect costs in Step 6. Be sure you see the parallel between the simple costing system overview diagram (Exhibit 1) and the costs calculated in Step 7. Exhibit 1 shows two direct-cost categories and one indirect-cost category. Therefore, the budgeted cost of each type of lens in Step 7 (Exhibit 2) has three line items: two for direct costs and one for allocated indirect costs. It is very helpful to draw overview diagrams to see the big picture of costing systems before getting into the detailed costing of products and services. The budgeted cost per S3 lens is $58.75, well above the $53 selling price quoted by Bandix. The budgeted cost per C5 lens is $97.

Applying the Five-Step Decision-Making Process at Plastim

To decide how it should respond to the threat that Bandix poses to its S3 lens business, Plastim's managers work through the five-step decision-making process.

Step 1: Identify the Problem and Uncertainties. The problem is clear: If Plastim wants to retain the Giovanni business for S3 lenses and make a profit, it must find a way to reduce the price and costs of the S3 lens. The two major uncertainties Plastim faces are (1) whether its technology and processes for the S3 lens are competitive with Bandix's and (2) whether Plastim's S3 lens is overcosted by the simple costing system.

Step 2: Obtain Information. Senior management asks a team of design and process engineers to analyze and evaluate the design, manufacturing, and distribution operations for the S3 lens. The team is very confident that the technology and processes for the S3 lens are not inferior to those of Bandix and other competitors because Plastim has many years of experience in manufacturing and distributing the S3 lens with a history and culture of continuous process improvements. The team is less certain about Plastim's capabilities in manufacturing and distributing complex lenses because it only recently started making this type of lens. Given these doubts, senior management is happy that Giovanni Motors considers the price of the C5 lens to be competitive. Plastim's managers are puzzled, though, by how, at the currently budgeted prices, Plastim is expected to earn a very large profit margin percentage (operating income ÷ revenues) on the C5 lenses and a small profit margin on the S3 lenses:

| | 60,000 Simple Lenses (S3) | | 15,000 Complex Lenses (C5) | | |
	Total (1)	per Unit (2) = (1) ÷ 60,000	Total (3)	per Unit (4) = (3) ÷ 15,000	Total (5) = (1) + (3)
Revenues	$3,780,000	$63.00	$2,055,000	$137.00	$5,835,000
Total costs	3,525,000	58.75	1,455,000	97.00	4,980,000
Operating income	$ 255,000	$ 4.25	$ 600,000	$ 40.00	$ 855,000
Profit margin percentage		6.75%		29.20%	

As they continue to gather information, Plastim's managers begin to ponder why the profit margins are under so much pressure for the S3 lens, where the company has strong capabilities, but are high on the newer, less-established C5 lens. Plastim is not deliberately charging a low price for S3, so managers begin to evaluate the costing system. Plastim's simple costing system may be overcosting the simple S3 lens (assigning too much cost to it) and undercosting the complex C5 lens (assigning too little cost to it).

Step 3: Make Predictions About the Future. Plastim's key challenge is to get a better estimate of what it will cost to design, make, and distribute the S3 and C5 lenses. Managers are fairly confident about the direct material and direct manufacturing labor cost of each lens because these costs are easily traced to the lenses. But managers are quite concerned about how accurately the simple costing system measures the indirect resources used by each type of lens. They believe the costing system can be substantially improved.

Even as they come to this conclusion, managers want to avoid biased thinking. In particular, they want to be careful that the desire to be competitive on the S3 lens does not lead to assumptions that bias them in favor of lowering costs of the S3 lens.

Step 4: Make Decisions by Choosing Among Alternatives. On the basis of predicted costs and taking into account how Bandix might respond, Plastim's managers must decide whether they should bid for Giovanni Motors' S3 lens business and, if they do bid, what price they should offer.

Step 5: Implement the Decision, Evaluate Performance, and Learn. If Plastim bids and wins Giovanni's S3 lens business, it must compare actual costs as it makes and ships S3 lenses to predicted costs and learn why actual costs deviate from predicted costs. Such evaluation and learning form the basis for future improvements.

The next few sections focus on Steps 3, 4, and 5: (3) how Plastim improves the allocation of indirect costs to the S3 and C5 lenses, (4) how it uses these predictions to bid for the S3 lens business, and (5) how it evaluates performance, makes product design and process improvements, and learns using the new system.

Refining a Costing System

A **refined costing system** reduces the use of broad averages for assigning the cost of resources to cost objects (such as jobs, products, and services) and provides better measurement of the costs of indirect resources used by different cost objects, no matter how differently various cost objects use indirect resources. Refining a costing system helps managers make better decisions about how to allocate resources and which products to produce.

Reasons for Refining a Costing System

Three principal reasons have accelerated the demand for refinements to the costing system.

1. **Increase in product diversity.** The growing demand for customized products has led managers to increase the variety of products and services their companies offer. Kanthal, a Swedish manufacturer of heating elements, for example, produces more than 10,000 different types of electrical heating wires and thermostats. Banks, such as Barclays Bank in the United Kingdom, offer many different types of accounts and services: special passbook accounts, ATMs, credit cards, and electronic banking products. Producing these products places different demands on resources because of differences in volume, process, technology, and complexity. For example, the computer and network resources needed to support electronic banking products are much greater than the computer and network resources needed to support a passbook savings account. The use of broad averages fails to capture these differences in demand and leads to distorted and inaccurate cost information.

2. **Increase in indirect costs.** The use of product and process technology such as computer-integrated manufacturing (CIM) and flexible manufacturing systems (FMS) has led to an increase in indirect costs and a decrease in direct costs, particularly direct manufacturing labor costs. In CIM and FMS, computers on the manufacturing floor instruct equipment to set up and run quickly and automatically. The computers accurately measure hundreds of production parameters and directly control the manufacturing processes to achieve high-quality output. Managing complex technology and producing diverse products also require additional support function resources for activities such as production scheduling, product and process design, and engineering. Because direct manufacturing labor is not a cost driver of these costs, allocating indirect costs on the basis of direct manufacturing labor (as in Plastim's simple costing system) does not accurately measure how resources are being used by different products.

3. **Competition in product markets.** As markets have become more competitive, managers have felt the need to obtain more accurate cost information to help them make important strategic decisions, such as how to price products and which products to sell. Making correct decisions about pricing and product mix is critical in competitive markets because competitors quickly capitalize on a manager's mistakes. For example, if Plastim overcosts the S3 lens and charges a higher price, a competitor aware of the true costs of making the lens could charge a lower price and gain the S3 business.

The preceding factors explain why managers want to refine cost systems. Refining costing systems requires gathering, validating, analyzing, and storing vast quantities of data. Advances in information technology have drastically reduced the costs of performing these activities.

Guidelines for Refining a Costing System

There are three main guidelines for refining a costing system:

1. **Direct-cost tracing.** Identify as many direct costs as is economically feasible. This guideline aims to reduce the amount of costs classified as indirect, thereby minimizing the extent to which costs have to be allocated rather than traced.

2. **Indirect-cost pools.** Expand the number of indirect-cost pools until each pool is more homogeneous. All costs in a *homogeneous cost pool* have the same or a similar

cause-and-effect (or benefits-received) relationship with a single cost driver that is used as the cost-allocation base. Consider, for example, a single indirect-cost pool containing both indirect machining costs and indirect distribution costs that are allocated to products using machine-hours. This pool is not homogeneous because machine-hours are a cost driver of machining costs but not of distribution costs, which has a different cost driver, number of shipments. If, instead, machining costs and distribution costs are separated into two indirect-cost pools, with machine-hours as the cost-allocation base for the machining cost pool and number of shipments as the cost-allocation base for the distribution cost pool, each indirect-cost pool would become homogeneous.

3. **Cost-allocation bases.** As we describe later in the chapter, whenever possible, managers should use the cost driver (the cause of indirect costs) as the cost-allocation base for each homogeneous indirect-cost pool (the effect).

Decision Point

How do managers refine a costing system?

Learning Objective 3

Distinguish between simple and activity-based costing systems

...unlike simple systems, activity-based costing systems calculate costs of individual activities to cost products

Activity-Based Costing Systems

One of the best tools for refining a costing system is *activity-based costing*. **Activity-based costing (ABC)** refines a costing system by identifying individual activities as the fundamental cost objects. An **activity** is an event, task, or unit of work with a specified purpose—for example, designing products, setting up machines, operating machines, and distributing products. More informally, activities are verbs; they are things that a firm does. To help make strategic decisions, ABC systems identify activities in all functions of the value chain, calculate costs of individual activities, and assign costs to cost objects such as products and services on the basis of the mix of activities needed to produce each product or service.[2]

Plastim's ABC System

After reviewing its simple costing system and the potential miscosting of product costs, Plastim's managers decide to implement an ABC system. Direct material costs and direct manufacturing labor costs can be traced to products easily, so the ABC system focuses on refining the assignment of indirect costs to departments, processes, products, or other cost objects. To identify activities, Plastim organizes a team of managers from design, manufacturing, distribution, accounting, and administration. Plastim's ABC system then uses these activities to break down its current single indirect cost pool into finer pools of costs related to the various activities.

Defining activities is difficult. The team evaluates hundreds of tasks performed at Plastim. It must decide which tasks should be classified as separate activities and which should be combined. For example, should maintenance of molding machines, operations of molding machines, and process control be regarded as separate activities or combined into a single activity? An activity-based costing system with many activities becomes overly detailed and unwieldy to operate. An activity-based costing system with too few activities may not be refined enough to measure cause-and-effect relationships between cost drivers and various indirect costs. To achieve an effective balance, Plastim's team

---

[2] For more details on ABC systems, see R. Cooper and R. S. Kaplan, *The Design of Cost Management Systems* (Upper Saddle River, NJ: Prentice Hall, 1999); G. Cokins, *Activity-Based Cost Management: An Executive's Guide* (Hoboken, NJ: John Wiley & Sons, 2001); and R. S. Kaplan and S. Anderson, *Time-Driven Activity-Based Costing: A Simpler and More Powerful Path to Higher Profits* (Boston: Harvard Business School Press, 2007).

focuses on activities that account for a sizable fraction of indirect costs and combines activities that have the same cost driver into a single activity. For example, the team decides to combine maintenance of molding machines, operations of molding machines, and process control into a single activity—molding machine operations—because all these activities have the same cost driver: molding machine-hours.

The team identifies the following seven activities by developing a flowchart of all the steps and processes needed to design, manufacture, and distribute S3 and C5 lenses.

a. Design products and processes

b. Set up molding machines to ensure that the molds are properly held in place and parts are properly aligned before manufacturing starts

c. Operate molding machines to manufacture lenses

d. Clean and maintain the molds after lenses are manufactured

e. Prepare batches of finished lenses for shipment

f. Distribute lenses to customers

g. Administer and manage all processes at Plastim

These activity descriptions (or *activity list* or *activity dictionary*) form the basis of the activity-based costing system. Compiling the list of tasks, however, is only the first step in implementing activity-based costing systems. Plastim must also identify the cost of each activity and the related cost driver by using the three guidelines for refining a costing system.

1. **Direct-cost tracing.** Plastim's ABC system subdivides the single indirect cost pool into seven smaller cost pools related to the different activities. The costs in the cleaning and maintenance activity cost pool (item d) consist of salaries and wages paid to workers who clean the mold. These costs are direct costs because they can be economically traced to a specific mold and lens.

2. **Indirect-cost pools.** The remaining six activity cost pools are indirect cost pools. Unlike the single indirect cost pool of Plastim's simple costing system, each of the activity-related cost pools is homogeneous. That is, each activity cost pool includes only those narrow and focused sets of costs that have the same cost driver. For example, the distribution cost pool includes only those costs (such as wages of truck drivers) that, over time, increase as the cost driver of distribution costs, cubic feet of packages delivered, increases. In the simple costing system, Plastim lumped all indirect costs together and the cost-allocation base, direct manufacturing labor-hours, was not a cost driver of the indirect costs. Managers were therefore unable to measure how different cost objects used resources.

   To determine the costs of activity pools, managers assign costs accumulated in various account classifications (such as salaries, wages, maintenance, and electricity) to each of the activity cost pools. This process is commonly called *first-stage allocation*. For example, as we will see later in the chapter, of the $2,385,000 in the total indirect-cost pool, Plastim identifies setup costs of $300,000. Setup costs include depreciation and maintenance costs of setup equipment, wages of setup workers, and allocated salaries of design engineers, process engineers, and supervisors. We focus here on the *second-stage allocation*, the allocation of costs of activity cost pools to products.

3. **Cost-allocation bases.** For each activity cost pool, Plastim uses the cost driver (whenever possible) as the cost-allocation base. To identify cost drivers, Plastim's managers consider various alternatives and use their knowledge of operations to choose among them. For example, Plastim's managers choose setup-hours rather than the number of setups as the cost driver of setup costs because Plastim's managers believe that more complex setups take more time and are more costly. Over time, Plastim's managers can use data to test their beliefs.

The logic of ABC systems is twofold. First, when managers structure activity cost pools more finely with cost drivers for each activity cost pool as the cost-allocation base, it leads to more accurate costing of activities. Second, allocating these costs to products by measuring the cost-allocation bases of different activities used by different products leads to more accurate product costs. We illustrate this logic by focusing on the setup activity at Plastim.

Setting up molding machines frequently entails trial runs, fine-tuning, and adjustments. Improper setups cause quality problems such as scratches on the surface of the lens. The resources needed for each setup depend on the complexity of the manufacturing operation. Complex lenses require more setup resources (setup-hours) per setup than simple lenses. Furthermore, complex lenses can be produced only in small batches because the molds for complex lenses need to be cleaned more often than molds for simple lenses. Relative to simple lenses, complex lenses therefore not only use more setup-hours per setup, but they also require more frequent setups.

Setup data for the simple S3 lens and the complex C5 lens are as follows.

		Simple S3 Lens	Complex C5 Lens	Total
1	Quantity of lenses produced	60,000	15,000	
2	Number of lenses produced per batch	240	50	
3 = (1) ÷ (2)	Number of batches	250	300	
4	Setup time per batch	2 hours	5 hours	
5 = (3) × (4)	Total setup-hours	500 hours	1,500 hours	2,000 hours

Recall that in its simple costing system, Plastim uses direct manufacturing labor-hours to allocate all $2,385,000 of indirect costs (which includes $300,000 of indirect setup costs) to products. The following table compares how setup costs allocated to simple and complex lenses will be different if Plastim allocates setup costs to lenses based on setup-hours rather than direct manufacturing labor-hours. Of the $60 total rate per direct manufacturing labor-hour, the setup cost per direct manufacturing labor-hour amounts to $7.54717 ($300,000 ÷ 39,750 total direct manufacturing labor-hours). The setup cost per setup-hour equals $150 ($300,000 ÷ 2,000 total setup-hours).

	Simple S3 Lens	Complex C5 Lens	Total
Setup cost allocated using direct manufacturing labor-hours:			
$7.54717 × 30,000; $7.54717 × 9,750	$226,415	$ 73,585	$300,000
Setup cost allocated using setup-hours:			
$150 × 500; $150 × 1,500	$ 75,000	$225,000	$300,000

ABC systems that use available time (setup-hours in our example) to calculate the cost of a resource and to allocate costs to cost objects are sometimes called *time-driven activity-based costing (TDABC) systems*. As we have already discussed when presenting guidelines 2 and 3, setup-hours, not direct manufacturing labor-hours, are the cost driver of setup costs. The C5 lens uses substantially more setup-hours than the S3 lens (1,500 hours ÷ 2,000 hours = 75% of the total setup-hours) because the C5 requires a greater number of setups (batches) and each setup is more challenging and requires more setup-hours.

The ABC system therefore allocates significantly more setup costs to C5 than to S3. When direct manufacturing labor-hours rather than setup-hours are used to allocate setup costs in the simple costing system, the S3 lens is allocated a very large share of the setup costs because the S3 lens uses a larger proportion of direct manufacturing labor-hours (30,000 ÷ 39,750 = 75.47%). As a result, the simple costing system overcosts the S3 lens with regard to setup costs.

As we will see later in the chapter, ABC systems provide valuable information to managers beyond more accurate product costs. For example, identifying setup-hours as the cost driver correctly orients managers' cost reduction efforts on reducing setup-hours and cost per setup-hour. Note that setup-hours are related to batches (or groups)

Decision Point
What is the difference between the design of a simple costing system and an activity-based costing (ABC) system?

of lenses made, not the number of individual lenses. Activity-based costing attempts to identify the most relevant cause-and-effect relationship for each activity pool without restricting the cost driver to only units of output or variables related to units of output (such as direct manufacturing labor-hours). As our discussion of setups illustrates, limiting cost-allocation bases to only units of output weakens the cause-and-effect relationship between the cost-allocation base and the costs in a cost pool.

Cost Hierarchies

A **cost hierarchy** categorizes various activity cost pools on the basis of the different types of cost drivers, cost-allocation bases, or different degrees of difficulty in determining cause-and-effect (or benefits-received) relationships. ABC systems commonly use a cost hierarchy with four levels to identify cost-allocation bases that are cost drivers of the activity cost pools: (1) output unit–level costs, (2) batch-level costs, (3) product-sustaining costs, and (4) facility-sustaining costs.

Output unit–level costs are the costs of activities performed on each individual unit of a product or service. Machine operations costs (such as the cost of energy, machine depreciation, and repair) related to the activity of running the automated molding machines are output unit–level costs because, over time, the cost of this activity increases with additional units of output produced (or machine-hours used). Plastim's ABC system uses molding machine-hours, an output unit–level cost-allocation base, to allocate machine operations costs to products.

Batch-level costs are the costs of activities related to a group of units of a product or service rather than each individual unit of product or service. In the Plastim example, setup costs are batch-level costs because, over time, the cost of this setup activity increases with setup-hours needed to produce batches (groups) of lenses. As described in the table, the S3 lens requires 500 setup-hours (2 setup-hours per batch × 250 batches). The C5 lens requires 1,500 setup-hours (5 setup-hours per batch × 300 batches). The total setup costs allocated to S3 and C5 depend on the total setup-hours required by each type of lens, not on the number of units of S3 and C5 produced. (Setup costs being a batch-level cost cannot be avoided by producing one less unit of S3 or C5.) Plastim's ABC system uses setup-hours, a batch-level cost-allocation base, to allocate setup costs to products. Other examples of batch-level costs are material-handling and quality-inspection costs associated with batches (not the quantities) of products produced and costs of placing purchase orders, receiving materials, and paying invoices related to the number of purchase orders placed rather than the quantity or value of materials purchased.

Product-sustaining costs (service-sustaining costs) are the costs of activities undertaken to support individual products or services regardless of the number of units or batches in which the units are produced. In the Plastim example, design costs are product-sustaining costs. Over time, design costs depend largely on the time designers spend on designing and modifying the product, the mold, and the process. These design costs are a function of the complexity of the mold, measured by the number of parts in the mold multiplied by the area (in square feet) over which the molten plastic must flow (12 parts × 2.5 square feet, or 30 parts-square feet for the S3 lens; and 14 parts × 5 square feet, or 70 parts-square feet for the C5 lens). As a result, the total design costs allocated to S3 and C5 depend on the complexity of the mold, regardless of the number of units or batches of production. Plastim can't avoid design costs by producing fewer units or running fewer batches. Plastim's ABC system uses parts-square feet, a product-sustaining cost-allocation base, to allocate design costs to products. Other examples of product-sustaining costs are product research and development costs, costs of making engineering changes, and marketing costs to launch new products.

Facility-sustaining costs are the costs of activities that managers cannot trace to individual products or services but that support the organization as a whole. In the Plastim example and at companies such as Volvo, Samsung, and General Electric, the general administration costs (including top management compensation, rent, and building security) are facility-sustaining costs. It is usually difficult to find a good cause-and-effect

Learning Objective 4

Describe a four-part cost hierarchy

…a four-part cost hierarchy is used to categorize costs based on different types of cost drivers—for example, costs that vary with each unit of a product versus costs that vary with each batch of products

Decision Point

What is a cost hierarchy?

relationship between these costs and the cost-allocation base, so some companies deduct facility-sustaining costs as a separate lump-sum amount from operating income rather than allocate them to products. Managers who follow this approach need to keep in mind that when making decisions based on costs (such as pricing), some lump-sum costs have not been allocated. They must set prices that are much greater than the allocated costs to recover some of the unallocated facility-sustaining costs. Other companies, such as Plastim, allocate facility-sustaining costs to products on some basis—for example, direct manufacturing labor-hours—because management believes all costs should be allocated to products even if it's done in a somewhat arbitrary way. Allocating all costs to products or services ensures that managers have taken into account all costs when making decisions based on costs (such as pricing). So long as managers are aware of the nature of facility-sustaining costs and the pros and cons of allocating them, which method a manager chooses is a matter of personal preference.

Learning Objective 5 ▶

Cost products or services using activity-based costing

...use cost rates for different activities to compute indirect costs of a product

Implementing Activity-Based Costing

Now that you understand the basic concepts of ABC, let's see how Plastim's managers refine the simple costing system, evaluate the two systems, and identify the factors to consider when deciding whether to develop the ABC system.

Implementing ABC at Plastim

To implement ABC, Plastim's managers follow the seven-step approach to costing and the three guidelines for refining costing systems (increase direct-cost tracing, create homogeneous indirect-cost pools, and identify cost-allocation bases that have cause-and-effect relationships with costs in the cost pool). Exhibit 3 shows an overview of Plastim's ABC system. Use this exhibit as a guide as you study the following steps, each of which is marked in Exhibit 3.

Exhibit 3	Overview of Plastim's Activity-Based Costing System

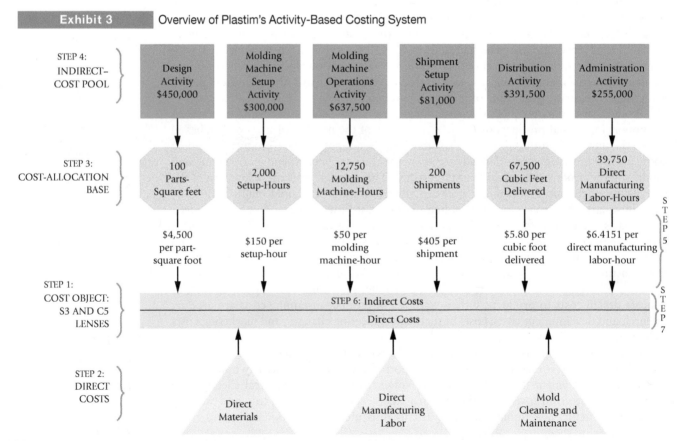

Step 1: Identify the Products That Are the Chosen Cost Objects. The cost objects are the 60,000 S3 and the 15,000 C5 lenses that Plastim will produce in 2014. Plastim's managers want to determine the total costs and then the per-unit cost of designing, manufacturing, and distributing these lenses.

Step 2: Identify the Direct Costs of the Products. The managers identify the following direct costs of the lenses because these costs can be economically traced to a specific mold and lens: direct material costs, direct manufacturing labor costs, and mold cleaning and maintenance costs.

Exhibit 5 shows the direct and indirect costs for the S3 and C5 lenses using the ABC system. The direct costs calculations appear on lines 6, 7, 8, and 9 in Exhibit 5. Plastim's managers classify all other costs as indirect costs, as we will see in Exhibit 4.

Step 3: Select the Activities and Cost-Allocation Bases to Use for Allocating Indirect Costs to the Products. Following guidelines 2 and 3 for refining a costing system, Plastim's managers identify six activities for allocating indirect costs to products: (a) design, (b) molding machine setups, (c) machine operations, (d) shipment setup, (e) distribution, and (f) administration. Exhibit 4, column 2, shows the cost hierarchy category, and column 4 shows the cost-allocation base and the budgeted quantity of the cost-allocation base for each activity described in column 1.

Identifying the cost-allocation bases defines the number of activity pools into which costs must be grouped in an ABC system. For example, rather than define the design activities of product design, process design, and prototyping as separate activities, Plastim's managers define these three activities together as a combined "design" activity and form a homogeneous design cost pool. Why? Because the same cost driver— the complexity of the mold— drives the costs of each design activity. A second consideration for choosing a cost-allocation base is the availability of reliable data and measures. For example, in its ABC system, Plastim's managers measure mold complexity in terms of the number of parts in the mold and the surface area of the mold (parts-square feet). If these data are difficult to obtain or measure, Plastim's managers may be forced to use some other measure of complexity, such as the amount of material flowing through the mold that may only be weakly related to the cost of the design activity.

Exhibit 4	Activity-Cost Rates for Indirect-Cost Pools

	Home	Insert	Page Layout	Formulas	Data	Review	View	
	A	B	C	D	E	F	G	H
1			(Step 4)	(Step 3)		(Step 5)		
2	Activity	Cost Hierarchy Category	Total Budgeted Indirect Costs	Budgeted Quantity of Cost-Allocation Base		Budgeted Indirect Cost Rate		Cause-and-Effect Relationship Between Allocation Base and Activity Cost
3	(1)	(2)	(3)	(4)		(5) = (3) ÷ (4)		(6)
4	Design	Product-sustaining	$450,000	100	parts-square feet	$ 4,500	per part-square foot	Design Department indirect costs increase with more complex molds (more parts, larger surface area).
5	Setup molding machines	Batch-level	$300,000	2,000	setup-hours	$ 150	per setup-hour	Indirect setup costs increase with setup-hours.
6	Machine operations	Output unit-level	$637,500	12,750	molding machine-hours	$ 50	per molding machine-hour	Indirect costs of operating molding machines increases with molding machine-hours.
7	Shipment setup	Batch-level	$ 81,000	200	shipments	$ 405	per shipment	Shipping costs incurred to prepare batches for shipment increase with the number of shipments.
8	Distribution	Output-unit-level	$391,500	67,500	cubic feet delivered	$ 5.80	per cubic foot delivered	Distribution costs increase with the cubic feet of packages delivered.
9	Administration	Facility sustaining	$255,000	39,750	direct manuf. labor-hours	$6.4151	per direct manuf. labor-hour	The demand for administrative resources increases with direct manufacturing labor-hours.

Step 4: Identify the Indirect Costs Associated with Each Cost-Allocation Base. In this step, Plastim's managers try to assign budgeted indirect costs for 2014 to activities (see Exhibit 4, column 3) on the basis of a cause-and-effect relationship between the cost-allocation base for an activity and the cost. For example, all costs that have a cause-and-effect relationship to cubic feet of packages moved are assigned to the distribution cost pool. Of course, the strength of the cause-and-effect relationship between the cost-allocation base and the cost of an activity varies across cost pools. For example, the cause-and-effect relationship between direct manufacturing labor-hours and administration activity costs, which as we discussed earlier is somewhat arbitrary, is not as strong as the relationship between setup-hours and setup activity costs, where setup-hours is the cost driver of setup costs.

Some costs can be directly identified with a particular activity. For example, salaries paid to design engineers and depreciation of equipment used in the design department are directly identified with the design activity. Other costs need to be allocated across activities. For example, on the basis of interviews or time records, manufacturing engineers and supervisors estimate the time they will spend on design, molding machine setup, and molding machine operations. If a manufacturing engineer spends 15% of her time on design, 45% of her time managing molding machine setups, and 40% of her time on molding operations, the company will allocate the manufacturing engineer's salary to each of these activities in proportion to the time spent. Still other costs are allocated to activity-cost pools using allocation bases that measure how these costs support different activities. For example, rent costs are allocated to activity cost pools on the basis of square-feet area used by different activities.

As you can see, all costs do not fit neatly into activity categories. Often, costs may first need to be allocated to activities (Stage 1 of the two-stage cost-allocation model) before the costs of the activities can be allocated to products (Stage 2).

The following table shows the assignment of costs to the seven activities identified earlier. Recall that Plastim's management accountants reclassify mold cleaning costs as a direct cost because these costs can be easily traced to a specific mold and lens.

	Design	Molding Machine Setups	Molding Operations	Mold Cleaning	Shipment Setup	Distribution	Administration	Total
Salaries (supervisors, design engineers, process engineers)	$320,000	$105,000	$137,500	$ 0	$21,000	$61,500	$165,000	$ 810,000
Wages of support staff	65,000	115,000	70,000	234,000	34,000	125,000	40,000	683,000
Depreciation	24,000	30,000	290,000	18,000	11,000	140,000	15,000	528,000
Maintenance	13,000	16,000	45,000	12,000	6,000	25,000	5,000	122,000
Power and fuel	18,000	20,000	35,000	6,000	5,000	30,000	10,000	124,000
Rent	10,000	14,000	60,000	0	4,000	10,000	20,000	118,000
Total	$450,000	$300,000	$637,500	$270,000	$81,000	$391,500	$255,000	$2,385,000

Step 5: Compute the Rate per Unit of Each Cost-Allocation Base. Exhibit 4, column 5, summarizes the calculation of the budgeted indirect-cost rates using the budgeted quantity of the cost-allocation base from Step 3 and the total budgeted indirect costs of each activity from Step 4.

Step 6: Compute the Indirect Costs Allocated to the Products. Exhibit 5 shows total budgeted indirect costs of $1,153,953 allocated to the simple lens and $961,047 allocated to the complex lens. Follow the budgeted indirect cost calculations for each lens in Exhibit 5. For each activity, Plastim's operations personnel indicate the total quantity of the cost-allocation base that will be used by each type of lens (recall that Plastim operates at capacity). For example, lines 15 and 16 in Exhibit 5 show that of the 2,000 total setup-hours, the S3 lens is budgeted to use 500 hours and the C5 lens 1,500 hours. The budgeted indirect cost rate is $150 per setup-hour (Exhibit 4, column 5, line 5). Therefore, the total budgeted cost of the setup activity allocated to the S3 lens is $75,000

Exhibit 5	Plastim's Product Costs Using Activity-Based Costing System

	A	B	C	D	E	F	G
		Home Insert Page Layout Formulas Data Review View					
1		60,000			15,000		
2		Simple Lenses (S3)			Complex Lenses (C5)		
3		Total	per Unit		Total	per Unit	Total
4	Cost Description	(1)	(2) = (1) ÷ 60,000		(3)	(4) = (3) ÷ 15,000	(5) = (1) + (3)
5	Direct costs						
6	Direct materials	$1,125,000	$18.75		$ 675,000	$ 45.00	$1,800,000
7	Direct manufacturing labor	600,000	10.00		195,000	13.00	795,000
8	Direct mold cleaning and maintenance costs	120,000	2.00		150,000	10.00	270,000
9	Total direct costs (Step 2)	1,845,000	30.75		1,020,000	68.00	2,865,000
10	Indirect Costs of Activities						
11	Design						
12	S3, 30 parts-sq.ft. × $4,500	135,000	2.25				} 450,000
13	C5, 70 parts-sq.ft. × $4,500				315,000	21.00	
14	Setup of molding machines						
15	S3, 500 setup-hours × $150	75,000	1.25				} 300,000
16	C5, 1,500 setup-hours × $150				225,000	15.00	
17	Machine operations						
18	S3, 9,000 molding machine-hours × $50	450,000	7.50				} 637,500
19	C5, 3,750 molding machine-hours × $50				187,500	12.50	
20	Shipment setup						
21	S3, 100 shipments × $405	40,500	0.67				} 81,000
22	C5, 100 shipments × $405				40,500	2.70	
23	Distribution						
24	S3, 45,000 cubic feet delivered × $5.80	261,000	4.35				} 391,500
25	C5, 22,500 cubic feet delivered × $5.80				130,500	8.70	
26	Administration						
27	S3, 30,000 dir. manuf. labor-hours × $6.4151	192,453	3.21				} 255,000
28	C5, 9,750 dir. manuf. labor-hours × $6.4151				62,547	4.17	
29	Total indirect costs allocated (Step 6)	1,153,953	19.23		961,047	64.07	2,115,000
30	Total Costs (Step 7)	$2,998,953	$49.98		$1,981,047	$132.07	$4,980,000
31							

(500 setup-hours × $150 per setup-hour) and to the C5 lens is $225,000 (1,500 setup-hours × $150 per setup-hour). Budgeted setup cost per unit equals $1.25 ($75,000 ÷ 60,000 units) for the S3 lens and $15 ($225,000 ÷ 15,000 units) for the C5 lens.

Step 7: Compute the Total Cost of the Products by Adding All Direct and Indirect Costs Assigned to the Products. Exhibit 5 presents the product costs for the simple and complex lenses. The direct costs are calculated in Step 2, and the indirect costs are calculated in Step 6. The ABC system overview in Exhibit 3 shows three direct-cost categories and six indirect-cost categories. The budgeted cost of each lens type in Exhibit 5 has nine line items, three for direct costs and six for indirect costs. The differences between the ABC product costs of S3 and C5 calculated in Exhibit 5 highlight how each of these products uses different amounts of direct and indirect costs in each activity area.

We emphasize two features of ABC systems. First, these systems identify all costs used by products, whether the costs are variable or fixed in the short run. When making long-run strategic decisions using ABC information, managers want revenues to exceed total costs. Otherwise, a company will make losses and will be unable to continue in business. Second, recognizing the hierarchy of costs is critical when allocating costs to products.

Decision Point

How do managers cost products or services using ABC systems?

Management accountants use the cost hierarchy to first calculate the total costs of each product. They then derive per-unit costs by dividing total costs by the number of units produced.

Comparing Alternative Costing Systems

Exhibit 6 compares the simple costing system using a single indirect-cost pool (Exhibits 1 and 2) that Plastim had been using and the ABC system (Exhibits 3 and 5). Note three points in Exhibit 6, consistent with the guidelines for refining a costing system: (1) ABC systems trace more costs as direct costs; (2) ABC systems create homogeneous cost pools linked to different activities; and (3) for each activity-cost pool, ABC systems seek a cost-allocation base that has a cause-and-effect relationship with costs in the cost pool.

The homogeneous cost pools and the choice of cost-allocation bases, tied to the cost hierarchy, give Plastim's managers greater confidence in the activity and product cost numbers from the ABC system. The bottom part of Exhibit 6 shows that allocating costs to lenses using only an output unit–level allocation base—direct manufacturing labor-hours, as in the single indirect-cost pool system used prior to ABC—overcosts the simple S3 lens by $8.77 per unit and undercosts the complex C5 lens by $35.07 per unit. The C5 lens uses a disproportionately larger amount of output unit–level, batch-level, and product-sustaining costs than is represented by the direct manufacturing labor-hour cost-allocation base. The S3 lens uses a disproportionately smaller amount of these costs.

Exhibit 6	Comparing Alternative Costing Systems

	Simple Costing System Using a Single Indirect-Cost Pool (1)	ABC System (2)	Difference (3) = (2) − (1)
Direct-cost categories	2	3	1
	Direct materials	Direct materials	
	Direct manufacturing labor	Direct manufacturing labor	
		Direct mold cleaning and maintenance labor	
Total direct costs	$2,595,000	$2,865,000	$270,000
Indirect-cost pools	1	6	5
	Single indirect-cost pool allocated using direct manufacturing labor-hours	Design (parts-square feet)[1]	
		Molding machine setup (setup-hours)	
		Machine operations (molding machine-hours)	
		Shipment setup (number of shipments)	
		Distribution (cubic feet delivered)	
		Administration (direct manufacturing labor-hours)	
Total indirect costs	$2,385,000	$2,115,000	($270,000)
Total costs assigned to simple (S3) lens	$3,525,000	$2,998,953	($526,047)
Cost per unit of simple (S3) lens	$58.75	$49.98	($8.77)
Total costs assigned to complex (C5) lens	$1,455,000	$1,981,047	$526,047
Cost per unit of complex (C5) lens	$97.00	$132.07	$35.07

[1]Cost drivers for the various indirect-cost pools are shown in parentheses.

The benefit of an ABC system is that it provides information to make better decisions. But managers must weigh this benefit against the measurement and implementation costs of an ABC system.

Considerations in Implementing Activity-Based Costing Systems

◄ Learning Objective 6

Evaluate the costs and benefits of implementing activity-based costing systems

…measurement difficulties versus more accurate costs that aid in decision making when products make diverse demands on indirect resources

Managers choose the level of detail to use in a costing system by evaluating the expected costs of the system against the expected benefits that result from better decisions.

Benefits and Costs of Activity-Based Costing Systems

Here are some of the telltale signs of when an ABC system is likely to provide the most benefits:

- Significant amounts of indirect costs are allocated using only one or two cost pools.

- All or most indirect costs are identified as output unit–level costs (few indirect costs are described as batch-level costs, product-sustaining costs, or facility-sustaining costs).

- Products make diverse demands on resources because of differences in volume, process steps, batch size, or complexity.

- Products that a company is well-suited to make and sell show small profits; whereas products that a company is less suited to make and sell show large profits.

- Operations staff has substantial disagreement with the reported costs of manufacturing and marketing products and services.

When managers decide to implement ABC, they must make important choices about the level of detail to use. Should managers choose many finely specified activities, cost drivers, and cost pools, or would a few suffice? For example, Plastim's managers could identify a different molding machine-hour rate for each different type of molding machine. In making such choices, managers weigh the benefits against the costs and limitations of implementing a more detailed costing system.

The main costs and limitations of an ABC system are the measurements necessary to implement it. ABC systems require managers to estimate costs of activity pools and to identify and measure cost drivers for these pools to serve as cost-allocation bases. Even basic ABC systems require many calculations to determine costs of products and services. These measurements are costly. Activity-cost rates also need to be updated regularly.

As ABC systems get very detailed and more cost pools are created, more allocations are necessary to calculate activity costs for each cost pool, which increases the chances of misidentifying the costs of different activity cost pools. For example, supervisors are more prone to incorrectly identify the time they spend on different activities if they have to allocate their time over five activities rather than only two activities.

Occasionally, managers are also forced to use allocation bases for which data are readily available rather than allocation bases they would have liked to use. For example, a manager might be forced to use the number of loads moved, instead of the degree of difficulty and distance of different loads moved, as the allocation base for material-handling costs because data on degree of difficulty and distance of moves are difficult to obtain. When incorrect cost-allocation bases are used, activity-cost information can be misleading. For example, if the cost per load moved decreases, a company may conclude that it has become more efficient in its materials-handling operations. In fact, the lower cost per load moved may have resulted solely from moving many lighter loads over shorter distances.

Many companies, such as Kanthal, a Swedish heating elements manufacturer, have found the strategic and operational benefits of a less-detailed ABC system to be good enough to not warrant incurring the costs and challenges of operating a more detailed system. Other organizations, such as Hewlett-Packard, have implemented ABC in only certain divisions (such as the Roseville Networks Division, which manufactures printed circuit boards) or functions (such as procurement and production). As improvements in information technology and accompanying declines in measurement costs continue, more detailed ABC systems have become a practical alternative in many companies. As these advancements become more widespread, more detailed ABC systems will be better able to pass the cost–benefit test.

Global surveys of company practice suggest that ABC implementation varies among companies. Nevertheless, its framework and ideas provide a standard for judging whether any simple costing system is good enough for a particular management's purposes. ABC thinking can help managers improve any simple costing system.

Behavioral Issues in Implementing Activity-Based Costing Systems

Successfully implementing ABC systems requires more than an understanding of the technical details. ABC implementation often represents a significant change in the costing system and, as the chapter indicates, requires a manager to choose how to define activities and the level of detail. What then are some of the behavioral issues that managers and management accountants must be sensitive to?

1. **Gaining support of top management and creating a sense of urgency for the ABC effort.** This requires managers and management accountants to clearly communicate the strategic benefits of ABC, such as improvements in product and process design. For example, at USAA Federal Savings Bank, managers calculated the cost of individual activities such as opening and closing accounts and demonstrated how the information gained from ABC provided insights into the efficiency of bank operations, which were previously unavailable.

2. **Creating a guiding coalition of managers throughout the value chain for the ABC effort.** ABC systems measure how the resources of an organization are used. Managers responsible for these resources have the best knowledge about activities and cost drivers. Getting managers to cooperate and take the initiative for implementing ABC is essential for gaining the required expertise, the proper credibility, greater commitment, valuable coordination, and the necessary leadership.

3. **Educating and training employees in ABC as a basis for employee empowerment.** Management accountants must disseminate information about ABC throughout the organization to enable employees in all areas of a business to use their knowledge of ABC to make improvements. For example, WS Industries, an Indian manufacturer of insulators, not only shared ABC information with its workers but also established an incentive plan that gave them a percentage of the cost savings. The results were dramatic because employees were empowered and motivated to implement numerous cost-saving projects.

4. **Seeking small short-run successes as proof that the ABC implementation is yielding results.** Too often, managers and management accountants seek big results and major changes far too quickly. In many situations, achieving a significant change overnight is difficult. However, showing how ABC information has helped improve a process and save costs, even if only in small ways, motivates the team to stay on course and build momentum. The credibility gained from small victories leads to additional and bigger improvements involving larger numbers of people and different parts of the organization. Eventually ABC becomes rooted in the culture of the organization. Sharing short-term successes also helps motivate employees to be innovative. At USAA Federal Savings Bank, managers created a "process improvement" mailbox in Microsoft Outlook to facilitate the sharing of process improvement ideas.

5. **Recognizing that ABC information is not perfect because it balances the need for better information against the costs of creating a complex system that few managers**

and employees can understand. The management accountant must help managers recognize both the value and the limitations of ABC and not oversell it. Open and honest communication about ABC ensures that managers use ABC thoughtfully to make good decisions. Managers can then make critical judgments without being adversarial and can ask tough questions to help drive better decisions about the system.

Decision Point

What should managers consider when deciding to implement ABC systems?

Activity-Based Management

The emphasis of this chapter so far has been on the role of ABC systems in obtaining better product costs. However, Plastim's managers must now use this information to make decisions (Step 4 of the five-step decision process) and to implement the decision, evaluate performance, and learn (Step 5). **Activity-based management (ABM)** is a method of management decision making that uses activity-based costing information to improve customer satisfaction and profitability. We define ABM broadly to include decisions about pricing and product mix, cost reduction, process improvement, and product and process design.

Learning Objective 7

Explain how managers use activity-based costing systems in activity-based management

...such as pricing decisions, product-mix decisions, and cost reduction

Pricing and Product-Mix Decisions

An ABC system gives managers information about the costs of making and selling diverse products. With this information, managers can make pricing and product-mix decisions. For example, the ABC system indicates that Plastim can match its competitor's price of $53 for the S3 lens and still make a profit because the ABC cost of S3 is $49.98 (see Exhibit 5).

Plastim's managers offer Giovanni Motors a price of $52 for the S3 lens. Plastim's managers are confident that they can use the deeper understanding of costs that the ABC system provides to improve efficiency and further reduce the cost of the S3 lens. Without information from the ABC system, Plastim managers might have erroneously concluded that they would incur an operating loss on the S3 lens at a price of $53. This incorrect conclusion would have probably caused Plastim to reduce or exit its business in simple lenses and focus instead on complex lenses, where its single indirect-cost-pool system indicated it is very profitable.

Focusing on complex lenses would have been a mistake. The ABC system indicates that the cost of making the complex lens is much higher—$132.07 versus $97 indicated by the direct manufacturing labor-hour-based costing system Plastim had been using. As Plastim's operations staff had thought all along, Plastim has no competitive advantage in making C5 lenses. At a price of $137 per lens for C5, the profit margin is very small ($137.00 − $132.07 = $4.93). As Plastim reduces its prices on simple lenses, it would need to negotiate a higher price for complex lenses with Giovanni Motors.

Cost Reduction and Process Improvement Decisions

Managers use ABC systems to focus on how and where to reduce costs. They set cost reduction targets for the cost per unit of the cost-allocation base in different activity areas. For example, the supervisor of the distribution activity area at Plastim could have a performance target of decreasing distribution cost per cubic foot of products delivered from $5.80 to $5.40 by reducing distribution labor and warehouse rental costs. The goal is to reduce these costs by improving the way work is done without compromising customer service or the actual or perceived value (usefulness) customers obtain from the product or service. That is, the supervisor will attempt to take out only those costs that are *nonvalue added.* Controlling physical cost drivers, such as setup-hours or cubic feet delivered, is another fundamental way that operating personnel manage costs. For example, the distribution department can decrease distribution costs by packing the lenses in a way that reduces the bulkiness of the packages delivered.

The following table shows the reduction in distribution costs of the S3 and C5 lenses as a result of actions that lower cost per cubic foot delivered (from $5.80 to $5.40) and total cubic feet of deliveries (from 45,000 to 40,000 for S3 and 22,500 to 20,000 for C5).

	60,000 (S3) Lenses		15,000 (C5) Lenses	
	Total (1)	per Unit (2) = (1) ÷ 60,000	Total (3)	per Unit (4) = (3) ÷ 15,000
Distribution costs (from Exhibit 5)				
S3: 45,000 cubic × $5.80/cubic foot	$261,000	$4.35		
C5: 22,500 cubic × $5.80/cubic foot			$130,500	$8.70
Distribution costs as a result of process improvements				
S3: 40,000 cubic × $5.40/cubic foot	216,000	3.60		
C5: 20,000 cubic × $5.40/cubic foot			108,000	7.20
Savings in distribution costs from process improvements	$ 45,000	$0.75	$ 22,500	$1.50

In the long run, total distribution costs will decrease from $391,500 ($261,000 + $130,500) to $324,000 ($216,000 + $108,000). In the short run, however, distribution costs may be fixed and may not decrease. Suppose all $391,500 of distribution costs are fixed costs in the short run. The efficiency improvements (using less distribution labor and space) mean that the same $391,500 of distribution costs can now be used to distribute

$$72,500 \left(= \frac{\$391,500}{\$5.40 \text{ per cubic feet}} \right)$$ cubic feet of lenses. In this case, how should costs be

allocated to the S3 and C5 lenses?

ABC systems distinguish costs incurred from resources used to design, manufacture, and deliver products and services. For the distribution activity, after process improvements,

Costs incurred = $391,500

Resources used = $216,000 (for S3 lens) + $108,000 (for CL5 lens) = $324,000

On the basis of the resources used by each product, Plastim's ABC system allocates $216,000 to S3 and $108,000 to C5 for a total of $324,000. The difference of $67,500 ($391,500 − $324,000) is shown as costs of unused but available distribution capacity. Plastim's ABC system does not allocate the costs of unused capacity to products so as not to burden the product costs of S3 and C5 with the cost of resources not used by these products. Instead, the system highlights the amount of unused capacity as a separate line item to alert managers to reduce these costs, such as by redeploying labor to other uses or laying off workers.

Design Decisions

ABC systems help managers to evaluate the effect of current product and process designs on activities and costs and to identify new designs to reduce costs. For example, design decisions that decrease the complexity of the mold reduce costs of design, but also materials, labor, machine setups, machine operations, and mold cleaning and maintenance because a less-complex design reduces scrap and the time for setups and operations of the molding machine. Plastim's customers may be willing to give up some features of the lens in exchange for a lower price. Note that Plastim's previous costing system, which used direct manufacturing labor-hours as the cost-allocation base for all indirect costs, would have mistakenly signaled that Plastim choose those designs that most reduce direct manufacturing labor-hours when, in fact, there is a weak cause-and-effect relationship between direct manufacturing labor-hours and indirect costs.

Planning and Managing Activities

Most managers implementing ABC systems for the first time start by analyzing actual costs to identify activity-cost pools and activity-cost rates. Managers then calculate a budgeted rate (as in the Plastim example) that they use for planning, making decisions, and managing activities. At year-end, managers compare budgeted costs and actual costs to evaluate how well activities were managed. Management accountants make adjustments for underallocated or overallocated indirect costs for each activity. As activities and processes change, managers calculate new activity-cost rates.

Decision Point
How can ABC systems be used to manage better?

Activity-Based Costing and Department Costing Systems

Learning Objective 8

Compare activity-based costing systems and department costing systems

...activity-based costing systems are a refinement of department costing systems into more-focused and homogenous cost pools

Companies often use costing systems that have features of ABC systems—such as multiple cost pools and multiple cost-allocation bases—but that do not emphasize individual activities. Many companies have evolved their costing systems from using a single indirect cost rate system to using separate indirect cost rates for each department (such as design, manufacturing, and distribution) or each subdepartment (such as machining and assembly departments within manufacturing) that can represent broad tasks. ABC systems, with its focus on specific activities, are a further refinement of department costing systems. In this section, we compare ABC systems and department costing systems.

Plastim uses the design department indirect cost rate to cost its design activity. Plastim calculates the design activity rate by dividing total design department costs by total parts-square feet, a measure of the complexity of the mold and the driver of design department costs. Plastim does not find it worthwhile to calculate separate activity rates within the design department for the different design activities, such as designing products, making temporary molds, and designing processes. The complexity of a mold is an appropriate cost-allocation base for costs incurred in each design activity because design department costs are homogeneous with respect to this cost-allocation base.

In contrast, the manufacturing department identifies two activity cost pools—a setup cost pool and a machine operations cost pool—instead of a single manufacturing department overhead cost pool. It identifies these activity cost pools for two reasons. First, each of these activities within manufacturing incurs significant costs and has a different cost driver, setup-hours for the setup cost pool and machine-hours for the machine operations cost pool. Second, the S3 and C5 lenses do not use resources from these two activity areas in the same proportion. For example, C5 uses 75% (1,500 ÷ 2,000) of the setup-hours but only 29.4% (3,750 ÷ 12,750) of the machine-hours. Using only machine-hours, say, to allocate all manufacturing department costs at Plastim would result in C5 being undercosted because it would not be charged for the significant amounts of setup resources it actually uses.

For the reasons we just explained, using department indirect cost rates to allocate costs to products results in similar information as activity cost rates if (1) a single activity accounts for a sizable proportion of the department's costs; or (2) significant costs are incurred on different activities within a department, but each activity has the same cost driver and therefore cost-allocation base (as was the case in Plastim's design department). From a purely product costing standpoint, department and activity indirect cost rates will also result in the same product costs if (1) significant costs are incurred for different activities with different cost-allocation bases within a department but (2) different products use resources from the different activity areas in the same proportions (for example, if C5 had used 65%, say, of the setup-hours and 65% of the machine-hours). In this case, though, not identifying activities and cost drivers within departments conceals activity cost information that would help managers manage costs and improve design and processes.

Decision Point

When can department costing systems be used instead of ABC systems?

We close this section with a note of caution: Do not assume that because department costing systems require the creation of multiple indirect cost pools that they properly recognize the drivers of costs within departments as well as how resources are used by products. As we have indicated, in many situations, department costing systems can be refined using ABC. Emphasizing activities leads to more-focused and homogeneous cost pools, aids in identifying cost-allocation bases for activities that have a better cause-and-effect relationship with the costs in activity cost pools, and leads to better design and process decisions. But these benefits of an ABC system would need to be balanced against its costs and limitations.

ABC in Service and Merchandising Companies

Although many early examples of ABC originated in manufacturing, managers also use ABC in service and merchandising companies. For instance, the Plastim example includes the application of ABC to a service activity—design—and to a merchandising activity—distribution. Companies such as the USAA Federal Savings Bank, Braintree Hospital, BCTel in the telecommunications industry, and Union Pacific in the railroad industry have implemented some form of ABC systems to identify profitable product mixes, improve efficiency, and satisfy customers. Similarly, many retail and wholesale companies—for example, Supervalu, a retailer and distributor of grocery store products, and Owens and Minor, a medical supplies distributor—have used ABC systems. A large number of financial services companies (as well as other companies) employ variations of ABC systems to analyze and improve the profitability of their customer interactions.

The widespread use of ABC systems in service and merchandising companies reinforces the idea that ABC systems are used by managers for strategic decisions rather than for inventory valuation. (Inventory valuation is fairly straightforward in merchandising companies and not needed in service companies.) Service companies, in particular, find great value from ABC because a vast majority of their cost structure is composed of indirect costs. After all, there are few direct costs when a bank makes a loan or when a representative answers a phone call at a call center. As we have seen, a major benefit of ABC is its ability to assign indirect costs to cost objects by identifying activities and cost drivers. As a result, ABC systems provide greater insight than traditional systems into the management of these indirect costs. The general approach to ABC in service and merchandising companies is similar to the ABC approach in manufacturing.

The USAA Federal Savings Bank followed the approach described in this chapter when it implemented ABC in its banking operations. Managers calculated the cost rates of various activities, such as performing ATM transactions, opening and closing accounts, administering mortgages, and processing Visa transactions by dividing the cost of these activities by the time available to do them. Managers used these time-based rates to cost individual products, such as checking accounts, mortgages, and Visa cards, and to calculate the costs of supporting different types of customers. Information from this time-driven activity-based costing system helped the USAA Federal Savings Bank to improve its processes and to identify profitable products and customer segments. Concepts in Action: Hospitals Use Time-Driven Activity-Based Costing to Reduce Costs and Improve Care describes how hospitals, such as the M.D. Anderson Cancer Research Center in Houston and Children's Hospital in Boston, have similarly benefited from using ABC analysis.

Activity-based costing raises some interesting issues when it is applied to a public service institution, such as the U.S. Postal Service. The costs of delivering mail to remote locations are far greater than the costs of delivering mail within urban areas. However, for fairness and community-building reasons, the Postal Service cannot charge higher prices to customers in remote areas. In this case, activity-based costing is valuable for understanding, managing, and reducing costs but not for pricing decisions.

Concepts in Action ▷ Hospitals Use Time-Driven Activity-Based Costing to Reduce Costs and Improve Care

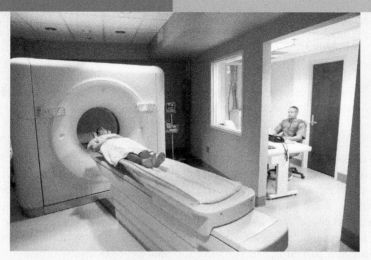

In the United States, health care costs in 2012 exceeded 17% of gross domestic product and are expected to rise to 19.6% by 2021. Several medical centers, such as the M.D. Anderson Cancer Center in Houston and Children's Hospital in Boston, are using time-driven activity-based costing (TDABC) to help bring accurate cost and value measurement practices into the health care delivery system.

TDABC assigns all of the organization's resource costs to cost objects using a framework that requires two sets of estimates. TDABC first calculates the cost of supplying resource capacity, such as a doctor's time. The total cost of resources—including personnel, supervision, insurance, space occupancy, technology, and supplies—is divided by the available capacity—the time available for doctors to do their work—to obtain the capacity cost rate. Next, TDABC uses the capacity cost rate to drive resource costs to cost objects, such as the number of patients seen, by estimating the demand for resource capacity (time) that the cost object requires.

Medical centers implementing TDABC have succeeded in reducing costs. For head and neck procedures at the M.D. Anderson Cancer Center, the TDABC-modified process resulted in a 16% reduction in process time, a 12% decrease in costs for technical staff, and a 36% reduction in total cost per patient. Prior to implementing TDABC, managers did not have the necessary information to make decisions to reduce costs.

More broadly, health care providers implementing TDABC have found that better outcomes for patients often go hand in hand with lower total costs. For example, spending more on early detection and better diagnosis of disease reduces patient suffering and often leads to less-complex and less-expensive care. With the insights from TDABC, health care providers can utilize medical staff, equipment, facilities, and administrative resources far more efficiently; streamline the path of patients through the system; and select treatment approaches that improve outcomes while eliminating services that do not.

Sources: Based on R. S. Kaplan and S. R. Anderson, "The Innovation of Time-Driven Activity-Based Costing," *Cost Management* (March-April 2007); R. S. Kaplan and S. R. Anderson, "Time-Drive Activity-Based Costing" (Boston, MA: Harvard Business School Press, 2007); and R. S. Kaplan and M. E. Porter, "How to Solve the Cost Crisis in Health Care," *Harvard Business Review* (September 2011); and Louise Radnofsky, "Steep Rise in Health Costs Projected," *The Wall Street Journal* (June 12, 2012).

Problem for Self-Study

Family Supermarkets (FS) has decided to increase the size of its Memphis store. It wants information about the profitability of individual product lines: soft drinks, fresh produce, and packaged food. FS provides the following data for 2014 for each product line:

	Soft Drinks	Fresh Produce	Packaged Food
Revenues	$317,400	$840,240	$483,960
Cost of goods sold	$240,000	$600,000	$360,000
Cost of bottles returned	$ 4,800	$ 0	$ 0
Number of purchase orders placed	144	336	144
Number of deliveries received	120	876	264
Hours of shelf-stocking time	216	2,160	1,080
Items sold	50,400	441,600	122,400

FS also provides the following information for 2014:

Activity (1)	Description of Activity (2)	Total Support Costs (3)	Cost-Allocation Base (4)
1. Bottle returns	Returning of empty bottles to store	$ 4,800	Direct tracing to soft-drink line
2. Ordering	Placing of orders for purchases	$ 62,400	624 purchase orders
3. Delivery	Physical delivery and receipt of merchandise	$100,800	1,260 deliveries
4. Shelf-stocking	Stocking of merchandise on store shelves and ongoing restocking	$ 69,120	3,456 hours of shelf-stocking time
5. Customer support	Assistance provided to customers, including checkout and bagging	$122,880	614,400 items sold
Total		$360,000	

Required

1. Family Supermarkets currently allocates store support costs (all costs other than cost of goods sold) to product lines on the basis of cost of goods sold of each product line. Calculate the operating income and operating income as a percentage of revenues for each product line.
2. If Family Supermarkets allocates store support costs (all costs other than cost of goods sold) to product lines using an ABC system, calculate the operating income and operating income as a percentage of revenues for each product line.
3. Comment on your answers in requirements 1 and 2.

Solution

1. The following table shows the operating income and operating income as a percentage of revenues for each product line. All store support costs (all costs other than cost of goods sold) are allocated to product lines using cost of goods sold of each product line as the cost-allocation base. Total store support costs equal $360,000 (cost of bottles returned, $4,800 + cost of purchase orders, $62,400 + cost of deliveries, $100,800 + cost of shelf-stocking, $69,120 + cost of customer support, $122,880). The allocation rate for store support costs = $360,000 ÷ $1,200,000 (soft drinks $240,000 + fresh produce $600,000 + packaged food, $360,000) = 30% of cost of goods sold. To allocate support costs to each product line, FS multiplies the cost of goods sold of each product line by 0.30.

	Soft Drinks	Fresh Produce	Packaged Food	Total
Revenues	$317,400	$840,240	$483,960	$1,641,600
Cost of goods sold	240,000	600,000	360,000	1,200,000
Store support cost				
($240,000; $600,000; $360,000) × 0.30	72,000	180,000	108,000	360,000
Total costs	312,000	780,000	468,000	1,560,000
Operating income	$ 5,400	$ 60,240	$ 15,960	$ 81,600
Operating income ÷ Revenues	1.70%	7.17%	3.30%	4.97%

2. The ABC system identifies bottle-return costs as a direct cost because these costs can be traced to the soft-drink product line. FS then calculates cost-allocation rates for each activity area (as in Step 5 of the seven-step costing system, described earlier). The activity rates are as follows.

Activity (1)	Cost Hierarchy (2)	Total Costs (3)	Quantity of Cost-Allocation Base (4)	Overhead Allocation Rate (5) = (3) ÷ (4)
Ordering	Batch-level	$ 62,400	624 purchase orders	$100 per purchase order
Delivery	Batch-level	$100,800	1,260 deliveries	$80 per delivery
Shelf-stocking	Output unit–level	$ 69,120	3,456 shelf-stocking hours	$20 per stocking-hour
Customer support	Output unit–level	$122,880	614,400 items sold	$0.20 per item sold

Store support costs for each product line by activity are obtained by multiplying the total quantity of the cost-allocation base for each product line by the activity cost rate. Operating income and operating income as a percentage of revenues for each product line are as follows.

	Soft Drinks	Fresh Produce	Packaged Food	Total
Revenues	$317,400	$840,240	$483,960	$1,641,600
Cost of goods sold	240,000	600,000	360,000	1,200,000
Bottle-return costs	4,800	0	0	4,800
Ordering costs				
(144; 336; 144) purchase orders × $100	14,400	33,600	14,400	62,400
Delivery costs				
(120; 876; 264) deliveries × $80	9,600	70,080	21,120	100,800
Shelf-stocking costs				
(216; 2,160; 1,080) stocking-hours × $20	4,320	43,200	21,600	69,120
Customer-support costs				
(50,400; 441,600; 122,400) items sold × $0.20	10,080	88,320	24,480	122,880
Total costs	283,200	835,200	441,600	1,560,000
Operating income	$ 34,200	$ 5,040	$ 42,360	$ 81,600
Operating income ÷ Revenues	10.78%	0.60%	8.75%	4.97%

3. Managers believe the ABC system is more credible than the simple costing system. The ABC system distinguishes the different types of activities at FS more precisely. It also tracks more accurately how individual product lines use resources. Rankings of relative profitability—operating income as a percentage of revenues—of the three product lines under the simple costing system and under the ABC system are as follows.

Simple Costing System		ABC Systemm	
1. Fresh produce	7.17%	1. Soft drinks	10.78%
2. Packaged food	3.30%	2. Packaged food	8.75%
3. Soft drinks	1.70%	3. Fresh produce	0.60%

The percentage of revenues, cost of goods sold, and activity costs for each product line are as follows.

	Soft Drinks	Fresh Produce	Packaged Food
Revenues	19.34%	51.18%	29.48%
Cost of goods sold	20.00	50.00	30.00
Bottle returns	100.00	0	0
Activity areas:			
Ordering	23.08	53.84	23.08
Delivery	9.53	69.52	20.95
Shelf-stocking	6.25	62.50	31.25
Customer support	8.20	71.88	19.92

Soft drinks have fewer deliveries and require less shelf-stocking time and customer support than either fresh produce or packaged food. Most major soft-drink suppliers deliver merchandise to the store shelves and stock the shelves themselves. In contrast, the fresh produce area has the most deliveries and consumes a large percentage of shelf-stocking time. It also has the highest number of individual sales items and so requires the most customer support. The simple costing system assumed that each product line used the resources in each activity area in the same ratio as their respective individual cost of goods sold to total cost of goods sold. Clearly, this assumption is incorrect. Relative to cost of goods sold, soft drinks and packaged food use fewer resources while fresh produce uses more resources. As a result, the ABC system reduces the costs assigned to soft drinks and packaged food and increases the costs assigned to fresh produce. The simple costing system is an example of averaging that is too broad.

FS managers can use the ABC information to guide decisions such as how to allocate a planned increase in floor space. An increase in the percentage of space allocated to soft drinks is warranted. Note, however, that ABC information is only one input into decisions about shelf-space allocation. In many situations, companies cannot make product decisions in isolation but must consider the effect that dropping or deemphasizing a product might have on customer demand for other products. For example, FS will have a minimum limit on the shelf space allocated to fresh produce because reducing the choice of fresh produce will lead to customers not shopping at FS, resulting in loss of sales of other, more profitable products.

Pricing decisions can also be made in a more informed way with ABC information. For example, suppose a competitor announces a 5% reduction in soft-drink prices. Given the 10.78% margin FS currently earns on its soft-drink product line, it has flexibility to reduce prices and still make a profit on this product line. In contrast, the simple costing system erroneously implied that soft drinks only had a 1.70% margin, leaving little room to counter a competitor's pricing initiatives.

▶ Decision Points

The following question-and-answer format summarizes the chapter's learning objectives. Each decision presents a key question related to a learning objective. The guidelines are the answer to that question.

Decision	Guidelines
1. When does product undercosting or overcosting occur?	Product undercosting (overcosting) occurs when a product or service consumes a high (low) level of resources but is reported to have a low (high) cost. Broad averaging, or peanut-butter costing, a common cause of undercosting or overcosting, is the result of using broad averages that uniformly assign, or spread, the cost of resources to products when the individual products use those resources in a nonuniform way. Product-cost cross-subsidization exists when one undercosted (overcosted) product results in at least one other product being overcosted (undercosted).
2. How do managers refine a costing system?	Refining a costing system means making changes that result in cost numbers that better measure the way different cost objects, such as products, use different amounts of resources of the company. These changes can require additional direct-cost tracing, the choice of more-homogeneous indirect cost pools, or the use of cost drivers as cost-allocation bases.
3. What is the difference between the design of a simple costing system and an activity-based costing (ABC) system?	The ABC system differs from the simple system by its fundamental focus on activities. The ABC system typically has more-homogeneous indirect-cost pools than the simple system, and more cost drivers are used as cost-allocation bases.
4. What is a cost hierarchy?	A cost hierarchy categorizes costs into different cost pools on the basis of the different types of cost-allocation bases or different degrees of difficulty in determining cause-and-effect (or benefits-received) relationships. A four-part hierarchy to cost products consists of output unit–level costs, batch-level costs, product-sustaining or service-sustaining costs, and facility-sustaining costs.
5. How do managers cost products or services using ABC systems?	In ABC, costs of activities are used to assign costs to other cost objects such as products or services based on the activities the products or services consume.
6. What should managers consider when deciding to implement ABC systems?	ABC systems are likely to yield the most decision-making benefits when indirect costs are a high percentage of total costs or when products and services make diverse demands on indirect resources. The main costs of ABC systems are the difficulties of the measurements necessary to implement and update the systems.

7. How can ABC systems be used to manage better?

Activity-based management (ABM) is a management method of decision making that uses ABC information to satisfy customers and improve profits. ABC systems are used for such management decisions as pricing, product-mix, cost reduction, process improvement, product and process redesign, and planning and managing activities.

8. When can department costing systems be used instead of ABC systems?

Activity-based costing systems are a refinement of department costing systems into more-focused and homogeneous cost pools. Cost information in department costing systems approximates cost information in ABC systems only when each department has a single activity (or a single activity accounts for a significant proportion of department costs) or a single cost driver for different activities or when different products use the different activities of the department in the same proportions.

Terms to Learn

This chapter contains definitions of the following important terms:

activity
activity-based costing (ABC)
activity-based management (ABM)
batch-level costs
cost hierarchy

facility-sustaining costs
output unit–level costs
product-cost cross-subsidization
product overcosting
product-sustaining costs

product undercosting
refined costing system
service-sustaining costs

Assignment Material

Questions

1 What is broad averaging, and what consequences can it have on costs?
2 Why should managers worry about product overcosting or undercosting?
3 What is costing system refinement? Describe three guidelines for refinement.
4 What is an activity-based approach to designing a costing system?
5 Describe four levels of a cost hierarchy.
6 Why is it important to classify costs into a cost hierarchy?
7 What are the key reasons for product cost differences between simple costing systems and ABC systems?
8 Describe four decisions for which ABC information is useful.
9 "Department indirect-cost rates are never activity-cost rates." Do you agree? Explain.
10 Describe four signs that help indicate when ABC systems are likely to provide the most benefits.
11 What are the main costs and limitations of implementing ABC systems?
12 "ABC systems only apply to manufacturing companies." Do you agree? Explain.
13 "Activity-based costing is the wave of the present and the future. All companies should adopt it." Do you agree? Explain.
14 "Increasing the number of indirect-cost pools is guaranteed to sizably increase the accuracy of product or service costs." Do you agree? Why?
15 The controller of a retail company has just had a $50,000 request to implement an ABC system quickly turned down. A senior vice president, in rejecting the request, noted, "Given a choice, I will always prefer a $50,000 investment in improving things a customer sees or experiences, such as our shelves or our store layout. How does a customer benefit by our spending $50,000 on a supposedly better accounting system?" How should the controller respond?

MyAccountingLab

Exercises

16 Cost hierarchy. Forrester, Inc., manufactures karaoke machines for several well-known companies. The machines differ significantly in their complexity and their manufacturing batch sizes. The following costs were incurred in 2014:

a. Indirect manufacturing labor costs such as supervision that supports direct manufacturing labor, $825,000

b. Procurement costs of placing purchase orders, receiving materials, and paying suppliers related to the number of purchase orders placed, $525,000

c. Cost of indirect materials, $160,000

d. Costs incurred to set up machines each time a different product needs to be manufactured, $365,000

e. Designing processes, drawing process charts, and making engineering process changes for products, $287,500

f. Machine-related overhead costs such as depreciation, maintenance, and production engineering, $950,000 (These resources relate to the activity of running the machines.)

g. Plant management, plant rent, and plant insurance, $512,000

Required

1. Classify each of the preceding costs as output unit–level, batch-level, product-sustaining, or facility-sustaining. Explain each answer.

2. Consider two types of karaoke machines made by Forrester, Inc. One machine, designed for professional use, is complex to make and is produced in many batches. The other machine, designed for home use, is simple to make and is produced in few batches. Suppose that Forrester needs the same number of machine-hours to make each type of karaoke machine and that Forrester allocates all overhead costs using machine-hours as the only allocation base. How, if at all, would the machines be miscosted? Briefly explain why.

3. How is the cost hierarchy helpful to Forrester in managing its business?

17 ABC, cost hierarchy, service. (CMA, adapted) Vineyard Test Laboratories does heat testing (HT) and stress testing (ST) on materials and operates at capacity. Under its current simple costing system, Vineyard aggregates all operating costs of $1,190,000 into a single overhead cost pool. Vineyard calculates a rate per test-hour of $17 ($1,190,000 ÷ 70,000 total test-hours). HT uses 40,000 test-hours, and ST uses 30,000 test-hours. Gary Celeste, Vineyard's controller, believes that there is enough variation in test procedures and cost structures to establish separate costing and billing rates for HT and ST. The market for test services is becoming competitive. Without this information, any miscosting and mispricing of its services could cause Vineyard to lose business. Celeste divides Vineyard's costs into four activity-cost categories.

a. Direct-labor costs, $146,000. These costs can be directly traced to HT, $100,000, and ST, $46,000.

b. Equipment-related costs (rent, maintenance, energy, and so on), $350,000. These costs are allocated to HT and ST on the basis of test-hours.

c. Setup costs, $430,000. These costs are allocated to HT and ST on the basis of the number of setup-hours required. HT requires 13,600 setup-hours, and ST requires 3,600 setup-hours.

d. Costs of designing tests, $264,000. These costs are allocated to HT and ST on the basis of the time required for designing the tests. HT requires 3,000 hours, and ST requires 1,400 hours.

Required

1. Classify each activity cost as output unit–level, batch-level, product- or service-sustaining, or facility-sustaining. Explain each answer.

2. Calculate the cost per test-hour for HT and ST. Explain briefly the reasons why these numbers differ from the $17 per test-hour that Vineyard calculated using its simple costing system.

3. Explain the accuracy of the product costs calculated using the simple costing system and the ABC system. How might Vineyard's management use the cost hierarchy and ABC information to better manage its business?

18 Alternative allocation bases for a professional services firm. The Walliston Group (WG) provides tax advice to multinational firms. WG charges clients for (a) direct professional time (at an hourly rate) and (b) support services (at 30% of the direct professional costs billed). The three professionals in WG and their rates per professional hour are as follows:

Professional	Billing Rate per Hour
Max Walliston	$640
Alexa Boutin	220
Jacob Abbington	100

WG has just prepared the May 2014 bills for two clients. The hours of professional time spent on each client are as follows:

	Hours per Client	
Professional	**San Antonio Dominion**	**Amsterdam Enterprises**
Walliston	26	4
Boutin	5	14
Abbington	39	52
Total	70	70

Required

1. What amounts did WG bill to San Antonio Dominion and Amsterdam Enterprises for May 2014?
2. Suppose support services were billed at $75 per professional labor-hour (instead of 30% of professional labor costs). How would this change affect the amounts WG billed to the two clients for May 2014? Comment on the differences between the amounts billed in requirements 1 and 2.
3. How would you determine whether professional labor costs or professional labor-hours is the more appropriate allocation base for WG's support services?

19 Plant-wide, department, and ABC indirect cost rates. Automotive Products (AP) designs and produces automotive parts. In 2014, actual variable manufacturing overhead is $308,600. AP's simple costing system allocates variable manufacturing overhead to its three customers based on machine-hours and prices its contracts based on full costs. One of its customers has regularly complained of being charged noncompetitive prices, so AP's controller Devon Smith realizes that it is time to examine the consumption of overhead resources more closely. He knows that there are three main departments that consume overhead resources: design, production, and engineering. Interviews with the department personnel and examination of time records yield the following detailed information.

	Home	Insert	Page Layout	Formulas	Data	Review	View	
	A	B	C	D	E	F	
1				Usage of Cost Drivers by Customer Contract			
2	**Department**	**Cost Driver**	**Manufacturing Overhead in 2014**	**United Motors**	**Holden Motors**	**Leland Auto**	
3	Design	CAD-design-hours	$ 39,000	110	200	80	
4	Production	Engineering-hours	29,600	70	60	240	
5	Engineering	Machine-hours	240,000	120	2,800	1,080	
6	Total		$308,600				

Required

1. Compute the manufacturing overhead allocated to each customer in 2014 using the simple costing system that uses machine-hours as the allocation base.
2. Compute the manufacturing overhead allocated to each customer in 2014 using department-based manufacturing overhead rates.
3. Comment on your answers in requirements 1 and 2. Which customer do you think was complaining about being overcharged in the simple system? If the new department-based rates are used to price contracts, which customer(s) will be unhappy? How would you respond to these concerns?
4. How else might AP use the information available from its department-by-department analysis of manufacturing overhead costs?
5. AP's managers are wondering if they should further refine the department-by-department costing system into an ABC system by identifying different activities within each department. Under what conditions would it not be worthwhile to further refine the department costing system into an ABC system?

20 Plant-wide, department, and activity-cost rates. Triumph Trophies makes trophies and plaques and operates at capacity. Triumph does large custom orders, such as the participant trophies for the Minnetonka Little League. The controller has asked you to compare plant-wide, department, and activity-based cost allocation.

Triumph Trophies Budgeted Information for the Year Ended November 30, 2014

Forming Department	Trophies	Plaques	Total
Direct materials	$26,000	$22,500	$48,500
Direct manufacturing labor	31,200	18,000	49,200
Overhead costs			
Set up			24,000
Supervision			20,772

Assembly Department	Trophies	Plaques	Total
Direct materials	$ 5,200	$18,750	$23,950
Direct manufacturing labor	15,600	21,000	36,600
Overhead costs			
Setup			46,000
Supervision			21,920

Other information follows:

Setup costs in each department vary with the number of batches processed in each department. The budgeted number of batches for each product line in each department is as follows:

	Trophies	Plaques
Forming department	40	116
Assembly department	43	103

Supervision costs in each department vary with direct manufacturing labor costs in each department.

Required

1. Calculate the budgeted cost of trophies and plaques based on a single plant-wide overhead rate, if total overhead is allocated based on total direct costs.
2. Calculate the budgeted cost of trophies and plaques based on departmental overhead rates, where forming department overhead costs are allocated based on direct manufacturing labor costs of the forming department and assembly department overhead costs are allocated based on total direct costs of the assembly department.
3. Calculate the budgeted cost of trophies and plaques if Triumph allocates overhead costs in each department using activity-based costing.
4. Explain how the disaggregation of information could improve or reduce decision quality.

21 ABC, process costing. Parker Company produces mathematical and financial calculators and operates at capacity. Data related to the two products are presented here:

	Mathematical	Financial
Annual production in units	50,000	100,000
Direct material costs	$150,000	$300,000
Direct manufacturing labor costs	$ 50,000	$100,000
Direct manufacturing labor-hours	2,500	5,000
Machine-hours	25,000	50,000
Number of production runs	50	50
Inspection hours	1,000	500

Total manufacturing overhead costs are as follows:

	Total
Machining costs	$375,000
Setup costs	120,000
Inspection costs	105,000

Required

1. Choose a cost driver for each overhead cost pool and calculate the manufacturing overhead cost per unit for each product.
2. Compute the manufacturing cost per unit for each product.
3. How might Parker's managers use the new cost information from its activity-based costing system to better manage its business?

22 Department costing, service company. CKM is an architectural firm that designs and builds buildings. It prices each job on a cost plus 20% basis. Overhead costs in 2014 are $4,011,780. CKM's simple costing system allocates overhead costs to its jobs based on number of jobs. There were three jobs in 2014. One customer, Sanders, has complained that the cost of its building in Chicago was not competitive. As a result, the controller has initiated a detailed review of the overhead allocation to determine if overhead costs are charged to jobs in proportion to consumption of overhead resources by jobs. She gathers the following information.

Department	Cost Driver	Overhead Costs in 2014	Quantity of Cost Drivers Used by Each Project		
			Sanders	Hanley	Stanley
Design	Design department hours	$ 1,500,000	1,000	5,000	4,000
Engineering	Number of engineers	$ 500,030	2,000	2,000	2,200
Construction	Labor-hours	$ 2,011,750	20,800	21,500	19,600
		$ 4,011,780			

Required

1. Compute the overhead allocated to each project in 2014 using the simple costing system.
2. Compute the overhead allocated to each project in 2014 using department overhead cost rates.
3. Do you think Sanders had a valid reason for dissatisfaction with the cost? How does the allocation based on department rates change costs for each project?
4. What value, if any, would CKM get by allocating costs of each department based on the activities done in that department?

23 Activity-based costing, service company. Speediprint Corporation owns a small printing press that prints leaflets, brochures, and advertising materials. Speediprint classifies its various printing jobs as standard jobs or special jobs. Speediprint's simple job-costing system has two direct-cost categories (direct materials and direct labor) and a single indirect-cost pool. Speediprint operates at capacity and allocates all indirect costs using printing machine-hours as the allocation base.

Speediprint is concerned about the accuracy of the costs assigned to standard and special jobs and therefore is planning to implement an activity-based costing system. Speediprint's ABC system would have the same direct-cost categories as its simple costing system. However, instead of a single indirect-cost pool there would now be six categories for assigning indirect costs: design, purchasing, setup, printing machine operations, marketing, and administration. To see how activity-based costing would affect the costs of standard and special jobs, Speediprint collects the following information for the fiscal year 2014 that just ended.

	A	B	C	D	E F G H
1		Standard Job	Special Job	Total	Cause-and-Effect Relationship Between Allocation Base and Activity Cost
2	Number of printing jobs	400	200		
3	Price per job	$ 600	$ 750		
4	Cost of supplies per job	$ 100	$ 125		
5	Direct labor costs per job	$ 90	$ 100		
6	Printing machine-hours per job	10	10		
7	Cost of printing machine operations			$ 75,000	Indirect costs of operating printing machines
8					increase with printing machine-hours
9	Setup-hours per job	4	7		
10	Setup costs			$ 45,000	Indirect setup costs increase with setup-hours
11	Total number of purchase orders	400	500		
12	Purchase order costs			$ 18,000	Indirect purchase order costs increase with
13					number of purchase orders
14	Design costs	$4,000	$16,000	$ 20,000	Design costs are allocated to standard and special
15					jobs based on a special study of the design department
16	Marketing costs as a percentage of revenues	5%	5%	$ 19,500	
17	Administration costs			$ 24,000	Demand for administrative resources increases with direct labor costs

1. Calculate the cost of a standard job and a special job under the simple costing system.
2. Calculate the cost of a standard job and a special job under the activity-based costing system.
3. Compare the costs of a standard job and a special job in requirements 1 and 2. Why do the simple and activity-based costing systems differ in the cost of a standard job and a special job?
4. How might Speediprint use the new cost information from its activity-based costing system to better manage its business?

24 Activity-based costing, manufacturing. Fancy Doors, Inc., produces two types of doors, interior and exterior. The company's simple costing system has two direct cost categories (materials and labor) and one indirect cost pool. The simple costing system allocates indirect costs on the basis of machine-hours. Recently, the owners of Fancy Doors have been concerned about a decline in the market share for their interior doors, usually their biggest seller. Information related to Fancy Doors production for the most recent year follows:

	Interior	Exterior
Units sold	3,200	1,800
Selling price	$ 250	$ 400
Direct material cost per unit	$ 60	$ 90
Direct manufacturing labor cost per hour	$ 32	$ 32
Direct manufacturing labor-hours per unit	1.50	2.25
Production runs	40	85
Material moves	72	168
Machine setups	45	155
Machine-hours	5,500	4,500
Number of inspections	250	150

The owners have heard of other companies in the industry that are now using an activity-based costing system and are curious how an ABC system would affect their product costing decisions. After analyzing the indirect cost pool for Fancy Doors, the owners identify six activities as generating indirect costs: production scheduling, material handling, machine setup, assembly, inspection, and marketing. Fancy Doors collected the following data related to the indirect cost activities:

Activity	Activity Cost	Activity Cost Driver
Production scheduling	$190,000	Production runs
Material handling	$ 90,000	Material moves
Machine setup	$ 50,000	Machine setups
Assembly	$120,000	Machine-hours
Inspection	$ 16,000	Number of inspections

Marketing costs were determined to be 3% of the sales revenue for each type of door.

1. Calculate the cost of an interior door and an exterior door under the existing simple costing system.
2. Calculate the cost of an interior door and an exterior door under an activity-based costing system.
3. Compare the costs of the doors in requirements 1 and 2. Why do the simple and activity-based costing systems differ in the cost of an interior and exterior door?
4. How might Fancy Door, Inc., use the new cost information from its activity-based costing system to address the declining market share for interior doors?

25 ABC, retail product-line profitability. Henderson Supermarkets (HS) operates at capacity and decides to apply ABC analysis to three product lines: baked goods, milk and fruit juice, and frozen foods. It identifies four activities and their activity cost rates as follows:

Ordering	$102 per purchase order
Delivery and receipt of merchandise	$ 78 per delivery
Shelf-stocking	$ 21 per hour
Customer support and assistance	$ 0.22 per item sold

The revenues, cost of goods sold, store support costs, activities that account for the store support costs, and activity-area usage of the three product lines are as follows:

	Baked Goods	Milk and Fruit Juice	Frozen Products
Financial data			
Revenues	$59,500	$66,000	$51,000
Cost of goods sold	$36,000	$48,000	$34,000
Store support	$10,800	$14,400	$10,200
Activity-area usage (cost-allocation base)			
Ordering (purchase orders)	25	20	15
Delivery (deliveries)	90	35	30
Shelf-stocking (hours)	190	180	40
Customer support (items sold)	13,500	17,500	8,000

Under its simple costing system, HS allocated support costs to products at the rate of 30% of cost of goods sold.

Required

1. Use the simple costing system to prepare a product-line profitability report for HS.
2. Use the ABC system to prepare a product-line profitability report for HS.
3. What new insights does the ABC system in requirement 2 provide to HS managers?

26 ABC, wholesale, customer profitability. Ramirez Wholesalers operates at capacity and sells furniture items to four department-store chains (customers). Mr. Ramirez commented, "We apply ABC to determine product-line profitability. The same ideas apply to customer profitability, and we should find out our customer profitability as well." Ramirez Wholesalers sends catalogs to corporate purchasing departments on a monthly basis. The customers are entitled to return unsold merchandise within a six-month period from the purchase date and receive a full purchase price refund. The following data were collected from last year's operations:

	Chain			
	1	2	3	4
Gross sales	$50,000	$30,000	$100,000	$70,000
Sales returns:				
Number of items	100	26	60	40
Amount	$10,000	$ 5,000	$ 7,000	$ 6,000
Number of orders:				
Regular	40	150	50	70
Rush	10	50	10	30

Ramirez has calculated the following activity rates:

Activity	Cost-Driver Rate
Regular order processing	$20 per regular order
Rush order processing	$100 per rush order
Returned items processing	$10 per item
Catalogs and customer support	$1,000 per customer

Customers pay the transportation costs. The cost of goods sold averages 80% of sales.

Determine the contribution to profit from each chain last year. Comment on your solution.

Required

27 ABC, activity area cost-driver rates, product cross-subsidization. Intex Potatoes (IP) operates at capacity and processes potatoes into potato cuts at its highly automated Pocatello plant. It sells potatoes to the retail consumer market and to the institutional market, which includes hospitals, cafeterias, and university dormitories.

IP's simple costing system, which does not distinguish between potato cuts processed for retail and institutional markets, has a single direct-cost category (direct materials; that is, raw potatoes) and a single indirect-cost pool (production support). Support costs, which include packaging materials, are allocated on the basis of pounds of potato cuts processed. The company uses 1,800,000 pounds of raw potatoes to process 1,600,000 pounds of potato cuts. At the end of 2014, IP unsuccessfully bid for a large institutional contract. Its bid was reported to be 30% above the winning bid. This feedback came as a shock because IP included only a minimum profit margin on its bid, and the Pocatello plant was acknowledged as the most efficient in the industry.

As a result of its review process of the lost contract bid, IP decided to explore ways to refine its costing system. The company determined that 90% of the direct materials (raw potatoes) related to the retail market and 10% to the institutional market. In addition, the company identified that packaging materials could be directly traced to individual jobs ($190,000 for retail and $9,000 for institutional). Also, the company used ABC to identify three main activity areas that generated support costs: cleaning, cutting, and packaging.

- **Cleaning Activity Area**—The cost-allocation base is pounds of raw potatoes cleaned.
- **Cutting Activity Area**—The production line produces (a) 150 pounds of retail potato cuts per cutting-hour and (b) 200 pounds of institutional potato cuts per cutting-hour. The cost-allocation base is cutting-hours on the production line.
- **Packaging Activity Area**—The packaging line packages (a) 25 pounds of retail potato cuts per packaging-hour and (b) 80 pounds of institutional potato cuts per packaging-hour. The cost-allocation base is packaging-hours on the production line.

The following table summarizes the actual costs for 2014 before and after the preceding cost analysis.

| | Before the Cost Analysis | After the Cost Analysis | | | |
		Production Support	Retail	Institutional	Total
Direct materials used					
Potatoes	$ 231,000		$207,900	$23,100	$ 231,000
Packaging			190,000	9,000	199,000
Production support	1,689,000				
Cleaning		$ 270,000			270,000
Cutting		624,000			624,000
Packaging		596,000			596,000
Total	$1,920,000	$1,490,000	$397,900	$32,100	$1,920,000

Required

1. Using the simple costing system, what is the cost per pound of potato cuts produced by IP?
2. Calculate the cost rate per unit of the cost driver in the (a) cleaning, (b) cutting, and (c) packaging activity areas.
3. Suppose IP uses information from its activity cost rates to calculate costs incurred on retail potato cuts and institutional potato cuts. Using the ABC system, what is the cost per pound of (a) retail potato cuts and (b) institutional potato cuts?
4. Comment on the cost differences between the two costing systems in requirements 1 and 3. How might IP use the information in requirement 3 to make better decisions?

28 Activity-based costing. The job costing system at Sheri's Custom Framing has five indirect cost pools (purchasing, material handling, machine maintenance, product inspection, and packaging). The company is in the process of bidding on two jobs: Job 215, an order of 15 intricate personalized frames, and Job 325, an order of 6 standard personalized frames. The controller wants you to compare overhead allocated under the current simple job-costing system and a newly designed activity-based job-costing system. Total budgeted costs in each indirect cost pool and the budgeted quantity of activity driver are as follows.

	Budgeted Overhead	Activity Driver	Budgeted Quantity of Activity Driver
Purchasing	$ 35,000	Purchase orders processed	2,000
Material handling	43,750	Material moves	5,000
Machine maintenance	118,650	Machine-hours	10,500
Product inspection	9,450	Inspections	1,200
Packaging	19,950	Units produced	3,800
	$226,800		

Information related to Job 215 and Job 325 follows. Job 215 incurs more batch-level costs because it uses more types of materials that need to be purchased, moved, and inspected relative to Job 325.

	Job 215	Job 325
Number of purchase orders	25	8
Number of material moves	10	4
Machine-hours	40	60
Number of inspections	9	3
Units produced	15	6

Required

1. Compute the total overhead allocated to each job under a simple costing system, where overhead is allocated based on machine-hours.
2. Compute the total overhead allocated to each job under an activity-based costing system using the appropriate activity drivers.
3. Explain why Sheri's Custom Framing might favor the ABC job-costing system over the simple job-costing system, especially in its bidding process.

29 ABC, product costing at banks, cross-subsidization. United Savings Bank (USB) is examining the profitability of its Premier Account, a combined savings and checking account. Depositors receive a 7% annual interest rate on their average deposit. USB earns an interest rate spread of 3% (the difference between the rate at which it lends money and the rate it pays depositors) by lending money for home-loan purposes at 10%. Thus, USB would gain $60 on the interest spread if a depositor had an average Premier Account balance of $2,000 in 2014 ($2,000 × 3% = $60).

The Premier Account allows depositors unlimited use of services such as deposits, withdrawals, checking accounts, and foreign currency drafts. Depositors with Premier Account balances of $1,000 or more receive unlimited free use of services. Depositors with minimum balances of less than $1,000 pay a $22-a-month service fee for their Premier Account.

USB recently conducted an activity-based costing study of its services. It assessed the following costs for six individual services. The use of these services in 2014 by three customers is as follows:

	Activity-Based Cost per "Transaction"	Account Usage Lindell	Account Usage Welker	Account Usage Colston
Deposit/withdrawal with teller	$ 2.50	44	49	4
Deposit/withdrawal with automatic teller machine (ATM)	0.80	12	24	13
Deposit/withdrawal on prearranged monthly basis	0.50	0	14	58
Bank checks written	8.20	8	2	3
Foreign currency drafts	12.10	6	1	5
Inquiries about account balance	1.70	7	16	6
Average Premier Account balance for 2013		$1,200	$700	$24,900

Assume Lindell and Colston always maintain a balance above $1,000, whereas Welker always has a balance below $1,000.

1. Compute the 2014 profitability of the Lindell, Welker, and Colston Premier Accounts at USB.
2. Why might USB worry about the profitability of individual customers if the Premier Account product offering is profitable as a whole?
3. What changes would you recommend for USB's Premier Account?

MyAccountingLab

Problems

30 Job costing with single direct-cost category, single indirect-cost pool, law firm. Bradley Associates is a recently formed law partnership. Emmit Harrington, the managing partner of Bradley Associates, has just finished a tense phone call with Martin Omar, president of Campa Coal. Omar strongly complained about the price Bradley charged for some legal work done for Campa Coal.

Harrington also received a phone call from its only other client (St. Edith's Glass), which was very pleased with both the quality of the work and the price charged on its most recent job.

Bradley Associates operates at capacity and uses a cost-based approach to pricing (billing) each job. Currently it uses a simple costing system with a single direct-cost category (professional labor-hours) and a single indirect-cost pool (general support). Indirect costs are allocated to cases on the basis of professional labor-hours per case. The job files show the following:

	Campa Coal	St. Edith's Glass
Professional labor	150 hours	100 hours

Professional labor costs at Bradley Associates are $80 an hour. Indirect costs are allocated to cases at $100 an hour. Total indirect costs in the most recent period were $25,000.

1. Why is it important for Bradley Associates to understand the costs associated with individual jobs?
2. Compute the costs of the Campa Coal and St. Edith's Glass jobs using Bradley's simple costing system.

31 Job costing with multiple direct-cost categories, single indirect-cost pool, law firm (continuation of 30). Harrington asks his assistant to collect details on those costs included in the $25,000 indirect-cost pool that can be traced to each individual job. After analysis, Bradley is able to reclassify $15,000 of the $25,000 as direct costs:

Other Direct Costs	Campa Coal	St. Edith's Glass
Research support labor	$1,800	$ 3,850
Computer time	400	1,600
Travel and allowances	700	4,200
Telephones/faxes	250	1,200
Photocopying	300	700
Total	$3,450	$11,550

Harrington decides to calculate the costs of each job as if Bradley had used six direct cost-pools and a single indirect-cost pool. The single indirect-cost pool would have $10,000 of costs and would be allocated to each case using the professional labor-hours base.

1. Calculate the revised indirect-cost allocation rate per professional labor-hour for Bradley Associates when total indirect costs are $10,000.
2. Compute the costs of the Campa and St. Edith's jobs if Bradley Associates had used its refined costing system with multiple direct-cost categories and one indirect-cost pool.
3. Compare the costs of Campa and St. Edith's jobs in requirement 2 with those in requirement 2 of Problem 30. Comment on the results.

32 Job costing with multiple direct-cost categories, multiple indirect-cost pools, law firm (continuation of 30 and 31). Bradley has two classifications of professional staff: partners and associates. Harrington asks his assistant to examine the relative use of partners and associates on the recent Campa Coal and St. Edith's jobs. The Campa job used 50 partner-hours and 100 associate-hours. The St. Edith's job used 75 partner-hours and 25 associate-hours. Therefore, totals of the two jobs together were 125 partner-hours and 125 associate-hours. Harrington decides to examine how using separate direct-cost rates for partners and associates and using separate indirect-cost pools for partners and associates would have affected the costs of the Campa and St. Edith's jobs. Indirect costs in each indirect-cost pool would be allocated on the basis of total hours of that category of professional labor. From the total indirect cost-pool of $10,000, $6,000 is attributable to the activities of partners and $4,000 is attributable to the activities of associates.

The rates per category of professional labor are as follows:

Category of Professional Labor	Direct Cost per Hour	Indirect Cost per Hour
Partner	$100	$6,000 ÷ 125 hours = $48
Associate	$ 60	$4,000 ÷ 125 hours = $32

Required

1. Compute the costs of the Campa and St. Edith's cases using Bradley's further refined system, with multiple direct-cost categories and multiple indirect-cost pools.
2. For what decisions might Bradley Associates find it more useful to use this job-costing approach rather than the approaches in Problem 30 or 31?

33 First-stage allocation, activity-based costing, manufacturing sector. Thurgood Devices uses activity-based costing to allocate overhead costs to customer orders for pricing purposes. Many customer orders are won through competitive bidding. Direct material and direct manufacturing labor costs are traced directly to each order. Thurgood's direct manufacturing labor rate is $20 per hour. The company reports the following yearly overhead costs:

Wages and salaries	$480,000
Depreciation	60,000
Rent	120,000
Other overhead	240,000
Total overhead costs	$900,000

Thurgood has established four activity cost pools:

Activity Cost Pool	Activity Measure	Total Activity for the Year
Direct manufacturing labor support	Number of direct manufacturing labor-hours	30,000 direct manufacturing labor-hours
Order processing	Number of customer orders	500 orders
Design support	Number of custom designs	100 custom designs
Other	Facility-sustaining costs allocated to orders based on direct manufacturing labor-hours	30,000 direct manufacturing labor-hours

Only about 20% of Thurgood's yearly orders require custom designs.

Paul Moeller, Thurgood's controller, has prepared the following estimates for distribution of the overhead costs across the four activity cost pools:

	Direct Manufacturing Labor Support	Order Processing	Design Support	Other	Total
Wages and salaries	40%	25%	30%	5%	100%
Depreciation	25%	10%	15%	50%	100%
Rent	30%	25%	10%	35%	100%
Other overhead	20%	30%	35%	15%	100%

Order 448200 required $4,550 of direct materials, 80 direct manufacturing labor-hours, and one custom design.

1. Allocate the overhead costs to each activity cost pool. Calculate the activity rate for each pool.
2. Determine the cost of Order 448200.
3. How does activity-based costing enhance Thurgood's ability to price its orders? Suppose Thurgood used a traditional costing system to allocate all overhead costs to orders on the basis of direct manufacturing labor-hours. How might this have affected Thurgood's pricing decisions?

34 First-stage allocation, activity-based costing, service sector. LawnCare USA provides lawn care and landscaping services to commercial clients. LawnCare USA uses activity-based costing to bid on jobs and to evaluate their profitability. LawnCare USA reports the following annual costs:

Wages and salaries	$360,000
Depreciation	72,000
Supplies	120,000
Other overhead	288,000
Total overhead costs	$840,000

John Gilroy, controller of LawnCare USA, has established four activity cost pools:

Activity Cost Pool	Activity Measure	Total Activity for the Year
Estimating jobs	Number of job estimates	250 estimates
Lawn care	Number of direct labor-hours	10,000 direct labor-hours
Landscape design	Number of design hours	500 design hours
Other	Facility-sustaining costs that are not allocated to jobs	Not applicable

Gilroy estimates that LawnCare USA's costs are distributed to the activity-cost pools as follows:

	Estimating Jobs	Lawn Care	Landscape Design	Other	Total
Wages and salaries	5%	70%	15%	10%	100%
Depreciation	10%	65%	10%	15%	100%
Supplies	0%	100%	0%	0%	100%
Other overhead	15%	50%	20%	15%	100%

Sunset Office Park, a new development in a nearby community, has contacted LawnCare USA to provide an estimate on landscape design and annual lawn maintenance. The job is estimated to require a single landscape design requiring 40 design hours in total and 250 direct labor-hours annually. LawnCare USA has a policy of pricing estimates at 150% of cost.

1. Allocate LawnCare USA's costs to the activity-cost pools and determine the activity rate for each pool.
2. Estimate total cost for the Sunset Office Park job.
3. How much should LawnCare USA bid to perform the job?
4. Sunset Office Park asks LawnCare USA to give an estimate for providing its services for a 2-year period. What are the advantages and disadvantages for LawnCare USA to provide a 2-year estimate?

35 Department and activity-cost rates, service sector. Raynham's Radiology Center (RRC) performs X-rays, ultrasounds, computer tomography (CT) scans, and magnetic resonance imaging (MRI). RRC has developed a reputation as a top radiology center in the state. RRC has achieved this status because it constantly reexamines its processes and procedures. RRC has been using a single, facility-wide overhead allocation rate. The vice president of finance believes that RRC can make better process improvements if it uses more disaggregated cost information. She says, "We have state-of-the-art medical imaging technology. Can't we have state-of-the-art accounting technology?"

Raynham's Radiology Center Budgeted Information for the Year Ended May 31, 2014

	X-rays	Ultrasound	CT Scan	MRI	Total
Technician labor	$ 62,000	$101,000	$155,000	$ 103,000	$ 421,000
Depreciation	42,240	256,000	424,960	876,800	1,600,000
Materials	22,600	16,400	23,600	31,500	94,100
Administration					20,000
Maintenance					250,000
Sanitation					252,500
Utilities					151,100
	$126,840	$373,400	$603,560	$1,011,300	$2,788,700
Number of procedures	3,842	4,352	2,924	2,482	
Minutes to clean after each procedure	5	5	15	35	
Minutes for each procedure	5	15	25	40	

RRC operates at capacity. The proposed allocation bases for overhead are:

Administration	Number of procedures
Maintenance (including parts)	Capital cost of the equipment (use Depreciation)
Sanitation	Total cleaning minutes
Utilities	Total procedure minutes

Required

1. Calculate the budgeted cost per service for X-rays, ultrasounds, CT scans, and MRI using direct technician labor costs as the allocation basis.
2. Calculate the budgeted cost per service of X-rays, ultrasounds, CT scans, and MRI if RRC allocated overhead costs using activity-based costing.
3. Explain how the disaggregation of information could be helpful to RRC's intention to continuously improve its services.

36 Activity-based costing, merchandising. Pharmahelp, Inc., a distributor of special pharmaceutical products, operates at capacity and has three main market segments:

a. General supermarket chains
b. Drugstore chains
c. Mom-and-pop single-store pharmacies

Rick Flair, the new controller of Pharmahelp, reported the following data for 2014

	A	B	C	D	E
1					
2	Pharmahelp, 2014	General			
3		Supermarket	Drugstore	Mom-and-Pop	
4		Chains	Chains	Single Stores	Pharmahelp
5	Revenues	$3,708,000	$3,150,000	$1,980,000	$8,838,000
6	Cost of goods sold	3,600,000	3,000,000	1,800,000	8,400,000
7	Gross margin	$ 108,000	$ 150,000	$ 180,000	438,000
8	Other operating costs				301,080
9	Operating income				$ 136,920

For many years, Pharmahelp has used gross margin percentage [(Revenue − Cost of goods sold) ÷ Revenue] to evaluate the relative profitability of its market segments. But Flair recently attended a seminar on activity-based costing and is considering using it at Pharmahelp to analyze and allocate "other operating costs." He meets with all the key managers and several of his operations and sales staff, and they agree that there are five key activities that drive other operating costs at Pharmahelp:

Activity Area	Cost Driver
Order processing	Number of customer purchase orders
Line-item processing	Number of line items ordered by customers
Delivering to stores	Number of store deliveries
Cartons shipped to store	Number of cartons shipped
Stocking of customer store shelves	Hours of shelf-stocking

Each customer order consists of one or more line items. A line item represents a single product (such as Extra-Strength Tylenol Tablets). Each product line item is delivered in one or more separate cartons. Each store delivery entails the delivery of one or more cartons of products to a customer. Pharmahelp's staff stacks cartons directly onto display shelves in customers' stores. Currently, there is no additional charge to the customer for shelf-stocking and not all customers use Pharmahelp for this activity. The level of each activity in the three market segments and the total cost incurred for each activity in 2014 is as follows:

Home	Insert	Page Layout	Formulas	Data	Review	View
	A	B	C	D	E
13					
14	Activity-based Cost Data		Activity Level		
15	Pharmahelp 2014	General			Total Cost
16		Supermarket	Drugstore	Mom-and-Pop	of Activity
17	Activity	Chains	Chains	Single Stores	in 2014
18	Orders processed (number)	140	360	1,500	$ 80,000
19	Line-items ordered (number)	1,960	4,320	15,000	63,840
20	Store deliveries made (number)	120	360	1,000	71,000
21	Cartons shipped to stores (number)	36,000	24,000	16,000	76,000
22	Shelf stocking (hours)	360	180	100	10,240
23					$301,080

Required

1. Compute the 2014 gross-margin percentage for each of Pharmahelp's three market segments.
2. Compute the cost driver rates for each of the five activity areas.
3. Use the activity-based costing information to allocate the $301,080 of "other operating costs" to each of the market segments. Compute the operating income for each market segment.
4. Comment on the results. What new insights are available with the activity-based costing information?

37 **Choosing cost drivers, activity-based costing, activity-based management.** Pastel Bags (PB) is a designer of high-quality backpacks and purses. Each design is made in small batches. Each spring, PB comes out with new designs for the backpack and for the purse. The company uses these designs for a year and then moves on to the next trend. The bags are all made on the same fabrication equipment that is expected to operate at capacity. The equipment must be switched over to a new design and set up to prepare for the production of each new batch of products. When completed, each batch of products is immediately shipped to a wholesaler. Shipping costs vary with the number of shipments. Budgeted information for the year is as follows:

Pastel Bags
Budget for Costs and Activities
For the Year Ended February 28, 2014

Direct materials—purses	$ 319,155
Direct materials—backpacks	454,995
Direct manufacturing labor—purses	99,000
Direct manufacturing labor—backpacks	113,000
Setup	64,000
Shipping	73,000
Design	169,000
Plant utilities and administration	221,000
Total	$1,513,150

Other budget information follows:

	Backpacks	Purses	Total
Number of bags	6,175	3,075	9,250
Hours of production	1,665	2,585	4,250
Number of batches	120	80	200
Number of designs	2	2	4

Required

1. Identify the cost hierarchy level for each cost category.
2. Identify the most appropriate cost driver for each cost category. Explain briefly your choice of cost driver.
3. Calculate the budgeted cost per unit of cost driver for each cost category.
4. Calculate the budgeted total costs and cost per unit for each product line.
5. Explain how you could use the information in requirement 4 to reduce costs.

38 **ABC, health care.** Crosstown Health Center runs two programs: drug addict rehabilitation and aftercare (counseling and support of patients after release from a mental hospital). The center's budget for 2014 follows.

Professional salaries:		
4 physicians × $150,000	$600,000	
12 psychologists × $75,000	900,000	
16 nurses × $30,000	480,000	$1,980,000
Medical supplies		242,000
Rent and clinic maintenance		138,600
Administrative costs to manage patient charts, food, laundry		484,000
Laboratory services		92,400
Total		$2,937,000

Kim Yu, the director of the center, is keen on determining the cost of each program. Yu compiled the following data describing employee allocations to individual programs:

	Drug	Aftercare	Total Employees
Physicians	4		4
Psychologists	4	8	12
Nurses	6	10	16

Yu has recently become aware of activity-based costing as a method to refine costing systems. She asks her accountant, Gus Gates, how she should apply this technique. Gates obtains the following budgeted information for 2014:

	Drug	Aftercare	Total
Square feet of space occupied by each program	9,000	12,000	21,000
Patient-years of service	50	60	110
Number of laboratory tests	1,400	700	2,100

Required

1. **a.** Selecting cost-allocation bases that you believe are the most appropriate for allocating indirect costs to programs, calculate the budgeted indirect cost rates for medical supplies; rent and clinic maintenance; administrative costs for patient charts, food, and laundry; and laboratory services.
   b. Using an activity-based costing approach to cost analysis, calculate the budgeted cost of each program and the budgeted cost per patient-year of the drug program.
   c. What benefits can Crosstown Health Center obtain by implementing the ABC system?

2. What factors, other than cost, do you think Crosstown Health Center should consider in allocating resources to its programs?

39 Unused capacity, activity-based costing, activity-based management. Zarson's Netballs is a manufacturer of high-quality basketballs and volleyballs. Setup costs are driven by the number of batches. Equipment and maintenance costs increase with the number of machine-hours, and lease rent is paid per square foot. Capacity of the facility is 14,000 square feet, and Zarson is using only 80% of this capacity. Zarson records the cost of unused capacity as a separate line item and not as a product cost. The following is the budgeted information for Zarson:

Zarson's Netballs
Budgeted Costs and Activities
For the Year Ended December 31, 2014

Direct materials—basketballs	$ 168, 100
Direct materials—volleyballs	303,280
Direct manufacturing labor—basketballs	111,800
Direct manufacturing labor—volleyballs	100,820
Setup	157,500
Equipment and maintenance costs	115,200
Lease rent	210,000
Total	$1,166,700

Other budget information follows:

	Basketballs	Volleyballs
Number of balls	58,000	85,000
Machine-hours	13,500	10,500
Number of batches	450	300
Square footage of production space used	3,200	8,000

Required

1. Calculate the budgeted cost per unit of cost driver for each indirect cost pool.
2. What is the budgeted cost of unused capacity?
3. What is the budgeted total cost and the cost per unit of resources used to produce (a) basketballs and (b) volleyballs?
4. Why might excess capacity be beneficial for Zarson? What are some of the issues Zarson should consider before increasing production to use the space?

40 Unused capacity, activity-based costing, activity-based management. Whitewater Adventures manufactures two models of kayaks, Basic and Deluxe, using a combination of machining and hand finishing. Machine setup costs are driven by the number of setups. Indirect manufacturing labor costs increase with direct manufacturing labor costs. Equipment and maintenance costs increase with the number of machine-hours, and facility rent is paid per square foot. Capacity of the facility is 6,250 square feet, and Whitewater is using only 80% of this capacity. Whitewater records the cost of unused capacity as a separate line item and not as a product cost. For the current year, Whitewater has budgeted the following:

Whitewater Adventures
Budgeted Costs and Activities
for the Year Ended December 31, 2014

Direct materials—Basic kayaks	$325,000
Direct materials—Deluxe kayaks	240,000
Direct manufacturing labor—Basic kayaks	110,000
Direct manufacturing labor—Deluxe kayaks	130,000
Indirect manufacturing labor costs	72,000
Machine setup costs	40,500
Equipment and maintenance costs	235,000
Facility rent	200,000
Total	$1,352,500

Other budget information follows:

	Basic	Deluxe
Number of kayaks	5,000	3,000
Machine-hours	11,000	12,500
Number of setups	300	200
Square footage of production space used	2,860	2,140

Required

1. Calculate the cost per unit of each cost-allocation base.
2. What is the budgeted cost of unused capacity?
3. Calculate the budgeted total cost and the cost per unit for each model.
4. Why might excess capacity be beneficial for Whitewater? What are some of the issues Whitewater should consider before increasing production to use the space?

41 ABC, implementation, ethics. (CMA, adapted) Plum Electronics, a division of Berry Corporation, manufactures two large-screen television models: the Mammoth, which has been produced since 2010 and sells for $990, and the Maximum, a newer model introduced in early 2012 that sells for $1,254. Based on the following income statement for the year ended November 30, 2014, senior management at Berry have decided to concentrate Plum's marketing resources on the Maximum model and to begin to phase out the Mammoth model because Maximum generates a much bigger operating income per unit.

Plum Electronics
Income Statement for the
Fiscal Year Ended November 30, 2014

	Mammoth	Maximum	Total
Revenues	$21,780,000	$5,016,000	$26,796,000
Cost of goods sold	13,794,000	3,511,200	17,305,200
Gross margin	7,986,000	1,504,800	9,490,800
Selling and administrative expense	6,413,000	1,075,800	7,488,800
Operating income	$ 1,573,000	$ 429,000	$ 2,002,000
Units produced and sold	22,000	4,000	
Operating income per unit sold	$ 71.50	$ 107.25	

Details for cost of goods sold for Mammoth and Maximum are as follows:

	Mammoth		Maximum	
	Total	Per Unit	Total	Per Unit
Direct materials	$ 5,033,600	$ 228.80	$2,569,600	$642.40
Direct manufacturing labor[a]	435,600	19.80	184,800	46.20
Machine costs[b]	3,484,800	158.40	316,800	79.20
Total direct costs	$ 8,954,000	$ 407.00	$3,071,200	$767.80
Manufacturing overhead costs[c]	$ 4,840,000	$ 220.00	$ 440,000	$110.00
Total cost of goods sold	$13,794,000	$ 627.00	$3,511,200	$877.80

[a] Mammoth requires 1.5 hours per unit and Maximum requires 3.5 hours per unit. The direct manufacturing labor cost is $13.20 per hour.

[b] Machine costs include lease costs of the machine, repairs, and maintenance. Mammoth requires 8 machine-hours per unit and Maximum requires 4 machine-hours per unit. The machine-hour rate is $19.80 per hour.

[c] Manufacturing overhead costs are allocated to products based on machine-hours at the rate of $27.50 per hour.

Plum's controller, Steve Jacobs, is advocating the use of activity-based costing and activity-based management and has gathered the following information about the company's manufacturing overhead costs for the year ended November 30, 2014.

		Units of the Cost-Allocation Base		
Activity Center (Cost-Allocation Base)	Total Activity Costs	Mammoth	Maximum	Total
Soldering (number of solder points)	$1,036,200	1,185,000	385,000	1,570,000
Shipments (number of shipments)	946,000	16,200	3,800	20,000
Quality control (number of inspections)	1,364,000	56,200	21,300	77,500
Purchase orders (number of orders)	1,045,440	80,100	109,980	190,080
Machine power (machine-hours)	63,360	176,000	16,000	192,000
Machine setups (number of setups)	825,000	16,000	14,000	30,000
Total manufacturing overhead	$5,280,000			

After completing his analysis, Jacobs shows the results to Charles Clark, the Plum division president. Clark does not like what he sees. "If you show headquarters this analysis, they are going to ask us to phase out the Maximum line, which we have just introduced. This whole costing stuff has been a major problem for us. First Mammoth was not profitable and now Maximum.

"Looking at the ABC analysis, I see two problems. First, we do many more activities than the ones you have listed. If you had included all activities, maybe your conclusions would be different. Second, you used number of setups and number of inspections as allocation bases. The numbers would be different had you used setup-hours and inspection-hours instead. I know that measurement problems precluded you from using these other cost-allocation bases, but I believe you ought to make some adjustments to our current numbers to compensate for these issues. I know you can do better. We can't afford to phase out either product."

Jacobs knows that his numbers are fairly accurate. As a quick check, he calculates the profitability of Maximum and Mammoth using more and different allocation bases. The set of activities and activity rates he had used results in numbers that closely approximate those based on more detailed analyses. He is confident that headquarters, knowing that Maximum was introduced only recently, will not ask Plum to phase it out. He is also aware that a sizable portion of Clark's bonus is based on division revenues.

Phasing out either product would adversely affect his bonus. Still, he feels some pressure from Clark to do something.

1. Using activity-based costing, calculate the gross margin per unit of the Maximum and Mammoth models.
2. Explain briefly why these numbers differ from the gross margin per unit of the Maximum and Mammoth models calculated using Plum's existing simple costing system.
3. Comment on Clark's concerns about the accuracy and limitations of ABC.
4. How might Plum find the ABC information helpful in managing its business?
5. What should Steve Jacobs do in response to Clark's comments?

42 Activity-based costing, activity-based management, merchandising. Main Street Books and Café (MSBC) is a large city bookstore that sells books and music CDs and has a café. MSBC operates at capacity and allocates selling, general, and administration (S, G & A) costs to each product line using the cost of merchandise of each product line. MSBC wants to optimize the pricing and cost management of each product line. MSBC is wondering if its accounting system is providing it with the best information for making such decisions.

Main Street Books and Café
Product Line Information
For the Year Ended December 31, 2014

	Books	CDs	Café
Revenues	$3,720,480	$2,315,360	$736,216
Cost of merchandise	$2,656,727	$1,722,311	$556,685
Cost of café cleaning	—	—	$ 18,250
Number of purchase orders placed	2,800	2,500	2,000
Number of deliveries received	1,400	1,700	1,600
Hours of shelf stocking time	15,000	14,000	10,000
Items sold	124,016	115,768	368,108

Main Street Books and Café incurs the following selling, general, and administration costs:

Main Street Books and Café
Selling, General, and Administration (S, G & A) Costs
For the Year Ended December 31, 2014

Purchasing department expense	$ 474,500
Receiving department expense	432,400
Shelf stocking labor expense	487,500
Customer support expense (cashiers and floor employees)	91,184
	$1,485,584

1. Suppose MSBC uses cost of merchandise to allocate all S, G & A costs. Prepare product line and total company income statements.
2. Identify an improved method for allocating costs to the three product lines. Explain. Use the method for allocating S, G & A costs that you propose to prepare new product line and total company income statements. Compare your results to the results in requirement 1.
3. Write a memo to MSBC management describing how the improved system might be useful for managing the store.

Glossary

Activity. An event, task, or unit of work with a specified purpose.

Activity-based costing (ABC). Approach to costing that focuses on individual activities as the fundamental cost objects. It uses the costs of these activities as the basis for assigning costs to other cost objects such as products or services.

Activity-based management (ABM). Method of management decision-making that uses activity-based costing information to improve customer satisfaction and profitability.

Batch-level costs. The costs of activities related to a group of units of products or services rather than to each individual unit of product or service.

Cost hierarchy. Categorization of indirect costs into different cost pools on the basis of the different types of cost drivers, or cost-allocation bases, or different degrees of difficulty in determining cause-and-effect (or benefits received) relationships.

Facility-sustaining costs. The costs of activities that cannot be traced to individual products or services but support the organization as a whole.

Output unit–level costs. The costs of activities performed on each individual unit of a product or service.

Product-cost cross-subsidization. Costing outcome where one undercosted (overcosted) product results in at least one other product being overcosted (undercosted).

Product overcosting. A product consumes a low level of resources but is reported to have a high cost per unit.

Product-sustaining costs. The costs of activities undertaken to support individual products regardless of the number of units or batches in which the units are produced.

Product undercosting. A product consumes a high level of resources but is reported to have a low cost per unit.

Refined costing system. Costing system that reduces the use of broad averages for assigning the cost of resources to cost objects (jobs, products, services) and provides better measurement of the costs of indirect resources used by different cost objects—no matter how differently various cost objects use indirect resources.

Service-sustaining costs. The costs of activities undertaken to support individual services.

Photo Credits

Chapter 7

Flexible Budgets, Direct-Cost Variances, and Management Control

From Chapter 7 of *Cost Accounting: A Managerial Emphasis,* Fifteenth Edition. Charles T. Horngren, Srikant M. Datar, Madhav V. Rajan. Copyright © 2015 by Pearson Education, Inc. All rights reserved.

Flexible Budgets, Direct-Cost Variances, and Management Control

Every organization, regardless of its profitability or growth, has to step back and take a hard look at its spending decisions.

And when customers are affected by a recession, the need for managers to use budgeting and variance analysis tools for cost control becomes especially critical. By studying variances, managers can focus on where specific performances have fallen short and use the information they learn to make corrective adjustments and achieve significant savings for their companies. The drive to achieve cost reductions might seem at odds with the growing push for organizations to pursue environmentally sound business practices. To the contrary, managers looking to be more efficient with their plants and operations have found that cornerstones of the sustainability movement, such as reducing waste and power usage, offer fresh ways to help them manage risk and control costs, as the following article shows.

Going for the (Other) Green: Reducing Standard Costs[1]

While Whole Foods and IKEA have long been associated with eco-friendliness, sustainable practices have been spreading far beyond these early adopters to a broad swath of businesses. In recent years, managers in some unlikely industries have discovered that the financial benefits of sustainability can manifest themselves in numerous ways. One surprising way involves companies going green to reduce their standard costs.

At APC Construction, a small road-builder in Colorado, the company increased the amount of recycled asphalt it uses in its production process—purely out of necessity. When the cost of standard asphalt cement skyrocketed from $180 per ton in 2003 to $600 per ton in 2008, the company needed to rein in its standard costs for cement. As a result, the company began increasing the amount of recycled ingredients in its product. "With a 30% recycled product, you're looking at a savings of almost $8 per ton," says Bob Stewart, the company's finance chief. "You're reducing the amount of energy you use to crush the rock and you're preserving natural resources."

Urschel Laboratories, a maker of capital equipment for the food processing and chemical industries, simultaneously reduced its freight costs and carbon footprint. With

---

[1] *Source:* Kate O'Sullivan, "Going for the Green" Sept. 01, 2011, CFO Magazine.

oil prices rising, some of Urschel's carriers began adding fuel surcharges to ship the company's machinery. Since much of what the company sells is heavy equipment, Urschel found that its customers often had enough lead time to wait 4 to 6 weeks for their orders to arrive by sea, a practice that costs the company half of what air freight—its former standard—costs. This lowered the company's standard costs for shipping while reducing the amount of fuel oil required to ship its equipment to customers around the world.

Understanding the behavior of costs, planning for them, performing variance analysis, and acting appropriately on the results are critical functions for managers. For retailers such as McDonald's and Dunkin' Donuts, an intricate understanding of direct costs is essential in order to make each high-quality food item and beverage at the lowest possible cost. Similarly, organizations ranging from General Electric and Bank of America to sports teams such as the Sacramento Kings have to manage costs and analyze variances for long-term sustainability.

Budgets help managers with their planning function. We now explain how budgets, specifically flexible budgets, are used to compute variances, which assist managers in their control function. Flexible budgets and variances enable managers to compare a firm's actual results with its planned performance, understand why the two differ, and learn what improvements can be made. Variance analysis supports the critical final function in the five-step decision-making process by enabling managers to *evaluate performance and learn* after decisions are implemented. In this chapter, we explain how.

Static Budgets and Variances

Learning Objective 1

Understand static budgets

...the master budget based on output planned at start of period

and static-budget variances

...the difference between the actual result and the corresponding budgeted amount in the static budget

A **variance** is the difference between actual results and expected performance. The expected performance is also called **budgeted performance,** which is a point of reference for making comparisons.

The Use of Variances

Variances bring together the planning and control functions of management and facilitate management by exception. **Management by exception** is a practice whereby managers focus more closely on areas that are not operating as expected and less closely on areas that are. Consider the scrap and rework costs at a Maytag appliances plant. If the plant's actual costs are much higher than originally budgeted, the variances will prompt managers to find out why and correct the problem so future operations result in less scrap and rework. Sometimes a large positive variance may occur, such as a significant decrease in the manufacturing costs of a product. Managers will try to understand the reasons for the decrease (better operator training or changes in manufacturing methods, for example) so these practices can be continued and implemented by other divisions within the organization.

Variances are also used for evaluating performance and to motivate managers. Production-line managers at Maytag may have quarterly efficiency incentives linked to achieving a budgeted amount of operating costs.

Sometimes variances suggest that the company should consider a change in strategy. For example, large negative variances caused by excessive defect rates for a new product may suggest a flawed product design. Managers may then want to investigate the product design and potentially change the mix of products being offered. Variances also help managers make more informed predictions about the future and thereby improve the quality of the five-step decision-making process.

The benefits of variance analysis are not restricted to companies. In today's difficult economic environment, public officials have realized that the ability to make timely tactical changes based on variance information can result in their having to make fewer draconian adjustments later. For example, the city of Scottsdale, Arizona, monitors its tax and fee performance against expenditures monthly. Why? One of the city's goals is to keep its water usage rates stable. By monitoring the extent to which the city's water revenues are matching its current expenses, Scottsdale can avoid sudden spikes in the rate it charges residents for water as well as finance water-related infrastructure projects.[2]

How important of a decision-making tool is variance analysis? Very. A recent survey by the United Kingdom's Chartered Institute of Management Accountants found that it was easily the most popular costing tool used by organizations of all sizes.

Static Budgets and Static-Budget Variances

We will take a closer look at variances by examining one company's accounting system. As you study the exhibits in this chapter, note that "level" followed by a number denotes the amount of detail shown by a variance analysis. Level 1 reports the least detail; level 2 offers more information; and so on.

Consider Webb Company, a firm that manufactures and sells jackets. The jackets require tailoring and many other hand operations. Webb sells exclusively to distributors, who in turn sell to independent clothing stores and retail chains. For simplicity, we assume the following:

1. Webb's only costs are in the manufacturing function; Webb incurs no costs in other value-chain functions, such as marketing and distribution.
2. All units manufactured in April 2014 are sold in April 2014.
3. There is no direct materials inventory at either the beginning or the end of the period. No work-in-process or finished goods inventories exist at either the beginning or the end of the period.

Webb has three variable-cost categories. The budgeted variable cost per jacket for each category is as follows:

Cost Category	Variable Cost per Jacket
Direct materials costs	$60
Direct manufacturing labor costs	16
Variable manufacturing overhead costs	12
Total variable costs	$88

The *number of units manufactured* is the cost driver for direct materials, direct manufacturing labor, and variable manufacturing overhead. The relevant range for the cost driver is from 0 to 12,000 jackets. Budgeted and actual data for April 2014 are:

Budgeted fixed costs for production between 0 and 12,000 jackets	$276,000
Budgeted selling price	$ 120 per jacket
Budgeted production and sales	12,000 jackets
Actual production and sales	10,000 jackets

---

[2] For an excellent discussion and other related examples from governmental settings, see Kavanagh S., and C. Swanson. 2009. Tactical financial management: Cash flow and budgetary variance analysis. *Government Finance Review*, October 1.

Level 1 Analysis

Exhibit 1

Static-Budget-Based Variance Analysis for Webb Company for April 2014[a]

	Actual Results (1)	Static-Budget Variances (2) = (1) – (3)	Static Budget (3)
Units sold	10,000	2,000 U	12,000
Revenues	$ 1,250,000	$190,000 U	$1,440,000
Variable costs			
Direct materials	621,600	98,400 F	720,000
Direct manufacturing labor	198,000	6,000 U	192,000
Variable manufacturing overhead	130,500	13,500 F	144,000
Total variable costs	950,100	105,900 F	1,056,000
Contribution margin	299,900	84,100 U	384,000
Fixed costs	285,000	9,000 U	276,000
Operating income	$ 14,900	$ 93,100 U	$ 108,000

$ 93,100 U

Static-budget variance

[a]F = favorable effect on operating income; U = unfavorable effect on operating income.

The **static budget,** or master budget, is based on the level of output planned at the start of the budget period. The master budget is called a static budget because the budget for the period is developed around a single (static) planned output level. Exhibit 1, column 3, presents the static budget for Webb Company for April 2014 that was prepared at the end of 2013. For each line item in the income statement, Exhibit 1, column 1, displays data for the actual April results. For example, actual revenues are $1,250,000, and the actual selling price is $1,250,000 ÷ 10,000 jackets = $125 per jacket—compared with the budgeted selling price of $120 per jacket. Similarly, actual direct materials costs are $621,600, and the direct material cost per jacket is $621,600 ÷ 10,000 = $62.16 per jacket—compared with the budgeted direct material cost per jacket of $60. We describe potential reasons and explanations for these differences as we discuss different variances throughout the chapter.

The **static-budget variance** (see Exhibit 1, column 2) is the difference between the actual result and the corresponding budgeted amount in the static budget.

A **favorable variance**—denoted F in this text—has the effect, when considered in isolation, of increasing operating income relative to the budgeted amount. For revenue items, F means actual revenues exceed budgeted revenues. For cost items, F means actual costs are less than budgeted costs. An **unfavorable variance**—denoted U in this text—has the effect, when viewed in isolation, of decreasing operating income relative to the budgeted amount. Unfavorable variances are also called *adverse variances* in some countries, such as the United Kingdom.

The unfavorable static-budget variance for operating income of $93,100 in Exhibit 1 is calculated by subtracting static-budget operating income of $108,000 from actual operating income of $14,900:

$$\text{Static-budget variance for operating income} = \text{Actual result} - \text{Static-budget amount}$$

$$= \$14,900 - \$108,000$$

$$= \$93,100 \text{ U.}$$

The analysis in Exhibit 1 provides managers with additional information on the static-budget variance for operating income of $93,100 U. The more detailed breakdown indicates how the line items that comprise operating income—revenues, individual variable costs, and fixed costs—add up to the static-budget variance of $93,100.

Decision Point

What are static budgets and static-budget variances?

Recall that Webb produced and sold only 10,000 jackets, although managers anticipated an output of 12,000 jackets in the static budget. *Managers want to know how much of the static-budget variance is due to Webb inaccurately forecasting what it expected to produce and sell and how much is due to how it actually performed manufacturing and selling 10,000 jackets.* Managers, therefore, create a flexible budget, which enables a more in-depth understanding of deviations from the static budget.

Learning Objective 2

Examine the concept of a flexible budget

...the budget that is adjusted (flexed) to recognize the actual output level

and learn how to develop it

...proportionately increase variable costs; keep fixed costs the same

Flexible Budgets

A **flexible budget** calculates budgeted revenues and budgeted costs based on *the actual output in the budget period*. The flexible budget is prepared at the end of the period (April 2014 for Webb), after managers know the actual output of 10,000 jackets. The flexible budget is the *hypothetical* budget that Webb would have prepared at the start of the budget period if it had correctly forecast the actual output of 10,000 jackets. In other words, the flexible budget is not the plan Webb initially had in mind for April 2014 (remember Webb planned for an output of 12,000 jackets). Rather, it is the budget Webb *would have* put together for April if it knew in advance that the output for the month would be 10,000 jackets. In preparing the flexible budget, note that:

- The budgeted selling price is the same $120 per jacket used in the static budget.
- The budgeted unit variable cost is the same $88 per jacket used in the static budget.
- The budgeted *total* fixed costs are the same static-budget amount of $276,000. Why? Because the 10,000 jackets produced falls within the relevant range of 0 to 12,000 jackets. Therefore, Webb would have budgeted the same amount of fixed costs, $276,000, whether it anticipated making 10,000 or 12,000 jackets.

The *only* difference between the static budget and the flexible budget is that the static budget is prepared for the planned output of 12,000 jackets, whereas the flexible budget is prepared retroactively based on the actual output of 10,000 jackets. In other words, the static budget is being "flexed," or adjusted, from 12,000 jackets to 10,000 jackets.[3] The flexible budget for 10,000 jackets assumes all costs are either completely variable or completely fixed with respect to the number of jackets produced.

Webb develops its flexible budget in three steps.

Step 1: Identify the Actual Quantity of Output. In April 2014, Webb produced and sold 10,000 jackets.

Step 2: Calculate the Flexible Budget for Revenues Based on the Budgeted Selling Price and Actual Quantity of Output.

$$\text{Flexible-budget revenues} = \$120 \text{ per jacket} \times 10,000 \text{ jackets}$$
$$= \$1,200,000$$

Step 3: Calculate the Flexible Budget for Costs Based on the Budgeted Variable Cost per Output Unit, Actual Quantity of Output, and Budgeted Fixed Costs.

Flexible-budget variable costs	
Direct materials, $60 per jacket $\times$ 10,000 jackets	$ 600,000
Direct manufacturing labor, $16 per jacket $\times$ 10,000 jackets	160,000
Variable manufacturing overhead, $12 per jacket $\times$ 10,000 jackets	120,000
Total flexible-budget variable costs	880,000
Flexible-budget fixed costs	276,000
Flexible-budget total costs	$1,156,000

---

[3] Suppose Webb, when preparing its annual budget for 2014 at the end of 2013, had perfectly anticipated that its output in April 2014 would equal 10,000 jackets. Then the flexible budget for April 2014 would be identical to the static budget.

| Exhibit 2 | Level 2 Flexible-Budget-Based Variance Analysis for Webb Company for April 2014[a] |

Level 2 Analysis

	Actual Results (1)	Flexible-Budget Variances (2) = (1) – (3)	Flexible Budget (3)	Sales-Volume Variances (4) = (3) – (5)	Static Budget (5)
Units sold	10,000	0	10,000	2,000 U	12,000
Revenues	$1,250,000	$50,000 F	$1,200,000	$240,000 U	$1,440,000
Variable costs					
Direct materials	621,600	21,600 U	600,000	120,000 F	720,000
Direct manufacturing labor	198,000	38,000 U	160,000	32,000 F	192,000
Variable manufacturing overhead	130,500	10,500 U	120,000	24,000 F	144,000
Total variable costs	950,100	70,100 U	880,000	176,000 F	1,056,000
Contribution margin	299,900	20,100 U	320,000	64,000 U	384,000
Fixed manufacturing costs	285,000	9,000 U	276,000	0	276,000
Operating income	$ 14,900	$29,100 U	$ 44,000	$ 64,000 U	$ 108,000

| **Level 2** | ↑ | $29,100 U | ↑ | $ 64,000 U | ↑ |
| | | Flexible-budget variance | | Sales-volume variance | |

| **Level 1** | ↑ | | $93,100 U | | ↑ |
| | | | Static-budget variance | | |

[a]F = favorable effect on operating income; U = unfavorable effect on operating income.

These three steps enable Webb to prepare a flexible budget, as shown in Exhibit 2, column 3. The flexible budget allows for a more detailed analysis of the $93,100 unfavorable static-budget variance for operating income.

Decision Point

How can managers develop a flexible budget and why is it useful to do so?

Flexible-Budget Variances and Sales-Volume Variances

Exhibit 2 shows the flexible-budget-based variance analysis for Webb, which subdivides the $93,100 unfavorable static-budget variance for operating income into two parts: a flexible-budget variance of $29,100 U and a sales-volume variance of $64,000 U. The **sales-volume variance** is the difference between a flexible-budget amount and the corresponding static-budget amount. The **flexible-budget variance** is the difference between an actual result and the corresponding flexible-budget amount.

Sales-Volume Variances

Keep in mind that the flexible-budget amounts in column 3 of Exhibit 2 and the static-budget amounts in column 5 are both computed using budgeted selling prices, budgeted variable cost per jacket, and budgeted fixed costs. The difference between the static-budget and the flexible-budget amounts is called the sales-volume variance because it arises *solely* from the difference between the 10,000 actual quantity (or volume) of jackets sold and the 12,000 quantity of jackets expected to be sold in the static budget.

Learning Objective 3

Calculate flexible-budget variances

...each flexible-budget variance is the difference between an actual result and a flexible-budget amount

and sales-volume variances

...each sales-volume variance is the difference between a flexible-budget amount and a static-budget amount

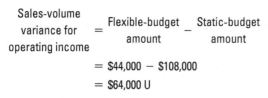

$$\text{Sales-volume variance for operating income} = \text{Flexible-budget amount} - \text{Static-budget amount}$$

$$= \$44,000 - \$108,000$$

$$= \$64,000 \text{ U}$$

The sales-volume variance in operating income for Webb measures the change in the budgeted contribution margin because Webb sold only 10,000 jackets rather than the budgeted 12,000.

$$\begin{aligned}
\begin{array}{c}\text{Sales-volume}\\ \text{variance for}\\ \text{operating income}\end{array} &= \left(\begin{array}{c}\text{Budgeted contribution}\\ \text{margin per unit}\end{array}\right) \times \left(\begin{array}{c}\text{Actual units}\\ \text{sold}\end{array} - \begin{array}{c}\text{Static-budget}\\ \text{units sold}\end{array}\right)\\[2ex]
&= \left(\begin{array}{c}\text{Budgeted selling}\\ \text{price}\end{array} - \begin{array}{c}\text{Budgeted variable}\\ \text{cost per unit}\end{array}\right) \times \left(\begin{array}{c}\text{Actual units}\\ \text{sold}\end{array} - \begin{array}{c}\text{Static-budget}\\ \text{units sold}\end{array}\right)\\[2ex]
&= (\$120 \text{ per jacket} - \$88 \text{ per jacket}) \times (10{,}000 \text{ jackets} - 12{,}000 \text{ jackets})\\[1ex]
&= \$32 \text{ per jacket} \times (-2{,}000 \text{ jackets})\\[1ex]
&= \$64{,}000 \text{ U}
\end{aligned}$$

Exhibit 2, column 4, shows the components of this overall variance by identifying the sales-volume variance for each of the line items in the income statement. The unfavorable sales-volume variance in operating income arises because of one or more of the following reasons:

1. Failure of Webb's managers to execute the sales plans
2. Weaker than anticipated overall demand for jackets
3. Competitors taking away market share from Webb
4. Unexpected changes in customer tastes and preferences away from Webb's designs
5. Quality problems leading to customer dissatisfaction with Webb's jackets

How Webb responds to the unfavorable sales-volume variance will depend on what its managers believe caused the variance. For example, if Webb's managers believe the unfavorable sales-volume variance was caused by market-related reasons (reasons 1, 2, 3, or 4), the sales manager would be in the best position to explain what happened and suggest corrective actions that may be needed, such as sales promotions, market studies, or changes to advertising plans. If, however, managers believe the unfavorable sales-volume variance was caused by unanticipated quality problems (reason 5), the production manager would be in the best position to analyze the causes and suggest strategies for improvement, such as changes in the manufacturing process or investments in new machines.

The static-budget variances compared actual revenues and costs for 10,000 jackets against budgeted revenues and costs for 12,000 jackets. A portion of this difference, the sales-volume variance, reflects the effects of selling fewer units or inaccurate forecasting of sales. By removing this component from the static-budget variance, managers can compare their firm's revenues earned and costs incurred for April 2014 against the flexible budget—the revenues and costs Webb would have budgeted for the 10,000 jackets actually produced and sold. *Flexible-budget variances are a better measure of sales price and cost performance than static-budget variances because they compare actual revenues to budgeted revenues and actual costs to budgeted costs for the same 10,000 jackets of output.* Concepts in Action: Flexible Budgets at Corning shows the importance of flexible budgets for conducting variance analysis and in enabling a company to manage its business in an uncertain environment.

Flexible-Budget Variances

The first three columns of Exhibit 2 compare Webb's actual results with its flexible-budget amounts. The flexible-budget variances for each line item in the income statement are shown in column 2:

$$\begin{array}{c}\text{Flexible-budget}\\ \text{variance}\end{array} = \begin{array}{c}\text{Actual}\\ \text{result}\end{array} - \begin{array}{c}\text{Flexible-budget}\\ \text{amount}\end{array}$$

The operating income line in Exhibit 2 shows the flexible-budget variance is $29,100 U ($14,900 − $44,000). The $29,100 U arises because the actual selling price, actual variable

Concepts in Action

Flexible Budgets at Corning

Historically, the rule of business budgeting was simple: Make a budget and stick to it. In today's fast-changing environment, however, many companies are pairing their annual "static" budget with a flexible budget that adjusts for changes in the volume of activity. Corning, the 160-year-old maker of specialty glass and ceramics, uses a flexible budget to quickly accommodate the impact of significant changes that affect its business.

Each year, Corning pulls together its annual budget. While managers still work to make sure that budget is achieved, it cannot predict the actions of Corning's customers and competitors with 100% accuracy. For instance, Apple uses the company's scratch-resistant Gorilla Glass on its iPhone screens. If Apple decides to expedite the production of its newest iPhone model, Corning may have to unexpectedly ramp up its Gorilla Glass manufacturing, which has both unexpected costs and revenues. At Corning, management accountants and finance executives produce rolling forecasts each month to address what the company thinks will happen for the rest of the quarter. According to Tony Tripeny, Corning's senior vice president and corporate controller, "Based on this analysis, we will go to the business units and say, 'What are you going to do differently? What actions are you going to take, and how is that different from what we had assumed with the budget?'"

By using a flexible budget, Corning managers can analyze uncertainty, improve performance evaluation, and conduct useful variance analysis that helps the company stay on track. So, why does Corning develop a detailed budget at all? It has specific benefits, explains Tripeny. As an example, he cites the relationship of a budget to Corning's resolve to be the lowest-cost producer in its markets. "During the budget process, we set up specific objectives, like targets for manufacturing costs," he says. "Even though the business might change during the year, it normally doesn't change enough to alter the manufacturing-performance targets. From a control standpoint, a budget still has value, but it shouldn't guide how you manage the business, which is about perceiving what's ahead and acting on it quicker than the competition."

Sources: Pogue, David. 2010. Gorilla Glass, the smartphone's unsung hero. Pogue's Posts (blog), *New York Times*, December 9. http://pogue.blogs.nytimes.com; Banham, Russ. 2011. Let it roll. *CFO Magazine*, May.

cost per unit, and actual fixed costs differ from their budgeted amounts. The actual results and budgeted amounts for the selling price and variable cost per unit are as follows:

	Actual Result	Budgeted Amount
Selling price	$125.00 ($1,250,000 ÷ 10,000 jackets)	$120.00 ($1,200,000 ÷ 10,000 jackets)
Variable cost per jacket	$ 95.01 ($ 950,100 ÷ 10,000 jackets)	$ 88.00 ($ 880,000 ÷ 10,000 jackets)

The flexible-budget variance for revenues is called the **selling-price variance** because it arises solely from the difference between the actual selling price and the budgeted selling price:

$$\text{Selling-price variance} = \left(\begin{array}{c} \text{Actual} \\ \text{selling price} \end{array} - \begin{array}{c} \text{Budgeted} \\ \text{selling price} \end{array} \right) \times \begin{array}{c} \text{Actual} \\ \text{units sold} \end{array}$$

$$= (\$125 \text{ per jacket} - \$120 \text{ per jacket}) \times 10,000 \text{ jackets}$$

$$= \$50,000 \text{ F}$$

Webb has a favorable selling-price variance because the $125 actual selling price exceeds the $120 budgeted amount, which increases operating income. Marketing managers are generally in the best position to understand and explain the reason for a selling price difference. For example, was the difference due to better quality? Or was it due to an overall increase in market prices? Webb's managers concluded it was due to a general increase in prices.

The flexible-budget variance for total variable costs is unfavorable ($70,100 U) for the actual output of 10,000 jackets. It's unfavorable because of one or both of the following:

- Webb used greater quantities of inputs (such as direct manufacturing labor-hours) compared to the budgeted quantities of inputs.
- Webb incurred higher prices per unit for the inputs (such as the wage rate per direct manufacturing labor-hour) compared to the budgeted prices per unit of the inputs.

Higher input quantities and/or higher input prices relative to the budgeted amounts could be the result of Webb deciding to produce a better product than what was planned or the result of inefficiencies related to Webb's manufacturing and purchasing operations or both. *You should always think of variance analysis as providing suggestions for further investigation rather than as establishing conclusive evidence of good or bad performance.*

The actual fixed costs of $285,000 are $9,000 more than the budgeted amount of $276,000. This unfavorable flexible-budget variance reflects unexpected increases in the cost of fixed indirect resources, such as the factory's rent or supervisors' salaries.

In the rest of this chapter, we will focus on variable direct-cost input variances.

Decision Point

How are flexible-budget and sales-volume variances calculated?

Learning Objective 4

Explain why standard costs are often used in variance analysis

...standard costs exclude past inefficiencies and take into account expected future changes

Standard Costs for Variance Analysis

To gain further insight, a company will subdivide the flexible-budget variance for its direct-cost inputs into two more-detailed variances:

1. A price variance that reflects the difference between an actual input price and a budgeted input price
2. An efficiency variance that reflects the difference between an actual input quantity and a budgeted input quantity

We will call these level 3 variances. Managers generally have more control over efficiency variances than price variances because the quantity of inputs used is primarily affected by factors inside the company (such as the efficiency with which operations are performed), whereas changes in the price of materials or in wage rates may be largely dictated by market forces outside the company.

Obtaining Budgeted Input Prices and Budgeted Input Quantities

To calculate price and efficiency variances, Webb needs to obtain budgeted input prices and budgeted input quantities. Webb's three main sources for this information are: (1) past data, (2) data from similar companies, and (3) standards. Each source has its advantages and disadvantages.

1. **Actual input data from past periods.** Most companies have past data on actual input prices and actual input quantities. These historical data could be analyzed for trends or patterns to obtain estimates of budgeted prices and quantities.

   Advantages: Past data represent quantities and prices that are real rather than hypothetical, so they can be very useful benchmarks for measuring improvements in performance. Moreover, past data are typically easy to collect at a low cost.

   Disadvantages: A firm's inefficiencies, such as the wastage of direct materials, are incorporated in past data. Consequently, the data do not represent the performance the firm could have ideally attained, only the performance it achieved in the past. Past data also do not incorporate any changes expected for the budget period, such as improvements resulting from new investments in technology.

2. **Data from other companies that have similar processes.** Another source of information is data from peer companies or companies that have similar processes, which can serve as a benchmark. For example, Baptist Healthcare System in Louisville, Kentucky, benchmarks its labor performance data against those of similar top-ranked hospitals.

   Advantages: Data from other companies can provide a firm useful information about how it's performing relative to its competitors.

   Disadvantages: Input-price and input-quantity data from other companies are often not available or may not be comparable to a particular company's situation. Consider American Apparel, which makes more than 1 million articles of clothing a week. At its sole factory, in Los Angeles, workers receive hourly wages, piece rates, and medical benefits well in excess of those paid by its competitors, virtually all of whom are offshore and have significantly lower production costs. (We will discuss benchmarking in more detail later in the chapter.)

3. **Standards developed by the firm itself.** A **standard** is a carefully determined price, cost, or quantity that is used as a benchmark for judging performance. Standards are usually expressed on a per-unit basis. Consider how Webb determines its direct manufacturing labor standards. Webb conducts engineering studies to obtain a detailed breakdown of the steps required to make a jacket. Each step is assigned a standard time based on work performed by a *skilled* worker using equipment operating in an *efficient* manner. Similarly, Webb determines the standard quantity of square yards of cloth based on what is required by a skilled operator to make a jacket.

   Advantages: Standard times (1) aim to exclude past inefficiencies and (2) take into account changes expected to occur in the budget period. An example of the latter would be a decision by Webb's managers to lease new, faster, and more accurate sewing machines. Webb would incorporate the resulting higher level of efficiency into the new standards it sets.

   Disdvantages: Because they are not based on realized benchmarks, the standards might not be achievable, and workers could get discouraged trying to meet them.

The term *standard* refers to many different things:

- A **standard input** is a carefully determined quantity of input, such as square yards of cloth or direct manufacturing labor-hours, required for one unit of output, such as a jacket.
- A **standard price** is a carefully determined price a company expects to pay for a unit of input. In the Webb example, the standard wage rate the firm expects to pay its operators is an example of a standard price of a direct manufacturing labor-hour.
- A **standard cost** is a carefully determined cost of a unit of output, such as the standard direct manufacturing labor cost of a jacket at Webb.

$$\begin{array}{c} \text{Standard cost per output unit for} \\ \text{each variable direct-cost input} \end{array} = \begin{array}{c} \text{Standard input allowed} \\ \text{for one output unit} \end{array} \times \begin{array}{c} \text{Standard price} \\ \text{per input unit} \end{array}$$

Standard direct material cost per jacket: 2 square yards of cloth input allowed per output unit (jacket) manufactured, at $30 standard price per square yard

Standard direct material cost per jacket = 2 square yards × $30 per square yard = $60

Standard direct manufacturing labor cost per jacket: 0.8 manufacturing labor-hour of input allowed per output unit manufactured, at $20 standard price per hour

Standard direct manufacturing labor cost per jacket = 0.8 labor-hour × $20 per labor-hour = $16

How are the words *budget* and *standard* related? Budget is the broader term. To clarify, budgeted input prices, input quantities, and costs need *not* be based on standards. As we saw previously, they could be based on past data or competitive benchmarks. However, when standards *are* used to obtain budgeted input quantities and prices, the terms *standard* and *budget* are used interchangeably. The standard cost of each input required for one unit of output is determined by the standard quantity of the input required for one unit of output and the standard price per input unit. Notice how the standard-cost computations shown previously for direct materials and direct manufacturing labor result in the budgeted direct material cost per jacket of $60 and the budgeted direct manufacturing labor cost of $16 referred to earlier.

In its standard costing system, Webb uses standards that are attainable by operating efficiently but that allow for normal disruptions. A normal disruption could include, for example, a short delay in the receipt of materials needed to produce the jackets or a production delay because a piece of equipment needed a minor repair. An alternative is to set more-challenging standards that are more difficult to attain. Setting challenging standards can increase the motivation of employees and a firm's performance. However, as we have indicated, if workers believe the standards are unachievable, they can become frustrated and the firm's performance could suffer.

Decision Point

What is a standard cost and what are its purposes?

Learning Objective 5

Compute price variances

...each price variance is the difference between an actual input price and a budgeted input price

and efficiency variances

...each efficiency variance is the difference between an actual input quantity and a budgeted input quantity for actual output

for direct-cost categories

Price Variances and Efficiency Variances for Direct-Cost Inputs

Consider Webb's two direct-cost categories. The actual cost for each of these categories for the 10,000 jackets manufactured and sold in April 2014 is as follows:

Direct Materials Purchased and Used[4]

1. Square yards of cloth input purchased and used	22,200
2. Actual price incurred per square yard	$ 28
3. Direct material costs (22,200 × $28) [shown in Exhibit 2, column 1]	$621,600

Direct manufacturing Labor used

1. Direct manufacturing labor-hours used	9,000
2. Actual price incurred per direct manufacturing labor-hour	$ 22
3. Direct manufacturing labor costs (9,000 × $22) [shown in Exhibit 2, column 1]	$198,000

Let's use the Webb Company data to illustrate the price variance and the efficiency variance for direct-cost inputs.

A **price variance** is the difference between actual price and budgeted price, multiplied by the actual input quantity, such as direct materials purchased. A price variance is sometimes called a **rate variance**, especially when it's used to describe the price variance for direct manufacturing labor. An **efficiency variance** is the difference between the actual input quantity used (such as square yards of cloth) and the budgeted input quantity allowed for actual output, multiplied by budgeted price. An efficiency variance is sometimes called a **usage variance**. Let's explore price and efficiency variances in greater detail so we can see how managers use them.

Price Variances

The formula for computing the price variance is as follows:

$$\frac{\text{Price}}{\text{variance}} = \left(\frac{\text{Actual price}}{\text{of input}} - \frac{\text{Budgeted price}}{\text{of input}}\right) \times \frac{\text{Actual quantity}}{\text{of input}}$$

The price variances for Webb's two direct-cost categories are as follows:

Direct-Cost Category	$\left(\dfrac{\text{Actual price}}{\text{of input}} - \dfrac{\text{Budgeted price}}{\text{of input}}\right) \times$	Actual quantity of input	=	Price Variance
Direct materials	($28 per sq. yard) − $30 per sq. yard) ×	22,200 square yards	=	$44,400 F
Direct manufacturing labor	($22 per hour − $20 per hour)	× 9,000 hours	=	$18,000 U

---

[4] The Problem for Self-Study relaxes the assumption that the quantity of direct materials used equals the quantity of direct materials purchased.

The direct materials price variance is favorable because the actual price of cloth is less than the budgeted price, resulting in an increase in operating income. The direct manufacturing labor price variance is unfavorable because the actual wage rate paid to labor is more than the budgeted rate, resulting in a decrease in operating income.

Managers should always consider a broad range of possible causes for a price variance. For example, Webb's favorable direct materials price variance could be due to one or more of the following:

- Webb's purchasing manager negotiated the direct materials prices more skillfully than was planned for in the budget.
- The purchasing manager switched to a lower-price supplier.
- The purchasing manager ordered larger quantities than the quantities budgeted, thereby obtaining quantity discounts.
- Direct materials prices decreased unexpectedly due to an oversupply of materials in the industry.
- The budgeted purchase prices of direct materials were set too high because managers did not carefully analyze market conditions.
- The purchasing manager negotiated favorable prices because he was willing to accept unfavorable terms on factors other than prices (such as agree to lower-quality material).

How Webb's managers respond to the direct materials price variance depends on what they believe caused it. For example, if they believe the purchasing manager received quantity discounts by ordering a larger amount of materials than budgeted, Webb could investigate whether the larger quantities resulted in higher storage costs for the firm. If the increase in storage and inventory holding costs exceeds the quantity discounts, purchasing in larger quantities is not beneficial. Some companies have reduced their materials storage areas to prevent their purchasing managers from ordering in larger quantities.

Efficiency Variance

For any actual level of output, the efficiency variance is the difference between the actual quantity of input used and the budgeted quantity of input allowed for that output level, multiplied by the budgeted input price:

$$\text{Efficiency variance} = \left(\begin{array}{c} \text{Actual} \\ \text{quantity of} \\ \text{input used} \end{array} - \begin{array}{c} \text{Budgeted quantity} \\ \text{of input allowed} \\ \text{for actual output} \end{array} \right) \times \begin{array}{c} \text{Budgeted price} \\ \text{of input} \end{array}$$

The idea here is that, given a certain output level, a company is inefficient if it uses a larger quantity of input than budgeted. Conversely, a company is efficient if it uses a smaller input quantity than was budgeted for that output level.

The efficiency variances for each of Webb's direct-cost categories are as follows:

Direct-Cost Category	$\left(\begin{array}{c} \text{Actual} \\ \text{quantity of} \\ \text{input used} \end{array} - \begin{array}{c} \text{Budgeted quantity} \\ \text{of input allowed} \\ \text{for actual output} \end{array} \right)$	$\times \begin{array}{c} \text{Budgeted price} \\ \text{of input} \end{array}$	$= \begin{array}{c} \text{Efficiency} \\ \text{variance} \end{array}$
Direct materials	[22,200 sq. yds. − (10,000 units × 2 sq. yds./unit)]	× $30 per sq. yard	
	= (22,200 sq. yds. − 20,000 sq. yds.)	× $30 per sq. yard	= $66,000 U
Direct manufacturing labor	[9,000 hours − (10,000 units × 0.8 hour/unit)]	× $20 per hour	
	= (9,000 hours − 8,000 hours)	× $20 per hour	= 20,000 U

The two manufacturing efficiency variances—the direct materials efficiency variance and the direct manufacturing labor efficiency variance—are each unfavorable. Why? Because given the firm's actual output, more of these inputs were used than were budgeted for. This lowered Webb's operating income.

As with price variances, there is a broad range of possible causes for these efficiency variances. For example, Webb's unfavorable efficiency variance for direct manufacturing labor could be because of one or more of the following:

- Webb's workers took longer to make each jacket because they worked more slowly or made poor-quality jackets that required reworking.
- Webb's personnel manager hired underskilled workers.
- Webb's production scheduler inefficiently scheduled work, resulting in more manufacturing labor time than budgeted being used per jacket.
- Webb's maintenance department did not properly maintain machines, resulting in more manufacturing labor time than budgeted being used per jacket.
- Webb's budgeted time standards were too tight because the skill levels of employees and the environment in which they operated weren't accurately evaluated.

Suppose Webb's managers determine that the unfavorable variance is due to poor machine maintenance. Webb could then establish a team consisting of plant engineers and machine operators to develop a maintenance schedule to reduce future breakdowns and prevent adverse effects on labor time and product quality.[5]

Exhibit 3 provides an alternative way to calculate price and efficiency variances. It shows how the price variance and the efficiency variance subdivide the flexible-budget variance. Consider direct materials. The direct materials flexible-budget variance of $21,600 U is the difference between the actual costs incurred (actual input quantity × actual price) of $621,600 shown in column 1 and the flexible budget (budgeted input quantity allowed

| Exhibit 3 | Columnar Presentation of Variance Analysis: Direct Costs for Webb Company for April 2014[a] |

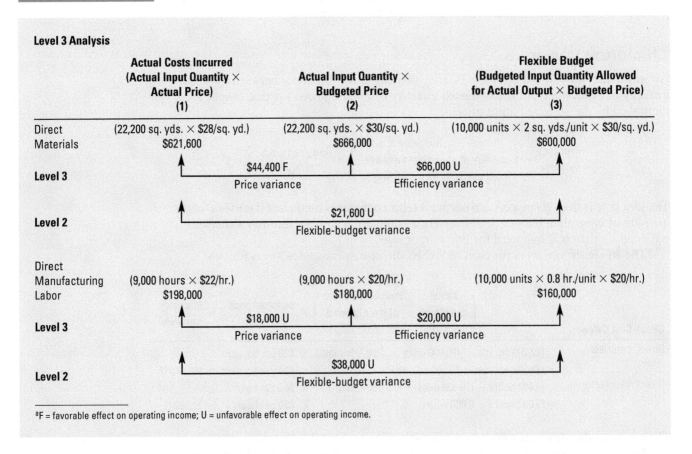

Level 3 Analysis

	Actual Costs Incurred (Actual Input Quantity × Actual Price) (1)	Actual Input Quantity × Budgeted Price (2)	Flexible Budget (Budgeted Input Quantity Allowed for Actual Output × Budgeted Price) (3)
Direct Materials	(22,200 sq. yds. × $28/sq. yd.) $621,600	(22,200 sq. yds. × $30/sq. yd.) $666,000	(10,000 units × 2 sq. yds./unit × $30/sq. yd.) $600,000
Level 3		$44,400 F Price variance	$66,000 U Efficiency variance
Level 2		$21,600 U Flexible-budget variance	
Direct Manufacturing Labor	(9,000 hours × $22/hr.) $198,000	(9,000 hours × $20/hr.) $180,000	(10,000 units × 0.8 hr./unit × $20/hr.) $160,000
Level 3		$18,000 U Price variance	$20,000 U Efficiency variance
Level 2		$38,000 U Flexible-budget variance	

[a]F = favorable effect on operating income; U = unfavorable effect on operating income.

_____

[5] When there are multiple inputs, such as different types of materials, that can be substituted for one another, the efficiency variance can be further decomposed into mix and yield variances. The appendix to this chapter describes how these variances are calculated.

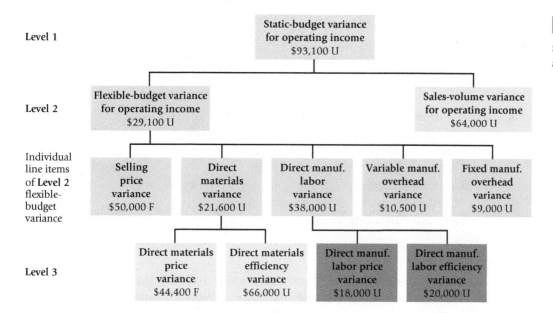

Level 1

Exhibit 4

Summary of Level 1, 2, and 3 Variance Analyses

for actual output × budgeted price) of $600,000 shown in column 3. Column 2 (actual input quantity × budgeted price) is inserted between column 1 and column 3. The difference between columns 1 and 2 is the price variance of $44,400 F. This price variance occurs because the same actual input quantity (22,200 sq. yds.) is multiplied by the *actual price* ($28) in column 1 and the *budgeted price* ($30) in column 2. The difference between columns 2 and 3 is the efficiency variance of $66,000 U because the same budgeted price ($30) is multiplied by the *actual input quantity* (22,200 sq. yds) in column 2 and the *budgeted input quantity allowed for actual output* (20,000 sq. yds.) in column 3. The sum of the direct materials price variance, $44,400 F, and the direct materials efficiency variance, $66,000 U, equals the direct materials flexible budget variance, $21,600 U.

Exhibit 4 provides a summary of the different variances. Note how the variances at each higher level provide disaggregated and more detailed information for evaluating performance.

We now present Webb's journal entries under its standard costing system.

Journal Entries Using Standard Costs

Our focus is on direct materials and direct manufacturing labor. All the numbers included in the following journal entries are found in Exhibit 3.

Note: In each of the following entries, unfavorable variances are always debits (they decrease operating income), and favorable variances are always credits (they increase operating income).

Journal Entry 1A

Isolate the direct materials price variance at the time the materials were purchased. This is done by increasing (debiting) the Direct Materials Control account by the standard price Webb established for purchasing the materials. This is the earliest time possible to isolate this variance.

1a.	Direct Materials Control		
	(22,200 square yards × $30 per square yard)	666,000	
	Direct Materials Price Variance		
	(22,200 square yards × $2 per square yard)		44,400
	Accounts Payable Control		
	(22,200 square yards × $28 per square yard)		621,600
	This records the direct materials purchased.		

Journal Entry 1B

Isolate the direct materials efficiency variance at the time the direct materials are used by increasing (debiting) the Work-in-Process Control account. Use the standard quantities allowed for the actual output units manufactured times their standard purchase prices.

1b.	Work-in-Process Control		
	(10,000 jackets × 2 yards per jacket × $30 per square yard)	600,000	
	Direct Materials Efficiency Variance		
	(2,200 square yards × $30 per square yard)	66,000	
	Direct Materials Control		
	(22,200 square yards × $30 per square yard)		666,000
	This records the direct materials used.		

Journal Entry 2

Isolate the direct manufacturing labor price variance and efficiency variance at the time the labor is used by increasing (debiting) the Work-in-Process Control by the standard hours and standard wage rates allowed for the actual units manufactured. Note that the Wages Payable Control account measures the actual amounts payable to workers based on the actual hours they worked and their actual wage rate.

2.	Work-in-Process Control		
	(10,000 jackets × 0.80 hour per jacket × $20 per hour)	160,000	
	Direct Manufacturing Labor Price Variance		
	(9,000 hours × $2 per hour)	18,000	
	Direct Manufacturing Labor Efficiency Variance		
	(1,000 hours × $20 per hour)	20,000	
	Wages Payable Control		
	(9,000 hours × $22 per hour)		198,000
	This records the liability for Webb's direct manufacturing labor costs.		

You have learned how standard costing and variance analysis help managers focus on areas not operating as expected. The journal entries here point to another advantage of standard costing systems: standard costs simplify product costing. As each unit is manufactured, costs are assigned to it using the standard cost of direct materials, the standard cost of direct manufacturing labor, and the standard manufacturing overhead cost.

From the perspective of control, all variances should be isolated at the earliest possible time. For example, by isolating the direct materials price variance at the time materials are purchased, managers can take corrective actions—such as trying to obtain cost reductions from the firm's current suppliers or obtaining price quotes from other potential suppliers—immediately when a large unfavorable variance is known rather than waiting until after the materials are used in production.

If the variance accounts are immaterial in amount at the end of the fiscal year, they are written off to the cost of goods sold. For simplicity, we assume that the balances in the different direct cost variance accounts as of April 2014 are also the balances at the end of 2014 and are immaterial in total. Webb would record the following journal entry to write off the direct cost variance accounts to the Cost of Goods Sold account.

Cost of Goods Sold	59,600	
Direct Materials Price Variance	44,400	
Direct Materials Efficiency Variance		66,000
Direct Manufacturing Labor Price Variance		18,000
Direct Manufacturing Labor Efficiency Variance		20,000

Alternatively, assuming Webb has inventories at the end of the fiscal year and the variances are material in their amounts, the variance accounts will be prorated among the cost of goods sold and various inventory accounts. For example, the Direct Materials Price Variance will be prorated among Materials Control, Work-in-Process Control, Finished Goods Control, and Cost of Goods Sold on the basis of the standard costs of direct materials in each account's ending balance. Direct Materials Efficiency Variance is prorated among Work-in-Process Control, Finished Goods Control, and Cost of Goods Sold on the basis of the direct material costs in each account's ending balance (after proration of the direct materials price variance).

Many accountants, industrial engineers, and managers argue that to the extent variances measure inefficiency during the year, they should be written off against income for that period instead of being prorated among inventories and the cost of goods sold. These people believe it's better to apply a combination of the write-off and proration methods for each individual variance. That way, unlike full proration, the firm doesn't end up carrying the costs of inefficiency as part of its inventoriable costs. Consider the efficiency variance: The portion of the variance due to avoidable inefficiencies should be written off to cost of goods sold. In contrast, the portion that is unavoidable should be prorated. Likewise, if a portion of the direct materials price variance is unavoidable because it is entirely caused by general market conditions, it too should be prorated.

Implementing Standard Costing

Standard costing provides valuable information that is used for the management and control of materials, labor, and other activities related to production.

Standard Costing and Information Technology

Both large and small firms are increasingly using computerized standard costing systems. For example, companies such as Sandoz, a maker of generic drugs, and Dell store standard prices and standard quantities in their computer systems. A bar code scanner records the receipt of materials, immediately costing each material using its stored standard price. The receipt of materials is then matched with the firm's purchase orders and recorded in accounts payable, and the direct material price variance is isolated.

The direct materials efficiency variance is calculated as output is completed by comparing the standard quantity of direct materials that should have been used with the computerized request for direct materials submitted by an operator on the production floor. Labor variances are calculated as employees log into production-floor terminals and punch in their employee numbers, start and end times, and the quantity of product they helped produce. Managers use this instantaneous feedback from variances to immediately detect and correct any cost-related problem.

Wide Applicability of Standard Costing

Manufacturing firms as well as firms in the service sector find standard costing to be a useful tool. Companies implementing total quality management programs use standard costing to control materials costs. Service-sector companies such as McDonald's are labor intensive and use standard costs to control labor costs. Companies that have implemented computer-integrated manufacturing (CIM), such as Toyota, use flexible budgeting and standard costing to manage activities such as materials handling and setups. The growing use of Enterprise Resource Planning (ERP) systems has made it easy for firms to keep track of the standard, average, and actual costs of items in inventory and to make real-time assessments of variances. Managers use variance information to identify areas of the firm's manufacturing or purchasing process that most need attention.

Decision Point

Why should a company calculate price and efficiency variances?

Concepts in Action ▶ Starbucks Reduces Direct-Cost Variances to Brew a Turnaround

Along with coffee, Starbucks brewed profitable growth for many years. But when consumers tightened their purse strings amid the recent recession, the company was in serious trouble. With customers cutting back and lower-priced competition—from Dunkin' Donuts and McDonald's among others—increasing, Starbucks' profit margins were under attack.

For Starbucks, profitability depends on making each beverage at the lowest possible cost. In each Starbucks store, the two key direct costs are materials and labor. Materials costs at Starbucks include coffee beans, milk, flavoring syrups, pastries, paper cups, and lids. To reduce budgeted costs for materials, Starbucks sought to avoid waste and spoilage by no longer brewing decaffeinated and darker coffee blends in the afternoon and evening, when store traffic is slower. With milk prices rising, the company switched to 2% milk, which is healthier and costs less, and redoubled efforts to reduce milk-related spoilage. To reduce labor costs, stores employed fewer baristas. In other stores, Starbucks adopted many "lean" production techniques to make its drink-making processes more efficient. While some changes seem small—keeping bins of coffee beans on top of the counter so baristas don't have to bend over and moving bottles of flavored syrups closer to where drinks are made—some stores experienced a 10% increase in transactions using the same number of workers or fewer.

Starbucks' focus on reducing direct-cost variances paid off. The company has reduced its store operating expenses from 36.1% of total net revenue in 2008 to 29.5% in 2012. Continued focus on direct-cost variances will remain critical to the company's future success in any economic climate.

Sources: Adamy, Janet. 2009. Starbucks brews up new cost cuts by putting lid on afternoon decaf. *Wall Street Journal,* January 28; Harris, Craig. 2007. Starbucks slips; lattes rise. *Seattle Post Intelligencer,* July 23; Jargon, Julie. 2010. Starbucks growth revives, perked by Via. *Wall Street Journal,* January 21; Jargon, Julie. 2009. Latest Starbucks buzzword: 'Lean' Japanese techniques. *Wall Street Journal,* August 4; Kesmodel, David. 2009. Starbucks sees demand stirring again. *Wall Street Journal,* November 6; Starbucks Corporation, 2012 Annual Report (Seattle: Starbucks Corporation, 2013); and Starbucks Corporation, 2008 Annual Report (Seattle: Starbucks Corporation, 2009).

Learning Objective 6 ▶

Understand how managers use variances

...managers use variances to improve future performance

Management's Use of Variances

Managers and management accountants use variances to evaluate performance after decisions are implemented, to trigger organization learning, and to make continuous improvements. Variances serve as an early warning system to alert managers to existing problems or to prospective opportunities. When done well, variance analysis enables managers to evaluate the effectiveness of the actions and performance of personnel in the current period, as well as to fine-tune strategies for achieving improved performance in the future. Concepts in Action: Starbucks Reduces Direct-Cost Variances to Brew a Turnaround shows the huge payoff the coffee retailing giant has reaped from paying careful attention to variance analysis wth respect to its direct costs.

Multiple Causes of Variances

To interpret variances correctly and make appropriate decisions based on them, managers need to recognize that variances can have multiple causes. Managers must not interpret variances in isolation of each other. The causes of variances in one part of the value chain can be the result of decisions made in another part of the value chain. Consider an unfavorable direct materials efficiency variance on Webb's production line. Possible operational causes of this variance across the value chain of the company are:

1. Poor design of products or processes
2. Poor work on the production line because of underskilled workers or faulty machines
3. Inappropriate assignment of labor or machines to specific jobs
4. Congestion due to scheduling a large number of rush orders placed by Webb's sales representatives
5. Webb's cloth suppliers not manufacturing materials of uniformly high quality

Item 5 offers an even broader reason for the cause of the unfavorable direct materials efficiency variance by considering inefficiencies in the supply chain of companies—in this case, by the cloth suppliers for Webb's jackets. Whenever possible, managers must attempt to understand the root causes of the variances.

When to Investigate Variances

Because a standard is not a single measure but rather a range of acceptable input quantities, costs, output quantities, or prices, managers should expect small variances to arise. A variance within an acceptable range is considered to be an "in-control occurrence" and calls for no investigation or action by managers. So when do managers need to investigate variances?

Frequently, managers investigate variances based on subjective judgments or rules of thumb. For critical items, such as product defects, even a small variance can prompt an investigation. For other items, such as direct material costs, labor costs, and repair costs, companies generally have rules such as "investigate all variances exceeding $5,000 or 20% of the budgeted cost, whichever is lower." The idea is that a 4% variance in direct material costs of $1 million—a $40,000 variance—deserves more attention than a 15% variance in repair costs of $10,000—a $1,500 variance. In other words, variance analysis is subject to the same cost–benefit test as all other phases of a management control system.

Using Variances for Performance Measurement

Managers often use variance analysis when evaluating the performance of their employees or business units. Two attributes of performance are commonly evaluated:

1. **Effectiveness:** the degree to which a predetermined objective or target is met, such as the sales, market share, and customer satisfaction ratings of Starbucks' VIA® Ready Brew line of instant coffees.
2. **Efficiency:** the relative amount of inputs used to achieve a given output level. For example, the smaller the quantity of Arabica beans used to make a given number of VIA packets or the greater the number of VIA packets made from a given quantity of beans, the greater the efficiency.

As we discussed earlier, it is important to understand the causes of a variance before using it for performance evaluation. Suppose a purchasing manager for Starbucks has just negotiated a deal that results in a favorable price variance for direct materials. The deal could have achieved a favorable variance for any or all of the following reasons:

1. The purchasing manager bargained effectively with suppliers.
2. The purchasing manager secured a discount for buying in bulk with fewer purchase orders. (However, buying larger quantities than necessary for the short run resulted in excessive inventory.)
3. The purchasing manager accepted a bid from the lowest-priced supplier without fully checking the supplier's quality-monitoring procedures.

If the purchasing manager's performance is evaluated solely on price variances, then the evaluation will be positive. Reason 1 would support this conclusion: The purchasing manager bargained effectively. Reasons 2 and 3, buying in bulk or buying without checking the supplier's quality-monitoring procedures, will lead to short-run gains. But should these lead to a positive evaluation for the purchasing manager? Not necessarily. These short-run gains could be offset by higher inventory storage costs or higher inspection costs and defect rates. Starbucks may ultimately lose more money because of reasons 2 and 3 than it gains from the favorable price variance.

Bottom line: Managers should not automatically interpret a favorable variance as "good news" or assume it means their subordinates performed well.

Firms benefit from variance analysis because it highlights individual aspects of performance. However, if any single performance measure (for example, achieving a certain labor efficiency variance or a certain consumer rating) is overemphasized, managers will tend to make decisions that will cause the particular performance measure to look good. These actions may conflict with the company's overall goals, inhibiting the goals from being achieved. This faulty perspective on performance usually arises when top management designs a performance evaluation and reward system that does not emphasize total company objectives.

Organization Learning

The goal of variance analysis is for managers to understand why variances arise, to learn, and to improve their firm's future performance. For instance, to reduce the unfavorable direct materials efficiency variance, Webb's managers may attempt to improve the design of its jackets, the commitment of its workers to do the job right the first time, and the quality of the materials. Sometimes an unfavorable direct materials efficiency variance may signal a need to change the strategy related to a product, perhaps because it cannot be made at a low enough cost. Variance analysis should not be used to "play the blame game" (find someone to blame for every unfavorable variance) but to help managers learn about what happened and how to perform better in the future.

Companies need to strike a delicate balance between using variances to evaluate the performance of managers and employees and improve learning within the organization. If the performance evaluation aspect is overemphasized, managers will focus on setting and meeting targets that are easy to attain rather than targets that are challenging, require creativity and resourcefulness, and result in continuous improvement. For example, Webb's manufacturing manager will prefer an easy standard that allows workers ample time to manufacture a jacket. But that will provide the manufacturing department little incentive to improve processes and identify methods to reduce production times and costs. Alternatively, the manufacturing manager might urge workers to produce jackets within the time allowed, even if this leads to poorer quality jackets being produced, which would later hurt revenues. If variance analysis is seen as a way to promote learning within the organization, negative effects such as these can be minimized.

Continuous Improvement

Managers can also use variance analysis to create a virtuous cycle of continuous improvement. How? By repeatedly identifying the causes of variances, taking corrective actions, and evaluating the results. Improvement opportunities are often easier to identify when the company first produces a product. Once managers identify easy improvements, much more ingenuity may be required to identify successive ones. Some companies use kaizen budgeting to specifically target reductions in budgeted costs over successive periods. The advantage of kaizen budgeting is that it makes continuous improvement goals explicit.

Financial and Nonfinancial Performance Measures

Almost all companies use a combination of financial and nonfinancial performance measures for planning and control rather than relying exclusively on either type of measure. To control a production process, supervisors cannot wait for an accounting report with variances reported in dollars. Instead, timely nonfinancial performance measures are frequently used for control purposes. For example, Nissan and many other manufacturers display real-time defect rates and production levels on large LED screens throughout their plants for workers and managers to see.

In Webb's cutting room, cloth is laid out and cut into pieces, which are then matched and assembled. Managers exercise control in the cutting room by observing workers and by focusing on *nonfinancial measures*, such as number of square yards of cloth used to produce 1,000 jackets or the percentage of jackets started and completed without requiring any rework. Webb's production workers find these nonfinancial measures easy to understand. Webb's managers also use *financial measures* to evaluate the overall cost efficiency with which operations are being run and to help guide decisions about, say, changing the mix of inputs used in manufacturing jackets. Financial measures are critical in a company because they indicate the economic impact of diverse physical activities. This knowledge allows managers to make trade-offs, such as increasing the costs of one physical activity (say, cutting) to reduce the costs of another physical measure (say, defects).

Decision Point

How do managers use variances?

Benchmarking and Variance Analysis

Webb Company based its budgeted amounts on analysis of its own operations. We now turn to the situation in which companies develop standards based on the operations of other companies. **Benchmarking** is the continuous process of comparing your firm's performance levels against the best levels of performance in competing companies or in companies having similar processes. When benchmarks are used as standards, managers and management accountants know that the company will be competitive in the marketplace if it can meet or beat those standards.

Companies develop benchmarks and calculate variances on items that are the most important to their businesses. A common unit of measurement used to compare the efficiency of airlines is cost per available seat mile. Available seat mile (ASM) is a measure of airline size and equals the total seats in a plane multiplied by the distance the plane traveled. Consider the cost per available seat mile for United. Assume United uses data from each of six competing U.S. airlines in its benchmark cost comparisons. Summary data are in Exhibit 5. The benchmark companies are in alphabetical order in column A. Also reported in Exhibit 5 are operating cost per ASM, operating revenue per ASM, operating income per ASM, fuel cost per ASM, labor cost per ASM, and total available seat miles for each airline. The slow recovery of the travel industry from the recession induced by the financial crisis is evident in the fact that only five of the seven airlines have positive levels of operating income.

How well did United manage its costs? The answer depends on which specific benchmark is being used for comparison. United's actual operating cost of 14.19 cents per ASM is above the average operating cost of 12.91 cents per ASM of the six other airlines. Moreover, United's operating cost per ASM is 24.2% higher than JetBlue Airways, the lowest-cost competitor at 11.42 cents per ASM $[(14.19 - 11.42) \div 11.42 = 0.242]$. So why is United's operating cost per ASM so high? Columns E and F suggest that both fuel cost and labor cost are possible reasons. These benchmarking data alert management at United that it needs to become more efficient in its use of both material and labor inputs to become more cost competitive.

It can be difficult for firms to find appropriate benchmarks such as those in Exhibit 5. Many companies purchase benchmark data from consulting firms. Another problem is ensuring the benchmark numbers are comparable. In other words, there needs to be an "apples to apples" comparison. Differences can exist across companies in their strategies, inventory costing methods, depreciation methods, and so on. For example, JetBlue serves fewer cities and flies mostly long-haul routes compared with United, which serves almost all major U.S. cities and several international cities and flies both long-haul and short-haul routes. Southwest Airlines differs from United because it specializes in short-haul direct flights and offers fewer services on board its planes. Because United's strategy is different from the strategies of JetBlue and Southwest, one might expect its cost per ASM to be different, too. United's strategy is more comparable to the strategies of American, Delta, and U.S. Airways. Note that its costs per ASM are relatively more competitive with these airlines. But United

Learning Objective 7

Describe benchmarking and explain its role in cost management

...benchmarking compares actual performance against the best levels of performance

Exhibit 5	Available Seat Mile (ASM) Benchmark Comparison of United Airlines with Six Other Airlines

Home	Insert	Page Layout	Formulas	Data	Review	View

	A	B	C	D	E	F	G
1		Operating Cost (Cents per ASM)	Operating Revenue (Cents per ASM)	Operating Income (Cents per ASM)	Fuel Cost (Cents per ASM)	Labor Cost (Cents per ASM)	Total ASMs (Millions)
2							
3	Airline	(1)	(2)	(3) = (2) − (1)	(4)	(5)	(6)
4							
5	United Airlines	14.19	13.10	- 1.09	4.90	4.24	216,299
6	Airlines used as benchmarks:						
7	Alaska Airlines	11.90	13.09	1.19	4.10	3.53	28,185
8	American Airlines	14.26	13.47	-0.79	4.90	4.28	152,627
9	Delta Airlines	13.80	14.48	0.68	5.00	3.86	200,880
10	JetBlue Airways	11.42	11.96	0.54	4.40	2.76	40,095
11	Southwest Airlines	12.83	13.29	0.46	4.60	3.90	128,272
12	U.S. Airways	13.25	13.49	0.24	4.60	3.54	74,204
13	Average of airlines						
14	used as benchmarks	12.91	13.30	0.39	4.60	3.65	104,044
15							
16	Source: 2012 data from the MIT Global Airline Industry Program						

Decision Point ▶

What is benchmarking and why is it useful?

competes head to head with JetBlue and Southwest in several cities and markets, so it still needs to benchmark against these carriers as well.

United's management accountants can use benchmarking data to address several questions. How do factors such as plane size and type or the duration of flights affect the cost per ASM? Do airlines differ in their fixed cost/variable cost structures? To what extent can United's performance be improved by rerouting flights, using different types of aircraft on different routes, or changing the frequency or timing of specific flights? What explains revenue differences per ASM across airlines? Is it differences in the service quality passengers perceive or differences in an airline's competitive power at specific airports? Management accountants are more valuable to managers when they use benchmarking data to provide insight into *why* costs or revenues differ across companies or within plants of the same company, as distinguished from simply reporting the magnitude of the differences.

Problem for Self-Study

O'Shea Company manufactures ceramic vases. It uses its standard costing system when developing its flexible-budget amounts. In September 2014, 2,000 finished units were produced. The following information relates to its two direct manufacturing cost categories: direct materials and direct manufacturing labor.

Direct materials used were 4,400 kilograms (kg). The standard direct materials input allowed for one output unit is 2 kilograms at $15 per kilogram. O'Shea purchased 5,000 kilograms of materials at $16.50 per kilogram, a total of $82,500. (This Problem for Self-Study illustrates how to calculate direct materials variances when the quantity of materials *purchased* in a period differs from the quantity of materials *used* in that period.)

Actual direct manufacturing labor-hours were 3,250, at a total cost of $66,300. Standard manufacturing labor time allowed is 1.5 hours per output unit, and the standard direct manufacturing labor cost is $20 per hour.

1. Calculate the direct materials price variance and efficiency variance and the direct manufacturing labor price variance and efficiency variance. Base the direct materials price variance on a flexible budget for *actual quantity purchased*, but base the direct materials efficiency variance on a flexible budget for *actual quantity used*.

2. Prepare journal entries for a standard costing system that isolates variances at the earliest possible time.

Solution

1. Exhibit 6 shows how the columnar presentation of variances introduced in Exhibit 3 can be adjusted for the difference in timing between purchase and use of materials. Note, in particular, the two sets of computations in column 2 for direct materials—the $75,000 for direct materials purchased and the $66,000 for direct materials used. The direct materials price variance is calculated on purchases so that managers responsible for the purchase can immediately identify and isolate reasons for the variance and initiate any desired corrective action. The efficiency variance is the responsibility of the production manager, so this variance is identified only at the time materials are used.

2.

Materials Control (5,000 kg × $15 per kg)	75,000	
Direct Materials Price Variance (5,000 kg × $1.50 per kg)	7,500	
Accounts Payable Control (5,000 kg × $16.50 per kg)		82,500
Work-in-Process Control (2,000 units × 2 kg per unit × $15 per kg)	60,000	
Direct Materials Efficiency Variance (400 kg × $15 per kg)	6,000	
Materials Control (4,400 kg × $15 per kg)		66,000
Work-in-Process Control (2,000 units × 1.5 hours per unit × $20 per hour)	60,000	
Direct Manufacturing Labor Price Variance (3,250 hours × $0.40 per hour)	1,300	
Direct Manufacturing Labor Efficiency Variance (250 hours × $20 per hour)	5,000	
Wages Payable Control (3,250 hours × $20.40 per hour)		66,300

Note: All the variances are debits because they are unfavorable and therefore reduce operating income.

Columnar Presentation of Variance Analysis for O'Shea Company: Direct Materials and Direct Manufacturing Labor for September 2014

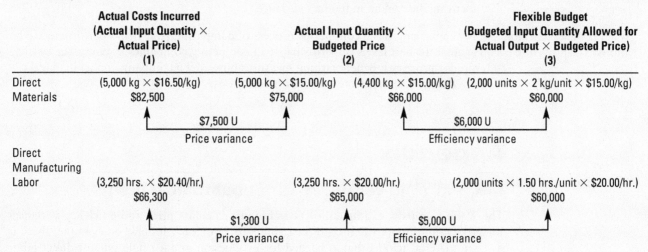

Level 3 Analysis

	Actual Costs Incurred (Actual Input Quantity × Actual Price) (1)	Actual Input Quantity × Budgeted Price (2)		Flexible Budget (Budgeted Input Quantity Allowed for Actual Output × Budgeted Price) (3)
Direct Materials	(5,000 kg × $16.50/kg) $82,500	(5,000 kg × $15.00/kg) $75,000	(4,400 kg × $15.00/kg) $66,000	(2,000 units × 2 kg/unit × $15.00/kg) $60,000
	↑ $7,500 U ↑ Price variance		↑ $6,000 U ↑ Efficiency variance	
Direct Manufacturing Labor	(3,250 hrs. × $20.40/hr.) $66,300	(3,250 hrs. × $20.00/hr.) $65,000		(2,000 units × 1.50 hrs./unit × $20.00/hr.) $60,000
	↑ $1,300 U ↑ Price variance		↑ $5,000 U ↑ Efficiency variance ↑	

[a]F = favorable effect on operating income; U = unfavorable effect on operating income.

▶ Decision Points

The following question-and-answer format summarizes the chapter's learning objectives. Each decision presents a key question related to a learning objective. The guidelines are the answer to that question.

Decision	Guidelines
1. What are static budgets and static-budget variances?	A static budget is based on the level of output planned at the start of the budget period. The static-budget variance is the difference between the actual result and the corresponding budgeted amount in the static budget.
2. How can managers develop a flexible budget, and why is it useful to do so?	A flexible budget is adjusted (flexed) to recognize the actual output level of the budget period. Managers use a three-step procedure to develop a flexible budget. When all costs are either variable or fixed with respect to output, these three steps require only information about the budgeted selling price, budgeted variable cost per output unit, budgeted fixed costs, and actual quantity of output units. Flexible budgets help managers gain more insight into the causes of variances than is available from static budgets.
3. How are flexible-budget and sales-volume variances calculated?	The static-budget variance can be subdivided into a flexible-budget variance (the difference between the actual result and the corresponding flexible-budget amount) and a sales-volume variance (the difference between the flexible-budget amount and the corresponding static-budget amount).
4. What is a standard cost and what are its purposes?	A standard cost is a carefully determined cost used as a benchmark for judging performance. The purposes of a standard cost are to exclude past inefficiencies and to take into account changes expected to occur in the budget period.
5. Why should a company calculate price and efficiency variables?	The computation of price and efficiency variances helps managers gain insight into two different—but not independent—aspects of performance. The price variance focuses on the difference between the actual input price and the budgeted input price. The efficiency variance focuses on the difference between the actual quantity of input and the budgeted quantity of input allowed for actual output.
6. How do managers use variances?	Managers use variances for control, decision-making, performance evaluation, organization learning, and continuous improvement. When using variances for these purposes, managers should consider several variances together rather than focusing only on an individual variance.
7. What is benchmarking and why is it useful?	Benchmarking is the continuous process of comparing your firm's performance against the best levels of performance in competing companies or companies with similar processes. Benchmarking measures how well a company and its managers are doing in comparison to other organizations.

Appendix

Mix and Yield Variances for Substitutable Inputs

The Webb Company example illustrates how to calculate price and efficiency variances for production inputs when there is a single form of each input. For example, there is a single material (cloth) that is needed for production and a single type of direct labor employed by Webb. But what if managers have leeway in combining and substituting inputs? For example, Del Monte can combine material inputs (such as pineapples, cherries, and grapes) in varying proportions for its cans of fruit cocktail. Within limits, these individual fruits are *substitutable inputs* in making the fruit cocktail.

We illustrate how the efficiency variance discussed in this chapter can be subdivided into variances that highlight the financial impact of input mix and input yield when inputs are substitutable. Consider Delpino Corporation, which makes tomato ketchup. Our example focuses on direct material inputs and substitution among three of these inputs. The same approach can also be used to examine substitutable direct manufacturing labor inputs.

To produce ketchup of a specified consistency, color, and taste, Delpino mixes three types of tomatoes grown in different regions: Latin American tomatoes (Latoms), California tomatoes (Caltoms), and Florida tomatoes (Flotoms). Delpino's production standards require 1.60 tons of tomatoes to produce 1 ton of ketchup; 50% of the tomatoes are budgeted to be Latoms, 30% Caltoms, and 20% Flotoms. The direct material inputs budgeted to produce 1 ton of ketchup are as follows:

0.80 (50% of 1.6) ton of Latoms at $70 per ton	$ 56.00
0.48 (30% of 1.6) ton of Caltoms at $80 per ton	38.40
0.32 (20% of 1.6) ton of Flotoms at $90 per ton	28.80
Total budgeted cost of 1.6 tons of tomatoes	$123.20

Budgeted average cost per ton of tomatoes is $123.20 ÷ 1.60 tons = $77 per ton.

Because Delpino uses fresh tomatoes to make ketchup, no inventories of tomatoes are kept. Purchases are made as needed, so all price variances relate to tomatoes purchased and used. Actual results for June 2014 show that a total of 6,500 tons of tomatoes were used to produce 4,000 tons of ketchup:

3,250	tons of Latoms at actual cost of $70 per ton	$227,500
2,275	tons of Caltoms at actual cost of $82 per ton	186,550
975	tons of Flotoms at actual cost of $96 per ton	93,600
6,500	tons of tomatoes	507,650
	Budgeted cost of 4,000 tons of ketchup at $123.20 per ton	492,800
	Flexible-budget variance for direct materials	$ 14,850 U

Given the standard ratio of 1.60 tons of tomatoes to 1 ton of ketchup, 6,400 tons of tomatoes should be used to produce 4,000 tons of ketchup. At standard mix, quantities of each type of tomato required are as follows:

Latoms:	0.50 × 6,400 = 3,200 tons
Caltoms:	0.30 × 6,400 = 1,920 tons
Flotoms:	0.20 × 6,400 = 1,280 tons

Direct Materials Price and Efficiency Variances

Exhibit 7 presents in columnar format the analysis of the flexible-budget variance for direct materials discussed in the body of the chapter. The materials price and efficiency variances are calculated separately for each input material and then added together. The variance analysis prompts Delpino to investigate the unfavorable price and efficiency variances. Why did it pay more for tomatoes and use greater quantities than it had budgeted? Were actual market prices of tomatoes higher, in general, or could the purchasing department have negotiated lower prices? Did the inefficiencies result from inferior tomatoes or from problems in processing?

Direct Materials Mix and Direct Materials Yield Variances

Managers sometimes have discretion to substitute one material for another. The manager of Delpino's ketchup plant has some leeway in combining Latoms, Caltoms, and Flotoms without affecting the ketchup's quality. We will assume that to maintain quality, mix percentages of each type of tomato can only vary up to 5% from standard mix. For example, the percentage of Caltoms in the mix can vary between 25% and 35% (30% ± 5%).

| | **Exhibit 7** | Direct Materials Price and Efficiency Variances for the Delpino Corporation for June 2014 |

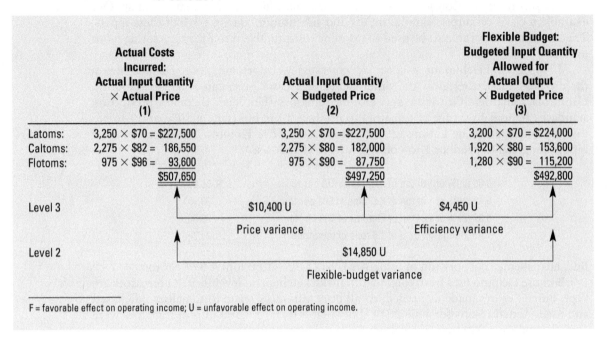

	Actual Costs Incurred: Actual Input Quantity × Actual Price (1)	**Actual Input Quantity × Budgeted Price (2)**	**Flexible Budget: Budgeted Input Quantity Allowed for Actual Output × Budgeted Price (3)**
Latoms:	3,250 × $70 = $227,500	3,250 × $70 = $227,500	3,200 × $70 = $224,000
Caltoms:	2,275 × $82 = 186,550	2,275 × $80 = 182,000	1,920 × $80 = 153,600
Flotoms:	975 × $96 = 93,600	975 × $90 = 87,750	1,280 × $90 = 115,200
	$507,650	$497,250	$492,800

Level 3 $10,400 U $4,450 U

      Price variance   Efficiency variance

Level 2 $14,850 U

      Flexible-budget variance

F = favorable effect on operating income; U = unfavorable effect on operating income.

When inputs are substitutable, direct materials efficiency improvement relative to budgeted costs can come from two sources: (1) using a cheaper mix to produce a given quantity of output, measured by the direct materials mix variance, and (2) using less input to achieve a given quantity of output, measured by the direct materials yield variance.

Holding actual total quantity of all direct materials inputs used constant, the total **direct materials mix variance** is the difference between (1) budgeted cost for actual mix of actual total quantity of direct materials used and (2) budgeted cost of budgeted mix of actual total quantity of direct materials used. Holding budgeted input mix constant, the **direct materials yield variance** is the difference between (1) budgeted cost of direct materials based on actual total quantity of direct materials used and (2) flexible-budget cost of direct materials based on budgeted total quantity of direct materials allowed for actual output produced. Exhibit 8 presents the direct materials mix and yield variances for the Delpino Corporation.

Direct Materials Mix Variance

The total direct materials mix variance is the sum of the direct materials mix variances for each input:

$$
\begin{array}{c}
\text{Direct} \\
\text{materials} \\
\text{mix variance} \\
\text{for each input}
\end{array}
=
\begin{array}{c}
\text{Actual total} \\
\text{quantity of all} \\
\text{direct materials} \\
\text{inputs used}
\end{array}
\times
\left(
\begin{array}{c}
\text{Actual} \\
\text{direct materials} \\
\text{input mix} \\
\text{percentage}
\end{array}
-
\begin{array}{c}
\text{Budgeted} \\
\text{direct materials} \\
\text{input mix} \\
\text{percentage}
\end{array}
\right)
\times
\begin{array}{c}
\text{Budegeted} \\
\text{price of} \\
\text{direct materials} \\
\text{input}
\end{array}
$$

The direct materials mix variances are as follows:

Latoms:	6,500 tons × (0.50 − 0.50) × $70 per ton = 6,500 × 0.00 × $70 =	$ 0
Caltoms:	6,500 tons × (0.35 − 0.30) × $80 per ton = 6,500 × 0.05 × $80 =	26,000 U
Flotoms:	6,500 tons × (0.15 − 0.20) × $90 per ton = 6,500 × −0.05 × $90 =	29,250 F
Total direct materials mix variance		$ 3,250 F

| Exhibit 8 | Total Direct Materials Yield and Mix Variances for the Delpino Corporation for June 2014 |

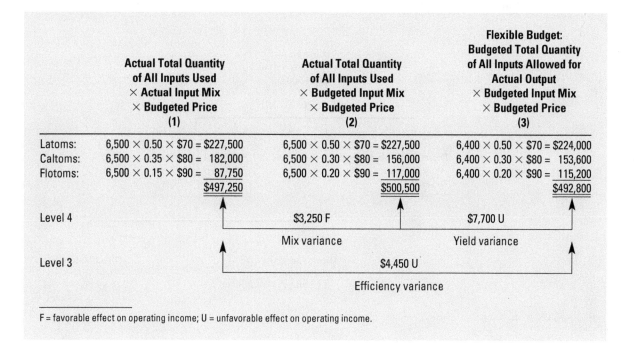

	Actual Total Quantity of All Inputs Used × Actual Input Mix × Budgeted Price (1)	Actual Total Quantity of All Inputs Used × Budgeted Input Mix × Budgeted Price (2)	Flexible Budget: Budgeted Total Quantity of All Inputs Allowed for Actual Output × Budgeted Input Mix × Budgeted Price (3)
Latoms:	6,500 × 0.50 × $70 = $227,500	6,500 × 0.50 × $70 = $227,500	6,400 × 0.50 × $70 = $224,000
Caltoms:	6,500 × 0.35 × $80 = 182,000	6,500 × 0.30 × $80 = 156,000	6,400 × 0.30 × $80 = 153,600
Flotoms:	6,500 × 0.15 × $90 = 87,750	6,500 × 0.20 × $90 = 117,000	6,400 × 0.20 × $90 = 115,200
	$497,250	$500,500	$492,800

Level 4 $3,250 F $7,700 U

                       Mix variance   Yield variance

Level 3 $4,450 U

                       Efficiency variance

F = favorable effect on operating income; U = unfavorable effect on operating income.

The total direct materials mix variance is favorable because relative to the budgeted mix, Delpino substitutes 5% of the cheaper Caltoms for 5% of the more-expensive Flotoms.

Direct Materials Yield Variance

The direct materials yield variance is the sum of the direct materials yield variances for each input:

$$
\begin{pmatrix} \text{Direct} \\ \text{materials} \\ \text{yield variance} \\ \text{for each input} \end{pmatrix} = \begin{pmatrix} \text{Actual total} & \text{Budgeted total} \\ \text{quantity of} & \text{quantity of all} \\ \text{all direct} - \text{direct materials} \\ \text{materials} & \text{input allowed} \\ \text{inputs used} & \text{for actual output} \end{pmatrix} \times \begin{pmatrix} \text{Budgeted} \\ \text{direct materials} \\ \text{input mix} \\ \text{percentage} \end{pmatrix} \times \begin{pmatrix} \text{Budegeted} \\ \text{price of} \\ \text{direct materials} \\ \text{input} \end{pmatrix}
$$

The direct materials yield variances are as follows:

Latoms:	(6,500 − 6,400) tons × 0.50 × $70 per ton = 100 × 0.50 × $70 = $3,500 U
Caltoms:	(6,500 − 6,400) tons × 0.30 × $80 per ton = 100 × 0.30 × $80 = 2,400 U
Flotoms:	(6,500 − 6,400) tons × 0.20 × $90 per ton = 100 × 0.20 × $90 = 1,800 U
Total direct materials yield variance	$7,700 U

The total direct materials yield variance is unfavorable because Delpino used 6,500 tons of tomatoes rather than the 6,400 tons that it should have used to produce 4,000 tons of ketchup. Holding the budgeted mix and budgeted prices of tomatoes constant, the budgeted cost per ton of tomatoes in the budgeted mix is $77 per ton. The unfavorable yield variance represents the budgeted cost of using 100 more tons of tomatoes, (6,500 − 6,400) tons × $77 per ton = $7,700 U. Delpino would want to investigate reasons for this unfavorable yield variance. For example, did the substitution of the cheaper Caltoms for Flotoms that resulted in the favorable mix variance also cause the unfavorable yield variance?

233

The direct materials variances computed in Exhibits 7 and 8 can be summarized as follows:

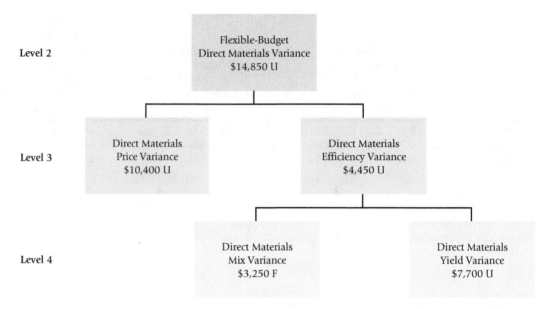

Terms to Learn

This chapter contains definitions of the following important terms:

benchmarking

budgeted performance

direct materials mix variance

direct materials yield variance

effectiveness

efficiency

efficiency variance

favorable variance

flexible budget

flexible-budget variance

management by exception

price variance

rate variance

sales-volume variance

selling-price variance

standard

standard cost

standard input

standard price

static budget

static-budget variance

unfavorable variance

usage variance

variance

Assignment Material

Questions

1 What is the relationship between management by exception and variance analysis?
2 What are two possible sources of information a company might use to compute the budgeted amount in variance analysis?
3 Distinguish between a favorable variance and an unfavorable variance.
4 What is the key difference between a static budget and a flexible budget?
5 Why might managers find a flexible-budget analysis more informative than a static-budget analysis?
6 Describe the steps in developing a flexible budget.
7 List four reasons for using standard costs.
8 How might a manager gain insight into the causes of a flexible-budget variance for direct materials?
9 List three causes of a favorable direct materials price variance.
10 Describe three reasons for an unfavorable direct manufacturing labor efficiency variance.
11 How does variance analysis help in continuous improvement?
12 Why might an analyst examining variances in the production area look beyond that business function for explanations of those variances?

13 Comment on the following statement made by a plant manager: "Meetings with my plant accountant are frustrating. All he wants to do is pin the blame on someone for the many variances he reports."

14 How can the sales-volume variance be decomposed further to obtain useful information?

15 "Benchmarking against other companies enables a company to identify the lowest-cost producer. This amount should become the performance measure for next year." Do you agree?

Exercises

MyAccountingLab

16 **Flexible budget.** Brabham Enterprises manufactures tires for the Formula I motor racing circuit. For August 2014, it budgeted to manufacture and sell 3,000 tires at a variable cost of $74 per tire and total fixed costs of $54,000. The budgeted selling price was $110 per tire. Actual results in August 2014 were 2,800 tires manufactured and sold at a selling price of $112 per tire. The actual total variable costs were $229,600, and the actual total fixed costs were $50,000.

1. Prepare a performance report (akin to Exhibit 2) that uses a flexible budget and a static budget.
2. Comment on the results in requirement 1.

Required

17 **Flexible budget.** Connor Company's budgeted prices for direct materials, direct manufacturing labor, and direct marketing (distribution) labor per attaché case are $40, $8, and $12, respectively. The president is pleased with the following performance report:

	Actual Costs	Static Budget	Variance
Direct materials	$364,000	$400,000	$36,000 F
Direct manufacturing labor	78,000	80,000	2,000 F
Direct marketing (distribution) labor	110,000	120,000	10,000 F

Actual output was 8,800 attaché cases. Assume all three direct-cost items shown are variable costs.

Is the president's pleasure justified? Prepare a revised performance report that uses a flexible budget and a static budget.

Required

18 **Flexible-budget preparation and analysis.** Bank Management Printers, Inc., produces luxury checkbooks with three checks and stubs per page. Each checkbook is designed for an individual customer and is ordered through the customer's bank. The company's operating budget for September 2014 included these data:

Number of checkbooks	15,000
Selling price per book	$ 20
Variable cost per book	$ 8
Fixed costs for the month	$145,000

The actual results for September 2014 were as follows:

Number of checkbooks produced and sold	12,000
Average selling price per book	$ 21
Variable cost per book	$ 7
Fixed costs for the month	$150,000

The executive vice president of the company observed that the operating income for September was much lower than anticipated, despite a higher-than-budgeted selling price and a lower-than-budgeted variable cost per unit. As the company's management accountant, you have been asked to provide explanations for the disappointing September results.

Bank Management develops its flexible budget on the basis of budgeted per-output-unit revenue and per-output-unit variable costs without detailed analysis of budgeted inputs.

1. Prepare a static-budget-based variance analysis of the September performance.
2. Prepare a flexible-budget-based variance analysis of the September performance.
3. Why might Bank Management find the flexible-budget-based variance analysis more informative than the static-budget-based variance analysis? Explain your answer.

Required

19 Flexible budget, working backward. The Clarkson Company produces engine parts for car manufacturers. A new accountant intern at Clarkson has accidentally deleted the calculations on the company's variance analysis calculations for the year ended December 31, 2014. The following table is what remains of the data.

	A	B	C	D	E	F
1	Performance Report, Year Ended December 31, 2014					
2						
3		Actual Results	Flexible-Budget Variances	Flexible Budget	Sales-Volume Variances	Static Budget
4	Units sold	130,000				120,000
5	Revenues (sales)	$715,000				$420,000
6	Variable costs	515,000				240,000
7	Contribution margin	200,000				180,000
8	Fixed costs	140,000				120,000
9	Operating income	$ 60,000				$ 60,000

Required

1. Calculate all the required variances. (If your work is accurate, you will find that the total static-budget variance is $0.)
2. What are the actual and budgeted selling prices? What are the actual and budgeted variable costs per unit?
3. Review the variances you have calculated and discuss possible causes and potential problems. What is the important lesson learned here?

20 Flexible-budget and sales volume variances. Luster, Inc., produces the basic fillings used in many popular frozen desserts and treats—vanilla and chocolate ice creams, puddings, meringues, and fudge. Luster uses standard costing and carries over no inventory from one month to the next. The ice-cream product group's results for June 2014 were as follows:

	A	B	C
1	Performance Report, June 2014		
2		Actual Results	Static Budget
3	Units (pounds)	350,000	335,000
4	Revenues	$2,012,500	$1,976,500
5	Variable manufacturing costs	1,137,500	1,038,500
6	Contribution margin	$875,000	$938,000

Sam Adler, the business manager for ice-cream products, is pleased that more pounds of ice cream were sold than budgeted and that revenues were up. Unfortunately, variable manufacturing costs went up, too. The bottom line is that contribution margin declined by $63,000, which is less than 3% of the budgeted revenues of $1,976,500. Overall, Adler feels that the business is running fine.

Required

1. Calculate the static-budget variance in units, revenues, variable manufacturing costs, and contribution margin. What percentage is each static-budget variance relative to its static-budget amount?
2. Break down each static-budget variance into a flexible-budget variance and a sales-volume variance.
3. Calculate the selling-price variance.
4. Assume the role of management accountant at Luster. How would you present the results to Sam Adler? Should he be more concerned? If so, why?

21 Price and efficiency variances. Peterson Foods manufactures pumpkin scones. For January 2014, it budgeted to purchase and use 15,000 pounds of pumpkin at $0.89 a pound. Actual purchases and usage for January 2014 were 16,000 pounds at $0.82 a pound. Peterson budgeted for 60,000 pumpkin scones. Actual output was 60,800 pumpkin scones.

1. Compute the flexible-budget variance.
2. Compute the price and efficiency variances.
3. Comment on the results for requirements 1 and 2 and provide a possible explanation for them.

22 Materials and manufacturing labor variances. Consider the following data collected for Great Homes, Inc.:

	Direct Materials	Direct Manufacturing Labor
Cost incurred: Actual inputs × actual prices	$200,000	$90,000
Actual inputs × standard prices	214,000	86,000
Standard inputs allowed for actual output × standard prices	225,000	80,000

Compute the price, efficiency, and flexible-budget variances for direct materials and direct manufacturing labor.

23 Direct materials and direct manufacturing labor variances. SallyMay, Inc., designs and manufactures T-shirts. It sells its T-shirts to brand-name clothes retailers in lots of one dozen. SallyMay's May 2013 static budget and actual results for direct inputs are as follows:

Static Budget

Number of T-shirt lots (1 lot = 1 dozen)	400

Per Lot of T-shirts:

Direct materials	14 meters at $1.70 per meter = $23.80
Direct manufacturing labor	1.6 hours at $8.10 per hour = $12.96

Actual Results

Number of T-shirt lots sold	450

Total Direct Inputs:

Direct materials	6,840 meters at $1.95 per meter = $13,338
Direct manufacturing labor	675 hours at $8.20 per hour = $5,535

SallyMay has a policy of analyzing all input variances when they add up to more than 10% of the total cost of materials and labor in the flexible budget, and this is true in May 2013. The production manager discusses the sources of the variances: "A new type of material was purchased in May. This led to faster cutting and sewing, but the workers used more material than usual as they learned to work with it. For now, the standards are fine."

1. Calculate the direct materials and direct manufacturing labor price and efficiency variances in May 2013. What is the total flexible-budget variance for both inputs (direct materials and direct manufacturing labor) combined? What percentage is this variance of the total cost of direct materials and direct manufacturing labor in the flexible budget?
2. Sally King, the CEO, is concerned about the input variances. But she likes the quality and feel of the new material and agrees to use it for one more year. In May 2014, SallyMay again produces 450 lots of T-shirts. Relative to May 2013, 2% less direct material is used, direct material price is down 5%, and 2% less direct manufacturing labor is used. Labor price has remained the same as in May 2013. Calculate the direct materials and direct manufacturing labor price and efficiency variances in May 2014. What is the total flexible-budget variance for both inputs (direct materials and direct manufacturing labor) combined? What percentage is this variance of the total cost of direct materials and direct manufacturing labor in the flexible budget?
3. Comment on the May 2014 results. Would you continue the "experiment" of using the new material?

24 Price and efficiency variances, journal entries. The Schuyler Corporation manufactures lamps. It has set up the following standards per finished unit for direct materials and direct manufacturing labor:

Direct materials: 10 lb. at $4.50 per lb.	$45.00
Direct manufacturing labor: 0.5 hour at $30 per hour	15.00

The number of finished units budgeted for January 2014 was 10,000; 9,850 units were actually produced.

Actual results in January 2014 were as follows:

Direct materials: 98,055 lb. used
Direct manufacturing labor: 4,900 hours $154,350

Assume that there was no beginning inventory of either direct materials or finished units.

During the month, materials purchased amounted to 100,000 lb., at a total cost of $465,000. Input price variances are isolated upon purchase. Input-efficiency variances are isolated at the time of usage.

Required

1. Compute the January 2014 price and efficiency variances of direct materials and direct manufacturing labor.
2. Prepare journal entries to record the variances in requirement 1.
3. Comment on the January 2014 price and efficiency variances of Schuyler Corporation.
4. Why might Schuyler calculate direct materials price variances and direct materials efficiency variances with reference to different points in time?

25 **Materials and manufacturing labor variances, standard costs.** Dunn, Inc., is a privately held furniture manufacturer. For August 2014, Dunn had the following standards for one of its products, a wicker chair:

	Standards per Chair
Direct materials	2 square yards of input at $5 per square yard
Direct manufacturing labor	0.5 hour of input at $10 per hour

The following data were compiled regarding *actual performance*: actual output units (chairs) produced, 2,000; square yards of input purchased and used, 3,700; price per square yard, $5.10; direct manufacturing labor costs, $8,820; actual hours of input, 900; labor price per hour, $9.80.

1. Show computations of price and efficiency variances for direct materials and direct manufacturing labor. Give a plausible explanation of why each variance occurred.
2. Suppose 6,000 square yards of materials were purchased (at $5.10 per square yard), even though only 3,700 square yards were used. Suppose further that variances are identified at their most timely control point; accordingly, direct materials price variances are isolated and traced at the time of purchase to the purchasing department rather than to the production department. Compute the price and efficiency variances under this approach.

26 **Journal entries and T-accounts (continuation of 25).** Prepare journal entries and post them to T-accounts for all transactions in Exercise 25, including requirement 2. Summarize how these journal entries differ from normal-costing entries.

27 **Price and efficiency variances, benchmarking.** Topiary Co. produces molded plastic garden pots and other plastic containers. In June 2014, Topiary produces 1,000 lots (each lot is 12 dozen pots) of its most popular line of pots, the 14-inch "Grecian urns," at each of its two plants, which are located in Mineola and Bayside. The production manager, Janice Roberts, asks her assistant, Alastair Ramy, to find out the precise per-unit budgeted variable costs at the two plants and the variable costs of a competitor, Land Art, who offers similar-quality pots at cheaper prices. Ramy pulls together the following information for each lot:

Per lot	Mineola Plant	Bayside Plant	Land Art
Direct materials	13.50 lbs. @ $9.20 per lb.	14.00 lbs. @ $9.00 per lb.	13.00 lbs. @ $8.80 per lb.
Direct labor	3 hrs. @ $10.15 per hr.	2.7 hrs. @ $10.20 per hr.	2.5 hrs. @ $10.00 per hr.
Variable overhead	$12 per lot	$11 per lot	$11 per lot

Required

1. What is the budgeted variable cost per lot at the Mineola Plant, the Bayside Plant, and at Land Art?
2. Using the Land Art data as the standard, calculate the direct materials and direct labor price and efficiency variances for the Mineola and Bayside plants.
3. What advantage does Topiary get by using Land Art's benchmark data as standards in calculating its variances? Identify two issues that Roberts should keep in mind in using the Land Art data as the standards.

28 **Static and flexible budgets, service sector.** Student Finance (StuFi) is a startup that aims to use the power of social communities to transform the student loan market. It connects participants through a dedicated lending pool, enabling current students to borrow from a school's alumni community. StuFi's revenue model is to take an upfront fee of 40 basis points (0.40%) *each* from the alumni investor and the student borrower for every loan originated on its platform.

StuFi hopes to go public in the near future and is keen to ensure that its financial results are in line with that ambition. StuFi's budgeted and actual results for the third quarter of 2014 are presented below.

	A	B	C	D	E
1		**Static Budget**		**Actual Results**	
2	New loans originated	8,200		10,250	
3	Average amount of loan	$145,000		$162,000	
4	Variable costs per loan:				
5	Professional labor	$360	(8 hrs at $45 per hour)	$475	(9.5 hrs at $50 per hour)
6	Credit verification	$100		$100	
7	Federal documentation fees	$120		$125	
8	Courier services	$50		$54	
9	Administrative costs (fixed)	$800,000		$945,000	
10	Technology costs (fixed)	$1,300,000		$1,415,000	

Required

1. Prepare StuFi's static budget of operating income for the third quarter of 2014.
2. Prepare an analysis of variances for the third quarter of 2014 along the lines of Exhibit 2; identify the sales volume and flexible budget variances for operating income.
3. Compute the professional labor price and efficiency variances for the third quarter of 2014.
4. What factors would you consider in evaluating the effectiveness of professional labor in the third quarter of 2014.

Problems

29 Flexible budget, direct materials, and direct manufacturing labor variances. Milan Statuary manufactures bust statues of famous historical figures. All statues are the same size. Each unit requires the same amount of resources. The following information is from the static budget for 2014:

Expected production and sales	6,100 units
Expected selling price per unit	$ 700
Total fixed costs	$1,350,000

Standard quantities, standard prices, and standard unit costs follow for direct materials and direct manufacturing labor:

	Standard Quantity	Standard Price	Standard Unit Cost
Direct materials	16 pounds	$14 per pound	$224
Direct manufacturing labor	3.8 hours	$ 30 per hour	$114

During 2014, actual number of units produced and sold was 5,100, at an average selling price of $730. Actual cost of direct materials used was $1,149,400, based on 70,000 pounds purchased at $16.42 per pound. Direct manufacturing labor-hours actually used were 17,000, at the rate of $33.70 per hour. As a result, actual direct manufacturing labor costs were $572,900. Actual fixed costs were $1,200,000. There were no beginning or ending inventories.

1. Calculate the sales-volume variance and flexible-budget variance for operating income.
2. Compute price and efficiency variances for direct materials and direct manufacturing labor.

Required

30 Variance analysis, nonmanufacturing setting. Marcus McQueen has run In-A-Flash Car Detailing for the past 10 years. His static budget and actual results for June 2014 are provided next. Marcus has one employee who has been with him for all 10 years that he has been in business. In addition, at any given time he also employs two other less experienced workers. It usually takes each employee 2 hours to detail a vehicle, regardless of his or her experience. Marcus pays his experienced employee $30 per vehicle and the other two employees $15 per vehicle. There were no wage increases in June.

In-A-Flash Car Detailing
Actual and Budgeted Income Statements
For the Month Ended June 30, 2014

	Budget	Actual
Cars detailed	280	320
Revenue	$53,200	$72,000
Variable costs		
Costs of supplies	1,260	1,360
Labor	6,720	8,400
Total variable costs	7,980	9,760
Contribution margin	45,220	62,240
Fixed costs	9,800	9,800
Operating income	$35,420	$52,440

Required

1. How many cars, on average, did Marcus budget for each employee? How many cars did each employee actually detail?
2. Prepare a flexible budget for June 2014.
3. Compute the sales price variance and the labor efficiency variance for each labor type.
4. What information, in addition to that provided in the income statements, would you want Marcus to gather, if you wanted to improve operational efficiency?

31 Comprehensive variance analysis, responsibility issues. (CMA, adapted) Ultra, Inc., manufactures a full line of well-known sunglasses frames and lenses. Ultra uses a standard costing system to set attainable standards for direct materials, labor, and overhead costs. Ultra reviews and revises standards annually as necessary. Department managers, whose evaluations and bonuses are affected by their department's performance, are held responsible to explain variances in their department performance reports.

Recently, the manufacturing variances in the Delta prestige line of sunglasses have caused some concern. For no apparent reason, unfavorable materials and labor variances have occurred. At the monthly staff meeting, John Puckett, manager of the Image line, will be expected to explain his variances and suggest ways of improving performance. Barton will be asked to explain the following performance report for 2014:

	Actual Results	Static-Budget Amounts
Units sold	7,300	7,800
Revenues	$576,700	$608,400
Variable manufacturing costs	346,604	273,000
Fixed manufacturing costs	111,000	114,000
Gross margin	119,096	221,400

Barton collected the following information:
Three items comprised the standard variable manufacturing costs in 2014:

- Direct materials: Frames. Static budget cost of $35,880. The standard input for 2014 is 2.00 ounces per unit.

- Direct materials: Lenses. Static budget costs of $96,720. The standard input for 2014 is 4.00 ounces per unit.

- Direct manufacturing labor: Static budget costs of $140,400. The standard input for 2014 is 1 hour per unit.

Assume there are no variable manufacturing overhead costs.
The actual variable manufacturing costs in 2014 were as follows:

- Direct materials: Frames. Actual costs of $70,080. Actual ounces used were 4.00 ounces per unit.

- Direct materials: Lenses. Actual costs of $131,400. Actual ounces used were 6.00 ounces per unit.

- Direct manufacturing labor: Actual costs of $145,124. The actual labor rate was $14.20 per hour.

Required

1. Prepare a report that includes the following:
   a. Selling-price variance
   b. Sales-volume variance and flexible-budget variance for operating income in the format of the analysis in Exhibit 2

   c. Price and efficiency variances for the following:
- Direct materials: frames
- Direct materials: lenses
- Direct manufacturing labor

2. Give three possible explanations for each of the three price and efficiency variances at Ultra in requirement 1c.

32 Possible causes for price and efficiency variances. You are a student preparing for a job interview with a *Fortune* 100 consumer products manufacturer. You are applying for a job in the finance department. This company is known for its rigorous case-based interview process. One of the students who successfully obtained a job with them upon graduation last year advised you to "know your variances cold!" When you inquired further, she told you that she had been asked to pretend that she was investigating wage and materials variances. Per her advice, you have been studying the causes and consequences of variances. You are excited when you walk in and find that the first case deals with variance analysis. You are given the following data for May for a detergent bottling plant located in Mexico:

Actual

Bottles filled	360,000
Direct materials used in production	6,300,000 oz.
Actual direct material cost	2,205,000 pesos
Actual direct manufacturing labor-hours	24,500 hours
Actual direct labor cost	739,165 pesos

Standards

Purchase price of direct materials	0.34 pesos/oz
Bottle size	15 oz.
Wage rate	29.30 pesos/hour
Bottles per minute	0.50

Please respond to the following questions as if you were in an interview situation:

Required

1. Calculate the materials efficiency and price variance and the wage and labor efficiency variances for the month of May.
2. You are given the following context: "Union organizers are targeting our detergent bottling plant in Puebla, Mexico, for a union." Can you provide a better explanation for the variances that you have calculated on the basis of this information?

33 Material cost variances, use of variances for performance evaluation. Katharine Johnson is the owner of Best Bikes, a company that produces high-quality cross-country bicycles. Best Bikes participates in a supply chain that consists of suppliers, manufacturers, distributors, and elite bicycle shops. For several years Best Bikes has purchased titanium from suppliers in the supply chain. Best Bikes uses titanium for the bicycle frames because it is stronger and lighter than other metals and therefore increases the quality of the bicycle. Earlier this year, Best Bikes hired Michael Bentfield, a recent graduate from State University, as purchasing manager. Michael believed that he could reduce costs if he purchased titanium from an online marketplace at a lower price.

Best Bikes established the following standards based upon the company's experience with previous suppliers. The standards are as follows:

Cost of titanium	$18 per pound
Titanium used per bicycle	8 lbs.

Actual results for the first month using the online supplier of titanium are as follows:

Bicycles produced	400
Titanium purchased	5,200 lb. for $88,400
Titanium used in production	4,700 lb.

Required

1. Compute the direct materials price and efficiency variances.
2. What factors can explain the variances identified in requirement 1? Could any other variances be affected?
3. Was switching suppliers a good idea for Best Bikes? Explain why or why not.

4. Should Michael Bentfield's performance evaluation be based solely on price variances? Should the production manager's evaluation be based solely on efficiency variances? Why is it important for Katharine Johnson to understand the causes of a variance before she evaluates performance?
5. Other than performance evaluation, what reasons are there for calculating variances?
6. What future problems could result from Best Bikes' decision to buy a lower quality of titanium from the online marketplace?

34 Direct manufacturing labor and direct materials variances, missing data. (CMA, heavily adapted) Young Bay Surfboards manufactures fiberglass surfboards. The standard cost of direct materials and direct manufacturing labor is $223 per board. This includes 40 pounds of direct materials, at the budgeted price of $2 per pound, and 10 hours of direct manufacturing labor, at the budgeted rate of $14.30 per hour. Following are additional data for the month of July:

Units completed	5,500 units
Direct material purchases	160,000 pounds
Cost of direct material purchases	$432,000
Actual direct manufacturing labor-hours	41,000 hours
Actual direct labor cost	$594,500
Direct materials efficiency variance	$ 1,700 F

There were no beginning inventories.

Required

1. Compute direct manufacturing labor variances for July.
2. Compute the actual pounds of direct materials used in production in July.
3. Calculate the actual price per pound of direct materials purchased.
4. Calculate the direct materials price variance.

35 Direct materials efficiency, mix, and yield variances. Nature's Best Nuts produces specialty nut products for the gourmet and natural foods market. Its most popular product is Zesty Zingers, a mixture of roasted nuts that are seasoned with a secret spice mixture and sold in 1-pound tins. The direct materials used in Zesty Zingers are almonds, cashews, pistachios, and seasoning. For each batch of 100 tins, the budgeted quantities and budgeted prices of direct materials are as follows:

	Quantity for One Batch	Price of Input
Almonds	180 cups	$1 per cup
Cashews	300 cups	$2 per cup
Pistachios	90 cups	$3 per cup
Seasoning	30 cups	$6 per cup

Changing the standard mix of direct material quantities slightly does not significantly affect the overall end product, particularly for the nuts. In addition, not all nuts added to production end up in the finished product, as some are rejected during inspection.

In the current period, Nature's Best made 2,500 tins of Zesty Zingers in 25 batches with the following actual quantity, cost, and mix of inputs:

	Actual Quantity	Actual Cost	Actual Mix
Almonds	5,280 cups	$ 5,280	33%
Cashews	7,520 cups	15,040	47%
Pistachios	2,720 cups	8,160	17%
Seasoning	480 cups	2,880	3%
Total actual	16,000 cups	$31,360	100%

Required

1. What is the budgeted cost of direct materials for the 2,500 tins?
2. Calculate the total direct materials efficiency variance.
3. Why is the total direct materials price variance zero?
4. Calculate the total direct materials mix and yield variances. What are these variances telling you about the 2,500 tins produced this period? Are the variances large enough to investigate?

36 Direct materials and manufacturing labor variances, solving unknowns. (CPA, adapted) On May 1, 2014, Lowell Company began the manufacture of a new paging machine known as Dandy. The company installed a standard costing system to account for manufacturing costs. The standard costs for a unit of Dandy follow:

Direct materials (2 lb. at $3 per lb.)	$6.00
Direct manufacturing labor (1/2 hour at $16 per hour)	8.00
Manufacturing overhead (80% of direct manufacturing labor costs)	6.40
	$20.40

The following data were obtained from Lowell's records for the month of May:

	Debit	Credit
Revenues		$150,000
Accounts payable control (for May's purchases of direct materials)		36,300
Direct materials price variance	$4,500	
Direct materials efficiency variance	2,900	
Direct manufacturing labor price variance	1,700	
Direct manufacturing labor efficiency variance		2,000

Actual production in May was 4,700 units of Dandy, and actual sales in May were 3,000 units.

The amount shown for direct materials price variance applies to materials purchased during May. There was no beginning inventory of materials on May 1, 2014.

Compute each of the following items for Lowell for the month of May. Show your computations.

Required

1. Standard direct manufacturing labor-hours allowed for actual output produced
2. Actual direct manufacturing labor-hours worked
3. Actual direct manufacturing labor wage rate
4. Standard quantity of direct materials allowed (in pounds)
5. Actual quantity of direct materials used (in pounds)
6. Actual quantity of direct materials purchased (in pounds)
7. Actual direct materials price per pound

37 Direct materials and manufacturing labor variances, journal entries. Zanella's Smart Shawls, Inc., is a small business that Zanella developed while in college. She began hand-knitting shawls for her dorm friends to wear while studying. As demand grew, she hired some workers and began to manage the operation. Zanella's shawls require wool and labor. She experiments with the type of wool that she uses, and she has great variety in the shawls she produces. Zanella has bimodal turnover in her labor. She has some employees who have been with her for a very long time and others who are new and inexperienced.

Zanella uses standard costing for her shawls. She expects that a typical shawl should take 3 hours to produce, and the standard wage rate is $9.00 per hour. An average shawl uses 13 skeins of wool. Zanella shops around for good deals and expects to pay $3.40 per skein.

Zanella uses a just-in-time inventory system, as she has clients tell her what type and color of wool they would like her to use.

For the month of April, Zanella's workers produced 200 shawls using 580 hours and 3,500 skeins of wool. Zanella bought wool for $9,000 (and used the entire quantity) and incurred labor costs of $5,520.

Required

1. Calculate the price and efficiency variances for the wool and the price and efficiency variances for direct manufacturing labor.
2. Record the journal entries for the variances incurred.
3. Discuss logical explanations for the combination of variances that Zanella experienced.

38 Use of materials and manufacturing labor variances for benchmarking. You are a new junior accountant at In Focus Corporation, maker of lenses for eyeglasses. Your company sells generic-quality lenses for a moderate price. Your boss, the controller, has given you the latest month's report for the lens trade association. This report includes information related to operations for your firm and three of your competitors within the trade association. The report also includes information related to the industry benchmark for each line item in the report. You do not know which firm is which, except that you know you are Firm A.

Unit Variable Costs
Member Firms
For the Month Ended September 30, 2014

	Firm A	Firm B	Firm C	Firm D	Industry Benchmark	
Materials input	2.15	2.00	2.20	2.60	2.15	oz. of glass
Materials price	$ 5.00	$ 5.25	$ 5.10	$ 4.50	$ 5.10	per oz.
Labor-hours used	0.75	1.00	0.65	0.70	0.70	hours
Wage rate	$14.50	$14.00	$14.25	$15.25	$12.50	per DLH
Variable overhead rate	$ 9.25	$14.00	$ 7.75	$11.75	$12.25	per DLH

Required

1. Calculate the total variable cost per unit for each firm in the trade association. Compute the percent of total for the material, labor, and variable overhead components.
2. Using the trade association's industry benchmark, calculate direct materials and direct manufacturing labor price and efficiency variances for the four firms. Calculate the percent over standard for each firm and each variance.
3. Write a brief memo to your boss outlining the advantages and disadvantages of belonging to this trade association for benchmarking purposes. Include a few ideas to improve productivity that you want your boss to take to the department heads' meeting.

39 Direct labor variances: price, efficiency, mix, and yield. Trevor Joseph employs two workers in his guitar-making business. The first worker, George, has been making guitars for 20 years and is paid $30 per hour. The second worker, Earl, is less experienced and is paid $20 per hour. One guitar requires, on average, 10 hours of labor. The budgeted direct labor quantities and prices for one guitar are as follows:

	Quantity	Price per Hour of Labor	Cost for One Guitar
George	6 hours	$30 per hour	$180
Earl	4 hours	$20 per hour	80

That is, each guitar is budgeted to require 10 hours of direct labor, composed of 60% of George's labor and 40% of Earl's, although sometimes Earl works more hours on a particular guitar and George less, or vice versa, with no obvious change in the quality or function of the guitar.

During the month of August, Joseph manufactures 25 guitars. Actual direct labor costs are as follows:

George (145 hours)	$4,350
Earl (108 hours)	2,160
Total actual direct labor cost	$6,510

Required

1. What is the budgeted cost of direct labor for 25 guitars?
2. Calculate the total direct labor price and efficiency variances.
3. For the 25 guitars, what is the total actual amount of direct labor used? What is the actual direct labor input mix percentage? What is the budgeted amount of George's and Earl's labor that should have been used for the 25 guitars?
4. Calculate the total direct labor mix and yield variances. How do these numbers relate to the total direct labor efficiency variance? What do these variances tell you?

40 Direct-cost and selling price variances. MicroDisk is the market leader in the Secure Digital (SD) card industry and sells memory cards for use in portable devices such as mobile phones, tablets, and digital cameras. Its most popular card is the Mini SD, which it sells to OEMs as well as through outlets such as Target and Walmart for an average selling price of $8. MicroDisk has a standard monthly production level of

420,000 Mini SDs in its Taiwan facility. The standard input quantities and prices for direct-cost inputs are as follows:

	Quantity per		Standard	
Cost Item	Mini SD card		Unit Costs	
Direct materials				
Specialty polymer	17	mm	$0.05	/mm
Connector pins	10	units	0.10	/unit
Wi-Fi transreceiver	1	unit	0.50	/unit
Direct manufacturing labor				
Setup	1	min.	24.00	/hr.
Fabrication	2	min.	30.00	/hr.

Phoebe King, the CEO, is disappointed with the results for June 2014, especially in comparison to her expectations based on the standard cost data.

Performance Report, June 2014					
	Actual		Budget		Variance	
Output units	462,000		420,000		42,000	F
Revenues	$3,626,700		$3,360,000		$266,700	F
Direct materials	1,200,000		987,000		213,000	U
Direct manufacturing labor	628,400		588,000		40,400	U

King observes that despite the significant increase in the output of Mini SDs in June, the product's contribution to the company's profitability has been lower than expected. She gathers the following information to help analyze the situation:

Input Usage Report, June 2014				
Cost Item	Quantity		Actual Cost	
Direct materials				
Specialty polymer	8,300,000	mm	$415,000	
Connector pins	5,000,000	units	550,000	
Wi-Fi transreceiver	470,000	units	235,000	
Direct manufacturing labor				
Setup	455,000	min.	182,000	
Fabrication	864,000	min.	446,400	

Calculate the following variances. Comment on the variances and provide potential reasons why they might have arisen, with particular attention to the variances that may be related to one another:

1. Selling-price variance
2. Direct materials price variance, for each category of materials
3. Direct materials efficiency variance, for each category of materials

4. Direct manufacturing labor price variance, for setup and fabrication

5. Direct manufacturing labor efficiency variance, for setup and fabrication.

41 Comprehensive variance analysis review. Vivus Bioscience produces a generic statin pill that is used to treat patients with high cholesterol. The pills are sold in blister packs of 10. Vivus employs a team of sales representatives who are paid varying amounts of commission.

Given the narrow margins in the generic drugs industry, Vivus relies on tight standards and cost controls to manage its operations. Vivus has the following budgeted standards for the month of April 2014:

Average selling price per pack	$ 7.20
Total direct materials cost per pack	$ 1.80
Direct manufacturing labor cost per hour	$ 14.40
Average labor productivity rate (packs per hour)	280
Sales commission cost per unit	$ 0.36
Fixed administrative and manufacturing overhead	$960,000

Vivus budgeted sales of 1,400,000 packs for April. At the end of the month, the controller revealed that actual results for April had deviated from the budget in several ways:

- Unit sales and production were 90% of plan.
- Actual average selling price increased to $7.30.
- Productivity dropped to 250 packs per hour.
- Actual direct manufacturing labor cost was $14.60 per hour.
- Actual total direct material cost per unit increased to $1.90.
- Actual sales commissions were $0.30 per unit.
- Fixed overhead costs were $12,000 above budget.

Calculate the following amounts for Vivus for April 2014:

Required

1. Static-budget and actual operating income

2. Static-budget variance for operating income

3. Flexible-budget operating income

4. Flexible-budget variance for operating income

5. Sales-volume variance for operating income

6. Price and efficiency variances for direct manufacturing labor

7. Flexible-budget variance for direct manufacturing labor

42 Price and efficiency variances, benchmarking and ethics. Sunto Scientific manufactures GPS devices for a chain of retail stores. Its most popular model, the Magellan XS, is assembled in a dedicated facility in Savannah, Georgia. Sunto is keenly aware of the competitive threat from smartphones that use Google Maps and has put in a standard cost system to manage production of the Magellan XS. It has also implemented a just-in-time system so the Savannah facility operates with no inventory of any kind.

Producing the Magellan XS involves combining a navigation system (imported from Sunto's plant in Dresden at a fixed price), an LCD screen made of polarized glass, and a casing developed from specialty plastic. The budgeted and actual amounts for Magellan XS for July 2014 were as follows:

	Budgeted Amounts	Actual Amounts
Magellan XS units produced	4,000	4,400
Navigation system cost	$81,600	$89,000
Navigation systems	4,080	4,450
Polarized glass cost	$40,000	$40,300
Sheets of polarized glass used	800	816
Plastic casing cost	$12,000	$12,500
Ounces of specialty plastic used	4,000	4,250
Direct manufacturing labor costs	$36,000	$37,200
Direct manufacturing labor-hours	2,000	2,040

The controller of the Savannah plant, Jim Williams, is disappointed with the standard costing system in place. The standards were developed on the basis of a study done by an outside consultant at the start of the year. Williams points out that he has rarely seen a significant unfavorable variance under this system. He observes that even at the present level of output, workers seem to have a substantial amount of idle time. Moreover, he is concerned that the production supervisor, John Kelso, is aware of the issue but is unwilling to tighten the standards because the current lenient benchmarks make his performance look good.

1. Compute the price and efficiency variances for the three categories of direct materials and for direct manufacturing labor in July 2014.
2. Describe the types of actions the employees at the Savannah plant may have taken to reduce the accuracy of the standards set by the outside consultant. Why would employees take those actions? Is this behavior ethical?
3. If Williams does nothing about the standard costs, will his behavior violate any of the standards of ethical conduct for practitioners described in the IMA Statement of Ethical Professional Practice?
4. What actions should Williams take?
5. Williams can obtain benchmarking information about the estimated costs of Sunto's competitors such as Garmin and TomTom from the Competitive Intelligence Institute (CII). Discuss the pros and cons of using the CII information to compute the variances in requirement 1.

Glossary

Benchmarking. The continuous process of comparing the levels of performance in producing products and services and executing activities against the best levels of performance in competing companies or in companies having similar processes.

Budgeted performance. Expected performance or a point of reference to compare actual results.

Direct materials mix variance. The difference between (1) budgeted cost for actual mix of the actual total quantity of direct materials used and (2) budgeted cost of budgeted mix of the actual total quantity of direct materials used.

Direct materials yield variance. The difference between (1) budgeted cost of direct materials based on the actual total quantity of direct materials used and (2) flexible-budget cost of direct materials based on the budgeted total quantity of direct materials allowed for the actual output produced.

Effectiveness. The degree to which a predetermined objective or target is met.

Efficiency. The relative amount of inputs used to achieve a given output level.

Efficiency variance. The difference between actual input quantity used and budgeted input quantity allowed for actual output, multiplied by budgeted price. Also called *usage variance*.

Favorable variance. Variance that has the effect of increasing operating income relative to the budgeted amount. Denoted F.

Flexible budget. Budget developed using budgeted revenues and budgeted costs based on the actual output in the budget period.

Flexible-budget variance. The difference between an actual result and the corresponding flexible-budget amount based on the actual output level in the budget period.

Management by exception. Practice of focusing management attention on areas not operating as expected and giving less attention to areas operating as expected.

Price variance. The difference between actual price and budgeted price multiplied by actual quantity of input. Also called *rate variance*.

Rate variance. See *price variance*.

Sales-volume variance. The difference between a flexible-budget amount and the corresponding static-budget amount.

Selling-price variance. The difference between the actual selling price and the budgeted selling price multiplied by the actual units sold.

Standard. A carefully determined price, cost, or quantity that is used as a benchmark for judging performance. It is usually expressed on a per unit basis.

Standard cost. A carefully determined cost of a unit of output.

Standard input.   A carefully determined quantity of input required for one unit of output.

Standard price.   A carefully determined price that a company expects to pay for a unit of input.

Static budget.   Budget based on the level of output planned at the start of the budget period.

Static-budget variance.   Difference between an actual result and the corresponding budgeted amount in the static budget.

Unfavorable variance.   Variance that has the effect of decreasing operating income relative to the budgeted amount. Denoted U.

Usage variance.   See *efficiency variance*.

Variance.   The difference between actual result and expected performance.

Photo Credits

Credits are listed in order of appearance.

Photo 1: Alexandru Magurean/Getty Images
Photo 2: Rachel Youdelman/Pearson Education, Inc
Photo 3: Soultana Koleska/Alamy

Chapter 8

Flexible Budgets, Overhead Cost Variances, and Management Control

From Chapter 8 of *Cost Accounting: A Managerial Emphasis*, Fifteenth Edition. Charles T. Horngren, Srikant M. Datar, Madhav V. Rajan. Copyright © 2015 by Pearson Education, Inc. All rights reserved.

Flexible Budgets, Overhead Cost Variances, and Management Control

What do this week's weather forecast and an organization's performance have in common?

Much of the time, reality doesn't match what people expect. Rain that results in a little league game being canceled may suddenly give way to sunshine. Business owners expecting to "whistle their way to the bank" may change their tune after tallying their monthly bills and discovering that skyrocketing operational costs have significantly reduced their profits. Differences, or variances, are all around us.

Analyzing variances is a valuable activity for firms because the process highlights the areas where performance most lags expectations. By using this information to make corrective adjustments, companies can achieve significant savings. Furthermore, the process of setting up standards requires firms to have a thorough understanding of their fixed and variable overhead costs, which brings its own benefits, as the following article shows.

Planning Fixed and Variable Overhead Costs at Tesla Motors[1]

Managers frequently review the differences, or variances, in overhead costs and make changes in the operations of a business. Sometimes staffing levels are increased or decreased, while at other times managers identify ways to use fewer resources like, say, office supplies and travel for business meetings that don't add value to the products and services that customers buy.

Tesla Motors is a Silicon Valley–based electric car manufacturer. To develop its renowned Model S all-electric plug-in sedan—*Consumer Reports* recently called it the best car it ever tested—Tesla Motors required an in-depth understanding of its fixed and variable overhead costs for planning and control purposes.

Automobile manufacturing is an industry with significant fixed overhead costs. As a new company, Tesla Motors made the strategic decision to make up-front fixed

---

[1] *Sources:* Ohnsman, Alan. 2012. Tesla Motors cuts factory cost to try to generate profit. *Bloomberg*, http://www.bloomberg.com/news/2012-04-12/tesla-motors-cuts-factory-cost-to-try-to-generate-profit.html, April 12; Tesla Motors, Inc. 2013. March 31, 2013 Form 10-Q (filed May 10); Valdes-Dapena, Peter. 2013. Tesla: Consumer Reports' best car ever tested. *CNNMoney.com*, http://money.cnn.com/2013/05/09/autos/tesla-models-consumer-reports/index.html, May 9; White, Joseph. 2013. Tesla has a fresh $1 billion—and lots of ways to spend it. *Corporate Intelligence (blog)*, *The Wall Street Journal*, http://blogs.wsj.com/corporate-intelligence/, May 17.

investments designed to benefit the company for many years. These resulted in various fixed overhead costs including depreciation and taxes on its new state-of-the-art factory, assembly line supervisors, insurance, and salaries for the engineers that design the battery packs and electric motors that power its specially designed vehicles. Variable costs for Tesla Motors include utilities, office supplies, advertising, and promotion costs among many others.

Understanding its fixed and variable overhead costs allows Tesla Motors' management accountants to develop the company's budgeted fixed and variable overhead cost rates for each Model S produced. Also, using flexible budgeting, the company can make strategic changes based on activity. For instance, when Tesla Motors began expanding sales beyond North America in early 2013, the company added new sales and marketing staff to support the growth of the business, which then resulted in a new variable overhead cost rate.

Companies such as DuPont, International Paper, and U.S. Steel, which invest heavily in capital equipment, and Amazon.com and Yahoo!, which invest large amounts in software, have high overhead costs. As the Tesla example suggests, understanding the behavior of overhead costs, planning for them, analyzing the variances related to them, and acting appropriately on the results are critical for a company.

Managers use flexible budgets and variance analysis to help plan and control the direct-cost categories of direct materials and direct manufacturing labor. In this chapter, you will learn how managers plan for and control the indirect-cost categories of variable manufacturing overhead and fixed manufacturing overhead. This chapter also explains why managers should be careful when interpreting variances based on overhead-cost concepts developed primarily for financial reporting purposes.

Planning of Variable and Fixed Overhead Costs

We'll use the Webb Company example to illustrate the planning and control of variable and fixed overhead costs. Webb manufactures jackets it sells to distributors, who in turn sell them to independent clothing stores and retail chains. Because we assume Webb's only costs are manufacturing costs, for simplicity we use the term "overhead costs" instead of "manufacturing overhead costs" in this chapter. Webb's variable overhead costs include energy, machine maintenance, engineering support, and indirect materials. Webb's fixed overhead costs include plant leasing costs, depreciation on plant equipment, and the salaries of the plant managers.

Planning Variable Overhead Costs

To effectively plan variable overhead costs for a product or service, managers must focus on the activities that create a superior product or service for their customers and eliminate activities that do not add value. For example, customers expect Webb's jackets to last, so

Learning Objective 1

Explain the similarities and differences in planning variable overhead costs and fixed overhead costs

...for both, plan only essential activities and be efficient; fixed overhead costs are usually determined well before the budget period begins

Webb's managers consider sewing to be an essential activity. Therefore, maintenance activities for sewing machines, which are included in Webb's variable overhead costs, are also essential activities for which management must plan. Such maintenance should be done in a cost-effective way, such as by scheduling periodic equipment maintenance rather than waiting for sewing machines to break down. For many companies today, it is critical to plan for ways to reduce the consumption of energy, a rapidly growing component of variable overhead costs. Webb installs smart meters in order to monitor energy use in real time and steer production operations away from peak consumption periods.

Planning Fixed Overhead Costs

Planning fixed overhead costs is similar to planning variable overhead costs—undertake only essential activities and then plan to be efficient in that undertaking. But there is an additional strategic issue when it comes to planning fixed overhead costs: choosing the appropriate level of capacity or investment that will benefit the company in the long run. Consider Webb's leasing of sewing machines, each of which has a fixed cost per year. Leasing too many machines will result in overcapacity and unnecessary fixed leasing costs. Leasing too few machines will result in an inability to meet demand, lost sales of jackets, and unhappy customers. Consider AT&T, which did not initially foresee the iPhone's appeal or the proliferation of "apps" and consequently did not upgrade its network sufficiently to handle the resulting data traffic. AT&T subsequently had to impose limits on how customers could use the iPhone (such as by curtailing tethering and the streaming of Webcasts). This explains why following the iPhone's release, at one point AT&T had the lowest customer satisfaction ratings among all major carriers.

The planning of fixed overhead costs differs from the planning of variable overhead costs in another regard as well: timing. At the start of a budget period, management will have made most of the decisions determining the level of fixed overhead costs to be incurred. But it's the day-to-day, ongoing operating decisions that mainly determine the level of variable overhead costs incurred in that period. For example, the variable overhead costs of hospitals, which include the costs of disposable supplies, doses of medication, suture packets, and medical waste disposal, are a function of the number and nature of procedures carried out, as well as the practice patterns of the physicians. However, most of the costs of providing hospital service are fixed overhead costs—those related to buildings, equipment, and salaried labor. These costs are unrelated to a hospital's volume of activity.[2]

Decision Point

How do managers plan variable overhead costs and fixed overhead costs?

Standard Costing at Webb Company

Learning Objective 2

Develop budgeted variable overhead cost rates

...budgeted variable costs divided by quantity of cost-allocation base

and budgeted fixed overhead cost rates

...budgeted fixed costs divided by quantity of cost-allocation base

Webb uses standard costing. This chapter explains how the standards for Webb's manufacturing overhead costs are developed. **Standard costing** is a costing system that (1) traces direct costs to output produced by multiplying the standard prices or rates by the standard quantities of inputs allowed for actual outputs produced and (2) allocates overhead costs on the basis of the standard overhead-cost rates times the standard quantities of the allocation bases allowed for the actual outputs produced.

The standard cost of Webb's jackets can be computed at the start of the budget period. This feature of standard costing simplifies record keeping because no record is needed of the actual overhead costs or of the actual quantities of the cost-allocation bases used for making the jackets. What managers *do* need are the standard overhead cost rates for Webb's variable and fixed overhead. Management accountants calculate these cost rates based on the planned amounts of variable and fixed overhead and the standard

---

[2] Free-standing surgery centers have thrived because they have lower fixed overhead costs compared to traditional hospitals. For an enlightening summary of costing issues in health care, see A. Macario. 2010. "What does one minute of operating room time cost?" *Journal of Clinical Anesthesia*, June.

quantities of the allocation bases. We describe these computations next. Note that once managers set these standards, the costs of using standard costing are low relative to the costs of using actual costing or normal costing.

Developing Budgeted Variable Overhead Rates

Budgeted variable overhead cost-allocation rates can be developed in four steps. Throughout the chapter, we use the broader term *budgeted rate* rather than *standard rate*. When standard costing is used, the budgeted rates are standard rates.

Step 1: Choose the Period to Be Used for the Budget. Webb uses a 12-month budget period. There are two reasons for using annual overhead rates rather than, say, monthly rates. The first relates to the numerator, such as reducing the influence of seasonality on the firm's cost structure. The second relates to the denominator, such as reducing the effect of varying output and number of days in a month. In addition, setting overhead rates once a year rather than 12 times a year saves managers time.

Step 2: Select the Cost-Allocation Bases to Use in Allocating the Variable Overhead Costs to the Output Produced. Webb's operating managers select machine-hours as the cost-allocation base because they believe that machine-hours is the only cost driver of variable overhead. Based on an engineering study, Webb estimates it will take 0.40 of a machine-hour per actual output unit. For its budgeted output of 144,000 jackets in 2014, Webb budgets 57,600 (0.40 × 144,000) machine-hours.

Step 3: Identify the Variable Overhead Costs Associated with Each Cost-Allocation Base. Webb groups all of its variable overhead costs, including the costs of energy, machine maintenance, engineering support, indirect materials, and indirect manufacturing labor, in a single cost pool. Webb's total budgeted variable overhead costs for 2014 are $1,728,000.

Step 4: Compute the Rate per Unit of Each Cost-Allocation Base Used to Allocate the Variable Overhead Costs to the Output Produced. Dividing the amount in Step 3 ($1,728,000) by the amount in Step 2 (57,600 machine-hours), Webb estimates a rate of $30 per standard machine-hour for allocating its variable overhead costs.

When standard costing is used, the variable overhead rate per unit of the cost-allocation base ($30 per machine-hour for Webb) is generally expressed as a standard rate per output unit. Webb calculates the budgeted variable overhead cost rate per output unit as follows:

$$\begin{array}{ccc} \text{Budgeted variable} & \text{Budgeted input} & \text{Budgeted variable} \\ \text{overhead cost rate} = & \text{allowed per} & \times \text{ overhead cost rate} \\ \text{per output unit} & \text{output unit} & \text{per input unit} \end{array}$$

$$= 0.40 \text{ hour per jacket} \times \$30 \text{ per hour}$$
$$= \$12 \text{ per jacket}$$

The $12-per-jacket rate is the budgeted variable overhead cost rate in Webb's static budget for 2014 as well as in the monthly performance reports the firm prepares during 2014.

The $12-per-jacket rate represents the amount by which managers expect Webb's variable overhead costs to change when the amount of output changes. As the number of jackets manufactured increases, the variable overhead costs allocated to output (for inventory costing) increase at the rate of $12 per jacket. The $12 per jacket represents the firm's total variable overhead costs per unit of output, including the costs of energy, repairs, indirect labor, and so on. Managers help control variable overhead costs by setting a budget for each of these line items and then investigating the possible causes of any significant variances.

Developing Budgeted Fixed Overhead Rates

Fixed overhead costs are, by definition, a lump sum of costs that remains unchanged for a given period, despite wide changes in a firm's level of activity or output. Fixed costs are included in flexible budgets, but they remain the same within the relevant range of activity regardless of the output level chosen to "flex" the variable costs and revenues. Webb's monthly fixed overhead costs of $276,000 are the same in the static budget as they are in the flexible budget. Do not assume, however, that these costs can never be changed. Managers can reduce them by selling equipment or laying off employees, for example. But the costs are fixed in the sense that, unlike variable costs such as direct material costs, fixed costs do not *automatically* increase or decrease with the level of activity within the relevant range.

The process of developing the budgeted fixed overhead rate is the same as the one for calculating the budgeted variable overhead rate. The steps are as follows:

Step 1: Choose the Period to Use for the Budget. As with variable overhead costs, the budget period for fixed overhead costs is typically one year, to help smooth out seasonal effects.

Step 2: Select the Cost-Allocation Bases to Use in Allocating the Fixed Overhead Costs to the Output Produced. Webb uses machine-hours as the only cost-allocation base for the firm's fixed overhead costs. Why? Because Webb's managers believe that, in the long run, the company's fixed overhead costs will increase or decrease to the levels needed to support the amount of machine-hours. Therefore, in the long run, the amount of machine-hours used is the only cost driver of fixed overhead costs. The number of machine-hours is the denominator in the budgeted fixed overhead rate computation and is called the **denominator level.** For simplicity, we assume Webb expects to operate at capacity in fiscal year 2014, with a budgeted usage of 57,600 machine-hours for a budgeted output of 144,000 jackets.[3]

Step 3: Identify the Fixed Overhead Costs Associated with Each Cost-Allocation Base. Because Webb identifies a single cost-allocation base—machine-hours—to allocate fixed overhead costs, it groups all such costs into a single cost pool. Costs in this pool include depreciation on plant and equipment, plant and equipment leasing costs, and the plant manager's salary. Webb's fixed overhead budget for 2014 is $3,312,000.

Step 4: Compute the Rate per Unit of Each Cost-Allocation Base Used to Allocate Fixed Overhead Costs to the Output Produced. By dividing the $3,312,000 from Step 3 by the 57,600 machine-hours from Step 2, Webb estimates a fixed overhead cost rate of $57.50 per machine-hour:

$$\begin{matrix} \text{Budgeted fixed} \\ \text{overhead cost per} \\ \text{unit of cost-allocation} \\ \text{base} \end{matrix} = \frac{\begin{matrix}\text{Budgeted total costs}\\\text{in fixed overhead cost pool}\end{matrix}}{\begin{matrix}\text{Budgeted total quantity of}\\\text{cost-allocation base}\end{matrix}} = \frac{\$3,312,000}{57,600} = \$57.50 \text{ per machine-hour}$$

Under standard costing, the $57.50 fixed overhead cost per machine-hour is usually expressed as a standard cost per output unit. Recall that Webb's engineering study estimates that it will take 0.40 machine-hour per output unit. Webb can now calculate the budgeted fixed overhead cost per output unit as follows:

$$\begin{matrix} \text{Budgeted fixed} \\ \text{overhead cost per} \\ \text{output unit} \end{matrix} = \begin{matrix}\text{Budgeted quantity}\\\text{of cost-allocation}\\\text{base allowed per}\\\text{output unit}\end{matrix} \times \begin{matrix}\text{Budgeted fixed}\\\text{overhead cost}\\\text{per unit of}\\\text{cost-allocation base}\end{matrix}$$

$$= 0.40 \text{ of a machine-hour per jacket} \times \$57.50 \text{ per machine-hour}$$

$$= \$23.00 \text{ per jacket}$$

Decision Point

How are budgeted variable overhead and fixed overhead cost rates calculated?

When preparing monthly budgets for 2014, Webb divides the $3,312,000 annual total fixed costs into 12 equal monthly amounts of $276,000.

---

[3] Because Webb plans its capacity over multiple periods, anticipated demand in 2014 could be such that budgeted output for 2014 is less than Webb's capacity. Companies vary in the denominator levels they choose. Some choose budgeted output and others choose capacity. In either case, the approach and analysis presented in this chapter is unchanged.

Variable Overhead Cost Variances

We now illustrate how the budgeted variable overhead rate is used to compute Webb's variable overhead cost variances. The following data are for April 2014, when Webb produced and sold 10,000 jackets:

	Actual Result	Flexible-Budget Amount
1. Output units (jackets)	10,000	10,000
2. Machine-hours per output unit	0.45	0.40
3. Machine-hours (1 × 2)	4,500	4,000
4. Variable overhead costs	$130,500	$120,000
5. Variable overhead costs per machine-hour (4 ÷ 3)	$ 29.00	$ 30.00
6. Variable overhead costs per output unit (4 ÷ 1)	$ 13.05	$ 12.00

The flexible budget enables Webb to highlight the differences between actual costs and actual quantities versus budgeted costs and budgeted quantities for the actual output level of 10,000 jackets.

Flexible-Budget Analysis

The **variable overhead flexible-budget variance** measures the difference between actual variable overhead costs incurred and flexible-budget variable overhead amounts.

$$\begin{array}{ll} \text{Variable overhead} \\ \text{flexible-budget variance} \end{array} = \begin{array}{l} \text{Actual costs} \\ \text{incurred} \end{array} - \begin{array}{l} \text{Flexible-budget} \\ \text{amount} \end{array}$$

$$= \$130,500 - \$120,000$$

$$= \$10,500 \text{ U}$$

This $10,500 unfavorable flexible-budget variance means Webb's actual variable overhead exceeded the flexible-budget amount by $10,500 for the 10,000 jackets actually produced and sold. Webb's managers would want to know why. Did Webb use more machine-hours than planned to produce the 10,000 jackets? If so, was it because workers were less skilled than expected in using machines? Or did Webb spend more on variable overhead costs, such as maintenance?

Webb's managers can get further insight into the reason for the $10,500 unfavorable variance by subdividing it into the efficiency variance and spending variance.

Variable Overhead Efficiency Variance

The **variable overhead efficiency variance** is the difference between actual quantity of the cost-allocation base used and budgeted quantity of the cost-allocation base that should have been used to produce the actual output, multiplied by the budgeted variable overhead cost per unit of the cost-allocation base.

$$\begin{array}{l} \text{Variable} \\ \text{overhead} \\ \text{efficiency} \\ \text{variance} \end{array} = \left(\begin{array}{l} \text{Actual quantity of} \\ \text{variable overhead} \\ \text{cost-allocation base} \\ \text{used for actual} \\ \text{output} \end{array} - \begin{array}{l} \text{Budgeted quantity of} \\ \text{variable overhead} \\ \text{cost-allocation base} \\ \text{allowed for} \\ \text{actual output} \end{array} \right) \times \begin{array}{l} \text{Budgeted variable} \\ \text{overhead cost per unit} \\ \text{of cost-allocation base} \end{array}$$

$$= (4,500 \text{ hours} - 0.40 \text{ hr./unit} \times 10,000 \text{ units}) \times \$30 \text{ per hour}$$

$$= (4,500 \text{ hours} - 4,000 \text{ hours}) \times \$30 \text{ per hour}$$

$$= \$15,000 \text{ U}$$

Columns 2 and 3 of Exhibit 1 depict the variable overhead efficiency variance. Note the variance arises solely because of the difference between the actual quantity (4,500 hours)

Learning Objective 3

Compute the variable overhead flexible-budget variance,

...difference between actual variable overhead costs and flexible-budget variable overhead amounts

the variable overhead efficiency variance,

...difference between actual quantity of cost-allocation base and budgeted quantity of cost-allocation base

and the variable overhead spending variance

...difference between actual variable overhead cost rate and budgeted variable overhead cost rate

Exhibit 1 Columnar Presentation of Variable Overhead Variance Analysis: Webb Company for April 2014[a]

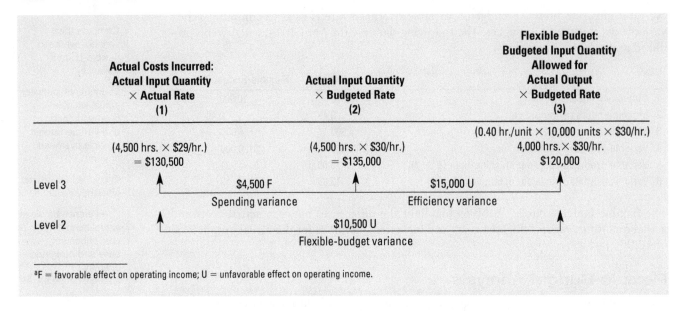

aF = favorable effect on operating income; U = unfavorable effect on operating income.

and budgeted quantity (4,000 hours) of the cost-allocation base. The variable overhead efficiency variance is computed the same way the efficiency variance for direct-cost items is. However, the interpretation of the variance is somewhat different. The efficiency variances for direct-cost items are based on the differences between the actual inputs used and the budgeted inputs allowed for the actual output produced. For example, a forensic laboratory (the kind popularized by television shows such as *CSI* and *Dexter*) would calculate a direct labor efficiency variance based on whether the lab used more or fewer hours than the standard hours allowed for the actual number of DNA tests. In contrast, the efficiency variance for variable overhead is based on the efficiency with which *the cost-allocation base* is used. Webb's unfavorable variable overhead efficiency variance of $15,000 means that the actual machine-hours (the cost-allocation base) of 4,500 hours was higher than the budgeted machine-hours of 4,000 hours allowed to manufacture 10,000 jackets and this, to the extent machine-hours are a cost driver for variable overhead, pushed up the potential spending on variable overhead.

The following table shows possible causes for Webb's actual machine-hours exceeding the budgeted machine-hours and Webb's potential responses to each of these causes.

Possible Causes for Exceeding Budget	Potential Management Responses
1. Workers were less efficient than expected in using machines.	1. Encourage the human resources department to implement better employee-hiring practices and training procedures.
2. The production scheduler inefficiently scheduled jobs, resulting in more machine-hours used than budgeted.	2. Improve plant operations by installing production-scheduling software.
3. Machines were not maintained in good operating condition.	3. Ensure preventive maintenance is done on all machines.
4. Webb's sales staff promised a distributor a rush delivery, which resulted in more machine-hours used than budgeted.	4. Coordinate production schedules with sales staff and distributors and share information with them.
5. Budgeted machine time standards were set too tight.	5. Commit more resources to develop appropriate standards.

Note how, depending on the cause(s) of the $15,000 U variance, corrective actions may need to be taken not just in manufacturing but also in other business functions of the value chain, such as sales and distribution.

Webb's managers discovered that one reason for the unfavorable variance was that workers were underskilled. As a result, Webb is improving its hiring and training practices. Insufficient maintenance performed in the 2 months prior to April 2014 was another reason. A former plant manager had delayed the maintenance in an attempt to meet Webb's monthly cost targets. Managers should not focus on meeting short-run cost targets if they are likely to result in harmful long-run consequences. For example, if Webb's employees were to hurt themselves while operating poorly maintained machinery, the consequences would not only be harmful, they could be deadly. Webb is now strengthening its internal maintenance procedures so that failure to do monthly maintenance as needed will raise a "red flag" that must be immediately explained to management. Webb is also taking a hard look at its evaluation practices to determine if they inadvertently pressure managers to fixate on short-term targets to the long-run detriment of the firm.

Variable Overhead Spending Variance

The **variable overhead spending variance** is the difference between the actual variable overhead cost per unit of the cost-allocation base and the budgeted variable overhead cost per unit of the cost-allocation base, multiplied by the actual quantity of variable overhead cost-allocation base used.

$$\begin{matrix} \text{Variable} \\ \text{overhead} \\ \text{spending} \\ \text{variance} \end{matrix} = \begin{pmatrix} \text{Actual variable} & \text{Budgeted variable} \\ \text{overhead cost per unit} - \text{overhead cost per unit} \\ \text{of cost-allocation base} & \text{of cost-allocation base} \end{pmatrix} \times \begin{matrix} \text{Actual quantity of} \\ \text{variable overhead} \\ \text{cost-allocation base} \\ \text{used} \end{matrix}$$

$$= (\$29 \text{ per machine-hour} - \$30 \text{ per machine-hour}) \times 4{,}500 \text{ machine-hours}$$

$$= (-\$1 \text{ per machine-hour}) \times 4{,}500 \text{ machine-hours}$$

$$= \$4{,}500 \text{ F}$$

Webb operated in April 2014 with a lower-than-budgeted variable overhead cost per machine-hour, so there is a favorable variable overhead spending variance. Columns 1 and 2 in Exhibit 1 depict this variance.

To understand why the favorable variable overhead spending variance occurred, Webb's managers need to recognize why *actual* variable overhead cost per unit of the cost-allocation base ($29 per machine-hour) is *lower* than the *budgeted* variable overhead cost per unit of the cost-allocation base ($30 per machine-hour).

Overall, Webb used 4,500 machine-hours, which is 12.5% greater than the flexible-budget amount of 4,000 machine-hours. However, actual variable overhead costs of $130,500 are only 8.75% greater than the flexible-budget amount of $120,000. Thus, relative to the flexible budget, the percentage increase in actual variable overhead costs is *less* than the percentage increase in machine-hours. Consequently, the actual variable overhead cost per machine-hour is lower than the budgeted amount, resulting in a favorable variable overhead spending variance.

Recall that variable overhead costs include costs of energy, machine maintenance, indirect materials, and indirect labor. Two possible reasons why the percentage increase in actual variable overhead costs is less than the percentage increase in machine-hours are as follows:

1. The actual prices of the individual inputs included in variable overhead costs, such as the price of energy, indirect materials, or indirect labor, are lower than budgeted prices of these inputs. For example, the actual price of electricity may only be $0.09 per kilowatt-hour, compared with a price of $0.10 per kilowatt-hour in the flexible budget.

2. Relative to the flexible budget, the percentage increase in the actual use of individual items in the variable overhead-cost pool is less than the percentage increase in machine-hours. Compared with the flexible-budget amount of 30,000 kilowatt-hours, suppose the actual energy use was 32,400 kilowatt-hours, or 8% higher. The fact that this is a smaller percentage increase than the 12.5% increase in machine-hours (4,500 actual

machine-hours versus a flexible budget of 4,000 machine-hours) will lead to a favorable variable overhead spending variance, which can be partially or completely traced to the efficient use of energy and other variable overhead items.

As part of the last stage of the five-step decision-making process, Webb's managers will need to examine the signals provided by the variable overhead variances to *evaluate the firm's performance and learn.* By understanding the reasons for these variances, Webb can take appropriate actions and make more precise predictions in order to achieve improved results in future periods.

For example, Webb's managers must examine why the actual prices of variable overhead cost items are different from the budgeted prices. The differences could be the result of skillful negotiation on the part of the purchasing manager, oversupply in the market, or lower quality of inputs such as indirect materials. Webb's response depends on what is believed to be the cause of the variance. If the concerns are about quality, for instance, Webb may want to put in place new quality management systems.

Similarly, Webb's managers should understand the possible causes for the efficiency with which variable overhead resources are used. These causes include the skill levels of workers, maintenance of machines, and the efficiency of the manufacturing process. Webb's managers discovered that Webb used fewer indirect labor resources per machine-hour because of manufacturing process improvements. As a result, the firm began organizing cross-functional teams to see if more process improvements could be achieved.

We emphasize that a manager should not always view a favorable variable overhead spending variance as desirable. For example, the variable overhead spending variance would be favorable if Webb's managers purchased lower-priced, poor-quality indirect materials, hired less-talented supervisors, or performed less machine maintenance. These decisions, however, are likely to hurt product quality and harm the long-run prospects of the business.

To clarify the concepts of variable overhead efficiency variance and variable overhead spending variance, consider the following example. Suppose that (a) energy is the only item of variable overhead cost and machine-hours is the cost-allocation base; (b) actual machine-hours used equals the number of machine-hours under the flexible budget; and (c) the actual price of energy equals the budgeted price. From (a) and (b), it follows that there is no efficiency variance—the company has been efficient with respect to the number of machine-hours (the cost-allocation base) used to produce the actual output. However, and despite (c), there could still be a spending variance. Why? Because even though the company used the correct number of machine-hours, the energy consumed *per machine-hour* could be higher than budgeted (for example, because the machines have not been maintained correctly). The cost of this higher energy usage would be reflected in an unfavorable spending variance.

Journal Entries for Variable Overhead Costs and Variances

We now prepare journal entries for the Variable Overhead Control account and the contra account Variable Overhead Allocated.

Entries for variable overhead for April 2014 (data from Exhibit 1) are as follows:

1. Variable Overhead Control	130,500	
Accounts Payable and various other accounts		130,500
To record actual variable overhead costs incurred.		
2. Work-in-Process Control	120,000	
Variable Overhead Allocated		120,000
To record variable overhead cost allocated		
(0.40 machine-hour/unit × 10,000 units × $30/machine-hour). (The costs accumulated in Work-in-Process Control are transferred to Finished Goods Control when production is completed and to Cost of Goods Sold when the products are sold.)		

3. Variable Overhead Allocated   120,000

    Variable Overhead Efficiency Variance   15,000

      Variable Overhead Control   130,500

      Variable Overhead Spending Variance   4,500

    This records the variances for the accounting period.

These variances are the underallocated or overallocated variable overhead costs. At the end of the fiscal year, the variance accounts are written off to cost of goods sold if immaterial in amount. If the variances are material in amount, they are prorated among the Work-in-Process Control, Finished Goods Control, and Cost of Goods Sold accounts on the basis of the variable overhead allocated to these accounts. Only unavoidable costs are prorated. Any part of the variances attributable to avoidable inefficiency is written off in the period. Assume that the balances in the variable overhead variance accounts as of April 2014 are also the balances at the end of the 2014 fiscal year and are immaterial in amount. The following journal entry records the write-off of the variance accounts to the cost of goods sold:

Cost of Goods Sold   10,500

    Variable Overhead Spending Variance   4,500

      Variable Overhead Efficiency Variance   15,000

Next we demonstrate how to calculate fixed overhead cost variances.

Decision Point

What variances can be calculated for variable overhead costs?

Fixed Overhead Cost Variances

Learning Objective 4

Compute the fixed overhead flexible-budget variance,

...difference between actual fixed overhead costs and flexible-budget fixed overhead amounts

the fixed overhead spending variance,

...same as the preceding explanation

and the fixed overhead production-volume variance

...difference between budgeted fixed overhead and fixed overhead allocated on the basis of actual output produced

The flexible-budget amount for a fixed-cost item is also the amount included in the static budget prepared at the start of the period. No adjustment is required for differences between actual output and budgeted output for fixed costs because fixed costs are unaffected by changes in the output level within the relevant range. At the start of 2014, Webb budgeted its fixed overhead costs to be $276,000 per month. The actual amount for April 2014 turned out to be $285,000. The **fixed overhead flexible-budget variance** is the difference between actual fixed overhead costs and fixed overhead costs in the flexible budget:

$$\text{Fixed overhead flexible-budget variance} = \frac{\text{Actual costs}}{\text{incurred}} - \frac{\text{Flexible-budget}}{\text{amount}}$$

$$= \$285{,}000 - \$276{,}000$$

$$= \$9{,}000 \text{ U}$$

The variance is unfavorable because the $285,000 actual fixed overhead costs exceed the $276,000 budgeted for April 2014, which decreases that month's operating income by $9,000.

The variable overhead flexible-budget variance described earlier in this chapter was subdivided into a spending variance and an efficiency variance. There is no efficiency variance for fixed overhead costs. That's because a given lump sum of fixed overhead costs will be unaffected by how efficiently machine-hours are used to produce output in a given budget period. As we will see later on, this does not mean that a company cannot be efficient or inefficient in its use of fixed-overhead-cost resources. As Exhibit 2 shows, because there is no efficiency variance, the **fixed overhead spending variance** is the same amount as the fixed overhead flexible-budget variance:

$$\text{Fixed overhead spending variance} = \frac{\text{Actual costs}}{\text{incurred}} - \frac{\text{Flexible-budget}}{\text{amount}}$$

$$= \$285{,}000 - \$276{,}000$$

$$= \$9{,}000 \text{ U}$$

Reasons for the unfavorable spending variance could be higher plant-leasing costs, higher depreciation on plant and equipment, or higher administrative costs, such as a higher-than-budgeted

| Exhibit 2 | Columnar Presentation of Fixed Overhead Variance Analysis: Webb Company for April 2014[a] |

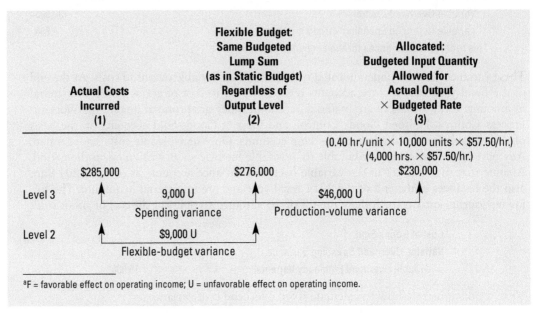

[a]F = favorable effect on operating income; U = unfavorable effect on operating income.

salary paid to the plant manager. Webb investigated this variance and found that there was a $9,000 per month unexpected increase in its equipment-leasing costs. However, managers concluded that the new lease rates were competitive with lease rates available elsewhere. If this were not the case, Webb would look to lease equipment from other suppliers.

Production-Volume Variance

The **production-volume variance** arises only for fixed costs. It is the difference between the budgeted fixed overhead and the fixed overhead allocated on the basis of actual output produced. Recall that at the start of the year, Webb calculated a budgeted fixed overhead rate of $57.50 per machine-hour based on monthly budgeted fixed overhead costs of $276,000. Under standard costing, Webb's fixed overhead costs are allocated to the actual output produced during each period at the rate of $57.50 per standard machine-hour, which is equivalent to a rate of $23 per jacket (0.40 machine-hour per jacket × $57.50 per machine-hour). If Webb produces 1,000 jackets, $23,000 ($23 per jacket × 1,000 jackets) out of April's budgeted fixed overhead costs of $276,000 will be allocated to the jackets. If Webb produces 10,000 jackets, $230,000 ($23 per jacket × 10,000 jackets) will be allocated. Only if Webb produces 12,000 jackets (that is, operates, as budgeted, at capacity) will all $276,000 ($23 per jacket × 12,000 jackets) of the budgeted fixed overhead costs be allocated to the jacket output. The key point here is that even though Webb budgeted its fixed overhead costs to be $276,000, it does not necessarily allocate all these costs to output. The reason is that Webb budgets $276,000 of fixed costs to support its planned production of 12,000 jackets. If Webb produces fewer than 12,000 jackets, it only allocates the budgeted cost of capacity actually needed and used to produce the jackets.

The production-volume variance, also referred to as the **denominator-level variance**, is the difference between the budgeted and allocated fixed overhead amounts. Note that the allocated overhead can be expressed in terms of allocation-base units (machine-hours for Webb) or in terms of the budgeted fixed cost per unit:

$$\frac{\text{Production}}{\text{volume variance}} = \frac{\text{Budgeted}}{\text{fixed overhead}} - \frac{\text{Fixed overhead allocated}}{\text{for actual output units produced}}$$

$$= \$276,000 - (0.40 \text{ hour per jacket} \times \$57.50 \text{ per hour} \times 10,000 \text{ jackets})$$

$$= \$276,000 - (\$23 \text{ per jacket} \times 10,000 \text{ jackets})$$

$$= \$276,000 - \$230,000$$

$$= \$46,000 \text{ U}$$

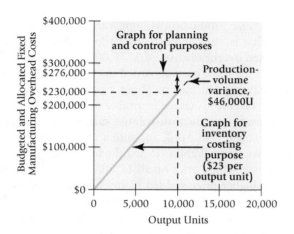

Exhibit 3

Behavior of Fixed Manufacturing Overhead Costs: Budgeted for Planning and Control Purposes and Allocated for Inventory Costing Purposes for Webb Company for April 2014

As shown in Exhibit 2, the budgeted fixed overhead ($276,000) will be the lump sum shown in the static budget and also in any flexible budget within the relevant range. The fixed overhead allocated ($230,000) is the amount of fixed overhead costs allocated; it is calculated by multiplying the number of output units produced during the budget period (10,000 units) by the budgeted cost per output unit ($23). The $46,000 U production-volume variance can also be thought of as $23 per jacket × 2,000 jackets that were *not* produced. We will explore possible causes for the unfavorable production-volume variance and its management implications in the following section.

Exhibit 3 shows Webb's production-volume variance. For planning and control purposes, Webb's fixed (manufacturing) overhead costs do not change in the 0- to 12,000-unit relevant range. Contrast this behavior of fixed costs with how these costs are depicted for the purpose of inventory costing in Exhibit 3. Under Generally Accepted Accounting Principles (GAAP), fixed (manufacturing) overhead costs are allocated as an inventoriable cost to the output units produced. Every output unit that Webb manufactures will increase the fixed overhead allocated to products by $23. That is, for purposes of allocating fixed overhead costs to jackets, these costs are viewed *as if* they had a variable-cost behavior pattern. As the graph in Exhibit 3 shows, the difference between the $276,000 in fixed overhead costs budgeted and the $230,000 of costs allocated is the $46,000 unfavorable production-volume variance.

Managers should always be careful to distinguish the true behavior of fixed costs from the manner in which fixed costs are assigned to products. In particular, although fixed costs are unitized and allocated for inventory costing purposes, managers should be wary of using the same unitized fixed overhead costs for planning and control purposes. When forecasting fixed costs, managers should concentrate on total lump-sum costs instead of unitized costs. Similarly, when managers are looking to assign costs for control purposes or identify the best way to use capacity resources fixed in the short run, the use of unitized fixed costs often leads to incorrect decisions.

Interpreting the Production-Volume Variance

Lump-sum fixed costs represent the costs of acquiring capacity. These costs do not decrease automatically if the capacity needed turns out to be less than the capacity acquired. Sometimes costs are fixed for a specific time period for contractual reasons, such as an annual lease contract for a plant. At other times, costs are fixed because capacity has to be acquired or disposed of in fixed increments, or lumps. For example, suppose that acquiring a sewing machine gives Webb the ability to produce 1,000 jackets. If it is not possible to buy or lease a fraction of a machine, Webb can add capacity only in increments of 1,000 jackets. That is, Webb may choose capacity levels of 10,000, 11,000, or 12,000 jackets, but nothing in between.

Webb's management would want to analyze the $46,000 unfavorable production-volume variance. Why did this overcapacity occur? Why were 10,000 jackets produced instead of 12,000? Is demand weak? Should Webb reevaluate its product and marketing strategies? Is there a quality problem? Or did Webb make a strategic mistake by acquiring too much capacity? The causes of the $46,000 unfavorable production-volume variance will determine the actions Webb's managers take in response to the variance.

In contrast, a favorable production-volume variance indicates an overallocation of fixed overhead costs. That is, the overhead costs allocated to the actual output produced exceed the budgeted fixed overhead costs of $276,000. The favorable production-volume variance is composed of the fixed costs recorded in excess of $276,000.

Be careful when drawing conclusions about a company's capacity planning whether the production-volume variance is either favorable or unfavorable. To correctly interpret Webb's $46,000 unfavorable production-volume variance, its managers should consider why it sold only 10,000 jackets in April. Suppose a new competitor gained market share by pricing its jackets lower than Webb's. To sell the budgeted 12,000 jackets, Webb might have had to reduce its own selling price on all 12,000 jackets. Suppose it decided that selling 10,000 jackets at a higher price yielded higher operating income than selling 12,000 jackets at a lower price. The production-volume variance does not take into account such information. The failure of the production-volume variance to consider such information is why Webb should not interpret the $46,000 U amount as the total economic cost of selling 2,000 jackets fewer than the 12,000 jackets budgeted. If, however, Webb's managers anticipate they will not need capacity beyond 10,000 jackets, they may reduce the excess capacity, say, by canceling the lease on some of the machines.

Companies plan their plant capacity strategically on the basis of market information about how much capacity will be needed over some future time horizon. For 2014, Webb's budgeted quantity of output is equal to the maximum capacity of the plant for that budget period. Actual demand (and quantity produced) turned out to be below the budgeted quantity of output, so Webb reports an unfavorable production-volume variance for April 2014. However, it would be incorrect to conclude that Webb's management made a poor planning decision regarding its plant capacity. The demand for Webb's jackets might be highly uncertain. Given this uncertainty and the cost of not having sufficient capacity to meet sudden demand surges (including lost contribution margins as well as reduced repeat business), Webb's management may have made a wise capacity choice for 2014.

So what should Webb's managers ultimately do about the unfavorable variance in April? Should they try to reduce capacity, increase sales, or do nothing? Based on their analysis of the situation, Webb's managers decided to reduce some capacity but continued to maintain some excess capacity to accommodate unexpected surges in demand. Concepts in Action: Variance Analysis and Standard Costing Help Sandoz Manage Its Overhead Costs highlights another example of managers using variances to help guide their decisions.

Next we describe the journal entries Webb would make to record fixed overhead costs using standard costing.

Journal Entries for Fixed Overhead Costs and Variances

We illustrate journal entries for fixed overhead costs for April 2014 using the Fixed Overhead Control account and the contra account Fixed Overhead Allocated (data from Exhibit 2).

1. Fixed Overhead Control 285,000
      Salaries Payable, Accumulated Depreciation, and various other accounts 285,000
     To record actual fixed overhead costs incurred.

2. Work-in-Process Control 230,000
      Fixed Overhead Allocated 230,000
     To record fixed overhead costs allocated.
       (0.40 machine-hour/unit × 10,000 units × $57.50/machine-hour). (The costs accumulated in Work-in-Process Control are transferred to Finished Goods Control when production is completed and to the Cost of Goods Sold when the products are sold.)

3. Fixed Overhead Allocated 230,000
     Fixed Overhead Spending Variance 9,000
     Fixed Overhead Production-Volume Variance 46,000
      Fixed Overhead Control 285,000
     To record variances for the accounting period.

Concepts in Action

Variance Analysis and Standard Costing Help Sandoz Manage Its Overhead Costs

Sandoz US, the $8.7 billion subsidiary of Swiss-based Novartis AG, is one of the world's largest generic drug manufacturers. Market pricing pressure means that Sandoz operates on razor-thin margins. As a result, Sandoz must tackle the challenge of accounting for overhead costs. Sandoz uses standard costing and variance analysis to manage its overhead costs.

Each year, Sandoz prepares an overhead budget based on a detailed production plan, planned overhead spending, and other factors. Sandoz then uses activity-based costing to assign budgeted overhead costs to different work centers (for example, mixing, blending, tableting, testing, and packaging). Finally, overhead costs are assigned to products based on the activity levels required by each product at each work center. The resulting standard product cost is used in product profitability analysis and as a basis for making pricing decisions. The two main focal points in Sandoz's performance analyses are overhead absorption analysis and manufacturing overhead variance analysis.

Each month, Sandoz uses absorption analysis to compare its actual production and actual costs to the standard costs of its processed inventory. The monthly analysis evaluates two key trends:

1. Are costs in line with the budget? If not, the reasons are examined and the accountable managers are notified.

2. Are production volume and product mix conforming to plan? If not, Sandoz reviews and adjusts the capacities of its machines, and the absorption trend is deemed to be permanent.

Manufacturing overhead variances are examined at the work center level. These variances help determine when equipment is not running as expected so it can be repaired or replaced. Variances also help in identifying inefficiencies in processing and setup and cleaning times, which leads to more efficient ways to use equipment. Sometimes, the manufacturing overhead variance analysis leads to the review and improvement of the standards themselves—a critical element in planning the level of plant capacity. Managers also review the company's current and future capacity on a monthly basis to identify constraints and future capital needs.

Sources: Novartis AG. 2013. December 31, 2012 Form 20-F (filed January 23, 2013), accessed May 2013; and conversations with and documents prepared by Eric Evans and Erich Erchr (of Sandoz US), 2004.

Overall, $285,000 of fixed overhead costs were incurred during April, but only $230,000 were allocated to jackets. The difference of $55,000 is the underallocated fixed overhead costs. The third entry illustrates how the fixed overhead spending variance of $9,000 and the fixed overhead production-volume variance of $46,000 together record this amount in a standard costing system.

At the end of the fiscal year, the fixed overhead spending variance is written off to the cost of goods sold if it is immaterial in amount or prorated among Work-in-Process Control, Finished Goods Control, and Cost of Goods Sold on the basis of the fixed overhead allocated to these accounts. Some companies combine the write-off and proration methods—that is, they write off the portion of the variance that is due to inefficiency and could have been avoided and prorate the portion of the variance that is unavoidable. Assume that the balance in the Fixed

Overhead Spending Variance account as of April 2014 is also the balance at the end of 2014 and is immaterial in amount. The following journal entry records the write-off to Cost of Goods Sold.

Cost of Goods Sold	9,000	
Fixed Overhead Spending Variance		9,000

We now consider the production-volume variance. Assume that the balance in the Fixed Overhead Production-Volume Variance account as of April 2014 is also the balance at the end of 2014. Also assume that some of the jackets manufactured during 2014 are in work-in-process and finished goods inventory at the end of the year. Many management accountants make a strong argument for writing off to Cost of Goods Sold and not prorating an unfavorable production-volume variance. Proponents of this argument contend that the unfavorable production-volume variance of $46,000 measures the cost of resources expended for 2,000 jackets that were not produced ($23 per jacket $\times$ 2,000 jackets = $46,000). Prorating these costs would inappropriately allocate the fixed overhead costs incurred for the 2,000 jackets not produced to the jackets that were produced. The jackets produced already bear their representative share of fixed overhead costs of $23 per jacket. Therefore, this argument favors charging the unfavorable production-volume variance against the year's revenues so that fixed costs of unused capacity are not carried in work-in-process inventory and finished goods inventory.

There is, however, an alternative view. This view regards the denominator level as a "soft" rather than a "hard" measure of the fixed resources required and needed to produce each jacket. Suppose that either because of the design of the jacket or the functioning of the machines, it took more machine-hours than previously thought to manufacture each jacket. Consequently, Webb could make only 10,000 jackets rather than the planned 12,000 in April. In this case, the $276,000 of budgeted fixed overhead costs support the production of the 10,000 jackets manufactured. Under this reasoning, prorating the fixed overhead production-volume variance would appropriately spread the fixed overhead costs among the Work-in-Process Control, Finished Goods Control, and Cost of Goods Sold accounts.

What about a favorable production-volume variance? Suppose Webb manufactured 13,800 jackets in April 2014.

$$\text{Production-volume variance} = \begin{matrix} \text{Budgeted} \\ \text{fixed} \\ \text{overhead} \end{matrix} - \begin{matrix} \text{Fixed overhead allocated using} \\ \text{budgeted cost per output unit overhead} \\ \text{allowed for actual output produced} \end{matrix}$$

$$= \$276,000 - (\$23 \text{ per jacket} \times 13,800 \text{ jackets})$$

$$= \$276,000 - \$317,400 = \$41,400 \text{ F}$$

Because actual production exceeded the planned capacity level, clearly the fixed overhead costs of $276,000 supported the production of all 13,800 jackets and should therefore be allocated to them. Prorating the favorable production-volume variance achieves this outcome and reduces the amounts in the Work-in-Process Control, Finished Goods Control, and Cost of Goods Sold accounts. Proration is also the more conservative approach in the sense that it results in a lower operating income than if the entire favorable production-volume variance were credited to Cost of Goods Sold.

Another point relevant to this discussion is that if variances are always written off to Cost of Goods Sold, a company could set its standards to either increase (for financial reporting purposes) or decrease (for tax purposes) its operating income. In other words, always writing off variances invites gaming behavior. For example, Webb could generate a favorable production-volume variance by setting the denominator level used to allocate the firm's fixed overhead costs low and thereby increase its operating income. Or the firm could do just the opposite if it wanted to decrease its operating income to lower its taxes. The proration method has the effect of approximating the allocation of fixed costs based on actual costs and actual output, so it is not susceptible to this type of manipulation.

There is no clear-cut or preferred approach for closing out the production-volume variance. The appropriate accounting procedure is a matter of judgment and depends on the circumstances of each case. Variations of the proration method may be desirable. For example, a company may choose to write off a portion of the production-volume variance and prorate the rest. The goal is to write off that part of the production-volume variance that represents the cost of capacity not used to support the production of output during the period. The rest of the production-volume variance is prorated to Work-in-Process Control, Finished Goods Control, and Cost of Goods Sold.

If Webb were to write off the production-volume variance to Cost of Goods Sold, it would make the following journal entry.

Cost of Goods Sold	46,000	
Fixed Overhead Production-Volume Variance		46,000

Decision Point

What variances can be calculated for fixed overhead costs?

Integrated Analysis of Overhead Cost Variances

Learning Objective 5

Show how the 4-variance analysis approach reconciles the actual overhead incurred with the overhead amounts allocated during the period

...the 4-variance analysis approach identifies spending and efficiency variances for variable overhead costs and spending and production-volume variances for fixed overhead costs

As our discussion indicates, the variance calculations for variable overhead and fixed overhead differ:

- Variable overhead has no production-volume variance.
- Fixed overhead has no efficiency variance.

Exhibit 4 presents an integrated summary of the variable overhead variances and the fixed overhead variances computed using standard costs for April 2014. Panel A shows the variances for variable overhead, whereas Panel B contains the fixed overhead variances. As you study Exhibit 4, note how the columns in Panels A and B are aligned to measure the different variances. In both Panels A and B,

- the difference between columns 1 and 2 measures the spending variance.
- the difference between columns 2 and 3 measures the efficiency variance (if applicable).
- the difference between columns 3 and 4 measures the production-volume variance (if applicable).

Panel A contains an efficiency variance; Panel B has no efficiency variance for fixed overhead. As we discussed, a lump-sum amount of fixed costs will be unaffected by the degree of operating efficiency in a given budget period.

Panel A does not have a production-volume variance because the amount of variable overhead allocated is always the same as the flexible-budget amount. Variable costs never have any unused capacity. When production and sales decline from 12,000 jackets to 10,000 jackets, budgeted variable overhead costs proportionately decline. Fixed costs are different. Panel B has a production-volume variance (see Exhibit 3) because Webb did not use some of the fixed overhead capacity it had acquired when it planned to produce 12,000 jackets.

4-Variance Analysis

When all of the overhead variances are presented together as in Exhibit 4, we refer to it as a 4-variance analysis:

4-Variance Analysis

	Spending Variance	Efficiency Variance	Production-Volume Variance
Variable overhead	$4,500 F	$15,000 U	Never a variance
Fixed overhead	$9,000 U	Never a variance	$46,000 U

Note that the 4-variance analysis provides the same level of information as the variance analysis carried out earlier for variable overhead and fixed overhead separately

Exhibit 4   Columnar Presentation of Integrated Variance Analysis: Webb Company for April 2014[a]

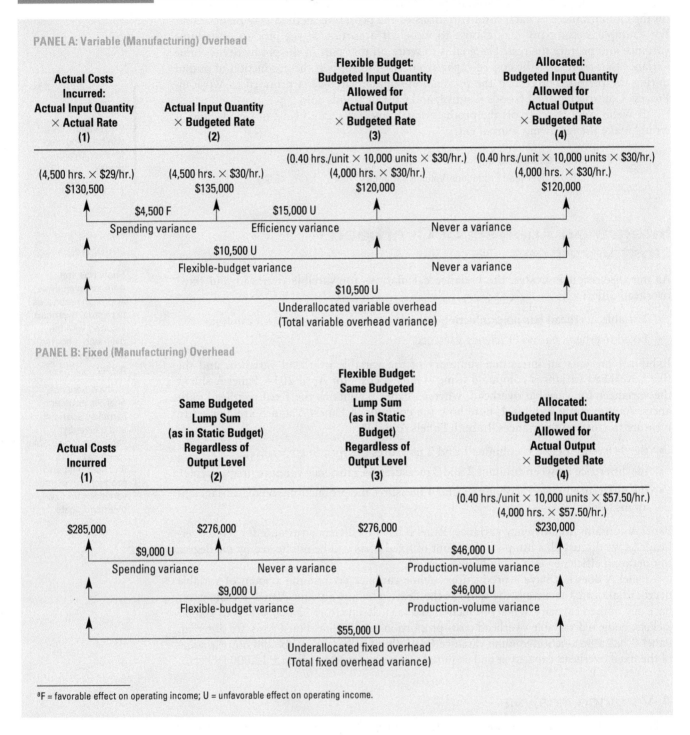

PANEL A: Variable (Manufacturing) Overhead

Actual Costs Incurred: Actual Input Quantity × Actual Rate (1)	Actual Input Quantity × Budgeted Rate (2)	Flexible Budget: Budgeted Input Quantity Allowed for Actual Output × Budgeted Rate (3)	Allocated: Budgeted Input Quantity Allowed for Actual Output × Budgeted Rate (4)
		(0.40 hrs./unit × 10,000 units × $30/hr.) (4,000 hrs. × $30/hr.)	(0.40 hrs./unit × 10,000 units × $30/hr.) (4,000 hrs. × $30/hr.)
(4,500 hrs. × $29/hr.) $130,500	(4,500 hrs. × $30/hr.) $135,000	$120,000	$120,000

$4,500 F ← Spending variance → $15,000 U ← Efficiency variance →   Never a variance

$10,500 U ← Flexible-budget variance →   Never a variance

$10,500 U ← Underallocated variable overhead (Total variable overhead variance)

PANEL B: Fixed (Manufacturing) Overhead

Actual Costs Incurred (1)	Same Budgeted Lump Sum (as in Static Budget) Regardless of Output Level (2)	Flexible Budget: Same Budgeted Lump Sum (as in Static Budget) Regardless of Output Level (3)	Allocated: Budgeted Input Quantity Allowed for Actual Output × Budgeted Rate (4)
			(0.40 hrs./unit × 10,000 units × $57.50/hr.) (4,000 hrs. × $57.50/hr.)
$285,000	$276,000	$276,000	$230,000

$9,000 U ← Spending variance →   Never a variance   → $46,000 U ← Production-volume variance

$9,000 U ← Flexible-budget variance → $46,000 U ← Production-volume variance

$55,000 U ← Underallocated fixed overhead (Total fixed overhead variance)

[a]F = favorable effect on operating income; U = unfavorable effect on operating income.

(in Exhibits 1 and 2, respectively), but it does so in a unified presentation that also indicates those variances that are never present.

As with other variances, the variances in Webb's 4-variance analysis are not necessarily independent of each other. For example, Webb may purchase lower-quality machine fluids (leading to a favorable variable overhead spending variance), which results in the machines taking longer to operate than budgeted (causing an unfavorable variable overhead efficiency variance), and producing less than budgeted output (causing an unfavorable production-volume variance).

Combined Variance Analysis

To keep track of all that is happening within their areas of responsibility, managers in large, complex businesses, such as General Electric and Disney, use detailed 4-variance analysis. Doing so helps them identify and focus attention on the areas not operating as expected. Managers of small businesses understand their operations better based on personal observations and nonfinancial measures. They find less value in doing the additional measurements required for 4-variance analyses. For example, to simplify their costing systems, small companies may not distinguish variable overhead incurred from fixed overhead incurred because making this distinction is often not clear-cut. Many costs such as supervision, quality control, and materials handling have both variable- and fixed-cost components that may not be easy to separate. Managers may therefore use a less detailed analysis that *combines* the variable overhead and fixed overhead into a single total overhead cost.

When a single total overhead cost category is used, it can still be analyzed in depth. The variances are now the sums of the variable overhead and fixed overhead variances for that level, as computed in Exhibit 4. The combined variance analysis looks as follows:

	Combined 3-Variance Analysis		
	Spending Variance	Efficiency Variance	Production-Volume Variance
Total overhead	$4,500 U	$15,000 U	$46,000 U

The accounting for 3-variance analysis is simpler than for 4-variance analysis, but some information is lost because the variable and fixed overhead spending variances are combined into a single total overhead spending variance.

Finally, the overall **total-overhead variance** is given by the sum of the preceding variances. In the Webb example, this equals $65,500 U. Note that this amount, which aggregates the flexible-budget and production-volume variances, equals the total amount of underallocated (or underapplied) overhead costs. Using figures from Exhibit 4, the $65,500 U total-overhead variance is the difference between (a) the total actual overhead incurred ($130,500 + $285,000 = $415,500) and (b) the overhead allocated ($120,000 + $230,000 = $350,000) to the actual output produced. If the total-overhead variance were favorable, it would have corresponded instead to the amount of overapplied overhead costs.

Decision Point

What is the most detailed way for a company to reconcile actual overhead incurred with the amount allocated during a period?

Production-Volume Variance and Sales-Volume Variance

Learning Objective 6

Explain the relationship between the sales-volume variance and the production-volume variance

...the production-volume and operating-income volume variances together comprise the sales-volume variance

As we complete our study of variance analysis for Webb Company, it is helpful to step back to see the "big picture" and to link the accounting and performance evaluation functions of standard costing. A static-budget variance of $93,100 U can be identified as the difference between the static budget operating income of $108,000 and the actual operating income of $14,900. That static-budget variance of $93,100 U can be subdivided into a flexible-budget variance of $29,100 U and a sales-volume variance of $64,000 U. More detailed variances subdivide, whenever possible, individual flexible-budget variances for the selling price, direct materials, direct manufacturing labor, and variable overhead. For the fixed overhead, we noted that the flexible-budget variance is the same as the spending variance. Where does the production-volume variance belong then? As you shall see, the production-volume variance is a component of the sales-volume variance. Under our assumption of actual production and sales of 10,000 jackets, Webb's costing system debits to Work-in-Process Control the standard costs of the 10,000 jackets produced. These amounts are then transferred to Finished Goods and finally to Cost of Goods Sold:

Direct materials	
($60 per jacket × 10,000 jackets)	$ 600,000
Direct manufacturing labor	
($16 per jacket × 10,000 jackets)	160,000
Variable overhead	
($12 per jacket × 10,000 jackets)	120,000
Fixed overhead	
($23 per jacket × 10,000 jackets)	230,000
Cost of goods sold at standard cost	
($111 per jacket × 10,000 jackets)	$1,110,000

Webb's costing system also records the revenues from the 10,000 jackets sold at the budgeted selling price of $120 per jacket. The net effect of these entries on Webb's budgeted operating income is as follows:

Revenues at budgeted selling price	
($120 per jacket × 10,000 jackets)	$1,200,000
Cost of goods sold at standard cost	
($111 per jacket × 10,000 jackets)	1,110,000
Operating income based on budgeted profit per jacket	
($9 per jacket × 10,000 jackets)	$ 90,000

A crucial point to keep in mind is that under standard costing, fixed overhead costs are treated as if they are a variable cost. That is, in determining the budgeted operating income of $90,000, only $230,000 ($23 per jacket × 10,000 jackets) of the fixed overhead costs are considered, whereas the budgeted fixed overhead costs are $276,000. Webb's accountants then record the $46,000 unfavorable production-volume variance (the difference between the budgeted fixed overhead costs, $276,000, and allocated fixed overhead costs, $230,000), as well as the various flexible-budget variances (including the fixed overhead spending variance) that total $29,100 unfavorable. This results in actual operating income of $14,900 as follows:

Operating income based on budgeted profit per jacket	
($9 per jacket × 10,000 jackets)	$ 90,000
Unfavorable production-volume variance	(46,000)
Flexible-budget operating income	44,000
Unfavorable flexible-budget variance for operating income	(29,100)
Actual operating income	$ 14,900

In contrast, the static-budget operating income of $108,000 is not entered in Webb's costing system because standard costing records budgeted revenues, standard costs, and variances only for the 10,000 jackets actually produced and sold, not for the 12,000 jackets that were *planned* to be produced and sold. As a result, the sales-volume variance of $64,000 U, which is the difference between the static-budget operating income of $108,000 and the flexible-budget operating income of $44,000, is never actually recorded under standard costing. Nevertheless, the sales-volume variance is useful because it helps managers understand the lost contribution margin from selling 2,000 fewer jackets (the sales-volume variance assumes fixed costs remain at the budgeted level of $276,000).

The sales-volume variance has two components. They are as follows:

1. A difference between the static-budget operating income of $108,000 for 12,000 jackets and the budgeted operating income of $90,000 for 10,000 jackets. This is the

operating-income volume variance of $18,000 U ($108,000 − $90,000). It reflects the fact that Webb produced and sold 2,000 fewer units than budgeted.

2. A difference between the budgeted operating income of $90,000 and the flexible budget operating income of $44,000 for the 10,000 actual units. This difference arises because Webb's costing system treats fixed costs as if they behave in a variable manner and assumes fixed costs equal the allocated amount of $230,000, rather than the budgeted fixed costs of $276,000. Of course, this difference is precisely the production-volume variance of $46,000 U.

In summary, we have the following:

	Operating-income volume variance	$18,000 U
(+)	Production-volume variance	46,000 U
Equals	Sales-volume variance	$64,000 U

We can now provide a summary (see Exhibit 5) that formally disaggregates the static-budget variance of $93,100 U into its components.

We next describe the use of variance analysis in activity-based costing systems.

> **Decision Point**
>
> What is the relationship between the sales-volume variance and the production-volume variance?

Variance Analysis and Activity-Based Costing

> **Learning Objective 7**
>
> Calculate variances in activity-based costing
>
> ...compare budgeted and actual overhead costs of activities

Activity-based costing (ABC) systems focus on individual activities as the fundamental cost objects. ABC systems classify the costs of various activities into a cost hierarchy— output unit-level costs, batch-level costs, product-sustaining costs, and facility-sustaining costs. In this section, we show how a company that has an ABC system and batch-level costs can benefit from variance analysis. Batch-level costs are the costs of activities related to a group of units of products or services rather than to each individual

---

Exhibit 5 Summary of Levels 1, 2, and 3 Variance Analysis: Webb Company for April 2014

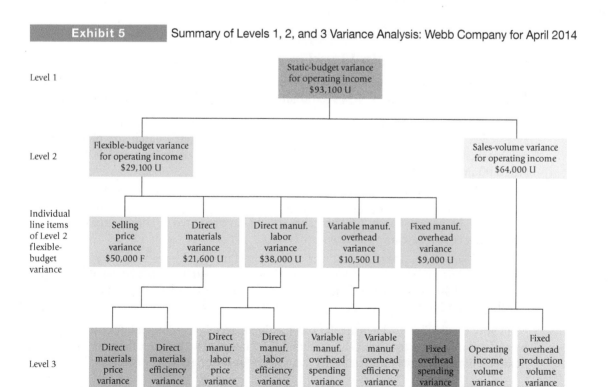

unit of product or service. We illustrate variance analysis for variable batch-level direct costs and fixed batch-level setup overhead costs.[4]

Consider Lyco Brass Works, which manufactures many different types of faucets and brass fittings. Because of the wide range of products it produces, Lyco uses an activity-based costing system. In contrast, Webb uses a simple costing system because it makes only one type of jacket. One of Lyco's products is Elegance, a decorative brass faucet for home spas. Lyco produces Elegance in batches.

For each product Lyco makes, it uses dedicated materials-handling labor to bring materials to the production floor, transport items in process from one work center to the next, and take the finished goods to the shipping area. Therefore, materials-handling labor costs for Elegance are direct costs of Elegance. Because the materials for a batch are moved together, materials-handling labor costs vary with number of batches rather than with number of units in a batch. Materials-handling labor costs are variable direct batch-level costs.

To manufacture a batch of Elegance, Lyco must set up the machines and molds. Employees must be highly skilled to set up the machines and molds. Hence, a separate setup department is responsible for setting up the machines and molds for different batches of products. Setup costs are overhead costs. For simplicity, assume that setup costs are fixed with respect to the number of setup-hours. The costs consist of salaries paid to engineers and supervisors and the costs of leasing setup equipment.

Information regarding Elegance for 2014 follows:

	Actual Result	Static-Budget Amount
1. Units of Elegance produced and sold	151,200	180,000
2. Batch size (units per batch)	140	150
3. Number of batches (Line 1 ÷ Line 2)	1,080	1,200
4. Materials-handling labor-hours per batch	5.25	5
5. Total materials-handling labor-hours (Line 3 $\times$ Line 4)	5,670	6,000
6. Cost per materials-handling labor-hour	$ 14.50	$ 14
7. Total materials-handling labor costs (Line 5 $\times$ Line 6)	$ 82,215	$ 84,000
8. Setup-hours per batch	6.25	6
9. Total setup-hours (Line 3 $\times$ Line 8)	6,750	7,200
10. Total fixed setup overhead costs	$220,000	$216,000

Flexible Budget and Variance Analysis for Direct Materials-Handling Labor Costs

To prepare the flexible budget for the materials-handling labor costs, Lyco starts with the actual units of output produced, 151,200 units, and proceeds with the following steps.

Step 1: Using the Budgeted Batch Size, Calculate the Number of Batches that Should Have Been Used to Produce the Actual Output. At the budgeted batch size of 150 units per batch, Lyco should have produced the 151,200 units of output in 1,008 batches (151,200 units ÷ 150 units per batch).

Step 2: Using the Budgeted Materials-Handling Labor-Hours per Batch, Calculate the Number of Materials-Handling Labor-Hours that Should Have Been Used. At the budgeted quantity of 5 hours per batch, 1,008 batches should have required 5,040 materials-handling labor-hours (1,008 batches × 5 hours per batch).

Step 3: Using the Budgeted Cost per Materials-Handling Labor-Hour, Calculate the Flexible-Budget Amount for the Materials-Handling Labor-Hours. The flexible-budget amount is 5,040 materials-handling labor-hours × the $14 budgeted cost per materials-handling labor-hour = $70,560.

Note how the flexible-budget calculations for the materials-handling labor costs focus on batch-level quantities (materials-handling labor-hours per batch rather than per unit). The flexible-budget quantity computations focus at the appropriate level of the cost hierarchy.

---

[4] The techniques we demonstrate can be applied to analyze variable batch-level overhead costs as well.

For example, because materials handling is a batch-level cost, the flexible-budget quantity calculations are made at the batch level—the quantity of materials-handling labor-hours that Lyco should have used based on the number of batches it should have used to produce the actual quantity of 151,200 units. If a cost had been a product-sustaining cost—such as product design cost—the flexible-budget quantity computations would focus at the product-sustaining level, for example, by evaluating the actual complexity of the product's design relative to the budget.

The flexible-budget variance for the materials-handling labor costs can now be calculated as follows:

$$\frac{\text{Flexible-budget}}{\text{variance}} = \text{Actual costs} - \text{Flexible-budget costs}$$

$$= (5{,}670 \text{ hours} \times \$14.50 \text{ per hour}) - (5{,}040 \text{ hours} \times \$14 \text{ per hour})$$

$$= \$82{,}215 - \$70{,}560$$

$$= \$11{,}655 \text{ U}$$

The unfavorable variance indicates that materials-handling labor costs were $11,655 higher than the flexible-budget target. We can get some insight into the possible reasons for this unfavorable outcome by examining the price and efficiency components of the flexible-budget variance. Exhibit 6 presents the variances in columnar form.

$$\frac{\text{Price}}{\text{variance}} = \left(\frac{\text{Actual price}}{\text{of input}} - \frac{\text{Budgeted price}}{\text{of input}}\right) \times \frac{\text{Actual quantity}}{\text{of input}}$$

$$= (\$14.50 \text{ per hour} - \$14 \text{ per hour}) \times 5{,}670 \text{ hours}$$

$$= \$0.50 \text{ per hour} \times 5{,}670 \text{ hours}$$

$$= \$2{,}835 \text{ U}$$

The unfavorable price variance for materials-handling labor indicates that the $14.50 actual cost per materials-handling labor-hour exceeds the $14.00 budgeted cost per materials-handling labor-hour. This variance could be the result of Lyco's human resources manager negotiating wage rates less skillfully or of wage rates increasing unexpectedly due to a scarcity of labor.

$$\frac{\text{Efficiency}}{\text{variance}} = \left(\begin{array}{c}\text{Actual} \\ \text{quantity of} \\ \text{input used}\end{array} - \begin{array}{c}\text{Budgeted quantity} \\ \text{of input allowed} \\ \text{for actual output}\end{array}\right) \times \frac{\text{Budgeted price}}{\text{of input}}$$

$$= (5{,}670 \text{ hours} - 5{,}040 \text{ hours}) \times \$14 \text{ per hour}$$

$$= 630 \text{ hours} \times \$14 \text{ per hour}$$

$$= \$8{,}820 \text{ U}$$

| Exhibit 6 | Columnar Presentation of Variance Analysis for Direct Materials-Handling Labor Costs: Lyco Brass Works for 2014[a] |

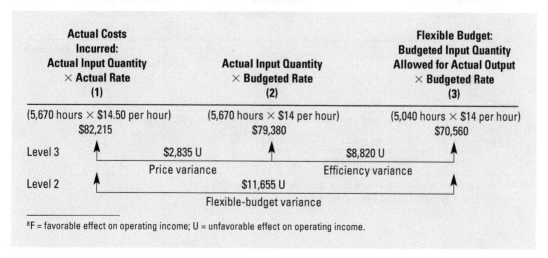

Actual Costs Incurred: Actual Input Quantity × Actual Rate (1)	Actual Input Quantity × Budgeted Rate (2)	Flexible Budget: Budgeted Input Quantity Allowed for Actual Output × Budgeted Rate (3)
(5,670 hours × $14.50 per hour) $82,215	(5,670 hours × $14 per hour) $79,380	(5,040 hours × $14 per hour) $70,560

Level 3   ↑ $2,835 U   ↑ $8,820 U   ↑

Price variance   Efficiency variance

Level 2   ↑ $11,655 U   ↑

Flexible-budget variance

[a]F = favorable effect on operating income; U = unfavorable effect on operating income.

The unfavorable efficiency variance indicates that the 5,670 actual materials-handling labor-hours exceeded the 5,040 budgeted materials-handling labor-hours for the actual output. Possible reasons for the unfavorable efficiency variance are as follows:

- Smaller actual batch sizes of 140 units, instead of the budgeted batch sizes of 150 units, resulted in Lyco producing the 151,200 units in 1,080 batches instead of 1,008 (151,200 ÷ 150) batches
- The actual materials-handling labor-hours per batch (5.25 hours) were higher than the budgeted materials-handling labor-hours per batch (5 hours)

Reasons for smaller-than-budgeted batch sizes could include quality problems when batch sizes exceed 140 faucets and high costs of carrying inventory.

Possible reasons for the larger actual materials-handling labor-hours per batch are as follows:

- Inefficient layout of the Elegance production line
- Materials-handling labor having to wait at work centers before picking up or delivering materials
- Unmotivated, inexperienced, and underskilled employees
- Very tight standards for materials-handling time

Identifying the reasons for the efficiency variance helps Lyco's managers develop a plan for improving its materials-handling labor efficiency and take corrective action that will be incorporated into future budgets.

We now consider fixed setup overhead costs.

Flexible Budget and Variance Analysis for Fixed Setup Overhead Costs

Exhibit 7 presents the variances for fixed setup overhead costs in columnar form.

| Exhibit 7 | Columnar Presentation of Fixed Setup Overhead Variance Analysis: Lyco Brass Works for 2014[a] |

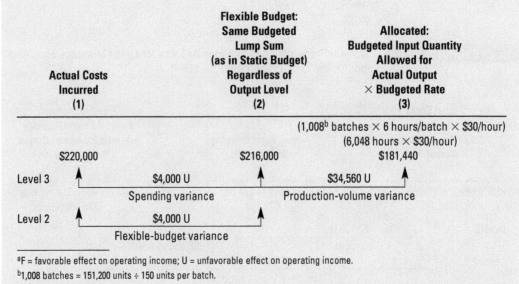

[a]F = favorable effect on operating income; U = unfavorable effect on operating income.
[b]1,008 batches = 151,200 units ÷ 150 units per batch.

Lyco's fixed setup overhead flexible-budget variance is calculated as follows:

$$\begin{array}{l} \text{Fixed-setup} \\ \text{overhead} \\ \text{flexible-budget} \\ \text{variance} \end{array} = \begin{array}{c} \text{Actual costs} \\ \text{incurred} \end{array} - \begin{array}{c} \text{Flexible-budget} \\ \text{costs} \end{array}$$

$$= \$220,000 - \$216,000$$

$$= \$4,000 \text{ U}$$

Note that the flexible-budget amount for the fixed setup overhead costs equals the static-budget amount of $216,000. That's because there is no "flexing" of fixed costs. Moreover, because the fixed overhead costs have no efficiency variance, the fixed setup overhead spending variance is the same as the fixed overhead flexible-budget variance. The spending variance could be unfavorable because of higher leasing costs of new setup equipment or higher salaries paid to engineers and supervisors. Lyco may have incurred these costs to alleviate some of the difficulties it was having in setting up machines.

To calculate the production-volume variance, Lyco first computes the budgeted cost-allocation rate for the fixed setup overhead costs using the same four-step approach.

Step 1:   Choose the Period to Use for the Budget. Lyco uses a period of 12 months (the year 2014).

Step 2:   Select the Cost-Allocation Base to Use in Allocating the Fixed Overhead Costs to the Output Produced. Lyco uses budgeted setup-hours as the cost-allocation base for fixed setup overhead costs. Budgeted setup-hours in the static budget for 2014 are 7,200 hours.

Step 3:   Identify the Fixed Overhead Costs Associated with the Cost-Allocation Base. Lyco's fixed setup overhead cost budget for 2014 is $216,000.

Step 4:   Compute the Rate per Unit of the Cost-Allocation Base Used to Allocate the Fixed Overhead Costs to the Output Produced. Dividing the $216,000 from Step 3 by the 7,200 setup-hours from Step 2, Lyco estimates a fixed setup overhead cost rate of $30 per setup-hour:

$$\begin{array}{l} \text{Budgeted fixed} \\ \text{setup overhead} \\ \text{cost per unit of} \\ \text{cost-allocation base} \end{array} = \dfrac{\begin{array}{c}\text{Budgeted total costs} \\ \text{in fixed overhead cost pool}\end{array}}{\begin{array}{c}\text{Budgeted total quantity of} \\ \text{cost-allocation base}\end{array}} = \dfrac{\$216,000}{7,200 \text{ setup hours}}$$

$$= \$30 \text{ per setup-hour}$$

$$\begin{array}{l} \text{Production-volume} \\ \text{variance for} \\ \text{fixed setup} \\ \text{overhead costs} \end{array} = \begin{array}{c} \text{Budgeted} \\ \text{fixed setup} \\ \text{overhead} \\ \text{costs} \end{array} - \begin{array}{c} \text{Fixed setup overhead} \\ \text{allocation using budgeted} \\ \text{input allowed for actual} \\ \text{output units produced} \end{array}$$

$$= \$216,000 - (1,008 \text{ batches} \times 6 \text{ hours/batch}) \times \$30/\text{hour}$$

$$= \$216,000 - (6,048 \text{ hours} \times \$30/\text{hour})$$

$$= \$216,000 - \$181,440$$

$$= \$34,560 \text{ U}$$

During 2014, Lyco planned to produce 180,000 units of Elegance but actually produced 151,200 units. The unfavorable production-volume variance measures the amount of extra fixed setup costs Lyco incurred for setup capacity it did not use. One interpretation is that the unfavorable $34,560 production-volume variance represents an inefficient use of the company's setup capacity. However, Lyco may have earned higher operating income by selling 151,200 units at a higher price than 180,000 units at a lower price. As a result, Lyco's managers should interpret the production-volume variance cautiously because it does not consider the effect of output on selling prices and operating income.

◀ Decision Point

How can variance analysis be used in an activity-based costing system?

Learning
Objective 8

Examine the use of
overhead variances
in nonmanufacturing
settings

...analyze
nonmanufacturing
variable overhead
costs for decision
making and cost
management; fixed
overhead variances
are especially impor-
tant in service settings

Overhead Variances in Nonmanufacturing Settings

Our Webb Company example examined variable and fixed manufacturing overhead costs. Managers can also use variance analysis to examine the overhead costs of the nonmanufacturing areas of the company and to make decisions about (1) pricing, (2) managing costs, and (3) the mix of products to make. For example, when product distribution costs are high, as they are in the automobile, consumer durables, cement, and steel industries, standard costing can provide managers with reliable and timely information on variable distribution overhead spending variances and efficiency variances.

What about service-sector companies such as airlines, hospitals, hotels, and railroads? How can they benefit from variance analyses? The output measures these companies commonly use are passenger-miles flown, patient days provided, room-days occupied, and ton-miles of freight hauled, respectively. Few costs can be traced to these outputs in a cost-effective way. Most of the costs are fixed overhead costs, such as the costs of equipment, buildings, and staff. Using capacity effectively is the key to profitability, and fixed overhead variances can help managers in this task. Retail businesses, such as Kmart, also have high capacity-related fixed costs (lease and occupancy costs). In the case of Kmart, sales declines resulted in unused capacity and unfavorable fixed-cost variances. Kmart reduced its fixed costs by closing some of its stores, but it also had to file for Chapter 11 bankruptcy.

Consider the following data for United Airlines for selected years from the past decade. Available seat miles (ASMs) are the actual seats in an airplane multiplied by the distance the plane traveled.

Year	Total ASMs (Millions) (1)	Operating Revenue per ASM (2)	Operating Cost per ASM (3)	Operating Income per ASM (4) = (2) – (3)
2000	175,493	10.2 cents	10.0 cents	0.2 cents
2003	136,566	8.6 cents	9.8 cents	−1.2 cents
2006	143,085	10.6 cents	10.8 cents	−0.2 cents
2008	135,859	11.9 cents	13.6 cents	−1.4 cents
2011	118,973	13.1 cents	13.5 cents	−0.4 cents

When air travel declined after terrorists hijacked a number of commercial jets on September 11, 2001, United's revenues fell. However most of the company's fixed costs—for its airport facilities, equipment, personnel, and so on—did not. United had a large unfavorable production-volume variance because its capacity was underutilized. As column 1 of the table indicates, United responded by reducing its capacity substantially over the next few years. Available seat miles (ASMs) declined from 175,493 million in 2000 to 136,566 million in 2003. Yet United was unable to fill even the planes it had retained, so its revenue per ASM declined (column 2) and its cost per ASM stayed roughly the same (column 3). United filed for Chapter 11 bankruptcy in December 2002 and began seeking government guarantees to obtain the loans it needed. Subsequently, strong demand for airline travel, as well as productivity improvements resulting from the more efficient use of resources and networks, led to increased traffic and higher average ticket prices. By maintaining a disciplined approach to capacity and tight control over growth, United saw over a 20% increase in its revenue per ASM between 2003 and 2006. The improvement in performance allowed United to come out of bankruptcy on February 1, 2006. In the past few years, however, the global recession and soaring jet fuel prices have had a significant negative impact on United's performance, as reflected in the continued negative operating incomes and the further decline in capacity. In May 2010, a merger agreement was reached between United and Continental Airlines, and Continental was dissolved in 2012.

Financial and Nonfinancial Performance Measures

The overhead variances discussed in this chapter are examples of financial performance measures. As the preceding examples illustrate, nonfinancial measures such as those related to capacity utilization and physical measures of input usage also provide useful information. The nonfinancial measures that managers of Webb would likely find helpful in planning and controlling its overhead costs include the following:

1. Quantity of actual indirect materials used per machine-hour, relative to the quantity of budgeted indirect materials used per machine-hour

2. Actual energy used per machine-hour, relative to the budgeted energy used per machine-hour

3. Actual machine-hours per jacket, relative to the budgeted machine-hours per jacket

These performance measures, like the financial variances discussed in this chapter, alert managers to problems and probably would be reported daily or hourly on the production floor. The overhead variances we discussed in this chapter capture the financial effects of items such as the three factors listed, which in many cases first appear as nonfinancial performance measures. An especially interesting example along these lines comes from Japan: Some Japanese companies have begun reining in their CO_2 emissions in part by doing a budgeted-to-actual variance analysis of the emissions. The goal is to make employees aware of the emissions and reduce them in advance of greenhouse-gas reduction plans being drawn up by the Japanese government.

Finally, both financial and nonfinancial performance measures are used to evaluate the performance of managers. Exclusive reliance on either is always too simplistic because each gives a different perspective on performance. Nonfinancial measures (such as those described previously) provide feedback on individual aspects of a manager's performance, whereas financial measures evaluate the overall effect of and the tradeoffs among different nonfinancial performance measures.

Decision Point

How are overhead variances useful in nonmanufacturing settings?

Problem for Self-Study

Nina Garcia is the newly appointed president of Laser Products. She is examining the May 2014 results for the Aerospace Products Division. This division manufactures wing parts for satellites. Garcia's current concern is with manufacturing overhead costs at the Aerospace Products Division. Both variable and fixed overhead costs are allocated to the wing parts on the basis of laser-cutting-hours. The following budget information is available:

Budgeted variable overhead rate	$200 per hour
Budgeted fixed overhead rate	$240 per hour
Budgeted laser-cutting time per wing part	1.5 hours
Budgeted production and sales for May 2014	5,000 wing parts
Budgeted fixed overhead costs for May 2014	$1,800,000

Actual results for May 2014 are as follows:

Wing parts produced and sold	4,800 units
Laser-cutting-hours used	8,400 hours
Variable overhead costs	$1,478,400
Fixed overhead costs	$1,832,200

1. Compute the spending variance and the efficiency variance for variable overhead.
2. Compute the spending variance and the production-volume variance for fixed overhead.
3. Give two explanations for each of the variances calculated in requirements 1 and 2.

Required

Solution

1 and 2. See Exhibit 8.

3. a. Variable overhead spending variance, $201,600 F. One possible reason for this variance is that the actual prices of individual items included in variable overhead (such as cutting fluids) are lower than budgeted prices. A second possible reason is that the percentage increase in the actual quantity usage of individual items in the variable overhead cost pool is less than the percentage increase in laser-cutting-hours compared to the flexible budget.

    b. Variable overhead efficiency variance, $240,000 U. One possible reason for this variance is inadequate maintenance of laser machines, causing them to take more

| **Exhibit 8** | Columnar Presentation of Integrated Variance Analysis: Laser Products for May 2014[a] |

PANEL A: Variable (Manufacturing) Overhead

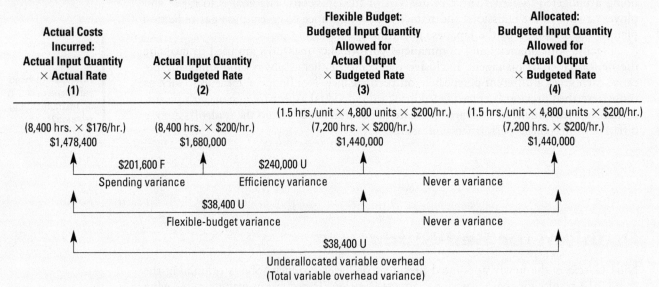

PANEL B: Fixed (Manufacturing) Overhead

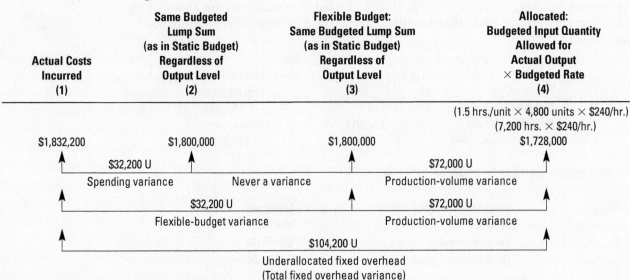

[a]F = favorable effect on operating income; U = unfavorable effect on operating income.

Source: Republished with permission of Strategic Finance by Paul Sherman. Copyright 2003 by Institute of Management Accountants. Permission conveyed through Copyright Clearance Center, Inc.

laser-cutting time per wing part. A second possible reason is use of undermotivated, inexperienced, or underskilled workers operating the laser-cutting machines, resulting in more laser-cutting time per wing part.

c. Fixed overhead spending variance, $32,200 U. One possible reason for this variance is that the actual prices of individual items in the fixed-cost pool unexpectedly increased from the prices budgeted (such as an unexpected increase in the cost of leasing each machine). A second possible reason is that the Aerospace Products Division had to lease more machines or hire more supervisors than had been budgeted.

d. Production-volume variance, $72,000 U. Actual production of wing parts is 4,800 units, compared with 5,000 units budgeted. One possible reason for this variance is demand factors, such as a decline in an aerospace program that led to a decline in demand for aircraft parts. A second possible reason is supply factors, such as a production stoppage due to labor problems or machine breakdowns.

▶ Decision Points

The following question-and-answer format summarizes the chapter's learning objectives. Each decision presents a key question related to a learning objective. The guidelines are the answer to that question.

Decision	Guidelines
1. How do managers plan variable overhead costs and fixed overhead costs?	Planning of both variable and fixed overhead costs involves undertaking only activities that add value and then being efficient in that undertaking. The key difference is that for variable-cost planning, ongoing decisions during the budget period play a much larger role; for fixed-cost planning, most key decisions are made before the start of the period.
2. How are budgeted variable overhead and fixed overhead cost rates calculated?	The budgeted variable (fixed) overhead cost rate is calculated by dividing the budgeted variable (fixed) overhead costs by the denominator level of the cost-allocation base.
3. What variances can be calculated for variable overhead costs?	When the flexible budget for variable overhead is developed, an overhead efficiency variance and an overhead spending variance can be computed. The variable overhead efficiency variance focuses on the difference between the actual quantity of the cost-allocation base used relative to the budgeted quantity of the cost-allocation base. The variable overhead spending variance focuses on the difference between the actual variable overhead cost per unit of the cost-allocation base relative to the budgeted variable overhead cost per unit of the cost-allocation base.
4. What variances can be calculated for fixed overhead costs?	For fixed overhead, the static and flexible budgets coincide. The difference between the budgeted and actual amount of fixed overhead is the flexible-budget variance, also referred to as the spending variance. The production-volume variance measures the difference between the budgeted fixed overhead and the fixed overhead allocated on the basis of actual output produced.
5. What is the most detailed way for a company to reconcile actual overhead incurred with the amount allocated during a period?	A 4-variance analysis presents spending and efficiency variances for variable overhead costs and spending and production-volume variances for fixed overhead costs. By analyzing these four variances together, managers can reconcile the actual overhead costs with the amount of overhead allocated to the output produced during a period.
6. What is the relationship between the sales-volume variance and the production-volume variance?	The production-volume variance is a component of the sales-volume variance. The production-volume and operating-income volume variances together comprise the sales-volume variance.

Decision	Guidelines
7. How can variance analysis be used in an activity-based costing system?	Flexible budgets in ABC systems give insight into why actual activity costs differ from budgeted activity costs. Using output and input measures for an activity, a comprehensive variance analysis can be conducted.
8. How are overhead variances useful in nonmanufacturing settings?	Managers can analyze variances for all variable overhead costs, including those outside the manufacturing function. The analysis can be used to make pricing and product mix decisions and to manage costs. Fixed overhead variances are especially important in service settings, where using capacity effectively is the key to profitability. In all cases, the information provided by variances can be supplemented by the use of suitable nonfinancial metrics.

Terms to Learn

The chapter contains definitions of the following important terms:

denominator level

denominator-level variance

fixed overhead flexible-budget variance

fixed overhead spending variance

operating-income volume variance

production-volume variance

standard costing

total-overhead variance

variable overhead efficiency variance

variable overhead flexible-budget variance

variable overhead spending variance

Assignment Material

Questions

1 How do managers plan for variable overhead costs?

2 How does the planning of fixed overhead costs differ from the planning of variable overhead costs?

3 How does standard costing differ from actual costing?

4 What are the steps in developing a budgeted variable overhead cost-allocation rate?

5 What are the factors that affect the spending variance for variable manufacturing overhead?

6 Assume variable manufacturing overhead is allocated using machine-hours. Give three possible reasons for a favorable variable overhead efficiency variance.

7 Describe the difference between a direct materials efficiency variance and a variable manufacturing overhead efficiency variance.

8 What are the steps in developing a budgeted fixed overhead rate?

9 Why is the flexible-budget variance the same amount as the spending variance for fixed manufacturing overhead?

10 Explain how the analysis of fixed manufacturing overhead costs differs for (a) planning and control and (b) inventory costing for financial reporting.

11 Provide one caveat that will affect whether a production-volume variance is a good measure of the economic cost of unused capacity.

12 "The production-volume variance should always be written off to Cost of Goods Sold." Do you agree? Explain.

13 What are the variances in a 4-variance analysis?

14 "Overhead variances should be viewed as interdependent rather than independent." Give an example.

15 Describe how flexible-budget variance analysis can be used in the control of costs of activity areas.

Exercises

16 **Variable manufacturing overhead, variance analysis.** Esquire Clothing is a manufacturer of designer suits. The cost of each suit is the sum of three variable costs (direct material costs, direct

manufacturing labor costs, and manufacturing overhead costs) and one fixed-cost category (manufacturing overhead costs). Variable manufacturing overhead cost is allocated to each suit on the basis of budgeted direct manufacturing labor-hours per suit. For June 2014, each suit is budgeted to take 4 labor-hours. Budgeted variable manufacturing overhead cost per labor-hour is $12. The budgeted number of suits to be manufactured in June 2014 is 1,040.

Actual variable manufacturing costs in June 2014 were $52,164 for 1,080 suits started and completed. There were no beginning or ending inventories of suits. Actual direct manufacturing labor-hours for June were 4,536.

1. Compute the flexible-budget variance, the spending variance, and the efficiency variance for variable manufacturing overhead.
2. Comment on the results.

Required

17 Fixed manufacturing overhead, variance analysis (continuation of 16). Esquire Clothing allocates fixed manufacturing overhead to each suit using budgeted direct manufacturing labor-hours per suit. Data pertaining to fixed manufacturing overhead costs for June 2014 are budgeted, $62,400, and actual, $63,916.

1. Compute the spending variance for fixed manufacturing overhead. Comment on the results.
2. Compute the production-volume variance for June 2014. What inferences can Esquire Clothing draw from this variance?

Required

18 Variable manufacturing overhead variance analysis. The French Bread Company bakes baguettes for distribution to upscale grocery stores. The company has two direct-cost categories: direct materials and direct manufacturing labor. Variable manufacturing overhead is allocated to products on the basis of standard direct manufacturing labor-hours. Following is some budget data for the French Bread Company:

Direct manufacturing labor use	0.02 hours per baguette
Variable manufacturing overhead	$10.00 per direct manufacturing labor-hour

The French Bread Company provides the following additional data for the year ended December 31, 2014:

Planned (budgeted) output	3,200,000 baguettes
Actual production	2,800,000 baguettes
Direct manufacturing labor	50,400 hours
Actual variable manufacturing overhead	$680,400

1. What is the denominator level used for allocating variable manufacturing overhead? (That is, for how many direct manufacturing labor-hours is French Bread budgeting?)
2. Prepare a variance analysis of variable manufacturing overhead. Use Exhibit 4 for reference.
3. Discuss the variances you have calculated and give possible explanations for them.

Required

19 Fixed manufacturing overhead variance analysis (continuation of 18). The French Bread Company also allocates fixed manufacturing overhead to products on the basis of standard direct manufacturing labor-hours. For 2014, fixed manufacturing overhead was budgeted at $4.00 per direct manufacturing labor-hour. Actual fixed manufacturing overhead incurred during the year was $272,000.

1. Prepare a variance analysis of fixed manufacturing overhead cost. Use Exhibit 4 as a guide.
2. Is fixed overhead underallocated or overallocated? By what amount?
3. Comment on your results. Discuss the variances and explain what may be driving them.

Required

20 Manufacturing overhead, variance analysis. The Principles Corporation is a manufacturer of centrifuges. Fixed and variable manufacturing overheads are allocated to each centrifuge using budgeted assembly-hours. Budgeted assembly time is 2 hours per unit. The following table shows the budgeted amounts and actual results related to overhead for June 2014.

	A	B	C	D	E	F	G
	Home	Insert	Page Layout	Formulas	Data	Review	View
1	The Principles Corporation (June 2014)					**Actual Results**	**Static Budget**
2	Number of centrifuges assembled and sold					225	110
3	Hours of assembly time					360	
4	Variable manufacturing overhead cost per hour of assembly time						$32.00
5	Variable manufacturing overhead costs					$11,933	
6	Fixed manufacturing overhead costs					$12,180	$10,780

Flexible Budgets, Overhead Cost Variances, and Management Control

1. Prepare an analysis of all variable manufacturing overhead and fixed manufacturing overhead variances using the columnar approach in Exhibit 4.
2. Prepare journal entries for Principles' June 2014 variable and fixed manufacturing overhead costs and variances; write off these variances to cost of goods sold for the quarter ending June 30, 2014.
3. How does the planning and control of variable manufacturing overhead costs differ from the planning and control of fixed manufacturing overhead costs?

21 **4-variance analysis, fill in the blanks.** Rozema, Inc., produces chemicals for large biotech companies. It has the following data for manufacturing overhead costs during August 2015:

	Variable	Fixed
Actual costs incurred	$31,000	$18,000
Costs allocated to products	33,000	14,600
Flexible budget	———	13,400
Actual input × budgeted rate	30,800	———

Use F for favorable and U for unfavorable:

	Variable	Fixed
(1) Spending variance	$_____	$_____
(2) Efficiency variance	_____	_____
(3) Production-volume variance	_____	_____
(4) Flexible-budget variance	_____	_____
(5) Underallocated (overallocated) manufacturing overhead	_____	_____

22 **Straightforward 4-variance overhead analysis.** The Lopez Company uses standard costing in its manufacturing plant for auto parts. The standard cost of a particular auto part, based on a denominator level of 4,000 output units per year, included 6 machine-hours of variable manufacturing overhead at $8 per hour and 6 machine-hours of fixed manufacturing overhead at $15 per hour. Actual output produced was 4,400 units. Variable manufacturing overhead incurred was $245,000. Fixed manufacturing overhead incurred was $373,000. Actual machine-hours were 28,400.

1. Prepare an analysis of all variable manufacturing overhead and fixed manufacturing overhead variances, using the 4-variance analysis in Exhibit 4.
2. Prepare journal entries using the 4-variance analysis.
3. Describe how individual fixed manufacturing overhead items are controlled from day to day.
4. Discuss possible causes of the fixed manufacturing overhead variances.

23 **Straightforward coverage of manufacturing overhead, standard-costing system.** The Singapore division of a Canadian telecommunications company uses standard costing for its machine-paced production of telephone equipment. Data regarding production during June are as follows:

Variable manufacturing overhead costs incurred	$618,840
Variable manufacturing overhead cost rate	$8 per standard machine-hour
Fixed manufacturing overhead costs incurred	$145,790
Fixed manufacturing overhead costs budgeted	$144,000
Denominator level in machine-hours	72,000
Standard machine-hour allowed per unit of output	1.2
Units of output	65,500
Actual machine-hours used	76,400
Ending work-in-process inventory	0

1. Prepare an analysis of all manufacturing overhead variances. Use the 4-variance analysis framework illustrated in Exhibit 4.
2. Prepare journal entries for manufacturing overhead costs and their variances.
3. Describe how individual variable manufacturing overhead items are controlled from day to day.
4. Discuss possible causes of the variable manufacturing overhead variances.

24 Overhead variances, service sector. Easy Meals Now (EMN) operates a meal home-delivery service. It has agreements with 20 restaurants to pick up and deliver meals to customers who phone or fax orders to EMN. EMN allocates variable and fixed overhead costs on the basis of delivery time. EMN's owner, Steve Roberts, obtains the following information for May 2014 overhead costs:

	A	B	C
	Home Insert Page Layout Formulas Data Review		
1	Easy Meals Now (May 2014)	Actual Results	Static Budget
2	Output units (number of deliveries)	8,600	12,000
3	Hours per delivery		0.70
4	Hours of delivery time	5,660	
5	Variable overhead cost per hour of delivery time		$1.75
6	Variable overhead costs	$11,320	
7	Fixed overhead costs	$39,600	$33,600

Required

1. Compute spending and efficiency variances for EMN's variable overhead in May 2014.
2. Compute the spending variance and production-volume variance for EMN's fixed overhead in May 2014.
3. Comment on EMN's overhead variances and suggest how Steve Roberts might manage EMN's variable overhead differently from its fixed overhead costs.

25 Total overhead, 3-variance analysis. Ames Air Force Base has a bay that specializes in maintenance for aircraft engines. It uses standard costing and flexible budgets to account for this activity. For 2014, budgeted variable overhead at a level of 8,000 standard monthly direct labor-hours was $64,000; budgeted total overhead at 10,000 standard monthly direct labor-hours was $197,600. The standard cost allocated to repair output included a total overhead rate of 120% of standard direct labor costs.

For February, Ames incurred total overhead of $249,000 and direct labor costs of $202,440. The direct labor price variance was $9,640 unfavorable. The direct labor flexible-budget variance was $14,440 unfavorable. The standard labor price was $16 per hour. The production-volume variance was $14,000 favorable.

Required

1. Compute the direct labor efficiency variance.
2. Compute the denominator level and the spending and efficiency variances for total overhead.
3. Describe how individual variable overhead items are controlled from day to day. Also, describe how individual fixed overhead items are controlled.

26 Production-volume variance analysis and sales volume variance. Marissa Designs, Inc., makes jewelry in the shape of geometric patterns. Each piece is handmade and takes an average of 1.5 hours to produce because of the intricate design and scrollwork. Marissa uses direct labor-hours to allocate the overhead cost to production. Fixed overhead costs, including rent, depreciation, supervisory salaries, and other production expenses, are budgeted at $10,800 per month. These costs are incurred for a facility large enough to produce 1,200 pieces of jewelry a month.

During the month of February, Marissa produced 720 pieces of jewelry and actual fixed costs were $11,400.

Required

1. Calculate the fixed overhead spending variance and indicate whether it is favorable (F) or unfavorable (U).
2. If Marissa uses direct labor-hours available at capacity to calculate the budgeted fixed overhead rate, what is the production-volume variance? Indicate whether it is favorable (F) or unfavorable (U).
3. An unfavorable production-volume variance could be interpreted as the economic cost of unused capacity. Why would Marissa be willing to incur this cost?
4. Marissa's budgeted variable cost per unit is $25, and it expects to sell its jewelry for $55 apiece. Compute the sales-volume variance and reconcile it with the production-volume variance calculated in requirement 2. What does each concept measure?

27 Overhead variances, service setting. Munich Partners provides a diverse array of back office services to its clients in the financial services industry, ranging from record keeping and compliance to order processing and trade settlement. Munich has grown increasingly reliant on technology to acquire, retain, and serve its clients. Worried that its spending on information technology is getting out of control, Munich has recently embraced variance analysis as a tool for cost management.

After some study, Munich determines that its variable and fixed technology overhead costs are both driven by the processing time involved in meeting client requests. This is typically measured in CPU units of usage of a high-performance computing cluster. Munich's primary measure of output is the number of client interactions its partners have in a given period.

The following information pertains to the first quarter of 2014 (dollars in thousands):

Budgeted Output Units	14,000 client interactions
Budgeted Fixed Technology Overhead	$ 11,200
Budgeted Variable Technology Overhead	$ 1.50 per CPU unit
Budgeted CPU units	0.2 units per client interaction
Fixed Technology Overhead incurred	$ 12,200
CPU Units used	4,000
Variable Technology Overhead incurred	$ 5,500
Actual Output Units	15,000 client interactions

1. Calculate the variable overhead spending and efficiency variances, and indicate whether each is favorable (F) or unfavorable (U).
2. Calculate the fixed overhead spending and production volume variances, and indicate whether each is favorable (F) or unfavorable (U).
3. Comment on Munich Partners' overhead variances. In your view, is the firm right to be worried about its control over technology spending?

28 Identifying favorable and unfavorable variances. Purdue, Inc., manufactures tires for large auto companies. It uses standard costing and allocates variable and fixed manufacturing overhead based on machine-hours. For each independent scenario given, indicate whether each of the manufacturing variances will be favorable or unfavorable or, in case of insufficient information, indicate "CBD" (cannot be determined).

Scenario	Variable Overhead Spending Variance	Variable Overhead Efficiency Variance	Fixed Overhead Spending Variance	Fixed Overhead Production-Volume Variance
Production output is 6% less than budgeted, and actual fixed manufacturing overhead costs are 5% more than budgeted				
Production output is 13% less than budgeted; actual machine-hours are 7% more than budgeted				
Production output is 10% more than budgeted				
Actual machine-hours are 20% less than flexible-budget machine-hours				
Relative to the flexible budget, actual machine-hours are 15% less, and actual variable manufacturing overhead costs are 20% greater				

29 Flexible-budget variances. Michael Roberts is a cost accountant and business analyst for Darby Design Company (DDC), which manufactures expensive brass doorknobs. DDC uses two direct cost categories: direct materials and direct manufacturing labor. Roberts feels that manufacturing overhead is most closely related to material usage. Therefore, DDC allocates manufacturing overhead to production based upon pounds of materials used.

At the beginning of 2014, DDC budgeted annual production of 410,000 doorknobs and adopted the following standards for each doorknob:

	Input	Cost/Doorknob
Direct materials (brass)	0.3 lb. @ $9/lb.	$ 2.70
Direct manufacturing labor	1.2 hours @ $16/hour	19.20
Manufacturing overhead:		
Variable	$4/lb. × 0.3 lb.	1.20
Fixed	$14/lb. × 0.3 lb.	4.20
Standard cost per doorknob		$27.30

Actual results for April 2014 were as follows:

Production	32,000 doorknobs
Direct materials purchased	12,900 lb. at $10/lb.
Direct materials used	9,000 lbs.
Direct manufacturing labor	29,600 hours for $621,600
Variable manufacturing overhead	$ 64,900
Fixed manufacturing overhead	$160,000

Required

1. For the month of April, compute the following variances, indicating whether each is favorable (F) or unfavorable (U):
   a. Direct materials price variance (based on purchases)
   b. Direct materials efficiency variance
   c. Direct manufacturing labor price variance
   d. Direct manufacturing labor efficiency variance
   e. Variable manufacturing overhead spending variance
   f. Variable manufacturing overhead efficiency variance
   g. Production-volume variance
   h. Fixed manufacturing overhead spending variance

2. Can Roberts use any of the variances to help explain any of the other variances? Give examples.

Problems

MyAccountingLab

30 **Comprehensive variance analysis.** Chef Whiz manufactures premium food processors. The following are some manufacturing overhead data for Chef Whiz for the year ended December 31, 2014:

Manufacturing Overhead	Actual Results	Flexible Budget	Allocated Amount
Variable	$51,480	$79,950	$79,950
Fixed	350,210	343,980	380,250

Budgeted number of output units: 588
Planned allocation rate: 3 machine-hours per unit
Actual number of machine-hours used: 1,170
Static-budget variable manufacturing overhead costs: $72,324

Compute the following quantities (you should be able to do so in the prescribed order):

Required

1. Budgeted number of machine-hours planned
2. Budgeted fixed manufacturing overhead costs per machine-hour
3. Budgeted variable manufacturing overhead costs per machine-hour
4. Budgeted number of machine-hours allowed for actual output produced
5. Actual number of output units
6. Actual number of machine-hours used per output unit

31 **Journal entries (continuation of 30).**

1. Prepare journal entries for variable and fixed manufacturing overhead (you will need to calculate the various variances to accomplish this).
2. Overhead variances are written off to the Cost of Goods Sold (COGS) account at the end of the fiscal year. Show how COGS is adjusted through journal entries.

Required

32 **Graphs and overhead variances.** Best Around, Inc., is a manufacturer of vacuums and uses standard costing. Manufacturing overhead (both variable and fixed) is allocated to products on the basis of budgeted machine-hours. In 2014, budgeted fixed manufacturing overhead cost was $17,000,000. Budgeted variable manufacturing overhead was $10 per machine-hour. The denominator level was 1,000,000 machine-hours.

1. Prepare a graph for fixed manufacturing overhead. The graph should display how Best Around, Inc.'s fixed manufacturing overhead costs will be depicted for the purposes of (a) planning and control and (b) inventory costing.

Required

2. Suppose that 1,125,000 machine-hours were allowed for actual output produced in 2014, but 1,200,000 actual machine-hours were used. Actual manufacturing overhead was $12,075,000, variable, and $17,100,000, fixed. Compute (a) the variable manufacturing overhead spending and efficiency variances and (b) the fixed manufacturing overhead spending and production-volume variances. Use the columnar presentation illustrated in Exhibit 4.

3. What is the amount of the under- or overallocated variable manufacturing overhead and the under- or overallocated fixed manufacturing overhead? Why are the flexible-budget variance and the under- or overallocated overhead amount always the same for variable manufacturing overhead but rarely the same for fixed manufacturing overhead?

4. Suppose the denominator level was 1,700,000 rather than 1,000,000 machine-hours. What variances in requirement 2 would be affected? Recompute them.

33 Overhead variance, missing information. Consider the following two situations—cases A and B—independently. Data refer to operations for April 2014. For each situation, assume standard costing. Also assume the use of a flexible budget for control of variable and fixed manufacturing overhead based on machine-hours.

		Cases	
		A	**B**
(1)	Fixed manufacturing overhead incurred	$ 84,920	$23,180
(2)	Variable manufacturing overhead incurred	$120,400	—
(3)	Denominator level in machine-hours	—	1,000
(4)	Standard machine-hours allowed for actual output achieved	6,200	—
(5)	Fixed manufacturing overhead (per standard machine-hour)	—	—
Flexible-Budget Data:			
(6)	Variable manufacturing overhead (per standard machine-hour)	—	$ 42.00
(7)	Budgeted fixed manufacturing overhead	$ 88,200	$20,000
(8)	Budgeted variable manufacturing overhead[a]	—	—
(9)	Total budgeted manufacturing overhead[a]	—	—
Additional Data:			
(10)	Standard variable manufacturing overhead allocated	$124,000	—
(11)	Standard fixed manufacturing overhead allocated	$ 86,800	—
(12)	Production-volume variance	—	$ 4,000 F
(13)	Variable manufacturing overhead spending variance	$ 5,000 F	$ 2,282 F
(14)	Variable manufacturing overhead efficiency variance	—	$ 2,478 F
(15)	Fixed manufacturing overhead spending variance	—	—
(16)	Actual machine-hours used	—	—

[a]For standard machine-hours allowed for actual output produced.

Required

Fill in the blanks under each case. [*Hint:* Prepare a worksheet similar to that in Exhibit 4. Fill in the knowns and then solve for the unknowns.]

34 Flexible budgets, 4-variance analysis. (CMA, adapted) Wilson Products uses standard costing. It allocates manufacturing overhead (both variable and fixed) to products on the basis of standard direct manufacturing labor-hours (DLH). Wilson Products develops its manufacturing overhead rate from the current annual budget. The manufacturing overhead budget for 2014 is based on budgeted output of 672,000 units, requiring 3,360,000 DLH. The company is able to schedule production uniformly throughout the year.

A total of 72,000 output units requiring 321,000 DLH was produced during May 2014. Manufacturing overhead (MOH) costs incurred for May amounted to $355,800. The actual costs, compared with the annual budget and 1/12 of the annual budget, are as follows:

Annual Manufacturing Overhead Budget 2014

	Total Amount	Per Output Unit	Per DLH Input Unit	Monthly MOH Budget May 2014	Actual MOH Costs for May 2014
Variable MOH					
Indirect manufacturing labor	$1,008,000	$1.50	$0.30	$ 84,000	$ 84,000
Supplies	672,000	1.00	0.20	56,000	117,000
Fixed MOH					
Supervision	571,200	0.85	0.17	47,600	41,000
Utilities	369,600	0.55	0.11	30,800	55,000
Depreciation	705,600	1.05	0.21	58,800	88,800
Total	$3,326,400	$4.95	$0.99	$277,200	$355,800

Calculate the following amounts for Wilson Products for May 2014:

Required

1. Total manufacturing overhead costs allocated
2. Variable manufacturing overhead spending variance
3. Fixed manufacturing overhead spending variance
4. Variable manufacturing overhead efficiency variance
5. Production-volume variance

Be sure to identify each variance as favorable (F) or unfavorable (U).

35 Activity-based costing, batch-level variance analysis. Audrina's Fleet Feet, Inc., produces dance shoes for stores all over the world. While the pairs of shoes are boxed individually, they are crated and shipped in batches. The shipping department records both variable direct batch-level costs and fixed batch-level overhead costs. The following information pertains to shipping department costs for 2014.

	Static-Budget Amounts	Actual Results
Pairs of shoes shipped	225,000	180,000
Average number of pairs of shoes per crate	15	10
Packing hours per crate	0.9 hours	1.1 hour
Variable direct cost per hour	$18	$16
Fixed overhead cost	$54,000	$56,500

Required

1. What is the static budget number of crates for 2014?
2. What is the flexible budget number of crates for 2014?
3. What is the actual number of crates shipped in 2014?
4. Assuming fixed overhead is allocated using crate-packing hours, what is the predetermined fixed overhead allocation rate?
5. For variable direct batch-level costs, compute the price and efficiency variances.
6. For fixed overhead costs, compute the spending and the production-volume variances.

36 Overhead variances and sales volume variance. Birken Company manufactures shopping bags made of recycled plastic that it plans to sell for $5 each. Birken budgets production and sales of 800,000 bags for 2014, with a standard of 400,000 machine-hours for the whole year. Budgeted fixed overhead costs are $500,000, and variable overhead cost is $1.60 per machine-hour.

Because of increased demand, Birken actually produced and sold 900,000 bags in 2014, using a total of 440,000 machine-hours. Actual variable overhead costs are $699,600 and actual fixed overhead is $501,900. Actual selling price is $6 per bag.

Direct materials and direct labor actual costs were the same as standard costs, which were $1.20 per unit and $1.80 per unit, respectively.

Required

1. Calculate the variable overhead and fixed overhead variances (spending, efficiency, spending, and volume).
2. Create a chart showing Flexible Budget Variances and Sales Volume Variances for revenues, costs, contribution margin, and operating income.
3. Calculate the operating income based on budgeted profit per shopping bag.

4. Reconcile the budgeted operating income from requirement 3 to the actual operating income from your chart in requirement 2.
5. Calculate the operating income volume variance and show how the sales volume variance is composed of the production volume variance and the operating income volume variance.

37 Activity-based costing, batch-level variance analysis. Rae Steven Publishing Company specializes in printing specialty textbooks for a small but profitable college market. Due to the high setup costs for each batch printed, Rae Steven holds the book requests until demand for a book is approximately 520. At that point Rae Steven will schedule the setup and production of the book. For rush orders, Rae Steven will produce smaller batches for an additional charge of $987 per setup.

Budgeted and actual costs for the printing process for 2014 were as follows:

	Static-Budget Amounts	Actual Results
Number of books produced	197,600	225,680
Average number of books per setup	520	496
Hours to set up printers	7 hours	7.5 hours
Direct variable cost per setup-hour	$130	$70
Total fixed setup overhead costs	$53,200	$68,000

1. What is the static budget number of setups for 2014?
2. What is the flexible budget number of setups for 2014?
3. What is the actual number of setups in 2014?
4. Assuming fixed setup overhead costs are allocated using setup-hours, what is the predetermined fixed setup overhead allocation rate?
5. Does Rae Steven's charge of $987 cover the budgeted direct variable cost of an order? The budgeted total cost?
6. For direct variable setup costs, compute the price and efficiency variances.
7. For fixed setup overhead costs, compute the spending and the production-volume variances.
8. What qualitative factors should Rae Steven consider before accepting or rejecting a special order?

38 Comprehensive review, working backward from given variances. The Gallo Company uses a flexible budget and standard costs to aid planning and control of its machining manufacturing operations. Its costing system for manufacturing has two direct-cost categories (direct materials and direct manufacturing labor—both variable) and two overhead-cost categories (variable manufacturing overhead and fixed manufacturing overhead, both allocated using direct manufacturing labor-hours).

At the 50,000 budgeted direct manufacturing labor-hour level for August, budgeted direct manufacturing labor is $1,250,000, budgeted variable manufacturing overhead is $500,000, and budgeted fixed manufacturing overhead is $1,000,000.

The following actual results are for August:

Direct materials price variance (based on purchases)	$179,300 F
Direct materials efficiency variance	75,900 U
Direct manufacturing labor costs incurred	535,500
Variable manufacturing overhead flexible-budget variance	10,400 U
Variable manufacturing overhead efficiency variance	18,100 U
Fixed manufacturing overhead incurred	957,550

The standard cost per pound of direct materials is $11.50. The standard allowance is 6 pounds of direct materials for each unit of product. During August, 20,000 units of product were produced. There was no beginning inventory of direct materials. There was no beginning or ending work in process. In August, the direct materials price variance was $1.10 per pound.

In July, labor unrest caused a major slowdown in the pace of production, resulting in an unfavorable direct manufacturing labor efficiency variance of $40,000. There was no direct manufacturing labor price variance. Labor unrest persisted into August. Some workers quit. Their replacements had to be hired at higher wage rates, which had to be extended to all workers. The actual average wage rate in August exceeded the standard average wage rate by $0.50 per hour.

1. Compute the following for August:
   a. Total pounds of direct materials purchased
   b. Total number of pounds of excess direct materials used
   c. Variable manufacturing overhead spending variance
   d. Total number of actual direct manufacturing labor-hours used
   e. Total number of standard direct manufacturing labor-hours allowed for the units produced
   f. Production-volume variance

2. Describe how Gallo's control of variable manufacturing overhead items differs from its control of fixed manufacturing overhead items.

39 Review, 3-variance analysis. (CPA, adapted) The Brown Manufacturing Company's costing system has two direct-cost categories: direct materials and direct manufacturing labor. Manufacturing overhead (both variable and fixed) is allocated to products on the basis of standard direct manufacturing labor-hours (DLH). At the beginning of 2014, Beal adopted the following standards for its manufacturing costs:

	Input	Cost per Output Unit
Direct materials	5 lb. at $4 per lb.	$ 20.00
Direct manufacturing labor	4 hrs. at $16 per hr.	64.00
Manufacturing overhead:		
Variable	$8 per DLH	32.00
Fixed	$9 per DLH	36.00
Standard manufacturing cost per output unit		$152.00

The denominator level for total manufacturing overhead per month in 2014 is 37,000 direct manufacturing labor-hours. Beal's flexible budget for January 2014 was based on this denominator level. The records for January indicated the following:

Direct materials purchased	40,300 lb. at $3.80 per lb.
Direct materials used	37,300 lb.
Direct manufacturing labor	31,400 hrs. at $16.25 per hr.
Total actual manufacturing overhead (variable and fixed)	$650,000
Actual production	7,600 output units

1. Prepare a schedule of total standard manufacturing costs for the 7,600 output units in January 2014.
2. For the month of January 2014, compute the following variances, indicating whether each is favorable (F) or unfavorable (U):
   a. Direct materials price variance, based on purchases
   b. Direct materials efficiency variance
   c. Direct manufacturing labor price variance
   d. Direct manufacturing labor efficiency variance
   e. Total manufacturing overhead spending variance
   f. Variable manufacturing overhead efficiency variance
   g. Production-volume variance

40 Non-financial variances. Max Canine Products produces high-quality dog food distributed only through veterinary offices. To ensure that the food is of the highest quality and has taste appeal, Max Canine has a rigorous inspection process. For quality control purposes, Max Canine has a standard based on the pounds of food inspected per hour and the number of pounds that pass or fail the inspection.

Max Canine expects that for every 13,000 pounds of food produced, 1,300 pounds of food will be inspected. Inspection of 1,300 pounds of dog food should take 1 hour. Max Canine also expects that 5% of the food inspected will fail the inspection. During the month of May, Supreme produced 2,990,000 pounds of food and inspected 292,500 pounds of food in 200 hours. Of the 292,500 pounds of food inspected, 15,625 pounds of food failed to pass the inspection.

1. Compute two variances that help determine whether the time spent on inspections was more or less than expected. (Follow a format similar to the one used for the variable overhead spending and efficiency variances, but without prices.)
2. Compute two variances that can be used to evaluate the percentage of the food that fails the inspection.

41 Overhead variances, service sector. Cavio is a cloud service provider that offers computing resources to handle enterprise-wide applications. For March 2014, Cavio estimates that it will provide 18,000 RAM hours of services to clients. The budgeted variable overhead rate is $6 per RAM hour.

At the end of March, there is a $500 favorable spending variance for variable overhead and a $1,575 unfavorable spending variance for fixed overhead. For the services actually provided during the month, 14,850 RAM hours are budgeted and 15,000 RAM hours are actually used. Total actual overhead costs are $119,875.

1. Compute efficiency and flexible-budget variances for Cavio's variable overhead in March 2014. Will variable overhead be over- or underallocated? By how much?
2. Compute production-volume and flexible-budget variances for Cavio's fixed overhead in March 2014. Will fixed overhead be over- or underallocated? By how much?

42 Direct-cost and overhead variances, income statement. The Kordell Company started business on January 1, 2013, in Raleigh. The company adopted a standard absorption costing system for its one product—a football for use in collegiate intramural sports. Because of the extensive handcrafting needed to do quality assurance on the final product, Kordell chose direct labor as the application base for overhead and decided to use the proration method to account for variances at year-end.

Kordell expected to make and sell 80,000 footballs the first year; each football was budgeted to use 1 pound of leather and require 15 minutes of direct labor work. The company expected to pay $1 for each pound of leather and compensate workers at an hourly wage of $16. Kordell has no variable overhead costs, but expected to spend $200,000 on fixed manufacturing overhead in 2013.

In 2013, Kordell actually made 100,000 footballs and sold 80,000 of them for a total revenue of $1 million. The expenses incurred were as follows:

Fixed manufacturing costs	$300,000
Leather costs (110,000 pounds bought and used)	$121,000
Direct labor costs (30,000 hours)	$465,000

1. Compute the following variances for 2013, and indicate whether each is favorable (F) or unfavorable (U):
   a. Direct materials efficiency variance
   b. Direct materials price variance
   c. Direct labor efficiency variance
   d. Direct labor price variance
   e. Total manufacturing overhead spending variance
   f. Fixed overhead flexible budget variance
   g. Fixed overhead production-volume variance
2. Compute Kordell Company's gross margin for its first year of operation.

43 Overhead variances, ethics. Hartmann Company uses standard costing. The company has two manufacturing plants, one in Georgia and the other in Alabama. For the Georgia plant, Hartmann has budgeted annual output of 2,000,000 units. Standard labor-hours per unit are 0.50, and the variable overhead rate for the Georgia plant is $3.30 per direct labor-hour. Fixed overhead for the Georgia plant is budgeted at $2,400,000 for the year.

For the Alabama plant, Hartmann has budgeted annual output of 2,100,000 units with standard labor-hours also 0.50 per unit. However, the variable overhead rate for the Alabama plant is $3.10 per hour, and the budgeted fixed overhead for the year is only $2,205,000.

Firm management has always used variance analysis as a performance measure for the two plants and has compared the results of the two plants.

Tom Saban has just been hired as a new controller for Hartmann. Tom is good friends with the Alabama plant manager and wants him to get a favorable review. Tom suggests allocating the firm's budgeted common fixed costs of $3,150,000 to the two plants, but on the basis of one-third to the Alabama plant and two-thirds to the Georgia plant. His explanation for this allocation base is that Georgia is a more expensive state than Alabama.

At the end of the year, the Georgia plant reported the following actual results: output of 1,950,000 using 1,020,000 labor-hours in total, at a cost of $3,264,000 in variable overhead and $2,440,000 in fixed overhead.

Actual results for the Alabama plant are an output of 2,175,000 units using 1,225,000 labor-hours with a variable cost of $3,920,000 and fixed overhead cost of $2,300,000. The actual common fixed costs for the year were $3,075,000.

1. Compute the budgeted fixed cost per labor-hour for the fixed overhead separately for each plant:
   a. Excluding allocated common fixed costs
   b. Including allocated common fixed costs
2. Compute the variable overhead spending variance and the variable overhead efficiency variance separately for each plant.
3. Compute the fixed overhead spending and volume variances for each plant:
   a. Excluding allocated common fixed costs
   b. Including allocated common fixed costs
4. Did Tom Saban's attempt to make the Alabama plant look better than the Georgia plant by allocating common fixed costs work? Why or why not?
5. Should common fixed costs be allocated in general when variances are used as performance measures? Why or why not?
6. What do you think of Tom Saban's behavior overall?

Glossary

Denominator level. The denominator in the budgeted fixed overhead rate computation.

Denominator-level variance. See *production-volume variance*.

Fixed overhead flexible-budget variance. The difference between actual fixed overhead costs and fixed overhead costs in the flexible budget.

Fixed overhead spending variance. Same as the fixed overhead flexible-budget variance. The difference between actual fixed overhead costs and fixed overhead costs in the flexible budget.

Operating-income volume variance. The difference between static-budget operating income and the operating income based on budgeted profit per unit and actual units of output.

Production-volume variance. The difference between budgeted fixed overhead and fixed overhead allocated on the basis of actual output produced. Also called *denominator-level variance*.

Standard costing. Costing system that traces direct costs to output produced by multiplying the standard prices or rates by the standard quantities of inputs allowed for actual outputs produced and allocates overhead costs on the basis of the standard overhead-cost rates times the standard quantities of the allocation bases allowed for the actual outputs produced.

Total-overhead variance. The sum of the flexible-budget variance and the production-volume variance.

Variable overhead efficiency variance. The difference between the actual quantity of variable overhead cost-allocation base used and budgeted quantity of variable overhead cost-allocation base that should have been used to produce actual output, multiplied by budgeted variable overhead cost per unit of cost-allocation base.

Variable overhead flexible-budget variance. The difference between actual variable overhead costs incurred and flexible-budget variable overhead amounts.

Variable overhead spending variance. The difference between actual variable overhead cost per unit and budgeted variable overhead cost per unit of the cost-allocation base, multiplied by actual quantity of variable overhead cost-allocation base used for actual output.

Photo Credits

Credits are listed in order of appearance.

Photo 1: MShieldsPhotos/Alamy
Photo 2: Liaison/Getty Images

Chapter 9

Inventory Costing and Capacity Analysis

From Chapter 9 of *Cost Accounting: A Managerial Emphasis*, Fifteenth Edition. Charles T. Horngren, Srikant M. Datar, Madhav V. Rajan. Copyright © 2015 by Pearson Education, Inc. All rights reserved.

Inventory Costing and Capacity Analysis

Few numbers capture the attention of managers and shareholders more than operating profits.

In industries that require significant upfront investments in capacity, two key decisions have a substantial impact on corporate profits: (1) How much money a firm spends on fixed investments and (2) the extent to which the firm eventually utilizes capacity to meet customer demand. Unfortunately, the compensation and reward systems of a firm, as well as the choice of inventory-costing methods, may induce managers to make decisions that benefit short-term earnings at the expense of a firm's long-term health. It may take a substantial external shock, like a sharp economic slowdown, to motivate managers to make the right capacity and inventory choices, as the following article illustrates.

Lean Manufacturing Helps Companies Reduce Inventory and Survive the Recession[1]

Can changing the way a mattress is pieced together help a company stay in business and remain profitable during a recession? For Sealy, the world's largest mattress manufacturer, the answer was a resounding "yes!"

Sealy used to manufacture as many mattresses as its resources allowed, regardless of customer orders. While factories operated at peak capacity, inventory often piled up, which cost the company millions of dollars each year. During the recent recession, Sealy was among thousands of manufacturers that remained profitable by changing its production plans to become more cost-efficient. Sealy adopted a policy of lean manufacturing, that is, producing only completed units and initiating production only in response to actual customer orders.

While Sealy launched its lean strategy in 2004, it intensified that strategy during the recession. The firm reconfigured old manufacturing processes to be more efficient. As a result:

- Each bed is now completed in 4 hours, down from 21.
- Median delivery times from Sealy to its retailers were cut to 60 hours, down from 72.

---

[1] *Sources:* Davidson, Paul. 2009. Lean manufacturing helps companies survive recession. *USA Today*, November 2; Sealy Corporation. 2011 Annual Report. Trinity, NC: Sealy Corporation, 2012; Sealy Corporation. 2009 Annual Report. Trinity, NC: Sealy Corporation, 2010; Hsu, Tiffany. 2012. Mattress mates: Tempur-Pedic buys Sealy for $1.3 billion. *The Los Angeles Times*, September 27.

- Raw-material inventories were cut by 50%.
- The company now adheres to a precise production schedule based on orders from retailers. While factories no longer run at full capacity, no mattress is made now until a customer orders it.

Sealy's manufacturing and inventory strategy was key to its survival during the recession and beyond. From 2008 to 2011, Sealy's lean manufacturing successfully reduced its inventory costs by 12%, or $7.6 million. This reduction enhanced the company's operations and made it an attractive acquisition target. In 2012, rival Tempur-Pedic purchased Sealy for $1.3 billion to create one of the largest companies in the competitive bedding industry.

Managers in industries with high fixed costs, like manufacturing, must manage capacity levels and make decisions about how to use available capacity. Managers must also decide on a production and inventory policy (as Sealy did). These decisions and the accounting choices managers make affect the operating incomes of manufacturing companies. This chapter focuses on two types of cost accounting choices:

1. *The inventory-costing choice* determines which manufacturing costs are treated as inventoriable costs. *Inventoriable costs* are all costs of a product that are regarded as assets when they are incurred and expensed as cost of goods sold when the product is sold. There are three types of inventory costing methods: absorption costing, variable costing, and throughput costing.

2. *The denominator-level capacity choice* focuses on the cost allocation base used to set budgeted fixed manufacturing cost rates. There are four possible choices of capacity levels: theoretical capacity, practical capacity, normal capacity utilization, and master-budget capacity utilization.

Variable and Absorption Costing

Learning Objective 1

Identify what distinguishes variable costing

...fixed manufacturing costs excluded from inventoriable costs

from absorption costing

...fixed manufacturing costs included in inventoriable costs

The two most common methods of costing inventories in manufacturing companies are *variable costing* and *absorption costing*. We describe each in this section and then discuss them in detail, using a hypothetical telescope-manufacturing company as an example.

Variable Costing

Variable costing is a method of inventory costing in which all variable manufacturing costs (direct and indirect) are included as inventoriable costs. All fixed manufacturing costs are excluded from inventoriable costs and are instead treated as costs of the period in which they are incurred. Note that *variable costing* is an imprecise term to describe this inventory-costing method because only variable manufacturing costs are inventoried; variable nonmanufacturing costs are still treated as period costs and are expensed. Another common term used to describe this method is **direct costing**. This term is also imprecise because variable costing considers variable manufacturing overhead (an indirect cost) as inventoriable, while excluding direct marketing costs, for example.

293

Absorption Costing

Absorption costing is a method of inventory costing in which all variable manufacturing costs and all fixed manufacturing costs are included as inventoriable costs. That is, inventory "absorbs" all manufacturing costs.

Under both variable costing and absorption costing, all variable manufacturing costs are inventoriable costs and all nonmanufacturing costs in the value chain (such as research and development and marketing), whether variable or fixed, are period costs and are recorded as expenses when incurred.

Comparing Variable and Absorption Costing

The easiest way to understand the difference between variable costing and absorption costing is with an example. In this chapter, we will study Stassen Company, an optical consumer-products manufacturer, and focus on its product line of high-end telescopes for aspiring astronomers.

Stassen uses standard costing:

- Direct costs are traced to products using standard prices and standard inputs allowed for actual outputs produced.

- Indirect (overhead) manufacturing costs are allocated using standard indirect rates times standard inputs allowed for actual outputs produced.

Stassen's management wants to prepare an income statement for 2014 (the fiscal year just ended) to evaluate the performance of the telescope product line. The operating information for the year is as follows:

	A	B
1		**Units**
2	Beginning inventory	0
3	Production	8,000
4	Sales	6,000
5	Ending inventory	2,000

Actual price and cost data for 2014 are as follows:

	A	B
10	Selling price	$ 1,000
11	Variable manufacturing cost per unit	
12	Direct material cost per unit	$ 110
13	Direct manufacturing labor cost per unit	40
14	Manufacturing overhead cost per unit	50
15	Total variable manufacturing cost per unit	$ 200
16	Variable marketing cost per unit sold	$ 185
17	Fixed manufacturing costs (all indirect)	$1,080,000
18	Fixed marketing costs (all indirect)	$1,380,000

For simplicity and to focus on the main ideas, we assume the following about Stassen:

- Stassen incurs manufacturing and marketing costs only. The cost driver for all variable manufacturing costs is units produced; the cost driver for variable marketing costs is units sold. There are no batch-level costs and no product-sustaining costs.

- There are no price variances, efficiency variances, or spending variances. Therefore, the *budgeted* (standard) price and cost data for 2014 are the same as the *actual* price and cost data.

- Work-in-process inventory is zero.

- Stassen budgeted production of 8,000 units for 2014. This was used to calculate the budgeted fixed manufacturing cost per unit of $135 ($1,080,000/8,000 units).[2]

- Stassen budgeted sales of 6,000 units for 2014, which is the same as the actual sales for 2014.

- The actual production for 2014 is 8,000 units. As a result, there is no production-volume variance for manufacturing costs in 2014. A later example, based on data for 2015, does include production-volume variances. However, even in that case, the income statement contains no variances other than the production-volume variance.

- Variances are written off to cost of goods sold in the period (year) in which they occur.

Based on the preceding information, Stassen's inventoriable costs per unit produced in 2014 under the two inventory costing methods are as follows:

	Variable Costing		Absorption Costing	
Variable manufacturing cost per unit produced:				
Direct materials	$110		$110	
Direct manufacturing labor	40		40	
Manufacturing overhead	50	$200	50	$200
Fixed manufacturing cost per unit produced		—		135
Total inventoriable cost per unit produced		$200		$335

To summarize, the main difference between variable costing and absorption costing is the accounting for fixed manufacturing costs:

- Under variable costing, fixed manufacturing costs are not inventoried; they are treated as an expense of the period.

- Under absorption costing, fixed manufacturing costs are inventoriable costs. In our example, the standard fixed manufacturing cost is $135 per unit ($1,080,000 ÷ 8,000 units) produced.

Decision Point

How does variable costing differ from absorption costing?

Variable vs. Absorption Costing: Operating Income and Income Statements

When comparing variable and absorption costing, we must also take into account whether we are looking at short- or long-term numbers. How does the data for a one-year period differ from that of a two-year period under variable and absorption costing?

Comparing Income Statements for One Year

What will Stassen's operating income be if it uses variable costing or absorption costing? The differences between these methods are apparent in Exhibit 1. Panel A shows the variable costing income statement and Panel B the absorption-costing income statement for Stassen's telescope product line for 2014. The variable-costing income statement uses the contribution-margin format. The absorption-costing income statement uses the gross-margin format. Why these different formats? The distinction between variable costs and fixed costs is central to

Learning Objective 2

Compute income under absorption costing

...using the gross-margin format

and variable costing,

...using the contribution-margin format

and explain the difference in income

...affected by the unit level of production and sales under absorption costing, but only the unit level of sales under variable costing

---

[2] Throughout this section, we use budgeted output as the basis for calculating the fixed manufacturing cost per unit for ease of exposition. In the latter half of this chapter, we consider the relative merits of alternative denominator-level choices for calculating this unit cost.

Exhibit 1	Comparison of Variable Costing and Absorption Costing for Stassen Company: Telescope Product-Line Income Statements for 2014

Home   Insert   Page Layout   Formulas   Data   Review   View

	A	B	C	D	E	F	G
1	Panel A: VARIABLE COSTING				Panel B: ABSORPTION COSTING		
2	Revenues: $1,000 × 6,000 units		$6,000,000		Revenues: $1,000 × 6,000 units		$6,000,000
3	Variable cost of goods sold:				Cost of goods sold:		
4	Beginning inventory	$ 0			Beginning inventory	$ 0	
5	Variable manufacturing costs: $200 × 8,000 units	1,600,000			Variable manufacturing costs: $200 × 8,000 units	1,600,000	
6					Allocated fixed manufacturing costs: $135 × 8,000 units	1,080,000	
7	Cost of goods available for sale	1,600,000			Cost of goods available for sale	2,680,000	
8	Deduct ending inventory: $200 × 2,000 units	(400,000)			Deduct ending inventory: $335 × 2,000 units	(670,000)	
9	Variable cost of goods sold		1,200,000		Cost of goods sold		2,010,000
10	Variable marketing costs: $185 × 6,000 units sold		1,110,000				
11	Contribution margin		3,690,000		Gross Margin		3,990,000
12	Fixed manufacturing costs		1,080,000		Variable marketing costs: $185 × 6,000 units sold		1,110,000
13	Fixed marketing costs		1,380,000		Fixed marketing costs		1,380,000
14	Operating income		$1,230,000		Operating Income		$1,500,000
15							
16	Manufacturing costs expensed in Panel A:				Manufacturing costs expensed in Panel B:		
17	Variable cost of goods sold		$1,200,000				
18	Fixed manufacturing costs		1,080,000				
19	Total		$2,280,000		Cost of goods sold		$2,010,000

variable costing, and it is highlighted by the contribution-margin format. Similarly, the distinction between manufacturing and nonmanufacturing costs is central to absorption costing, and it is highlighted by the gross-margin format.

Absorption-costing income statements do not need to differentiate between variable and fixed costs. However, we will make this distinction between variable and fixed costs in the Stassen example to show how individual line items are classified differently under variable costing and absorption costing. In Exhibit 1, Panel B, note that inventoriable cost is $335 per unit under absorption costing: allocated fixed manufacturing costs of $135 per unit plus variable manufacturing costs of $200 per unit.

Notice how the fixed manufacturing costs of $1,080,000 are accounted for under variable costing and absorption costing in Exhibit 1. The income statement under variable costing deducts the $1,080,000 lump sum as an expense for 2014. In contrast, under absorption costing, the $1,080,000 ($135 per unit × 8,000 units) is initially treated as an inventoriable cost in 2014. Of this $1,080,000, $810,000 ($135 per unit × 6,000 units sold) subsequently becomes a part of cost of goods sold in 2014, and $270,000 ($135 per unit × 2,000 units) remains an asset—part of ending finished goods inventory on December 31, 2014.

Operating income is $270,000 higher under absorption costing compared with variable costing because only $810,000 of fixed manufacturing costs are expensed under absorption costing, whereas all $1,080,000 of fixed manufacturing costs are expensed under variable costing. Note that the variable manufacturing cost of $200 per unit is accounted for the same way in both income statements in Exhibit 1.

These points can be summarized as follows:

	Variable Costing	Absorption Costing
Variable manufacturing costs: $200 per telescope produced	Inventoriable	Inventoriable
Fixed manufacturing costs: $1,080,000 per year	Deducted as an expense of the period	Inventoriable at $135 per telescope produced using budgeted denominator level of 8,000 units produced per year ($1,080,000 ÷ 8,000 units = $135 per unit)

The basis of the difference between variable costing and absorption costing is how fixed manufacturing costs are accounted for. If inventory levels change, operating income will differ between the two methods because of the difference in accounting for fixed manufacturing costs. To see this difference, let's compare telescope sales of 6,000, 7,000, and 8,000 units by Stassen in 2014, when 8,000 units were produced. Of the $1,080,000 total fixed manufacturing costs, the amount expensed in the 2014 income statement under each of these scenarios would be as follows:

	A	B	C	D	E	G	H
1			Variable Costing			Absorption Costing	
2						Fixed Manufacturing Costs	
3	Units	Ending	Fixed Manufacturing Costs			Included in Inventory	Amount Expensed
4	Sold	Inventory	Included in Inventory	Amount Expensed		=$135 × Ending Inv.	=$135 × Units Sold
5	6,000	2,000	$0	$1,080,000		$270,000	$ 810,000
6	7,000	1,000	$0	$1,080,000		$135,000	$ 945,000
7	8,000	0	$0	$1,080,000		$ 0	$1,080,000

In the last scenario, where 8,000 units are produced and sold, both variable and absorption costing report the same net income because inventory levels are unchanged. This chapter's appendix describes how the choice of variable costing or absorption costing affects the breakeven quantity of sales when inventory levels are allowed to vary.

Comparing Income Statements for Multiple Years

To get a more comprehensive view of the effects of variable costing and absorption costing, Stassen's management accountants prepare income statements for two years of operations, starting with 2014. The data are given in units in the following table:

	E	F	G
1		2014	2015
2	Budgeted production	8,000	8,000
3	Beginning inventory	0	2,000
4	Actual production	8,000	5,000
5	Sales	6,000	6,500
6	Ending inventory	2,000	500

All other 2014 data given earlier for Stassen also apply for 2015.

In 2015, Stassen has a production-volume variance because actual telescope production differs from the budgeted level of production of 8,000 units per year used to calculate the budgeted fixed manufacturing cost per unit. The actual quantity sold for 2015 is 6,500 units, which is the same as the sales quantity budgeted for that year.

Exhibit 2 presents the income statement under variable costing in Panel A and the income statement under absorption costing in Panel B for 2014 and 2015. As you study Exhibit 2, note that the 2014 columns in both Panels A and B show the same figures as Exhibit 1. The 2015 column is similar to 2014 *except for the production-volume variance line item under absorption costing in Panel B*. Keep in mind the following points about absorption costing as you study Panel B of Exhibit 2:

1. The $135 fixed manufacturing cost rate is based on the budgeted denominator capacity level of 8,000 units in 2014 and 2015 ($1,080,000 ÷ 8,000 units = $135 per unit). Whenever production (the quantity produced, not the quantity sold) deviates from the denominator level, there will be a production-volume variance. The amount of Stassen's production-volume variance is determined by multiplying $135 per unit by the difference between the actual level of production and the denominator level.

Exhibit 2	Comparison of Variable Costing and Absorption Costing for Stassen Company: Telescope Product-Line Income Statements for 2014 and 2015

	A	B	C	D	E
1	**Panel A: VARIABLE COSTING**				
2			**2014**		**2015**
3	Revenues: $1,000 × 6,000; 6,500 units		$6,000,000		$6,500,000
4	Variable cost of goods sold:				
5	Beginning inventory: $200 × 0; 2,000 units	$ 0		$ 400,000	
6	Variable manufacturing costs: $200 × 8,000; 5,000 units	1,600,000		1,000,000	
7	Cost of goods available for sale	1,600,000		1,400,000	
8	Deduct ending inventory: $200 × 2,000; 500 units	(400,000)		(100,000)	
9	Variable cost of goods sold		1,200,000		1,300,000
10	Variable marketing costs: $185 × 6,000; 6,500 units		1,110,000		1,202,500
11	Contribution margin		3,690,000		3,997,500
12	Fixed manufacturing costs		1,080,000		1,080,000
13	Fixed marketing costs		1,380,000		1,380,000
14	Operating income		$1,230,000		$1,537,500
15					
16	**Panel B: ABSORPTION COSTING**				
17			**2014**		**2015**
18	Revenues: $1,000 × 6,000; 6,500 units		$6,000,000		$6,500,000
19	Cost of goods sold:				
20	Beginning inventory: $335 × 0; 2,000 units	0		670,000	
21	Variable manufacturing costs: $200 × 8,000; 5,000 units	1,600,000		1,000,000	
22	Allocated fixed manufacturing costs: $135 × 8,000; 5,000 units	1,080,000		675,000	
23	Cost of goods available for sale	2,680,000		2,345,000	
24	Deduct ending inventory: $335 × 2,000; 500 units	(670,000)		(167,500)	
25	Adjustment for production-volume variance[a]	$ 0		$ 405,000	U
26	Cost of goods sold		2,010,000		2,582,500
27	Gross Margin		3,990,000		3,917,500
28	Variable marketing costs: $185 × 6,000; 6,500 units		1,110,000		1,202,500
29	Fixed marketing costs		1,380,000		1,380,000
30	Operating Income		$1,500,000		$1,335,000
31					
32	[a]Production-volume variance = Budgeted fixed manufacturing costs − Fixed manufacturing overhead allocated using budgeted cost per output unit allowed for actual output produced (Panel B, line 22)				
33	2014: $1,080,000 − ($135 × 8,000) = $1,080,000 − $1,080,000 = $0				
34	2015: $1,080,000 − ($135 × 5,000) = $1,080,000 − $675,000 = $405,000 U				
35					
36	Production-volume variance can also be calculated as follows:				
37	Fixed manufacturing cost per unit × (Denominator level − Actual output units produced)				
38	2014: $135 × (8,000 − 8,000) units = $135 × 0 = $0				
39	2015: $135 × (8,000 − 5,000) units = $135 × 3,000 = $405,000 U				

Recall how standard costing works under absorption costing. Each time a unit is manufactured, $135 of fixed manufacturing costs is included in the cost of goods manufactured and available for sale. In 2015, when 5,000 units are manufactured, $675,000 ($135 per unit × 5,000 units) of fixed manufacturing costs is included in the cost of goods available for sale (see Exhibit 2, Panel B, line 22). Total fixed manufacturing costs for 2015 are $1,080,000. The production-volume variance of $405,000 U equals the difference between $1,080,000 and $675,000. In Panel B, note how, for each year, the fixed manufacturing costs included in the cost of goods available for sale plus the production-volume variance always equals $1,080,000.

2. As a result of the production-volume variance, note that the absorption costing income is lower in 2015 than in 2014 even though Stassen sold 500 more units. We explore the impact of production levels on income under absorption costing in greater detail later in this chapter.

3. The production-volume variance, which relates only to fixed manufacturing overhead, exists under absorption costing but not under variable costing. Under variable costing, fixed manufacturing costs of $1,080,000 are always treated as an expense of the period, regardless of the level of production (and sales).

Here's a summary (using information from Exhibit 2) of the operating-income differences for Stassen Company during 2014 and 2015:

	2014	2015
1. Absorption-costing operating income	$1,500,000	$1,335,000
2. Variable-costing operating income	$1,230,000	$1,537,500
3. Difference: (1) – (2)	$ 270,000	$ (202,500)

The sizeable differences in the preceding table illustrate why managers whose performance is measured by reported income are concerned about the choice between variable costing and absorption costing.

Why do variable costing and absorption costing report different operating income numbers? In general, if inventory increases during an accounting period, less operating income will be reported under variable costing than absorption costing. Conversely, if inventory decreases, more operating income will be reported under variable costing than absorption costing. The difference in reported operating income is due solely to (a) moving fixed manufacturing costs into inventories as inventories increase and (b) moving fixed manufacturing costs out of inventories as inventories decrease under absorption costing.

The difference between operating income under absorption costing and variable costing can be computed by formula 1, which focuses on fixed manufacturing costs in beginning inventory and ending inventory:

	A	B	C	D	E	F	G	H
1	Formula 1							
2						Fixed manufacturing		Fixed manufacturing
3		Absorption-costing	–	Variable-costing	=	costs in ending inventory	–	costs in beginning inventory
4		operating income		operation income		under absorption costing		under absorption costing
5	2014	$1,500,000	–	$1,230,000	=	($135 × 2,000 units)	–	($135 × 0 units)
6		$270,000			=	$270,000		
7								
8	2015	$1,335,000	–	$1,537,500	=	($135 × 500 units)	–	($135 × 2,000 units)
9		($202,500)			=	($202,500)		

Fixed manufacturing costs in ending inventory are deferred to a future period under absorption costing. For example, $270,000 of fixed manufacturing overhead is deferred to 2015 at December 31, 2014. Under variable costing, all $1,080,000 of fixed manufacturing costs are treated as an expense of 2014.

Recall that

$$\frac{\text{Beginning}}{\text{inventory}} + \frac{\text{Cost of goods}}{\text{manufactured}} = \frac{\text{Cost of goods}}{\text{sold}} + \frac{\text{Ending}}{\text{Inventory}}$$

Therefore, instead of focusing on fixed manufacturing costs in ending and beginning inventory (as in formula 1), we could alternatively look at fixed manufacturing costs in units produced and units sold. The latter approach (see formula 2) highlights how fixed manufacturing costs move between units produced and units sold during the fiscal year.

	A	B	C	D	E	F	G	H
12	**Formula 2**							
13						**Fixed manufacturing costs**		**Fixed manufacturing costs**
14		**Absorption-costing**	**–**	**Variable-costing**	**=**	**inventoried in units produced**	**–**	**in cost of goods sold**
15		**operating income**		**operation income**		**under absorption costing**		**under absorption costing**
16	**2014**	$1,500,000	–	$1,230,000	=	($135 × 8,000 units)	–	($135 × 6,000 units)
17		$270,000			=	$270,000		
18								
19	**2015**	$1,335,000	–	$1,537,500	=	($135 × 5,000 units)	–	($135 × 6,500 units)
20		($202,500)			=	($202,500)		

Managers face increasing pressure to reduce inventory levels. Some companies are achieving steep reductions in inventory levels using policies such as just-in-time production—a production system under which products are manufactured only when needed. Formula 1 illustrates that, as Stassen reduces its inventory levels, operating income differences between absorption costing and variable costing become immaterial. Consider, for example, the formula for 2014. If instead of 2,000 units in ending inventory, Stassen had only 2 units in ending inventory, the difference between absorption-costing operating income and variable-costing operating income would drop from $270,000 to just $270.

Variable Costing and the Effect of Sales and Production on Operating Income

Given a constant contribution margin per unit and constant fixed costs, the period-to-period change in operating income under variable costing is *driven solely by changes in the quantity of units actually sold.* Consider the variable-costing operating income of Stassen in 2015 versus 2014. Recall the following:

$$\frac{\text{Contribution}}{\text{margin per unit}} = \text{Selling price} - \frac{\text{Variable manufacturing}}{\text{cost per unit}} - \frac{\text{Variable marketing}}{\text{cost per unit}}$$

$$= \$1,000 \text{ per unit} - \$200 \text{ per unit} - \$185 \text{ per unit}$$

$$= \$615 \text{ per unit}$$

$$\begin{array}{c}\text{Change in}\\ \text{variable-costing}\\ \text{operating income}\end{array} = \begin{array}{c}\text{Contribution}\\ \text{margin}\\ \text{per unit}\end{array} \times \begin{array}{c}\text{Change in quantity}\\ \text{of units sold}\end{array}$$

2015 vs. 2014: $1,537,500 − $1,230,000 = $615 per unit × (6,500 unit − 6,000 units)

$307,500 = $307,500

Decision Point

How does income differ under variable and absorption costing?

Under variable costing, Stassen managers cannot increase operating income by "producing for inventory." Why not? Because, as you can see from the preceding computations, when using variable costing, only the quantity of units sold drives operating income. We'll explain later in this chapter that absorption costing enables managers to increase operating income by increasing the unit level of sales, as well as by producing more units. Before you proceed to the next section, make sure that you examine Exhibit 3 for a detailed comparison of the differences between variable costing and absorption costing.

| Exhibit 3 | Comparative Income Effects of Variable Costing and Absorption Costing

Question	Variable Costing	Absorption Costing	Comment
Are fixed manufacturing costs inventoried?	No	Yes	Basic theoretical question of when these costs should be expensed
Is there a production-volume variance?	No	Yes	Choice of denominator level affects measurement of operating income under absorption costing only
Are classifications between variable and fixed costs routinely made?	Yes	Infrequently	Absorption costing can be easily modified to obtain subclassifications for variable and fixed costs, if desired (for example, see Exhibit 1, Panel B)
How do changes in unit inventory levels affect operating income?[a]			Differences are attributable to the timing of when fixed manufacturing costs are expensed
Production = sales	Equal	Equal	
Production > sales	Lower[b]	Higher[c]	
Production < sales	Higher	Lower	
What are the effects on cost-volume-profit relationship (for a given level of fixed costs and a given contribution margin per unit)?	Driven by unit level of sales	Driven by (a) unit level of sales, (b) unit level of production, and (c) chosen denominator level	Management control benefit: Effects of changes in production level on operating income are easier to understand under variable costing

[a]Assuming that all manufacturing variances are written off as period costs, that no change occurs in work-in-process inventory, and no change occurs in the budgeted fixed manufacturing cost rate between accounting periods.

[b]That is, lower operating income than under absorption costing.

[c]That is, higher operating income than under variable costing.

Absorption Costing and Performance Measurement

Absorption costing is the required inventory method for external financial reporting in most countries (we provide potential reasons for this rule later in the chapter). Many companies use absorption costing for internal accounting as well because:

- It is cost-effective and less confusing for managers to use one common method of inventory costing for both external and internal reporting and performance evaluation.

- It can help prevent managers from taking actions that make their performance measure look good but that hurt the income they report to shareholders.

- It measures the cost of all manufacturing resources, whether variable or fixed, necessary to produce inventory. Many companies use inventory costing information for long-run decisions, such as pricing and choosing a product mix. For these long-run decisions, inventory costs should include both variable *and* fixed costs.

An important attribute of absorption costing is that it enables a manager to increase margins and operating income by producing more ending inventory. Producing for inventory is justified when a firm's managers anticipate rapid growth in demand and want to produce and store additional units to deal with possible production shortages in the next year. For example, with the recent improvement in the national economy, manufacturers of energy-efficient doors and windows are stepping up production in order to take advantage of an anticipated rebound in the housing market. But, under absorption costing, Stassen's managers may be tempted to produce inventory even when they *do not* anticipate customer demand to grow. The reason is that this production leads to higher operating income, which can benefit managers in two ways: directly, because higher incomes typically result in a higher bonus for the manager, and indirectly, because greater income levels have a positive effect on stock price, which increases managers'

Learning Objective 3

Understand how absorption costing can provide undesirable incentives for managers to build up inventory

...producing more units for inventory absorbs fixed manufacturing costs and increases operating income

301

stock-based compensation. But higher income results in the company paying higher taxes. Shareholders and supporters of good corporate governance would also argue that it is unethical for managers to take actions that are intended solely to increase their compensation rather than to improve the company. Producing for inventory is a risky strategy, especially in industries with volatile demand or high risk of product obsolescence because of the pace at which innovation is occuring. For example, the new BlackBerry Z10 smartphone has seen declining sell-through rates and higher levels of inventory and is being sold at deeply discounted prices in the United Kingdom. Concepts in Action: Absorption Costing and the Bankruptcy of U.S. Automakers illustrates the dramatic negative impact of producing for inventory in the auto industry.

To reduce the undesirable incentives to build up inventories that absorption costing can create, a number of companies use variable costing for internal reporting. Variable costing focuses attention on distinguishing variable manufacturing costs from fixed manufacturing costs. This distinction is important for short-run decision making.

Companies that use both methods for internal reporting—variable costing for short-run decisions and performance evaluation and absorption costing for long-run decisions—benefit from the different advantages of both. Surveys sponsored by Chartered Institute of Management Accountants (United Kingdom), the world's largest professional body of management accountants, have shown that while most organizations employ absorption costing systems, more than 75% indicate the use of variable costing information as either the most important or second most important measure for decision-making purposes.

In the next section, we explore in more detail the challenges that arise from absorption costing.

Concepts in Action

Absorption Costing and the Bankruptcy of U.S. Automakers

In the years leading up to the 2008 recession, General Motors, Ford, and Chrysler were producing new vehicles in excess of market demand. This led to large inventories on car dealers' lots across the United States. At the same time, profits were rising and executives at these three companies were achieving their short-term incentive targets. How is this possible? Absorption costing may hold the answer.

In 2009, General Motors and Chrysler filed for bankruptcy and appealed for government aid. Yet these automakers had abundant excess capacity. They also had enormous fixed costs, from factories and machinery to workers whose contracts protected them from layoffs when demand was low. To "absorb" these costs, the automakers produced more cars while using absorption costing. The more vehicles they made, the lower the cost per vehicle, and the higher the profits on their income statements. In effect, the automakers shifted costs from their income statements to their balance sheets.

Ultimately, this practice hurt the automakers by driving up advertising and inventory costs. "When the dealers couldn't sell the cars, they would sit on the lots," says Dr. Karen Sedatole, a Michigan State professor who recently co-authored a study on the topic. "They'd have to go in and replace the tires, and there were costs associated with that." The companies also had to pay to advertise their cars, often at discounted prices using rebates, employee pricing, and 0% financing promotions. General Motors and Chrysler ran out of cash for operations and making loans available for car buyers. In January 2009, the U.S. government used $24.9 billion in bailout funds to rescue General Motors and Chrysler.

Sources: Based on Marielle Segarra, "Lots of Trouble," *CFO Magazine* (March 2012); and Bruggen, A., R. Krishnan, and K. L. Sedatole. 2011. Drivers and Consequences of Short-Term Production Decisions: Evidence from the Auto Industry. *Contemporary Accounting Research* 28 (1):83–123.

Undesirable Buildup of Inventories

If a manager's bonus is based on reported absorption-costing operating income, that manager may be motivated to build up an undesirable level of inventories. Assume that Stassen's managers have such a bonus plan. Exhibit 4 shows how Stassen's absorption costing operating income for 2015 changes as the production level changes. This exhibit assumes that the production-volume variance is written off to cost of goods sold at the end of each year. Beginning inventory of 2,000 units and sales of 6,500 units for 2015 are unchanged from the case shown in Exhibit 2. *As you review* Exhibit 4, *keep in mind that the computations are basically the same as those in* Exhibit 2.

Exhibit 4 shows that production of 4,500 units meets the 2015 sales budget of 6,500 units (2,000 units from beginning inventory +4,500 units produced). Operating income at this production level is $1,267,500. By producing more than 4,500 units, commonly referred to as *producing for inventory*, Stassen increases absorption-costing operating income. Each additional unit in 2015 ending inventory will increase operating income by $135. For example, if 9,000 units are produced (column H in Exhibit 4), ending inventory will be 4,500 units and operating income increases to $1,875,000. This amount is $607,500 more than the operating income with zero ending inventory ($1,875,000 – $1,267,500, or 4,500 units × $135 per unit = $607,500). By producing 4,500 units for inventory, the company using absorption costing includes $607,500 of fixed manufacturing costs in finished goods inventory, so those costs are not expensed in 2015.

The scenarios outlined in Exhibit 4 raise three other important points. First, column D is the base-case setting and just restates the 2015 absorption costing results from Panel B of Exhibit 2. Second, column F highlights that when inventory levels are unchanged, that is, production equals sales, the absorption costing income equals the income under variable costing (see Panel A of Exhibit 2 for comparison). Third, the example in Exhibit 4 focuses on one year, 2015. A Stassen manager who built up an inventory of 4,500 telescopes at the end of 2015 would have to further increase ending inventories in 2016 to increase that year's operating income by producing for inventory. There are limits to how much inventory levels can be increased over time because of physical constraints

Exhibit 4	Effect on Absorption-Costing Operating Income of Different Production Levels for Stassen Company: Telescope Product-Line Income Statement for 2015 at Sales of 6,500 Units

	Home	Insert	Page Layout	Formulas	Data	Review	View			
	A	B	C	D	E	F	G	H	I
1	Unit Data								
2	Beginning inventory	2,000		2,000		2,000		2,000	
3	Production	4,500		5,000		6,500		9,000	
4	Goods available for sale	6,500		7,000		8,500		11,000	
5	Sales	6,500		6,500		6,500		6,500	
6	Ending inventory	0		500		2,000		4,500	
7									
8	Income Statement								
9	Revenues	$6,500,000		$6,500,000		$6,500,000		$6,500,000	
10	Cost of goods sold:								
11	Beginning inventory: $335 × 2,000	670,000		670,000		670,000		670,000	
12	Variable manufacturing costs: $200 × production	900,000		1,000,000		1,300,000		1,800,000	
13	Allocated fixed manufacturing costs: $135 × production	607,500		675,000		877,500		1,215,000	
14	Cost of goods available for sale	2,177,500		2,345,000		2,847,500		3,685,000	
15	Deduct ending inventory: $335 × ending inventory	0		(167,500)		(670,000)		(1,507,500)	
16	Adjustment for production-volume variance[a]	472,500 U		405,000 U		202,500 U		(135,000) F
17	Cost of goods sold	2,650,000		2,582,500		2,380,000		2,042,500	
18	Gross Margin	3,850,000		3,917,500		4,120,000		4,457,500	
19	Marketing costs: $1,380,000 + ($185 per unit × 6,500 units sold)	2,582,500		2,582,500		2,582,500		2,582,500	
20	Operating Income	$1,267,500		$1,335,000		$1,537,500		$1,875,000	
21									
22	[a]Production-volume variance = Budgeted fixed manufacturing costs – Allocated fixed manufacturing costs (Income Statement, line 13)								
23	At production of 4,500 units: $1,080,000 – $607,500 = $472,500 U								
24	At production of 5,000 units: $1,080,000 – $675,000 = $405,000 U								
25	At production of 6,500 units: $1,080,000 – $877,500 = $202,500 U								
26	At production of 9,000 units: $1,080,000 – $1,215,000 = ($135,000) F								

on storage space and management controls. Such limits reduce the likelihood of incurring some of absorption costing's undesirable effects. Nevertheless, managers do have the ability and incentive to move costs in and out of inventory in order to manage operating income under absorption costing.

Top management can implement checks and balances that limit managers from producing for inventory under absorption costing. However, the practice cannot be completely prevented. There are many subtle ways a manager can produce for inventory that may not be easy to detect. For example, consider the following scenarios:

- A plant manager may switch to manufacturing products that absorb the highest amount of fixed manufacturing costs, regardless of the customer demand for these products (called "cherry picking" the production line). Delaying the production of items that absorb the least or lower fixed manufacturing costs could lead to failure to meet promised customer delivery dates (which, over time, can result in unhappy customers).

- A plant manager may accept a particular order to increase production, even though another plant in the same company is better suited to handle that order.

- To increase production, a manager may defer maintenance of equipment beyond the current period. Although operating income in this period may increase as a result, future operating income could decrease by a larger amount if repair costs increase and equipment becomes less efficient.

Proposals for Revising Performance Evaluation

Top management, with help from the controller and management accountants, can take several steps to reduce the undesirable effects of absorption costing.

- Focus on careful budgeting and inventory planning to reduce management's freedom to build up excess inventory. For example, the budgeted monthly balance sheets have estimates of the dollar amount of inventories. If actual inventories exceed these dollar amounts, top management can investigate the inventory buildups.

- Incorporate a carrying charge for inventory in the internal accounting system. For example, the company could assess an inventory carrying charge of 1% per month on the investment tied up in inventory and for spoilage and obsolescence when it evaluates a manager's performance. An increasing number of companies are beginning to adopt this inventory carrying charge.

- Change the period used to evaluate performance. Critics of absorption costing give examples in which managers take actions that maximize quarterly or annual income at the potential expense of long-run income. When their performance is evaluated over a three- to five-year period, managers will be less tempted to produce for inventory.

- Include nonfinancial as well as financial variables in the measures used to evaluate performance. Examples of nonfinancial measures that can be used to monitor the performance of Stassen's managers in 2015 (see column H of Exhibit 4) are as follows:

(a) $\dfrac{\text{Ending inventory in units in 2015}}{\text{Beginning inventory in units in 2015}} = \dfrac{4,500}{2,000} = 2.25$

(b) $\dfrac{\text{Units produced in 2015}}{\text{Units sold in 2015}} = \dfrac{9,000}{6,500} = 1.38$

Decision Point
Why might managers build up finished goods inventory if they use absorption costing?

Top management would want to see production equal to sales and relatively stable levels of inventory. Companies that manufacture or sell several products could report these two measures for each of the products they manufacture and sell.

Besides the formal performance measurement systems, companies develop codes of conduct to discourage behavior that benefits managers but not the company and build values and cultures that focus on behaving ethically.

Comparing Inventory Costing Methods

Before we begin our discussion of capacity, we will look at *throughput costing*, a variation of variable costing, and compare the various costing methods.

Throughput Costing

Some managers believe that even variable costing promotes an excessive amount of costs being inventoried. They argue that only direct materials, such as the lenses, casing, scope, and mount in the case of Stassen's telescopes, are "truly variable" in output. **Throughput costing**, which is also called **super-variable costing**, is an extreme form of variable costing in which only direct material costs are included as inventoriable costs. All other costs are costs of the period in which they are incurred. In particular, variable direct manufacturing labor costs and variable manufacturing overhead costs are regarded as period costs and are deducted as expenses of the period.

Exhibit 5 is the throughput-costing income statement for Stassen Company for 2014 and 2015. *Throughput margin* equals revenues minus all direct material cost of the goods sold. Compare the operating income amounts reported in Exhibit 5 with those for absorption costing and variable costing:

	2014	2015
Absorption-costing operating income	$1,500,000	$1,335,000
Variable-costing operating income	$1,230,000	$1,537,500
Throughput-costing operating income	$1,050,000	$1,672,500

Only the $110 direct material cost per unit is inventoriable under throughput costing, compared with $335 per unit for absorption costing and $200 per unit for variable costing. When the production quantity exceeds sales, as in 2014, throughput costing results in the largest amount of expenses in the current period's income statement. Advocates of throughput costing say it provides managers less incentive to produce for inventory than either variable costing or, especially, absorption costing. Throughput costing is a more

Exhibit 5

Throughput Costing for Stassen Company: Telescope Product-Line Income Statements for 2014 and 2015

	A	B	C
1		**2014**	**2015**
2	Revenues: $1,000 × 6,000; 6,500 units	$6,000,000	$6,500,000
3	Direct material cost of goods sold		
4	Beginning inventory: $110 × 0; 2,000 units	0	220,000
5	Direct materials: $110 × 8,000; 5,000 units	880,000	550,000
6	Cost of goods available for sale	880,000	770,000
7	Deduct ending inventory: $110 × 2,000; 500 units	(220,000)	(55,000)
8	Direct material cost of goods sold	660,000	715,000
9	Throughput margin[a]	5,340,000	5,785,000
10	Manufacturing costs (other than direct materials)[b]	1,800,000	1,530,000
11	Marketing costs[c]	2,490,000	2,582,500
12	Operating income	$1,050,000	$1,672,500
13			
14	[a]Throughput margin equals revenues minus all direct material cost of goods sold		
15	[b]Fixed manuf. costs + [(variable manuf. labor cost per unit + variable manuf. overhead cost per unit) × units produced]; $1,080,000 + [($40 + $50) × 8,000; 5,000 units]		
16	[c]Fixed marketing costs + (variable marketing cost per unit × units sold);		
17	$1,380,000 + ($185 × 6,000; 6,500 units)		

recent phenomenon in comparison with variable costing and absorption costing and has avid supporters, but so far it has not been widely adopted.[3]

A Comparison of Alternative Inventory-Costing Methods

Variable costing and absorption costing may be combined with actual, normal, or standard costing. Exhibit 6 compares product costing under these six alternative inventory-costing systems.

Variable costing has been controversial among accountants because of how it affects *external reporting*, not because of disagreement about the need to delineate between variable and fixed costs for internal planning and control. Accountants who favor variable costing for external reporting maintain that the fixed portion of manufacturing costs is more closely related to the capacity to produce than to the actual production of specific units. Fixed costs should therefore be expensed, not inventoried.

Accountants who support absorption costing for *external reporting* maintain that inventories should carry a fixed-manufacturing-cost component because both variable manufacturing costs and fixed manufacturing costs are necessary to produce goods. Therefore, both types of costs should be inventoried in order to match all manufacturing costs to revenues, regardless of their different behavior patterns. For external reporting to shareholders, companies around the globe tend to follow the generally accepted accounting principle that all manufacturing costs are inventoriable. This also eases the burden on firms and auditors to attempt to disentangle fixed and variable costs of production, a distinction that is not always clear-cut in practice.

Similarly, for tax reporting in the United States, managers must take direct production costs, as well as fixed and variable indirect production costs, into account in the computation of inventoriable costs in accordance with the "full absorption" method of inventory costing. Indirect production costs include items such as rent, utilities, maintenance, repair

Exhibit 6	Comparison of Alternative Inventory-Costing Systems

			Actual Costing	Normal Costing	Standard Costing
Absorption Costing	Variable Costing	Variable Direct Manufacturing Cost	Actual prices × Actual quantity of inputs used	Actual prices × Actual quantity of inputs used	Standard prices × Standard quantity of inputs allowed for actual output achieved
		Variable Manufacturing Overhead Costs	Actual variable overhead rates × Actual quantity of cost-allocation bases used	Budgeted variable overhead rates × Actual quantity of cost-allocation bases used	Standard variable overhead rates × Standard quantity of cost-allocation bases allowed for actual output achieved
		Fixed Direct Manufacturing Costs	Actual prices × Actual quantity of inputs used	Actual prices × Actual quantity of inputs used	Standard prices × Standard quantity of inputs allowed for actual output achieved
		Fixed Manufacturing Overhead Costs	Actual fixed overhead rates × Actual quantity of cost-allocation bases used	Budgeted fixed overhead rates × Actual quantity of cost-allocation bases used	Standard fixed overhead rates × Standard quantity of cost-allocation bases allowed for actual output achieved

---

[3] See E. Goldratt, *The Theory of Constraints* (New York: North River Press, 1990); E. Noreen, D. Smith, and J. Mackey, *The Theory of Constraints and Its Implications for Management Accounting* (New York: North River Press, 1995).

expenses, indirect materials, and indirect labor. For other indirect cost categories (including depreciation, insurance, taxes, officers' salaries, factory administrative expenses, and strike-related costs), the portion of the cost that is "incident to and necessary for production or manufacturing operations or processes" is inventoriable for tax purposes *only* if it is treated as inventoriable for the purposes of financial reporting. Accordingly, managers must often allocate costs between those portions related to manufacturing activities and those not related to manufacturing.[4]

Denominator-Level Capacity Concepts and Fixed-Cost Capacity Analysis

We have seen that the difference between variable and absorption costing methods arises solely from the treatment of fixed manufacturing costs. Spending on fixed manufacturing costs enables firms to obtain the scale or capacity needed to satisfy the expected market demand from customers. Determining the "right" amount of spending, or the appropriate level of capacity, is one of the most strategic and most difficult decisions managers face. Having too much capacity to produce relative to that needed to meet market demand means firms will incur some costs of unused capacity. Having too little capacity to produce means that demand from some customers may be unfilled. These customers may go to other sources of supply and never return. Both managers and accountants must understand these issues that arise with capacity costs.

We start this section by analyzing a key question in absorption costing: Given a firm's level of spending on fixed manufacturing costs, what capacity level should managers and accountants use to compute the fixed manufacturing cost per unit produced? We then study the broader question of how a firm should decide on its level of capacity investment.

Absorption Costing and Alternative Denominator-Level Capacity Concepts

Normal costing and standard costing report costs in an ongoing timely manner throughout a fiscal year. The choice of the capacity level used to allocate budgeted fixed manufacturing costs to products can greatly affect the operating income reported under normal costing or standard costing and the product-cost information available to managers.

Consider the Stassen Company example again. Recall that the annual fixed manufacturing costs of the production facility are $1,080,000. Stassen currently uses absorption costing with standard costs for external reporting purposes, and it calculates its budgeted fixed manufacturing rate on a per unit basis. We will now examine four different capacity levels used as the denominator to compute the budgeted fixed manufacturing cost rate: theoretical capacity, practical capacity, normal capacity utilization, and master-budget capacity utilization.

Theoretical Capacity and Practical Capacity

In business and accounting, capacity ordinarily means a "constraint," an "upper limit." **Theoretical capacity** is the level of capacity based on producing at full efficiency all the time. Stassen can produce 25 units per shift when the production lines are operating at maximum speed. If we assume 360 days per year, the theoretical annual capacity for 2 shifts per day is as follows:

25 units per shift $\times$ 2 shifts per day $\times$ 360 days = 18,000 units

---

[4] Details regarding tax rules can be found in Section 1.471-11 of the U.S. Internal Revenue Code: Inventories of Manufacturers (see http://ecfr.gpoaccess.gov). Costs not related to production, such as marketing, distribution, or research expenses, are treated as period expenses for financial reporting. Under U.S. tax rules, a firm can still consider these costs as inventoriable for tax purposes provided that it does so consistently.

Theoretical capacity is theoretical in the sense that it does not allow for any slowdowns due to plant maintenance, shutdown periods, or interruptions because of downtime on the assembly lines. Theoretical capacity levels are unattainable in the real world, but they represent the ideal goal of capacity utilization a company can aspire to.

Practical capacity is the level of capacity that reduces theoretical capacity by considering unavoidable operating interruptions, such as scheduled maintenance time and shutdowns for holidays. Assume that practical capacity is the practical production rate of 20 units per shift (as opposed to 25 units per shift under theoretical capacity) for 2 shifts per day for 300 days a year (as opposed to 360 days a year under theoretical capacity). The practical annual capacity is as follows:

$$20 \text{ units per shift} \times 2 \text{ shifts per day} \times 300 \text{ days} = 12,000 \text{ units}$$

Engineering and human resource factors are both important when estimating theoretical or practical capacity. Engineers at the Stassen facility can provide input on the technical capabilities of machines for cutting and polishing lenses. Human resources can evaluate employee safety factors, such as increased injury risk when the line operates at faster speeds.

Normal Capacity Utilization and Master-Budget Capacity Utilization

Both theoretical capacity and practical capacity measure capacity levels in terms of what a plant can *supply*—available capacity. In contrast, normal capacity utilization and master-budget capacity utilization measure capacity levels in terms of *demand* for the output of the plant, that is, the amount of available capacity the plant expects to use based on the demand for its products. In many cases, budgeted demand is well below production capacity available.

Normal capacity utilization is the level of capacity utilization that satisfies average customer demand over a period (say, two to three years) that includes seasonal, cyclical, and trend factors. **Master-budget capacity utilization** is the level of capacity utilization that managers expect for the current budget period, which is typically one year. These two capacity-utilization levels can differ quite significantly in industries that face cyclical demand patterns. For example:

- The automobile industry may have a period of high demand due to low interest rates or a period of low demand due to a recession.
- The semiconductor industry may have a period of high demand if companies update employee computers or a period of low demand if companies downsize.

Consider Stassen's master budget for 2014, based on production of 8,000 telescopes per year. Despite using this master-budget capacity-utilization level of 8,000 telescopes for 2014, top management believes that over the next three years the normal (average) annual production level will be 10,000 telescopes. It views 2014's budgeted production level of 8,000 telescopes to be "abnormally" low because a major competitor has been sharply reducing its selling price and spending a lot of money on advertising. Stassen expects that the competitor's lower price and advertising blitz will not be a long-run phenomenon and that, by 2015 and beyond, Stassen's production and sales will be higher.

Effect on Budgeted Fixed Manufacturing Cost Rate

We now illustrate how each of these four denominator levels affects the budgeted fixed manufacturing cost rate. Stassen has budgeted (standard) fixed manufacturing overhead costs of $1,080,000 for 2014. This lump-sum is incurred to provide the capacity to produce telescopes. The amount includes, among other costs, leasing costs for the facility and the compensation of the facility managers. The budgeted fixed manufacturing cost rates for 2014 for each of the four capacity-level concepts are as follows:

	A	B	C	D
1		Budgeted Fixed	Budget	Budgeted Fixed
2	Denominator-Level	Manufacturing	Capacity Level	Manufacturing
3	Capacity Concept	Costs per Year	(in units)	Cost per Unit
4	(1)	(2)	(3)	(4) = (2)/(3)
5	Theoretical capacity	$1,080,000	18,000	$ 60
6	Practical capacity	$1,080,000	12,000	$ 90
7	Normal capacity utilization	$1,080,000	10,000	$108
8	Master-budget capacity utilization	$1,080,000	8,000	$135

The significant difference in cost rates (from $60 to $135) arises because of large differences in budgeted capacity levels under the different capacity concepts.

Budgeted (standard) variable manufacturing cost is $200 per unit. The total budgeted (standard) manufacturing cost per unit for alternative capacity-level concepts is as follows:

	A	B	C	D
1		Budgeted Variable	Budgeted Fixed	Budgeted Total
2	Denominator-Level	Manufacturing	Manufacturing	Manufacturing
3	Capacity Concept	Cost per Unit	Cost per Unit	Cost per Unit
4	(1)	(2)	(3)	(4) = (2) + (3)
5	Theoretical capacity	$200	$ 60	$260
6	Practical capacity	$200	$ 90	$290
7	Normal capacity utilization	$200	$108	$308
8	Master-budget capacity utilization	$200	$135	$335

Because different denominator-level capacity concepts yield different budgeted fixed manufacturing costs per unit, Stassen must decide which capacity level to use. Stassen is not required to use the same capacity-level concept, say, for management planning and control, external reporting to shareholders, and income tax purposes.

Choosing a Capacity Level

As we just saw, at the start of each fiscal year, managers determine different denominator levels for the different capacity concepts and calculate different budgeted fixed manufacturing costs per unit. We now discuss different denominator-level choices for different purposes, including (a) product costing and capacity management, (b) pricing, (c) performance evaluation, (d) external reporting, and (e) tax requirements.

Product Costing and Capacity Management

Data from normal costing or standard costing are often used in pricing or product-mix decisions. As the Stassen example illustrates, use of theoretical capacity results in an unrealistically small fixed manufacturing cost per unit because it is based on an idealistic and unattainable level of capacity. Theoretical capacity is rarely used to calculate budgeted fixed manufacturing cost per unit because it departs significantly from the real capacity available to a company.

Decision Point

What are the various capacity levels a company can use to compute the budgeted fixed manufacturing cost rate?

Learning Objective 6

Examine the key factors in choosing a capacity level to compute the budgeted fixed manufacturing cost rate

...managers must consider the effect a capacity level has on product costing, pricing decisions, performance evaluation, and financial and tax statements

Many companies favor practical capacity as the denominator to calculate budgeted fixed manufacturing cost per unit. Practical capacity in the Stassen example represents the maximum number of units (12,000) that Stassen can reasonably expect to produce per year for the $1,080,000 it will spend annually on capacity. If Stassen had consistently planned to produce fewer units, say 6,000 telescopes each year, it would have built a smaller plant and incurred lower costs.

Stassen budgets $90 in fixed manufacturing cost per unit based on the $1,080,000 it costs to acquire the capacity to produce 12,000 units. This level of plant capacity is an important strategic decision that managers make well before Stassen uses the capacity and even before Stassen knows how much of the capacity it will actually use. That is, budgeted fixed manufacturing cost of $90 per unit measures the *cost per unit of supplying the capacity*.

Demand for Stassen's telescopes in 2014 is expected to be 8,000 units, which is 4,000 units lower than the practical capacity of 12,000 units. However, it costs Stassen $1,080,000 per year to acquire the capacity to make 12,000 units, so the cost of *supplying* the capacity needed to make 12,000 units is still $90 per unit. The capacity and its cost are fixed *in the short run*; unlike variable costs, the capacity supplied does not automatically reduce to match the capacity needed in 2014. As a result, not all of the capacity supplied at $90 per unit will be needed or used in 2014. Using practical capacity as the denominator level, managers can subdivide the cost of resources supplied into used and unused components. At the supply cost of $90 per unit, the manufacturing resources that Stassen will use equal $720,000 ($90 per unit × 8,000 units). Manufacturing resources that Stassen will not use are $360,000 [$90 per unit × (12,000 − 8,000) units].

Using practical capacity as the denominator level sets the cost of capacity at the cost of supplying the capacity, regardless of the demand for the capacity. Highlighting the cost of capacity acquired but not used directs managers' attention toward managing unused capacity, perhaps by designing new products to fill unused capacity, by leasing unused capacity to others, or by eliminating unused capacity. In contrast, using either of the capacity levels based on the demand for Stassen's telescopes—master-budget capacity utilization or normal capacity utilization—hides the amount of unused capacity. If Stassen had used master-budget capacity utilization as the capacity level, it would have calculated budgeted fixed manufacturing cost per unit as $135 ($1,080,000 ÷ 8,000 units). This calculation does not use data about practical capacity, so it does not separately identify the cost of unused capacity. Note, however, that the cost of $135 per unit includes a charge for unused capacity: It is composed of the $90 fixed manufacturing resource that would be used to produce each unit at practical capacity plus the cost of unused capacity allocated to each unit, $45 per unit ($360,000 ÷ 8,000 units).

From the perspective of long-run product costing, which cost of capacity should Stassen use for pricing purposes or for benchmarking its product cost structure against competitors: $90 per unit based on practical capacity or $135 per unit based on master-budget capacity utilization? Probably the $90 per unit based on practical capacity. Why? Because $90 per unit represents the budgeted cost per unit of only the capacity used to produce the product, and it explicitly excludes the cost of any unused capacity. Stassen's customers will be willing to pay a price that covers the cost of the capacity actually used but will not want to pay for unused capacity that provides no other benefits to them. Customers expect Stassen to manage its unused capacity or to bear the cost of unused capacity, not pass it along to them. Moreover, if Stassen's competitors manage unused capacity more effectively, the cost of capacity in the competitors' cost structures (which guides competitors' pricing decisions) is likely to approach $90. In the next section, we show how using normal capacity utilization or master-budget capacity utilization can result in managers setting selling prices that are not competitive.

Pricing Decisions and the Downward Demand Spiral

The **downward demand spiral** for a company is the continuing reduction in the demand for its products that occurs when competitor prices are not met; as demand drops further, higher and higher unit costs result in greater reluctance to meet competitors' prices.

The easiest way to understand the downward demand spiral is with an example. Assume Stassen uses master-budget capacity utilization of 8,000 units for product costing in 2014. The resulting manufacturing cost is $335 per unit ($200 variable manufacturing cost per unit + $135 fixed manufacturing cost per unit). Assume that in December 2013, a competitor offers to supply a major customer of Stassen (a customer who was expected to purchase 2,000 units in 2014) telescopes at $300 per unit. The Stassen manager doesn't want to show a loss on the account and wants to recoup all costs in the long run, so the manager declines to match the competitor's price. The account is lost. The loss means budgeted fixed manufacturing costs of $1,080,000 will be spread over the remaining master-budget volume of 6,000 units at a rate of $180 per unit ($1,080,000 ÷ 6,000 units).

Suppose yet another Stassen customer, who also accounts for 2,000 units of budgeted volume, receives a bid from a competitor at a price of $350 per unit. The Stassen manager compares this bid with his revised unit cost of $380 ($200 + $180) and declines to match the competition, and the account is lost. Planned output would shrink further to 4,000 units. Budgeted fixed manufacturing cost per unit for the remaining 4,000 telescopes would now be $270 ($1,080,000 ÷ 4,000 units). The following table shows the effect of spreading fixed manufacturing costs over a shrinking amount of master-budget capacity utilization:

	A	B	C	D
	Home Insert Page Layout Formulas Data Review View			
1	Master-Budget		Budgeted Fixed	
2	Capacity Utilization	Budgeted Variable	Manufacturing	Budgeted Total
3	Denominator Level	Manufacturing Cost	Cost per Unit	Manufacturing
4	(Units)	per Unit	[$1,080,000 ÷ (1)]	Cost per Unit
5	(1)	(2)	(3)	(4) = (2) + (3)
6	8,000	$200	$135	$335
7	6,000	$200	$180	$380
8	4,000	$200	$270	$470
9	3,000	$200	$360	$560

Practical capacity, by contrast, is a stable measure. The use of practical capacity as the denominator to calculate budgeted fixed manufacturing cost per unit avoids the recalculation of unit costs when expected demand levels change because the fixed cost rate is calculated based on *capacity available* rather than *capacity used to meet demand*. Managers who use reported unit costs in a mechanical way to set prices are less likely to promote a downward demand spiral when they use practical capacity than when they use normal capacity utilization or master-budget capacity utilization.

Using practical capacity as the denominator level also gives the manager a more accurate idea of the resources needed and used to produce a unit by excluding the cost of unused capacity. As discussed earlier, the cost of manufacturing resources supplied to produce a telescope is $290 ($200 variable manufacturing cost per unit plus $90 fixed manufacturing cost per unit). This cost is lower than the prices Stassen's competitors offer and would have correctly led the manager to match the prices and retain the accounts (assuming for purposes of this discussion that Stassen has no other costs). If, however, the prices competitors offered were lower than $290 per unit, the Stassen manager would not recover the cost of resources used to supply telescopes. This would signal to the manager that Stassen was noncompetitive even if it had no unused capacity. The only way for Stassen to be profitable and retain customers in the long run would be to reduce its manufacturing cost per unit.[5]

Performance Evaluation

Consider how the choice among normal capacity utilization, master-budget capacity utilization, and practical capacity affects how a company evaluates its marketing manager. Normal capacity utilization is often used as a basis for long-run plans. Normal

---

[5] The downward demand spiral is currently at work in the traditional landline phone industry. As more telephone customers shift services to wireless or Internet-based options, Verizon and AT&T, the two largest telephone service providers in the United States, are reducing their focus on providing copper-wire telephone service to homes and business. As AT&T told the U.S. Federal Communications Commission, "The business model for legacy phone services is in a death spiral."

capacity utilization depends on the time span selected and the forecasts made for each year. *However, normal capacity utilization is an average that provides no meaningful feedback to the marketing manager for a particular year.* Using normal capacity utilization to judge current performance of a marketing manager is an example of a company misusing a long-run measure for a short-run purpose. The company should use master-budget capacity utilization, rather than normal capacity utilization or practical capacity, to evaluate a marketing manager's performance in the current year because the master budget is the principal short-run planning and control tool. Managers feel more obligated to reach the levels specified in the master budget, which the company should have carefully set in relation to the maximum opportunities for sales in the current year.

When large differences exist between practical capacity and master-budget capacity utilization, several companies (such as Texas Instruments, Polysar, and Sandoz) classify the difference as *planned unused capacity.* One reason for this approach is performance evaluation. Consider our Stassen telescope example. The managers in charge of capacity planning usually do not make pricing decisions. Top management decided to build a production facility with 12,000 units of practical capacity, focusing on demand over the next five years. But Stassen's marketing managers, who are mid-level managers, make the pricing decisions. These marketing managers believe they should be held accountable only for the manufacturing overhead costs related to their potential customer base in 2014. The master-budget capacity utilization suggests a customer base in 2014 of 8,000 units (2/3 of the 12,000 practical capacity). Using responsibility accounting principles, only 2/3 of the budgeted total fixed manufacturing costs ($1,080,000 × 2/3 = $720,000) would be attributed to the fixed capacity costs of meeting 2014 demand. The remaining 1/3 of the numerator ($1,080,000 × 1/3 = $360,000) would be separately shown as the capacity cost of meeting increases in long-run demand expected to occur beyond 2014.[6]

External Reporting

The magnitude of the favorable/unfavorable production-volume variance under absorption costing is affected by the choice of the denominator level used to calculate the budgeted fixed manufacturing cost per unit. Assume the following actual operating information for Stassen in 2014:

	A	B	C
1	Beginning inventory	0	
2	Production	8,000	units
3	Sales	6,000	units
4	Ending inventory	2,000	units
5	Selling price	$ 1,000	per unit
6	Variable manufacturing cost	$ 200	per unit
7	Fixed manufacturing costs	$ 1,080,000	
8	Variable marketing cost	$ 185	per unit sold
9	Fixed marketing costs	$ 1,380,000	

Note that this is the same data used to calculate the income under variable and absorption costing for Stassen in Exhibit 1. As before, we assume that there are no price, spending, or efficiency variances in manufacturing costs.

---

[6] For further discussion, see T. Klammer, *Capacity Measurement and Improvement* (Chicago: Irwin, 1996). This research was facilitated by CAM-I, an organization promoting innovative cost management practices. CAM-I's research on capacity costs explores how companies can identify types of capacity costs that can be reduced (or eliminated) without affecting the required output to meet customer demand. An example is improving processes to successfully eliminate the costs of capacity held in anticipation of handling difficulties due to imperfect coordination with suppliers and customers.

The equation used to calculate the production-volume variance is:

$$\text{Production-volume variance} = \left(\begin{array}{c}\text{Budgeted}\\\text{fixed}\\\text{manufacturing}\\\text{overhead}\end{array}\right) - \left(\begin{array}{c}\text{Fixed manufacturing overhead allocated using}\\\text{budgeted cost per output unit}\\\text{allowed for actual output produced}\end{array}\right)$$

The four different capacity-level concepts result in four different budgeted fixed manufacturing overhead cost rates per unit. The different rates will result in different amounts of fixed manufacturing overhead costs allocated to the 8,000 units actually produced and different amounts of production-volume variance. Using the budgeted fixed manufacturing costs of $1,080,000 (equal to actual fixed manufacturing costs) and the rates calculated for different denominator levels, the production-volume variance computations are as follows:

Production-volume variance (theoretical capacity) = $1,080,000 − (8,000 units × $60 per unit)
= $1,080,000 − 480,000
= $600,000 U

Production-volume variance (practical capacity) = $1,080,000 − (8,000 units × $90 per unit)
= $1,080,000 − 720,000
= $360,000 U

Production-volume variance (normal capacity utilization) = $1,080,00 − (8,000 units × $108 per unit)
= $1,080,000 − 864,000
= $216,000 U

Production-volume variance (master-budget capacity utilization)
= $1,080,000 − (8,000 units × $135 per unit)
= $1,080,000 − 1,080,000
= $0

How Stassen disposes of its production-volume variance at the end of the fiscal year will determine the effect this variance has on the company's operating income. We now discuss the three alternative approaches Stassen can use to dispose of the production-volume variance.

1. **Adjusted allocation-rate approach.** This approach restates all amounts in the general and subsidiary ledgers by using actual rather than budgeted cost rates. Given that actual fixed manufacturing costs are $1,080,000 and actual production is 8,000 units, the recalculated fixed manufacturing cost is $135 per unit ($1,080,000 ÷ 8,000 actual units). Under the adjusted allocation-rate approach, the choice of the capacity level used to calculate the budgeted fixed manufacturing cost per unit has no impact on year-end financial statements. In effect, actual costing is adopted at the end of the fiscal year.

2. **Proration approach.** The underallocated or overallocated overhead is spread among ending balances in Work-in-Process Control, Finished Goods Control, and Cost of Goods Sold. The proration restates the ending balances in these accounts to what they would have been if actual cost rates had been used rather than budgeted cost rates. The proration approach also results in the choice of the capacity level used to calculate the budgeted fixed manufacturing cost per unit having no effect on year-end financial statements.

3. **Write-off variances to cost of goods sold approach.** Exhibit 7 shows how use of this approach affects Stassen's operating income for 2014. Recall that the ending inventory on December 31, 2014, is 2,000 units. Using master-budget capacity utilization as the denominator level results in assigning the highest amount of fixed manufacturing cost per unit to the 2,000 units in ending inventory (see the line item "deduct ending inventory" in Exhibit 7). Accordingly, operating income is highest using master-budget capacity utilization. The differences in operating income for the four denominator-level

concepts in Exhibit 7 are due to these different amounts of fixed manufacturing overhead being inventoried at the end of 2014:

Fixed Manufacturing Overhead in December 31, 2014, Inventory

Theoretical capacity	2,000 units × $60 per unit = $120,000
Practical capacity	2,000 units × $90 per unit = $180,000
Normal capacity utilization	2,000 units × $108 per unit = $216,000
Master-budget capacity utilization	2,000 units × $135 per unit = $270,000

In Exhibit 7, for example, the $54,000 difference ($1,500,000 − $1,446,000) in operating income between master-budget capacity utilization and normal capacity utilization is due to the difference in fixed manufacturing overhead inventoried ($270,000 − $216,000).

To summarize, the common factor behind the increasing operating-income numbers in Exhibit 4 and Exhibit 7 is the increasing amount of fixed manufacturing costs incurred that is included in ending inventory. The amount of fixed manufacturing costs inventoried depends on two factors: the number of units in ending inventory and the rate at which fixed manufacturing costs are allocated to each unit. Exhibit 4 shows the effect on operating income of increasing the number of units in ending inventory (by increasing production). Exhibit 7 shows the effect on operating income of increasing the

---

Exhibit 7   Income-Statement Effects of Using Alternative Capacity-Level Concepts: Stassen Company for 2014

	A	B	C	D	E	F	G	H	I
		Theoretical Capacity		Practical Capacity		Normal Capacity Utilization		Master-Budget Capacity Utilization	
2	Denominator level in units	18,000		12,000		10,000		8,000	
3	Revenues[a]	$6,000,000		$6,000,000		$6,000,000		$6,000,000	
4	Cost of goods sold								
5	Beginning inventory	0		0		0		0	
6	Variable manufacturing costs[b]	1,600,000		1,600,000		1,600,000		1,600,000	
7	Fixed manufacturing costs[c]	480,000		720,000		864,000		1,080,000	
8	Cost of goods available for sale	2,080,000		2,320,000		2,464,000		2,680,000	
9	Deduct ending inventory[d]	(520,000)		(580,000)		(616,000)		(670,000)	
10	Cost of goods sold (at standard cost)	1,560,000		1,740,000		1,848,000		2,010,000	
11	Adjustment for production-volume variance	600,000	U	360,000	U	216,000	U	0	
12	Cost of goods sold	2,160,000		2,100,000		2,064,000		2,010,000	
13	Gross margin	3,840,000		3,900,000		3,936,000		3,990,000	
14	Marketing costs[e]	2,490,000		2,490,000		2,490,000		2,490,000	
15	Operating income	$1,350,000		$1,410,000		$1,446,000		$1,500,000	
16									
17	[a]$1,000 × 6,000 units = $6,000,000			[d]Ending inventory costs:					
18	[b]$200 × 8,000 units = $1,600,000			($200 + $60) × 2,000 units = $520,000					
19	[c]Fixed manufacturing overhead costs:			($200 + $90) × 2,000 units = $580,000					
20	$60 × 8,000 units = $ 480,000			($200 + $108) × 2,000 units = $616,000					
21	$90 × 8,000 units = $ 720,000			($200 + $135) × 2,000 units = $670,000					
22	$108 × 8,000 units = $ 864,000			[e]Marketing costs:					
23	$135 × 8,000 units = $1,080,000			$1,380,000 + ($185 × 6,000 units) = $2,490,000					

fixed manufacturing cost allocated per unit (by decreasing the denominator level used to calculate the rate).

Managers and management accountants must consider various issues when deciding whether to prorate the production-volume variance among inventories and cost of goods sold or to simply write off the variance to cost of goods sold. The objective is to write off the portion of the production-volume variance that represents the cost of capacity not used to support the production of output during the period. Determining this amount is almost always a matter of judgment.

Tax Requirements

For tax reporting purposes in the United States, the Internal Revenue Service (IRS) requires companies to assign inventoriable indirect production costs by a "method of allocation which fairly apportions such costs among the various items produced." The IRS accepts approaches that involve the use of either overhead rates (which the IRS terms the "manufacturing burden rate method") or standard costs. Under either approach, U.S. tax reporting requires end-of-period reconciliation between actual and applied indirect costs using the adjusted allocation-rate method or the proration method.[7] More interestingly, under either approach, the IRS permits the use of practical capacity to calculate budgeted fixed manufacturing cost per unit. Further, the production-volume variance generated this way can be deducted for tax purposes in the year in which the cost is incurred. The tax benefits from this policy are evident from Exhibit 7. Note that the operating income when the denominator is set to practical capacity (column D, where the production volume variance of $360,000 is written off to cost of goods sold) is lower than those under normal capacity utilization (column F) or master-budget capacity utilization (column H).

Decision Point

What are the major factors managers consider in choosing the capacity level to compute the budgeted fixed manufacturing cost rate?

Planning and Control of Capacity Costs

In addition to the issues previously discussed, managers must take a variety of other factors into account when planning capacity levels and in deciding how best to control and assign capacity costs. These other factors include the level of uncertainty about both the expected costs and the expected demand for the installed capacity; the presence of capacity-related issues in nonmanufacturing settings; and the potential use of activity-based costing techniques in allocating capacity costs.

Learning Objective 7

Understand other issues that play an important role in capacity planning and control

...uncertainty regarding the expected spending on capacity costs and the demand for installed capacity, the role of capacity-related issues in nonmanufacturing areas, and the possible use of activity-based costing techniques in allocating capacity costs

Difficulties in Forecasting Chosen Denominator-Level Concept

Practical capacity measures the available supply of capacity. Managers can usually use engineering studies and human resource considerations (such as worker safety) to obtain a reliable estimate of this denominator level for the budget period. It is more difficult to obtain reliable estimates of demand-side denominator-level concepts, especially longer-term normal capacity utilization figures. For example, many U.S. steel companies in the 1980s believed they were in the downturn of a demand cycle that would have an upturn within two or three years. After all, steel had been a cyclical business in which upturns followed downturns, making the notion of normal capacity utilization appear reasonable. Unfortunately, the steel cycle in the 1980s did not turn up, resulting in some companies and numerous plants closing. The recent global economic slowdown demonstrated the extent to which demand projections could be inaccurate. Consider that in 2006 auto analysts forecast that annual demand in India for cars and passenger vehicles would hit 1.92 million in the year 2009–2010. In early 2009, the forecast for the same period was revised downward to 1.37 million vehicles. Inaccurate forecasts are not exclusive to the auto industry. In April

---

[7] For example, Section 1.471-11 of the U.S. Internal Revenue Code states, "The proper use of the standard cost method... requires that a taxpayer must reallocate to the goods in ending inventory a pro rata portion of any net negative or net positive overhead variances." Of course, if the variances are not material in amount, they can be expensed (i.e., written off to cost of goods sold), provided the same treatment is carried out in the firm's financial reports.

2013, the world's largest miner, BHP Billiton, scrapped plans for projects worth $40 billion in Australia to reflect dropping prices for major metals in response to slowing demand from China, the largest commodities consumer. In addition to dealing with economic cycles and inaccurate forecasts, companies also face the problem of marketing managers who may overestimate their ability to regain lost sales and market share. Their estimate of "normal" demand for their product may consequently be based on an overly optimistic outlook. Master-budget capacity utilization focuses only on the expected demand for the next year. Therefore, companies can more reliably estimate master-budget capacity utilization than normal capacity utilization. However, master-budget capacity utilization is still just a forecast, and the true demand realization can be either higher or lower than this estimate.

It is important to understand that costing systems, such as normal costing or standard costing, do not recognize uncertainty the way managers recognize it. A single amount, rather than a range of possible amounts, is used as the denominator level when calculating the budgeted fixed manufacturing cost per unit in absorption costing. Consider Stassen's facility, which has an estimated practical capacity of 12,000 units. The estimated master-budget capacity utilization for 2014 is 8,000 units. However, there is still substantial doubt about the actual number of units Stassen will have to manufacture in 2014 and in future years. Managers recognize uncertainty in their capacity-planning decisions. Stassen built its current plant with a 12,000-unit practical capacity in part to provide the capability to meet possible demand surges. Even if such surges do not occur in a given period, do not conclude that capacity unused in a given period is wasted resources. The gains from meeting sudden demand surges may well require having unused capacity in some periods.

Difficulties in Forecasting Fixed Manufacturing Costs

The fixed manufacturing cost rate is based on a numerator (budgeted fixed manufacturing costs) and a denominator (some measure of capacity or capacity utilization). Our discussion so far has emphasized issues concerning the choice of the denominator. Challenging issues also arise in measuring the numerator. For example, deregulation of the U.S. electric utility industry has resulted in many electric utilities becoming unprofitable. This situation has led to write-downs in the values of the utilities' plants and equipment. The write-downs reduce the numerator because there is less depreciation expense included in the calculation of fixed capacity cost per kilowatt-hour of electricity produced. The difficulty that managers face in this situation is that the amount of write-downs is not clear-cut but, rather, a matter of judgment. In several industries, the increased emphasis on sustainability and attention to the environment has led to unexpected increases in the fixed costs of operations. On the other hand, infrastructure costs for information technology have continued to plummet and have moved from fixed to variable costs in many cases because of the capabilities offered by providers such as Amazon Web Services.

Nonmanufacturing Costs

Capacity costs also arise in nonmanufacturing parts of the value chain. Stassen may acquire a fleet of vehicles capable of distributing the practical capacity of its production facility. When actual production is below practical capacity, there will be unused-capacity cost issues with the distribution function, as well as with the manufacturing function.

Capacity cost issues are prominent in many service-sector companies, such as airlines, hospitals, and railroads—even though these companies carry no inventory and so have no inventory costing problems. For example, in calculating the fixed overhead cost per patient-day in its obstetrics and gynecology department, a hospital must decide which denominator level to use: practical capacity, normal capacity utilization, or master-budget capacity utilization. The hospital's decision may have implications for capacity management, as well as pricing and performance evaluation.

Activity-Based Costing

To maintain simplicity, the Stassen example in this chapter assumed that all costs were either variable or fixed. In particular, there were no batch-level costs and no product-sustaining costs. It is easy to see that the distinction between variable and absorption costing carries over directly into activity-based costing systems, with batch-level costs acting as variable costs and product-sustaining ones as fixed costs, as a function of the number of units produced.

In order to focus on the choice of denominator to calculate the budgeted fixed manufacturing cost rate, our Stassen example assumed that all fixed manufacturing costs had a single cost driver: telescope units produced. Activity-based costing systems have multiple overhead cost pools at the output-unit, batch, product-sustaining, and facility-sustaining levels—each with its own cost driver. In calculating activity cost rates (for fixed costs of setups and material handling, say), management must choose a capacity level for the quantity of the cost driver (setup-hours or loads moved). Should management use practical capacity, normal capacity utilization, or master-budget capacity utilization? For all the reasons described in this chapter (such as pricing and capacity management), most proponents of activity-based costing argue that managers should use practical capacity as the denominator level to calculate activity cost rates.

> **Decision Point**
>
> What issues must managers take into account when planning capacity levels and for assigning capacity costs?

Problem for Self-Study

Assume Stassen Company on January 1, 2014, decides to contract with another company to preassemble a large percentage of the components of its telescopes. The revised manufacturing cost structure during the 2014–2015 period is as follows:

Variable manufacturing cost per unit produced	
Direct materials	$ 250
Direct manufacturing labor	20
Manufacturing overhead	5
Total variable manufacturing cost per unit produced	$ 275
Fixed manufacturing costs	$480,000

Under the revised cost structure, a larger percentage of Stassen's manufacturing costs are variable for units produced. The denominator level of production used to calculate budgeted fixed manufacturing cost per unit in 2014 and 2015 is 8,000 units. Assume no other change from the data underlying Exhibits 1 and 2. Summary information pertaining to absorption-costing operating income and variable-costing operating income with this revised cost structure are as follows:

	2014	2015
Absorption-costing operating income	$1,500,000	$1,560,000
Variable-costing operating income	1,380,000	1,650,000
Difference	$ 120,000	$ (90,000)

1. Compute the budgeted fixed manufacturing cost per unit in 2014 and 2015.
2. Explain the difference between absorption-costing operating income and variable-costing operating income in 2014 and 2015, focusing on fixed manufacturing costs in beginning and ending inventory.
3. Why are these differences smaller than the differences in Exhibit 2?
4. Assume the same preceding information, except that for 2014, the master-budget capacity utilization is 10,000 units instead of 8,000. How would Stassen's absorption-costing income for 2014 differ from the $1,500,000 shown previously? Show your computations.

> **Required**

Solution

1. $$\text{Budgeted fixed manufacturing cost per unit} = \frac{\text{Budgeted fixed manufacturing costs}}{\text{Budgeted production units}}$$

$$= \frac{\$480,000}{8,000 \text{ units}}$$

$$= \$60 \text{ per unit}$$

2.
Absorption-costing operating income	−	Variable-costing operating income	=	Fixed manufacturing costs in ending inventory under absorption costing	−	Fixed manufacturing costs in beginning inventory under absorption costing

2014: $1,500,000 − $1,380,000 = ($60 per unit × 2,000 units) − ($60 per unit × 0 units)

$120,000 = $120,000

2015: $1,560,000 − $1,650,000 = ($60 per unit × 500 units) − ($60 per unit × 2,000 units)

−$90,000 = −$90,000

3. Subcontracting a large part of manufacturing has greatly reduced the magnitude of fixed manufacturing costs. This reduction, in turn, means differences between absorption costing and variable costing are much smaller than in Exhibit 2.

4. Given the higher master-budget capacity utilization level of 10,000 units, the budgeted fixed manufacturing cost rate for 2014 is now as follows:

$$\frac{\$480,000}{10,000 \text{ units}} = \$48 \text{ per unit}$$

The manufacturing cost per unit is $323 ($275 + $48). So, the production-volume variance for 2014 is

$$(10,000 \text{ units} - 8,000 \text{ units}) \times \$48 \text{ per unit} = \$96,000 \text{ U}$$

The absorption-costing income statement for 2014 is as follows:

Revenues: $1,000 per unit × 6,000 units	$6,000,000
Cost of goods sold:	
Beginning inventory	0
Variable manufacturing costs: $275 per unit × 8,000 units	2,200,000
Fixed manufacturing costs: $48 per unit × 8,000 units	384,000
Cost of goods available for sale	2,584,000
Deduct ending inventory: $323 per unit × 2,000 units	(646,000)
Cost of goods sold (at standard costs)	1,938,000
Adjustment for production-volume variance	96,000 U
Cost of goods sold	2,034,000
Gross margin	3,966,000
Marketing costs: $1,380,000 fixed + ($185 per unit × 6,000 units sold)	2,490,000
Operating income	$1,476,000

The higher denominator level used to calculate the budgeted fixed manufacturing cost per unit means that fewer fixed manufacturing costs are inventoried ($48 per unit × 2,000 units = $96,000) than when the master-budget capacity utilization was 8,000 units ($60 per unit × 2,000 units = $120,000). This difference of $24,000 ($120,000 − $96,000) results in operating income being lower by $24,000 relative to the prior calculated income level of $1,500,000.

▶ Decision Points

The following question-and-answer format summarizes the chapter's learning objectives. Each decision presents a key question related to a learning objective. The guidelines are the answer to that question.

Decision	Guidelines
1. How does variable costing differ from absorption costing?	Variable costing and absorption costing differ in only one respect: how to account for fixed manufacturing costs. Under variable costing, fixed manufacturing costs are excluded from inventoriable costs and are a cost of the period in which they are incurred. Under absorption costing, fixed manufacturing costs are inventoriable and become a part of cost of goods sold in the period when sales occur.
2. How does income differ under variable and absorption costing?	The variable-costing income statement is based on the contribution-margin format. Under it, operating income is driven by the unit level of sales. Under absorption costing, the income statement follows the gross-margin format. Operating income is driven by the unit level of production, the unit level of sales, and the denominator level used for assigning fixed costs.
3. Why might managers build up finished goods inventory if they use absorption costing?	When absorption costing is used, managers can increase current operating income by producing more units for inventory. Producing for inventory absorbs more fixed manufacturing costs into inventory and reduces costs expensed in the period. Critics of absorption costing label this manipulation of income as the major negative consequence of treating fixed manufacturing costs as inventoriable costs.
4. How does throughput costing differ from variable costing and absorption costing?	Throughput costing treats all costs except direct materials as costs of the period in which they are incurred. Throughput costing results in a lower amount of manufacturing costs being inventoried than either variable or absorption costing.
5. What are the various capacity levels a company can use to compute the budgeted fixed manufacturing cost rate?	Capacity levels can be measured in terms of capacity supplied—theoretical capacity or practical capacity. Capacity can also be measured in terms of output demanded—normal capacity utilization or master-budget capacity utilization.
6. What are the major factors managers consider in choosing the capacity level to compute the budgeted fixed manufacturing cost rate?	The major factors managers consider in choosing the capacity level to compute the budgeted fixed manufacturing cost rate are (a) effect on product costing and capacity management, (b) effect on pricing decisions, (c) effect on performance evaluation, (d) effect on financial statements, and (e) regulatory requirements.
7. What issues must managers take into account when planning capacity levels and for assigning capacity costs?	Critical factors when planning capacity levels and for assigning capacity costs include the uncertainty about the expected spending on capacity costs and the demand for the installed capacity; the role of capacity-related issues in nonmanufacturing areas; and the possible use of activity-based costing techniques in allocating capacity costs.

Appendix

Breakeven Points in Variable Costing and Absorption Costing

If variable costing is used, the breakeven point (that's where operating income is $0) is computed in the usual manner. There is only one breakeven point in this case, and it depends on (1) fixed (manufacturing and operating) costs and (2) contribution margin per unit.

The formula for computing the breakeven point under variable costing is a special case of the more general target operating income formula:

$$\text{Let } Q = \text{Number of units sold to earn the target operating income}$$

$$\text{Then } Q = \frac{\text{Total fixed costs} + \text{Target operating income}}{\text{Contribution margin per unit}}$$

Breakeven occurs when the target operating income is $0. In our Stassen illustration for 2014 (see Exhibit 1):

$$Q = \frac{(\$1,080,000 + \$1,380,000) + \$0}{(\$1,000 - (\$200 + \$185))} = \frac{\$2,460,000}{\$615}$$

$$= 4,000 \text{ units}$$

We now verify that Stassen will achieve breakeven under variable costing by selling 4,000 units:

Revenues, $1,000 × 4,000 units	$4,000,000
Variable costs, $385 × 4,000 units	1,540,000
Contribution margin, $615 × 4,000 units	2,460,000
Fixed costs	2,460,000
Operating income	$ 0

If absorption costing is used, the required number of units to be sold to earn a specific target operating income is not unique because of the number of variables involved. The following formula shows the factors that will affect the target operating income under absorption costing:

$$Q = \frac{\begin{array}{c}\text{Total} \\ \text{fixed} \\ \text{costs}\end{array} + \begin{array}{c}\text{Target} \\ \text{operating} \\ \text{income}\end{array} + \left[\begin{array}{c}\text{Fixed} \\ \text{manufacturing} \\ \text{cost rate}\end{array} \times \left(\begin{array}{c}\text{Breakeven} \\ \text{sales} \\ \text{in units}\end{array} - \begin{array}{c}\text{Units} \\ \text{produced}\end{array}\right)\right]}{\text{Contribution margin per unit}}$$

In this formula, the numerator is the sum of three terms (from the perspective of the two "+" signs), compared with two terms in the numerator of the variable-costing formula stated earlier. The additional term in the numerator under absorption costing is as follows:

$$\left[\begin{array}{c}\text{Fixed manufacturing} \\ \text{cost rate}\end{array} \times \left(\begin{array}{c}\text{Breakeven sales} \\ \text{in units}\end{array} - \begin{array}{c}\text{Units} \\ \text{produced}\end{array}\right)\right]$$

This term reduces the fixed costs that need to be recovered when units produced exceed the breakeven sales quantity. When production exceeds the breakeven sales quantity, some of the fixed manufacturing costs that are expensed under variable costing are not expensed under absorption costing; they are instead included in finished goods inventory. The breakeven sales quantity under absorption costing is correspondingly lower than under variable costing.[8]

---

[8] The reverse situation, where production is lower than the breakeven sales quantity, is not possible unless the firm has opening inventory. In that case, provided the variable manufacturing cost per unit and the fixed manufacturing cost rate are constant over time, the breakeven formula given is still valid. The breakeven sales quantity under absorption costing would then exceed that under variable costing.

For Stassen Company in 2014, suppose that actual production is 5,280 units. Then one breakeven point, Q, under absorption costing is as follows:

$$Q = \frac{(\$1,080,000 + \$1,380,000) + \$0 + [\$135 \times (Q - 5,280)]}{(\$1,000 - (\$200 + \$185))}$$

$$= \frac{(\$2,460,000 + \$135Q - \$712,800)}{\$615}$$

$$\$615Q = \$1,747,200 + \$135Q$$

$$\$480Q = \$1,747,200$$

$$Q = 3,640$$

We next verify that production of 5,280 units and sales of 3,640 units will lead Stassen to break even under absorption costing:

Revenues, $1,000 × 3,640 units		$3,640,000
Cost of goods sold:		
Cost of goods sold at standard cost, $335 × 3,640 units	$1,219,400	
Production-volume variance, $135 × (8,000 − 5,280) units	367,200 U	1,586,600
Gross margin		2,053,400
Marketing costs:		
Variable marketing costs, $185 × 3,640 units	673,400	
Fixed marketing costs	1,380,000	2,053,400
Operating income		$ 0

The breakeven point under absorption costing depends on (1) fixed manufacturing costs, (2) fixed operating (marketing) costs, (3) contribution margin per unit, (4) unit level of production, and (5) the capacity level chosen as the denominator to set the fixed manufacturing cost rate. For Stassen in 2014, a combination of 3,640 units sold, fixed manufacturing costs of $1,080,000, fixed marketing costs of $1,380,000, contribution margin per unit of $615, an 8,000-unit denominator level, and production of 5,280 units would result in an operating income of $0. *Note, however, that there are many combinations of these five factors that would give an operating income of $0.* For example, holding all other factors constant, a combination of 6,240 units produced and 3,370 units sold also results in an operating income of $0 under absorption costing. We provide verification of this alternative breakeven point next:

Revenues, $1,000 × 3,370 units		$3,370,000
Cost of goods sold:		
Cost of goods sold at standard cost, $335 × 3,370 units	$1,128,950	
Production-volume variance, $135 × (8,000 − 6,240) units	237,600 U	1,366,550
Gross margin		2,003,450
Marketing costs:		
Variable marketing costs, $185 × 3,370 units	623,450	
Fixed marketing costs	1,380,000	2,003,450
Operating income		$ 0

Suppose actual production in 2014 was equal to the denominator level, 8,000 units, and there were no units sold and no fixed marketing costs. All the units produced would be placed in inventory, so all the fixed manufacturing costs would be included in inventory. There would be no production-volume variance. Under these conditions, the company could break even under absorption costing with no sales whatsoever! In contrast, under variable costing, the operating loss would be equal to the fixed manufacturing costs of $1,080,000.

Terms to Learn

This chapter contains definitions of the following important terms:

absorption costing

direct costing

downward demand spiral

master-budget capacity utilization

normal capacity utilization

practical capacity

super-variable costing

theoretical capacity

throughput costing

variable costing

Assignment Material

MyAccountingLab

Questions

1 Differences in operating income between variable costing and absorption costing are due solely to accounting for fixed costs. Do you agree? Explain.

2 Why is the term *direct costing* a misnomer?

3 Do companies in either the service sector or the merchandising sector make choices about absorption costing versus variable costing?

4 Explain the main conceptual issue under variable costing and absorption costing regarding the timing for the release of fixed manufacturing overhead as expense.

5 "Companies that make no variable-cost/fixed-cost distinctions must use absorption costing, and those that do make variable-cost/fixed-cost distinctions must use variable costing." Do you agree? Explain.

6 The main trouble with variable costing is that it ignores the increasing importance of fixed costs in manufacturing companies. Do you agree? Why?

7 Give an example of how, under absorption costing, operating income could fall even though the unit sales level rises.

8 What are the factors that affect the breakeven point under (a) variable costing and (b) absorption costing?

9 Critics of absorption costing have increasingly emphasized its potential for leading to undesirable incentives for managers. Give an example.

10 What are two ways of reducing the negative aspects associated with using absorption costing to evaluate the performance of a plant manager?

11 What denominator-level capacity concepts emphasize the output a plant can supply? What denominator-level capacity concepts emphasize the output customers demand for products produced by a plant?

12 Describe the downward demand spiral and its implications for pricing decisions.

13 Will the financial statements of a company always differ when different choices at the start of the accounting period are made regarding the denominator-level capacity concept?

14 What is the IRS's requirement for tax reporting regarding the choice of a denominator-level capacity concept?

15 "The difference between practical capacity and master-budget capacity utilization is the best measure of management's ability to balance the costs of having too much capacity and having too little capacity." Do you agree? Explain.

MyAccountingLab

Exercises

16 **Variable and absorption costing, explaining operating-income differences.** Nascar Motors assembles and sells motor vehicles and uses standard costing. Actual data relating to April and May 2014 are as follows:

	A	B	C	D
		April		**May**
1				
2	Unit data			
3	Beginning inventory	0		150
4	Production	500		400
5	Sales	350		520
6	Variable costs			
7	Manufacturing cost per unit produced	$ 10,000		$ 10,000
8	Operating (marketing) cost per unit sold	3,000		3,000
9	Fixed costs			
10	Manufacturing costs	$2,000,000		$2,000,000
11	Operating (marketing) costs	600,000		600,000

The selling price per vehicle is $24,000. The budgeted level of production used to calculate the budgeted fixed manufacturing cost per unit is 500 units. There are no price, efficiency, or spending variances. Any production-volume variance is written off to cost of goods sold in the month in which it occurs.

Required

1. Prepare April and May 2014 income statements for Nascar Motors under (a) variable costing and (b) absorption costing.
2. Prepare a numerical reconciliation and explanation of the difference between operating income for each month under variable costing and absorption costing.

17 Throughput costing (continuation of 16). The variable manufacturing costs per unit of Nascar Motors are as follows:

	A	B	C
1		**April**	**May**
7	Direct material cost per unit	$6,700	$6,700
8	Direct manufacturing labor cost per unit	1,500	1,500
9	Manufacturing overhead cost per unit	1,800	1,800

Required

1. Prepare income statements for Nascar Motors in April and May 2014 under throughput costing.
2. Contrast the results in requirement 1 with those in requirement 1 of Exercise 16.
3. Give one motivation for Nascar Motors to adopt throughput costing.

18 Variable and absorption costing, explaining operating-income differences. Crystal Clear Corporation manufactures and sells 50-inch television sets and uses standard costing. Actual data relating to January, February, and March 2014 are as follows:

	January	February	March
Unit data			
Beginning inventory	0	100	100
Production	1,400	1,375	1,430
Sales	1,300	1,375	1,455
Variable costs			
Manufacturing cost per unit produced	$ 950	$ 950	$ 950
Operating (marketing) cost per unit sold	$ 725	$ 725	$ 725
Fixed costs			
Manufacturing costs	$490,000	$490,000	$490,000
Operating (marketing) costs	$120,000	$120,000	$120,000

The selling price per unit is $3,500. The budgeted level of production used to calculate the budgeted fixed manufacturing cost per unit is 1,400 units. There are no price, efficiency, or spending variances. Any production-volume variance is written off to cost of goods sold in the month in which it occurs.

1. Prepare income statements for Crystal Clear in January, February, and March 2014 under (a) variable costing and (b) absorption costing.
2. Explain the difference in operating income for January, February, and March under variable costing and absorption costing.

19 Throughput costing (continuation of 18). The variable manufacturing costs per unit of Crystal Clear Corporation are as follows:

	January	February	March
Direct material cost per unit	$550	$550	$550
Direct manufacturing labor cost per unit	175	175	175
Manufacturing overhead cost per unit	225	225	225
	$950	$950	$950

Required

1. Prepare income statements for Crystal Clear in January, February, and March 2014 under throughput costing.
2. Contrast the results in requirement 1 with those in requirement 1 of Exercise 18.
3. Give one motivation for Crystal Clear to adopt throughput costing.

20 Variable versus absorption costing. The Zwatch Company manufactures trendy, high-quality, moderately priced watches. As Zwatch's senior financial analyst, you are asked to recommend a method of inventory costing. The CFO will use your recommendation to prepare Zwatch's 2014 income statement. The following data are for the year ended December 31, 2014:

Beginning inventory, January 1, 2014	85,000 units
Ending inventory, December 31, 2014	34,500 units
2014 sales	345,400 units
Selling price (to distributor)	$22.00 per unit
Variable manufacturing cost per unit, including direct materials	$5.10 per unit
Variable operating (marketing) cost per unit sold	$1.10 per unit sold
Fixed manufacturing costs	$1,440,000
Denominator-level machine-hours	6,000
Standard production rate	50 units per machine-hour
Fixed operating (marketing) costs	$1,080,000

Required

Assume standard costs per unit are the same for units in beginning inventory and units produced during the year. Also, assume no price, spending, or efficiency variances. Any production-volume variance is written off to cost of goods sold in the month in which it occurs.

1. Prepare income statements under variable and absorption costing for the year ended December 31, 2014.
2. What is Zwatch's operating income as percentage of revenues under each costing method?
3. Explain the difference in operating income between the two methods.
4. Which costing method would you recommend to the CFO? Why?

21 Absorption and variable costing. (CMA) Osawa, Inc., planned and actually manufactured 200,000 units of its single product in 2014, its first year of operation. Variable manufacturing cost was $20 per unit produced. Variable operating (nonmanufacturing) cost was $10 per unit sold. Planned and actual fixed manufacturing costs were $600,000. Planned and actual fixed operating (nonmanufacturing) costs totaled $400,000. Osawa sold 120,000 units of product at $40 per unit.

Required

1. Osawa's 2014 operating income using absorption costing is (a) $440,000, (b) $200,000, (c) $600,000, (d) $840,000, or (e) none of these. Show supporting calculations.
2. Osawa's 2014 operating income using variable costing is (a) $800,000, (b) $440,000, (c) $200,000, (d) $600,000, or (e) none of these. Show supporting calculations.

22 Absorption versus variable costing. Regina Company manufacturers a professional-grade vacuum cleaner and began operations in 2014. For 2014, Regina budgeted to produce and sell 20,000 units. The company had no price, spending, or efficiency variances and writes off production-volume variance to cost of goods sold. Actual data for 2014 are given as follows:

	A	B
	Home Insert Page Layout Formulas Data	
	A	B
1	Units produced	18,000
2	Units sold	17,500
3	Selling price	$ 450
4	Variable costs:	
5	Manufacturing cost per unit produced	
6	Direct materials	$ 30
7	Direct manufacturing labor	25
8	Manufacturing overhead	60
9	Marketing cost per unit sold	45
10	Fixed costs:	
11	Manufacturing costs	$1,200,000
12	Administrative costs	965,450
13	Marketing	1,366,400

1. Prepare a 2014 income statement for Regina Company using variable costing.
2. Prepare a 2014 income statement for Regina Company using absorption costing.
3. Explain the differences in operating incomes obtained in requirements 1 and 2.
4. Regina's management is considering implementing a bonus for the supervisors based on gross margin under absorption costing. What incentives will this bonus plan create for the supervisors? What modifications could Regina management make to improve such a plan? Explain briefly.

Required

23 Variable and absorption costing, sales, and operating-income changes. Smart Safety, a three-year-old company, has been producing and selling a single type of bicycle helmet. Smart Safety uses standard costing. After reviewing the income statements for the first three years, Stuart Weil, president of Smart Safety, commented, "I was told by our accountants—and in fact, I have memorized—that our breakeven volume is 52,000 units. I was happy that we reached that sales goal in each of our first two years. But here's the strange thing: In our first year, we sold 52,000 units and indeed we broke even. Then in our second year we sold the same volume and had a positive operating income. I didn't complain, of course...but here's the bad part. In our third year, we *sold 20% more* helmets, but our *operating income fell by more than 80%* relative to the second year! We didn't change our selling price or cost structure over the past three years and have no price, efficiency, or spending variances...so what's going on?!"

	A	B	C	D
	Home Insert Page Layout Formulas Data Review View			
1	**Absorption Costing**			
2		**2013**	**2014**	**2015**
3	Sales (units)	52,000	52,000	62,400
4	Revenues	$2,236,000	$2,236,000	$2,683,200
5	Cost of goods sold			
6	Beginning inventory	0	0	405,600
7	Production	2,028,000	2,433,600	2,028,000
8	Available for sale	2,028,000	2,433,600	2,433,600
9	Deduct ending inventory	0	(405,600)	0
10	Adjustment for production-volume variance	0	(260,600)	0
11	Cost of goods sold	2,028,000	1,768,000	2,433,600
12	Gross margin	208,000	468,600	249,600
13	Selling and administrative expenses (all fixed)	208,000	208,000	208,000
14	Operating income	$ 0	$ 260,000	$ 41,600
15				
16	Beginning inventory	0	0	10,400
17	Production (units)	52,000	62,400	52,000
18	Sales (units)	52,000	52,000	62,400
19	Ending inventory	0	10,400	0
20	Variable manufacturing cost per unit	$ 14	$ 14	$ 14
21	Fixed manufacturing overhead costs	$1,300,000	$1,300,000	$1,300,000
22	Fixed manuf. costs allocated per unit produced	$ 25	$ 25	$ 25

Required

1. What denominator level is Smart Safety using to allocate fixed manufacturing costs to the bicycle helmets? How is Smart Safety disposing of any favorable or unfavorable production-volume variance at the end of the year? Explain your answer briefly.
2. How did Smart Safety's accountants arrive at the breakeven volume of 52,000 units?
3. Prepare a variable costing-based income statement for each year. Explain the variation in variable costing operating income for each year based on contribution margin per unit and sales volume.
4. Reconcile the operating incomes under variable costing and absorption costing for each year, and use this information to explain to Stuart Weil the positive operating income in 2014 and the drop in operating income in 2015.

24 Capacity management, denominator-level capacity concepts. Match each of the following numbered descriptions with one or more of the denominator-level capacity concepts by putting the appropriate letter(s) by each item:

a. Theoretical capacity
b. Practical capacity
c. Normal capacity utilization
d. Master-budget capacity utilization

1. Measures the denominator level in terms of what a plant can supply
2. Is based on producing at full efficiency all the time
3. Represents the expected level of capacity utilization for the next budget period
4. Measures the denominator level in terms of demand for the output of the plant
5. Takes into account seasonal, cyclical, and trend factors
6. Should be used for performance evaluation in the current year
7. Represents an ideal benchmark
8. Highlights the cost of capacity acquired but not used
9. Should be used for long-term pricing purposes
10. Hides the cost of capacity acquired but not used
11. If used as the denominator-level concept, would avoid the restatement of unit costs when expected demand levels change

25 Denominator-level problem. Thunder Bolt, Inc., is a manufacturer of the very popular G36 motorcycles. The management at Thunder Bolt has recently adopted absorption costing and is debating which denominator-level concept to use. The G36 motorcycles sell for an average price of $8,200. Budgeted fixed manufacturing overhead costs for 2014 are estimated at $6,480,000. Thunder Bolt, Inc., uses subassembly operators that provide component parts. The following are the denominator-level options that management has been considering:

a. Theoretical capacity—based on three shifts, completion of five motorcycles per shift, and a 360-day year—$3 \times 5 \times 360 = 5,400$.
b. Practical capacity—theoretical capacity adjusted for unavoidable interruptions, breakdowns, and so forth—$3 \times 4 \times 320 = 3,840$.
c. Normal capacity utilization—estimated at 3,240 units.
d. Master-budget capacity utilization—the strengthening stock market and the growing popularity of motorcycles have prompted the marketing department to issue an estimate for 2014 of 3,600 units.

Required

1. Calculate the budgeted fixed manufacturing overhead cost rates under the four denominator-level concepts.
2. What are the benefits to Thunder Bolt, Inc., of using either theoretical capacity or practical capacity?
3. Under a cost-based pricing system, what are the negative aspects of a master-budget denominator level? What are the positive aspects?

26 Variable and absorption costing and breakeven points. Artesa, a leading firm in the semiconductor industry, produces digital integrated circuits (ICs) for the communications and defense markets.

For the year ended December 31, 2013, Artesa sold 242,400 ICs at an average selling price of $47 per unit. The following information also relates to 2013 (assume constant unit costs and no variances of any kind):

Inventory, January 1, 2013:	32,600 ICs
Inventory, December 31, 2013:	24,800 ICs
Fixed manufacturing costs:	$1,876,800
Fixed administrative costs:	$3,284,400
Direct materials costs:	$13 per IC
Direct labor costs:	$11 per IC

Required

1. How many integrated circuits did Artesa produce in 2013?
2. Calculate the breakeven point (number of ICs sold) in 2013 under:
   a. Variable costing
   b. Absorption costing
3. Due to difficulties in obtaining high-quality silicon, Artesa expects that direct materials costs will increase to $15 per IC in 2014. Assuming all other data are the same, calculate the minimum number of ICs Artesa must sell in 2014 to break even under:
   a. Variable costing
   b. Absorption costing

27 Variable costing versus absorption costing. The Mavis Company uses an absorption-costing system based on standard costs. Total variable manufacturing cost, including direct material cost, is $3 per unit; the standard production rate is 10 units per machine-hour. Total budgeted and actual fixed manufacturing overhead costs are $420,000. Fixed manufacturing overhead is allocated at $7 per machine-hour ($420,000 ÷ 60,000 machine-hours of denominator level). Selling price is $5 per unit. Variable operating (nonmanufacturing) cost, which is driven by units sold, is $1 per unit. Fixed operating (nonmanufacturing) costs are $120,000. Beginning inventory in 2014 is 30,000 units; ending inventory is 40,000 units. Sales in 2014 are 540,000 units. The same standard unit costs persisted throughout 2013 and 2014. For simplicity, assume that there are no price, spending, or efficiency variances.

Required

1. Prepare an income statement for 2014 assuming that the production-volume variance is written off at year-end as an adjustment to cost of goods sold.
2. The president has heard about variable costing. She asks you to recast the 2014 statement as it would appear under variable costing.
3. Explain the difference in operating income as calculated in requirements 1 and 2.
4. Graph how fixed manufacturing overhead is accounted for under absorption costing. That is, there will be two lines: one for the budgeted fixed manufacturing overhead (which is equal to the actual fixed manufacturing overhead in this case) and one for the fixed manufacturing overhead allocated. Show the production-volume variance in the graph.

5. Critics have claimed that a widely used accounting system has led to undesirable buildups of inventory levels. (a) Is variable costing or absorption costing more likely to lead to such buildups? Why? (b) What can managers do to counteract undesirable inventory buildups?

MyAccountingLab

Problems

28 Variable costing and absorption costing, the All-Fixed Company. (R. Marple, adapted) It is the end of 2013. The All-Fixed Company began operations in January 2012. The company is so named because it has no variable costs. All its costs are fixed; they do not vary with output.

The All-Fixed Company is located on the bank of a river and has its own hydroelectric plant to supply power, light, and heat. The company manufactures a synthetic fertilizer from air and river water and sells its product at a price that is not expected to change. It has a small staff of employees, all paid fixed annual salaries. The output of the plant can be increased or decreased by adjusting a few dials on a control panel.

The following budgeted and actual data are for the operations of the All-Fixed Company. All-Fixed uses budgeted production as the denominator level and writes off any production-volume variance to cost of goods sold.

	2012	2013[a]
Sales	10,000 tons	10,000 tons
Production	20,000 tons	0 tons
Selling price	$ 30 per ton	$ 30 per ton
Costs (all fixed):		
Manufacturing	$280,000	$280,000
Operating (nonmanufacturing)	$ 40,000	$ 40,000

[a] Management adopted the policy, effective January 1, 2013, of producing only as much product as needed to fill sales orders. During 2013, sales were the same as for 2012 and were filled entirely from inventory at the start of 2013.

Required

1. Prepare income statements with one column for 2012, one column for 2013, and one column for the two years together using (a) variable costing and (b) absorption costing.
2. What is the breakeven point under (a) variable costing and (b) absorption costing?
3. What inventory costs would be carried in the balance sheet on December 31, 2012 and 2013, under each method?
4. Assume that the performance of the top manager of the company is evaluated and rewarded largely on the basis of reported operating income. Which costing method would the manager prefer? Why?

29 Comparison of variable costing and absorption costing. Gammaro Company uses standard costing. Tim Sweeney, the new president of Gammaro Company, is presented with the following data for 2014:

	A	B	C
	Home Insert Page Layout Formulas Data Review View		
1	**Gammaro Company**		
2	**Income Statements for the Year Ended December 31, 2014**		
3		**Variable**	**Absorption**
4		**Costing**	**Costing**
5	Revenues	$9,350,000	$9,350,000
6	Cost of goods sold (at standard costs)	4,695,000	5,855,000
7	Fixed manufacturing overhead (budgeted)	1,350,000	-
8	Fixed manufacturing overhead variances (all unfavorable):		
9	Spending	125,000	125,000
10	Production volume	-	405,000
11	Total marketing and administrative costs (all fixed)	1,570,000	1,570,000
12	Total costs	7,740,000	7,955,000
13	Operating income	$1,610,000	$1,395,000
14			
15	Inventories (at standard costs)		
16	December 31, 2013	$1,345,000	$1,730,000
17	December 31, 2014	45,000	215,000

1. At what percentage of denominator level was the plant operating during 2014?
2. How much fixed manufacturing overhead was included in the 2013 and the 2014 ending inventory under absorption costing?
3. Reconcile and explain the difference in 2014 operating incomes under variable and absorption costing.
4. Tim Sweeney is concerned: He notes that despite an increase in sales over 2013, 2014 operating income has actually declined under absorption costing. Explain how this occurred.

30 Effects of differing production levels on absorption costing income: Metrics to minimize inventory buildups. Horizon Press produces textbooks for college courses. The company recently hired a new editor, Billie White, to handle production and sales of books for an introduction to accounting course. Billie's compensation depends on the gross margin associated with sales of this book. Billie needs to decide how many copies of the book to produce. The following information is available for the fall semester 2013:

Estimated sales	26,000 books
Beginning inventory	0 books
Average selling price	$ 81 per book
Variable production costs	$ 45 per book
Fixed production costs	$416,000 per semester

The fixed cost allocation rate is based on expected sales and is therefore equal to $416,000/26,000 books = $16 per book.

Billie has decided to produce either 26,000, 32,500, or 33,800 books.

1. Calculate expected gross margin if Billie produces 26,000, 32,500, or 33,800 books. (Make sure you include the production-volume variance as part of cost of goods sold.)
2. Calculate ending inventory in units and in dollars for each production level.
3. Managers who are paid a bonus that is a function of gross margin may be inspired to produce a product in excess of demand to maximize their own bonus. The chapter suggested metrics to discourage managers from producing products in excess of demand. Do you think the following metrics will accomplish this objective? Show your work.

   a. Incorporate a charge of 5% of the cost of the ending inventory as an expense for evaluating the manager.
   b. Include nonfinancial measures (such as the ones recommended earlier) when evaluating management and rewarding performance.

31 Alternative denominator-level capacity concepts, effect on operating income. Castle Lager has just purchased the Jacksonville Brewery. The brewery is two years old and uses absorption costing. It will "sell" its product to Castle Lager at $47 per barrel. Peter Bryant, Castle Lager's controller, obtains the following information about Jacksonville Brewery's capacity and budgeted fixed manufacturing costs for 2014:

	A	B	C	D	E
1		**Budgeted Fixed**	**Days of**	**Hours of**	
2	**Denominator-Level**	**Manufacturing**	**Production**	**Production**	**Barrels**
3	**Capacity Concept**	**Overhead per Period**	**per Period**	**per Day**	**per Hour**
4	Theoretical capacity	$27,900,000	358	22	545
5	Practical capacity	$27,900,000	348	20	510
6	Normal capacity utilization	$27,900,000	348	20	410
7	Master-budget capacity for each half year				
8	(a) January–June 2014	$13,950,000	174	20	315
9	(b) July–December 2014	$13,950,000	174	20	505

1. Compute the budgeted fixed manufacturing overhead rate per barrel for each of the denominator-level capacity concepts. Explain why they are different.

2. In 2014, the Jacksonville Brewery reported these production results:

	Home	Insert	Page Layout	Formulas	Data
	A				B
12	Beginning inventory in barrels, 1-1-2014				0
13	Production in barrels				2,670,000
14	Ending inventory in barrels, 12-31-2014				210,000
15	Actual variable manufacturing costs				$80,634,000
16	Actual fixed manufacturing overhead costs				$26,700,000

There are no variable cost variances. Fixed manufacturing overhead cost variances are written off to cost of goods sold in the period in which they occur. Compute the Jacksonville Brewery's operating income when the denominator-level capacity is (a) theoretical capacity, (b) practical capacity, and (c) normal capacity utilization.

32 Motivational considerations in denominator-level capacity selection (continuation of 31).

Required

1. If the plant manager of the Jacksonville Brewery gets a bonus based on operating income, which denominator-level capacity concept would he prefer to use? Explain.
2. What denominator-level capacity concept would Castle Lager prefer to use for U.S. income-tax reporting? Explain.
3. How might the IRS limit the flexibility of an absorption-costing company like Castle Lager attempting to minimize its taxable income?

33 Denominator-level choices, changes in inventory levels, effect on operating income. Donaldson Corporation is a manufacturer of computer accessories. It uses absorption costing based on standard costs and reports the following data for 2014:

	Home	Insert	Page Layout	Formulas	Data	Review
	A				B	C
1	Theoretical capacity				275,000	units
2	Practical capacity				265,000	units
3	Normal capacity utilization				233,200	units
4	Selling price				$ 39	per unit
5	Beginning inventory				35,000	units
6	Production				235,000	units
7	Sales volume				250,000	units
8	Variable budgeted manufacturing cost				$ 8	per unit
9	Total budgeted fixed manufacturing costs				$2,915,000	
10	Total budgeted operating (nonmanuf.) costs (all fixed)				$ 200,000	

There are no price, spending, or efficiency variances. Actual operating costs equal budgeted operating costs. The production-volume variance is written off to cost of goods sold. For each choice of denominator level, the budgeted production cost per unit is also the cost per unit of beginning inventory.

Required

1. What is the production-volume variance in 2014 when the denominator level is (a) theoretical capacity, (b) practical capacity, and (c) normal capacity utilization?
2. Prepare absorption costing–based income statements for Donaldson Corporation using theoretical capacity, practical capacity, and normal capacity utilization as the denominator levels.
3. Why is the operating income under normal capacity utilization lower than the other two scenarios?
4. Reconcile the difference in operating income based on theoretical capacity and practical capacity with the difference in fixed manufacturing overhead included in inventory.

34 Variable and absorption costing and breakeven points. Whistler, Inc., manufactures a specialized snowboard made for the advanced snowboarder. Whistler began 2014 with an inventory of 240 snowboards. During the year, it produced 900 boards and sold 995 for $750 each. Fixed production costs were $280,000, and variable production costs were $325 per unit. Fixed advertising, marketing, and other general and administrative expenses were $112,000, and variable shipping costs were $15 per board. Assume that the cost of each unit in beginning inventory is equal to 2014 inventory cost.

Required

1. Prepare an income statement assuming Whistler uses variable costing.
2. Prepare an income statement assuming Whistler uses absorption costing. Whistler uses a denominator level of 1,000 units. Production-volume variances are written off to cost of goods sold.
3. Compute the breakeven point in units sold assuming Whistler uses the following:
   a. Variable costing   **b.** Absorption costing (Production = 900 boards)

4. Provide proof of your preceding breakeven calculations.

5. Assume that $20,000 of fixed administrative costs were reclassified as fixed production costs. Would this reclassification affect breakeven point using variable costing? What if absorption costing were used? Explain.

6. The company that supplies Whistler with its specialized impact-resistant material has announced a price increase of $30 for each board. What effect would this have on the breakeven points previously calculated?

35 Downward demand spiral. Gostkowski Company is about to enter the highly competitive personal electronics market with a new optical reader. In anticipation of future growth, the company has leased a large manufacturing facility and has purchased several expensive pieces of equipment. In 2013, the company's first year, Gostkowski budgets for production and sales of 24,000 units, compared with its practical capacity of 48,000. The company's cost data are as follows:

	A	B
1	Variable manufacturing costs per unit:	
2	Direct materials	$ 20
3	Direct manufacturing labor	35
4	Manufacturing overhead	9
5	Fixed manufacturing overhead	$576,000

Required

1. Assume that Gostkowski uses absorption costing and uses budgeted units produced as the denominator for calculating its fixed manufacturing overhead rate. Selling price is set at 130% of manufacturing cost. Compute Gostkowski's selling price.

2. Gostkowski enters the market with the selling price computed previously. However, despite growth in the overall market, sales are not as robust as the company had expected, and a competitor has priced its product $16 lower than Gostkowski's. Enrico Gostkowski, the company's president, insists that the competitor must be pricing its product at a loss and that the competitor will be unable to sustain that. In response, Gostkowski makes no price adjustments but budgets production and sales for 2014 at 18,000 units. Variable and fixed costs are not expected to change. Compute Gostkowski's new selling price. Comment on how Gostkowski's choice of budgeted production affected its selling price and competitive position.

3. Recompute the selling price using practical capacity as the denominator level of activity. How would this choice have affected Gostkowski's position in the marketplace? Generally, how would this choice affect the production-volume variance?

36 Absorption costing and production-volume variance—alternative capacity bases. Planet Light First (PLF), a producer of energy-efficient light bulbs, expects that demand will increase markedly over the next decade. Due to the high fixed costs involved in the business, PLF has decided to evaluate its financial performance using absorption costing income. The production-volume variance is written off to cost of goods sold. The variable cost of production is $2.40 per bulb. Fixed manufacturing costs are $1,170,000 per year. Variable and fixed selling and administrative expenses are $0.20 per bulb sold and $220,000, respectively. Because its light bulbs are currently popular with environmentally conscious customers, PLF can sell the bulbs for $9.80 each.

PLF is deciding among various concepts of capacity for calculating the cost of each unit produced. Its choices are as follows:

Theoretical capacity   900,000 bulbs
Practical capacity   520,000 bulbs
Normal capacity   260,000 bulbs (average expected output for the next three years)
Master budget capacity   225,000 bulbs expected production this year

Required

1. Calculate the inventoriable cost per unit using each level of capacity to compute fixed manufacturing cost per unit.

2. Suppose PLF actually produces 300,000 bulbs. Calculate the production-volume variance using each level of capacity to compute the fixed manufacturing overhead allocation rate.

3. Assume PLF has no beginning inventory. If this year's actual sales are 225,000 bulbs, calculate operating income for PLF using each type of capacity to compute fixed manufacturing cost per unit.

37 Operating income effects of denominator-level choice and disposal of production-volume variance (continuation of 36).

1. If PLF sells all 300,000 bulbs produced, what would be the effect on operating income of using each type of capacity as a basis for calculating manufacturing cost per unit?

Required

2. Compare the results of operating income at different capacity levels when 225,000 bulbs are sold and when 300,000 bulbs are sold. What conclusion can you draw from the comparison?

3. Using the original data (that is, 300,000 units produced and 225,000 units sold) if PLF had used the pro-ration approach to allocate the production-volume variance, what would operating income have been under each level of capacity? (Assume that there is no ending work in process.)

38 **Variable and absorption costing, actual costing.** The Iron City Company started business on January 1, 2014. Iron City manufactures a specialty honey beer, which it sells directly to state-owned distributors in Pennsylvania. Honey beer is produced and sold in six-packs, and in 2014, Iron City produced more six-packs than it was able to sell. In addition to variable and fixed manufacturing overhead, Iron City incurred direct materials costs of $880,000, direct manufacturing labor costs of $400,000, and fixed marketing and administrative costs of $295,000. For the year, Iron City sold a total of 180,000 six-packs for a sales revenue of $2,250,000.

Iron City's CFO is convinced that the firm should use an actual costing system but is debating whether to follow variable or absorption costing. The controller notes that Iron City's operating income for the year would be $438,000 under variable costing and $461,000 under absorption costing. Moreover, the ending finished goods inventory would be valued at $7.15 under variable costing and $8.30 under absorption costing.

Iron City incurs no variable nonmanufacturing expenses.

Required

1. What is Iron City's total contribution margin for 2014?
2. Iron City incurs fixed manufacturing costs in addition to its fixed marketing and administrative costs. How much did Iron City incur in fixed manufacturing costs in 2014?
3. How many six-packs did Iron City produce in 2014?
4. How much in variable manufacturing overhead did Iron City incur in 2014?
5. For 2014, how much in total manufacturing overhead is expensed under variable costing, either through Cost of Goods Sold or as a period expense?

39 **Cost allocation, downward demand spiral.** Top Catering operates a chain of 10 hospitals in the Los Angeles area. Its central food-catering facility, Topman, prepares and delivers meals to the hospitals. It has the capacity to deliver up to 1,025,000 meals a year. In 2014, based on estimates from each hospital controller, Topman budgeted for 925,000 meals a year. Budgeted fixed costs in 2014 were $1,517,000. Each hospital was charged $6.24 per meal—$4.60 variable costs plus $1.64 allocated budgeted fixed cost.

Recently, the hospitals have been complaining about the quality of Topman's meals and their rising costs. In mid-2014, Top Catering's president announces that all Top Catering hospitals and support facilities will be run as profit centers. Hospitals will be free to purchase quality-certified services from outside the system. Ron Smith, Topman's controller, is preparing the 2015 budget. He hears that three hospitals have decided to use outside suppliers for their meals, which will reduce the 2015 estimated demand to 820,000 meals. No change in variable cost per meal or total fixed costs is expected in 2015.

Required

1. How did Smith calculate the budgeted fixed cost per meal of $1.64 in 2014?
2. Using the same approach to calculating budgeted fixed cost per meal and pricing as in 2014, how much would hospitals be charged for each Topman meal in 2015? What would the reaction of the hospital controllers be to the price?
3. Suggest an alternative cost-based price per meal that Smith might propose and that might be more acceptable to the hospitals. What can Topman and Smith do to make this price profitable in the long run?

40 **Cost allocation, responsibility accounting, ethics (continuation of 39).** In 2015, only 740,000 Topman meals were produced and sold to the hospitals. Smith suspects that hospital controllers had systematically inflated their 2015 meal estimates.

Required

1. Recall that Topman uses the master-budget capacity utilization to allocate fixed costs and to price meals. What was the effect of production-volume variance on Topman's operating income in 2015?
2. Why might hospital controllers deliberately overestimate their future meal counts?
3. What other evidence should Top Catering's president seek to investigate Smith's concerns?
4. Suggest two specific steps that Smith might take to reduce hospital controllers' incentives to inflate their estimated meal counts.

41 **Absorption, variable, and throughput costing.** Tesla Motors assembles the fully electric Model S-85 automobile at its Fremont, California, plant. The standard variable manufacturing cost per vehicle in 2014 is $58,800, which consists of:

Direct materials	$36,000
Direct manufacturing labor	$10,800
Variable manufacturing overhead	$12,000

Variable manufacturing overhead is allocated to vehicles on the basis of assembly time. The standard assembly time per vehicle is 20 hours.

The Fremont plant is highly automated and has a practical capacity of 4,000 vehicles per month. The budgeted monthly fixed manufacturing overhead is $45 million. Fixed manufacturing overhead is allocated on the basis of the standard assembly time for the budgeted normal capacity utilization of the plant. For 2014, the budgeted normal capacity utilization is 3,000 vehicles per month.

Tesla started production of the Model S-85 in 2014. The actual production and sales figures for the first three months of the year are:

	January	February	March
Production	3,200	2,400	3,800
Sales	2,000	2,900	3,200

Franz Holzhausen is SVP of Tesla and director of the Fremont plant. His compensation includes a bonus that is 0.25% of quarterly operating income, calculated using absorption costing. Tesla prepares absorption-costing income statements monthly, which include an adjustment for the production-volume variance occurring in that month. There are no variable cost variances or fixed overhead spending variances in the first three months of 2014.

The Fremont plant is credited with revenue (net of marketing costs) of $96,000 for the sale of each Tesla S-85 vehicle.

Required

1. Compute (a) the fixed manufacturing cost per unit and (b) the total manufacturing cost per unit.
2. Compute the monthly operating income for January, February, and March under absorption costing. What amount of bonus is paid each month to Franz Holzhausen?
3. How much would the use of variable costing change Holzhausen's bonus each month if the same 0.25% figure were applied to variable-costing operating income?
4. Explain the differences in Holzhausen's bonuses in requirements 2 and 3.
5. How much would the use of throughput costing change Holzhausen's bonus each month if the same 0.25% figure were applied to throughput-costing operating income?
6. What are the different approaches Tesla Motors could take to reduce possible undesirable behavior associated with the use of absorption costing at its Fremont plant?

42 Costing methods and variances, comprehensive. Rob Kapito, the controller of Blackstar Paint Supply Company, has been exploring a variety of internal accounting systems. Rob hopes to get the input of Blackstar's board of directors in choosing one. To prepare for his presentation to the board, Rob applies four different cost accounting methods to the firm's operating data for 2013. The four methods are actual absorption costing, normal absorption costing, standard absorption costing, and standard variable costing.

With the help of a junior accountant, Rob prepares the following alternative income statements:

	A	B	C	D
Sales Revenue	$ 900,000	$ 900,000	$ 900,000	$ 900,000
Cost of Goods Sold	$ 375,000	$ 250,000	$ 420,000	$ 395,000
(+) Variances:				
Direct Materials	15,000	15,000	—	—
Direct Labor	5,000	5,000	—	—
Manufacturing Overhead	25,000	—	—	25,000
(+) Other Costs (All Fixed)	350,000	475,000	350,000	350,000
Total Costs	$ 770,000	$ 745,000	$ 770,000	$ 770,000
Net Income	$ 130,000	$ 155,000	$ 130,000	$ 130,000

Where applicable, Rob allocates both fixed and variable manufacturing overhead using direct labor hours as the driver. Blackstar carries no work-in-process inventory. Standard costs have been stable over time, and Rob writes off all variances to cost of goods sold. For 2013, there was no flexible budget variance for fixed overhead. In addition, the direct labor variance represents a price variance.

Required

1. Match each method below with the appropriate income statement (A, B, C, or D):

   Actual Absorption costing _____
   Normal Absorption costing _____
   Standard Absorption costing _____
   Standard Variable costing _____

2. During 2013, how did Blackstar's level of finished goods inventory change? In other words, is it possible to know whether Blackstar's finished goods inventory increased, decreased, or stayed constant during the year?
3. From the four income statements, can you determine how the actual volume of production during the year compared to the denominator (expected) volume level?
4. Did Blackstar have a favorable or unfavorable variable overhead spending variance during 2013?

Glossary

Absorption costing. Method of inventory costing in which all variable manufacturing costs and all fixed manufacturing costs are included as inventoriable costs.

Direct costing. See *variable costing*.

Downward demand spiral. Pricing context where prices are raised to spread capacity costs over a smaller number of output units. Continuing reduction in the demand for products that occurs when the prices of competitors' products are not met and, as demand drops further, higher and higher unit costs result in more and more reluctance to meet competitors' prices.

Master-budget capacity utilization. The expected level of capacity utilization for the current budget period (typically one year).

Normal capacity utilization. The level of capacity utilization that satisfies average customer demand over a period (say, two to three years) that includes seasonal, cyclical, and trend factors.

Practical capacity. The level of capacity that reduces theoretical capacity by unavoidable operating interruptions such as scheduled maintenance time, shutdowns for holidays, and so on.

Super-variable costing. See *throughput costing*.

Theoretical capacity. The level of capacity based on producing at full efficiency all the time.

Throughput costing. Method of inventory costing in which only variable direct material costs are included as inventoriable costs. Also called *super-variable costing*.

Variable costing. Method of inventory costing in which only all variable manufacturing costs are included as inventoriable costs. Also called *direct costing*.

Photo Credits

Credits are listed in order of appearance.

Photo 1: Bloomberg/Getty Images;
Photo 2: Paul Sakuma/AP Images

Chapter 17

Process Costing

From Chapter 17 of *Cost Accounting: A Managerial Emphasis*, Fifteenth Edition. Charles T. Horngren, Srikant M. Datar, Madhav V. Rajan. Copyright © 2015 by Pearson Education, Inc. All rights reserved.

Process Costing

Many companies use mass-production techniques to produce identical or similar units of a product or service:

Apple (smartphones), Coca-Cola (soft drinks), ExxonMobil (gasoline), JP MorganChase (processing of checks), and Novartis (pharmaceuticals). Managerial accountants at companies like these use process costing because it helps them (1) determine how many units of the product the firm has on hand at the end of an accounting reporting period, (2) evaluate the units' stages of completion, and (3) assign costs to units produced and in inventory. There are different methods for process costing (for example, the FIFO or weighted-average methods) that are based on different assumptions about the flow of product costs. As you learned in your financial accounting class, the choice of method results in different operating income and affects the taxes a company pays and the performance evaluation of managers. At times, variations in international rules and customs also determine the method chosen. In the case of ExxonMobil, differences in inventory accounting rules for the United States versus Europe have a large impact on the company's profits and tax liability.

ExxonMobil and Accounting Differences in the Oil Patch[1]

In 2013, ExxonMobil was ranked second in the *Fortune* 500 annual ranking of the largest U.S. companies, with revenue of $453 billion and more than $44 billion in profits. Believe it or not, however, by one measure ExxonMobil's profits are *understated*.

ExxonMobil, like most U.S. energy companies, uses last-in, first-out (LIFO) accounting for financial reporting. Under LIFO, ExxonMobil records its cost of inventory at the latest price paid for crude oil in the open market, even though it is often selling oil produced at a much lower cost. This increases the company's cost of goods sold, which in turn reduces profit and tax payments.

Assigning costs to inventory is a critical part of process costing, and a company's choice of method can result in substantially different profits. For instance, ExxonMobil's 2012 net income would have been $4.3 billion lower under FIFO. However, if ExxonMobil had used FIFO accounting in prior years, its operating income over the years would have been higher by $21.3 billion. Assuming a marginal tax rate of 35%, this would have resulted in an incremental tax burden of almost $7.5 billion.

It is interesting to note that International Financial Reporting Standards (IFRS) do not permit the use of LIFO accounting. European oil companies such as Royal Dutch Shell and British Petroleum must use the first-in, first-out (FIFO) methodology instead

---

[1] *Source:* Exxon Mobil Corporation, 2012 Annual Report (Irving, TX: Exxon Mobil Corporation, 2013); Izabella Kaminska, "Shell, BP, and the Increasing Cost of Inventory," *Financial Times.* "FT Alphaville" blog (April 29, 2010); David Reilly, "Big Oil's Accounting Methods Fuel Criticism," *Wall Street Journal* (August 8, 2006).

when accounting for inventory, thereby preventing them from receiving the favorable inventory accounting treatment enjoyed by ExxonMobil.

Companies such as ExxonMobil, Kellogg (cereals), and AB InBev (beer) produce many identical or similar units of a product using mass-production techniques. The focus of these companies on individual production processes gives rise to process costing. This chapter describes how companies use process-costing methods to determine the costs of products or services and to value inventory and the cost of goods sold.

Illustrating Process Costing

Learning Objective 1

Identify the situations in which process-costing systems are appropriate

...when masses of identical or similar units are produced

Before examining process costing in more detail, let's briefly discuss the distinction between job costing and process costing. Job-costing and process-costing systems are best viewed as ends of a continuum:

Job-costing system   Process-costing system

Distinct, identifiable units of a product or service (for example, custom-made machines and houses)   Masses of identical or similar units of a product or service (for example, food or chemicals)

In a *process-costing system*, the unit cost of a product or service is obtained by assigning total costs to many identical or similar units of output. In other words, unit costs are calculated by dividing total costs incurred by the number of units of output from the production process. In a manufacturing process-costing setting, each unit receives the same or similar amounts of direct material costs, direct manufacturing labor costs, and indirect manufacturing costs (manufacturing overhead).

The main difference between process costing and job costing is the *extent of averaging* used to compute the unit costs of products or services. In a job-costing system, individual jobs use different quantities of resources, so it would be incorrect to cost each job at the same average production cost. In contrast, when identical or similar units of products or services are mass-produced rather than processed as individual jobs, process costing is used to calculate an average production cost for all units produced. Some processes such as clothes manufacturing have aspects of both process costing (the cost per unit of each operation, such as cutting or sewing, is identical) and job costing (different materials are used in different batches of clothing, say, wool versus cotton). The final section in this chapter describes "hybrid" costing systems that combine elements of both job and process costing.

Consider the following example: Suppose that Pacific Electronics manufactures a variety of cell phone models. These models are assembled in the assembly department. Upon completion, units are transferred to the testing department. We focus on the assembly department process for one model, SG-40. All units of SG-40 are identical and must meet a set of demanding performance specifications. The process-costing system for SG-40 in the assembly department has a single direct-cost category—direct materials—and a single indirect-cost category—conversion costs. Conversion costs are all manufacturing costs other than direct material costs, including manufacturing labor, energy, plant depreciation, and so on. As the following figure shows, direct materials, such as a phone's circuit board, antenna, and microphone, are added at the beginning of the assembly process. Conversion costs are added evenly during assembly.

The following graphic represents these facts:

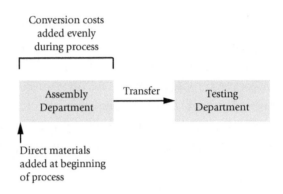

Process-costing systems separate costs into cost categories according to *when costs are introduced into the process.* Often, as in our Pacific Electronics example, only two cost classifications—direct materials and conversion costs—are necessary to assign costs to products. Why only two? Because *all* direct materials are added to the process at one time and all conversion costs generally are added to the process evenly through time. Sometimes the situation is different.

1. If two different direct materials—such as the circuit board and microphone—are added to the process at different times, two different direct-materials categories would be needed to assign these costs to products.

2. If manufacturing labor costs are added to the process at a different time compared to other conversion costs, an additional cost category—direct manufacturing labor costs—would be needed to assign these costs to products.

We illustrate process costing using three cases of increasing complexity:

- **Case 1**—Process costing with zero beginning and zero ending work-in-process inventory of SG-40. (That is, all units are started and fully completed within the accounting period.) *This case presents the most basic concepts of process costing and illustrates the averaging of costs.*

- **Case 2**—Process costing with zero beginning work-in-process inventory and some ending work-in-process inventory of SG-40. (That is, some units of SG-40 started during the accounting period are incomplete at the end of the period.) *This case introduces the five steps of process costing and the concept of equivalent units.*

- **Case 3**—Process costing with both some beginning and some ending work-in-process inventory of SG-40. *This case adds more complexity and illustrates the effects the weighted-average and first-in, first-out (FIFO) methods have on the cost of units completed and the cost of work-in-process inventory.*

Decision Point
Under what conditions is a process-costing system used?

Learning Objective 2
Understand the basic concepts of process-costing and compute average unit costs
...divide total costs by total units in a given accounting period

Case 1: Process Costing with No Beginning or Ending Work-in-Process Inventory

On January 1, 2014, there was no beginning inventory of SG-40 units in the assembly department. During the month of January, Pacific Electronics started, completely assembled, and transferred 400 units to the testing department.

Data for the assembly department for January 2014 are as follows:

Physical Units for January 2014

Work in process, beginning inventory (January 1)	0 units
Started during January	400 units
Completed and transferred out during January	400 units
Work in process, ending inventory (January 31)	0 units

Physical units refer to the number of output units, whether complete or incomplete. In January 2014, all 400 physical units started were completed.

Total Costs for January 2014

Direct materials costs added during January	$32,000
Conversion costs added during January	24,000
Total assembly department costs added during January	$56,000

Pacific Electronics records direct materials costs and conversion costs in the assembly department as these costs are incurred. The cost per unit is then calculated by dividing the total costs incurred in a given accounting period by the total units produced in that period. So, the assembly department cost of an SG-40 is $56,000 ÷ 400 units = $140 per unit:

Direct material cost per unit ($32,000 ÷ 400 units)	$ 80
Conversion cost per unit ($24,000 ÷ 400 units)	60
Assembly department cost per unit	$140

Case 1 applies whenever a company produces a homogeneous product or service but has no incomplete units when each accounting period ends, which is a common situation in service-sector organizations. For example, a bank can adopt this process-costing approach to compute the unit cost of processing 100,000 customer deposits made in a month because each deposit is processed in the same way regardless of the amount of the deposit.

Decision Point

How are average unit costs computed when no inventories are present?

Learning Objective 3

Describe the five steps in process costing

...to assign total costs to units completed and to units in work in process

and calculate equivalent units

...output units adjusted for incomplete units

Case 2: Process Costing with Zero Beginning and Some Ending Work-in-Process Inventory

In February 2014, Pacific Electronics places another 400 units of SG-40 into production. Because all units placed into production in January were completely assembled, there is no beginning inventory of partially completed units in the assembly department on February 1. Some customers order late, so not all units started in February are completed by the end of the month. Only 175 units are completed and transferred to the testing department.

Data for the assembly department for February 2014 are as follows:

		Home	Insert	Page Layout	Formulas	Data	Review	View	

	A	Physical Units (SG-40s) (1)	Direct Materials (2)	Conversion Costs (3)	Total Costs (4) = (2) + (3)
1					
2	Work in process, beginning inventory (February 1)	0			
3	Started during February	400			
4	Completed and transferred out during February	175			
5	Work in process, ending inventory (February 28)	225			
6	Degree of completion of ending work in process		100%	60%	
7	Total costs added during February		$32,000	$18,600	$50,600

The 225 partially assembled units as of February 28, 2014, are fully processed for direct materials because all direct materials in the assembly department are added at the beginning of the assembly process. Conversion costs, however, are added evenly during assembly.

An assembly department supervisor estimates that the partially assembled units are, on average, 60% complete with respect to conversion costs.

The accuracy of the completion estimate of conversion costs depends on the care, skill, and experience of the estimator and the nature of the conversion process. Estimating the degree of completion is usually easier for direct material costs than for conversion costs because the quantity of direct materials needed for a completed unit and the quantity of direct materials in a partially completed unit can be measured more accurately. In contrast, the conversion sequence usually consists of a number of operations, each for a specified period of time, at various steps in the production process.[2] The degree of completion for conversion costs depends on the proportion of the total conversion costs needed to complete one unit (or a batch of production) that has already been incurred on the units still in process.

Department supervisors and line managers are most familiar with the conversion process, so they most often estimate completion rates for conversion costs. However, in some industries, such as semiconductor manufacturing, no exact estimate is possible because manufacturing occurs inside sealed environments that can be opened only when the process is complete. In other settings, such as the textile industry, vast quantities of unfinished products such as shirts and pants make the task of estimation too costly. In these cases, to calculate the conversion costs, managers assume that all work in process in a department is complete to some preset degree (for example, one-third, one-half, or two-thirds).

Because some units are fully assembled and some are only partially assembled, a common metric is needed to compare the work that's been done on them and, more importantly, obtain a total measure of the work done. The concept we will use in this regard is that of *equivalent units*. We will explain this concept in greater detail next as part of the set of five steps required to calculate (1) the cost of fully assembled units in February 2014 and (2) the cost of partially assembled units still in process at the end of that month, for Pacific Electronics. The five steps of process costing are as follows:

Step 1: Summarize the flow of physical units of output.

Step 2: Compute output in terms of equivalent units.

Step 3: Summarize the total costs to account for.

Step 4: Compute the cost per equivalent unit.

Step 5: Assign the total costs to the units completed and to the units in ending work-in-process inventory.

Summarizing the Physical Units and Equivalent Units (Steps 1 and 2)

In **Step 1,** managers track the physical units of output. Recall that physical units are the number of output units, whether complete or incomplete. The physical-units column of Exhibit 1 tracks where the physical units came from (400 units started) and where they went (175 units completed and transferred out and 225 units in ending inventory). Remember that when there is no beginning inventory, the number of units started must equal the sum of units transferred out and ending inventory.

Because not all 400 physical units are fully completed, in **Step 2,** managers compute the output in *equivalent units*, not in *physical units*. **Equivalent units** are a derived measure of output calculated by (1) taking the quantity of each input (factor of production) in units completed and in incomplete units of work in process and (2) converting the quantity of input into the amount of completed output units that could be produced with that quantity of input. To see what is meant by equivalent units, suppose that during a month, 50 physical units were started but not completed. Managers estimate that the 50 units in ending inventory are 70% complete for conversion costs. Now, suppose all the conversion costs represented in these units were used to make fully completed units instead. How many completed units would that have resulted in? The answer is 35 units.

[2] For example, consider the conventional tanning process for converting hide to leather. Obtaining 250–300 kg of leather requires putting one metric ton of raw hide through as many as 15 steps: from soaking, liming, and pickling to tanning, dyeing, and fatliquoring, the step in which oils are introduced into the skin before the leather is dried.

Exhibit 1

	Home	Insert	Page Layout	Formulas	Data	Review	View		
	A				B	C		D	
1					(Step 1)	(Step 2)			
2						Equivalent Units			
3	Flow of Production				Physical Units	Direct Materials		Conversion Costs	
4	Work in process, beginning				0				
5	Started during current period				400				
6	To account for				400				
7	Completed and transferred out during current period				175	175		175	
8	Work in process, ending^a				225				
9	(225 × 100%; 225 × 60%)					225		135	
10	Accounted for				400				
11	Equivalent units of work done in current period					400		310	
12									
13	^aDegree of completion in this department; direct materials, 100%; conversion costs, 60%.								

Summarize the Flow of Physical Units and Compute Output in Equivalent Units for the Assembly Department for February 2014

Why? Because the conversion costs incurred to produce 50 units that are each 70% complete could have instead generated 35 (0.70×50) units that are 100% complete. The 35 units are referred to as *equivalent units* of output. That is, in terms of the work done on them, the 50 partially completed units are considered equivalent to 35 completed units.

Note that equivalent units are calculated separately for each input (such as direct materials and conversion costs). Moreover, every completed unit, by definition, is composed of one equivalent unit of each input required to make it. This chapter focuses on equivalent-unit calculations in manufacturing settings, but the calculations can be used in nonmanufacturing settings as well. For example, universities convert their part-time student enrollments into "full-time student equivalents" to get a better measure of faculty–student ratios over time. Without this adjustment, an increase in part-time students would lead to a lower faculty–student ratio. This would erroneously suggest a decline in the quality of instruction when, in fact, part-time students take fewer academic courses and do not need the same number of instructors as full-time students do.

When calculating the equivalent units in Step 2, focus on quantities. Disregard dollar amounts until after the equivalent units are computed. In the Pacific Electronics example, all 400 physical units—the 175 fully assembled units and the 225 partially assembled units—are 100% complete with respect to direct materials because all direct materials are added in the assembly department at the start of the process. Therefore, Exhibit 1 shows that the output is 400 *equivalent units* for direct materials: 175 equivalent units for the 175 physical units assembled and transferred out and 225 equivalent units for the 225 physical units in ending work-in-process inventory.

The 175 fully assembled units have also incurred all of their conversion costs. The 225 partially assembled units in ending work in process are 60% complete (on average). Therefore, their conversion costs are *equivalent* to the conversion costs incurred by 135 fully assembled units ($225 \times 60\% = 135$). Hence, Exhibit 1 shows that the output is a total of 310 *equivalent units* for the conversion costs: 175 equivalent units for the 175 physical units assembled and transferred out and 135 equivalent units for the 225 physical units in ending work-in-process inventory.

Calculating Product Costs (Steps 3, 4, and 5)

Exhibit 2 shows Steps 3, 4, and 5. Together, they are called the *production cost worksheet.*

In **Step 3**, managers summarize the total costs to account for. Because the beginning balance of work-in-process inventory is zero on February 1, the total costs to account for (that is, the total charges or debits to the Work in Process—Assembly account) consist only of costs added during February: $32,000 in direct materials and $18,600 in conversion costs, for a total of $50,600.

Exhibit 2	Summarize the Total Costs to Account For, Compute the Cost per Equivalent Unit, and Assign Costs to the Units Completed and Units in Ending Work-in-Process Inventory for the Assembly Department for February 2014

	A	B	C	D	E
			Total Production Costs	Direct Materials	Conversion Costs
1					
2	(Step 3)	Costs added during February	$50,600	$32,000	$18,600
3		Total costs to account for	$50,600	$32,000	$18,600
4					
5	(Step 4)	Costs added in current period	$50,600	$32,000	$18,600
6		Divide by equivalent units of work done in current period (Exhibit 17-1)		÷ 400	÷ 310
7		Cost per equivalent unit		$ 80	$ 60
8					
9	(Step 5)	Assignment of costs:			
10		Completed and transferred out (175 units)	$24,500	$(175^a \times \$80)$	$+ (175^a \times \$60)$
11		Work in process, ending (225 units):	26,100	$(225^b \times \$80)$	$+ (135^b \times \$60)$
12		Total costs accounted for	$50,600	$32,000	$+ $18,600
13					
14	[a] Equivalent units completed and transferred out from Exhibit 17-1, step 2.				
15	[b] Equivalent units in ending work in process from Exhibit 17-1, step 2.				

In **Step 4**, managers calculate the cost per equivalent unit separately for the direct materials costs and conversion costs. This is done by dividing the direct material costs and conversion costs added during February by their related quantities of equivalent units of work done in February (as calculated in Exhibit 1).

To see why it is important to understand equivalent units in unit-cost calculations, compare the conversion costs for January and February 2014. The $18,600 in total conversion costs for the 400 units worked on during February are lower than the $24,000 in total conversion costs for the 400 units worked on in January. However, the conversion costs to fully assemble a unit are the same: $60 per unit in both January and February. Total conversion costs are lower in February because fewer equivalent units of conversion-costs work were completed in that month than in January (310 in February versus 400 in January). Note that using physical units instead of equivalent units would have resulted in a conversion cost per unit of just $46.50 ($18,600 ÷ 400 units) for February, which is down from $60 in January. This incorrect costing might lead the firm's managers to believe that the assembly department achieved efficiencies that lowered the conversion costs of the SG-40 when in fact the costs had not declined.

Once the cost per equivalent unit is calculated for both the direct materials and conversion costs, managers can move to **Step 5**: assigning the total direct materials and conversion costs to the units completed and transferred out and to the units still in process at the end of February 2014. As Exhibit 2 shows, this is done by multiplying the equivalent output units for each input by the cost per equivalent unit. For example, the total costs (direct materials and conversion costs assigned to the 225 physical units in ending work-in-process inventory are as follows:

Direct material costs of 225 equivalent units (calculated in Step 2) ×	
$80 cost per equivalent unit of direct materials (calculated in Step 4)	$18,000
Conversion costs of 135 equivalent units (calculated in Step 2) ×	
$60 cost per equivalent unit of conversion costs (calculated in Step 4)	8,100
Total cost of ending work-in-process inventory	$26,100

Note that the total costs to account for in Step 3 ($50,600) equal the total costs accounted for in Step 5.

Journal Entries

Journal entries in process-costing systems are similar to the entries made in job-costing systems with respect to direct materials and conversion costs. The main difference is that, when process costing is used, there is one Work in Process account for each process. In our example, there are accounts for (1) Work in Process—Assembly and (2) Work in Process—Testing. Pacific Electronics purchases direct materials as needed. These materials are delivered directly to the assembly department. Using the amounts from Exhibit 2, the summary journal entries for February are as follows:

1. Work in Process—Assembly   32,000
       Accounts Payable Control   32,000
   To record the direct materials purchased and used in production during February.
2. Work in Process—Assembly   18,600
       Various accounts such as Wages Payable Control and Accumulated Depreciation   18,600
   To record the conversion costs for February; examples include energy, manufacturing supplies, all manufacturing labor, and plant depreciation.
3. Work in Process—Testing   24,500
       Work in Process—Assembly   24,500
   To record the cost of goods completed and transferred from assembly to testing during February.

Exhibit 3 shows a general framework for the flow of costs through T-accounts. Notice how entry 3 for $24,500 follows the physical transfer of goods from the assembly to the testing department. The T-account Work in Process—Assembly shows February 2014's ending balance of $26,100, which is the beginning balance of Work in Process—Assembly in March 2014. It is important to ensure that all costs have been accounted for and that the ending inventory of the current month is the beginning inventory of the following month.

    Earlier, we discussed the importance of accurately estimating the completion percentages for conversion costs. We can now calculate the effect of incorrect estimates of the degree of completion of units in ending work in process. Suppose, for example, that Pacific

> **Decision Point**
>
> What are the five steps in a process-costing system and how are equivalent units calculated?

| Exhibit 3 | Flow of Costs in a Process-Costing System for the Assembly Department for February 2014 |

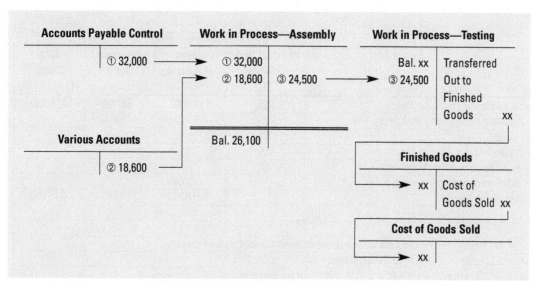

Electronics' managers overestimate the degree of completion for conversion costs at 80% instead of 60%. The computations would change as follows:

- Exhibit 1, Step 2
    Equivalent units of conversion costs in ending Work in Process—Assembly = 80% × 225 = 180
    Equivalent units of conversion costs for work done in the current period = 175 + 180 = 355

- Exhibit 2, Step 4
    Cost per equivalent unit of conversion costs = $18,600 ÷ 355 = $52.39
    Cost per equivalent unit of direct materials is the same, $80

- Exhibit 2, Step 5
    Cost of 175 units of goods completed and transferred out = 175 × $80 + 175 × $52.39 = $23,168.25

This amount is lower than the $24,500 of costs assigned to goods completed and transferred out calculated in Exhibit 2. Overestimating the degree of completion decreases the costs assigned to goods transferred out and eventually to cost of goods sold and increases operating income.

Managers must ensure that department supervisors avoid introducing personal biases into estimates of degrees of completion. To show better performance, for example, a department supervisor might report a higher degree of completion resulting in overstated operating income. If performance for the period is very good, the department supervisor may be tempted to report a lower degree of completion, reducing income in the current period. This has the effect of reducing the costs carried in ending inventory and the costs carried to the following year in beginning inventory. In other words, estimates of degree of completion can help to smooth earnings from one period to the next.

To guard against the possibility of bias, managers should ask supervisors specific questions about the process they followed to prepare estimates. Top management should always emphasize obtaining the correct answer, regardless of how it affects reported performance. This emphasis drives ethical actions throughout the organization.

Learning Objective 4

Use the weighted-average method of process costing

...assigns costs based on total costs and equivalent units completed to date

and the first-in, first-out (FIFO) method of process costing

...to assign costs based on costs and equivalent units of work done in the current period

Case 3: Process Costing with Some Beginning and Some Ending Work-in-Process Inventory

At the beginning of March 2014, Pacific Electronics had 225 partially assembled SG-40 units in the assembly department. It started production of another 275 units in March. The data for the assembly department for March are as follows:

	A	B	C	D	E
1		Physical Units (SG-40s) (1)	Direct Materials (2)	Conversion Costs (3)	Total Costs (4) = (2) + (3)
2	Work in process, beginning inventory (March 1)	225	$18,000[a]	$8,100[a]	$26,100
3	Degree of completion of beginning work in process		100%	60%	
4	Started during March	275			
5	Completed and transferred out during March	400			
6	Work in process, ending inventory (March 31)	100			
7	Degree of completion of ending work in process		100%	50%	
8	Total costs added during March		$19,800	$16,380	$36,180
9					
10					
11	[a]Work in process, beginning inventory (equals work in process, ending inventory for February)				
12	Direct materials: 225 physical units × 100% completed × $80 per unit = $18,000				
13	Conversion costs: 225 physical units × 60% completed × $60 per unit = $8,100				

Pacific Electronics now has incomplete units in both beginning work-in-process inventory and ending work-in-process inventory for March 2014. We can still use the five steps described earlier to calculate (1) the cost of units completed and transferred out and (2) the cost of ending work-in-process inventory. To assign costs to each of these categories, however, we first need to choose an inventory-valuation method. We next describe the five-step approach for two key methods—the *weighted-average method* and the *first-in, first-out method*. These different valuation methods produce different costs for the units completed and for the ending work-in-process inventory when the unit cost of inputs changes from one period to the next.

Weighted-Average Method

The **weighted-average process-costing method** calculates the cost per equivalent unit of all *work done to date* (regardless of the accounting period in which it was done) and assigns this cost to equivalent units completed and transferred out of the process and to equivalent units in ending work-in-process inventory. The weighted-average cost is the total of all costs entering the Work in Process account (whether the costs are from beginning work in process or from work started during the current period) divided by total equivalent units of work done to date. We now describe the weighted-average method using the five-step procedure.

Step 1: **Summarize the Flow of Physical Units of Output.** The physical-units column in Exhibit 4 shows where the units came from—225 units from beginning inventory and 275 units started during the current period—and where the units went—400 units completed and transferred out and 100 units in ending inventory.

Step 2: **Compute the Output in Terms of Equivalent Units.** We use the relationship shown in the following equation:

$$\begin{array}{l}\text{Equivalent units} \\ \text{in beginning work} \\ \text{in process}\end{array} + \begin{array}{l}\text{Equivalent units} \\ \text{of work done in} \\ \text{current period}\end{array} = \begin{array}{l}\text{Equivalent units} \\ \text{completed and transferred} \\ \text{out in current period}\end{array} + \begin{array}{l}\text{Equivalent units} \\ \text{in ending work} \\ \text{in process}\end{array}$$

Although we are interested in calculating the left side of the preceding equation, it is easier to calculate this sum using the equation's right side: (1) the equivalent units completed and transferred out in the current period plus (2) the equivalent units in ending work in process. *Note that the stage of completion of the current-period beginning work in process is not used in this computation.*

The equivalent-units columns in Exhibit 4 show the equivalent units of work done to date: 500 equivalent units of direct materials and 450 equivalent units of conversion

Exhibit 4

Summarize the Flow of Physical Units and Compute Output in Equivalent Units Using the Weighted-Average Method for the Assembly Department for March 2014

	A	B	C	D
		(Step 1)	(Step 2)	
1			Equivalent Units	
2				
3	**Flow of Production**	**Physical Units**	**Direct Materials**	**Conversion Costs**
4	Work in process, beginning (given)	225		
5	Started during current period (given)	275		
6	To account for	500		
7	Completed and transferred out during current period	400	400	400
8	Work in process, ending[a] (given)	100		
9	(100 × 100%; 100 × 50%)		100	50
10	Accounted for	500		
11	Equivalent units of work done to date		500	450
12				
13	[a]Degree of completion in this department; direct materials, 100%; conversion costs, 50%.			

Exhibit 5	Summarize the Total Costs to Account For, Compute the Cost per Equivalent Unit, and Assign Costs to the Units Completed and Units in Ending Work-in-Process Inventory Using the Weighted-Average Method for the Assembly Department for March 2014

	Home	Insert	Page Layout	Formulas	Data	Review	View		
	A	B					C	D	E
1							Total Production Costs	Direct Materials	Conversion Costs
2	(Step 3)	Work in process, beginning (given, p. 672)					$26,100	$18,000	$ 8,100
3		Costs added in current period (given, p. 672)					36,180	19,800	16,380
4		Total costs to account for					$62,280	$37,800	$24,480
5									
6	(Step 4)	Costs incurred to date						$37,800	$24,480
7		Divide by equivalent units of work done to date (Exhibit 17-4)						÷ 500	÷ 450
8		Cost per equivalent unit of work done to date						$ 75.60	$ 54.40
9									
10	(Step 5)	Assignment of costs:							
11		Completed and transferred out (400 units)					$52,000	(400[a] × $75.60) +	(400[a] × $54.40)
12		Work in process, ending (100 units):					10,280	(100[b] × $75.60) +	(50[b] × $54.40)
13		Total costs accounted for					$62,280	$37,800 +	$24,480
14									
15	[a]Equivalent units completed and transferred out from Exhibit 17-4, Step 2.								
16	[b]Equivalent units in ending work in process from Exhibit 17-4, Step 2.								

costs. All completed and transferred-out units are 100% complete with regard to both their direct materials and conversion costs. Partially completed units in ending work in process are 100% complete with regard to their direct materials costs (because the direct materials are introduced at the beginning of the process) and 50% complete with regard to their conversion costs, based on estimates from the assembly department manager.

Step 3: **Summarize the Total Costs to Account For.** Exhibit 5 presents Step 3. The total costs to account for in March 2014 are described in the example data:

Beginning work in process (direct materials, $18,000 + conversion costs, $8,100)	$26,100
Costs added during March (direct materials, $19,800 + conversion costs, $16,380)	36,180
Total costs to account for in March	$62,280

Step 4: **Compute the Cost per Equivalent Unit.** Exhibit 5, Step 4, shows how the weighted-average cost per equivalent unit for direct materials and conversion costs is computed. The weighted-average cost per equivalent unit is obtained by dividing the sum of the costs for beginning work in process plus the costs for work done in the current period by the total equivalent units of work done to date. For example, we calculate the weighted-average conversion cost per equivalent unit in Exhibit 5 as follows:

Total conversion costs (beginning work in process, $8,100 + work done in current period, $16,380)	$24,480
Divided by the total equivalent units of work done to date (equivalent units of conversion costs in beginning work in process and in work done in current period)	÷450
Weighted-average cost per equivalent unit	$ 54.40

Step 5: Assign Costs to the Units Completed and to Units in Ending Work-in-Process Inventory. Step 5 in Exhibit 5 takes the equivalent units completed and transferred out and the equivalent units in ending work in process (calculated in Exhibit 4, Step 2) and assigns dollar amounts to them using the weighted-average cost per equivalent unit for the direct materials and conversion costs calculated in Step 4. For example, the total costs of the 100 physical units in ending work in process are as follows:

Direct materials:

100 equivalent units × weighted-average cost per equivalent unit of $75.60	$ 7,560

Conversion costs:

50 equivalent units × weighted-average cost per equivalent unit of $54.40	2,720
Total costs of ending work in process	$10,280

The following table summarizes total costs to account for ($62,280) and how they are accounted for in Exhibit 5. The arrows indicate that the costs of units completed and transferred out and units in ending work in process are calculated using weighted-average total costs obtained after merging costs of beginning work in process and costs added in the current period.

Costs to Account For		Costs Accounted for Calculated on a Weighted-Average Basis	
Beginning work in process	$26,100	Completed and transferred out	$52,000
Costs added in current period	36,180	Ending work in process	10,280
Total costs to account for	$62,280	Total costs accounted for	$62,280

Before proceeding, review Exhibits 4 and 5 to check your understanding of the weighted-average method. Note: Exhibit 4 deals with only physical and equivalent units, not costs. Exhibit 5 shows the cost amounts.

Using amounts from Exhibit 5, the summary journal entries under the weighted-average method for March 2014 are as follows:

1. Work in Process—Assembly	19,800	
Accounts Payable Control		19,800

To record the direct materials purchased and used in production during March.

2. Work in Process—Assembly	16,380	
Various accounts such as Wages Payable Control and Accumulated Depreciation		16,380

To record the conversion costs for March; examples include energy, manufacturing supplies, all manufacturing labor, and plant depreciation.

3. Work in Process—Testing	52,000	
Work in Process—Assembly		52,000

To record the cost of goods completed and transferred from assembly to testing during March.

The T-account Work in Process—Assembly, under the weighted-average method, is as follows:

Work in Process—Assembly

Beginning inventory, March 1	26,100	③ Completed and transferred	52,000
① Direct materials	19,800	out to Work in Process—	
② Conversion costs	16,380	Testing	
Ending inventory, March 31	10,280		

First-In, First-Out Method

The **first-in, first-out (FIFO) process-costing method** (1) assigns the cost of the previous accounting period's equivalent units in beginning work-in-process inventory to the first units completed and transferred out of the process and (2) assigns the cost of equivalent units worked on during the *current* period first to complete the beginning inventory, next to start and complete new units, and finally to units in ending work-in-process inventory. The FIFO method assumes that the earliest equivalent units in work in process are completed first.

A distinctive feature of the FIFO process-costing method is that work done on the beginning inventory before the current period is kept separate from work done in the current period. The costs incurred and units produced in the current period are used to calculate the cost per equivalent unit of work done in the current period. In contrast, the equivalent-unit and cost-per-equivalent-unit calculations under the weighted-average method *merge* the units and costs in beginning inventory with the units and costs of work done in the current period.

We now describe the FIFO method using the five-step procedure.

Step 1: **Summarize the Flow of Physical Units of Output.** Exhibit 6, Step 1, traces the flow of the physical units of production and explains how they are calculated under the FIFO method.

- The first physical units assumed to be completed and transferred out during the period are 225 units from beginning work-in-process inventory.
- The March data indicate that 400 physical units were completed during March. The FIFO method assumes that of these 400 units, 175 units (400 units − 225 units from beginning work-in-process inventory) must have been started and completed during March.
- The ending work-in-process inventory consists of 100 physical units—the 275 physical units started minus the 175 units that were started and completed.
- The physical units "to account for" equal the physical units "accounted for" (500 units).

Step 2: **Compute the Output in Terms of Equivalent Units.** Exhibit 6 also presents the computations for Step 2 under the FIFO method. *The equivalent-unit calculations for each cost category focus on equivalent units of work done in the current period (March) only.*

Exhibit 6

Summarize the Flow of Physical Units and Compute Output in Equivalent Units Using the FIFO Method for the Assembly Department for March 2014

	Home Insert Page Layout Formulas Data Review View			
	A	B	C	D
1		(Step 1)	(Step 2)	
2			Equivalent Units	
3	**Flow of Production**	**Physical Units**	**Direct Materials**	**Conversion Costs**
4	Work in process, beginning (given, p. 673)	225	(work done before current period)	
5	Started during current period (given, p. 673)	275		
6	To account for	500		
7	Completed and transferred out during current period:			
8	From beginning work in process[a]	225		
9	[225 × (100% − 100%); 225 × (100% − 60%)]		0	90
10	Started and completed	175[b]		
11	(175 × 100%; 175 × 100%)		175	175
12	Work in process, ending[c] (given, p. 673)	100		
13	(100 × 100%; 100 × 50%)		100	50
14	Accounted for	500		
15	Equivalent units of work done in current period		275	315
16				
17	[a]Degree of completion in this department; direct materials, 100%; conversion costs, 60%.			
18	[b]400 physical units completed and transferred out minus 225 physical units completed and			
19	transferred out from beginning work-in-process inventory.			
20	[c]Degree of completion in this department: direct materials, 100%; conversion costs, 50%.			

Under the FIFO method, the equivalent units of work done in March on the beginning work-in-process inventory equal 225 physical units times *the percentage of work remaining to be done in March to complete these units*: 0% for direct materials, because the beginning work in process is 100% complete for direct materials, and 40% for conversion costs, because the beginning work in process is 60% complete for conversion costs. The results are 0 (0% × 225) equivalent units of work for direct materials and 90 (40% × 225) equivalent units of work for conversion costs.

The equivalent units of work done on the 175 physical units started and completed equals 175 units times 100% for both direct materials and conversion costs because all work on these units is done in the current period.

The equivalent units of work done on the 100 units of ending work in process equal 100 physical units times 100% for direct materials (because all direct materials for these units are added in the current period) and 50% for conversion costs (because 50% of the conversion-costs work on these units is done in the current period).

Step 3: Summarize the Total Costs to Account For. Exhibit 7 presents Step 3 and summarizes the $62,280 in total costs to account for in March 2014 (the costs of the beginning work in process, $26,100, and the costs added in the current period, $36,180).

Step 4: Compute the Cost per Equivalent Unit. Exhibit 7 shows the Step 4 computation of the cost per equivalent unit of *work done in the current period only* for the direct materials and conversion costs. For example, the conversion cost per equivalent

Exhibit 7	Summarize the Total Costs to Account For, Compute the Cost per Equivalent Unit, and Assign Costs to the Units Completed and Units in Ending Work-in-Process Inventory Using the FIFO Method for the Assembly Department for March 2014

	A	B	C	D	E
			Total Production Costs	Direct Material	Conversion Costs
1					
2	(Step 3)	Work in process, beginning (given, p. 672)	$26,100	$18,000	$ 8,100
3		Costs added in current period (given, p. 672)	36,180	19,800	16,380
4		Total costs to account for	$62,280	$37,800	$24,480
5					
6	(Step 4)	Costs added in current period		$19,800	$16,380
7		Divide by equivalent units of work done in current period (Exhibit 17-6)		÷ 275	÷ 315
8		Cost per equivalent unit of work done in current period		$ 72	$ 52
9					
10	(Step 5)	Assignment of costs:			
11		Completed and transferred out (400 units):			
12		Work in process, beginning (225 units)	$26,100	$18,000 + $8,100	
13		Costs added to beginning work in process in current period	4,680	(0[a] × $72) + (90[a] × $52)	
14		Total from beginning inventory	30,780		
15		Started and completed (175 units)	21,700	(175[b] × $72) + (175[b] × $52)	
16		Total costs of units completed and transferred out	52,480		
17		Work in process, ending (100 units):	9,800	(100[c] × $72) + (50[c] × $52)	
18		Total costs accounted for	$62,280	$37,800 + $24,480	
19					
20		[a]Equivalent units used to complete beginning work in process from Exhibit 17-6, Step 2.			
21		[b]Equivalent units started and completed from Exhibit 17-6, Step 2.			
22		[c]Equivalent units in ending work in process from Exhibit 17-6, Step 2.			

unit of $52 is obtained by dividing the current-period conversion costs of $16,380 by the current-period conversion-costs equivalent units of 315.

Step 5: Assign Costs to the Units Completed and Units in Ending Work-in-Process Inventory. Exhibit 7 shows the assignment of costs under the FIFO method. The costs of work done in the current period are assigned (1) first to the additional work done to complete the beginning work-in-process inventory, then (2) to work done on units started and completed during the current period, and finally (3) to ending work-in-process inventory. *Step 5 takes each quantity of equivalent units calculated in Exhibit 6, Step 2, and assigns dollar amounts to them (using the cost-per-equivalent-unit calculations in Step 4).* The goal is to use the cost of work done in the current period to determine the total costs of all units completed from beginning inventory and from work started and completed in the current period and the costs of ending work-in-process inventory.

Of the 400 completed units, 225 units are from beginning inventory and 175 units are started and completed during March. The FIFO method starts by assigning the costs of the beginning work-in-process inventory of $26,100 to the first units completed and transferred out. As we saw in Step 2, an additional 90 equivalent units of conversion costs are needed to complete these units in the current period. The current-period conversion cost per equivalent unit is $52, so $4,680 (90 equivalent units × $52 per equivalent unit) of additional costs are incurred to complete the beginning inventory. The total production costs for units in beginning inventory are $26,100 + $4,680 = $30,780. The 175 units started and completed in the current period consist of 175 equivalent units of direct materials and 175 equivalent units of conversion costs. These units are costed at the cost per equivalent unit in the current period (direct materials, $72, and conversion costs, $52) for a total production cost of $21,700 [175 × ($72 + $52)].

Under FIFO, the ending work-in-process inventory comes from units that were started but not fully completed during the current period. The total costs of the 100 partially assembled physical units in ending work in process are as follows:

Direct materials:	
100 equivalent units × $72 cost per equivalent unit in March	$7,200
Conversion costs:	
50 equivalent units × $52 cost per equivalent unit in March	2,600
Total cost of work in process on March 31	$9,800

The following table summarizes the total costs to account for and the costs accounted for under FIFO, which are $62,280 in Exhibit 7. Notice how the FIFO method keeps separate the layers of the beginning work-in-process costs and the costs added in the current period. The arrows indicate where the costs in each layer go—that is, to units completed and transferred out or to ending work in process. Be sure to include the costs of the beginning work-in-process inventory ($26,100) when calculating the costs of units completed.

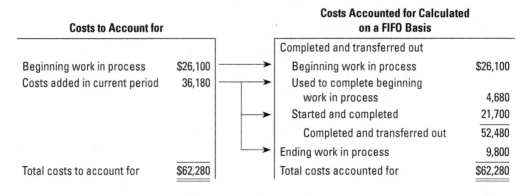

Costs to Account for			Costs Accounted for Calculated on a FIFO Basis	
			Completed and transferred out	
Beginning work in process	$26,100		Beginning work in process	$26,100
Costs added in current period	36,180		Used to complete beginning work in process	4,680
			Started and completed	21,700
			Completed and transferred out	52,480
			Ending work in process	9,800
Total costs to account for	$62,280		Total costs accounted for	$62,280

Before proceeding, review Exhibits 6 and 7 to check your understanding of the FIFO method. Note: Exhibit 6 deals with only physical and equivalent units, not costs. Exhibit 7 shows the cost amounts.

The journal entries under the FIFO method are identical to the journal entries under the weighted-average method except for one difference. The entry to record the cost of goods completed and transferred out would be $52,480 under the FIFO method instead of $52,000 under the weighted-average method.

Keep in mind that FIFO is applied within each department to compile the cost of units *transferred out*. As a practical matter, however, units *transferred in* during a given period usually are carried at a single average unit cost. For example, in the preceding example, the assembly department uses FIFO to distinguish between monthly batches of production. The resulting average cost of each SG-40 unit transferred out of the assembly department is $52,480 ÷ 400 units = $131.20. The testing department, however, costs these units (which consist of costs incurred in both February and March) at one average unit cost ($131.20 in this example). If this averaging were not done, the attempt to track costs on a pure FIFO basis throughout a series of processes would be cumbersome. As a result, the FIFO method should really be called a *modified* or *department* FIFO method.

Comparing the Weighted-Average and FIFO Methods

Consider the summary of the costs assigned to units completed and to units still in process under the weighted-average and FIFO process-costing methods in our example for March 2014:

	Weighted Average (from Exhibit 5)	FIFO (from Exhibit 7)	Difference
Cost of units completed and transferred out	$52,000	$52,480	+ $480
Work in process, ending	10,280	9,800	− $480
Total costs accounted for	$62,280	$62,280	

The weighted-average ending inventory is higher than the FIFO ending inventory by $480, or 4.9% ($480 ÷ $9,800 = 0.049, or 4.9%). This would be a significant difference when aggregated over the many thousands of products Pacific Electronics makes. When completed units are sold, the weighted-average method in our example leads to a lower cost of goods sold and, therefore, higher operating income than the FIFO method does. To see why, recall the data. For the beginning work-in-process inventory, the direct materials cost per equivalent unit is $80 and the conversion cost per equivalent unit is $60. These costs are greater, respectively, than the $72 direct materials cost and the $52 conversion cost per equivalent unit of work done during the current period. The current-period costs could be lower due to a decline in the prices of direct materials and conversion-cost inputs or as a result of Pacific Electronics becoming more efficient in its processes by using smaller quantities of inputs per unit of output or both.

FIFO assumes that (1) all the higher-cost units from the previous period in beginning work in process are the first to be completed and transferred out of the process and (2) the ending work in process consists of only the lower-cost current-period units. The weighted-average method, however, smooths out the cost per equivalent unit by assuming that (1) more of the lower-cost units are completed and transferred out and (2) some of the higher-cost units are placed in ending work in process. The decline in the current-period cost per equivalent unit results in a lower cost of units completed and transferred out and a higher ending work-in-process inventory under the weighted-average method relative to FIFO.

Managers use information from process-costing systems to make pricing and product-mix decisions and understand how well a firm's processes are performing. FIFO provides managers with information about changes in the costs per unit from one period to the next. Managers can use this data to adjust selling prices based on current conditions (for example, based on the $72 direct material cost and $52 conversion cost in March). The managers can also more easily evaluate the firm's cost performance relative to either a budget or the previous period (for example, both unit direct materials and conversion costs have declined relative to the prior period). By focusing on the work done and the costs of work done during the current period, the FIFO method provides valuable information for these planning and control purposes.

The weighted-average method merges unit costs from different accounting periods, obscuring period-to-period comparisons. For example, the weighted-average method would lead managers at Pacific Electronics to make decisions based on the $75.60 direct materials and $54.40 conversion costs, rather than the costs of $72 and $52 prevailing in the current period. However, costs are relatively easy to compute using the weighted-average method, and it results in a more-representative average unit cost when input prices fluctuate markedly from month to month.

The cost of units completed and, hence, a firm's operating income differ materially between the weighted-average and FIFO methods when (1) the direct materials or conversion cost per equivalent unit varies significantly from period to period and (2) the physical-inventory levels of the work in process are large relative to the total number of units transferred out of the process. As changes in unit costs and inventory levels across periods decrease, the difference in the costs of units completed under the weighted-average and FIFO methods also decreases.[3]

When the cost of units completed under the weighted-average and FIFO methods differs substantially, which method should a manager choose? In a period of falling prices, as in the Pacific Electronics case, the higher cost of goods sold under the FIFO method will lead to lower operating income and lower tax payments, saving the company cash and increasing the company's value. FIFO is the preferred choice, but managers may not make this choice. If the manager's compensation, for instance, is based on operating income, the manager may prefer the weighted-average method, which increases operating income even though it results in higher tax payments. Top managers must carefully design compensation plans to encourage managers to take actions that increase a company's value. For example, the compensation plan might reward after-tax cash flow metrics, in addition to operating income metrics, to align decision making and performance evaluation.

Occasionally, choosing a process-costing method can be more difficult. Suppose, for example, that by using FIFO a company would violate its debt covenants (agreements between a company and its creditors that the company will maintain certain financial ratios) resulting in its loans coming due. In this case, a manager may prefer the weighted-average method even though it results in higher taxes because the company does not have the liquidity to repay its loans.

In a period of rising prices, the weighted-average method will decrease taxes because cost of goods sold will be higher and operating income lower. Recall the vignette at the start of this chapter that describes how ExxonMobil uses the last-in, first-out (LIFO) method (not presented in this chapter) to save taxes.[4]

Finally, how is activity-based costing related to process costing? Like activity-based processing, each process—assembly, testing, and so on—can be considered a different (production) activity. However, no additional activities need to be identified within each process to use process costing. That's because products are homogeneous and use the resources of each process in a uniform way. The bottom line is that activity-based costing has less applicability in process-costing environments, especially when compared to the significant role it plays in job costing. *The appendix illustrates the use of the standard costing method for the assembly department.*

Decision Point

What are the weighted-average and first-in, first-out (FIFO) methods of process costing? Under what conditions will they yield different levels of operating income?

---

[3] For example, suppose the beginning work-in-process inventory for March was 125 physical units (instead of 225), and suppose the costs per equivalent unit of work done in the current period (March) were direct materials, $75, and conversion costs, $55. Assume that all other data for March are the same as in our example. In this case, the cost of units completed and transferred out would be $52,833 under the weighted-average method and $53,000 under the FIFO method. The work-in-process ending inventory would be $10,417 under the weighted-average method and $10,250 under the FIFO method (calculations not shown). These differences are much smaller than in the chapter example. The weighted-average ending inventory is higher than the FIFO ending inventory by only $167 ($10,417 − $10,250), or 1.6% ($167 ÷ $10,250 = 0.016), compared with 4.9% higher in the chapter example.

[4] Students not familiar with the LIFO method need only note that in a period of rising prices, the LIFO method reduces operating income and taxes even more than the weighted-average method.

Transferred-In Costs in Process Costing

Learning Objective 5

Apply process-costing methods to situations with transferred-in costs

...using weighted-average and FIFO methods

Many process-costing systems have two or more departments or processes in the production cycle. As units move from department to department, the related costs are also transferred by monthly journal entries. **Transferred-in costs** (also called **previous-department costs**) are costs incurred in previous departments that are carried forward as the product's cost when it moves to a subsequent process in the production cycle.

We now extend our Pacific Electronics example to the testing department. As the assembly process is completed, the assembly department of Pacific Electronics immediately transfers SG-40 units to the testing department. Conversion costs are added evenly during the testing department's process. At the *end of the testing process*, the units receive additional direct materials, including crating and other packing materials to prepare them for shipment. As units are completed in testing, they are immediately transferred to Finished Goods. The testing department costs consist of transferred-in costs, as well as direct materials and conversion costs added during testing.

The following diagram represents these facts:

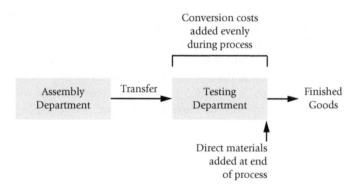

The data for the testing department for March 2014 are as follows:

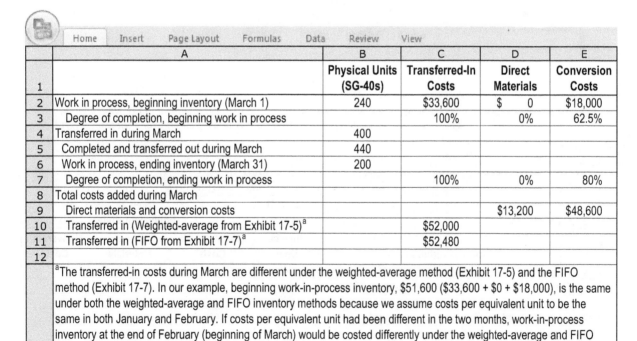

	Physical Units (SG-40s)	Transferred-In Costs	Direct Materials	Conversion Costs
2	Work in process, beginning inventory (March 1)	240	$33,600	$ 0	$18,000
3	Degree of completion, beginning work in process		100%	0%	62.5%
4	Transferred in during March	400			
5	Completed and transferred out during March	440			
6	Work in process, ending inventory (March 31)	200			
7	Degree of completion, ending work in process		100%	0%	80%
8	Total costs added during March				
9	Direct materials and conversion costs			$13,200	$48,600
10	Transferred in (Weighted-average from Exhibit 17-5)[a]		$52,000		
11	Transferred in (FIFO from Exhibit 17-7)[a]		$52,480		
12					

[a]The transferred-in costs during March are different under the weighted-average method (Exhibit 17-5) and the FIFO method (Exhibit 17-7). In our example, beginning work-in-process inventory, $51,600 ($33,600 + $0 + $18,000), is the same under both the weighted-average and FIFO inventory methods because we assume costs per equivalent unit to be the same in both January and February. If costs per equivalent unit had been different in the two months, work-in-process inventory at the end of February (beginning of March) would be costed differently under the weighted-average and FIFO methods. The basic approach to process costing with transferred-in costs, however, would still be the same as what we describe in this section.

Transferred-in costs are treated as if they are a separate type of direct material added at the beginning of the process. That is, the transferred-in costs are always 100% complete at the beginning of the process in the new department. When successive departments are involved, the transferred units from one department become all or a part of the direct materials of the next department; however, they are called transferred-in costs, not direct material costs.

Transferred-In Costs and the Weighted-Average Method

To examine the weighted-average process-costing method with transferred-in costs, we use the five-step procedure described earlier to assign the costs of the testing department to units completed and transferred out and to the units in ending work in process.

Exhibit 8 shows Steps 1 and 2. The computations are similar to the calculations of equivalent units under the weighted-average method for the assembly department in Exhibit 4. The one difference here is that we have transferred-in costs as an additional input. All units, whether completed and transferred out during the period or in ending work in process, are always fully complete with respect to transferred-in costs. The reason is that the transferred-in costs are the costs incurred in the assembly department, and any units received in the testing department must have first been completed in the assembly department. However, the direct material costs have a zero degree of completion in both beginning and ending work-in-process inventories because, in the testing department, direct materials are introduced at the *end* of the process.

Exhibit 9 describes Steps 3, 4, and 5 for the weighted-average method. Beginning work in process and work done in the current period are combined for the purposes of computing the cost per equivalent unit for the transferred-in costs, direct materials costs, and conversion costs.

The journal entry for the transfer from testing to Finished Goods (see Exhibit 9) is as follows:

Finished Goods Control	120,890	
Work in Process—Testing		120,890
To record cost of goods completed and transferred from testing to Finished Goods.		

Exhibit 8   Summarize the Flow of Physical Units and Compute Output in Equivalent Units Using the Weighted-Average Method for the Testing Department for March 2014

	A	B	C	D	E
1		**(Step 1)**		**(Step 2)**	
2				**Equivalent Units**	
3	**Flow of Production**	**Physical Units**	**Transferred-In Costs**	**Direct Materials**	**Conversion Costs**
4	Work in process, beginning (given, p. 681)	240			
5	Transferred in during current period (given, p. 681)	400			
6	To account for	640			
7	Completed and transferred out during current period	440	440	440	440
8	Work in process, ending[a] (given, p. 681)	200			
9	(200 × 100%; 200 × 0%; 200 × 80%)		200	0	160
10	Accounted for	640			
11	Equivalent units of work done to date		640	440	600
12					
13	[a]Degree of completion in this department; transferred-in costs, 100%; direct materials, 0%; conversion costs, 80%.				

| | | Exhibit 9 | | | Summarize the Total Costs to Account For, Compute the Cost per Equivalent Unit, and Assign Costs to the Units Completed and Units in Ending Work-in-Process Inventory Using the Weighted-Average Method for the Testing Department for March 2014 |

| | Home | Insert | Page Layout | Formulas | Data | Review | View |

	A	B	C	D	E	F
1			Total Production Costs	Transferred-In Costs	Direct Materials	Conversion Costs
2	(Step 3)	Work in process, beginning (given, p. 681)	$ 51,600	$33,600	$ 0	$18,000
3		Costs added in current period (given, p. 681)	113,800	52,000	13,200	48,600
4		Total costs to account for	$165,400	$85,600	$13,200	$66,600
5						
6	(Step 4)	Costs incurred to date		$85,600	$13,200	$66,600
7		Divide by equivalent units of work done to date (Exhibit 17-8)		÷ 640	÷ 440	÷ 600
8		Cost per equivalent unit of work done to date		$133.75	$ 30.00	$111.00
9						
10	(Step 5)	Assignment of costs:				
11		Completed and transferred out (440 units)	$120,890	$(440^a \times \$133.75)$ +	$(440^a \times \$30)$ +	$(440^a \times \$111)$
12		Work in process, ending (200 units):	44,510	$(200^b \times \$133.75)$ +	$(0^b \times \$30)$ +	$(160^b \times \$111)$
13		Total costs accounted for	$165,400	$85,600 +	$13,200 +	$66,600
14						
15	^{a}Equivalent units completed and transferred out from Exhibit 17-8, Step 2.					
16	^{b}Equivalent units in ending work in process from Exhibit 17-8, Step 2.					

Entries in the Work in Process—Testing account (see Exhibit 9) are as follows:

Work in Process—Testing

Beginning inventory, March 1	51,600	Transferred out	120,890
Transferred-in costs	52,000		
Direct materials	13,200		
Conversion costs	48,600		
Ending inventory, March 31	44,510		

Transferred-In Costs and the FIFO Method

To examine the FIFO process-costing method with transferred-in costs, we again use the five-step procedure. Exhibit 10 shows Steps 1 and 2. Other than accounting for transferred-in costs, computing the equivalent units is the same as under the FIFO method for the assembly department (see Exhibit 6).

Exhibit 11 describes Steps 3, 4, and 5. In Step 3, the $165,880 in total costs to account for under the FIFO method differ from the total costs under the weighted-average method, which are $165,400. This is because of the difference in the costs of completed units transferred in from the assembly department under the two methods—$52,480 under FIFO and $52,000 under the weighted-average method. The cost per equivalent unit for the current period in Step 4 is calculated on the basis of costs transferred in and work done in the current period only. Step 5 then accounts for the total costs of $165,880 by assigning them to the units transferred out and those in ending work-in-process inventory. Again, other than considering transferred-in costs, the calculations mirror those under the FIFO method for the assembly department (in Exhibit 7).

| Exhibit 10 | Summarize the Flow of Physical Units and Compute Output in Equivalent Units Using the FIFO Method for the Testing Department for March 2014 |

	A	B	C	D	E
	Home Insert Page Layout Formulas Data Review View				
1		**(Step 1)**	**(Step 2)**		
2			**Equivalent Units**		
3	**Flow of Production**	**Physical Units**	**Transferred-In Costs**	**Direct Materials**	**Conversion Costs**
4	Work in process, beginning (given, p. 681)	240	(work done before current period)		
5	Transferred in during current period (given, p. 681)	400			
6	To account for	640			
7	Completed and transferred out during current period:				
8	From beginning work in process[a]	240			
9	[240 × (100% − 100%); 240 × (100% − 0%); 240 × (100% − 62.5%)]		0	240	90
10	Started and completed	200[b]			
11	(200 × 100%; 200 × 100%; 200 × 100%)		200	200	200
12	Work in process, ending[c] (given, p. 681)	200			
13	(200 × 100%; 200 × 0%; 200 × 80%)		200	0	160
14	Accounted for	640			
15	Equivalent units of work done in current period		400	440	450
16					
17	[a]Degree of completion in this department: transferred-in costs, 100%; direct materials, 0%; conversion costs, 62.5%.				
18	[b]440 physical units completed and transferred out minus 240 physical units completed and transferred out from beginning				
19	work-in-process inventory.				
20	[c]Degree of completion in this department: transferred-in costs, 100%; direct materials, 0%; conversion costs, 80%.				

Remember that in a series of interdepartmental transfers, each department is regarded as separate and distinct for accounting purposes. The journal entry for the transfer from testing to Finished Goods (see Exhibit 11) is as follows:

Finished Goods Control	122,360	
Work in Process—Testing		122,360

To record the cost of goods completed and transferred from testing to Finished Goods.

The entries in the Work in Process—Testing account (see Exhibit 11) are as follows:

Work in Process—Testing

Beginning inventory, March 1	51,600	Transferred out	122,360
Transferred-in costs	52,480		
Direct materials	13,200		
Conversion costs	48,600		
Ending inventory, March 31	43,520		

Points to Remember About Transferred-In Costs

Some points to remember when accounting for transferred-in costs are as follows:

1. Be sure to include the transferred-in costs from previous departments in your calculations.

2. When calculating the costs to be transferred using the FIFO method, do not overlook costs assigned in the previous period to units that were in process at the beginning of the current period but are now included in the units transferred. For example, do not overlook the $51,600 in Exhibit 11.

Exhibit 11	Summarize the Total Costs to Account For, Compute the Cost per Equivalent Unit, and Assign Costs to the Units Completed and Units in Ending Work-in-Process Inventory Using the FIFO Method for the Testing Department for March 2014

	A	B	C	D	E	F
1			Total Production Costs	Transferred-In Cost	Direct Material	Conversion Costs
2	(Step 3)	Work in process, beginning (given, p. 681)	$ 51,600	$33,600	$ 0	$18,000
3		Costs added in current period (given, p. 681)	114,280	52,480	13,200	48,600
4		Total costs to account for	$165,880	$86,080	$13,200	$66,600
5						
6	(Step 4)	Costs added in current period		$52,480	$13,200	$48,600
7		Divide by equivalent units of work done in current period (Exhibit 17-10)		÷ 400	÷ 440	÷ 450
8		Cost per equivalent unit of work done in current period		$131.20	$ 30	$ 108
9						
10	(Step 5)	Assignment of costs:				
11		Completed and transferred out (440 units)				
12		Work in process, beginning (240 units)	$ 51,600	$33,600 +	$0 +	$18,000
13		Costs added to beginning work in process in current period	16,920	(0^a × $131.20) +	(240^a × $30) +	(90^a × $108)
14		Total from beginning inventory	68,520			
15		Started and completed (200 units)	53,840	(200^b × $131.20) +	(200^b × $30) +	(200^b × $108)
16		Total costs of units completed and transferred out	122,360			
17		Work in process, ending (200 units):	43,520	(200^c × $131.20) +	(0^c × $30) +	(160^c × $108)
18		Total costs accounted for	$165,880	$86,080 +	$13,200 +	$66,600
19						
20	^{a}Equivalent units used to complete beginning work in process from Exhibit 17-10, Step 2.					
21	^{b}Equivalent units started and completed from Exhibit 17-10, Step 2.					
22	^{c}Equivalent units in ending work in process from Exhibit 17-10, Step 2.					

3. Unit costs may fluctuate between periods. Therefore, transferred units may contain batches accumulated at different unit costs. For example, the 400 units transferred in at $52,480 in Exhibit 11 using the FIFO method consist of units that have different unit costs of direct materials and conversion costs when these units were worked on in the assembly department (see Exhibit 7). Remember, however, that when these units are transferred to the testing department, they are costed at *one average unit cost* of $131.20 ($52,480 ÷ 400 units), as in Exhibit 11.

4. Units may be measured in different denominations in different departments. Consider each department separately. For example, unit costs could be based on kilograms in the first department and liters in the second department. Accordingly, as units are received in the second department, their measurements must be converted to liters.

Decision Point

How are the weighted-average and FIFO process-costing methods applied to transferred-in costs?

Hybrid Costing Systems

Product-costing systems do not always fall neatly into either job-costing or process-costing categories. Many production systems are hybrid systems in which both mass production and customization occur. Consider Ford Motor Company. Automobiles are manufactured in a continuous flow (suited to process costing), but individual units may be customized with different engine sizes, transmissions, music systems, and so on (which requires job costing). A **hybrid-costing system** blends characteristics from both job-costing and process-costing systems. Managers must design product-costing systems to fit the particular characteristics of different production systems.

Firms that manufacture closely related standardized products (for example, various types of televisions, dishwashers, washing machines, and shoes) tend to use hybrid-costing

Learning Objective 6

Understand the need for hybrid-costing systems such as operation costing

...when product-costing does not fall into job-costing or process-costing categories

Concepts in Action ▶ Hybrid Costing for Customized Shoes at Adidas

Adidas has been designing and manufacturing athletic footwear for nearly 90 years. Although shoemakers have long individually crafted shoes for professional athletes, Adidas took this concept a step further when it initiated the *mi adidas* program.

The mi adidas customization offering is available online and in retail stores around the world. Consumers can choose from more than 200 styles across seven sports and lifestyle categories. Along with competitors Nike and New Balance, mi adidas offers the opportunity to create individual, custom shoes for performance, fit, and design. Once the designs are created and purchased, the design and product data are transferred to manufacturing plants where the product is then built to order and shipped directly to the consumer.

Adidas uses a hybrid-costing system. Accounting for individual customization requires job costing, but the similar process used to make sneakers lends itself to process costing. The cost of making each pair of shoes is calculated by accumulating all production costs and dividing by the number of shoes made. In other words, even though each pair of shoes is different, the conversion cost is roughly the same.

The combination of customization with certain features of mass production is called mass customization. It is the consequence of being able to digitize information that individual customers indicate is important to them. Various products that companies can customize within a mass-production setting (including personal computers, jeans, and bicycles) still require job costing of materials and considerable human intervention. However, as manufacturing systems become flexible, companies are also using process costing to account for the standardized conversion costs.

Sources: Tien, Ellen. 2011. These (custom) colors do run. *New York Times*, April 7; Kamenev, Marina. 2006. Adidas' high tech footwear. *Bloomberg Businessweek*, November 3; Seifert, Ralf. 2003. The "mi adidas" mass customization initiative. IMD No. 159. Lausanne, Switzerland: International Institute for Management Development.

systems. They use process costing to account for the conversion costs and job costing for the material and customizable components. Consider Nike, which has a message for shoppers looking for the hottest new shoe design: Just do it … yourself! Athletic apparel manufacturers have long individually crafted shoes for professional athletes. Now, Nike is making it possible for other customers to design their own shoes and clothing. Using the Internet and mobile applications, Nike's customers can personalize with their own colors and patterns for Jordan-brand sneakers and other apparel. Concepts in Action: Hybrid Costing for Customized Shoes at Adidas describes customization and the use of a hybrid-costing system at Nike's main rival, Adidas. The next section explains *operation costing*, a common type of hybrid-costing system.

Overview of Operation-Costing Systems

An **operation** is a standardized method or technique performed repetitively, often on different materials, resulting in different finished goods. Multiple operations are usually conducted within a department. For instance, a suit maker may have a cutting operation and a hemming operation within a single department. The term *operation*, however, is often used loosely. It may be a synonym for a department or process. For example, some companies may call their finishing department a finishing process or a finishing operation.

An **operation-costing system** is a hybrid-costing system applied to batches of similar, but not identical, products. Each batch of products is often a variation of a single design, and it proceeds through a sequence of operations. Within each operation, all product units are treated exactly alike, using identical amounts of the operation's resources. A key point in the operation system is that each batch does not necessarily move through the same operations as other batches. Batches are also called production runs.

In a company that makes suits, managers may select a single basic design for every suit to be made, but depending on specifications, each batch of suits varies somewhat from other batches. Batches may vary with respect to the material used or the type of stitching. Semiconductors, textiles, and shoes are also manufactured in batches and may have similar variations from batch to batch.

An operation-costing system uses work orders that specify the needed direct materials and step-by-step operations. Product costs are compiled for each work order. Direct materials that are unique to different work orders are specifically identified with the appropriate work order, as in job costing. However, each unit is assumed to use an identical amount of conversion costs for a given operation, as in process costing. A single average conversion cost per unit is calculated for each operation. This is done by dividing the total conversion costs for that operation by the number of units that pass through it. This average cost is then assigned to each unit passing through the operation. Units that do not pass through an operation are not allocated any costs for that operation. There were only two cost categories—direct materials and conversion costs—in the examples we have discussed. However, operation costing can have more than two cost categories. The costs in each category are identified with specific work orders using job-costing or process-costing methods as appropriate.

Managers find operation costing useful in cost management because operation costing focuses on control of physical processes, or operations, of a given production system. For example, in clothing manufacturing, managers are concerned with fabric waste, how many fabric layers can be cut at one time, and so on. Operation costing measures, in financial terms, how well managers have controlled physical processes.

Illustrating an Operation-Costing System

The Baltimore Clothing Company, a clothing manufacturer, produces two lines of blazers for department stores: those made of wool and those made of polyester. Wool blazers use better-quality materials and undergo more operations than polyester blazers do. The operations information on work order 423 for 50 wool blazers and work order 424 for 100 polyester blazers is as follows:

	Work Order 423	Work Order 424
Direct materials	Wool	Polyester
	Satin full lining	Rayon partial lining
	Bone buttons	Plastic buttons
Operations		
1. Cutting cloth	Use	Use
2. Checking edges	Use	Do not use
3. Sewing body	Use	Use
4. Checking seams	Use	Do not use
5. Machine sewing of collars and lapels	Do not use	Use
6. Hand sewing of collars and lapels	Use	Do not use

The cost data for these work orders, started and completed in March 2014, are as follows:

	Work Order 423	Work Order 424
Number of blazers	50	100
Direct materials costs	$ 6,000	$3,000
Conversion costs allocated:		
Operation 1	580	1,160
Operation 2	400	—
Operation 3	1,900	3,800
Operation 4	500	—
Operation 5	—	875
Operation 6	700	—
Total manufacturing costs	$10,080	$8,835

As in process costing, all product units in any work order are assumed to consume identical amounts of conversion costs of a particular operation. Baltimore's operation-costing system uses a budgeted rate to calculate the conversion costs of each operation. The budgeted rate for Operation 1 (amounts assumed) is as follows:

$$\begin{array}{l} \text{Operation 1 budgeted} \\ \text{conversion-cost} \\ \text{rate for 2014} \end{array} = \frac{\begin{array}{c} \text{Operation 1 budgeted} \\ \text{conversion costs for 2014} \end{array}}{\begin{array}{c} \text{Operation 1 budgeted} \\ \text{product units for 2014} \end{array}}$$

$$= \frac{\$232,000}{20,000 \text{ units}}$$

$$= \$11.60 \text{ per unit}$$

The budgeted conversion costs of Operation 1 include labor, power, repairs, supplies, depreciation, and other overhead of this operation. If some units have not been completed (so all units in Operation 1 have not received the same amounts of conversion costs), the conversion-cost rate is computed by dividing the budgeted conversion costs by the *equivalent units* of the conversion costs, as in process costing.

As the company manufactures blazers, managers allocate the conversion costs to the work orders processed in Operation 1 by multiplying the $11.60 conversion cost per unit by the number of units processed. Conversion costs of Operation 1 for 50 wool blazers (Work Order 423) are $11.60 per blazer × 50 blazers = $580 and for 100 polyester blazers (Work Order 424) are $11.60 per blazer × 100 blazers = $1,160. When equivalent units are used to calculate the conversion-cost rate, costs are allocated to work orders by multiplying the conversion cost per equivalent unit by the number of equivalent units in the work order. The direct material costs of $6,000 for the 50 wool blazers (Work Order 423) and $3,000 for the 100 polyester blazers (Work Order 424) are specifically identified with each order, as in job costing. The basic point of operation costing is this: Operation unit costs are assumed to be the same regardless of the work order, but direct material costs vary across orders when the materials for each work order vary.

Journal Entries

The actual conversion costs for Operation 1 in March 2014—assumed to be $24,400, including the actual costs incurred for work order 423 and work order 424—are entered into a Conversion Costs Control account:

1. Conversion Costs Control	24,400	
Various accounts (such as Wages Payable		
Control and Accumulated Depreciation)		24,400

The summary journal entries for assigning the costs to polyester blazers (work order 424) follow. Entries for wool blazers would be similar. Of the $3,000 of direct materials for work order 424, $2,975 are used in Operation 1, and the remaining $25 of materials are used in another operation. The journal entry to record direct materials used for the 100 polyester blazers in March 2014 is as follows:

2. Work in Process, Operation 1	2,975	
Materials Inventory Control		2,975

The journal entry to record the allocation of conversion costs to products uses the budgeted rate of $11.60 per blazer times the 100 polyester blazers processed, or $1,160:

3. Work in Process, Operation 1	1,160	
Conversion Costs Allocated		1,160

The journal entry to record the transfer of the 100 polyester blazers (at a cost of $2,975 + $1,160) from Operation 1 to Operation 3 (polyester blazers do not go through Operation 2) is as follows:

4. Work in Process, Operation 3	4,135	
Work in Process, Operation 1		4,135

After posting these entries, the Work in Process, Operation 1, account appears as follows:

Work in Process, Operation 1

② Direct materials	2,975	④ Transferred to Operation 3	4,135
③ Conversion costs allocated	1,160		
Ending inventory, March 31	0		

The costs of the blazers are transferred through the operations in which blazers are worked on and then to finished goods in the usual manner. Costs are added throughout the fiscal year in the Conversion Costs Control account and the Conversion Costs Allocated account. Any overallocation or underallocation of conversion costs is disposed of in the same way as overallocated or underallocated manufacturing overhead in a job-costing system.

Decision Point

What is an operation-costing system and when is it a better approach to product costing?

Problem for Self-Study

Allied Chemicals operates a thermo-assembly process as the second of three processes at its plastics plant. Direct materials in thermo-assembly are added at the end of the process. Conversion costs are added evenly during the process. The following data pertain to the thermo-assembly department for June 2014:

	A	B	C	D	E
1		Physical Units	Transferred-In Costs	Direct Materials	Conversion Costs
2	Work in process, beginning inventory	50,000			
3	Degree of completion, beginning work in process		100%	0%	80%
4	Transferred in during current period	200,000			
5	Completed and transferred out during current period	210,000			
6	Work in process, ending inventory	?			
7	Degree of completion, ending work in process		100%	0%	40%

Compute equivalent units under (1) the weighted-average method and (2) the FIFO method.

Required

Solution

1. The weighted-average method uses equivalent units of work done to date to compute cost per equivalent unit. The calculations of equivalent units follow:

	A	B	C	D	E
		(Step 1)		**(Step 2)**	
1					
2				**Equivalent Units**	
3	**Flow of Production**	**Physical Units**	**Transferred-In Costs**	**Direct Materials**	**Conversion Costs**
4	Work in process, beginning (given)	50,000			
5	Transferred in during current period (given)	200,000			
6	To account for	250,000			
7	Completed and transferred out during current period	210,000	210,000	210,000	210,000
8	Work in process, ending[a]	40,000[b]			
9	(40,000 × 100%; 40,000 × 0%; 40,000 × 40%)		40,000	0	16,000
10	Accounted for	250,000			
11	Equivalent units of work done to date		250,000	210,000	226,000
12					
13	[a]Degree of completion in this department: transferred-in costs, 100%; direct materials, 0%; conversion costs, 40%.				
14	[b]250,000 physical units to account for minus 210,000 physical units completed and transferred out.				

2. The FIFO method uses equivalent units of work done in the current period only to compute cost per equivalent unit. The calculations of equivalent units follow:

	A	B	C	D	E
		(Step 1)		**(Step 2)**	
1					
2				**Equivalent Units**	
3	**Flow of Production**	**Physical Units**	**Transferred-In Costs**	**Direct Materials**	**Conversion Costs**
4	Work in process, beginning (given)	50,000			
5	Transferred in during current period (given)	200,000			
6	To account for	250,000			
7	Completed and transferred out during current period:				
8	From beginning work in process[a]	50,000			
9	[50,000 × (100% − 100%); 50,000 × (100% − 0%); 50,000 × (100% − 80%)]		0	50,000	10,000
10	Started and completed	160,000[b]			
11	(160,000 × 100%; 160,000 × 100%; 160,000 × 100%)		160,000	160,000	160,000
12	Work in process, ending[c]	40,000[d]			
13	(40,000 × 100%; 40,000 × 0%; 40,000 × 40%)		40,000	0	16,000
14	Accounted for	250,000			
15	Equivalent units of work done in current period		200,000	210,000	186,000
16					
17	[a]Degree of completion in this department: transferred-in costs, 100%; direct materials, 0%; conversion costs, 80%.				
18	[b]210,000 physical units completed and transferred out minus 50,000 physical units completed and transferred out from beginning work-in-process inventory.				
19	[c]Degree of completion in this department: transferred-in costs, 100%; direct materials, 0%; conversion costs, 40%.				
20	[d]250,000 physical units to account for minus 210,000 physical units completed and transferred out.				

▶ Decision Points

The following question-and-answer format summarizes the chapter's learning objectives.
Each decision presents a key question related to a learning objective. The guidelines are
the answer to that question.

Decision	Guidelines
1. Under what conditions is a process-costing system used?	A process-costing system is used to determine cost of a product or service when masses of identical or similar units are produced. Industries using process-costing systems include the food, textiles, and oil-refining industries.
2. How are average unit costs computed when no inventories are present?	Average unit costs are computed by dividing the total costs in a given accounting period by the total units produced in that period.
3. What are the five steps in a process-costing system, and how are equivalent units calculated?	The five steps in a process-costing system are (1) summarize the flow of physical units of output, (2) compute the output in terms of equivalent units, (3) summarize the total costs to account for, (4) compute the cost per equivalent unit, and (5) assign the total costs to units completed and to units in ending work-in-process inventory. An equivalent unit is a derived measure of output that (a) takes the quantity of each input (factor of production) in units completed or in incomplete units in work in process and (b) converts the quantity of input into the amount of completed output units that could be made with that quantity of input.
4. What are the weighted-average and first-in, first-out (FIFO) methods of process costing? Under what conditions will they yield different levels of operating income?	The weighted-average method computes unit costs by dividing total costs in the Work in Process account by total equivalent units completed to date and assigns this average cost to units completed and to units in ending work-in-process inventory. The first-in, first-out (FIFO) method computes unit costs based on costs incurred during the current period and equivalent units of work done in the current period. Operating income can differ materially between the two methods when (1) direct material or conversion cost per equivalent unit varies significantly from period to period and (2) physical-inventory levels of work in process are large in relation to the total number of units transferred out of the process.
5. How are the weighted-average and FIFO process-costing methods applied to transferred-in costs?	The weighted-average method computes transferred-in costs per unit by dividing the total transferred-in costs to date by the total equivalent transferred-in units completed to date and assigns this average cost to units completed and to units in ending work-in-process inventory. The FIFO method computes the transferred-in costs per unit based on the costs transferred in during the current period and equivalent units of transferred-in costs of work done in the current period. The FIFO method assigns transferred-in costs in the beginning work-in-process inventory to units completed and costs transferred in during the current period first to complete the beginning inventory, next to start and complete new units, and finally to units in ending work-in-process inventory.
6. What is an operation-costing system, and when is it a better approach to product costing?	Operation costing is a hybrid-costing system that blends characteristics from both job-costing (for direct materials) and process-costing systems (for conversion costs). It is a better approach to product costing when production systems share some features of custom-order manufacturing and other features of mass-production manufacturing.

Appendix

Standard-Costing Method of Process Costing

Accounting in a standard-costing system involves making entries using standard costs and then isolating variances from these standards in order to support management control. This appendix describes how the principles of standard costing can be employed in process-costing systems.

Benefits of Standard Costing

Companies that use process-costing systems produce masses of identical or similar units of output. In such companies, it is fairly easy to budget for the quantities of inputs needed to produce a unit of output. Standard cost per input unit can then be multiplied by input quantity standards to develop a standard cost per output unit.

The weighted-average and FIFO methods become very complicated when used in process industries, such as textiles, ceramics, paints, and packaged food, that produce a wide variety of similar products. For example, a steel-rolling mill uses various steel alloys and produces sheets of varying sizes and finishes. The different types of direct materials used and the operations performed are few, but used in various combinations, they yield a wide variety of products. In these cases, if the broad averaging procedure of *actual* process costing were used, the result would be inaccurate costs for each product. Therefore, managers in these industries typically use the standard-costing method of process costing.

Under the standard-costing method, teams of design and process engineers, operations personnel, and management accountants work together to determine *separate* standard costs per equivalent unit on the basis of different technical processing specifications for each product. Identifying standard costs for each product overcomes the disadvantage of costing all products at a single average amount, as under actual costing.

Computations Under Standard Costing

We return to the assembly department of Pacific Electronics, but this time we use standard costs. Assume the same standard costs apply in February and March 2014. Data for the assembly department are as follows:

	A	B	C	D	E
		Physical Units (SG-40s) (1)	Direct Materials (2)	Conversion Costs (3)	Total Costs (4) = (2) + (3)
2	Standard cost per unit		$ 74	$ 54	
3	Work in process, beginning inventory (March 1)	225			
4	Degree of completion of beginning work in process		100%	60%	
5	Beginning work in process inventory at standard costs		$16,650[a]	$ 7,290[a]	$23,940
6	Started during March	275			
7	Completed and transferred out during March	400			
8	Work in process, ending inventory (March 31)	100			
9	Degree of completion of ending work in process		100%	50%	
10	Actual total costs added during March		$19,800	$16,380	$36,180
11					
12	[a]Work in process, beginning inventory at standard costs				
13	Direct materials: 225 physical units × 100% completed × $74 per unit = $16,650				
14	Conversion costs: 225 physical units × 60% completed × $54 per unit = $7,290				

We illustrate the standard-costing method of process costing using the five-step procedure.

Exhibit 12

Summarize the Flow of Physical Units and Compute Output in Equivalent Units Using the Standard-Costing Method for the Assembly Department for March 2014

	A	B	C	D
		(Step 1)	**(Step 2)**	
1				
2			**Equivalent Units**	
3	**Flow of Production**	**Physical Units**	**Direct Materials**	**Conversion Costs**
4	Work in process, beginning (given, p. 692)	225		
5	Started during current period (given, p. 692)	275		
6	To account for	500		
7	Completed and transferred out during current period:			
8	From beginning work in process[a]	225		
9	[225 × (100% − 100%); 225 × (100% − 60%)]		0	90
10	Started and completed	175[b]		
11	(175 × 100%; 175 × 100%)		175	175
12	Work in process, ending[c] (given, p. 692)	100		
13	(100 × 100%; 100 × 50%)		100	50
14	Accounted for	500		
15	Equivalent units of work done in current period		275	315
16				
17	[a]Degree of completion in this department: direct materials, 100%; conversion costs, 60%.			
18	[b]400 physical units completed and transferred out minus 225 physical units completed and transferred out from beginning work-in-process inventory.			
19	[c]Degree of completion in this department: direct materials, 100%; conversion costs, 50%.			

Exhibit 12 presents Steps 1 and 2. These steps are identical to the steps described for the FIFO method in Exhibit 6 because, as in FIFO, the standard-costing method also assumes that the earliest equivalent units in beginning work in process are completed first. Work done in the current period for direct materials is 275 equivalent units. Work done in the current period for conversion costs is 315 equivalent units.

Exhibit 13 describes Steps 3, 4, and 5. In Step 3, total costs to account for (that is, the total debits to Work in Process—Assembly) differ from total debits to Work in Process—Assembly under the actual-cost-based weighted-average and FIFO methods. That's because, as in all standard-costing systems, the debits to the Work in Process account are at standard costs, rather than actual costs. These standard costs total $61,300 in Exhibit 13. In Step 4, costs per equivalent unit are standard costs: direct materials, $74, and conversion costs, $54. *Therefore, costs per equivalent unit do not have to be computed as they were for the weighted-average and FIFO methods.*

Exhibit 13, Step 5, assigns total costs to units completed and transferred out and to units in ending work-in-process inventory, as in the FIFO method. Step 5 assigns amounts of standard costs to equivalent units calculated in Exhibit 12. These costs are assigned (1) first to complete beginning work-in-process inventory, (2) next to start and complete new units, and (3) finally to start new units that are in ending work-in-process inventory. Note how the $61,300 total costs accounted for in Step 5 of Exhibit 13 equal total costs to account for.

Accounting for Variances

Process-costing systems using standard costs record actual direct material costs in Direct Materials Control and actual conversion costs in Conversion Costs Control (similar to Variable and Fixed Overhead Control). In the journal entries that follow, the first two record these *actual costs*. In entries 3 and 4a, the Work-in-Process—Assembly account accumulates direct material costs and conversion costs at *standard*

Exhibit 13	Summarize the Total Costs to Account For, Compute the Cost per Equivalent Unit, and Assign Costs to the Units Completed and Units in Ending Work-in-Process Inventory Using the Standard-Costing Method for the Assembly Department for March 2014

	A	B	C	D	E	F	G
1			Total Production Costs	Direct Materials		Conversion Costs	
2	**(Step 3)**	Work in process, beginning (given, p. 692)					
3		Direct materials, 225 × $74; Conversion costs, 135 × $54	$23,940	$16,650		$ 7,290	
4		Costs added in current period at standard costs					
5		Direct materials, 275 × $74; Conversion costs, 315 × $54	37,360	20,350		17,010	
6		Total costs to account for	$61,300	$37,000		$24,300	
7							
8	**(Step 4)**	Standard cost per equivalent unit (given, p. 692)		$ 74		$ 54	
9							
10	**(Step 5)**	Assignment of costs at standard costs:					
11		Completed and transferred out (400 units):					
12		Work in process, beginning (225 units)	$23,940	$16,650	+	$ 7,290	
13		Costs added to beginning work in process in current period	4,860	(0^a × $74)	+	(90^a × $54)	
14		Total from beginning inventory	28,800				
15		Started and completed (175 units)	22,400	(175^b × $74)	+	(175^b × $54)	
16		Total costs of units completed and transferred out	51,200				
17		Work in process, ending (100 units):	10,100	(100^c × $74)	+	(50^c × $54)	
18		Total costs accounted for	$61,300	$37,000	+	$24,300	
19							
20		Summary of variances for current performance:					
21		Costs added in current period at standard costs (see Step 3 above)		$20,350		$17,010	
22		Actual costs incurred (given, p. 692)		$19,800		$16,380	
23		Variance		$ 550	F	$ 630	F
24							
25		^{a}Equivalent units used to complete beginning work in process from Exhibit 17-12, Step 2.					
26		^{b}Equivalent units started and completed from Exhibit 17-12, Step 2.					
27		^{c}Equivalent units in ending work in process from Exhibit 17-12, Step 2.					

costs. Entries 3 and 4b isolate total variances. The final entry transfers out completed goods at standard costs.

1. Assembly Department Direct Materials Control (at actual costs)	19,800	
Accounts Payable Control		19,800

To record the direct materials purchased and used in production during March. This cost control account is debited with actual costs.

2. Assembly Department Conversion Costs Control (at actual costs)	16,380	
Various accounts such as Wages Payable Control and Accumulated Depreciation		16,380

To record the assembly department conversion costs for March. This cost control account is debited with actual costs.

Entries 3, 4, and 5 use standard cost amounts from Exhibit 13.

3. Work in Process—Assembly (at standard costs)	20,350	
Direct Materials Variances		550
Assembly Department Direct Materials Control		19,800

To record the standard costs of direct materials assigned to units worked on and total direct materials variances.

4a. Work in Process—Assembly (at standard costs)   17,010
        Assembly Department Conversion Costs Allocated   17,010
    To record the conversion costs allocated at standard rates to the units
    worked on during March.

4b. Assembly Department Conversion Costs Allocated   17,010
        Conversion Costs Variances   630
        Assembly Department Conversion Costs Control   16,380
    To record the total conversion costs variances.

5. Work in Process—Testing (at standard costs)   51,200
        Work in Process—Assembly (at standard costs)   51,200
    To record the standard costs of units completed and transferred out from
    assembly to testing.

Variances arise under standard costing, as in entries 3 and 4b. That's because the standard costs assigned to products on the basis of work done in the current period do not equal actual costs incurred in the current period. Recall that variances that result in higher income than expected are termed favorable, while those that reduce income are unfavorable. From an accounting standpoint, favorable cost variances are credit entries, while unfavorable ones are debits. In the preceding example, both direct materials and conversion cost variances are favorable. This is also reflected in the "F" designations for both variances in Exhibit 13.

Variances can be analyzed in little or great detail for planning and control purposes. Sometimes direct materials price variances are isolated at the time direct materials are purchased and only efficiency variances are computed in entry 3. Exhibit 14 shows how the costs flow through the general-ledger accounts under standard costing.

Exhibit 14   Flow of Standard Costs in a Process-Costing System for the Assembly Department for March 2014

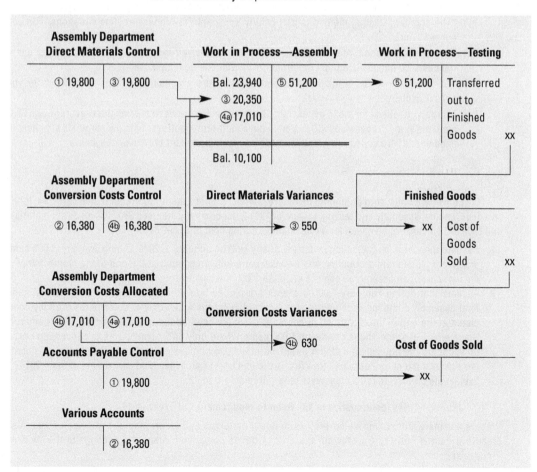

Terms to Learn

This chapter contains definitions of the following important terms:

equivalent units

first-in, first-out (FIFO) process-costing
  method

hybrid-costing system

operation

operation-costing system

previous-department costs

transferred-in costs

weighted-average process-costing
  method

Assignment Material

MyAccountingLab

Questions

1 Give three examples of industries that use process-costing systems.

2 In process costing, why are costs often divided into two main classifications?

3 Explain equivalent units. Why are equivalent-unit calculations necessary in process costing?

4 What problems might arise in estimating the degree of completion of semiconductor chips in a semiconductor plant?

5 Name the five steps in process costing when equivalent units are computed.

6 Name the three inventory methods commonly associated with process costing.

7 Describe the distinctive characteristic of weighted-average computations in assigning costs to units completed and to units in ending work in process.

8 Describe the distinctive characteristic of FIFO computations in assigning costs to units completed and to units in ending work in process.

9 Why should the FIFO method be called a modified or department FIFO method?

10 Identify a major advantage of the FIFO method for purposes of planning and control.

11 Identify the main difference between journal entries in process costing and job costing.

12 "The standard-costing method is particularly applicable to process-costing situations." Do you agree? Why?

13 Why should the accountant distinguish between transferred-in costs and additional direct material costs for each subsequent department in a process-costing system?

14 "Transferred-in costs are those costs incurred in the preceding accounting period." Do you agree? Explain.

15 "There's no reason for me to get excited about the choice between the weighted-average and FIFO methods in my process-costing system. I have long-term contracts with my materials suppliers at fixed prices." Do you agree with this statement made by a plant controller? Explain.

MyAccountingLab

Exercises

16 Equivalent units, zero beginning inventory. Candid, Inc., is a manufacturer of digital cameras. It has two departments: assembly and testing. In January 2014, the company incurred $800,000 on direct materials and $805,000 on conversion costs, for a total manufacturing cost of $1,605,000.

Required

1. Assume there was no beginning inventory of any kind on January 1, 2014. During January, 5,000 cameras were placed into production and all 5,000 were fully completed at the end of the month. What is the unit cost of an assembled camera in January?

2. Assume that during February 5,000 cameras are placed into production. Further assume the same total assembly costs for January are also incurred in February, but only 4,000 cameras are fully completed at the end of the month. All direct materials have been added to the remaining 1,000 cameras. However, on average, these remaining 1,000 cameras are only 60% complete as to conversion costs. (a) What are the equivalent units for direct materials and conversion costs and their respective costs per equivalent unit for February? (b) What is the unit cost of an assembled camera in February 2014?

3. Explain the difference in your answers to requirements 1 and 2.

17 Journal entries (continuation of 16). Refer to requirement 2 of Exercise 16.

Required

Prepare summary journal entries for the use of direct materials and incurrence of conversion costs. Also prepare a journal entry to transfer out the cost of goods completed. Show the postings to the Work in Process account.

18 Zero beginning inventory, materials introduced in middle of process. Pilar Chemicals has a mixing department and a refining department. Its process-costing system in the mixing department has two direct materials cost categories (chemical P and chemical Q) and one conversion costs pool. The following data pertain to the mixing department for July 2014:

Units	
Work in process, July 1	0
Units started	100,000
Completed and transferred to refining department	70,000
Costs	
Chemical P	$600,000
Chemical Q	140,000
Conversion costs	360,000

Chemical P is introduced at the start of operations in the mixing department, and chemical Q is added when the product is three-fourths completed in the mixing department. Conversion costs are added evenly during the process. The ending work in process in the mixing department is two-thirds complete.

1. Compute the equivalent units in the mixing department for July 2014 for each cost category.
2. Compute (a) the cost of goods completed and transferred to the refining department during July and (b) the cost of work in process as of July 31, 2014.

19 Weighted-average method, equivalent units. The assembly division of Fenton Watches, Inc., uses the weighted-average method of process costing. Consider the following data for the month of May 2014:

	Physical Units (Watches)	Direct Materials	Conversion Costs
Beginning work in process (May 1)[a]	80	$ 493,360	$ 91,040
Started in May 2014	500		
Completed during May 2014	460		
Ending work in process (May 31)[b]	120		
Total costs added during May 2014		$3,220,000	$1,392,000

[a]Degree of completion: direct materials, 90%; conversion costs, 40%.
[b]Degree of completion: direct materials, 60%; conversion costs, 30%.

Compute equivalent units for direct materials and conversion costs. Show physical units in the first column of your schedule.

20 Weighted-average method, assigning costs (continuation of 19).

For the data in Exercise 19, summarize the total costs to account for, calculate the cost per equivalent unit for direct materials and conversion costs, and assign costs to the units completed (and transferred out) and units in ending work in process.

21 FIFO method, equivalent units. Refer to the information in Exercise 19. Suppose the assembly division at Fenton Watches, Inc., uses the FIFO method of process costing instead of the weighted-average method.

Compute equivalent units for direct materials and conversion costs. Show physical units in the first column of your schedule.

22 FIFO method, assigning costs (continuation of 21).

For the data in Exercise 19, use the FIFO method to summarize the total costs to account for, calculate the cost per equivalent unit for direct materials and conversion costs, and assign costs to units completed (and transferred out) and to units in ending work in process.

23 Operation costing. Whole Goodness Bakery needs to determine the cost of two work orders for the month of June. Work order 215 is for 2,400 packages of dinner rolls, and work order 216 is for 2,800 loaves of multigrain bread. Dinner rolls are mixed and cut into individual rolls before being baked and then packaged. Multigrain loaves are mixed and shaped before being baked, sliced, and packaged. The following information applies to work order 215 and work order 216:

	Work Order 215	Work Order 216
Quantity (packages)	2,400	2,800
Operations		
1. Mix	Use	Use
2. Shape loaves	Do not use	Use
3. Cut rolls	Use	Do not use
4. Bake	Use	Use
5. Slice loaves	Do not use	Use
6. Package	Use	Use

Selected budget information for June follows:

	Dinner Rolls	**Multigrain Loaves**	**Total**
Packages	9,600	13,000	22,600
Direct material costs	$5,280	$11,700	$ 16,980

Budgeted conversion costs for each operation for June follow:

Mixing	$18,080
Shaping	3,250
Cutting	1,440
Baking	14,690
Slicing	1,300
Packaging	16,950

Required

1. Using budgeted number of packages as the denominator, calculate the budgeted conversion-cost rates for each operation.
2. Using the information in requirement 1, calculate the budgeted cost of goods manufactured for the two June work orders.
3. Calculate the cost per package of dinner rolls and multigrain loaves for work order 215 and 216.

24 Weighted-average method, assigning costs. Tomlinson Corporation is a biotech company based in Milpitas. It makes a cancer-treatment drug in a single processing department. Direct materials are added at the start of the process. Conversion costs are added evenly during the process. Tomlinson uses the weighted-average method of process costing. The following information for July 2014 is available.

		Equivalent Units	
	Physical Units	**Direct Materials**	**Conversion Costs**
Work in process, July 1	8,700[a]	8,700	2,175
Started during July	34,500		
Completed and transferred out during July	32,000	32,000	32,000
Work in process, July 31	11,200[b]	11,200	7,840

[a]Degree of completion: direct materials, 100%; conversion costs, 25%.
[b]Degree of completion: direct materials, 100%; conversion costs, 70%.

Total Costs for July 2014		
Work in process, beginning		
Direct materials	$61,500	
Conversion costs	43,200	$104,700
Direct materials added during July		301,380
Conversion costs added during July		498,624
Total costs to account for		$904,704

1. Calculate the cost per equivalent unit for direct materials and conversion costs.

2. Summarize the total costs to account for, and assign them to units completed (and transferred out) and to units in ending work in process.

Required

25 FIFO method, assigning costs.

1. Do Exercise 24 using the FIFO method.

2. Tomlinson's management seeks to have a more consistent cost per equivalent unit. Which method of process costing should the company choose and why?

Required

26 Transferred-in costs, weighted-average method. Trendy Clothing, Inc., is a manufacturer of winter clothes. It has a knitting department and a finishing department. This exercise focuses on the finishing department. Direct materials are added at the end of the process. Conversion costs are added evenly during the process. Trendy uses the weighted-average method of process costing. The following information for June 2014 is available.

	A	B	C	D	E
1		Physical Units (tons)	Transferred-In Costs	Direct Materials	Conversion Costs
2	Work in process, beginning inventory (June 1)	60	$ 60,000	$ 0	$24,000
3	Degree of completion, beginning work in process		100%	0%	50%
4	Transferred in during June	100			
5	Completed and transferred out during June	120			
6	Work in process, ending inventory (June 30)	40			
7	Degree of completion, ending work in process		100%	0%	75%
8	Total costs added during June		$117,000	$27,000	$62,400

1. Calculate equivalent units of transferred-in costs, direct materials, and conversion costs.

2. Summarize the total costs to account for, and calculate the cost per equivalent unit for transferred-in costs, direct materials, and conversion costs.

3. Assign costs to units completed (and transferred out) and to units in ending work in process.

Required

27 Transferred-in costs, FIFO method. Refer to the information in Exercise 26. Suppose that Trendy uses the FIFO method instead of the weighted-average method in all of its departments. The only changes to Exercise 26 under the FIFO method are that total transferred-in costs of beginning work in process on June 1 are $45,000 (instead of $60,000) and total transferred-in costs added during June are $114,000 (instead of $117,000).

Do Exercise 26 using the FIFO method. Note that you first need to calculate equivalent units of work done in the current period (for transferred-in costs, direct materials, and conversion costs) to complete beginning work in process, to start and complete new units, and to produce ending work in process.

Required

28 Operation costing. Purex produces three different types of detergents: Breeze, Fresh, and Joy. The company uses four operations to manufacture the detergents: spray drying, mixing, blending, and packaging. Breeze and Fresh are produced in powder form in the mixing department, while Joy is produced in liquid form in the blending department. The powder detergents are packed in 50-ounce paperboard cartons, and the liquid detergent is packed in 50-ounce bottles made of recycled plastic.

Purex applies conversion costs based on labor-hours in the spray drying department. It takes 1½ minutes to mix the ingredients for a 50-ounce container for each product. Conversion costs are applied based on the number of containers in the mixing and blending departments and on the basis of machine-hours in the packaging department. It takes 0.3 minutes of machine time to fill a 50-ounce container, regardless of the product.

The budgeted number of containers and expected direct materials cost for each type of detergent are as follows:

	Breeze	Fresh	Joy
Number of 50-ounce containers	11,000	8,000	21,000
Direct materials cost	$21,450	$20,000	$52,500

The budgeted conversion costs for each department for July are as follows:

Department	Budgeted Conversion Cost
Spray Drying	$ 8,000
Mixing	22,800
Blending	30,450
Packaging	1,000

Required

1. Calculate the conversion cost rates for each department.
2. Calculate the budgeted cost of goods manufactured for Breeze, Fresh, and Joy for the month of July.
3. Calculate the cost per 50-ounce container for each type of detergent for the month of July.

29 **Standard-costing with beginning and ending work in process.** Priscilla's Pearls Company (PPC) is a manufacturer of knock-off jewelry. Priscilla attends Fashion Week in New York City every September and February to gauge the latest fashion trends in jewelry. She then makes jewelry at a fraction of the cost of those designers who participate in Fashion Week. This fall's biggest item is triple-stranded pearl necklaces. Because of her large volume, Priscilla uses process costing to account for her production. In October, she had started some of the triple strands. She continued to work on those in November. Costs and output figures are as follows:

Priscilla's Pearls Company Process Costing
For the Month Ended November 30, 2014

	Units	Direct Materials	Conversion Costs
Standard cost per unit		$ 2.40	$ 9.00
Work in process, beginning inventory (Nov. 1)	29,000	$ 69,600	$ 156,600
Degree of completion of beginning work in process		100%	60%
Started during November	124,200		
Completed and transferred out	127,000		
Work in process, ending inventory (Nov. 30)	26,200		
Degree of completion of ending work in process		100%	40%
Total costs added during November		$327,500	$1,222,000

Required

1. Compute equivalent units for direct materials and conversion costs. Show physical units in the first column of your schedule.
2. Compute the total standard costs of pearls transferred out in November and the total standard costs of the November 30 inventory of work in process.
3. Compute the total November variances for direct materials and conversion costs.

MyAccountingLab   Problems

30 **Equivalent units, comprehensive.** Louisville Sports manufactures baseball bats for use by players in the major leagues. A critical requirement for elite players is that each bat they use have an identical look and feel. As a result, Louisville uses a dedicated process to produce bats to each player's specifications.

One of Louisville's key clients is Ryan Brown of the Green Bay Brewers. Producing his bat involves the use of three materials—ash, cork, and ink—and a sequence of 20 standardized steps. Materials are added as follows:

Ash: This is the basic wood used in bats. Eighty percent of the ash content is added at the start of the process; the rest is added at the start of the 16th step of the process.

Cork: This is inserted into the bat in order to increase Ryan's bat speed. Half of the cork is introduced at the beginning of the seventh step of the process; the rest is added at the beginning of the 14th step.

Ink: This is used to stamp Ryan's name on the finished bat and is added at the end of the process.

Of the total conversion costs, 6% are added during each of the first 10 steps of the process, and 4% are added at each of the remaining 10 steps.

On May 1, 2014, Louisville had 100 bats in inventory. These bats had completed the ninth step of the process as of April 30, 2014. During May, Louisville put another 60 bats into production. At the end of May, Louisville was left with 40 bats that had completed the 12th step of the production process.

1. Under the weighted-average method of process costing, compute equivalent units of work done for each relevant input for the month of May.
2. Under the FIFO method of process costing, compute equivalent units of work done for each relevant input for the month of May.

Required

31 Weighted-average method. Larsen Company manufactures car seats in its San Antonio plant. Each car seat passes through the assembly department and the testing department. This problem focuses on the assembly department. The process-costing system at Larsen Company has a single direct-cost category (direct materials) and a single indirect-cost category (conversion costs). Direct materials are added at the beginning of the process. Conversion costs are added evenly during the process. When the assembly department finishes work on each car seat, it is immediately transferred to testing.

Larsen Company uses the weighted-average method of process costing. Data for the assembly department for October 2014 are as follows:

	Physical Units (Car Seats)	Direct Materials	Conversion Costs
Work in process, October 1[a]	5,000	$1,250,000	$ 402,750
Started during October 2014	20,000		
Completed during October 2014	22,500		
Work in process, October 31[b]	2,500		
Total costs added during October 2014		$4,500,000	$2,337,500

[a]Degree of completion: direct materials,?%; conversion costs, 60%.
[b]Degree of completion: direct materials,?%; conversion costs, 70%.

1. For each cost category, compute equivalent units in the assembly department. Show physical units in the first column of your schedule.
2. What issues should the manager focus on when reviewing the equivalent units calculation?
3. For each cost category, summarize total assembly department costs for October 2014 and calculate the cost per equivalent unit.
4. Assign costs to units completed and transferred out and to units in ending work in process.

Required

32 Journal entries (continuation of 31).

Prepare a set of summarized journal entries for all October 2014 transactions affecting Work in Process—Assembly. Set up a T-account for Work in Process—Assembly and post your entries to it.

Required

33 FIFO method (continuation of 31).

1. Do Problem 31 using the FIFO method of process costing. Explain any difference between the cost per equivalent unit in the assembly department under the weighted-average method and the FIFO method.
2. Should Larsen's managers choose the weighted-average method or the FIFO method? Explain briefly.

Required

34 Transferred-in costs, weighted-average method (related to 31 to 33). Larsen Company, as you know, is a manufacturer of car seats. Each car seat passes through the assembly department and testing department. This problem focuses on the testing department. Direct materials are added when the testing department process is 90% complete. Conversion costs are added evenly during the testing department's process. As work in assembly is completed, each unit is immediately transferred to testing. As each unit is completed in testing, it is immediately transferred to Finished Goods.

Larsen Company uses the weighted-average method of process costing. Data for the testing department for October 2014 are as follows:

	Physical Units (Car Seats)	Transferred-In Costs	Direct Materials	Conversion Costs
Work in process, October 1[a]	7,500	$2,932,500	$ 0	$ 835,460
Transferred in during October 2014	?			
Completed during October 2014	26,300			
Work in process, October 31[b]	3,700			
Total costs added during October 2014		$7,717,500	$9,704,700	$3,955,900

[a]Degree of completion: transferred-in costs,?%; direct materials,?%; conversion costs, 70%.
[b]Degree of completion: transferred-in costs,?%; direct materials,?%; conversion costs, 60%.

1. What is the percentage of completion for (a) transferred-in costs and direct materials in beginning work-in-process inventory and (b) transferred-in costs and direct materials in ending work-in-process inventory?
2. For each cost category, compute equivalent units in the testing department. Show physical units in the first column of your schedule.
3. For each cost category, summarize total testing department costs for October 2014, calculate the cost per equivalent unit, and assign costs to units completed (and transferred out) and to units in ending work in process.
4. Prepare journal entries for October transfers from the assembly department to the testing department and from the testing department to Finished Goods.

35 Transferred-in costs, FIFO method (continuation of 34). Refer to the information in Problem 34. Suppose that Larsen Company uses the FIFO method instead of the weighted-average method in all of its departments. The only changes to Problem 34 under the FIFO method are that total transferred-in costs of beginning work in process on October 1 are $2,800,000 (instead of $2,932,500) and that total transferred-in costs added during October are $7,735,250 (instead of $7,717,500).

Using the FIFO process-costing method, complete Problem 34.

36 Weighted-average method. McKnight Handcraft is a manufacturer of picture frames for large retailers. Every picture frame passes through two departments: the assembly department and the finishing department. This problem focuses on the assembly department. The process-costing system at McKnight has a single direct-cost category (direct materials) and a single indirect-cost category (conversion costs). Direct materials are added when the assembly department process is 10% complete. Conversion costs are added evenly during the assembly department's process.

McKnight uses the weighted-average method of process costing. Consider the following data for the assembly department in April 2014:

	Physical Unit (Frames)	Direct Materials	Conversion Costs
Work in process, April 1[a]	60	$ 1,530	$ 156
Started during April 2014	510		
Completed during April 2014	450		
Work in process, April 30[b]	120		
Total costs added during April 2014		$17,850	$11,544

[a]Degree of completion: direct materials, 100%; conversion costs, 40%.
[b]Degree of completion: direct materials, 100%; conversion costs, 15%.

1. Summarize the total assembly department costs for April 2014, and assign them to units completed (and transferred out) and to units in ending work in process.
2. What issues should a manager focus on when reviewing the equivalent units calculation?

37 FIFO method (continuation of 36).

1. Complete Problem 36 using the FIFO method of process costing.
2. If you did Problem 36, explain any difference between the cost of work completed and transferred out and the cost of ending work in process in the assembly department under the weighted-average method and the FIFO method. Should McKnight's managers choose the weighted-average method or the FIFO method? Explain briefly.

38 Transferred-in costs, weighted-average method. Publishers, Inc., has two departments: printing and binding. Each department has one direct-cost category (direct materials) and one indirect-cost category (conversion costs). This problem focuses on the binding department. Books that have undergone the printing process are immediately transferred to the binding department. Direct material is added when the binding process is 70% complete. Conversion costs are added evenly during binding operations. When those operations are done, the books are immediately transferred to Finished Goods. Publishers, Inc., uses the weighted-average method of process costing. The following is a summary of the April 2014 operations of the binding department.

	A	B	C	D	E
1		Physical Units (books)	Transferred-In Costs	Direct Materials	Conversion Costs
2	Beginning work in process	1,260	$ 39,060	$ 0	$16,380
3	Degree of completion, beginning work in process		100%	0%	50%
4	Transferred in during April 2014	2,880			
5	Completed and transferred out during April	3,240			
6	Ending work in process (April 30)	900			
7	Degree of completion, ending work in process		100%	0%	70%
8	Total costs added during April		$155,520	$28,188	$84,240

Required

1. Summarize total binding department costs for April 2014, and assign these costs to units completed (and transferred out) and to units in ending work in process.
2. Prepare journal entries for April transfers from the printing department to the binding department and from the binding department to Finished Goods.

39 Transferred-in costs, FIFO method. Refer to the information in Problem 38. Suppose that Publishers, Inc., uses the FIFO method instead of the weighted-average method in all of its departments. The only changes to Problem 38 under the FIFO method are that total transferred-in costs of beginning work in process on April 1 are $44,100 (instead of $39,060) and that total transferred-in costs added during April are $149,760 (instead of $155,520).

Required

1. Using the FIFO process-costing method, complete Problem 38.
2. If you did Problem 38, explain any difference between the cost of work completed and transferred out and the cost of ending work in process in the binding department under the weighted-average method and the FIFO method.

40 Transferred-in costs, weighted-average and FIFO methods. Portland Pale Ale, Inc., makes a variety of specialty beers at its main brewery in Oregon. Production of beer occurs in three main stages: mashing, boiling, and fermenting. Consider the fermenting department, where direct materials (bottles and other packaging) are added at the end of the process. Conversion costs are added evenly during the process.

Portland Pale Ale provides the following information related to its top-selling Gypsum Ale for the fermenting department for the month of July:

	Physical Units (Cases)	Transferred-In Costs	Direct Materials	Conversion Costs
Beginning work in process	2,500	$116,000	$ 0	$ 37,500
Transferred in during July from boiling department	10,000			
Completed during July	10,500			
Ending work in process, July 31	2,000			
Total costs added during July		$384,000	$110,775	$152,250

The units in beginning work in process are 25% complete for conversion costs, while the units in ending inventory are 50% complete for conversion costs.

Required

1. Using the weighted-average method, summarize the total fermenting department costs for July, and assign costs to units completed (and transferred out) and to units in ending work in process.
2. Assume that the FIFO method is used for the fermenting department. Under FIFO, the transferred-in costs for work-in-process beginning inventory in July are $115,680 (instead of $116,000 under the weighted-average method), and the transferred-in costs during July from the boiling department are $376,000 (instead of $384,000 under the weighted-average method). All other data are unchanged. Summarize the total fermenting department costs for July, and assign costs to units completed and transferred out and to units in ending work in process using the FIFO method.

41 Multiple processes or operations, costing. The Sedona Company is dedicated to making products that meet the needs of customers in a sustainable manner. Sedona is best known for its KLN water bottle, which is a BPA-free, dishwasher-safe, bubbly glass bottle in a soft silicone sleeve.

The production process consists of three basic operations. In the first operation, the glass is formed by remelting cullets (broken or refuse glass). In the second operation, the glass is assembled with the silicone gasket and sleeve. The resulting product is finished in the final operation with the addition of the polypropylene cap.

Consulting studies have indicated that of the total conversion costs required to complete a finished unit, the forming operation requires 60%, the assembly 30%, and the finishing 10%.

The following data are available for March 2014 (there is no opening inventory of any kind):

Cullets purchased	$67,500
Silicone purchased	$24,000
Polypropylene used	$ 6,000
Total conversion costs incurred	$68,850
Ending inventory, cullets	$ 4,500
Ending inventory, silicone	$ 3,000
Number of bottles completed and transferred	12,000
Inventory in process at the end of the month:	
Units formed but not assembled	4,000
Units assembled but not finished	2,000

Required

1. What is the cost per equivalent unit for conversion costs for KLN bottles in March 2014?
2. Compute the cost per equivalent unit with respect to each of the three materials: cullets, silicone, and polypropylene.
3. What is the cost of goods completed and transferred out?
4. What is the cost of goods formed but not assembled?
5. What is the cost of goods assembled but not finished?

42 Benchmarking, ethics. Amanda McNall is the corporate controller of Scott Quarry. Scott Quarry operates 12 rock-crushing plants in Scott County, Kentucky, that process huge chunks of limestone rock extracted from underground mines.

Given the competitive landscape for pricing, Scott's managers pay close attention to costs. Each plant uses a process-costing system, and at the end of every quarter, each plant manager submits a production report and a production-cost report. The production report includes the plant manager's estimate of the percentage of completion of the ending work in process as to direct materials and conversion costs, as well as the level of processed limestone inventory. McNall uses these estimates to compute the cost per equivalent unit of work done for each input for the quarter. Plants are ranked from 1 to 12, and the three plants with the lowest cost per equivalent unit for direct materials and conversion costs are each given a bonus and recognized in the company newsletter.

McNall has been pleased with the success of her benchmarking program. However, she has recently received anonymous emails that two plant managers have been manipulating their monthly estimates of percentage of completion in an attempt to obtain the bonus.

Required

1. Why and how might managers manipulate their monthly estimates of percentage of completion and level of inventory?
2. McNall's first reaction is to contact each plant controller and discuss the problem raised by the anonymous communications. Is that a good idea?
3. Assume that each plant controller's primary reporting responsibility is to the plant manager and that each plant controller receives the phone call from McNall mentioned in requirement 2. What is the ethical responsibility of each plant controller (a) to Amanda McNall and (b) to Scott Quarry in relation to the equivalent-unit and inventory information each plant provides?
4. How might McNall learn whether the data provided by particular plants are being manipulated?

43 Standard-costing method. Hi-sense Technologies produces stripped-down phones for sale to customers in frontier economies. The firm purchases used or obsolete models of specific smartphone models. It removes nonstandard applications, installs open source Android software, and unlocks the phone so it can operate on GSM networks. Hi-sense's most popular offering is the iZoom phone.

Given the importance of scaling and cost control for the success of its business model, Hi-sense uses a standard-costing system. The following information is available for the second quarter of 2014 (April 1–June 30):

Physical and Equivalent Units for iZoom
For the Second Quarter of 2014

	Physical Units	Equivalent Units	
		Direct Materials	Conversion Costs
Completion of beginning work in process	1,158,000	—	521,100
Started and completed	1,014,000	1,014,000	1,014,000
Work on ending work in process	2,180,400	2,180,400	1,308,240
Units to account for	4,352,400	3,194,400	2,843,340

	Costs
Cost of units completed from beginning work in process	$ 9,206,100
Cost of new units started and completed	8,061,300
Cost of units completed in the second quarter	17,267,400
Cost of ending work in process	14,630,484
Total costs accounted for	$31,897,884

Required

1. What are the completion percentages of iZoom phones in beginning work-in-process inventory with respect to the two inputs?
2. What are the completion percentages of iZoom phones in ending work-in-process inventory with respect to the two inputs?
3. What are the standard costs per unit for direct materials and conversion costs?
4. What is the total cost of work-in-process inventory as of April 1, 2014 (the start of the second quarter)?

Glossary

Equivalent units. Derived amount of output units that (a) takes the quantity of each input (factor of production) in units completed and in incomplete units of work in process and (b) converts the quantity of input into the amount of completed output units that could be produced with that quantity of input.

First-in, first-out (FIFO) process-costing method. Method of process costing that assigns the cost of the previous accounting period's equivalent units in beginning work-in-process inventory to the first units completed and transferred out of the process, and assigns the cost of equivalent units worked on during the current period first to complete beginning inventory, next to start and complete new units, and finally to units in ending work-in-process inventory.

Hybrid-costing system. Costing system that blends characteristics from both job-costing systems and process-costing systems.

Operation. A standardized method or technique that is performed repetitively, often on different materials, resulting in different finished goods.

Operation-costing system. Hybrid-costing system applied to batches of similar, but not identical, products. Each batch of products is often a variation of a single design, and it proceeds through a sequence of operations, but each batch does not necessarily move through the same operations as other batches. Within each operation, all product units use identical amounts of the operation's resources.

Previous-department costs. See *transferred-in costs*.

Transferred-in costs. Costs incurred in previous departments that are carried forward as the product's costs when it moves to a subsequent process in the production cycle. Also called *previous department costs*.

Weighted-average process-costing method. Method of process costing that assigns the equivalent-unit cost of the work done to date (regardless of the accounting period in which it was done) to equivalent units completed and transferred out of the process and to equivalent units in ending work-in-process inventory.

Photo Credits

Credits are listed in order of appearance.

Photo 1: Roberta Sherman/Pearson Education, Inc.
Photo 2: AP Images

Index